UNITED STATES MILITARY ROAD ATLAS

COMPACT TRAVEL EDITION

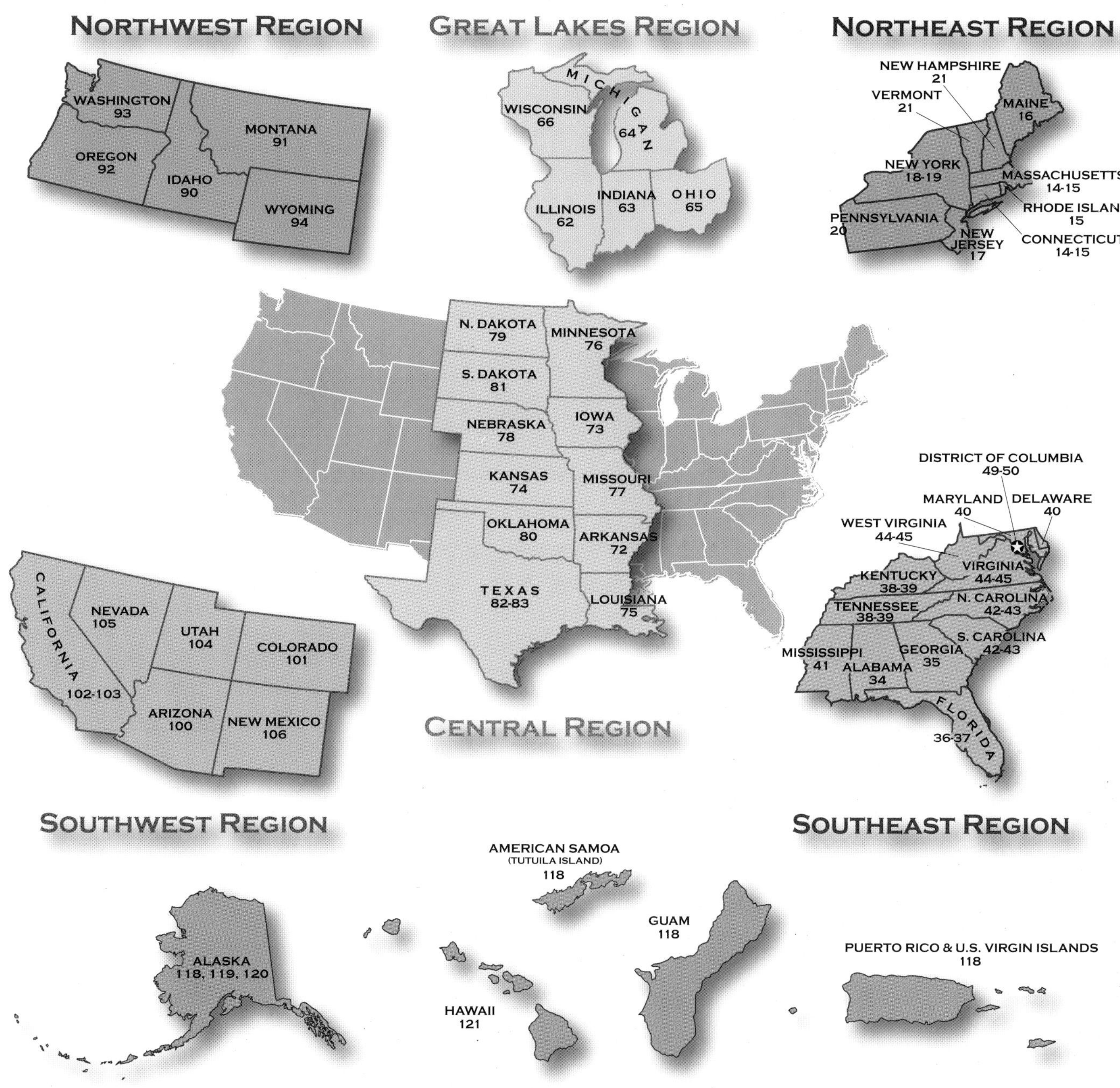

NORTHWEST REGION
WASHINGTON 93
MONTANA 91
OREGON 92
IDAHO 90
WYOMING 94
GREAT LAKES REGION
MICHIGAN 64
WISCONSIN 66
ILLINOIS 62
INDIANA 63
OHIO 65
NORTHEAST REGION
NEW HAMPSHIRE 21
VERMONT 21
MAINE 16
NEW YORK 18-19
MASSACHUSETTS 14-15
RHODE ISLAND 15
PENNSYLVANIA 20
NEW JERSEY 17
CONNECTICUT 14-15
N. DAKOTA 79
MINNESOTA 76
S. DAKOTA 81
NEBRASKA 78
IOWA 73
KANSAS 74
MISSOURI 77
OKLAHOMA 80
ARKANSAS 72
TEXAS 82-83
LOUISIANA 75
CENTRAL REGION
DISTRICT OF COLUMBIA 49-50
MARYLAND 40
DELAWARE 40
WEST VIRGINIA 44-45
VIRGINIA 44-45
KENTUCKY 38-39
N. CAROLINA 42-43
TENNESSEE 38-39
S. CAROLINA 42-43
MISSISSIPPI 41
GEORGIA 35
ALABAMA 34
FLORIDA 36-37
SOUTHEAST REGION
CALIFORNIA 102-103
NEVADA 105
UTAH 104
COLORADO 101
ARIZONA 100
NEW MEXICO 106
SOUTHWEST REGION
AMERICAN SAMOA (TUTUILA ISLAND) 118
GUAM 118
ALASKA 118, 119, 120
HAWAII 121
PUERTO RICO & U.S. VIRGIN ISLANDS 118

FAR WEST REGION & U. S. POSS[illegible]

Acknowledgments

William "Roy" Crawford, Ph.D.
Chief Executive Officer, Military Marketing Services, Inc.
and Military Living Publications

L. Ann Crawford
Executive Vice-President, Military Marketing Services, Inc.
and Publisher, Military Living Publications

R.J. Crawford
President, Military Marketing Services, Inc.
and Military Living Publications

Editorial Manager - J.J. Caddell

Cover Photo Credits:

Front Cover - Photo courtesy of
Shades of Green® on Walt Disney World® Resort

All photos within text are courtesy of the facility shown, unless otherwise noted.

About the Publisher

Military Living Publications
P.O. Box 2347
Falls Church, Virginia 22042-0347
Tel: 703-237-0203, ext 1
Fax: 703-997-8861
Website: www.militaryliving.com
E-mail: sales@militaryliving.com

ISBN 1-931424-21-7

Notice

This United States Military Road Atlas and all information herein was developed, produced and funded by Military Living Publications (Military Marketing Services, Inc.) and the Copyright Owners. Military Living Publications is a private company, in no way connected with the Department of Defense or any other government agency.

The information contained in this atlas has been compiled from sources believed to be reliable and to represent the latest facts available regarding this subject. Information about the installations and facilities listed including addresses, contact phone numbers and facilities could change. Roads can also change. This atlas should be used as a guide to the listed facilities with this understanding. No warranty, guarantee or representation is made, however, as to the correctness of information in this atlas or in any other publication, and Military Living Publications can assume no responsibility for incorrect information.

Base Closures

On 13 May 2005, the Defense Realignment and Base Closure (BRAC) Commission received the list of bases suggested by the Department of Defense for realignment and closure. The BRAC Commission was required to perform an independent analysis and evaluation of the list, including public input. President Bush received the Commission's final report on 8 September 2005. The President was required by the BRAC law to forward the report to the Congress or return it to the Commission for further evaluation. On 15 September 2005 President Bush concurred with and sent the 2005 BRAC report to Congress. The Congress had 45 legislative days to accept or reject the report in its entirety. Congress cannot make changes to the final report. The Congress allowed the report to pass into law at the mandatory 8 November 2005 deadline. The Commission approved 119 of the 190 DoD recommendations with no change and accepted another 45 with amendments. The Commission rejected in their entirety 13 DoD recommendations and significantly modified 13 other recommendations. The closure or realignment of five additional bases were recommended by the commission. Of DoD's recommended 33 "major" base closures, the Commission approved 21, recommended realignment of seven, and rejected five. In addition, the commission recommended one base for closure rather than realignment, for a total of 22 closures. We have noted in the text section of the atlas 16 of the 22 "major" bases which have been recommended for closure. The other 6 bases are industrial facilities which do not offer support services for military travelers and are not listed in this atlas.

Sample Page:

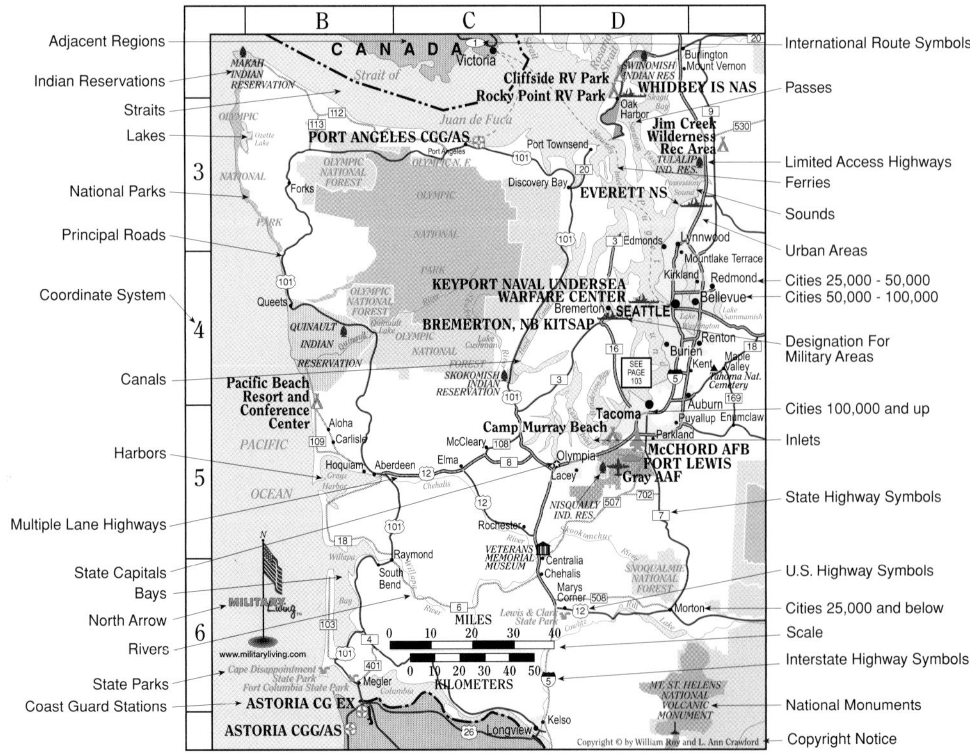

Explanation of Map Symbols

- ARMY
- NAVY
- AIR FORCE
- MARINE CORPS
- COAST GUARD
- NASA
- DoD or Commercial Facility
- UNITED STATES MERCHANT MARINE ACADEMY
- RECREATION AREA
- AIRPORT or AIRFIELD *with Military Significance*
- MUSEUM *with Military Significance*
- Military Area
- Temporary Military Lodging *(Off-Base)*
- International Airport
- International Airport *with Military Significance*
- Airport
- Stadium *for Military Academy Athletics*
- Interstate Highways
- U.S. Highways
- State Highways
- International Routes
- Limited Access Highways
- Multi Lane Highways
- Toll Roads
- Principal Roads
- Other Roads
- Seasonal Roads
- Tunnels
- State Capital
- City population 25,000 and below
- City popluation 25,000 - 50,000
- City population 50,000 - 100,000
- City population 100,000 and up
- International Border
- State Border
- Ferries
- Time Zones
- City Map Detail Reference
- INDIAN RESERVATION
- State Park
- NATIONAL MONUMENTS
- National Battlefields
- Urban Areas
- INDIAN RESERVATION
- NATIONAL FOREST
- NATIONAL PARKS

You deserve the
Military Savings

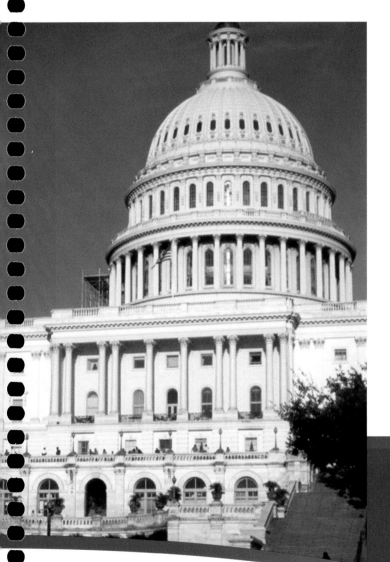

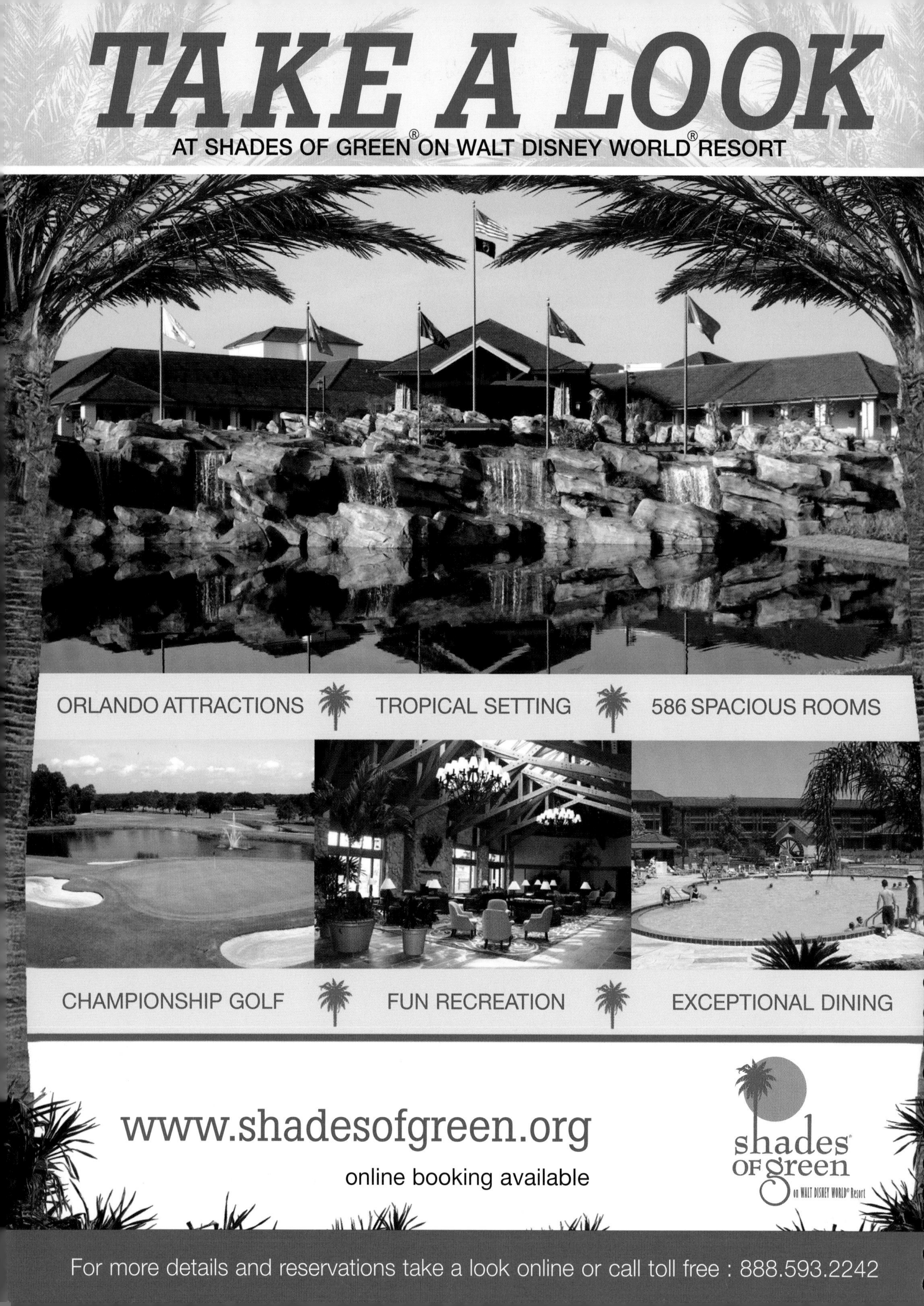
TAKE A LOOK
AT SHADES OF GREEN® ON WALT DISNEY WORLD® RESORT
ORLANDO ATTRACTIONS
TROPICAL SETTING
586 SPACIOUS ROOMS
CHAMPIONSHIP GOLF
FUN RECREATION
EXCEPTIONAL DINING
www.shadesofgreen.org
online booking available
shades OF green
on WALT DISNEY WORLD® Resort
For more details and reservations take a look online or call toll free : 888.593.2242

NORTHEAST REGION

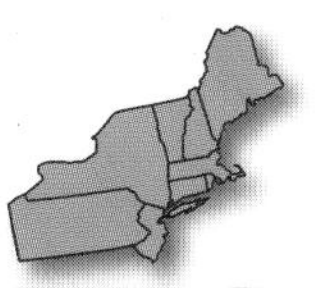

SOUTHEAST REGION

GREAT LAKES REGION

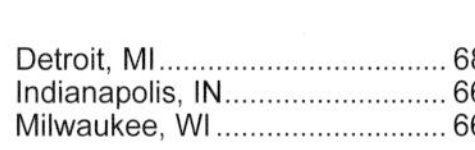

CENTRAL REGION

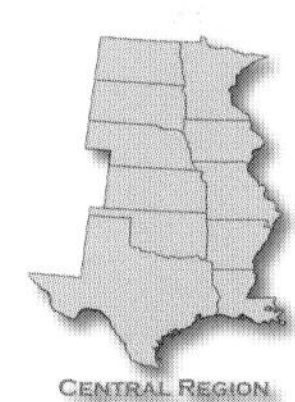

NORTHWEST REGION

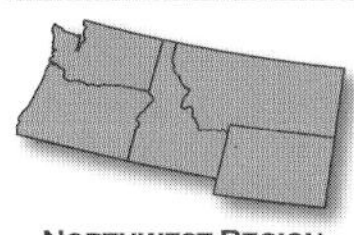

SOUTHWEST REGION

FAR WEST & U. S. POSSESSIONS REGION

OTHER ITEMS OF INTEREST

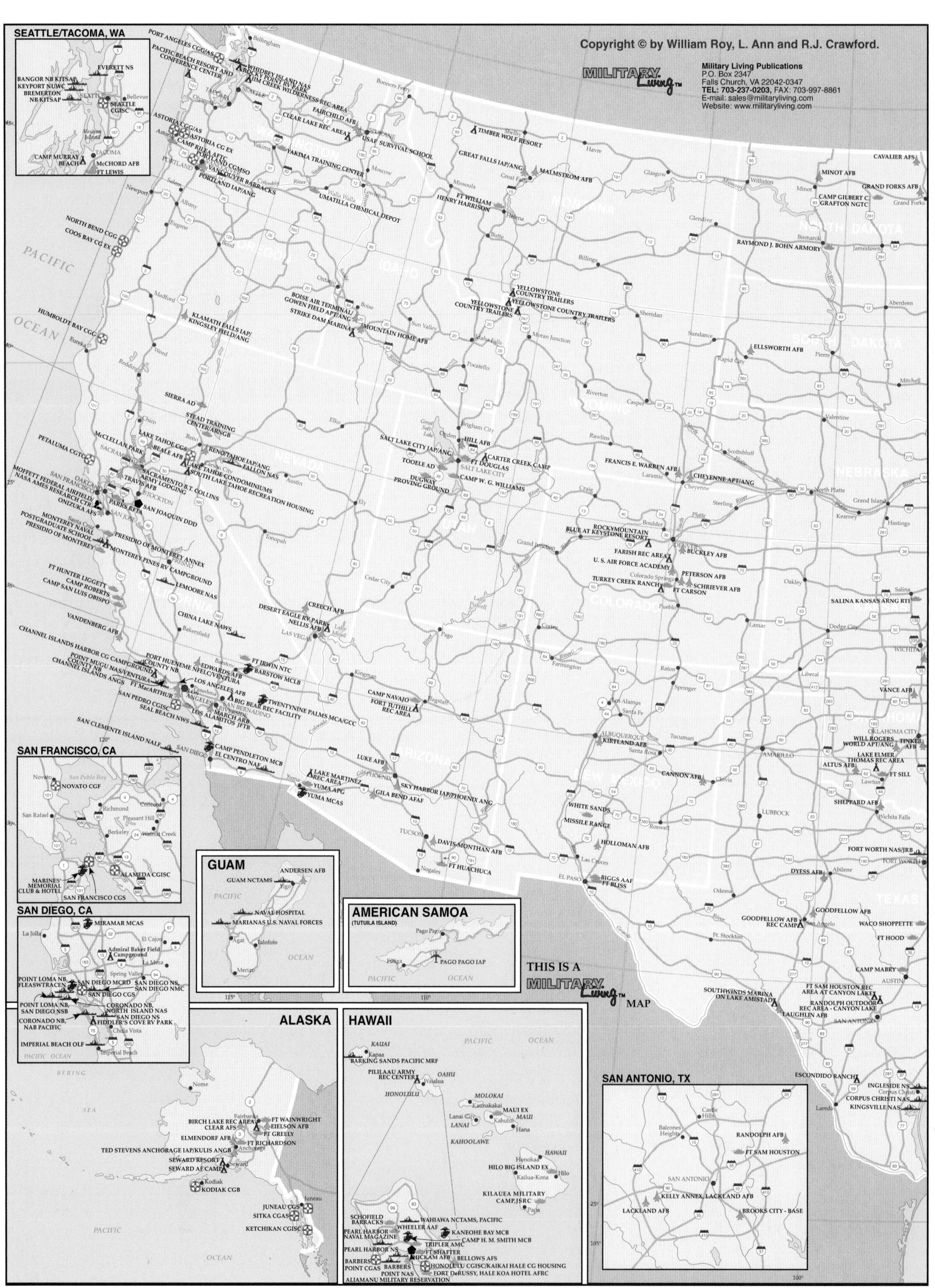

Copyright © by William Roy, L. Ann and R.J. Crawford.
MILITARY Living
Military Living Publications
P.O. Box 2347
Falls Church, VA 22042-0347
TEL: 703-237-0203, FAX: 703-997-8861
E-mail: sales@militaryliving.com
Website: www.militaryliving.com
SEATTLE/TACOMA, WA
EVERETT NS
BANGOR NB KITSAP
KEYPORT NUWC
BREMERTON NB KITSAP
SEATTLE CGISC
CAMP MURRAY BEACH
McCHORD AFB
FT LEWIS
PORT ANGELES CGG/AS
PACIFIC BEACH RESORT AND CONFERENCE CENTER
WHIDBEY ISLAND NAS
ROCKY POINT RV PARK
JIM CREEK WILDERNESS REC AREA
FAIRCHILD AFB
CLEAR LAKE REC AREA
USAF SURVIVAL SCHOOL
YAKIMA TRAINING CENTER
UMATILLA CHEMICAL DEPOT
ASTORIA CGG/AS
ASTORIA CG EX
CAMP RILEA AFTC
PORTLAND CGMSO
VANCOUVER BARRACKS
PORTLAND IAP/ANG
NORTH BEND CGG
COOS BAY CG EX
PACIFIC
OCEAN
HUMBOLDT BAY CGG
KLAMATH FALLS IAP/KINGSLEY FIELD/ANG
BOISE AIR TERMINAL/GOWEN FIELD APT/ANG
STRIKE DAM MARINA
MOUNTAIN HOME AFB
TIMBER WOLF RESORT
GREAT FALLS IAP/ANG
MALMSTROM AFB
FT WILLIAM HENRY HARRISON
YELLOWSTONE COUNTRY TRAILERS
YELLOWSTONE COUNTRY TRAILERS
YELLOWSTONE COUNTRY TRAILERS
CAVALIER AFS
MINOT AFB
GRAND FORKS AFB
CAMP GILBERT C GRAFTON NGTC
RAYMOND J. BOHN ARMORY
ELLSWORTH AFB
SIERRA AD
STEAD TRAINING CENTER/ARNGB
LAKE TAHOE CGS
McCLELLAN PARK
BEALE AFB
RENO/TAHOE IAP/ANG
FALLON NAS
LAKE TAHOE CONDOMINIUMS
SOUTH LAKE TAHOE RECREATION HOUSING
SACRAMENTO B.T. COLLINS ARMY LODGING
TRAVIS AFB
PETALUMA CGTC
MOFFETT FEDERAL AIRFIELD
NASA AMES RESEARCH CTR
ONIZUKA AFS
PARKS RFTA
SAN JOAQUIN DDD
MONTEREY NAVAL POSTGRADUATE SCHOOL
PRESIDIO OF MONTEREY
PRESIDIO OF MONTEREY ANNEX
MONTEREY PINES RV CAMPGROUND
LEMOORE NAS
FT HUNTER LIGGETT
CAMP ROBERTS
CAMP SAN LUIS OBISPO
VANDENBERG AFB
CHINA LAKE NAWS
SALT LAKE CITY IAP/ANG
HILL AFB
TOOELE AD
CARTER CREEK CAMP
FT DOUGLAS
DUGWAY PROVING GROUND
CAMP W. G. WILLIAMS
FRANCIS E. WARREN AFB
CHEYENNE APT/ANG
ROCKYMOUNTAIN BLUE AT KEYSTONE RESORT
FARISH REC AREA
BUCKLEY AFB
U. S. AIR FORCE ACADEMY
PETERSON AFB
SCHRIEVER AFB
TURKEY CREEK RANCH
FT CARSON
SALINA KANSAS ARNG RTI
CREECH AFB
DESERT EAGLE RV PARK
NELLIS AFB
CHANNEL ISLANDS HARBOR CG CAMPGROUND
PORT HUENEME NFELC/VENTURA COUNTY NB
POINT MUGU NAS/VENTURA COUNTY NB
CHANNEL ISLANDS ANGS
FT IRWIN NTC
BARSTOW MCLB
EDWARDS AFB
LOS ANGELES AFB
FT MacARTHUR
BIG BEAR REC FACILITY
MARCH ARB
TWENTYNINE PALMS MCA/GCC
SAN PEDRO CGISC
SEAL BEACH NWS
LOS ALAMITOS JFTB
SAN CLEMENTE ISLAND NALF
CAMP PENDLETON MCB
EL CENTRO NAF
CAMP NAVAJO
FORT TUTHILL REC AREA
LUKE AFB
LAKE MARTINEZ REC AREA
YUMA APG
YUMA MCAS
GILA BEND AFAF
SKY HARBOR IAP/PHOENIX ANG
DAVIS-MONTHAN AFB
FT HUACHUCA
KIRTLAND AFB
CANNON AFB
WHITE SANDS MISSILE RANGE
HOLLOMAN AFB
BIGGS AAF
FT BLISS
VANCE AFB
WILL ROGERS WORLD APT/ANG
TINKER AFB
LAKE ELMER THOMAS REC AREA
ALTUS AFB
FT SILL
SHEPPARD AFB
FORT WORTH NAS/JRB
DYESS AFB
GOODFELLOW AFB
GOODFELLOW AFB REC CAMP
WACO SHOPPETTE
FT HOOD
CAMP MABRY
FT SAM HOUSTON REC AREA AT CANYON LAKE
RANDOLPH OUTDOOR REC AREA - CANYON LAKE
SOUTHWINDS MARINA ON LAKE AMISTAD
LAUGHLIN AFB
ESCONDIDO RANCH
INGLESIDE NS
CORPUS CHRISTI NAS
KINGSVILLE NAS
WASHINGTON
OREGON
IDAHO
MONTANA
WYOMING
NEVADA
UTAH
COLORADO
CALIFORNIA
ARIZONA
NEW MEXICO
NORTH DAKOTA
SOUTH DAKOTA
NEBRASKA
KANSAS
OKLAHOMA
TEXAS
SAN FRANCISCO, CA
NOVATO CGF
MARINES' MEMORIAL CLUB & HOTEL
SAN FRANCISCO CGS
ALAMEDA CGISC
SAN DIEGO, CA
MIRAMAR MCAS
Admiral Baker Field Campground
POINT LOMA NB FLEASWTRACEN
SAN DIEGO MCRD
SAN DIEGO NS
SAN DIEGO NMC
SAN DIEGO CGS
POINT LOMA NB SAN DIEGO NSB
CORONADO NB NORTH ISLAND NAS
SAN DIEGO NS FIDDLER'S COVE RV PARK
CORONADO NB NAB PACIFIC
IMPERIAL BEACH OLF
GUAM
ANDERSEN AFB
GUAM NCTAMS
NAVAL HOSPITAL
MARIANAS U.S. NAVAL FORCES
AMERICAN SAMOA
(TUTUILA ISLAND)
PAGO PAGO IAP
THIS IS A MILITARY Living MAP
ALASKA
BIRCH LAKE REC AREA
CLEAR AFS
FT WAINWRIGHT
EIELSON AFB
FT GREELY
ELMENDORF AFB
FT RICHARDSON
TED STEVENS ANCHORAGE IAP/KULIS ANGB
SEWARD RESORT
SEWARD AF CAMP
KODIAK CGB
JUNEAU CGS
SITKA CGAS
KETCHIKAN CGISC
HAWAII
BARKING SANDS PACIFIC MRF
PILILAAU ARMY REC CENTER
MAUI EX
HILO BIG ISLAND EX
KILAUEA MILITARY CAMP, JSRC
SCHOFIELD BARRACKS
WAHIAWA NCTAMS, PACIFIC
WHEELER AAF
PEARL HARBOR NAVAL MAGAZINE
KANEOHE BAY MCB
CAMP H. M. SMITH MCB
TRIPLER AMC
FT SHAFTER
PEARL HARBOR NS
HICKAM AFB
BELLOWS AFS
BARBERS POINT CGAS
BARBERS POINT NAS
HONOLULU CGISC/KAIKAI HALE CG HOUSING
FORT DeRUSSY, HALE KOA HOTEL AFRC
ALIAMANU MILITARY RESERVATION
SAN ANTONIO, TX
RANDOLPH AFB
FT SAM HOUSTON
KELLY ANNEX, LACKLAND AFB
LACKLAND AFB
BROOKS CITY - BASE

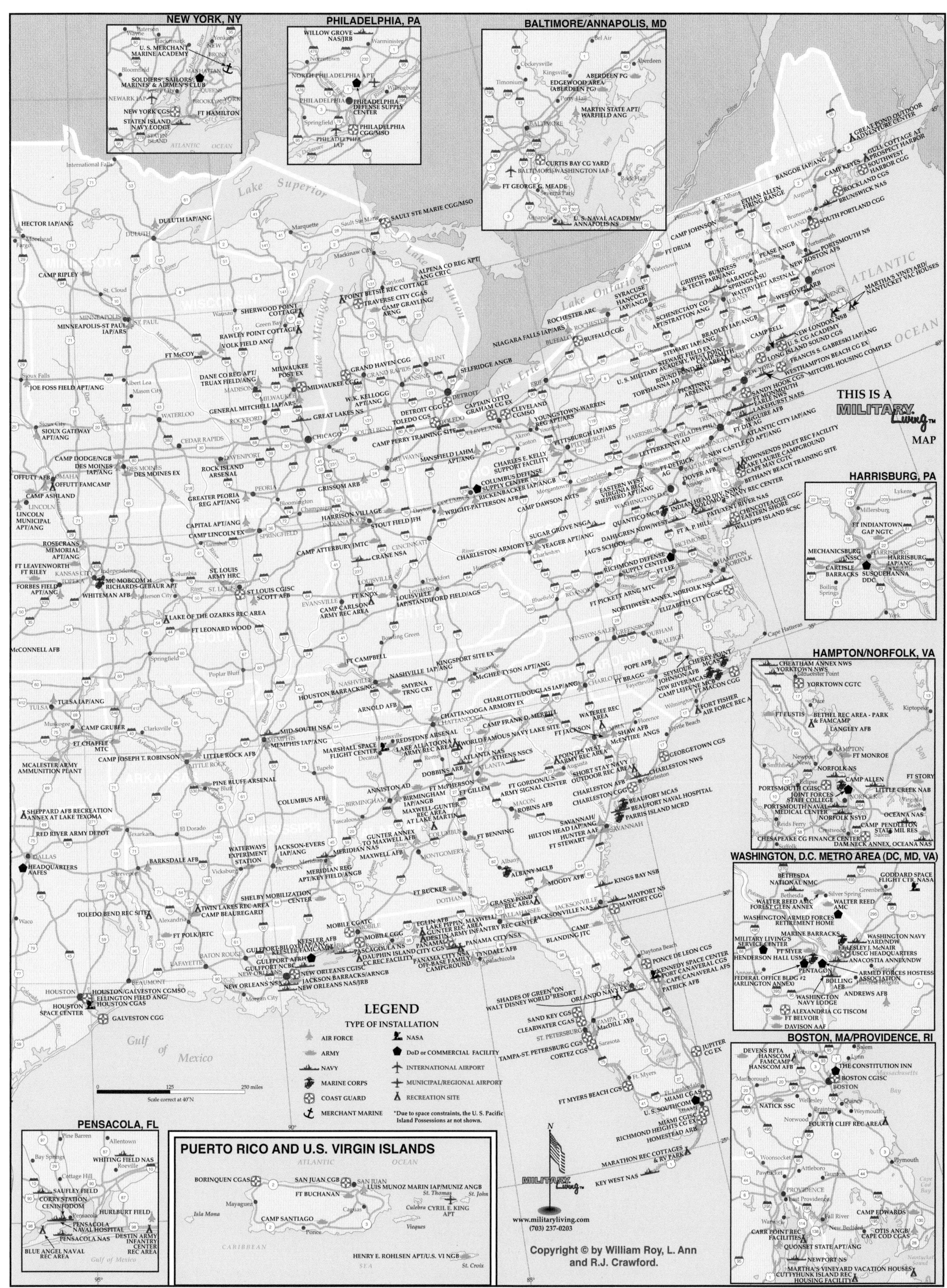
NEW YORK, NY
U. S. MERCHANT MARINE ACADEMY
SOLDIERS', SAILORS', MARINES' & AIRMEN'S CLUB
NEWARK IAP
NEW YORK CGS
FT HAMILTON
STATEN ISLAND NAVY LODGE
PHILADELPHIA, PA
WILLOW GROVE NAS/JRB
NORTH PHILADELPHIA APT
PHILADELPHIA DEFENSE SUPPLY CENTER
PHILADELPHIA IAP
PHILADELPHIA CGG/MSO
BALTIMORE/ANNAPOLIS, MD
ABERDEEN PG
EDGEWOOD AREA (ABERDEEN PG)
MARTIN STATE APT/ WARFIELD ANG
CURTIS BAY CG YARD
BALTIMORE-WASHINGTON IAP
FT GEORGE G. MEADE
U. S. NAVAL ACADEMY/ ANNAPOLIS NS
THIS IS A MILITARY Living MAP
HARRISBURG, PA
FT INDIANTOWN GAP NGTC
MECHANICSBURG NSSC
CARLISLE BARRACKS
HARRISBURG IAP/ANG
SUSQUEHANNA DDC
HAMPTON/NORFOLK, VA
CHEATHAM ANNEX NWS
YORKTOWN NWS
YORKTOWN CGTC
FT EUSTIS
BETHEL REC AREA - PARK & FAMCAMP
LANGLEY AFB
FT MONROE
NORFOLK NS
CAMP ALLEN
FT STORY
PORTSMOUTH CGISC
JOINT FORCES STAFF COLLEGE
LITTLE CREEK NAB
PORTSMOUTH NAVAL MEDICAL CENTER
NORFOLK NSYD
OCEANA NAS
CAMP PENDLETON STATE MIL RES
CHESAPEAKE CG FINANCE CENTER
DAM NECK ANNEX, OCEANA NAS
WASHINGTON, D.C. METRO AREA (DC, MD, VA)
BETHESDA NATIONAL NMC
GODDARD SPACE FLIGHT CTR, NASA
WALTER REED AMC FOREST GLEN ANNEX
WALTER REED AMC
WASHINGTON ARMED FORCES RETIREMENT HOME
MARINE BARRACKS
WASHINGTON NAVY YARD/NDW
MILITARY LIVING'S SERVICE CENTER
FT MYER
HENDERSON HALL USMC
BEASLEY J. McNAIR
USCG HEADQUARTERS
ANACOSTIA ANNEX/NDW
PENTAGON
FEDERAL OFFICE BLDG #2 (ARLINGTON ANNEX)
ARMED FORCES HOSTESS ASSOCIATION
BOLLING AFB
WASHINGTON NAVY LODGE
ANDREWS AFB
ALEXANDRIA CG TISCOM
FT BELVOIR
DAVISON AAF
BOSTON, MA/PROVIDENCE, RI
DEVENS RFTA
HANSCOM FAMCAMP
HANSCOM AFB
THE CONSTITUTION INN
BOSTON CGISC
NATICK SSC
FOURTH CLIFF REC AREA
CAMP EDWARDS
OTIS ANGB/ CAPE COD CGAS
CARR POINT REC FACILITIES
QUONSET STATE APT/ANG
NEWPORT NS
MARTHA'S VINEYARD VACATION HOUSES
CUTTYHUNK ISLAND REC HOUSING FACILITY
PENSACOLA, FL
WHITING FIELD NAS
SAUFLEY FIELD
CORRY STATION CENINFODOM
HURLBURT FIELD
PENSACOLA NAVAL HOSPITAL
PENSACOLA NAS
DESTIN ARMY INFANTRY CENTER REC AREA
BLUE ANGEL NAVAL REC AREA
PUERTO RICO AND U.S. VIRGIN ISLANDS
BORINQUEN CGAS
SAN JUAN CGB
LUIS MUNOZ MARIN IAP/MUNIZ ANGB
FT BUCHANAN
CYRIL E. KING APT
CAMP SANTIAGO
HENRY E. ROHLSEN APT/U.S. VI NGB
LEGEND
TYPE OF INSTALLATION
AIR FORCE
ARMY
NAVY
MARINE CORPS
COAST GUARD
MERCHANT MARINE
NASA
DoD or COMMERCIAL FACILITY
INTERNATIONAL AIRPORT
MUNICIPAL/REGIONAL AIRPORT
RECREATION SITE
*Due to space constraints, the U. S. Pacific Island Possessions are not shown.
Scale correct at 40°N
0 125 250 miles
Lake Superior
Lake Michigan
Lake Huron
Lake Ontario
Lake Erie
ATLANTIC OCEAN
Gulf of Mexico
HECTOR IAP/ANG
DULUTH IAP/ANG
SAULT STE MARIE CGG/MSO
CAMP RIPLEY
MINNEAPOLIS-ST PAUL IAP/ARS
FT McCOY
JOE FOSS FIELD APT/ANG
SIOUX GATEWAY APT/ANG
CAMP DODGE/NGB
DES MOINES IAP/ANG
DES MOINES EX
OFFUTT AFB
OFFUTT FAMCAMP
CAMP ASHLAND
LINCOLN MUNICIPAL APT/ANG
ROSECRANS MEMORIAL APT/ANG
FT LEAVENWORTH
FT RILEY
MC MOBCOM at RICHARDS-GEBAUR APT
WHITEMAN AFB
FORBES FIELD APT/ANG
McCONNELL AFB
LAKE OF THE OZARKS REC AREA
FT LEONARD WOOD
TULSA IAP/ANG
CAMP GRUBER
FT CHAFFEE MTC
McALESTER ARMY AMMUNITION PLANT
CAMP JOSEPH T. ROBINSON
LITTLE ROCK AFB
PINE BLUFF ARSENAL
SHEPPARD AFB RECREATION ANNEX AT LAKE TEXOMA
RED RIVER ARMY DEPOT
HEADQUARTERS AAFES
BARKSDALE AFB
TOLEDO BEND REC SITE
TWIN LAKES REC AREA
CAMP BEAUREGARD
FT POLK/JRTC
HOUSTON/GALVESTON CGMSO
ELLINGTON FIELD ANG/ HOUSTON CGAS
HOUSTON SPACE CENTER
GALVESTON CGG
SHERWOOD POINT COTTAGE
RAWLEY POINT COTTAGE
VOLK FIELD ANG
DANE CO REG APT/ TRUAX FIELD ANG
MILWAUKEE POST EX
MILWAUKEE CGG
GENERAL MITCHELL IAP/ARS
GREAT LAKES NS
ROCK ISLAND ARSENAL
GREATER PEORIA REG APT/ANG
CAPITAL APT/ANG
CAMP LINCOLN EX
ST. LOUIS ARMY HRC
ST LOUIS CGISC
SCOTT AFB
POINT BETSIE REC COTTAGE
TRAVERSE CITY CGAS
CAMP GRAYLING/ ARNG
ALPENA CO REG APT/ ANG CRTC
GRAND HAVEN CGG
W.K. KELLOGG APT/ANG
SELFRIDGE ANGB
DETROIT CGG
TOLEDO CGS
CAPTAIN OTTO GRAHAM CG EX
CLEVELAND CGMSO
CAMP PERRY TRAINING SITE
GRISSOM ARB
HARRISON VILLAGE
STOUT FIELD JFH
CAMP ATTERBURY JMTC
CRANE NSA
MANSFIELD LAHM APT/ANG
CHARLES E. KELLY SUPPORT FACILITY
COLUMBUS DEFENSE SUPPLY CENTER
RICKENBACKER IAP/ANGB
WRIGHT-PATTERSON AFB
YOUNGSTOWN-WARREN REG APT/ARS
PITTSBURGH IAP/ARS
FT KNOX
LOUISVILLE IAP/STANDIFORD FIELD/AGS
CAMP CARLSON ARMY REC AREA
FT CAMPBELL
NASHVILLE IAP/ANG
KINGSPORT SITE EX
McGHEE-TYSON APT/ANG
SMYRNA TRNG CRT
HOUSTON BARRACKS/NG
ARNOLD AFB
CHATTANOOGA ARMORY EX
MID-SOUTH NSA
MEMPHIS IAP/ANG
REDSTONE ARSENAL
MARSHALL SPACE FLIGHT CENTER
LAKE ALLATOONA ARMY REC AREA
WORLD FAMOUS NAVY LAKE SITE
ATLANTA NAS
DOBBINS ARB
ATHENS NSCS
FT McPHERSON
FT GILLEM
ANNISTON AD
BIRMINGHAM IAP/ANGB
MAXWELL-GUNTER REC AREA AT LAKE MARTIN
COLUMBUS AFB
GUNTER ANNEX TO MAXWELL AFB
MAXWELL AFB
JACKSON-EVERS IAP/ANG
MERIDIAN NAS
MERIDIAN REG APT/KEY FIELD/ANGB
WATERWAYS EXPERIMENT STATION
SHELBY MOBILIZATION CENTER
FT BENNING
FT RUCKER
MOBILE CGATC
MOBILE CGG
KEESLER AFB
KEESLER FAMCAMP
GULFPORT-BILOXI IAP/ANG
GULFPORT AFRH
GULFPORT NCBC
NEW ORLEANS CGISC
JACKSON BARRACKS/ARNGB
NEW ORLEANS NAS/JRB
NEW ORLEANS NSA
PASCAGOULA NS
DAUPHIN ISLAND CC REC FACILITY
EGLIN AFB
LAKE PIPPIN, MAXWELL GUNTER REC AREA
DESTIN ARMY INFANTRY REC CENTER
PANAMA CITY CGS
PANAMA CITY NSA
PANAMA CITY OFF-BASE FAMILY CAMPGROUND
TYNDALL AFB
ALBANY MCLB
MOODY AFB
GRASSY POND REC AREA
FT GORDON/U.S. ARMY SIGNAL CENTER
ROBINS AFB
POINTES WEST ARMY REC AREA
SHORT STAY NAVY OUTDOOR REC AREA
CHARLESTON AFB
CHARLESTON CGG
CHARLESTON NWS
BEAUFORT MCAS
BEAUFORT NAVAL HOSPITAL
PARRIS ISLAND MCRD
SAVANNAH/ HILTON HEAD IAP/ANG
HUNTER AAF
FT STEWART
KINGS BAY NSB
MAYPORT NS
MAYPORT CGG
JACKSONVILLE NAS
CAMP BLANDING JTC
PONCE DE LEON CGS
KENNEDY SPACE CENTER
PORT CANAVERAL CGS
CAPE CANAVERAL AFS
PATRICK AFB
SHADES OF GREEN ON WALT DISNEY WORLD RESORT
ORLANDO NAVY EX
SAND KEY CGS
CLEARWATER CGAS
MacDILL AFB
TAMPA-ST PETERSBURG CGS
CORTEZ CGS
JUPITER CG EX
FT MYERS BEACH CGS
MIAMI CGAS
U. S. SOUTHCOM
MIAMI CGB
RICHMOND HEIGHTS CG EX
HOMESTEAD ARB
MARATHON REC COTTAGES & RV PARK
KEY WEST NAS
WATEREE REC AREA
SHAW AFB
McENTIRE ANGS
GEORGETOWN CGS
CHARLOTTE/DOUGLAS IAP/ANG
CAMP FRANK D. MERRILL
FT JACKSON
POPE AFB
FT BRAGG
SEYMOUR JOHNSON AFB
CHERRY POINT MCAS
NEW RIVER MCAS
CAMP LEJEUNE MCB
FT MACON CGG
FORT FISHER AIR FORCE REC AREA
FT PICKETT ARNG MTC
NORTHWEST ANNEX, NORFOLK NSA
ELIZABETH CITY CGSC
RICHMOND DEFENSE SUPPLY CENTER
FT LEE
FT A. P. HILL
QUANTICO MCB
DAHLGREN NDW/WEST
JAG'S SCHOOL
CHARLESTON ARMORY EX
YEAGER APT/ANG
SUGAR GROVE NSGA
CAMP DAWSON ARTS
EASTERN WEST VIRGINIA REG APT/ANG
SHEPHERD APT/ANG
INDIAN HEAD DIV, NSWC
SOLOMONS NAVY REC CENTER
PATUXENT RIVER NAS
CHINCOTEAGUE CGG-EASTERN SHORE
WALLOPS ISLAND SCSC
LETTERKENNY AD
FT DETRICK
DOVER AFB
TOWNSENDS INLET REC FACILITY
LAKE LAURIE CAMPGROUND
CAPE MAY CGTC
BETHANY BEACH TRAINING SITE
NEW CASTLE CO APT/ANG
ATLANTIC CITY IAP/ANG
FT DIX
McGUIRE AFB
LAKEHURST NAES
EARLE NWS
FT MONMOUTH
SANDY HOOK CGS
PICATINNY ARSENAL
TOBYHANNA AD
ROUND POND REC AREA
U. S. MILITARY ACADEMY, WEST POINT
STEWART FIELD EX
STEWART IAP/ANG
CAMP SMITH
BRADLEY IAP/ANGB
LONG ISLAND SOUND CGS
U. S. CG ACADEMY
NEW LONDON NSB
FRANCIS S. GABRESKI IAP/ANG
WESTHAMPTON BEACH CG EX
MITCHEL HOUSING COMPLEX
CAMP RELL
SCHENECTADY CO APT/STRATTON ANG
WATERVLIET ARSENAL
SARATOGA SPRINGS NSU
GRIFFISS BUSINESS & TECH PARK/ANG
SYRACUSE HANCOCK IAP/ANGB
ROCHESTER ARC
NIAGARA FALLS IAP/ARS
BUFFALO CGG
FT DRUM
CAMP JOHNSON
ETHAN ALLEN FIRING RANGE
WESTOVER ARB
NEW BOSTON AFS
PEASE ANGB
PORTSMOUTH NS
MARTHA'S VINEYARD/ NANTUCKET VAC HOUSES
SOUTH PORTLAND CGG
BRUNSWICK NAS
ROCKLAND CGS
SOUTHWEST HARBOR CGG
GULL COTTAGE AT PROSPECT HARBOR
CAMP KEYES
BANGOR IAP/ANG
GREAT POND OUTDOOR ADVENTURE CENTER
www.militaryliving.com
(703) 237-0203
Copyright © by William Roy, L. Ann and R.J. Crawford.

NATIONAL DEFENSE TRANSPORTATION ASSOCIATION

Serving professionals in Distribution, Transportation, Logistics, Travel, and Related services. Membership available to Individuals, Military, Government, and Industry.

Networking...Education...Meetings...Trade Shows...Discounts...Bi-monthly Journal... Join today to enjoy these benefits and more!

In addition to the *Defense Transportation Journal*, published bi-monthly, you'll receive discounts on hotel stays, car rentals and insurance. We also offer options for legal aid with will preparation, small claims and other services. Members are eligible for college scholarship assistance, mentoring programs and educational opportunities. But the biggest benefit of all is your chance to meet with other professionals in the transportation industry. NDTA hosts a number of events throughout the year:

Forums in the US and Europe, Five major trade shows per year, Cooperative workshops with SDDC, NOLSC and the DoT, National Transportation Week (NTW) Co-Sponsor with the DoT Defense Transportation Day/Week activities

8,800 members in 31 countries; 61 Chapters with regular meetings and programs; 6 national committees: Military Airlift, Military Sealift, Surface Transportation, Passenger Travel Service, Security Best Practices, Military Distribution

NDTA Annual Transportation and Logistics Forum and Exposition Schedule
2005 San Diego, CA; 2006 Memphis, TN; 2007 Charleston, SC; 2008 Reno, NV

Join today! Call 703-751-5011

For information on corporate membership, contact Denny Edwards; For information on individual membership, contact Mark Victorson

50 South Pickett Street, Suite 220, Alexandria, VA 22304-7296, 703-751-5011, Visit NDTA on-line at www.ndtahq.com

Order Military Living's R&R Travel News®

for 3, 5 or 7 years and get one of our maps, travel guides or atlases

ABSOLUTELY FREE!

MILITARY Living's R&R Travel News®

HIGHLIGHTS
Our military travelers visit . . .
- Timbuktu, Mali, Part II
- Hawaii, Guam, Yokota & Singapore
- Slovenia and Hungary
- Retiree Living in Korea
- PLUS Tag Along with Ann

STAN & DEE INK'S SPACE-A ADVENTURE

TO HAWAII, GUAM, YOKOTA & SINGAPORE

. . . AND NEXT ISSUE, ON TO AUSTRALIA!

TUESDAY, NOV. 29, 2005- Dee and I (Stan) are off again this morning. We were going to fly our small plane to Jacksonville, FL, but the weather did not cooperate. We are now driving to Interlachen, FL. Dee's brother, Guy, is taking us to Jacksonville Naval Air Station and bringing the car back to his house until we return. We expect to catch a Navy 737 Space-A flight tomorrow morning from Jacksonville to Kaneohe Bay Marine Corps Base, HI which begins this trip that we hope will get us to Australia. We hope to make it all the way on Space-A flights.

We checked on our flight at the terminal, then Guy dropped us at the Navy Lodge. We walked a bit, exploring the woods and a walkway along St. John's Bay, and then had dinner at a sports bar at the golf club.

WEDNESDAY, NOVEMBER 30- We called about 0600 and a Duty Driver took us to the terminal. Nice service. ***Editor's Note: This service is usually only offered to duty passengers, so don't expect it!*** We checked in and took a bus to the plane by 0800. We were airborne before 0900 in a 72-seat Navy C-40 plane. It is configured to be a half-cargo plane. The seats were spaced so that we had lots of leg room. There were only 25 passengers. It was five and a half hours to North Island NAS, San Diego. We stayed for about one and a half hours for refueling. The flight to Kaneohe took six hours. We picked up snacks at the terminal, including a cheeseburger that we heated in the plane's microwave. The pilot had to do a "go around" when landing, reversing the end of the runway.

We got to Kaneohe about 1600 local time (2100 EST). Enterprise Rent-A-Car was waiting for us to go to their office for a car that I had reserved. By

Stan & Dee Ink with Ted and Sandy Finnerty

Continued on page 10

WHERE IN THE WORLD DO YOU WANT TO RETIRE?

In this issue, we have a feature by Jack Terwiel, the director of Osan AB Retiree office. Jack gives us a heads up on what it is like to retire to South Korea.

With Jack's feature in mind, I selected one of our favorite places for possible retirement. We currently live in the Washington, DC area. The place that we keep going to for R&R is Virginia Beach, VA, which is in the area called Hampton Roads. If we love to go there to have a bit of relaxation, surely we would love to live in that area.

Virginia Beach has miles of oceanfront and even more waterfront property located on lakes, rivers and the Chesapeake Bay, Back Bay, Broad Bay, Lynnhaven Bay and others. It also has the intracoastal waterway which avid boaters find to be ideal.

Continued on page 2

See page 16 to find out about our new

Military Space-A Air Travel Map and Pocket Directory™

Our subscribers travel on less per day . . . the military way!™ 1 R&R Travel News® Report 207 Mar-Apr 2006 Volume 36, No. 2

R&R Travel News® is published 6 times per year by Military Living Publications

3 Years Standard Mail $56 First Class $84
Choose your ***FREE*** Map below:
United States Military Road Map™—Paper ($11.20) or Plastic ($13.70)*
Military Space-A Air Travel Map & Pocket Directory™—Plastic ($17.20)*

5 Years Standard Mail $84 First Class $134
Choose you ***FREE*** Travel Guide below:
European Military Travel Guide™ ($26.75)*
Military RV, Camping & Outdoor Recreation Around the World™ ($21.30)*
Military Travel Guide U.S.A.™ ($19.05)
Temporary Military Lodging Around the World™ ($23.75)*

7 Years Standard Mail $106 First Class $181
*Choose your **FREE** Atlas below:*
United States Military Road Atlas™ ($27.55)*
United States Military Road Atlas, Compact Edition™ (Spiral Binding)

** Military Living Mail Order Value ** Offer expires 12/31/2006. After this date visit our website at www.militaryliving.com for 2007 special offers.*

CALL (703) 237-0203 Ext 1 and place your order today!

We accept Visa, Mastercard, American Express and Discover. Sorry, no billing.

PREMIER EDITION!

Military Space-A Air Travel Map and Pocket Directory™

Sturdy plastic map is an easy-to-use 36.5"W x 20"H and folds to a convenient 4"W x 10"H. Available ***NOW*** directly from Military Living. Call 703-237-0203 Ext. 1 and order with your credit card for $17.20 (includes first class mail shipping & handling!) Or, order at www.militaryliving.com at the ***ORDER FORM*** button. (VA orders will be charged VA 5% sales tax). Also available at military exchanges worldwide and online at **www.aafes.com** or by calling the AAFES at (800) 527-2345 and use order code **Q103Z.**

The Constitution Inn & Fitness Center

- 147 Newly Remodeled Guest Rooms-many with kitchenettes
- Fitness Center, Sauna & Indoor Pool
- Basketball Court
- Massage Therapy
- Jump into our ongoing classes. Yoga, Aerobics, Pilates, Stability Ball
- Discounted Parking
- Function Rooms
- Discounted Rates for Active, Retired, Reserve and Veteran Military
- Nearby TD BankNorth Garden, Freedom Trail, Faneuil Hall, USS Constitution, Many Museums, & Fabulous Restaurants!

150 Third Ave., Charlestown Navy Yard
Boston MA 02129
1.800.495.9622 or 617.241.8400

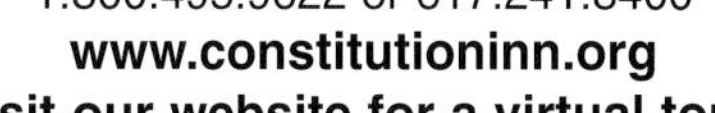

www.constitutioninn.org
Visit our website for a virtual tour!

HANSCOM FAMCAMP

MASSACHUSETTS

FAMCAMP Office

Parking Facility

- Visit historical sites
- A short drive to Boston
- Two miles to Hanscom AFB
- Many Leisure and Outdoor Recreation Activities

Call 781-377-4670 for more information.

Military RV Camping & Outdoor Recreation

Around the World - Including Golf Courses and Marinas

To order directly from Military Living, call 703-237-0203, Ext. 1 and order with a major credit card. $21.30 includes first-class postage and handling! Please include 5% sales tax with Virginia orders.

Or, order from AAFES for under $12.50 plus postage (Order Code T060F). Call toll-free 1-800-527-2345 or order online at www.AAFES.com.

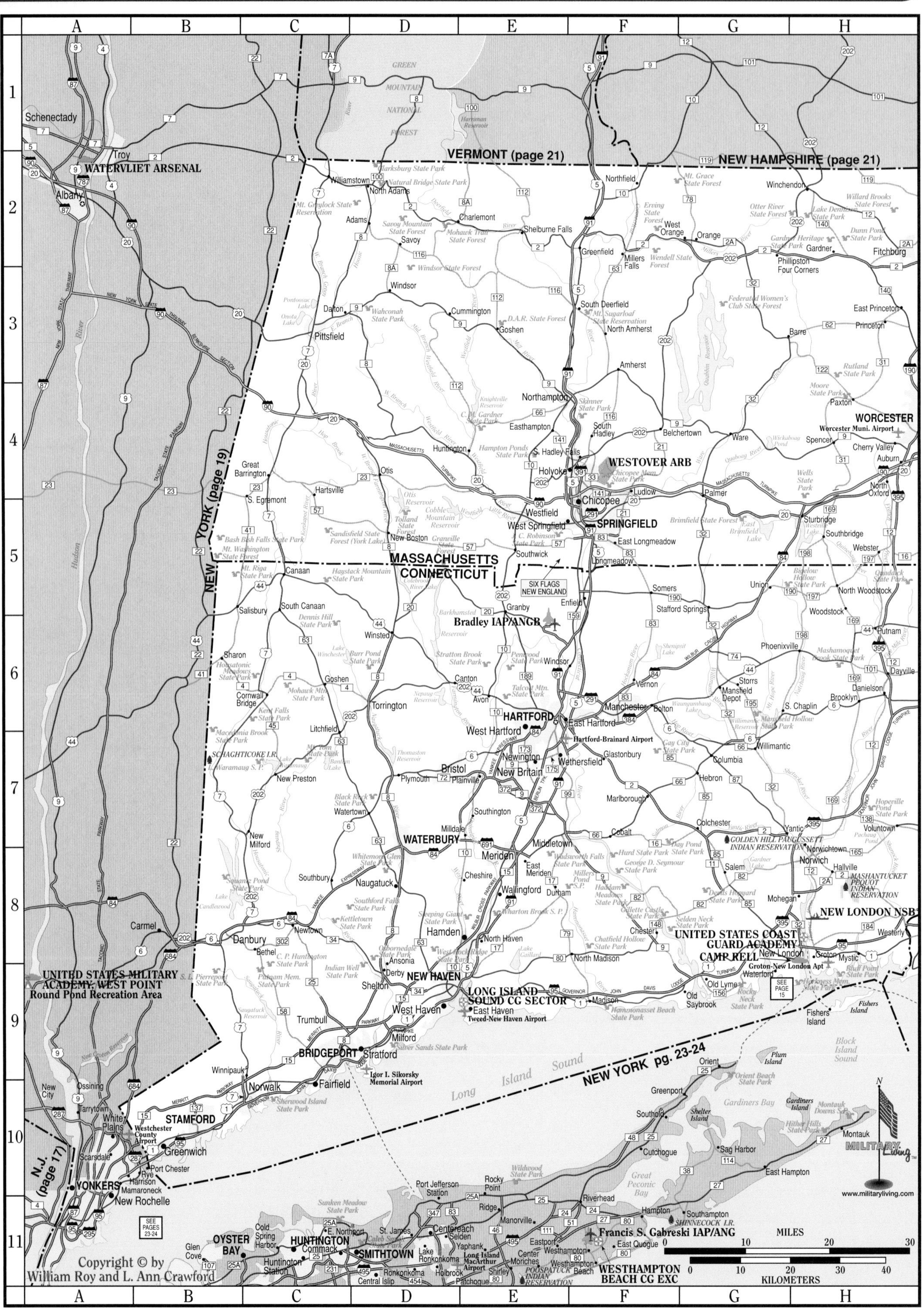

A
B
C
D
E
F
G
H
1
2
3
4
5
6
7
8
9
10
11
VERMONT (page 21)
NEW HAMPSHIRE (page 21)
NEW YORK (page 19)
MASSACHUSETTS
CONNECTICUT
NEW YORK pg. 23-24
N.J. (page 17)
GREEN MOUNTAIN NATIONAL FOREST
Schenectady
Troy
WATERVLIET ARSENAL
Albany
Williamstown
North Adams
Adams
Charlemont
Shelburne Falls
Northfield
Greenfield
Millers Falls
Winchendon
Orange
Gardner
Fitchburg
Phillipston Four Corners
Savoy
Windsor
Dalton
Pittsfield
Cummington
Goshen
South Deerfield
North Amherst
Amherst
Barre
East Princeton
Princeton
Northampton
Easthampton
South Hadley
Belchertown
Ware
Paxton
WORCESTER
Worcester Muni. Airport
Spencer
Cherry Valley
Auburn
North Oxford
Huntington
S. Hadley Falls
Holyoke
WESTOVER ARB
Great Barrington
Otis
Chicopee
Ludlow
Palmer
Hartsville
S. Egremont
Westfield
West Springfield
SPRINGFIELD
Sturbridge
Southbridge
New Boston
Southwick
East Longmeadow
Longmeadow
Webster
Canaan
SIX FLAGS NEW ENGLAND
Enfield
Somers
Stafford Springs
Union
North Woodstock
Woodstock
Salisbury
South Canaan
Granby
Bradley IAP/ANGB
Winsted
Putnam
Sharon
Goshen
Canton
Windsor
Vernon
Storrs
Phoenixville
Dayville
Danielson
Cornwall Bridge
Torrington
Avon
HARTFORD
Manchester
Bolton
Mansfield Depot
S. Chaplin
Brooklyn
Litchfield
West Hartford
East Hartford
Hartford-Brainard Airport
Willimantic
SCHAGHTICOKE I.R.
Bristol
Newington
Wethersfield
Glastonbury
Columbia
New Preston
Plymouth
Plainville
New Britain
Hebron
Marlborough
Watertown
Southington
Colchester
Yantic
Voluntown
New Milford
Milldale
WATERBURY
Middletown
Cobalt
GOLDEN HILL PAUGUSSETT INDIAN RESERVATION
Norwichtown
Norwich
Meriden
East Meriden
Salem
Hallville
MASHANTUCKET PEQUOT INDIAN RESERVATION
Southbury
Naugatuck
Cheshire
Wallingford
Durham
Mohegan
NEW LONDON NSB
Carmel
Danbury
Newtown
Bethel
Hamden
North Haven
Chester
UNITED STATES COAST GUARD ACADEMY
CAMP RELL
New London
Groton
Mystic
Westerly
Groton-New London Apt
North Madison
Ansonia
Derby
Shelton
NEW HAVEN
LONG ISLAND SOUND CG SECTOR
Madison
Old Lyme
Waterford
Old Saybrook
UNITED STATES MILITARY ACADEMY, WEST POINT
Round Pond Recreation Area
Trumbull
West Haven
East Haven
Tweed-New Haven Airport
Fishers Island
Milford
BRIDGEPORT
Stratford
Winnipauk
Norwalk
Fairfield
Igor I. Sikorsky Memorial Airport
Long Island Sound
Orient
Plum Island
Block Island Sound
Ossining
New City
Tarrytown
White Plains
Westchester County Airport
STAMFORD
Greenwich
Scarsdale
Rye
Port Chester
Harrison
Mamaroneck
YONKERS
New Rochelle
Greenport
Southold
Shelter Island
Gardiners Bay
Gardiners Island
Montauk
Cutchogue
Sag Harbor
East Hampton
Port Jefferson Station
Rocky Point
Riverhead
Hampton
Southampton
SHINNECOCK I.R.
Ridge
Manorville
Cold Spring Harbor
OYSTER BAY
HUNTINGTON
Commack
E. Northport
St. James
Centereach
Selden
Yaphank
Eastport
Francis S. Gabreski IAP/ANG
East Quogue
Glen Cove
Huntington Station
SMITHTOWN
Lake Ronkonkoma
Long Island MacArthur Airport
Center Moriches
Westhampton
Westhampton Beach
POOSPATUCK INDIAN RESERVATION
WESTHAMPTON BEACH CG EXC
Central Islip
Holbrook
Patchogue
Shirley
SEE PAGES 23-24
SEE PAGE 15
MILITARY Living
www.militaryliving.com
MILES
KILOMETERS
0
10
20
30
40
Copyright © by William Roy and L. Ann Crawford

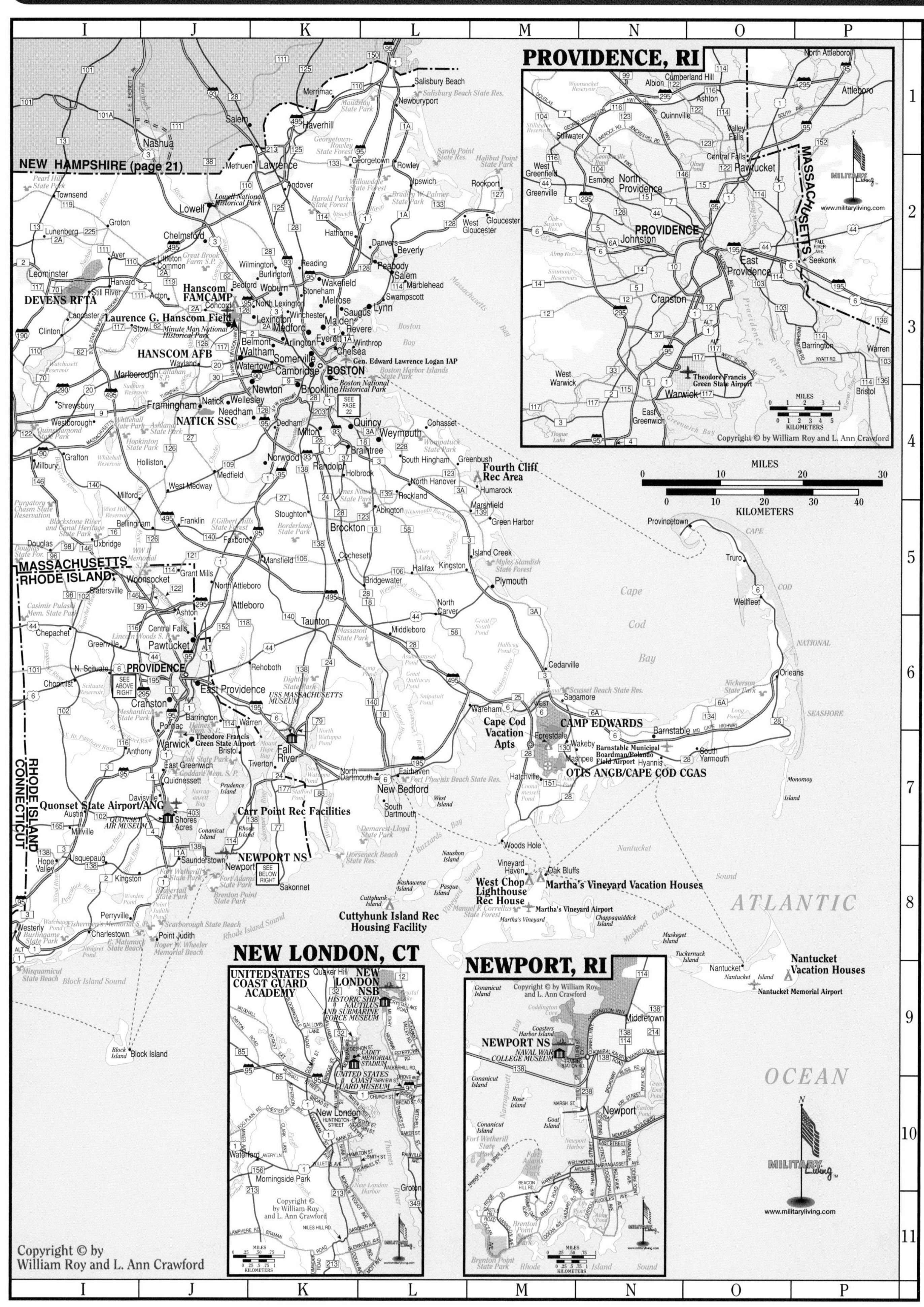
PROVIDENCE, RI
NEW LONDON, CT
NEWPORT, RI
NEW HAMPSHIRE (page 21)
MASSACHUSETTS
RHODE ISLAND
CONNECTICUT
DEVENS RFTA
Hanscom FAMCAMP
Laurence G. Hanscom Field
HANSCOM AFB
NATICK SSC
BOSTON
Gen. Edward Lawrence Logan IAP
Fourth Cliff Rec Area
CAMP EDWARDS
Cape Cod Vacation Apts
OTIS ANGB/CAPE COD CGAS
Quonset State Airport/ANG
Carr Point Rec Facilities
NEWPORT NS
Cuttyhunk Island Rec Housing Facility
West Chop Lighthouse Rec House
Martha's Vineyard Vacation Houses
Nantucket Vacation Houses
Nantucket Memorial Airport
Theodore Francis Green State Airport
UNITEDSTATES COAST GUARD ACADEMY
NEW LONDON NSB
Cape Cod Bay
ATLANTIC OCEAN
MILES
KILOMETERS
www.militaryliving.com
Copyright © by William Roy and L. Ann Crawford

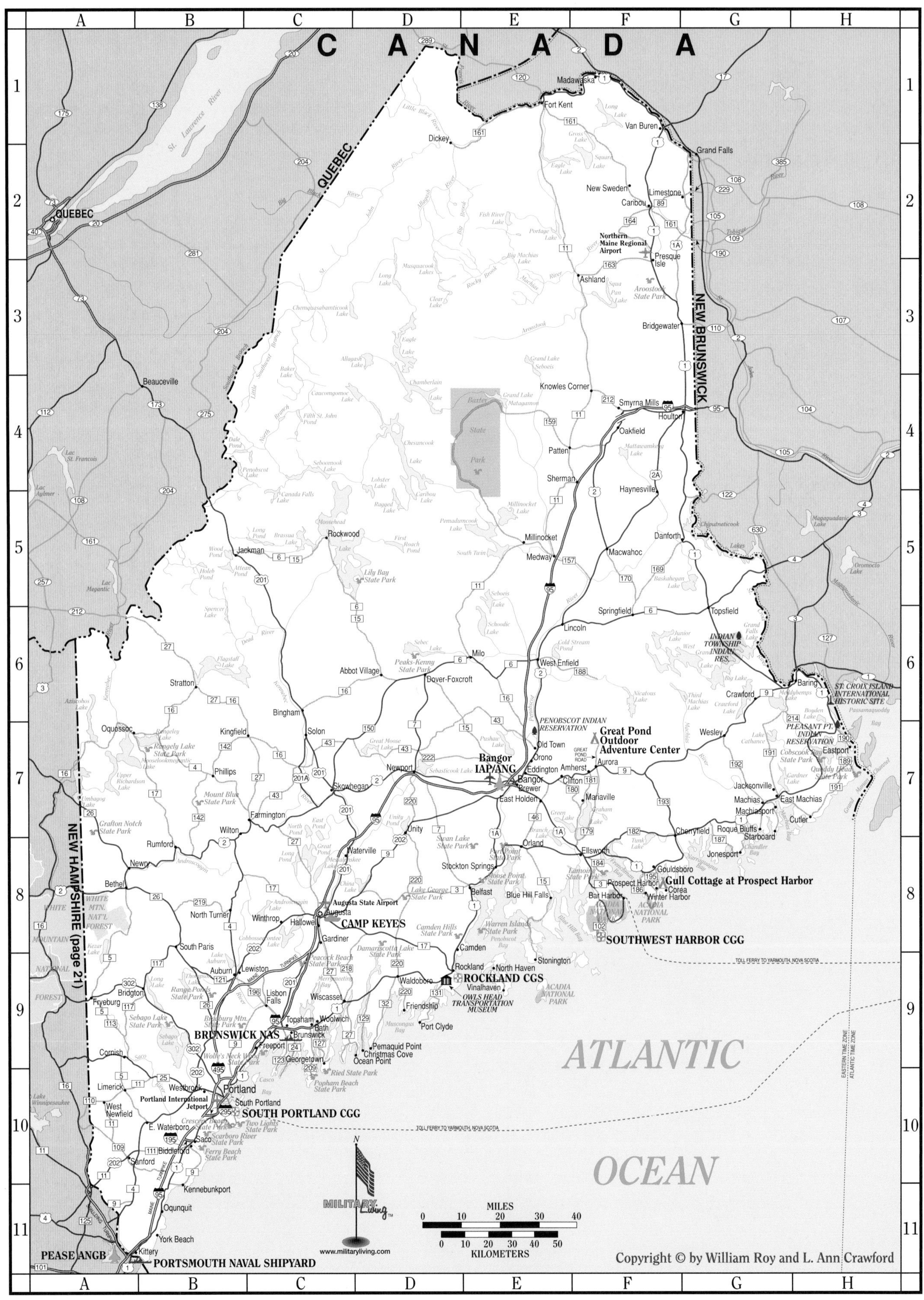
CANADA
QUEBEC
NEW BRUNSWICK
NEW HAMPSHIRE (page 21)
ATLANTIC
OCEAN
Quebec
Beauceville
Madawaska
Fort Kent
Van Buren
Grand Falls
Dickey
New Sweden
Limestone
Caribou
Northern Maine Regional Airport
Presque Isle
Ashland
Aroostook State Park
Bridgewater
Knowles Corner
Smyrna Mills
Houlton
Oakfield
Patten
Sherman
Haynesville
Baxter State Park
Millinocket
Medway
Danforth
Macwahoc
Rockwood
Jackman
Lily Bay State Park
Springfield
Topsfield
Lincoln
INDIAN TOWNSHIP INDIAN RES.
Milo
Abbot Village
Peaks-Kenny State Park
Dover-Foxcroft
West Enfield
Baring
ST. CROIX ISLAND INTERNATIONAL HISTORIC SITE
Crawford
Stratton
Bingham
Solon
Kingfield
Oquossoc
Rangeley Lake State Park
PENOBSCOT INDIAN RESERVATION
Great Pond Outdoor Adventure Center
Old Town
Orono
Wesley
PLEASANT PT. INDIAN RESERVATION
Eastport
Cobscook Bay State Park
Quoddy Head State Park
Bangor IAP/ANG
Newport
Skowhegan
Phillips
Eddington
Amherst
Aurora
Brewer
Clifton
Jacksonville
Machias
East Machias
Machiasport
Cutler
East Holden
Mariaville
Farmington
Grafton Notch State Park
Mount Blue State Park
Wilton
Rumford
Unity
Waterville
Swan Lake State Park
Orland
Ellsworth
Cherryfield
Roque Bluffs
Starboard
Jonesport
Newry
Bethel
Stockton Springs
Fort Point State Park
Gouldsboro
Prospect Harbor
Gull Cottage at Prospect Harbor
Corea
Winter Harbor
Bar Harbor
ACADIA NATIONAL PARK
Belfast
Blue Hill Falls
Lamoine State Park
Moose Point State Park
Augusta State Airport
Augusta
CAMP KEYES
Hallowell
Winthrop
North Turner
Gardiner
Camden Hills State Park
Camden
Warren Island State Park
SOUTHWEST HARBOR CGG
WHITE MTN. NAT'L FOREST
South Paris
Lewiston
Auburn
Peacock Beach State Park
Damariscotta Lake State Park
Rockland
North Haven
Stonington
Waldoboro
ROCKLAND CGS
Vinalhaven
OWLS HEAD TRANSPORTATION MUSEUM
Bridgton
Range Ponds State Park
Lisbon Falls
Wiscasset
Friendship
Port Clyde
Fryeburg
Sebago Lake State Park
Topsham
Woolwich
Bath
BRUNSWICK NAS
Brunswick
Freeport
Bradbury Mtn. State Park
Wolfe's Neck Woods State Park
Georgetown
Pemaquid Point
Christmas Cove
Ocean Point
Reid State Park
Popham Beach State Park
Cornish
Limerick
Westbrook
Portland
Portland International Jetport
South Portland
SOUTH PORTLAND CGG
West Newfield
E. Waterboro
Crescent Beach State Park
Two Lights State Park
Scarboro River State Park
Saco
Biddeford
Ferry Beach State Park
Sanford
Kennebunkport
Ogunquit
York Beach
Kittery
PEASE ANGB
PORTSMOUTH NAVAL SHIPYARD
TOLL FERRY TO YARMOUTH, NOVA SCOTIA
EASTERN TIME ZONE
ATLANTIC TIME ZONE
MILITARY Living
www.militaryliving.com
MILES
0 10 20 30 40
0 10 20 30 40 50
KILOMETERS
A B C D E F G H
1 2 3 4 5 6 7 8 9 10 11

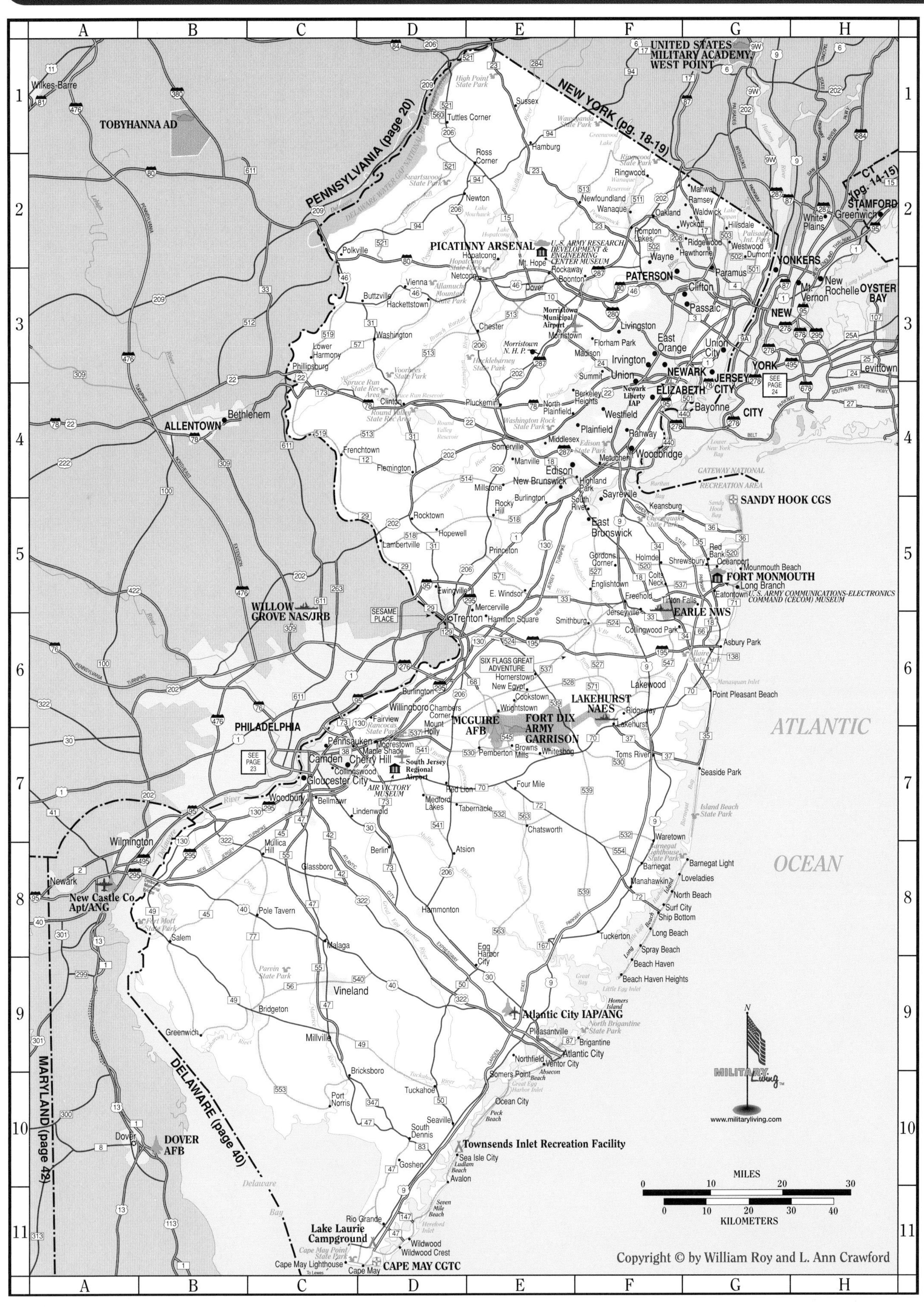

NEW YORK (pg. 18-19)
PENNSYLVANIA (page 20)
CT (pg. 14-15)
MARYLAND (page 42)
DELAWARE (page 40)
UNITED STATES MILITARY ACADEMY, WEST POINT
TOBYHANNA AD
PICATINNY ARSENAL
U.S. ARMY RESEARCH, DEVELOPMENT & ENGINEERING CENTER MUSEUM
Morristown Municipal Airport
Morristown N.H.P.
Newark Liberty IAP
SEE PAGE 24
GATEWAY NATIONAL RECREATION AREA
SANDY HOOK CGS
FORT MONMOUTH
U.S. ARMY COMMUNICATIONS-ELECTRONICS COMMAND (CECOM) MUSEUM
EARLE NWS
WILLOW GROVE NAS/JRB
SESAME PLACE
SIX FLAGS GREAT ADVENTURE
LAKEHURST NAES
MCGUIRE AFB
FORT DIX ARMY GARRISON
PHILADELPHIA
SEE PAGE 23
South Jersey Regional Airport
AIR VICTORY MUSEUM
New Castle Co Apt/ANG
ATLANTIC OCEAN
Atlantic City IAP/ANG
DOVER AFB
Townsends Inlet Recreation Facility
Lake Laurie Campground
CAPE MAY CGTC
ALLENTOWN
Bethlehem
Wilkes-Barre
Trenton
NEWARK
PATERSON
ELIZABETH
JERSEY CITY
YONKERS
NEW YORK CITY
STAMFORD
Wilmington
Vineland
Atlantic City
Camden
MILES
KILOMETERS
MILITARY Living
www.militaryliving.com

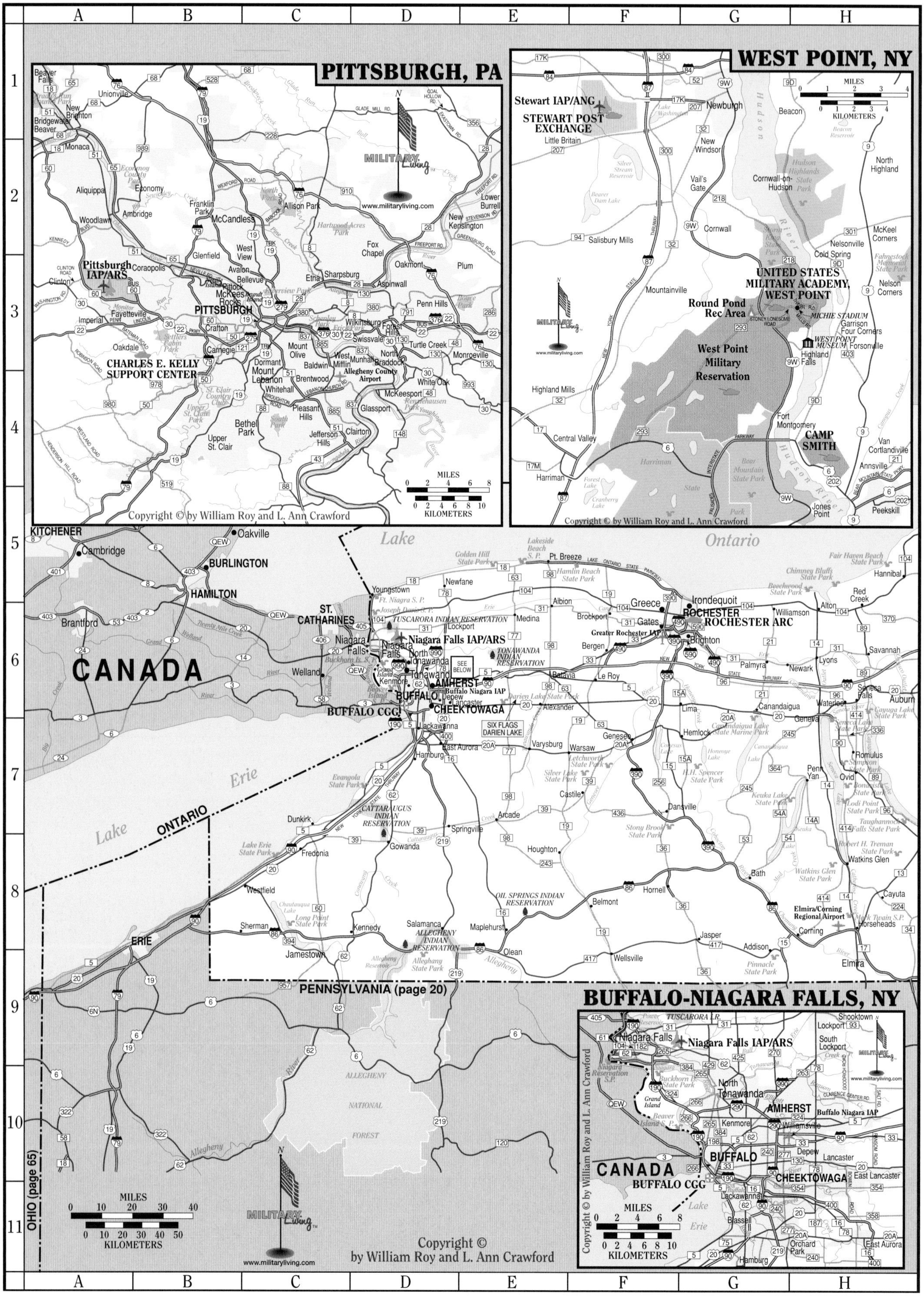

PITTSBURGH, PA

WEST POINT, NY

BUFFALO-NIAGARA FALLS, NY

PENNSYLVANIA (page 20)

OHIO (page 65)

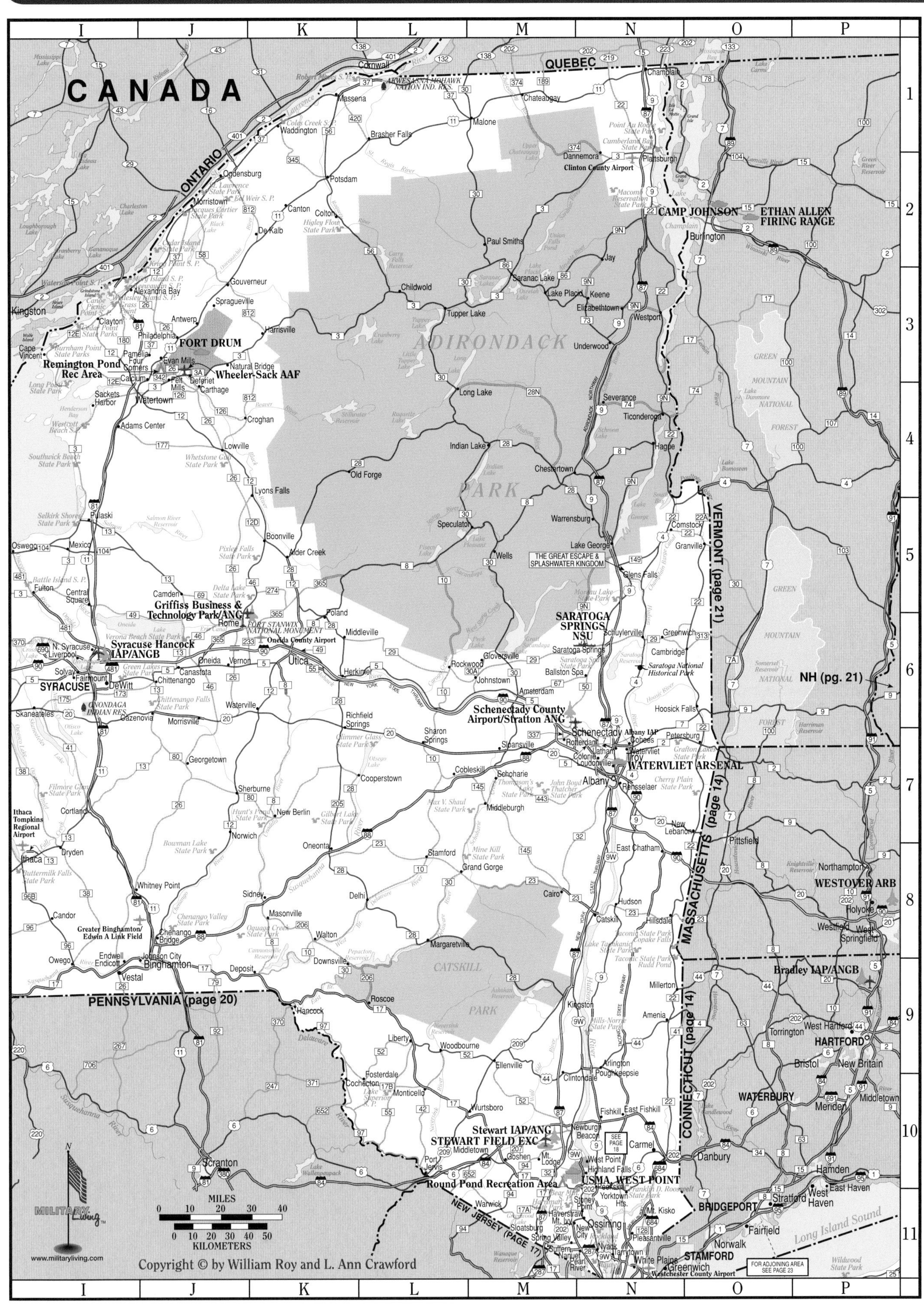
CANADA
QUEBEC
ONTARIO
ADIRONDACK PARK
CATSKILL PARK
FORT DRUM
Wheeler-Sack AAF
Griffiss Business & Technology Park/ANG
Syracuse Hancock IAP/ANGB
SARATOGA SPRINGS NSU
Schenectady County Airport/Stratton ANG
WATERVLIET ARSENAL
CAMP JOHNSON
ETHAN ALLEN FIRING RANGE
WESTOVER ARB
Bradley IAP/ANGB
Stewart IAP/ANG
STEWART FIELD EXC
USMA, WEST POINT
Round Pond Recreation Area
VERMONT (page 21)
NH (pg. 21)
MASSACHUSETTS (page 14)
CONNECTICUT (page 14)
PENNSYLVANIA (page 20)
NEW JERSEY (PAGE 17)
FOR ADJOINING AREA SEE PAGE 23
SEE PAGE 18
MILES 0 10 20 30 40
KILOMETERS 0 10 20 30 40 50
www.militaryliving.com
Copyright © by William Roy and L. Ann Crawford

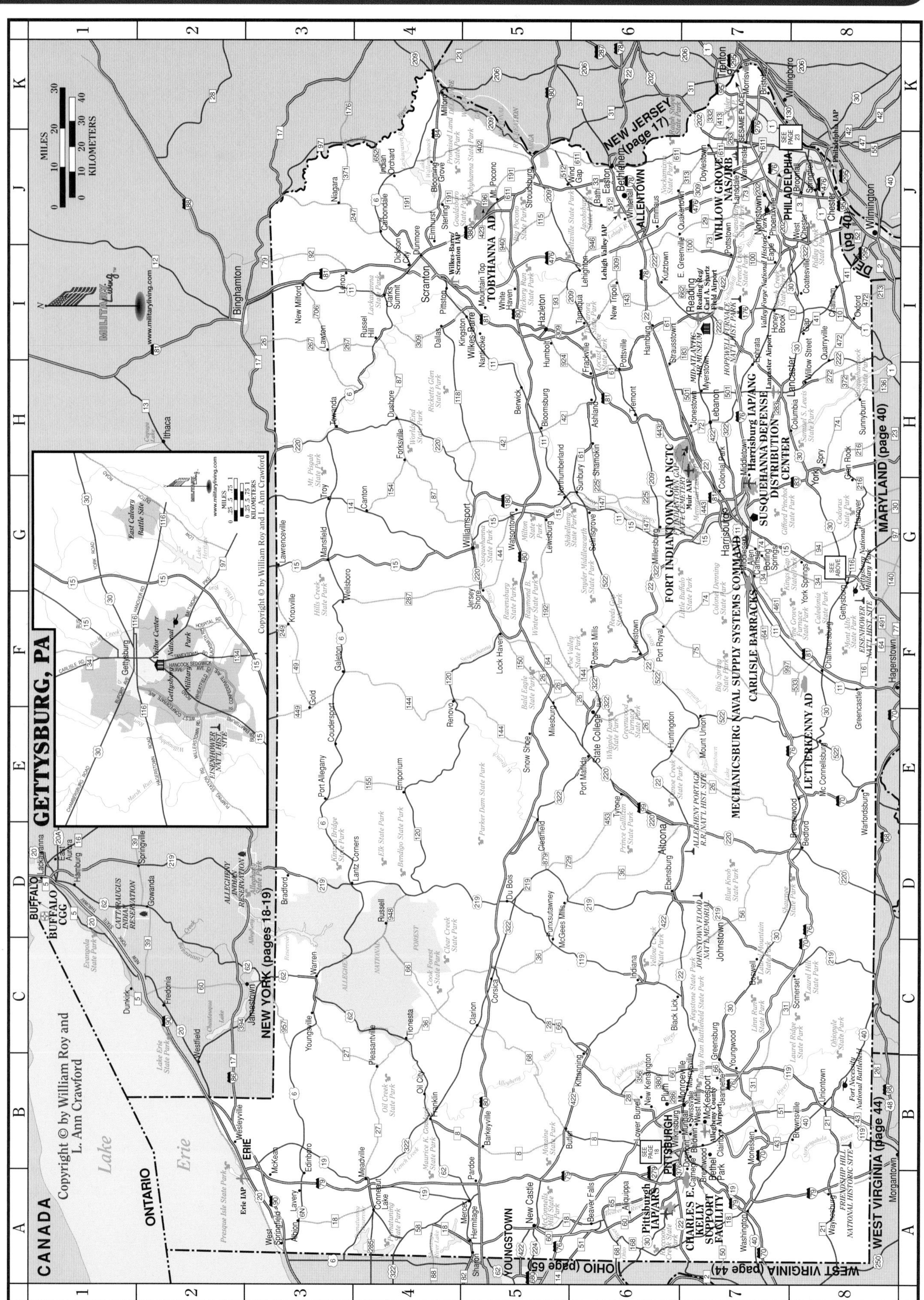
Copyright © by William Roy and L. Ann Crawford
MILES
KILOMETERS
www.militaryliving.com
GETTYSBURG, PA
Copyright © by William Roy and L. Ann Crawford
CANADA
ONTARIO
Lake Erie
NEW YORK (pages 18-19)
NEW JERSEY (page 17)
OHIO (page 65)
WEST VIRGINIA (page 44)
MARYLAND (page 40)
DEL (pg 40)
BUFFALO CGG
ERIE
Erie IAP
PITTSBURGH
Pittsburgh IAP/ARS
CHARLES E. KELLY SUPPORT FACILITY
TOBYHANNA AD
Wilkes-Barre/Scranton IAP
ALLENTOWN
Lehigh Valley IAP
WILLOW GROVE NAS/JRB
PHILADELPHIA
FORT INDIANTOWN GAP NGTC
Harrisburg IAP/ANG
SUSQUEHANNA DEFENSE DISTRIBUTION CENTER
MECHANICSBURG NAVAL SUPPLY SYSTEMS COMMAND
CARLISLE BARRACKS
LETTERKENNY AD
YOUNGSTOWN
Binghamton
Scranton
Harrisburg
Altoona
Williamsport
State College
Johnstown
Reading
Lancaster
Gettysburg
Hagerstown
Wilmington
Trenton

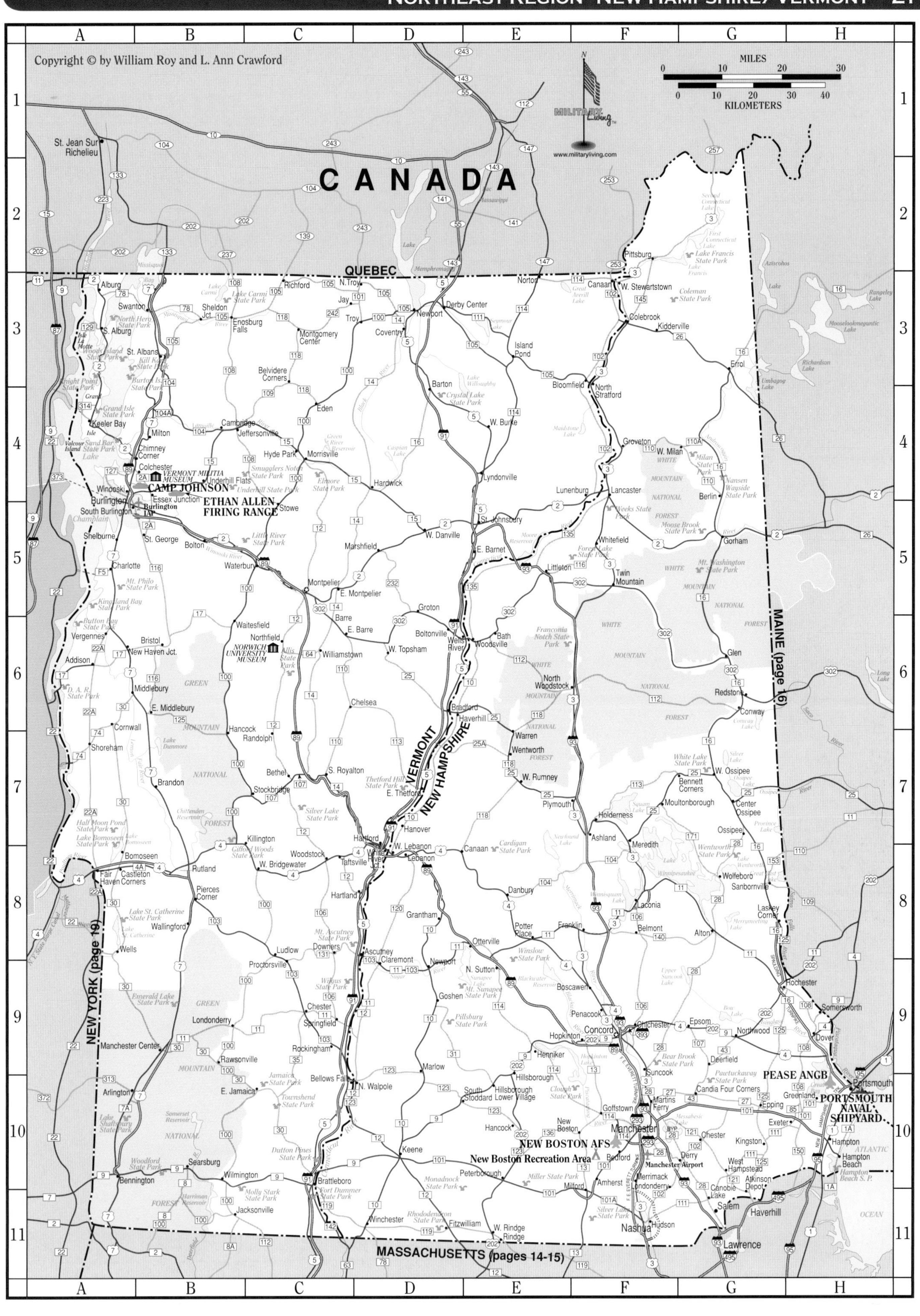
Copyright © by William Roy and L. Ann Crawford
MILES
KILOMETERS
www.militaryliving.com
CANADA
QUEBEC
VERMONT
NEW HAMPSHIRE
MAINE (page 16)
NEW YORK (page 19)
MASSACHUSETTS (pages 14-15)
VERMONT MILITIA MUSEUM
CAMP JOHNSON
ETHAN ALLEN FIRING RANGE
Burlington IAP
NORWICH UNIVERSITY MUSEUM
PEASE ANGB
PORTSMOUTH NAVAL SHIPYARD
NEW BOSTON AFS
New Boston Recreation Area
Manchester Airport
St. Jean Sur Richelieu
Swanton
St. Albans
Burlington
South Burlington
Montpelier
Barre
Newport
St. Johnsbury
Middlebury
Rutland
White River Jct.
Bennington
Brattleboro
Pittsburg
Colebrook
Berlin
Littleton
Conway
Laconia
Concord
Manchester
Nashua
Keene
Rochester
Dover
Portsmouth
Hampton
Lawrence
Haverhill

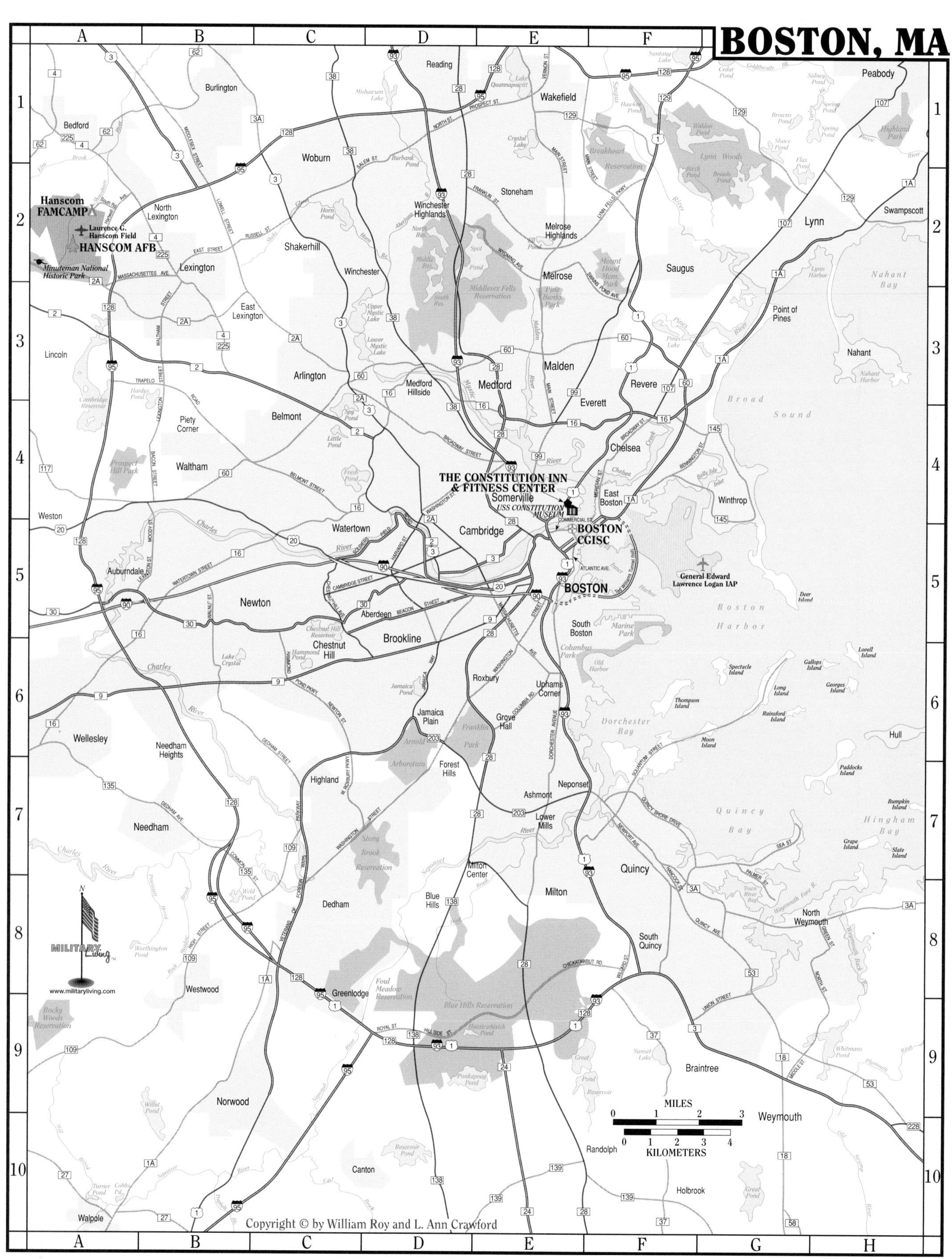
BOSTON, MA
THE CONSTITUTION INN & FITNESS CENTER
USS CONSTITUTION MUSEUM
BOSTON CGISC
HANSCOM AFB
Hanscom FAMCAMP
Laurence G. Hanscom Field
Minuteman National Historic Park
General Edward Lawrence Logan IAP
Burlington
Bedford
Woburn
Reading
Wakefield
Peabody
Lynn
Swampscott
Saugus
Stoneham
Melrose
Malden
Medford
Everett
Revere
Chelsea
Winthrop
East Boston
Somerville
Cambridge
Arlington
Lexington
Lincoln
Belmont
Waltham
Watertown
Newton
Brookline
Weston
Wellesley
Needham
Dedham
Roxbury
Jamaica Plain
Dorchester Bay
Quincy
Milton
Braintree
Weymouth
Randolph
Holbrook
Canton
Norwood
Westwood
Walpole
Nahant
Hull
Boston Harbor
MILES
KILOMETERS
www.militaryliving.com
Copyright © by William Roy and L. Ann Crawford

PHILADELPHIA, PA

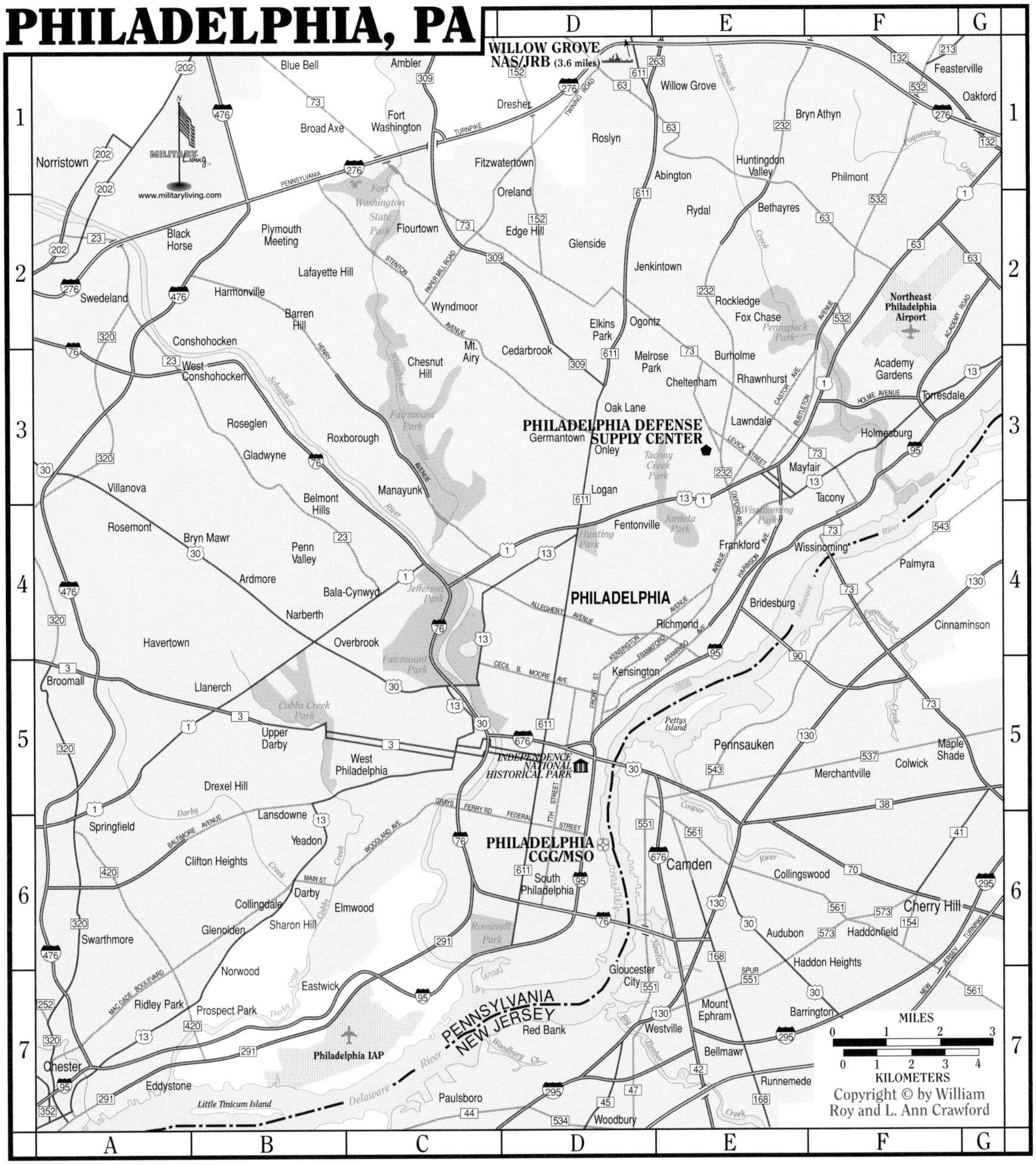

WILLOW GROVE NAS/JRB (3.6 miles)

Blue Bell
Ambler
Broad Axe
Fort Washington
Dresher
Willow Grove
Feasterville
Oakford
Bryn Athyn
Roslyn
Norristown
Fitzwatertown
Abington
Huntingdon Valley
Philmont
Oreland
Rydal
Bethayres
Fort Washington State Park
Plymouth Meeting
Flourtown
Edge Hill
Glenside
Black Horse
Jenkintown
Lafayette Hill
Swedeland
Harmonville
Wyndmoor
Rockledge
Fox Chase
Pennypack Park
Northeast Philadelphia Airport
Barren Hill
Elkins Park
Ogontz
Conshohocken
West Conshohocken
Chestnut Hill
Mt. Airy
Cedarbrook
Melrose Park
Burholme
Cheltenham
Rhawnhurst
Academy Gardens
Torresdale
Fairmount Park
Oak Lane
Roseglen
Roxborough
PHILADELPHIA DEFENSE SUPPLY CENTER
Germantown
Olney
Lawndale
Holmesburg
Gladwyne
Tacony Creek Park
Mayfair
Villanova
Manayunk
Logan
Tacony
Belmont Hills
Fentonville
Juniata Park
Wissinoming Park
Rosemont
Bryn Mawr
Hunting Park
Frankford
Wissinoming
Palmyra
Penn Valley
Ardmore
Bala-Cynwyd
Jefferson Park
PHILADELPHIA
Bridesburg
Narberth
Richmond
Cinnaminson
Havertown
Overbrook
Kensington
Broomall
Llanerch
Cobbs Creek Park
Pettys Island
Upper Darby
West Philadelphia
Pennsauken
Maple Shade
INDEPENDENCE NATIONAL HISTORICAL PARK
Colwick
Merchantville
Drexel Hill
Springfield
Lansdowne
Yeadon
PHILADELPHIA CGG/MSO
Clifton Heights
Camden
Collingswood
South Philadelphia
Darby
Cherry Hill
Collingdale
Elmwood
Glenolden
Sharon Hill
Swarthmore
Roosevelt Park
Audubon
Haddonfield
Norwood
Gloucester City
Haddon Heights
Eastwick
Ridley Park
Prospect Park
PENNSYLVANIA
NEW JERSEY
Red Bank
Westville
Mount Ephram
Barrington
Philadelphia IAP
Bellmawr
Chester
Eddystone
Runnemede
Little Tinicum Island
Paulsboro
Woodbury
Delaware River
Schuylkill River

MILES 0 1 2 3
0 1 2 3 4 KILOMETERS

A B C D E F G
1 2 3 4 5 6 7

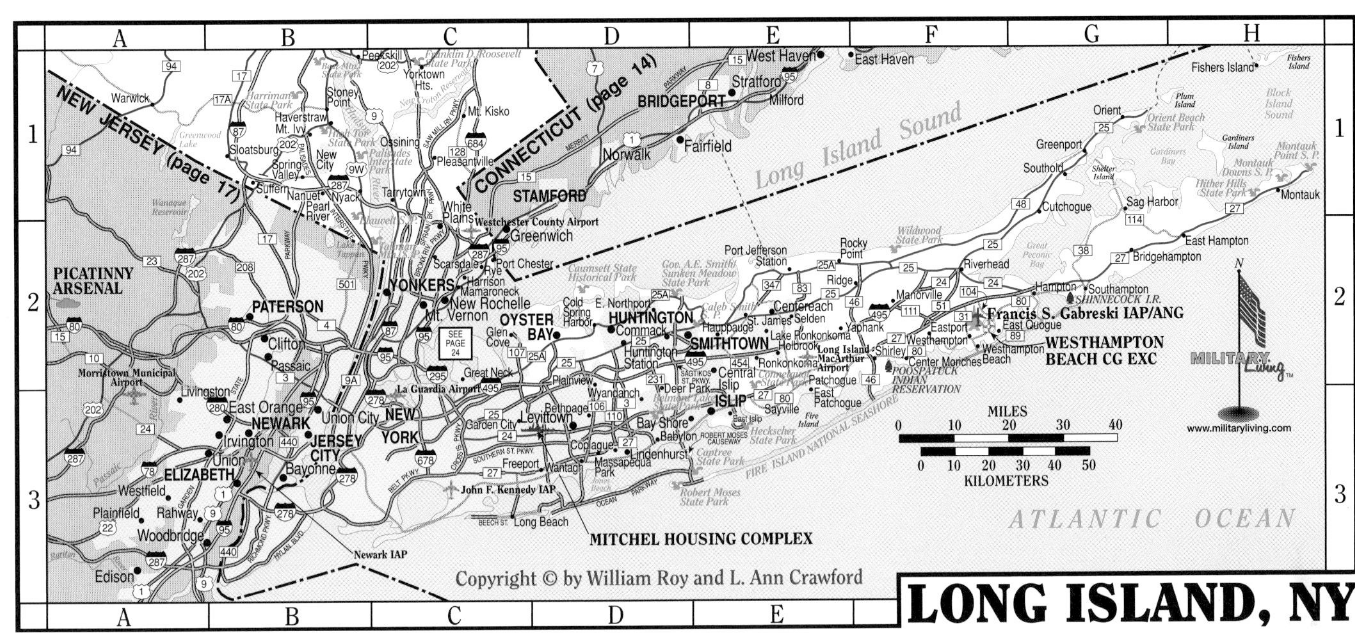

LONG ISLAND, NY

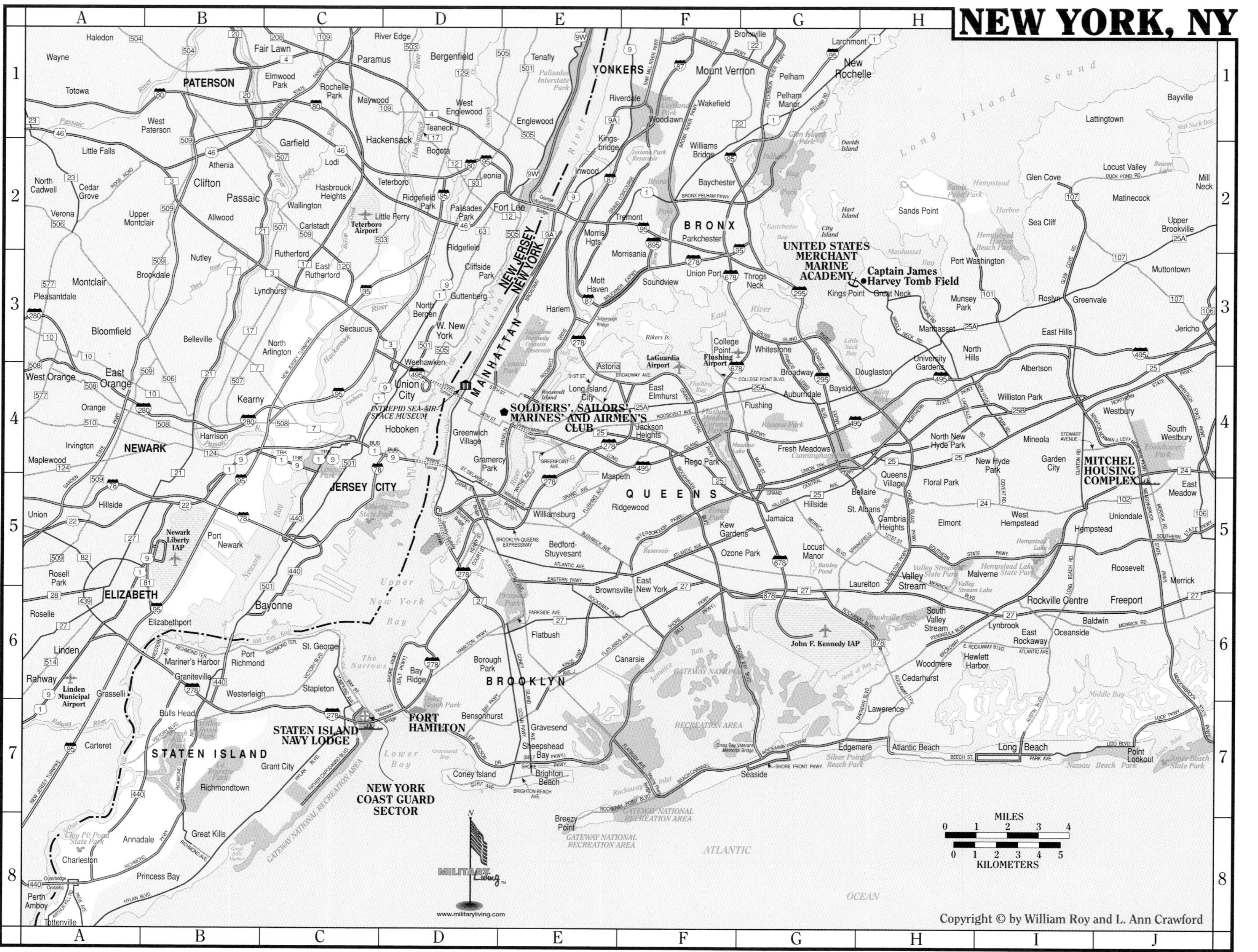
NEW YORK, NY
MANHATTAN
BRONX
QUEENS
BROOKLYN
STATEN ISLAND
NEW JERSEY
NEW YORK
NEWARK
JERSEY CITY
PATERSON
ELIZABETH
YONKERS
UNITED STATES MERCHANT MARINE ACADEMY
Captain James Harvey Tomb Field
MITCHEL HOUSING COMPLEX
SOLDIERS', SAILORS', MARINES' AND AIRMEN'S CLUB
INTREPID SEA-AIR-SPACE MUSEUM
FORT HAMILTON
NEW YORK COAST GUARD SECTOR
STATEN ISLAND NAVY LODGE
LaGuardia Airport
John F. Kennedy IAP
Newark Liberty IAP
Teterboro Airport
Linden Municipal Airport
Flushing Airport
Long Island Sound
Upper New York Bay
Lower Bay
ATLANTIC
OCEAN
GATEWAY NATIONAL RECREATION AREA
MILES
KILOMETERS
MILITARY Living
www.militaryliving.com
Copyright © by William Roy and L. Ann Crawford

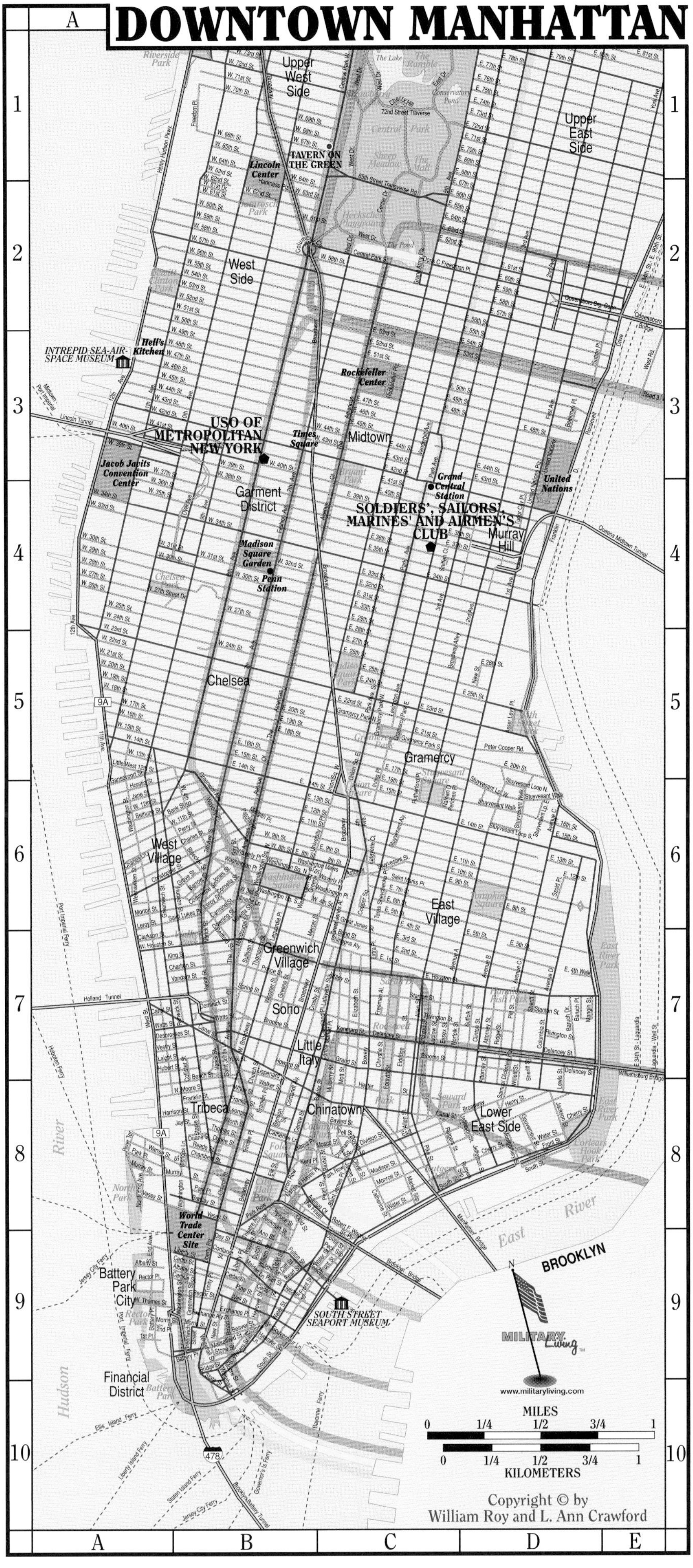

DOWNTOWN MANHATTAN

to visit New York City but not the high hotel rates?

Here's your passport to military $avings— two ways to save on your lodging costs when visiting NYC!

STATEN ISLAND NAVY LODGE
Bldg 408, North Path Road, Staten Island, NY 10305
C-718-442-0413 or or 800-NAVY-INN
WEB: http://www.navy-lodge.com/united_states/new_york/staten_island.html

Soldiers', Sailors', Marines' & Airmen's Club

SOLDIERS', SAILORS', MARINES' & AIRMEN'S CLUB
283 Lexington Avenue, New York, NY 10016
C-212-683-4353, Fax: C-212-683-4374
WEB: www.ssmaclub.org
NOTE: The Soldiers', Sailors', Marines' and Airmen's Club is a tax exempt, not-for-profit organization founded in 1919 to serve the needs of service personnel, veterans and reserves while visiting New York City. This club is not U.S. Military/Government lodging.

CONNECTICUT, pg. 14-15
New London, pg. 15

BRADLEY INTERNATIONAL AIRPORT/ AIR NATIONAL GUARD BASE
100 Nicholson Road, East Granby, CT 06026-9390
C-860-292-2310, DSN-312-220-2310, Police-292-2312
LOCATION: Take I-91 north or south to exit 40 west. Merge onto CT-20. Exit the Bradley Airport Connector onto CT-20 toward East Granby. Take a right onto Bradley Park Road, follow to end and take a right onto Nicholson Road. USMRA: CT/MA/RI map (E-5,6). NMC: Hartford, ten miles south.
RETAIL & DINING: EX-653-6994
Ten-digit dialing required for local calls.

CAMP RELL
38 Smith Street, Niantic, CT 06357-2597
C-860-691-4306/4314, DSN-312-636-7314,Police-739-5900
WEB: www.ct.ngb.army.mil
LOCATION: From I-95 north or south, take exit 74 and follow CT-161 south toward Niantic Center, then turn left onto Smith Street. USMRA: CT/MA/RI map (H-8).NMC: New London, 11 miles north.
RECREATION & TRAVEL: TML-691-4314
RETAIL & DINING: EX-739-9672

LONG ISLAND SOUND COAST GUARD SECTOR
120 Woodward Avenue, New Haven, CT 06512-3698
C-203-468-4444, Police-468-4401
WEB: www.uscg.mil/d1/units/grumsolis
LOCATION: From I-95 north to exit 50, right at light onto Woodward Avenue. Unit is one mile on the right. From I-95 south to the New Haven Airport exit 51 (Frontage Road), left at the second light onto Woodward Avenue. Unit is one mile on the right. USMRA: CT/MA/RI map (E-9). NMC: New Haven, within city limits. NMI: United States Coast Guard Academy, 48 miles north.
RETAIL & DINING: EX-468-2712

NEW LONDON NAVAL SUBMARINE BASE
Route 12 and Crystal Lake Road, P. O. Box 100
Groton, CT 06349-5044
C-860-694-3011, DSN-312-694-3011, Police-694-3777
WEB: www.subasenlon.navy.mil
LOCATION: From I-95 north or south, take exit 86 and turn right onto CT-12. Head north toward Crystal Lake Road. Turn left (west) on Crystal Lake Road, Main Gate is on the right. Clearly marked. USMRA: CT/MA/RI map (H-8); New London, CT map (L-9).
NMC: Providence, RI, 55 miles northeast.
RECREATION & TRAVEL: Golf-694-3763 Marina-694-3164 TML-694-3416 Navy Lodge-800-NAVY-INN or 446-1160
RETAIL & DINING: Clubs-CPO-694-3721 EMC-694-3050 Com-694-2244 Dining-Enlisted Galley-694-3997 Cross Hall Galley-694-3997 EX-446-5400 Gas-694-5203
SUPPORT & FAMILY: Med-628-9633

UNITED STATES COAST GUARD ACADEMY
15 Mohegan Avenue, New London, CT 06320-4195
C-860-444-8444 or 800-883-8724, Police-444-8597
WEB: www.cga.edu
LOCATION: From southbound I-95, take exit 83 in New London. From northbound I-95, take exit 82A. Follow signs; CT-32 (Mohegan Drive) clearly marked. USMRA: CT/MA/RI map (H-8); New London, CT map (K-9). NMC: New London, within city limits. NMI: New London NSB, across the Thames.
RECREATION & TRAVEL: TML-444-8664
RETAIL & DINING: Clubs-EMC-444-8456 OC-444-8458 Dining-444-8148 EX-444-8487/8 Gas-444-8494
SUPPORT & FAMILY: Med-444-8402

MAINE, pg. 16

BANGOR INTERNATIONAL AIRPORT/ AIR NATIONAL GUARD
101 ARW, MeANG, 103 Maineiac Avenue, Suite 505
Bangor, ME 04401-8099
C-207-990-7700 (ask for extensions), DSN-312-698-7700, Police-990-7311, e-mail: pa.101arw@mebngr.ang.af.mil
WEB: www.mebngr.ang.af.mil
LOCATION: Located in Bangor city limits. Northbound from I-95 take exit 184, Union Street (ME-222), left toward Airport. Travel 1.3 miles and turn left onto Griffin Road; entrance is on right. USMRA: ME map (E-7). NMC: Bangor, within city limits.
RECREATION & TRAVEL: SPA-990-7612 TML-942-2081
RETAIL & DINING: Com-990-7751 EX-942-1809

BRUNSWICK NAVAL AIR STATION
1251 Orion Street, Brunswick, ME 04011-5009
C-207-921-1110, DSN-312-476-1110, Police-921-2487/2587
WEB: www.nasb.navy.mil
LOCATION: From I-95, take exit 28 to US-1 (Pleasant Street). Exit US-1 onto Maine Street. Make a left at Dunlap Street, a right onto Federal Street and a left onto Bath Road to the main entrance of the base. USMRA: ME map (C-9). NMC: Portland, 30 miles southwest.
RECREATION & TRAVEL: Golf-921-2155 RVC-584-2000 SPA-990-7018 TML-921-2386 Navy Lodge-800-NAVY-INN or 725-6268
RETAIL & DINING: Galley-921-2293/2870 Clubs-EMC-921-2588 Irv's Blue & Gold Club-921-2591 Com-921-2536/2971 Dining-Galley-921-1663 Mess Hall-921-2293/2881 EX-921-2387 Gas-921-2586/2623
SUPPORT & FAMILY: Med-921-2956/67/87
NOTE: *The 2005 BRAC report recommended this base for closure. As required by Federal law, the DoD has until 15 September 2007 to begin closing and realigning the bases as called for in the approved report. This process must be completed by 15 September 2011.*

CAMP KEYES
Heaqdquarters Maine National Guard, Bldg 7
Augusta, ME 04333-0033
C-207-626-4271, DSN-312-476-4214, Police (Security)-626-4214
WEB: www.me.ngb.army.mil
LOCATION: From I-95 north or south, take exit 30 (Western Avenue). Make a left onto Airport Road and veer right onto Winthrop Street. Camp Keyes entrance is on right. USMRA: ME map (C-8). NMC: Augusta, within city limits.
RETAIL & DINING: Clubs-NCO-626-4405 EX-626-4213

GREAT POND OUTDOOR ADVENTURE CENTER
9 Dow Pines Road, Great Pond, ME 04408-3024
C-207-584-2000, Police-667-7575
LOCATION: Off base. From I-95 north or south, take exit 182A onto I-395. Travel south to exit 6A. Take Alternate US-1 and drive southeast to ME-46. Turn left on ME-46. Proceed to ME-9 and make a right. Travel east approximately 14 miles. Turn left at the Great Pond Business District sign (first left after Rt. 179) and proceed for 1.4 miles. Turn left on Great Pond Road and travel seven miles to the end of the road. USMRA: ME map (F-7). NMC: Bangor, 30 miles northwest. NMI: Brunswick NAS, 110 miles southwest.
NOTE: *For detailed information about this off-base recreation facility, as well as on-base recreation facilities, golf courses and marinas, consult Military Living's "Military RV, Camping and Outdoor Recreation Around the World".*

GULL COTTAGE AT PROSPECT HARBOR
Naval Satellite Operations Center Detachment ALFA
P.O. Box 229, Prospect Harbor, ME 04669-0229
C-207-963-7700, Police-963-7700
LOCATION: On base. From I-95 north or south at Bangor, ME, take Bangor/Brewer exit onto I-395. Take exit 6A onto Alternate US-1 southeast through Ellsworth. Take left at fourth light to stay on US-1. Follow US-1 into Gouldsboro to ME-195 (Pond Road) to Prospect Harbor and NAVSOC Detachment ALFA. USMRA: ME map (F-8). NMC: Bangor, 60 miles northwest. NMI: Brunswick NAS, 60 miles southwest.
RECREATION & TRAVEL: TML-963-7700
NOTE: *For detailed information about this, as well as other recreation facilities, golf courses and marinas, consult Military Living's "Temporary Military Lodging Around the World".*

ROCKLAND COAST GUARD STATION
54 Tillson Avenue, Rockland, ME 04841-3498
C-207-596-6667, Police-594-5656
WEB: www.uscg.mil/d1/units/gruswh/grpunits/starockland.htm
LOCATION: Take US-1 north into Rockland, go past Trade Winds Hotel, take a left onto Main Street and a right at next stop sign onto Tillson Avenue. Follow road to Coast Guard Station. USMRA: ME map (D,E-9). NMC: Rockland, within city limits.
RETAIL & DINING: EX-594-7731

SOUTH PORTLAND COAST GUARD GROUP
259 High Street, South Portland, ME 04106-0007
C-207-767-0320, Police-911
WEB: www.uscg.mil/d1/units/gruport
LOCATION: Exit I-95 east to I-295 north, exit onto I-295 south to Broadway, east to South Portland. Take a left onto Mussey Street and a right onto High Street. USMRA: ME map (B,C-10). NMC: Portland, two miles northwest. NMI: Brunswick NAS, 30 miles north.
RETAIL & DINING: Clubs-CC-767-0374 Dining-767-0379 EX-842-9197

SOUTHWEST HARBOR COAST GUARD GROUP
Commander, Coast Guard Group Southwest Harbor
184 Clark Point Road, Southwest Harbor, ME 04679-4466
C-207-244-5517, Police-911
WEB: www.uscg.mil/d1/units/gruswh
LOCATION: Take Alternate US-1 south to Ellsworth, ME-3 south to Mount Desert Island, ME-102 to downtown Southwest Harbor, second left onto Clark Point Road to end. USMRA: ME map (F-8). NMC: Bangor, 60 miles northwest.
RETAIL & DINING: EX-244-5670

MASSACHUSETTS, pg. 14-15
Boston, pg. 22

BOSTON COAST GUARD INTEGRATED SUPPORT COMMAND
427 Commercial Street, Boston, MA 02109-1027
C-617-223-3333, Boston Police-343-4200
WEB: http://www.uscgnewengland.com
LOCATION: From the south on MA-93 or I-90 (Massachusetts Turnpike), exit at Atlantic Avenue (which becomes Commercial Street), follow for one mile. Center is on the right. Or from the north on I-93, take Charlestown/Sommerville exit, cross Charlestown Bridge, take first left onto Commercial Street. Center is on the left. USMRA: Boston, MA map (E-5). NMC: Boston, within city limits.
RECREATION & TRAVEL: TML-Cuttyhunk Island-223-3181
RETAIL & DINING: Clubs-CC-All Hands-223-3266 Galley-223-3267 EX-223-3133/67
SUPPORT & FAMILY: Med-223-3250
Ten-digit dialing required for local calls.

CAMP EDWARDS
Bldg 3468, Camp Edwards, MA 02542-5003
C-508-968-5887 or 888-301-3103, Police (Security)-968-5997
WEB: www.mass.gov/guard/units/Cp_Ed/index.htm
LOCATION: Off MA-28 (MacArthur Blvd) at the base of Cape Cod. From I-495 south, exit to MA-25 east, continue over the Bourne Bridge, drive south on MA-28. Continue approximately four miles to the traffic circle. Follow it around to the sign for the Massachusetts Military Reservation. USMRA: CT/MA/RI map (M-6,7). NMC: Boston, 70 miles northwest.
RECREATION & TRAVEL: Golf-968-6453 TML-968-5915/6
RETAIL & DINING: EX-563-2495 Gas-564-5486/6153
Ten-digit dialing required for local calls.

THE CONSTITUTION INN & FITNESS CENTER
150 Second Avenue, Charlestown Navy Yard, MA 02129-4410
C-800-495-9622 or C-617-241-8400, Fax: C-617-241-2856
Police-343-4200
WEB: www.constitutioninn.com
LOCATION: From I-90 (Massachusetts Turnpike) to Boston, take I-93, exit 23, following signs to North Station. Proceed straight onto N. Washington Street and across the bridge. Continue along Chelsea Street to the third traffic light and turn right into the Charlestown Navy Yard. Turn left on First Avenue, take first left onto Sixth Street and follow to end. From I-93 south, take exit 28 toward Sullivan Square, to Rutherford Avenue, left on Chelsea Street, then follow signs to USS Constitution. Clearly marked. Also accessible from public transportation. USMRA: Boston, MA map (E-4). NMC: Boston, within city limits.
RECREATION & TRAVEL: TML-241-8400 or 800-495-9622
RETAIL & DINING: Dining-Atrium Cafe-241-5528
The Bistro-242-0036
NOTE: *For detailed information about this lodging facility, consult Military Living's "Temporary Military Lodging Around the World". Ten digit dialing required for local calls.*

CUTTYHUNK ISLAND RECREATIONAL HOUSING FACILITY
Commander (APS), ISC, 427 Commercial Street
Boston, MA 02109-1027
C-617-223-3181, Police-911
WEB: www.uscg.mil/mwr/cottages/cuttyhunkrecreationfacility.htm
LOCATION: Off base. On Cuttyhunk Island. From I-195, take exit 14/15 south on MA-18. Exit toward Elm Street onto North Water Street. Make a left onto Union Street and another left onto MacArthur Drive. Make a right into Fisherman's Wharf Ferry Station. Transportation to the island is via ferry M/V ALERT (508-992-1432). USMRA: CT/MA/RI map (L-8). NMC: Boston, approximately 65 miles north.
RECREATION & TRAVEL: RVC-223-3181 TML-223-3181
NOTE: *Facility only open from Memorial Day to 15 Oct. For detailed information about this off-base recreation facility, as well as on-base recreation facilities, golf courses and marinas, consult Military Living's "Military RV, Camping and Outdoor Recreation Around the World". Ten-digit dialing required for local calls.*

DEVENS RESERVE FORCES TRAINING AREA
Attn: AFRC-FAD-CO, Box 1130 Quebec Street
Devens, MA 01434-4479
C-978-796-2126, DSN-312-225-2126, Police/Fire-796-3333
WEB: www.devens.army.mil
LOCATION: Take MA-2 (west from I-495, or east from Leominster) to exit 37B to Devens/Jackson Road exit, to end of Jackson Road, right onto Givry. Continue straight to the fork in the road. Take the second left onto Queens Blvd. Main Gate is clearly marked.

USMRA: CT/MA/RI map (I-3). NMC: Boston, 35 miles northwest.
RECREATION & TRAVEL: TML-772-4300
RETAIL & DINING: Clubs-CC-772-2822 Dining-796-3074 EX-796-2065
SUPPORT & FAMILY: Med-796-2577(Open May-September)
Ten-digit dialing required for local calls.

FOURTH CLIFF RECREATION AREA

P.O. Box 479, Humarock, MA 02047-0479
C-800-468-9547 or 781-837-6785, Police-781-545-1212
WEB: www.hanscom.af.mil/SVS/fourth.aspx
LOCATION: Off base. I-95 or I-93 to MA-3, approximately ten miles south of Boston, south to exit 12, MA-139 east to Marshfield. Go straight through the traffic lights for 1.5 miles to Furnace Street, turn left. Continue to 'T' intersection, left on Ferry Street. From Ferry Street, make a right onto Sea Street, right over South River Bridge, left on Central Avenue, bear left at fork. (Do not go straight up hill on Cliff Road.) Proceed to gate. USMRA: CT/MA/RI map (M-4). NMC: Boston, 30 miles north. NMI: Hanscom AFB, 46 miles northwest.
RECREATION & TRAVEL: RVC-800-468-9547 or 781-837-9269 TML-800-468-9547 or 837-9269
NOTE: *For detailed information about this off-base recreation facility, as well as on-base recreation facilities, golf courses and marinas, consult Military Living's "Military RV, Camping and Outdoor Recreation Around the World".*
Ten-digit dialing required for local calls.

HANSCOM AIR FORCE BASE

66 ABW/PA, 20 Schilling Circle
Hanscom Air Force Base, MA 01731-2118
C-781-377-4441, DSN-312-478-4441, Police-377-2314/4357
WEB: www.hanscom.af.mil
LOCATION: From I-95/MA-128, take exit 30B (Hanscom Field exit), go 1.5 miles to the blinking light, take a right. Proceed for 0.25 miles straight, bear right to Hanscom AFB, Vandenberg Gate. After 2200 hours, take exit 31B off I-95/MA-128. Exit to the right, and follow to the jughandle turn located just past the Massachusetts Army National Guard Bldg on the right. Take the jughandle. This is Hartwell Avenue, follow road to Hartwell Gate. USMRA: CT/MA/RI map (J-3), Boston, MA map (A-2). NMC: Boston, 20 miles southeast.
RECREATION & TRAVEL: Golf-687-2396 Miniature Golf-377-3901 RVC-377-4670 SPA-377-1143 TML-377-2112, ext. 0
RETAIL & DINING: Clubs-EMC-377-2123 OC-377-5740 Com-377-2544 EX-377-5258 Gas-377-5155
SUPPORT & FAMILY: Med-888-628-9633
Ten-digit dialing required for local calls.

HANSCOM FAMCAMP

66 SVS, 20 Schilling Circle, Hanscom AFB, MA 01731-1807
C-781-377-4670, DSN-312-478-4670, Police (Security)-377-2315 Bedford Police-275-1212
WEB: http://www.hanscom.af.mil/svs/outdoor.aspx
LOCATION: Off base. From I-95, exit 31B west to MA-4/225. Travel 0.6 miles to right exit onto circle to Hartwell Avenue going southwest. Continue on Hartwell Avenue for 0.5 miles, turn right on McGuire Road and continue for 0.3 miles, then turn left onto Summer Street for 0.4 miles. Turn left onto South Street for 0.4 miles to FAMCAMP. USMRA: CT/MA/RI map (J-3); Boston, MA map (A-2). NMC: Boston, 20 miles southeast. NMI: Hanscom AFB, two miles southwest.
RECREATION & TRAVEL: RVC-377-4670 or 5316 off season
NOTE: *For detailed information about this off-base recreation facility, as well as on-base recreation facilities, golf courses and marinas, consult Military Living's "Military RV, Camping and Outdoor Recreation Around the World".*
Ten-digit dialing required for local calls.

MARTHA'S VINEYARD/NANTUCKET VACATION HOUSES

USCG Air Station Cape Cod, Bldg 3172
Air Station Cape Cod, MA 02542-5024
C-508-968-6461 Fax: C-508-968-6637
WEB: http://www.uscg.mil/d1/units/ascapecod/MWR/RF/recfacilities.htm
LOCATION: Off base. One house on Nantucket, three houses on Martha's Vineyard. Island accessible via ferry from West Yarmouth, Cape Cod. From US-6, take MA-132 exit and follow this road past the airport. Take a right onto Yarmouth Road, another right onto Main Street and a left onto Pleasant Street to the ferries. USMRA: CT/MA/RI map (M-8, O-9). NMC: Boston, 80 miles northwest. NMI: Otis ANGB/Cape Cod CGAS, 21 miles south of Martha's Vineyard and 48 miles southeast of Nantucket Vacation Houses.
RECREATION & TRAVEL: TML-968-6461
NOTE: *For detailed information about this off-base recreation facility, as well as on-base recreation facilities, golf courses and marinas, consult Military Living's "Military RV, Camping and Outdoor Recreation Around the World".*
Ten-digit dialing required for local calls.

NATICK SOLDIER SYSTEMS CENTER

15 Kansas Street, Natick, MA 01760-5012
C-508-233-4000, DSN-312-256-4000, Police-233-4201
WEB: www.natick.army.mil
LOCATION: From I-90 (Massachusetts Turnpike), exit 13 toward Natick to MA-30 east to MA-27 south. Or, exit MA-9 west for 6 miles to MA-27 south. Watch for signs to the Center's main entrance off Kansas Street. Please call for more specific instructions. USMRA: CT/MA/RI map (J-4). NMC: Boston, MA 20 miles northeast.
RETAIL & DINING: Cafeteria-233-5627 Clubs-OC-233-4791 Dining-233-4765 EX-233-4797
SUPPORT & FAMILY: Med-233-4155
Ten-digit dialing required for local calls.

OTIS AIR NATIONAL GUARD BASE/ CAPE COD COAST GUARD AIR STATION

102 Fighter Wing (ANG), Massachusetts Military Reservation
Coast Guard Air Station Cape Cod, MA 02542-5024
C-508-968-1000, Police-968-6690
WEB: www.uscg.mil/d1/units/ascapecod
LOCATION: Southeast of Plymouth, MA. South on MA-28 (MacArthur Blvd) to Otis Rotary. Take third right off rotary onto Connery Avenue, past Cape Cod National Cemetery approximately 1.5 miles to Main Gate (Bourne/Buzzards Bay Gate). From east or west on US-6, take exit 2 south onto MA-130. Go south approximately 4.3 miles to right (west) on Snake Pond Road approximately 1.5 miles to Sandwich Gate. From east or west on MA-151, turn north on Old Sandwich Road, go approximately 1.7 miles to Falmouth Gate. USMRA: CT/MA/RI map (M-7). NMC: Boston, 60 miles northwest.
RECREATION & TRAVEL: Golf (9 hole)-968-6453 RVC-968-6447 SPA-508-968-4831/2 TML-968-6461
RETAIL & DINING: Clubs-CPO-563-3747 Com-563-2587 Galley-968-6425 EX-563-2495 Gas-564-5486
SUPPORT & FAMILY: Med-968-6572
Ten-digit dialing required for local calls.

WESTOVER AIR RESERVE BASE

439 Airlift Wing (AFRC)
Westover Air Reserve Base, MA 01022-1825
C-413-557-1110, DSN-312-589-1110, Police-557-3557
WEB: www.afrc.af.mil/439aw/default.htm
LOCATION: From Boston, take I-90 west (Massachusetts Turnpike) to exit 5 in Chicopee; bear right after toll booth to traffic light; take a left onto Memorial Drive (MA-33) and follow signs to Westover ARB. USMRA: CT/MA/RI map (F-4). NMC: Springfield, eight miles south.
RECREATION & TRAVEL: RVC-557-2974 SPA-557-2622/3453 TML-557-2700
RETAIL & DINING: Clubs-557-5531 EX-557-2902 Gas-557-3869
SUPPORT & FAMILY: Med-557-3565

NEW HAMPSHIRE, pg. 21

NEW BOSTON AIR FORCE STATION

23 Space Operations Squadron, 317 Chestnut Hill Road
New Boston, NH 03070-5125
C-603-471-2000, DSN-312-489-2000, Police-471-2285
LOCATION: From I-93 north, take I-293 west to NH-114 north. Take a left on New Boston Road, drive approximately seven to eight miles. New Boston Air Station is on your right. USMRA: NH, VT map (F-10). NMC: Manchester, eight miles northeast. NMI: Hanscom AFB, 50 miles south.
RECREATION & TRAVEL: RVC-471-2234/2452

PEASE AIR NATIONAL GUARD BASE

157 Air Refueling Wing, 302 Newmarket Street
Newington, NH 03803-0157
C-603-430-2453, DSN-312-852-2453, Police-911
WEB: www.nhpeas.ang.af.mil
LOCATION: Take I-95, exit onto the US-4/NH-16 (Spaulding Turnpike) northwest, then follow signs. Base is at intersection of Spaulding Turnpike and Gosling Road. USMRA: NH, VT map (H-9,10). NMC: Portsmouth, three miles northeast.
RECREATION & TRAVEL: SPA-430-3323
RETAIL & DINING: EX-436-0302

PORTSMOUTH NAVAL SHIPYARD

Attn: Code 800, Bldg 86
Portsmouth Naval Shipyard, NH 03804-5000
C-207-438-1000, DSN-312-684-1000, Police-438-2230 Emergency-438-2444
WEB: www.ports.navy.mil
LOCATION: From I-95 north, cross Piscataqua River Bridge into Maine. Take exit 2 to NH-236 to US-1 south to US-203, and turn left onto Walker Street to Gate 1. From I-95 south, take exit 2, follow above directions. Located on an island on Piscataqua River between Portsmouth and Kittery, ME. USMRA: NH, VT map (H-10). NMC: Portsmouth, within city limits.
RECREATION & TRAVEL: Marina-438-2351 TML-438-1513
RETAIL & DINING: Clubs-CC-438-2269 OC-438-2269 Com-438-5532 EX-438-3024
SUPPORT & FAMILY: Med-438-4940

NEW JERSEY, pg. 17

ATLANTIC CITY INTERNATIONAL AIRPORT/ AIR NATIONAL GUARD

177 FW, 400 Langley Road
Egg Harbor Township, NJ 08234-9500
C-609-645-6000, DSN-312-455-6000, Police (Security)-645-6222
WEB: www.njatla.ang.af.mil
LOCATION: Take NJ-50 (Atlantic City Expressway) to exit 12 east, go east, follow signs to airport. USMRA: NJ map (E-9). NMC: Atlantic City, within city limits.
RETAIL & DINING: EX-383-6336

CAPE MAY COAST GUARD TRAINING CENTER

1 Munro Avenue, Cape May, NJ 08204-5002
C-609-898-6900, Police-898-6225
WEB: www.uscg.mil/hq/capemay
LOCATION: Take Garden State Parkway or US-9 to Cape May. In Cape May, take Pittsburgh Avenue to Pennsylvania Avenue to Main Gate. USMRA: NJ map (D-11). NMC: Atlantic City, 45 miles northeast.
RECREATION & TRAVEL: TML-898-6922
RETAIL & DINING: Clubs-CC-898-6937 CPO-898-6344 Com-898-6940 EX-898-6940
SUPPORT & FAMILY: Med-898-6959

EARLE NAVAL WEAPONS STATION

201 State Highway 34 South, Colts Neck, NJ 07722-5007
C-732-866-2000, DSN-312-449-2000, Police-866-2291
WEB: www.cnrne.navy.mil/alist/earle/earle.htm
LOCATION: From I-95 (New Jersey Turnpike), take exit 8 to NJ-33, east through Freehold to NJ-34, north to Main Gate. From Garden State Parkway to NJ-33, west to NJ-34, north to Station. USMRA: NJ map (F-5). NMC: Newark, 50 miles north.
RECREATION & TRAVEL: TML-866-2167
RETAIL & DINING: Clubs-Windjammer-866-2002 EX-866-2893
SUPPORT & FAMILY: Med-866-2300
Ten-digit dialing required for local calls.

FORT DIX ARMY GARRISON

Attn: AFZT-PAZ, 5417 Alabama Avenue, Fort Dix, NJ 08640-5002 **C-609-562-1011,** DSN-312-944-1110, Police-562-6001
WEB: www.dix.army.mil
LOCATION: From I-95 (NJ Turnpike), exit 7, right onto US-206, short distance left on NJ-68, continue to General Circle and Main Gate. USMRA: NJ map (E-7). NMC: Trenton, 17 miles northwest.
RECREATION & TRAVEL: Golf-562-4043/5443 TML-562-3188 or 723-2026
RETAIL & DINING: Clubs-723-3272 Com-754-4154 EX-723-6100 Gas-723-0044
SUPPORT & FAMILY: Med-888-999-5195

FORT MONMOUTH

Attn: PAO/AMSEL-IO, Fort Monmouth, NJ 07703-5016
C-732-532-9000, DSN-312-992-9110, Police-532-3882
WEB: www.monmouth.army.mil
LOCATION: Take I-95 (New Jersey Turnpike) to Garden State Parkway, exit 105 for Eatontown, NJ-35 north to Main Gate. USMRA: NJ map (G-5). NMC: Long Branch, seven miles southeast.
RECREATION & TRAVEL: Golf-389-9211 or 532-4307 Marina-532-4079 TML-532-1092/1635/5510 or 935-2000
RETAIL & DINING: Cafeteria-532-2761 Clubs-OC-532-4520 Lane Hall-532-3892 Com-532-1260 Dining-532-0311 EX-542-7235 Gas-542-7417
SUPPORT & FAMILY: Med-532-1764
NOTE: *The 2005 BRAC report recommended this base for closure. As required by Federal law, the DoD has until 15 September 2007 to begin closing and realigning the bases as called for in the approved report. This process must be completed by 15 September 2011.*
Ten-digit dialing required for local calls.

LAKE LAURIE CAMPGROUND

669 Route 9, Cape May, NJ 08204-4637
C-215-443-1000, DSN-312-991-1000, Police-911
LOCATION: Off base. Operated by Willow Grove NAS, PA. Campground entrance is on US-9, two miles north of junction with end of Garden State Parkway. USMRA: NJ map (D-11). NMC: Vineland, approximately 50 miles northwest. NMI: Cape May Coast Guard Training Center, five miles southeast.
RECREATION & TRAVEL: RVC-609-884-3567
NOTE: *For detailed information about this off-base recreation facility, as well as on-base recreation facilities, golf courses and marinas, consult Military Living's "Military RV, Camping and Outdoor Recreation Around the World".*
Ten-digit dialing required for local calls.

LAKEHURST NAVAL AIR ENGINEERING STATION

Code 75000B/150-2, Highway 547, Lakehurst, NJ 08733-5041
C-732-323-2011, DSN-312-624-1110, Police-323-2332/2457
WEB: www.lakehurst.navy.mil
LOCATION: Take the Garden State Parkway to exit 88. Take NJ-70 west to junction of NJ-547, turn right and proceed one mile to base. USMRA: NJ map (F-6,7). NMC: Trenton, 30 miles northwest.
RECREATION & TRAVEL: Golf-323-7483 SPA-323-2438 TML-323-2266
RETAIL & DINING: Com-323-2516 EX-323-7680/3
SUPPORT & FAMILY: Med-323-1223/4
Ten-digit dialing required for local calls.

MCGUIRE AIR FORCE BASE

2901 Falcon Lane, McGuire Air Force Base, NJ 08641-5002
C-609-754-1100, DSN-312-650-1100, Police-754-2001
WEB: http://public.mcguire.amc.af.mill
LOCATION: From I-95 (New Jersey Turnpike), take exit 7 to NJ-206 south to NJ-68 south, then to NJ-537, turn left. Take NJ-537 northeast to intersection (traffic light) of NJ-545 and NJ-680, turn right. Take NJ-680 to base's Main Gate, about two miles. Clearly marked. USMRA: NJ map (E-6,7). NMC: Trenton, 18 miles northwest. NMI: Fort Dix AG, adjacent.
RECREATION & TRAVEL: Golf-754-2169 SPA-754-2749/2864/5023 TML-754-4667/4853 or 888-AF-LODGE
RETAIL & DINING: Clubs-NCO-754-2396 OC-754-3294 Com-754-4155 Dining-754-2450 EX-723-6100 Gas-754-4608
SUPPORT & FAMILY: Med-888-999-5195

PICATINNY ARSENAL

U.S. Army TACOM/ARDEC, Route 15, Bldg 1
Picatinny Arsenal, NJ 07806-5736
C-973-724-4021 or C-800-831-2759, DSN-312-880-4021
Police-724-6666
WEB: www.pica.army.mil
LOCATION: From I-80 west, take exit 34B to NJ-15 north. Follow signs to Center, one mile north. From I-80 east, exit 34 to NJ-15, follow signs to Center. USMRA: NJ map (E-2). NMC: Newark, 30 miles east.
RECREATION & TRAVEL: Golf-724-4430 TML-724-4186/8855
RETAIL & DINING: Catering-724-2582 Clubs-OC-989-2460 Com-724-2918 EX-989-2466
SUPPORT & FAMILY: Med-724-2113
Ten-digit dialing required for local calls.

SANDY HOOK COAST GUARD STATION

20 Crispin Road, Sandy Hook, NJ 07732-4999
C-732-872-3428, Police-911
WEB: www.uscg.mil
LOCATION: From Garden State Parkway to exit 117, take NJ-36 south 15 miles. Take first right after drawbridge onto Hartshome Drive into Gateway National Recreation Area. Go straight six miles, veer right onto Crispin Road. Clearly marked. USMRA: NJ map (G-5). NMC: New Brunswick, 25 miles west. NMI: Fort Monmouth, 15 miles southwest.
RETAIL & DINING: EX-291-1080
Ten-digit dialing required for local calls.

TOWNSENDS INLET RECREATION FACILITY

8101 Landis Avenue, Sea Isle City, NJ 08243-1145
C-609-677-2028, Police-911
WEB: http://www.uscg.mil/d5/airstation/atlanticcity/htmls/about_us/mwr/mwr.html
LOCATION: Off base. Old Coast Guard lifesaving station in Sea Isle City, NJ. Two blocks from beach. From Garden State Parkway exit 17 to NJ-625 east. Turn south on NJ-49 (Landis Avenue). USMRA: NJ map (D-10). NMC: Atlantic City, 25 miles north.
RECREATION & TRAVEL: RVC-263-3722 (Mar-Oct) or 677-2028 (Nov-Feb) TML-263-3722 (Mar-Oct) or 677-2028 (Nov-Feb)
NOTE: *For detailed information about this off-base recreation facility, as well as on-base recreation facilities, golf courses and marinas, consult Military Living's "Military RV, Camping and Outdoor Recreation Around the World".*

NEW YORK, pg. 18-19, 23
Buffalo/Niagara Falls, pg. 18
Downtown Manhattan, pg. 25
Long Island, pg. 23
New York City, pg. 24
West Point, pg. 18

BUFFALO COAST GUARD GROUP

1 Fuhrmann Blvd, Buffalo, NY 14203-3189
C-716-843-9505, Police-843-9525/9527
WEB: www.uscg.mil
LOCATION: From NY-5 (Fuhrmann Blvd) toward Buffalo, take exit marked Buffalo Coast Guard west to CGG. USMRA: NY map (D-6, G-10). NMC: Buffalo, within city limits.

CAMP SMITH

Bldg 501, Cortlandt Manor, NY 10567-5000
C-914-788-7324, DSN-312-489-7373, Police-734-1621
WEB: www.dmna.state.ny.us/rental/cp-smith.html
LOCATION: From US-9 north or south at Peekskill, take US-6, two miles northwest to base. USMRA: West Point, NY map (H-4). NMC: Peekskill, three miles east.
RECREATION & TRAVEL: TML-788-7395
RETAIL & DINING: Clubs-EMC-788-7414

FORT DRUM

Public Affairs Office, 10000 10th Mountain Division Drive
Room 108, Fort Drum, NY 13602-5028
C-315-772-6011, DSN-772-6011, Police-772-5156/7
e-mail: PAO@drum.army.mil
WEB: www.drum.army.mil
LOCATION: From Interstate 81, take exit 48 (Black River/Fort Drum). Bear right off of the exit (coming from Interstate I-81 south) or left off the exit (coming from I-81 north) onto NYS Route 342. Go straight approximately five miles to the NYS Route 11 junction. Take a left onto Route 11 north. Follow signs to Fort Drum. North Gate is on the right. Stop at the Visitor Center before the gate and get a pass. Visitors must have ID card, driver's license, proof of registration and insurance. USMRA: NY map (J-3). NMC: Watertown, six miles south.
RECREATION & TRAVEL: RVC-772-5435 SPA-772-5681 TML-772-5435 or 773-7777
RETAIL & DINING: Clubs-CC-772-6222 Benway's Tavern-772-2736 Christie's-772-2734 Pennants-773-8003 Spinners-772-8970 Winner's Circle-772-7673 Com-772-5294/7457 EX-773-0061 Gas-773-4149
SUPPORT & FAMILY: Med-772-4615

FORT HAMILTON

U.S. Army Garrison, Fort Hamilton, Attn: ANFH-PA
114 White Avenue, Suite 2-39, Brooklyn, NY 11252-5700
C-718-630-4101, DSN-312-232-4101, Police-630-4456
WEB: www.hamilton.army.mil
LOCATION: From Belt Parkway exit 2 (Fort Hamilton Parkway) to 100th Street, take right to Fort Hamilton Parkway, left to Main Gate at 101st Street. USMRA: New York, NY map (D-7). NMC: New York City, within city limits.
RECREATION & TRAVEL: TML-630-4052/4564/4892
RETAIL & DINING: Clubs-CC-630-4903 Com-630-4591 EX-748-3440 Gas-680-2723
SUPPORT & FAMILY: Med-630-4129
Ten-digit dialing required for local calls.

FRANCIS S. GABRESKI INTERNATIONAL AIRPORT/AIR NATIONAL GUARD

150 Riverhead Road, Bldg 345, Westhampton Beach, NY 11978-1201
C-631-723-7400, DSN-312-456-7400, Police-723-7478
WEB: www.nysuff.ang.af.mil
LOCATION: Go east on Sunrise Highway to exit 63 south (Old Riverhead Road, County Route 31). The base entrance will be on your left about two miles down the road. Don't mistake the country airport entrance at the traffic light for the base, the base is another half mile past the traffic light. Look for the F-102 (Fighter Aircraft) in front of the gate. USMRA: Long Island, NY map (F-2). NMC: New York City, 60 miles west.
RECREATION & TRAVEL: SPA-723-7362
RETAIL & DINING: Clubs-CC-723-7481 EX-723-7557
SUPPORT & FAMILY: Med-723-7447

GRIFFISS BUSINESS AND TECHNOLOGY PARK/AIR NATIONAL GUARD

Northeast Air Defense Sector (NEADS)
387 Hangar Road, Rome, NY 13441-4507
C-315-334-6011/6515 or 800-223-5612, DSN-312-587-6515, Police-911, e-mail: pa@neads.ang.af.mil
WEB: www.neads.ang.af.mil
LOCATION: From I-90 east or west, take exit 33 to NY-365 toward Rome. Follow signs to Griffiss Park exit. Continue north around the traffic roundabout. Take a right onto Hangar Road. Just past Chappie James Blvd (which is blocked off), there will be a sign for 387 Hangar Road. Take a right into NEADS' Headquarters parking lot. In the lobby, call ext. 6515 for entry. USMRA: NY map (J,K-5,6). NMC: Syracuse, 45 miles west.
RETAIL & DINING: EX-330-7597

MITCHEL HOUSING COMPLEX

82B Mitchel Avenue, East Meadow, NY 11554-2214
C-516-486-2022, Police-222-1285
WEB: www.housing.navy.mil
LOCATION: From north, take Northern State Parkway to Senator Norman J. Levy Memorial Parkway south, take exit M5 and turn right at Merrick Avenue, right on Front Street, left at Mitchel Avenue. From south, take I-95 north, take I-278 east. Once past the Verrazano Bridge, go east on Belt Parkway, stay left to Southern State Parkway to Senator Norman J. Levy Memorial Parkway (exit 22 S) north to exit M5 and follow the directions as above. USMRA: New York, NY map (J-4). NMC: New York City, 27 miles west. NMI: Fort Hamilton, 20 miles southwest.
RETAIL & DINING: Com-222-0880 EX-222-1293/4
SUPPORT & FAMILY: Med-222-0228

NEW YORK COAST GUARD SECTOR

212 Coast Guard Drive, Staten Island, NY 10305-5005
C-718-354-4037, Police (Security)-354-4398
WEB: www.uscg.mil/d1/units/actny
LOCATION: Take I-95 north or south to exit 13 east to Goethals Bridge (I-278 east) to Staten Island. Last exit before Verrazano Bridge (Lily Pond Avenue). At light, turn left onto School Road, follow School Road to next light, turn right onto Bay Street to Main Gate. USMRA: New York, NY map (C-7). NMC: New York, within city limits.
RECREATION & TRAVEL: TML-354-4407 Navy Lodge-800-NAVY-INN or 442-0413
RETAIL & DINING Dining-354-4360 EX-354-6519
SUPPORT & FAMILY: Med (Information)-354-4414
Ten-digit dialing required for local calls.

NIAGARA FALLS INTERNATIONAL AIRPORT/ AIR RESERVE STATION

914 AW/PA, 2720 Kirkbridge Drive
Niagara Falls ARS, NY 14304-5001
C-716-236-2000/2136, DSN-312-238-2000, Police-236-2280
e-mail: 914awpa@niagarafalls.af.mil
WEB: http://www.afrc.af.mil/914aw/
LOCATION: Take I-190 north or south to Niagara Falls, exit 23 Porter/Packard Road east. Stay straight on NY-182 (Packard Road) east past five traffic lights until it becomes Lockport Road. Turn right at Main Gate. USMRA: NY map (D-6, F,G-9). NMC: Buffalo, sixteen miles south.
RECREATION & TRAVEL: SPA-236-2475/2534 TML-236-2014 or 800-546-4990 or 888-AF-LODGE
RETAIL & DINING: Clubs-CC-236-2027 EX-236-2100
SUPPORT & FAMILY: Med-236-2301

ROCHESTER ARMY RESERVE CENTER

2035 Goodman Street North, Rochester, NY 14609-1032
C-585-338-7400 or 800-238-3138, Fax-585-544-9724
WEB: www.usarc.army.mil/98thDIV
LOCATION: Take I-590 north to exit 10-A, NY-104 west to Goodman Street exit. Turn left on Goodman Street. The ARC is 0.25 miles south. USMRA: NY map (G-6). NMC: Rochester, within city limits.
RETAIL & DINING: EX-338-7400, ext. 320

ROUND POND RECREATION AREA

Army Community Service Division (ACS), Building 622
Swift Road, West Point, NY 10996-1926
C-845-938-2503 Fax: C-845-938-3019, DSN-312-688-3019; Police-938-3333
WEB: http://www.usma.edu/mwr/
LOCATION: Off post. Three miles west of West Point on NY-293. Exit 16 from I-87, follow US-6 east to NY-293, continue east to recreation area. USMRA: NY map (M-10), West Point, NY map (G-3). NMC: New York, 50 miles southeast. NMI: U.S. Military Academy, West Point, three miles east.
RECREATION & TRAVEL: RVC-938-2503
NOTE: *For detailed information about this off-base recreation facility, as well as on-base recreation facilities, golf courses and marinas, consult Military Living's "Military RV, Camping and Outdoor Recreation Around the World".*

SARATOGA SPRINGS NAVAL SUPPORT UNIT

197 J.F. King Drive, Saratoga Springs, NY 12866-9267
C-518-886-0200, ext. 9105, Police-581-0046
WEB: www.navsuppusaratoga.com
LOCATION: Take I-87 north to exit 13 onto US-9 and head toward Saratoga Springs. Turn left on NY-29 (Washington Street).Turn right on J.F. King Drive. USMRA: NY map (M,N-6). NMC: Albany, 30 miles south.
RETAIL & DINING: Com-370-5935 EX-377-6440
SUPPORT & FAMILY: Med-583-5300

SCHENECTADY COUNTY AIRPORT/ STRATTON AIR NATIONAL GUARD

109 Airlift Wing, 1 Air National Guard Road, Stratton ANG
Scotia, NY 12302-9460
C-518-344-2300, DSN-312-974-2300, Police (Security)-344-2400
WEB: www.dmna.state.ny.us/ang/109.html

LOCATION: From I-87 north or south, exit 89 to NY-146 west. Continue to Maple Avenue, left onto Ronald Reagan Way, then left onto Air National Guard Road to Main Gate. USMRA: NY map (M,N-6). NMC: Schenectady, three miles south.
RECREATION & TRAVEL: SPA-344-2326/2489

SOLDIERS', SAILORS', MARINES' & AIRMEN'S CLUB

283 Lexington Avenue, New York, NY 10016-3540
C-212-683-4353, Fax: C-212-683-4374, Police-911
WEB: www.ssmaclub.org
LOCATION: Midtown Manhattan, on Lexington Avenue between 36th (one way eastbound) and 37th Streets (one way westbound); five blocks from Grand Central Terminal at 42nd Street and Lexington Avenue. Exit the FDR onto 42nd Street. Make a left onto Lexington Avenue to the club. USMRA: New York, NY map (D,E-4); Downtown Manhattan map (C,D-4). NMC: New York, within city limits.
RECREATION & TRAVEL: TML-683-4353 or 800-678-8443
NOTE: *The Soldiers', Sailors', Marines' and Airmen's Club is a tax exempt, not-for-profit organization founded in 1919 to serve the needs of service personnel, veterans and reserves while visiting New York City. This club is not U.S. Military/Government lodging. Ten-digit dialing required for local calls.*

STATEN ISLAND NAVY LODGE

Bldg 408, North Path Road, Staten Island, NY 10305-5000
C-718-442-0413, Fax: C-718-816-0830, Police-354-4399/8
WEB: http://www.navy-lodge.com/united_states/new_york/staten_island.html
LOCATION: Take I-95 north or south to exit 13 east to I-278 east (Goethals Bridge) to Staten Island. Take exit 15 to Lily Pond Avenue South (last exit before the Verrazano Bridge). Make a left onto McClean Avenue and a right onto North Path Road. USMRA: New York, NY map (C,D-7). NMC: New York City, within city limits.
RECREATION & TRAVEL: TML-442-0413 or 800-NAVY-INN
Ten-digit dialing required for local calls.

STEWART FIELD EXCHANGE

AAFES/Stewart PX, Bldg 271, Breunig Road
New Windsor, NY 12553-4812
C-845-564-7600/1, Police-567-1033
LOCATION: From I-87, take exit 17 toward Newburg east to Union Avenue, south to NY-207 west. Follow signs to Stewart Airport and Subpost. USMRA: NY map (M-10); West Point, NY map (F-1). NMC: New York City, 60 miles south.
RETAIL & DINING: EX-564-7601

STEWART INTERNATIONAL AIRPORT/ AIR NATIONAL GUARD

Stewart ANGB, 218 Militia Way, Newburg, NY 12550-5042
C-845-563-1000, DSN-312-636-1000, Police-567-1033
WEB: www.nystew.ang.af.mil/
LOCATION: From I-84 or I-87, take exit 17 to Union Avenue south to NY-17-K west for three miles. Make a right onto Militia Way. Clearly marked. Co-located with Stewart IAP. USMRA: NY map (M-10). NMC: New York City, 60 miles south.
RECREATION & TRAVEL: SPA-563-2965/8
RETAIL & DINING: EX-564-7601
SUPPORT & FAMILY: Med-563-2113

SYRACUSE HANCOCK INTERNATIONAL AIRPORT/AIR NATIONAL GUARD BASE

174 FW, 6001 East Molloy Road, Syracuse, NY 13211-7099
C-315-233-2100 or C-800-982-3696, DSN-312-489-9651
Police-233-2199
WEB: http://www.nysyra.ang.af.mil/
LOCATION: Merge onto NY State Thruway N/I-87N toward Albany (portions toll). NY State Thruway N/I-87N becomes NY State Thruway W/1-90W (portions toll). Take exit 35 toward RT-298/Syracuse/East Syracuse. Enter next roundabout and take the first exit onto Thompson Rd/CR-13 N. Turn left onto E. Molloy Road/CR-71. Visitors may enter through the Main Gate. USMRA: NY map (I-6). NMC: Syracuse, four miles west.
RECREATION & TRAVEL: SPA-454-6100
RETAIL & DINING: Clubs-CC-454-6200 EX-454-6440

UNITED STATES MERCHANT MARINE ACADEMY

300 Steamboat Road,Kings Point, NY 11024-1699
C-516-773-5000, Police-773-5303
WEB: www.usmma.edu
LOCATION: Take I-495 east Long Island Expressway (portions toll) to exit 33 north. Follow Lakeville which will become Middle Neck Road. Take left on Steamboat Road. USMRA: New York, NY map (G-3). NMC: New York City, approximately three miles west.
RECREATION & TRAVEL: Marina-773-5396
RETAIL & DINING: Cafeteria-773-5557 Clubs-OC-773-5411 Com-773-5372

UNITED STATES MILITARY ACADEMY, WEST POINT

Bldg 600, Room A, West Point, NY 10996-1781
C-845-938-4011, DSN-312-688-4011, Police-446-5555
WEB: www.usma.edu
LOCATION: Off I-87 north or south or US-9W. From I-81, take exit 16 west on US-6 east to US-9W, north to Main Gate. From the north, take US-9W, go south to Highland Falls/Thayer Gate. From the south, take Palisades Interstate Parkway to US-9W north to Highland Falls/Thayer Gate. From the west, US-6 East to US-293 to US-9W South to Highland Falls/Thayer Gate. Clearly marked. USMRA: West Point, NY map (G-3); NY map (M,N-10). NMC: West Point, within city limits.
RECREATION & TRAVEL: Golf-938-2435 Marina-938-3011 RVC-938-2503 TML-Five Star Inn-938-6816 or 800-GO-ARMY Hotel Thayer-446-4731 or 800-247-5047
RETAIL & DINING: Clubs-OC-938-5120 Com-938-3663 EX-446-5406 Gas-446-3666
SUPPORT & FAMILY: Med-938-2273 or 938-4004/5/6
Ten-digit dialing required for local calls.

WATERVLIET ARSENAL

Attn: AMSTA-WV-CO, Watervliet, NY 12189-4050
C-518-266-5111, DSN-312-975-5111, Police-266-5520
WEB: www.wva.army.mil
LOCATION: From I-87 north, take exit 23, take I-787 north to NY-378 west 0.5 miles to NY-32 north (2nd Avenue) 1.5 miles to Arsenal on west side of NY-32. From I-87 south, exit 6 east on NY-2 (19th Street), go 3.5 miles to NY-32 south (Second Avenue) for one mile to Arsenal on west side of NY-32. USMRA: NY map (N-7). NMC: Albany, six miles south.
RETAIL & DINING: Cafeteria-266-5473 Clubs-CC-266-3617 EX-266-5371
SUPPORT & FAMILY: Med-266-4195

WESTHAMPTON BEACH COAST GUARD EXCHANGE

106 NYANG Base, Bldg 230, 150 Riverhead Road
Westhampton Beach, NY 11978-1201
C-631-723-7557, Police-395-4421
LOCATION: On Long Island, east one mile south of NY-27 (Sunrise Highway). Exit 63 south onto NY-31 south (Old Riverhead Road) to entrance. USMRA: Long Island, NY map (F-2). NMC: Westhampton Beach, within the city.
RETAIL & DINING: EX-723-7557
SUPPORT & FAMILY: Med-723-7447

PENNSYLVANIA, pg. 20
Gettysburg, pg. 20
Philadelphia, pg. 23
Pittsburgh, pg. 18

CARLISLE BARRACKS

U.S. Army War College, 122 Forbes Avenue, Carlisle, PA 17013-5234
C-717-245-3131, DSN-312-242-3131, Police-245-4115
WEB: www.carlisle.army.mil
LOCATION: From I-81 north or south take exit 49 onto PA-641. Make a right onto US-11. Signs clearly marked to Carlisle Barracks and Army War College. USMRA: PA map (G-7). NMC: Harrisburg, 18 miles northeast.
RECREATION & TRAVEL: Golf- 243-3262 TML-245-4245
RETAIL & DINING Com-245-3105 EX-243-2463
SUPPORT & FAMILY: Med-245-3915

CHARLES E. KELLY SUPPORT FACILITY

6 Lobaugh Street, Oakdale, PA 15071-5005
C-724-693-1844, Police (Security)-693-1848
WEB: http://www.dix.army.mil/cekelly/homepage.htm
LOCATION: From I-279 east or west, take I-79 south to exit 57 (Carnegie exit). Bear right (left, if coming from the south) on Noblestown Road and travel approximately 2.5 miles through town of Rennerdale. Make a left onto Nike Site Road and a right onto Lobaugh Street. Facility clearly marked. USMRA: PA map (A-7). NMC: Pittsburgh, 13 miles east.
RETAIL & DINING: Com-693-2463/5 EX- 693-2434
Ten-digit dialing required for all calls.

FORT INDIANTOWN GAP NATIONAL GUARD TRAINING CENTER

1 Garrison Road, Bldg T-0-1, Annville, PA 17003-5002
C-717-861-2000, DSN-491-2000, Police-861-2727
WEB: www.ftig.state.pa.us
LOCATION: From I-81 take the Fort Indiantown Gap exit (from northbound, take exit 85B. From southbound, take exit 85) onto Route 934 North. Pass entrance to Indiantown Gap National Cemetery. The entrance will be straight ahead. USMRA: PA map (G,H-6,7). NMC: Harrisburg, 18 miles southwest. NMI: Carlisle Barracks, 40 miles south.
RECREATION & TRAVEL: SPA-861-8963 TML-861-2512/2540/8158
RETAIL & DINING: Cafeteria-861-8538 Clubs-CC-861-2450 EX-861-2058 Gas-865-6938
SUPPORT & FAMILY: Med-861-2091

HARRISBURG INTERNATIONAL AIRPORT/ AIR NATIONAL GUARD

Bldg 81, Constellation Court, Middletown, PA 17057-5086
C-717-948-2200, Police (Security)-948-2454
WEB: www.paharr.ang.af.mil
LOCATION: From I-76 east or west, take exit 19 south onto PA-230 (Second Street) south to IAP on right. USMRA: PA map (G-7). NMC: Harrisburg, five miles northwest.
RETAIL & DINING: EX-948-2415
SUPPORT & FAMILY: Med-948-2235/57

LETTERKENNY ARMY DEPOT

Attn: AMSAM-LE-CO, Bldg 10, Overcash Avenue
Chambersburg, PA 17201-4150
C-717-267-8111, Police-267-8800
WEB: www.lead.army.mil
LOCATION: From I-81 north or south, take exit 20 toward Scotland to PA-997 north. Proceed on PA-997 for about five miles to enter depot at Gate 6 (located near the traffic signal two miles past the intersection of PA-997 and PA-11). USMRA: PA map (F-8). NMC: Harrisburg, 55 miles northeast.
RETAIL & DINING: Cafeteria-267-5320 EX-264-1713
SUPPORT & FAMILY: Med-267-8416

MECHANICSBURG NAVAL SUPPLY SYSTEMS COMMAND

5450 Carlisle Pike, P.O. Box 2050, Mechanicsburg, PA 17055-0791
C-717-605-1543, DSN-312-430-1543, Police-605-3351
WEB: www.navsup.navy.mil
LOCATION: From I-83 north or south, take exit 41B to US-11 west. Travel four miles to Main Gate on left (south). Or, from I-76 (Pennsylvania Turnpike), exit 16 (Carlisle) eight miles on PA-641 east to installation. USMRA: PA map (G-7). NMC: Harrisburg, ten miles northeast.
RECREATION & TRAVEL: Golf-605-3948
RETAIL & DINING: Cafeteria-605-3537 Clubs-OC-605-3505 EX-605-2608
SUPPORT & FAMILY: Med-605-3409
NOTE: *Anyone without NSSC Mechanicsburg stickers will be stopped and required to obtain a visitor's pass.*

PHILADELPHIA COAST GUARD GROUP/ MARINE SAFETY OFFICE

1 Washington Avenue, Philadelphia, PA 19147-4395
C-215-271-4800, Fax: C-215-271-4919, Police-271-4971
LOCATION: From I-95 South, take exit 20 (Columbus Blvd) south, take left (east) onto Washington Avenue. From I-95 North, take exit 20 (Columbus Blvd)) north, take right (east) onto Washington Avenue. USMRA: Philadelphia, PA/Long Island, NY map (D-6). NMC: Philadelphia, within city limits.
RETAIL & DINING: Dining Galley-271-4822 EX-271-4921
SUPPORT & FAMILY: Med-271-4816
Ten-digit dialing required for local calls.

PHILADELPHIA DEFENSE SUPPLY CENTER

700 Robbins Avenue, Philadelphia, PA 19111-5092
C-215-737-2000, DSN-312-444-2000, Police-737-2609
WEB: www.dscp.dla.mil/index.htm
LOCATION: From I-76 north or south, exit 34 to US-1. Go four miles east to PA-232 (Oxford Avenue). Turn left onto Oxford and follow for 1.3 miles to gate. Located in NAVICP compound. USMRA: Philadelphia, PA/Long Island, NY map (E-3). NMC: Philadelphia, within city limits.
RETAIL & DINING: Cafeteria-697-3704 EX-697-3703
SUPPORT & FAMILY: Med-697-3333
Ten-digit dialing required for local calls.

PITTSBURGH INTERNATIONAL AIRPORT/ AIR RESERVE STATION

911th Airlift Wing, 2475 Defense Avenue, Suite 227
Coraopolis, PA 15108-4403
C-412-474-8000, DSN-312-277-8000, Police-474-8255
WEB: http://www.afreserve.com/bases.asp?id=71
LOCATION: US-22 west toward I-279 S to US-30 west. Becomes PA-60 north. Take exit 3 toward Moon, merge onto Airport Parkway. Take the ramp toward Coraopolis/Sewickley, then take the ramp toward Air Force Reserve Base. Turn right onto Thorn Run Road, turn slight right onto Cliff MLS. Then turn left onto Defense Avenue. USMRA: PA map (A-6). NMC: Pittsburgh, 16 miles southeast.
RECREATION & TRAVEL: SPA-474-8163 TML-474-8229/30 or 888-AF-LODGE
RETAIL & DINING: Clubs-CC-474-8187 Dining-474-8058 EX-474-8207
Ten-digit dialing required for local calls.

SUSQUEHANNA DEFENSE DISTRIBUTION CENTER

2001 Mission Drive, New Cumberland, PA 17070-5001
C-717-770-6011, DSN-312-771-1110, Police-770-6270
WEB: www.ddc.dla.mil
LOCATION: From the Pennsylvania Turnpike, take exit 242 to PA-114. At the end of the ramp, turn right. Follow 114 to 'T', then turn right at the 'T.' Take the first left on Old Depot Road. Entrance Gate will be on the left at the end of the road. USMRA: PA map (G-7). NMC: Harrisburg, three miles northeast.
RECREATION & TRAVEL: Golf-770-5893 TML-770-7035
RETAIL & DINING: Cafeteria-770-5125 Clubs-CC-770-7802 Susquehanna-770-3030 Dining-770-7915 EX-774-4066 Gas-774-4066
SUPPORT & FAMILY: Med-728-1770

TOBYHANNA ARMY DEPOT

AMSEL-TY-CS, 11 Hap Arnold Blvd, Tobyhanna, PA 18466-5076
C-570-895-7000, DSN-312-795-7000, Police-895-7550
WEB: www.tobyhanna.army.mil
LOCATION: Take I-80 east or west to I-380 north, exit 8 to PA-507/Midway Road and one mile to depot. USMRA: PA map (J-5). NMC: Scranton, 20 miles northwest.
RECREATION & TRAVEL: TML-895-7584/8529
RETAIL & DINING: Cafeteria-895-7998 Clubs-CC-894-8478 Com-895-7709 Dining-895-7998 EX-895-7030 Gas-895-7030
SUPPORT & FAMILY: Med-895-7121
NOTE: *Visitor's Gate: Visitors can enter through the Main Gate and must have a photo ID. All vehicles are subject to search.*

WILLOW GROVE NAVAL AIR STATION/ JOINT RESERVE BASE

Bldg 1, NASJRB, Willow Grove, PA 19090-5001
C-215-443-1000, DSN-312-991-1000, Police-443-6000
LOCATION: Take I-276 (Pennsylvania Turnpike) to PA-611 exit 343 Willow Grove north, approximately three or four miles on PA-611 to NAS/JRB. USMRA: PA map (J-7). NMC: Philadelphia, 19 miles south.
RECREATION & TRAVEL: RVC-443-6087 SPA-443-6215/6/7 TML-442-5800/1 or 800-227-9472 Navy Lodge-800-NAVY-INN or 328-7800
RETAIL & DINING: Cafeteria-443-6282 Clubs-Orion's-443-6081 EX-443-6028
SUPPORT & FAMILY: Med-Naval Health Clinic-443-6379
NOTE: *The 2005 BRAC report recommended this base for closure. As required by Federal law, the DoD has until 15 September 2007 to begin closing and realigning the bases as called for in the approved report. This process must be completed by 15 September 2011. Ten-digit dialing required for local calls.*

RHODE ISLAND, pg. 15
Newport, pg. 15
Providence, pg. 15

CARR POINT RECREATION FACILITIES

ITT Office, BLDG 1121 Meyerkord Avenue
Naval Station Newport, Newport, RI 02841-1613
C-401-841-1369/7196, DSN-312-948-1369, Police-841-3241
WEB: www.nsnpt.navy.mil/mwr/rv_picnic.htm
LOCATION: From north and east, at the junction of RI-24 and RI-114, take RI-114 south for 1.7 miles to Stringham Road. From south and west, take I-95 to RI-138 east to RI-114 north. Follow RI-114 for 4.7 miles to Stringham Road. Follow Stringham for 2.3 miles to the turn into the facility. Clearly marked. USMRA: CT/MA/RI map (J,K-7). NMC: Providence, 30 miles northwest.
RECREATION & TRAVEL: RVC-841-3116
NOTE: *Fitness Center handles recreational activities.*

NEWPORT NAVAL STATION

690 Peary Street, Newport, RI 02841-1522
C-401-841-2311, DSN-312-948-2311, Police-841-3241/2
WEB: www.nsnpt.navy.mil
LOCATION: From US-1, exit to RI-138 east over Jamestown/Newport bridge (toll) to Newport. Bear right off of the bridge, enter the rotary, follow around to the other side and continue straight after the stop light to Gate 1. Visitors must make a right turn into the Security parking lot to receive a pass. USMRA: CT/MA/RI map (J-8; M,N-9). NMC: Newport, adjacent.
RECREATION & TRAVEL: Marina-841-3283 RVC-841-3116 TML-841-7900 Navy Lodge-800-NAVY-INN or 849-4500
RETAIL & DINING: Cafeteria-841-4445 Clubs-CPO/EMC-841-3054 OC-846-4821 Com-841-2111 EX-841-1399 Gas-841-3958
SUPPORT & FAMILY: Med-841-3771/2

QUONSET STATE AIRPORT/ AIR NATIONAL GUARD

1 Minuteman Way, North Kingstown, RI 02852-7502
C-401-886-1200, DSN-312-476-3319, Police (Security)-886-1245
WEB: www.riguard.com
LOCATION: From US-1, exit to RI-403 south or I-95 north or south, exit 9 to RI-4 south to exit 7 on RI-403 southwest. Airport is clearly marked. USMRA: CT/MA/RI map (J-7). NMC: Providence, 20 miles north.
RECREATION & TRAVEL: SPA-886-1518
RETAIL & DINING: Clubs-NCO-886-1003

VERMONT, pg. 21

CAMP JOHNSON

Green Mountain Armory, 789 Vermont National Guard Road
Colchester, VT 05446-3006
C-802-338-3000, DSN-312-636-3000, Police-338-3000
LOCATION: From I-89 north or south, take exit 15 east on VT-15 (College Parkway), approximately two miles to entrance on left. USMRA: NH, VT map (B-4). NMC: Burlington, six miles southwest.
RETAIL & DINING: EX-655-3030

ETHAN ALLEN FIRING RANGE

Training Site Detachment, 113 Ethan Allen Road
Jericho, VT 05465-9706
C-802-899-7000, DSN-312-636-3000, Police-338-3000
LOCATION: I-89 north or south, take exit 11 to VT-117. Make a right onto Barber Farm Road, continue straight, then make a left onto Brown's Trace Road. Take a right onto Ethan Allen Road. Clearly marked. USMRA: NH, VT map (B-4). NMC: Burlington, 15 miles west.
RETAIL & DINING: EX-655-3030
NOTE: *Open only when units are in field for annual training, approximately eight to ten weeks.*

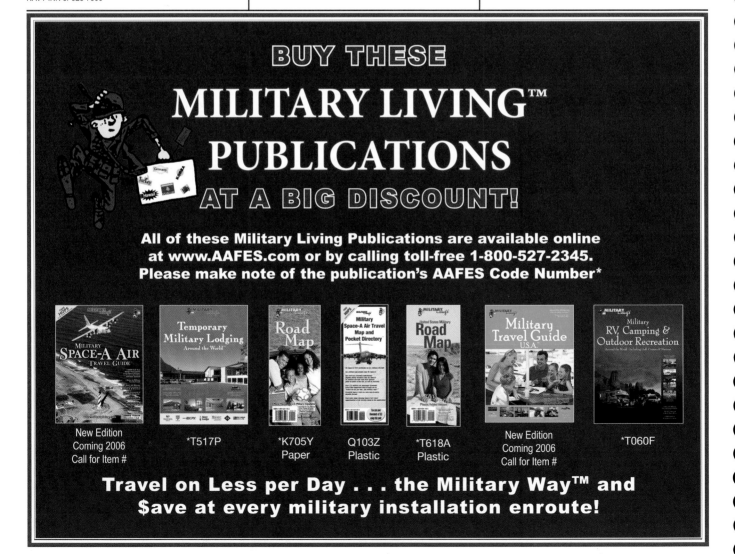

Shades of Green®

on Walt Disney World® Resort

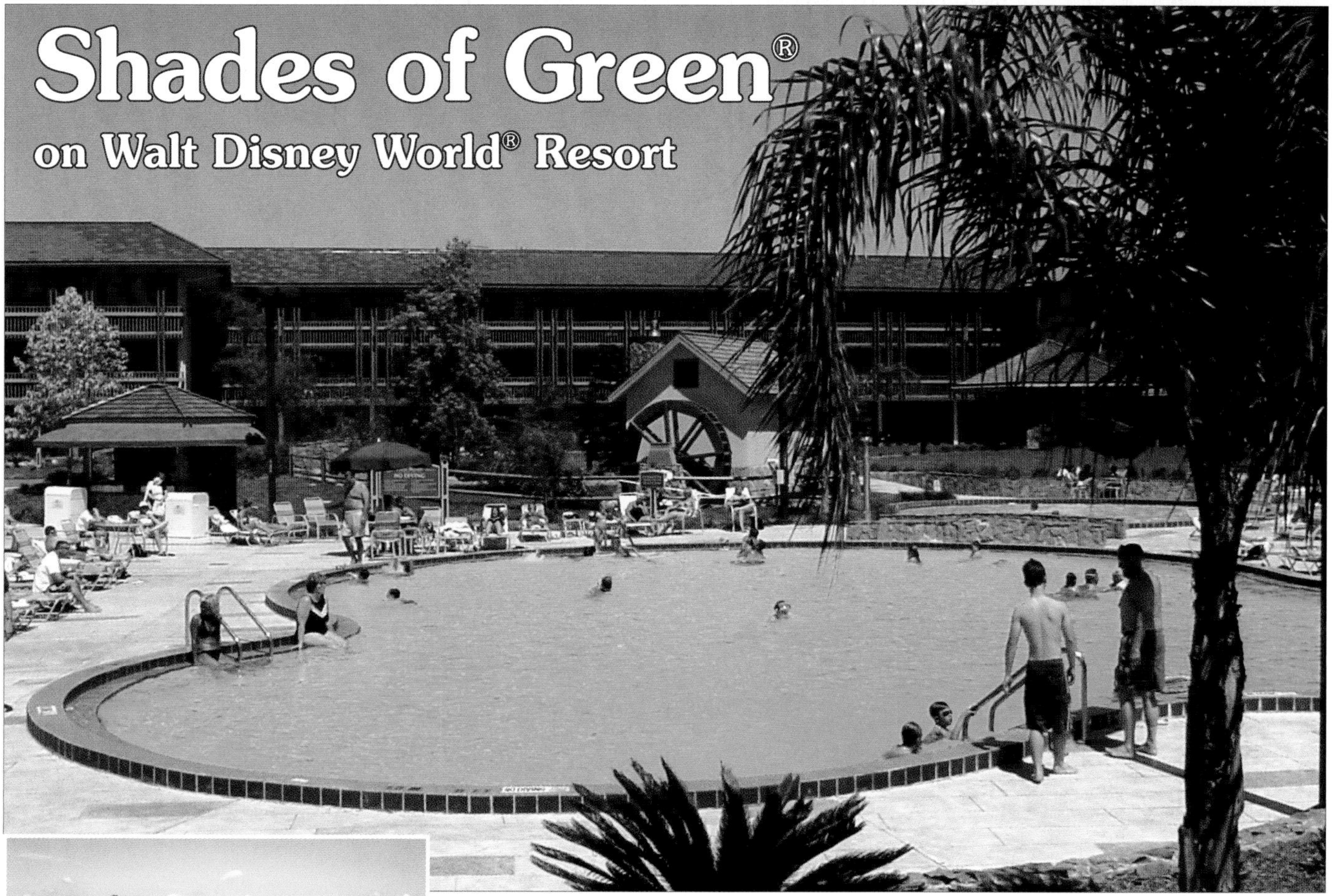

Shades of Green® on WALT DISNEY WORLD® Resort is one of four Armed Forces Recreation Centers around the world designed to give military personnel and their families all the comforts and benefits of a resort vacation while specifically catering to their needs and rewarding them for their service to our country.

As the only AFRC in the continental United States, Shades of Green, has delivered exceptional service to guests for over a decade. In response to ever-increasing demand, the resort launched a massive renovation and expansion in 2002. Over the course of 23 months, the resort underwent a complete transformation in order to create extraordinary facilities that would further accommodate their guests.

In March of 2004, Shades of Green re-opened its doors as a full service, guest-oriented, spectacular resort. Located in Orlando, Florida, in the heart of Walt Disney World, the resort is situated between two of Disney's PGA professional golf courses, the Palm and Magnolia. With an ideal location and stunning list of amenities, Shades of Green has truly emerged as a premier vacation destination.

The sheer size of the resort more than doubled, as it increased the guest room count to 586 rooms, also adding 10 junior and family suites. Each well-appointed guest room features a private patio or balcony and guests have their choice of views, either poolside or overlooking the stunning golf courses.

A multi-purpose banquet facility was also constructed in the new Palm Wing of the resort, with over 7,400 square feet of versatile event space. Intended to host a variety of functions, the space can be divided into four separate quadrants ideal for reunions, meetings, parties, conferences and banquets. The casually elegant décor makes the space ideal for weddings, award ceremonies and receptions.

The beautifully landscaped grounds also include a picturesque gazebo perfect for special events and ceremonies, with the breathtaking backdrop of the verdant Palm and Magnolia golf courses set against the lush woods.

Expanding upon the existing restaurants, Shades of Green introduced their signature dining experience, Mangino's, a northern Italian restaurant modeled after a traditional Tuscan trattoria. Mangino's is a delightful blend of familiar fine dining that accommodates Shades of Green guests. The authentic style of the restaurant and impeccable service are welcoming and impressive. The menu was developed by their award-winning culinary team and features dishes reflective of traditional Tuscan cuisine. The selection offers an array of antipasti, pasta, entrees and decadent desserts. By creating nightly specials, the chefs identify with changing trends and guest requests. The wine list is equally notable, highlighting a fine selection of Castello Banfi wines from Tuscany and also featuring other wines from around the world.

In addition to serving dinner seven nights a week, Mangino's functions as a remarkable location for private dinners, wine tastings, cooking demonstrations and other special events. Guests dining at Mangino's enjoy all the flavor and flair of Italy without ever leaving the resort.

The amenities offered at Shades of Green include increased transportation options for guests during their stay, with a new multi-level parking garage with valet services and complimentary bus and shuttle services. A state of the art fitness center, two heated recreational pools, a hot tub, tennis courts and video arcades also offer guests more recreational options at the resort.

Shades of Green offers great diversity in shopping as well; from the convenient and well-stocked AAFES General Store to the East Meets West gift shop guests can browse through unique items like jewelry, art, pottery, and clothing and also pick up essentials like sunscreen, snacks, and newspapers or magazines. The shops offer souvenirs from Disney and more, including gifts from AFRCs around the globe.

The Mill Pond Shoppe sells poolside gear like swimsuits, goggles, flip flops and underwater cameras, while serving up delicious ice cream treats, refreshing smoothies and other light snacks. With so many different options, guests have access to everything they could possibly need to fully enjoy their vacation.

A talented and knowledgeable Guest Services staff is available seven days a week to assist guests in planning their vacation. Always helpful, they can offer advice on local attractions and shows, make dinner reservations, schedule taxi and car rental services and arrange child care. The equally friendly staff in the Attraction Ticket Office sells discounted tickets to dozens of locations including all Walt Disney World theme parks, Universal Studios, Sea World Orlando and Kennedy Space Center. Additional discounts and special offers are available exclusively for Shades of Green guests, like extra magic hours at the parks and greatly reduced rates at area golf courses.

Seasonal celebrations abound at the resort where poolside barbeques, holiday parties, Oktoberfest, Thanksgiving, Christmas and New Year's festivities offer guests fun opportunities to be a part of the family at Shades of Green.

The peaceful wooded setting allows guests to relax amidst the constant excitement of Walt Disney World. The professional and courteous staff at Shades of Green remain dedicated to serving those who serve. Shades of Green has truly come a long way from its beginnings as a modest lodge in 1994, but nonetheless remains a "home away from home" for all members of the military and their families.

Don't miss the opportunity to enjoy a memorable vacation at the resort designed especially for you. Take advantage of additional discounts and great deals with our Fun & Sun Packages, a great way to extend the fun of summer. From short getaways to all-inclusive vacations, we have something to fit your plans and your budget. Reserve rooms at unbelievable rates and extend the savings to your friends and family. For more information or to get started planning the vacation of a lifetime, call today at 1.888.593.2242 or you can reserve online at www.shadesofgreen.org and take a virtual tour through the new Shades of Green!

Oak Grove Park

Naval Air Station Pensacola, Florida

Oak Grove Park has primitive camp sites, RV sites with water, sewer and electric hook-up and fully equipped cottages nestled in the trees along the beach.

Some amenities to make your stay enjoyable and relaxing are:

- ★ Waterfront view
- ★ Walking distance to the beach/water
- ★ Restrooms & showers
- ★ Washer & dryer
- ★ Cable TV
- ★ Walking/Jogging Trail
- ★ Walking distance to the Pensacola Bay Lighthouse

Check out our web site: www.naspensacola@navy.mil/mwr

OPEN TO ALL ACTIVE DUTY, RETIRED & RESERVISTS, MILITARY, DOD EMPLOYEES, FAMILY MEMBERS & GUESTS

ON BASE:

- ~ Several Restaurants
- ~ Officers' Club & CPO Club
- ~ A.C. Read Golf Club
- ~ Stars & Strikes Bowling Center
- ~ NEX
- ~ Barrancas Beach - Pensacola Bay
- ~ Bayou Grande Sailing Facility
- ~ Sherman Cove Marina
- ~ National Museum of Naval Aviation
- ~ Fort Redoubt and Fort Barrancas
- ~ Portside Cinema

OFF BASE IN DRIVING DISTANCE:

- ~ Corry Station Bingo
- ~ Navy Hospital
- ~ NEX & Commissary/ITT Office
- ~ Pensacola Beach - Gulf Of Mexico
- ~ Johnson Beach - Gulf Of Mexico
- ~ Ice Pilots Hockey - Seasonal
- ~ Barracudas Arena Football - Seasonal
- ~ Pensacola Pelicans Baseball - Seasonal

For reservations or information:
Com: 1-850-452-2535 FAX: 1-850-452-4366
E-mail: lance.don@cnet.navy.mil
Visit our website at www.naspensacola.navy.mil/mwr

Mail to:
Oak Grove Park
Bldg. 4137, Radford Blvd.
Naval Air Station
Pensacola, FL 32508-5217

Blue Angel Naval Recreation Area

Pensacola ★ Florida

Visit our updated facilities located on beautiful Perdido Bay. Blue Angel Recreation Park is open for RV, primitive, group and day camping plus group and family picnics.

More great features:

- ★ 4 mile Mountain Bike Trail
- ★ 18 hole Disc Golf Course
- ★ 3 playground areas
- ★ Complete boat & gear rental
- ★ 15 two-bedroom trailers for rent
- ★ Daily & weekly dry storage
- ★ Fishing
- ★ Kountry Store
- ★ Laundry
- ★ 18 hole Navy theme Mini Golf Course
- ★ Handicap accessible
- ★ Pay phone
- ★ Dumping station
- ★ Danger Zone Paintball

OPEN TO ALL ACTIVE DUTY, RETIRED & RESERVISTS, MILITARY, DOD EMPLOYEES, FAMILY MEMBERS & GUESTS

For Information and Reservations
Call 1-850-453-1147
Visit our website at
www.naspensacola.navy.mil/mwr
E-mail: bluaglpk@aol.com

Mail to:
Blue Angel Naval Recreation Area
2100 Bronson Road
Pensacola, Florida 32506

Order Military Living's R&R Travel News®

for 3, 5 or 7 years and get one of our maps, travel guides or atlases

MILITARY Living's®

R&R Travel News®

HIGHLIGHTS
Our military travelers visit . . .
- Timbuktu, Mali, Part II
- Hawaii, Guam, Yokota & Singapore
- Slovenia and Hungary
- Retiree Living in Korea
- PLUS Tag Along with Ann

A worldwide travel newsletter published ©2006 Military Living Publications www.militaryliving.com

STAN & DEE INK'S SPACE-A ADVENTURE

TO HAWAII, GUAM, YOKOTA & SINGAPORE

. . . AND NEXT ISSUE, ON TO AUSTRALIA!

TUESDAY, NOV. 29, 2005- Dee and I (Stan) are off again this morning. We were going to fly our small plane to Jacksonville, FL, but the weather did not cooperate. We are now driving to Interlachen, FL. Dee's brother, Guy, is taking us to Jacksonville Naval Air Station and bringing the car back to his house until we return. We expect to catch a Navy 737 Space-A flight tomorrow morning from Jacksonville to Kaneohe Bay Marine Corps Base, HI which begins this trip that we hope will get us to Australia. We hope to make it all the way on Space-A flights.

We checked on our flight at the terminal, then Guy dropped us at the Navy Lodge. We walked a bit, exploring the woods and a walkway along St. John's Bay, and then had dinner at a sports bar at the golf club.

WEDNESDAY, NOVEMBER 30- We called about 0600 and a Duty Driver took us to the terminal. Nice service. *Editor's Note: This service is usually only offered to duty passengers, so don't expect it!* We checked in and took a bus to the plane by 0800. We were airborne before 0900 in a 72-seat Navy C-40 plane. It is configured to be a half-cargo plane. The seats were spaced so that we had lots of leg room. There were only 25 passengers. It was five and a half hours to North Island NAS, San Diego. We stayed for about one and a half hours for refueling. The flight to Kaneohe took six hours. We picked up snacks at the terminal, including a cheeseburger that we heated in the plane's microwave. The pilot had to do a "go around" when landing, reversing the end of the runway.

We got to Kaneohe about 1600 local time (2100 EST). Enterprise Rent-A-Car was waiting for us to go to their office for a car that I had reserved. By

Stan & Dee Ink with Ted and Sandy Finnerty

Continued on page 10

WHERE IN THE WORLD DO YOU WANT TO RETIRE?

In this issue, we have a feature by Jack Terwiel, the director of Osan AB Retiree office. Jack gives us a heads up on what it is like to retire to South Korea.

With Jack's feature in mind, I selected one of our favorite places for possible retirement. We currently live in the Washington, DC area. The place that we keep going to for R&R is Virginia Beach, VA, which is in the area called Hampton Roads. If we love to go there to have a bit of relaxation, surely we would love to live in that area.

Virginia Beach has miles of oceanfront and even more waterfront property located on lakes, rivers and the Chesapeake Bay, Back Bay, Broad Bay, Lynnhaven Bay and others. It also has the intracoastal waterway which avid boaters find to be ideal.

Continued on page 2

See page 16 to find out about our new

Military Space-A Air Travel Map and Pocket Directory™

Our subscribers travel on less per day . . . the military way!™ 1 R&R Travel News® Report 207 Mar-Apr 2006 Volume 36, No. 2

R&R Travel News® is published 6 times per year by Military Living Publications

ABSOLUTELY FREE!

3 Years Standard Mail $56 First Class $84

Choose your **FREE** Map below:
United States Military Road Map™—Paper ($11.20) or Plastic ($13.70*)
Military Space-A Air Travel Map & Pocket Directory™—Plastic ($17.20*)

5 Years Standard Mail $84 First Class $134

Choose you **FREE** Travel Guide below:
European Military Travel Guide™ ($26.75*)
Military RV, Camping & Outdoor Recreation Around the World™ ($21.30*)
Military Travel Guide U.S.A.™ ($19.05)
Temporary Military Lodging Around the World™ ($23.75*)

7 Years Standard Mail $106 First Class $181

Choose your **FREE** Atlas below:
United States Military Road Atlas™ ($27.55*)
United States Military Road Atlas, Compact Edition™ (Spiral Binding)

* Military Living Mail Order Value ** Offer expires 12/31/2006. After this date visit our website at www.militaryliving.com for 2007 special offers.

CALL (703) 237-0203 Ext 1 and place your order today!

We accept Visa, Mastercard, American Express and Discover. Sorry, no billing.

Orlando's

Best Vacation Value

This beautiful all suite hotel is conveniently located just off International Dr. in ***"The Heart of The Magic",*** *only 1/2 mile from Sea World, 5 miles from Disney World, 4 miles from Universal Studios, and 1/2 mile from the Orange County Convention Center.*

- Spacious one bedroom suite (sleeps up to 6)
- Complimentary **full hot** breakfast buffet daily
- Fully equipped kitchens
- Heated pool, children's pool, and whirlpool spa
- Exercise room and 24 hour convenience store
- Video cassette player and Nintendo64®
- Free high speed wireless internet
- **Free scheduled transportation** to Disney Theme Parks

Special military rates from **$80.00** per night

Call 407-351-6600 or 1-800-331-5530

Hawthorn Suites - Orlando
6435 Westwood Blvd.
Orlando, Florida 32821
Fax: 407-351-1977
E-mail: Hawthorno@hsorlando.com
Website: **www.hawthorn.com**

HAWTHORN SUITES

As Good As It Can Be!

SURFSIDE

On the ocean at the north end of Miami Beach across from Bal Harbour Shops

Minutes away from South Beach, night-clubs and all tourist attractions.

Beautiful hotel apartments
reasonably priced,
complete with kitchenette.
Motel & Hotel rooms at sensible rates.

Gourmet restaurants and shopping boutiques on Harding Ave.

See your Travel Agent or call
Toll Free 1-800-327-4557

Surfside Tourist Bureau
(305) 864-0722
9301 Collins Avenue, Surfside, FL 33154
Web Site: www.townofsurfsidefl.gov

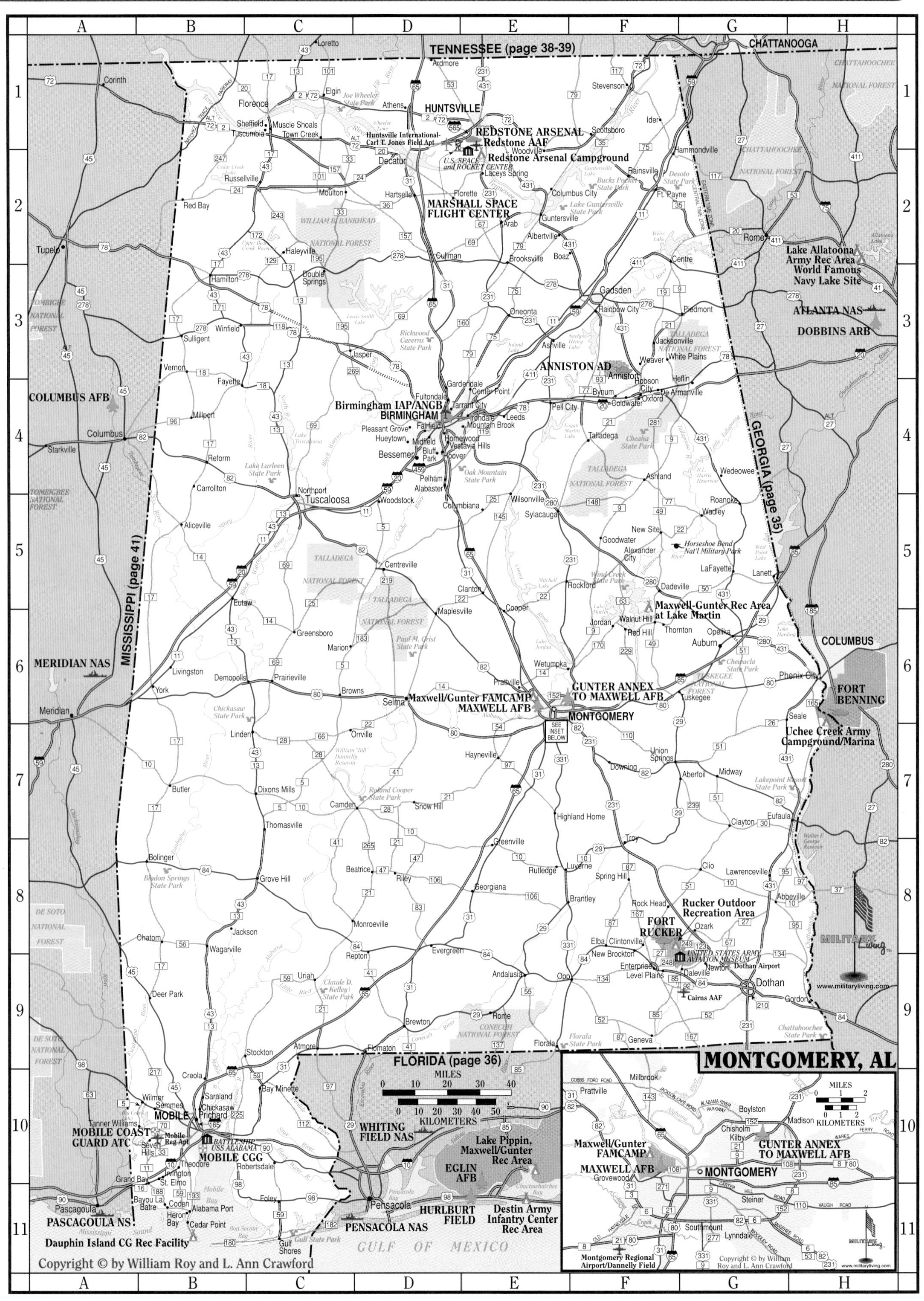

TENNESSEE (page 38-39)
CHATTANOOGA
GEORGIA (page 35)
MISSISSIPPI (page 41)
FLORIDA (page 36)
GULF OF MEXICO
HUNTSVILLE
REDSTONE ARSENAL
Redstone AAF
Redstone Arsenal Campground
Huntsville International-Carl T. Jones Field Apt
U.S. SPACE and ROCKET CENTER
MARSHALL SPACE FLIGHT CENTER
Lake Allatoona Army Rec Area
World Famous Navy Lake Site
ATLANTA NAS
DOBBINS AFB
ANNISTON AD
COLUMBUS AFB
Birmingham IAP/ANGB
BIRMINGHAM
Tuscaloosa
Maxwell-Gunter Rec Area at Lake Martin
COLUMBUS
FORT BENNING
MERIDIAN NAS
GUNTER ANNEX TO MAXWELL AFB
Maxwell/Gunter FAMCAMP
MAXWELL AFB
MONTGOMERY
SEE INSET BELOW
Uchee Creek Army Campground/Marina
Rucker Outdoor Recreation Area
FORT RUCKER
UNITED STATES ARMY AVIATION MUSEUM
Dothan Airport
Dothan
Cairns AAF
MOBILE
MOBILE COAST GUARD ATC
Mobile Reg Apt
BATTLESHIP USS ALABAMA
MOBILE CGG
WHITING FIELD NAS
Lake Pippin, Maxwell/Gunter Rec Area
EGLIN AFB
HURLBURT FIELD
Destin Army Infantry Center Rec Area
PENSACOLA NAS
Pensacola
PASCAGOULA NS
Dauphin Island CG Rec Facility
MILES
0 10 20 30 40
0 10 20 30 40 50
KILOMETERS
MONTGOMERY, AL
Prattville
Millbrook
Boylston
Chisholm
Kilby
Madison
Maxwell/Gunter FAMCAMP
MAXWELL AFB
Grovewood
GUNTER ANNEX TO MAXWELL AFB
MONTGOMERY
Steiner
Southmont
Lynndale
Montgomery Regional Airport/Dannelly Field
Copyright © by William Roy and L. Ann Crawford
www.militaryliving.com
Copyright © by William Roy and L. Ann Crawford

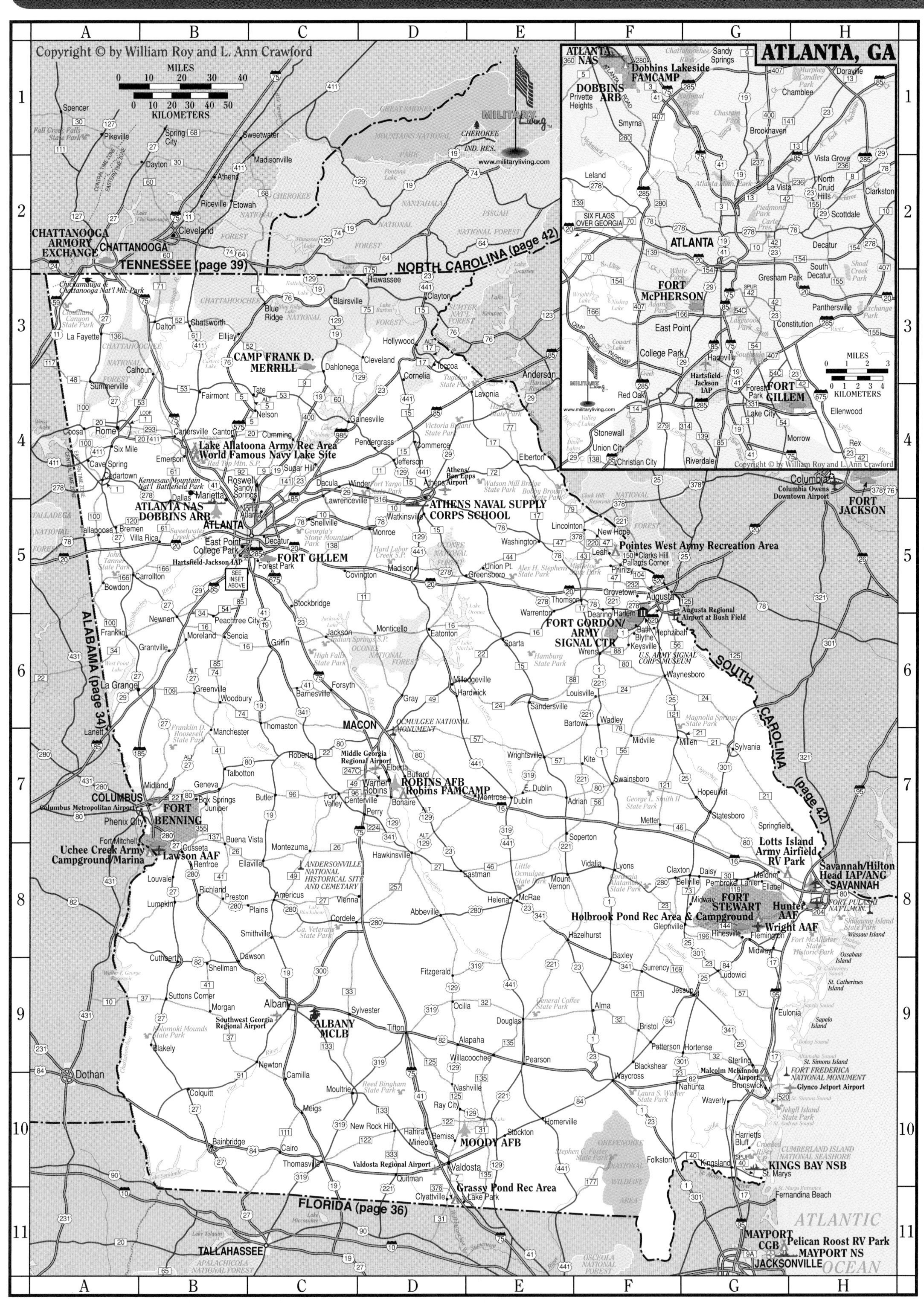

A B C D E F G H
1 2 3 4 5 6 7 8 9 10 11
Copyright © by William Roy and L. Ann Crawford
MILES
0 10 20 30 40
0 10 20 30 40 50
KILOMETERS
MILITARY Living
www.militaryliving.com
ATLANTA, GA
Atlanta NAS
Dobbins Lakeside FAMCAMP
DOBBINS ARB
Sandy Springs
Doraville
Chamblee
Privette Heights
Smyrna
Brookhaven
Vista Grove
North Druid Hills
Clarkston
Leland
La Vista
Scottdale
SIX FLAGS OVER GEORGIA
ATLANTA
Decatur
FORT McPHERSON
Gresham Park
South Decatur
Panthersville
East Point
Constitution
College Park
Hapeville
Hartsfield-Jackson IAP
FORT GILLEM
Forest Park
Red Oak
Lake City
Ellenwood
Stonewall
Union City
Morrow
Rex
Christian City
Riverdale
Copyright © by William Roy and L. Ann Crawford
CHATTANOOGA ARMORY EXCHANGE
CHATTANOOGA
TENNESSEE (page 39)
NORTH CAROLINA (page 42)
Spencer
Pikeville
Spring City
Sweetwater
Madisonville
Dayton
Athens
Riceville
Etowah
Cleveland
CHEROKEE IND. RES.
Hiawassee
Clayton
Blairsville
Blue Ridge
Dalton
Chatsworth
La Fayette
Ellijay
CAMP FRANK D. MERRILL
Dahlonega
Cleveland
Toccoa
Cornelia
Anderson
Calhoun
Summerville
Fairmont
Tate
Nelson
Gainesville
Lavonia
Rome
Cartersville
Canton
Cumming
Lake Allatoona Army Rec Area
World Famous Navy Lake Site
Pendergrass
Commerce
Elberton
Six Mile
Cave Spring
Cedartown
Emerson
Jefferson
Roswell
Sandy Springs
Dacula
Winder
Athens
Marietta
Dallas
ATLANTA NAS
DOBBINS ARB
Lawrenceville
ATHENS NAVAL SUPPLY CORPS SCHOOL
Watkinsville
Snellville
ATLANTA
Tallapoosa
Bremen
Villa Rica
Monroe
Lincolnton
East Point
College Park
Decatur
FORT GILLEM
Forest Park
Hartsfield-Jackson IAP
Washington
Pointes West Army Recreation Area
Carrollton
Madison
Union Pt.
Greensboro
Covington
Bowdon
Stockbridge
Grovetown
Augusta
Newnan
Peachtree City
Thomson
Warrenton
FORT GORDON/ ARMY SIGNAL CTR
Augusta Regional Airport at Bush Field
Franklin
Moreland
Senoia
Jackson
Monticello
Eatonton
Grantville
Griffin
Sparta
Wrens
Hephzibah
U.S. ARMY SIGNAL CORPS MUSEUM
Waynesboro
ALABAMA (page 34)
SOUTH CAROLINA (page 42)
La Grange
Greenville
Woodbury
Forsyth
Barnesville
Milledgeville
Hardwick
Louisville
Gray
Sandersville
Thomaston
MACON
Manchester
Bartow
Wadley
Midville
Millen
Sylvania
Lanett
Roberta
Middle Georgia Regional Airport
Wrightsville
Kite
Talbotton
ROBINS AFB
Robins FAMCAMP
Warner Robins
Bonaire
E. Dublin
Dublin
Swainsboro
Midland
Geneva
COLUMBUS
Columbus Metropolitan Airport
FORT BENNING
Box Springs
Juniper
Butler
Fort Valley
Centerville
Perry
Adrian
Statesboro
Springfield
Phenix City
Fort Mitchell
Buena Vista
Montezuma
Soperton
Lotts Island Army Airfield RV Park
Uchee Creek Army Campground/Marina
Lawson AAF
Cusseta
Renfroe
Ellaville
Hawkinsville
ANDERSONVILLE NATIONAL HISTORICAL SITE AND CEMETERY
Eastman
Vidalia
Lyons
Claxton
Daisy
Pembroke
Savannah/Hilton Head IAP/ANG
SAVANNAH
Louvale
Richland
Preston
Americus
Plains
Vienna
Mount Vernon
Helena
McRae
FORT STEWART
Hunter AAF
Wright AAF
Holbrook Pond Rec Area & Campground
Glennville
Hinesville
Lumpkin
Cordele
Abbeville
Hazlehurst
Flemington
Midway
Smithville
Cuthbert
Shellman
Dawson
Fitzgerald
Baxley
Surrency
Ludowici
Jesup
Suttons Corner
Morgan
Albany
Sylvester
Southwest Georgia Regional Airport
ALBANY MCLB
Tifton
Ocilla
Douglas
Alma
Eulonia
Blakely
Alapaha
Willacoochee
Pearson
Bristol
Patterson
Hortense
Newton
Camilla
Dothan
Moultrie
Nashville
Blackshear
Waycross
Malcolm McKinnon Airport
Brunswick
Glynco Jetport Airport
Nahunta
Sterling
Colquitt
Meigs
Ray City
Waverly
New Rock Hill
Hahira
Bemiss
Mineola
MOODY AFB
Stockton
Homerville
Bainbridge
Cairo
Thomasville
Valdosta Regional Airport
Valdosta
Quitman
Folkston
KINGS BAY NSB
Kingsland
St. Marys
Grassy Pond Rec Area
Clyattville
Lake Park
Fernandina Beach
FLORIDA (page 36)
ATLANTIC OCEAN
MAYPORT CGB
Pelican Roost RV Park
MAYPORT NS
JACKSONVILLE
TALLAHASSEE

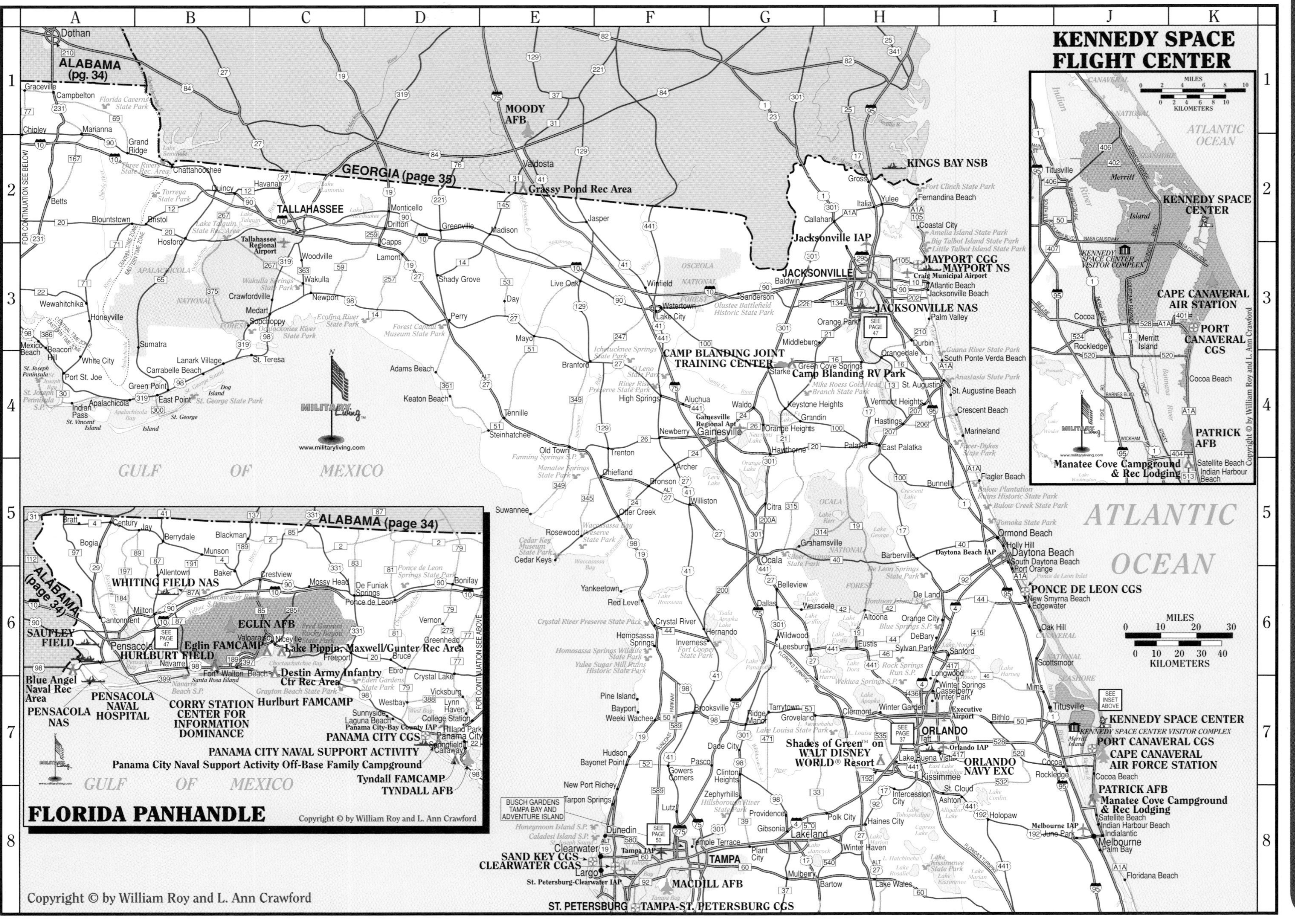
KENNEDY SPACE FLIGHT CENTER
KENNEDY SPACE CENTER
KENNEDY SPACE CENTER VISITOR COMPLEX
CAPE CANAVERAL AIR STATION
PORT CANAVERAL CGS
PATRICK AFB
Manatee Cove Campground & Rec Lodging
Copyright © by William Roy and L. Ann Crawford
ATLANTIC OCEAN
GULF OF MEXICO
ALABAMA (pg. 34)
GEORGIA (page 35)
MOODY AFB
Grassy Pond Rec Area
KINGS BAY NSB
TALLAHASSEE
Jacksonville IAP
JACKSONVILLE
MAYPORT CGG
MAYPORT NS
JACKSONVILLE NAS
CAMP BLANDING JOINT TRAINING CENTER
Camp Blanding RV Park
PONCE DE LEON CGS
KENNEDY SPACE CENTER
PORT CANAVERAL CGS
CAPE CANAVERAL AIR FORCE STATION
PATRICK AFB
Manatee Cove Campground & Rec Lodging
ORLANDO
ORLANDO NAVY EXC
Shades of Green™ on WALT DISNEY WORLD® Resort
TAMPA
MACDILL AFB
SAND KEY CGS
CLEARWATER CGAS
ST. PETERSBURG
TAMPA-ST. PETERSBURG CGS
FLORIDA PANHANDLE
ALABAMA (page 34)
WHITING FIELD NAS
SAUFLEY FIELD
EGLIN AFB
Eglin FAMCAMP
HURLBURT FIELD
Lake Pippin, Maxwell/Gunter Rec Area
Destin Army Infantry Ctr Rec Area
Blue Angel Naval Rec Area
PENSACOLA NAS
PENSACOLA NAVAL HOSPITAL
CORRY STATION CENTER FOR INFORMATION DOMINANCE
Hurlburt FAMCAMP
PANAMA CITY CGS
PANAMA CITY NAVAL SUPPORT ACTIVITY
Panama City Naval Support Activity Off-Base Family Campground
Tyndall FAMCAMP
TYNDALL AFB
Copyright © by William Roy and L. Ann Crawford
Copyright © by William Roy and L. Ann Crawford

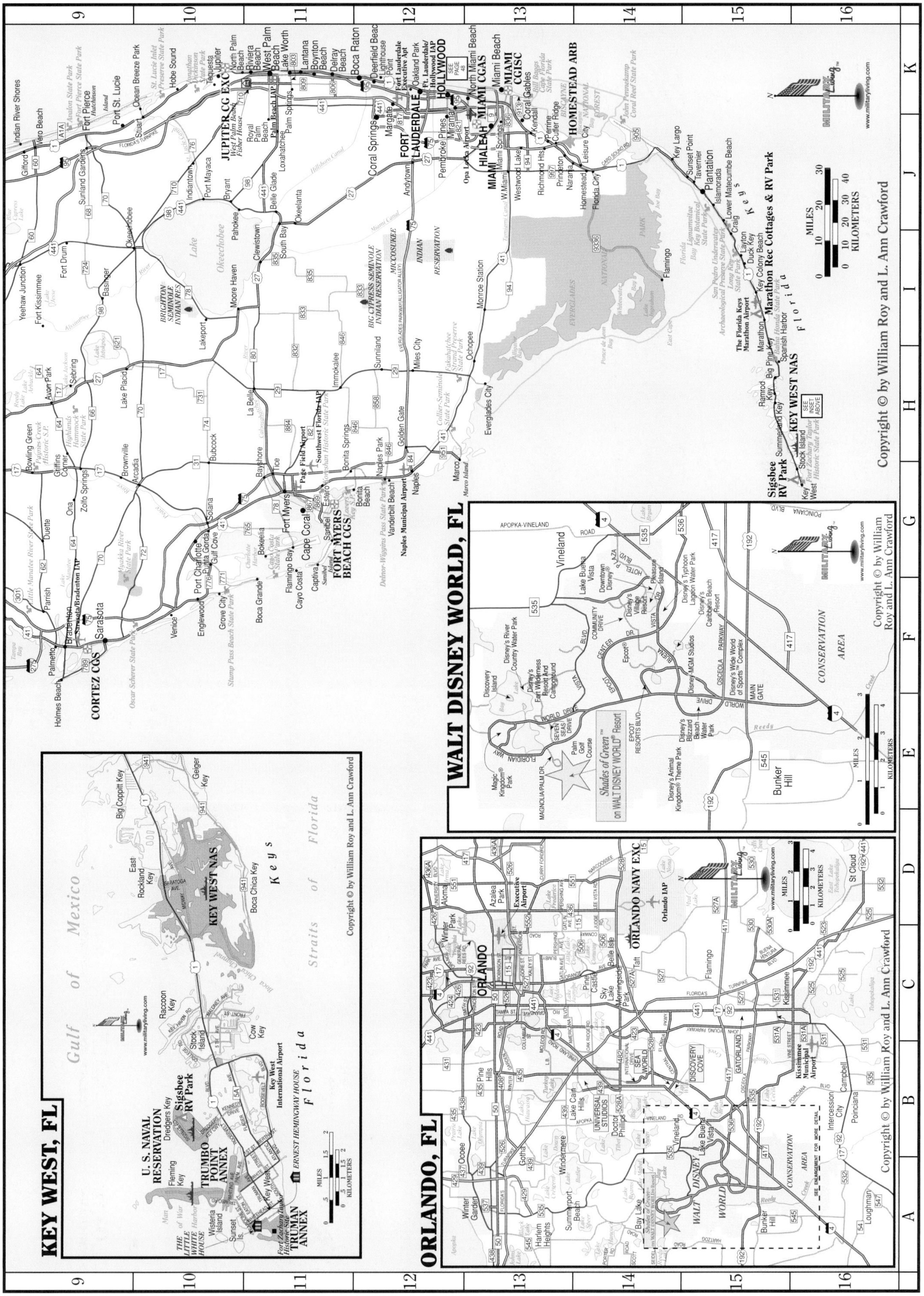

KEY WEST, FL

ORLANDO, FL

WALT DISNEY WORLD, FL

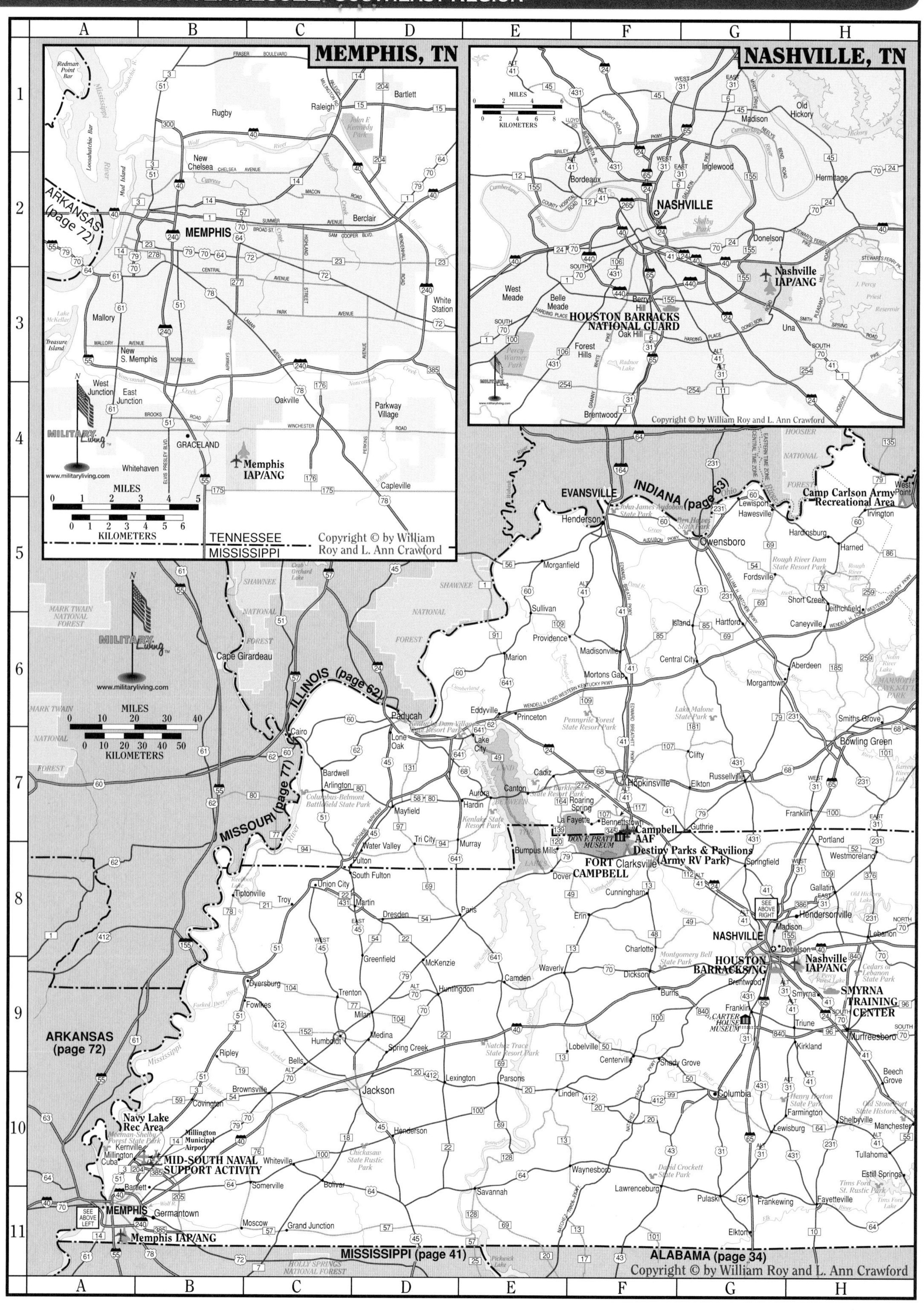
MEMPHIS, TN
NASHVILLE, TN
Memphis
Memphis IAP/ANG
Nashville
Nashville IAP/ANG
HOUSTON BARRACKS NATIONAL GUARD
Campbell AAF
FORT CAMPBELL
Destiny Parks & Pavilions (Army RV Park)
Camp Carlson Army Recreational Area
MID-SOUTH NAVAL SUPPORT ACTIVITY
Navy Lake Rec Area
SMYRNA TRAINING CENTER
DON F. PRATT MUSEUM
CARTER HOUSE MUSEUM
ILLINOIS (page 62)
INDIANA (page 63)
MISSOURI (page 77)
ARKANSAS (page 72)
MISSISSIPPI (page 41)
ALABAMA (page 34)
TENNESSEE
MISSISSIPPI
Paducah
Evansville
Owensboro
Bowling Green
Hopkinsville
Clarksville
Jackson
Murfreesboro
Columbia
Copyright © by William Roy and L. Ann Crawford
www.militaryliving.com

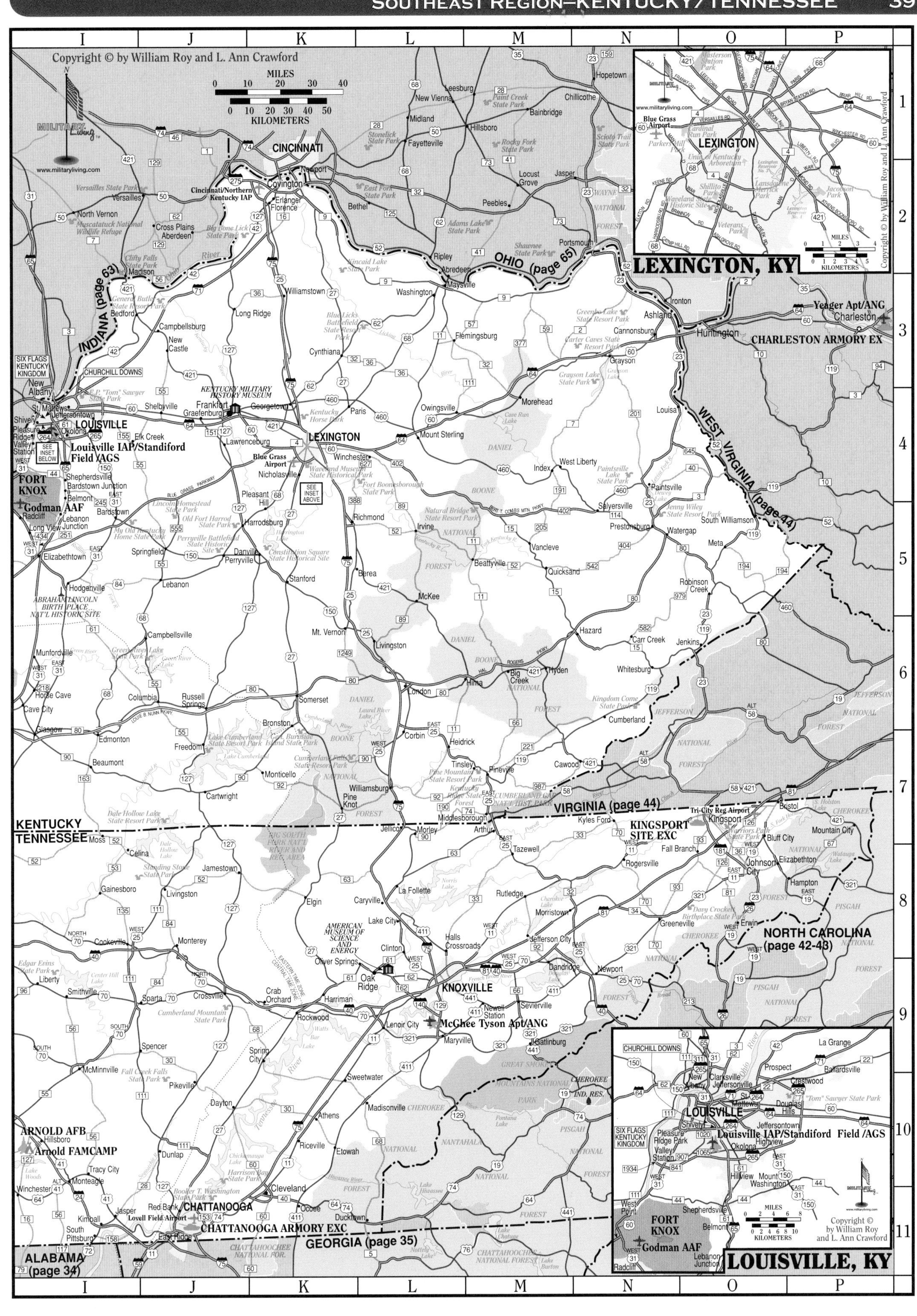
Copyright © by William Roy and L. Ann Crawford
MILES
KILOMETERS
www.militaryliving.com
CINCINNATI
Cincinnati/Northern Kentucky IAP
Covington
Newport
Erlanger
Florence
LEXINGTON
Blue Grass Airport
Frankfort
KENTUCKY MILITARY HISTORY MUSEUM
LOUISVILLE
Louisville IAP/Standiford Field /AGS
SEE INSET BELOW
SEE INSET ABOVE
FORT KNOX
Godman AAF
SIX FLAGS KENTUCKY KINGDOM
CHURCHILL DOWNS
INDIANA (page 63)
OHIO (page 65)
WEST VIRGINIA (page 44)
VIRGINIA (page 44)
NORTH CAROLINA (page 42-43)
GEORGIA (page 35)
ALABAMA (page 34)
KENTUCKY
TENNESSEE
Yeager Apt/ANG
Charleston
CHARLESTON ARMORY EX
Huntington
Ashland
Maysville
Richmond
Somerset
London
Corbin
Middlesborough
Hazard
Pikeville
Bowling Green
Tri-City Reg Airport
Kingsport
KINGSPORT SITE EXC
Bristol
Johnson City
KNOXVILLE
McGhee Tyson Apt/ANG
AMERICAN MUSEUM OF SCIENCE AND ENERGY
Oak Ridge
CHATTANOOGA
Lovell Field Airport
CHATTANOOGA ARMORY EXC
ARNOLD AFB
Arnold FAMCAMP
Cleveland
Gatlinburg
LEXINGTON, KY
LOUISVILLE, KY

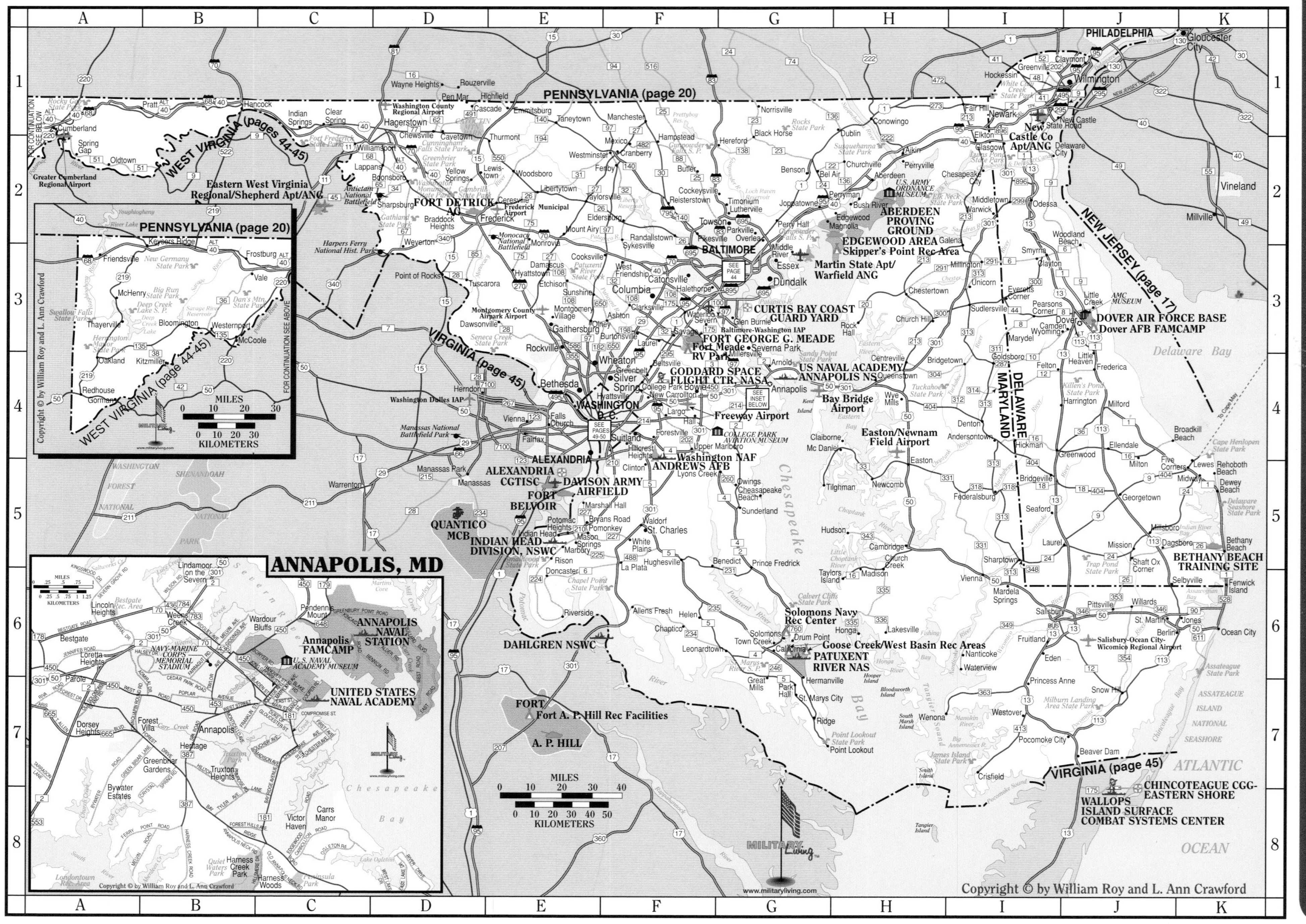
PENNSYLVANIA (page 20)
WEST VIRGINIA (pages 44-45)
NEW JERSEY (page 17)
DELAWARE
MARYLAND
VIRGINIA (page 45)
PHILADELPHIA
Wilmington
BALTIMORE
WASHINGTON D.C.
ALEXANDRIA
Annapolis
Eastern West Virginia Regional/Shepherd Apt/ANG
FORT DETRICK AG
Frederick Municipal Airport
ABERDEEN PROVING GROUND
EDGEWOOD AREA Skipper's Point Rec Area
Martin State Apt/ Warfield ANG
CURTIS BAY COAST GUARD YARD
FORT GEORGE G. MEADE
Fort Meade RV Park
GODDARD SPACE FLIGHT CTR. NASA
US NAVAL ACADEMY/ ANNAPOLIS NS
Bay Bridge Airport
Freeway Airport
Easton/Newnam Field Airport
Washington NAF ANDREWS AFB
ALEXANDRIA CGTISC
DAVISON ARMY AIRFIELD
FORT BELVOIR
QUANTICO MCB
INDIAN HEAD DIVISION, NSWC
DAHLGREN NSWC
FORT Fort A. P. Hill Rec Facilities
A. P. HILL
Solomons Navy Rec Center
Goose Creek/West Basin Rec Areas
PATUXENT RIVER NAS
New Castle Co Apt/ANG
DOVER AIR FORCE BASE Dover AFB FAMCAMP
BETHANY BEACH TRAINING SITE
Salisbury-Ocean City-Wicomico Regional Airport
CHINCOTEAGUE CGG-EASTERN SHORE
WALLOPS ISLAND SURFACE COMBAT SYSTEMS CENTER
Chesapeake Bay
Delaware Bay
ATLANTIC OCEAN
MILES 0 10 20 30 40
0 10 20 30 40 50 KILOMETERS
www.militaryliving.com
Copyright © by William Roy and L. Ann Crawford
PENNSYLVANIA (page 20)
WEST VIRGINIA (page 44-45)
FOR CONTINUATION SEE ABOVE
Copyright © by William Roy and L. Ann Crawford
ANNAPOLIS, MD
ANNAPOLIS NAVAL STATION
Annapolis FAMCAMP
U. S. NAVAL ACADEMY MUSEUM
UNITED STATES NAVAL ACADEMY
NAVY-MARINE CORPS MEMORIAL STADIUM
Copyright © by William Roy and L. Ann Crawford

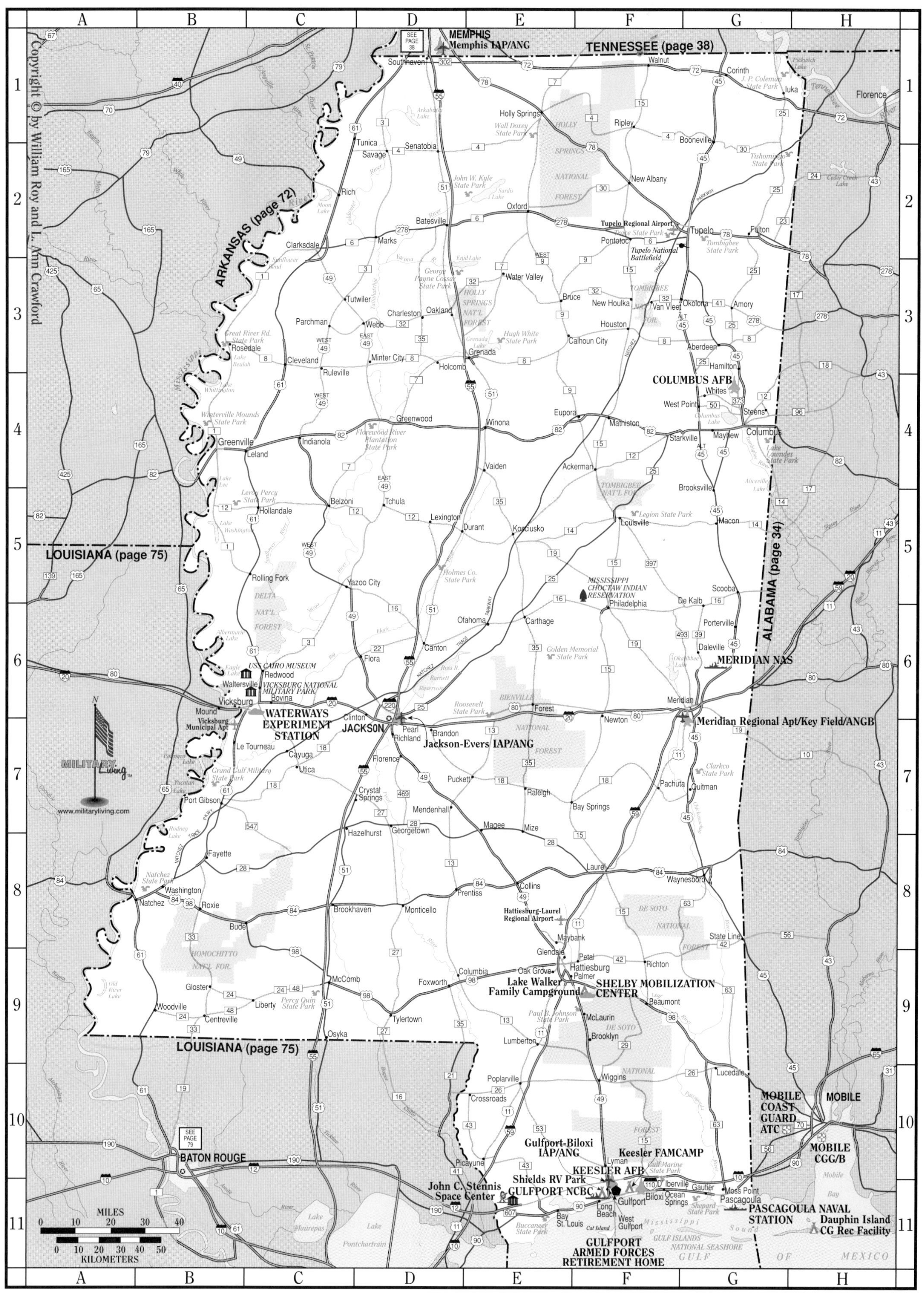
Copyright © by William Roy and L. Ann Crawford
TENNESSEE (page 38)
ARKANSAS (page 72)
LOUISIANA (page 75)
ALABAMA (page 34)
SEE PAGE 38
SEE PAGE 79
MEMPHIS
Memphis IAP/ANG
Southhaven
Walnut
Corinth
Iuka
Florence
Tunica
Savage
Senatobia
Holly Springs
Ripley
Booneville
New Albany
Rich
Oxford
Batesville
Tupelo Regional Airport
Tupelo
Fulton
Pontotoc
Tupelo National Battlefield
Clarksdale
Marks
Water Valley
Tutwiler
Bruce
New Houlka
Van Vleet
Okolona
Amory
Parchman
Webb
Charleston
Oakland
Houston
Rosedale
Cleveland
Minter City
Holcomb
Grenada
Calhoun City
Aberdeen
Hamilton
Ruleville
COLUMBUS AFB
Whites
West Point
Steens
Greenwood
Winona
Eupora
Mathiston
Starkville
Mayhew
Columbus
Greenville
Leland
Indianola
Vaiden
Ackerman
Brooksville
Belzoni
Tchula
Hollandale
Lexington
Durant
Kosciusko
Louisville
Macon
Rolling Fork
Yazoo City
Scooba
De Kalb
Philadelphia
Ofahoma
Carthage
Porterville
Dalleville
Canton
Flora
MERIDIAN NAS
USS CAIRO MUSEUM
Redwood
VICKSBURG NATIONAL MILITARY PARK
Waltersville
Bovina
Vicksburg
Mound
Vicksburg Municipal Apt
WATERWAYS EXPERIMENT STATION
Clinton
JACKSON
Pearl
Richland
Brandon
Jackson-Evers IAP/ANG
Forest
Newton
Meridian
Meridian Regional Apt/Key Field/ANGB
Le Tourneau
Cayuga
Utica
Florence
Puckett
Raleigh
Pachuta
Quitman
Port Gibson
Crystal Springs
Mendenhall
Bay Springs
Hazelhurst
Georgetown
Magee
Mize
Fayette
Laurel
Waynesboro
Washington
Natchez
Roxie
Prentiss
Collins
Brookhaven
Monticello
Hattiesburg-Laurel Regional Airport
Bude
Maybank
State Line
Glendale
Petal
Hattiesburg
Palmer
Richton
Oak Grove
Columbia
Foxworth
McComb
Gloster
Liberty
Lake Walker Family Campground
SHELBY MOBILIZATION CENTER
Beaumont
Woodville
Centreville
Tylertown
McLaurin
Brooklyn
Osyka
Lumberton
Poplarville
Wiggins
Lucedale
Crossroads
MOBILE COAST GUARD ATC
MOBILE
MOBILE CGG/B
BATON ROUGE
Picayune
Gulfport-Biloxi IAP/ANG
Keesler FAMCAMP
Lyman
KEESLER AFB
Shields RV Park
GULFPORT NCBC
John C. Stennis Space Center
Gulfport
Biloxi
D'Iberville
Gautier
Ocean Springs
Moss Point
Pascagoula
PASCAGOULA NAVAL STATION
Dauphin Island CG Rec Facility
Bay St. Louis
Long Beach
West Gulfport
GULFPORT ARMED FORCES RETIREMENT HOME
GULF OF MEXICO
MILES
KILOMETERS
MILITARY Living
www.militaryliving.com

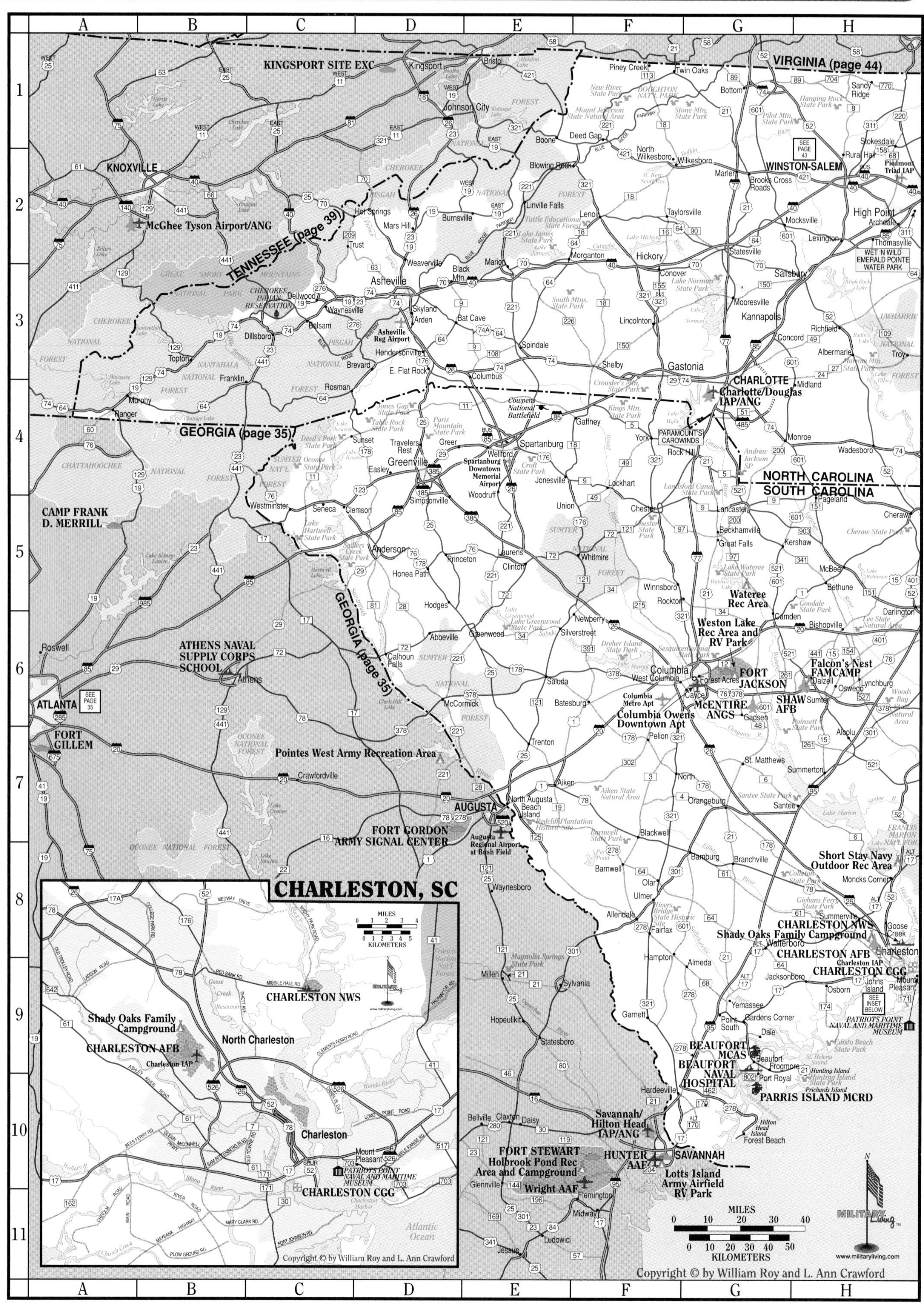

KINGSPORT SITE EXC
KNOXVILLE
McGhee Tyson Airport/ANG
TENNESSEE (page 39)
VIRGINIA (page 44)
GEORGIA (page 35)
NORTH CAROLINA
SOUTH CAROLINA
WINSTON-SALEM
Piedmont Triad IAP
High Point
WET 'N WILD EMERALD POINTE WATER PARK
Asheville
Asheville Reg Airport
CHARLOTTE
Charlotte/Douglas IAP/ANG
PARAMOUNT'S CAROWINDS
Gastonia
Spartanburg
Spartanburg Downtown Memorial Airport
Greenville
CAMP FRANK D. MERRILL
ATHENS NAVAL SUPPLY CORPS SCHOOL
ATLANTA
FORT GILLEM
Pointes West Army Recreation Area
AUGUSTA
FORT GORDON ARMY SIGNAL CENTER
Augusta Regional Airport at Bush Field
Wateree Rec Area
Weston Lake Rec Area and RV Park
Columbia
FORT JACKSON
Falcon's Nest FAMCAMP
SHAW AFB
McENTIRE ANGS
Columbia Metro Apt
Columbia Owens Downtown Apt
Short Stay Navy Outdoor Rec Area
CHARLESTON NWS
Shady Oaks Family Campground
CHARLESTON AFB
Charleston IAP
CHARLESTON CGG
PATRIOTS POINT NAVAL AND MARITIME MUSEUM
SEE INSET BELOW
BEAUFORT MCAS
BEAUFORT NAVAL HOSPITAL
PARRIS ISLAND MCRD
Savannah/Hilton Head IAP/ANG
HUNTER AAF
SAVANNAH
Lotts Island Army Airfield RV Park
FORT STEWART Holbrook Pond Rec Area and Campground
Wright AAF
CHARLESTON, SC
North Charleston
Charleston
Atlantic Ocean
MILES
KILOMETERS
Copyright © by William Roy and L. Ann Crawford
www.militaryliving.com

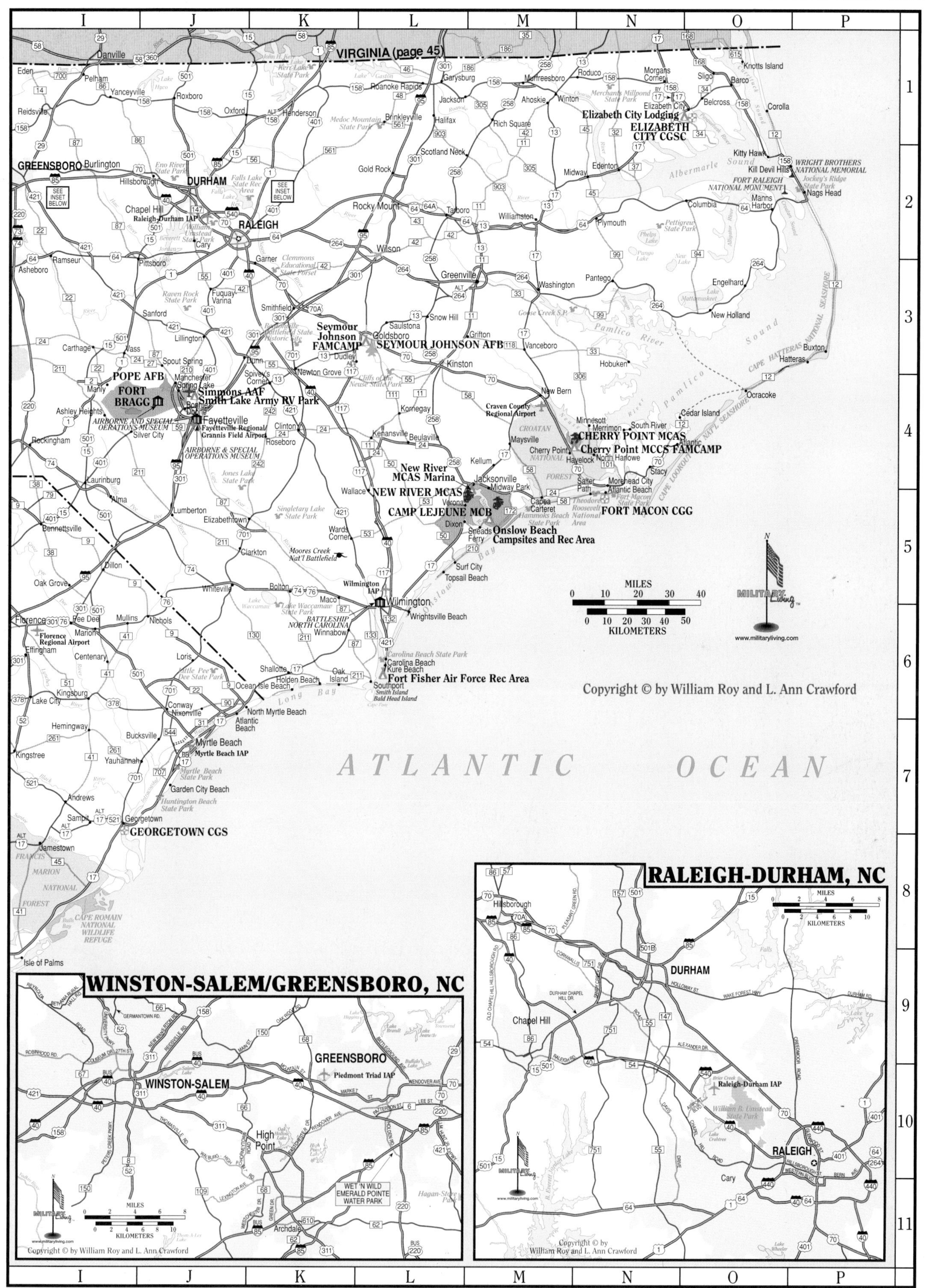

I J K L M N O P
1 2 3 4 5 6 7 8 9 10 11
VIRGINIA (page 45)
Danville
Eden
Pelham
Yanceyville
Roxboro
Reidsville
Oxford
Henderson
John H. Kerr Lake
Kerr Lake State Park
Roanoke Rapids
Garysburg
Murfreesboro
Roduco
Morgans Corner
Sligo
Barco
Knotts Island
Jackson
Ahoskie
Winton
Merchants Millpond State Park
Elizabeth City
Belcross
Corolla
Elizabeth City Lodging
ELIZABETH CITY CGSC
Medoc Mountain State Park
Brinkleyville
Halifax
Rich Square
GREENSBORO
Burlington
Eno River State Park
Hillsborough
DURHAM
Falls Lake State Rec Area
SEE INSET BELOW
Scotland Neck
Gold Rock
Edenton
Midway
Albemarle Sound
Kitty Hawk
Kill Devil Hills
WRIGHT BROTHERS NATIONAL MEMORIAL
Jockey's Ridge State Park
Nags Head
FORT RALEIGH NATIONAL MONUMENT
Manns Harbor
Columbia
Chapel Hill
Raleigh-Durham IAP
RALEIGH
William B. Umstead State Park
Cary
Rocky Mount
Tarboro
Williamston
Plymouth
Pettigrew State Park
Asheboro
Ramseur
Pittsboro
Garner
Clemmons Educational State Forest
Wilson
Greenville
Washington
Pantego
Engelhart
New Holland
Raven Rock State Park
Fuquay-Varina
Sanford
Smithfield
Bentonville Battlefield State Historic Site
Seymour Johnson FAMCAMP
SEYMOUR JOHNSON AFB
Goldsboro
Saulstona
Snow Hill
Grifton
Vanceboro
Goose Creek S.P.
Pamlico River
Pamlico Sound
CAPE HATTERAS NATIONAL SEASHORE
Buxton
Hatteras
Ocracoke
Carthage
Vass
Lillington
Spout Spring
Dunn
Dudley
Kinston
Hobuken
POPE AFB
FORT BRAGG
Manly
Manchester
Spring Lake
Simmons AAF
Smith Lake Army RV Park
Fayetteville
Fayetteville Regional/Grannis Field Airport
AIRBORNE AND SPECIAL OPERATIONS MUSEUM
Spivey's Corner
Newton Grove
Cliffs of the Neuse State Park
New Bern
Craven County Regional Airport
Ashley Heights
Rockingham
Silver City
Clinton
Roseboro
Kornegay
Kenansville
Beulaville
CROATAN NATIONAL FOREST
Maysville
Minnesott
Merrimon
South River
Cedar Island
CHERRY POINT MCAS
Cherry Point MCCS FAMCAMP
Cherry Point
Havelock
North Harlowe
Stacy
Laurinburg
Jones Lake State Park
Kellum
New River MCAS Marina
Jacksonville
Midway Park
NEW RIVER MCAS
Wallace
Morehead City
Atlantic Beach
Salter Path
Cape Carteret
Fort Macon State Park
Theodore Roosevelt Natural Area
Hammocks Beach State Park
FORT MACON CGG
CAPE LOOKOUT NATL SEASHORE
Lumberton
Elizabethtown
Singletary Lake State Park
Verona
CAMP LEJEUNE MCB
Dixon
Sneads Ferry
Onslow Beach Campsites and Rec Area
Bennettsville
Wards Corner
Clarkton
Moores Creek Nat'l Battlefield
Surf City
Topsail Beach
Onslow Bay
Dillon
Oak Grove
Whiteville
Bolton
Lake Waccamaw
Lake Waccamaw State Park
Maco
Wilmington IAP
Wilmington
Wrightsville Beach
BATTLESHIP NORTH CAROLINA
Winnabow
Florence
Florence Regional Airport
Effingham
Marion
Mullins
Nichols
Centenary
Loris
Little Pee Dee State Park
Shallotte
Holden Beach
Ocean Isle Beach
Oak Island
Carolina Beach State Park
Carolina Beach
Kure Beach
Fort Fisher Air Force Rec Area
Southport
Smith Island
Bald Head Island
Long Bay
Kingsburg
Lake City
Conway
Nixonville
North Myrtle Beach
Atlantic Beach
Hemingway
Bucksville
Myrtle Beach
Myrtle Beach IAP
Kingstree
Yauhannah
Myrtle Beach State Park
Garden City Beach
Huntington Beach State Park
Andrews
Sampit
Georgetown
GEORGETOWN CGS
Jamestown
FRANCIS MARION NATIONAL FOREST
CAPE ROMAIN NATIONAL WILDLIFE REFUGE
Isle of Palms
ATLANTIC OCEAN
MILES 0 10 20 30 40
0 10 20 30 40 50 KILOMETERS
MILITARY Living
www.militaryliving.com
Copyright © by William Roy and L. Ann Crawford
WINSTON-SALEM/GREENSBORO, NC
GREENSBORO
Piedmont Triad IAP
WINSTON-SALEM
High Point
Archdale
WET 'N WILD EMERALD POINTE WATER PARK
Hagan-Stone Park
MILES 0 2 4 6 8
0 2 4 6 8 10 KILOMETERS
Copyright © by William Roy and L. Ann Crawford
RALEIGH-DURHAM, NC
Hillsborough
DURHAM
Chapel Hill
Raleigh-Durham IAP
William B. Umstead State Park
RALEIGH
Cary
MILES 0 2 4 6 8
0 2 4 6 8 10 KILOMETERS
Copyright © by William Roy and L. Ann Crawford

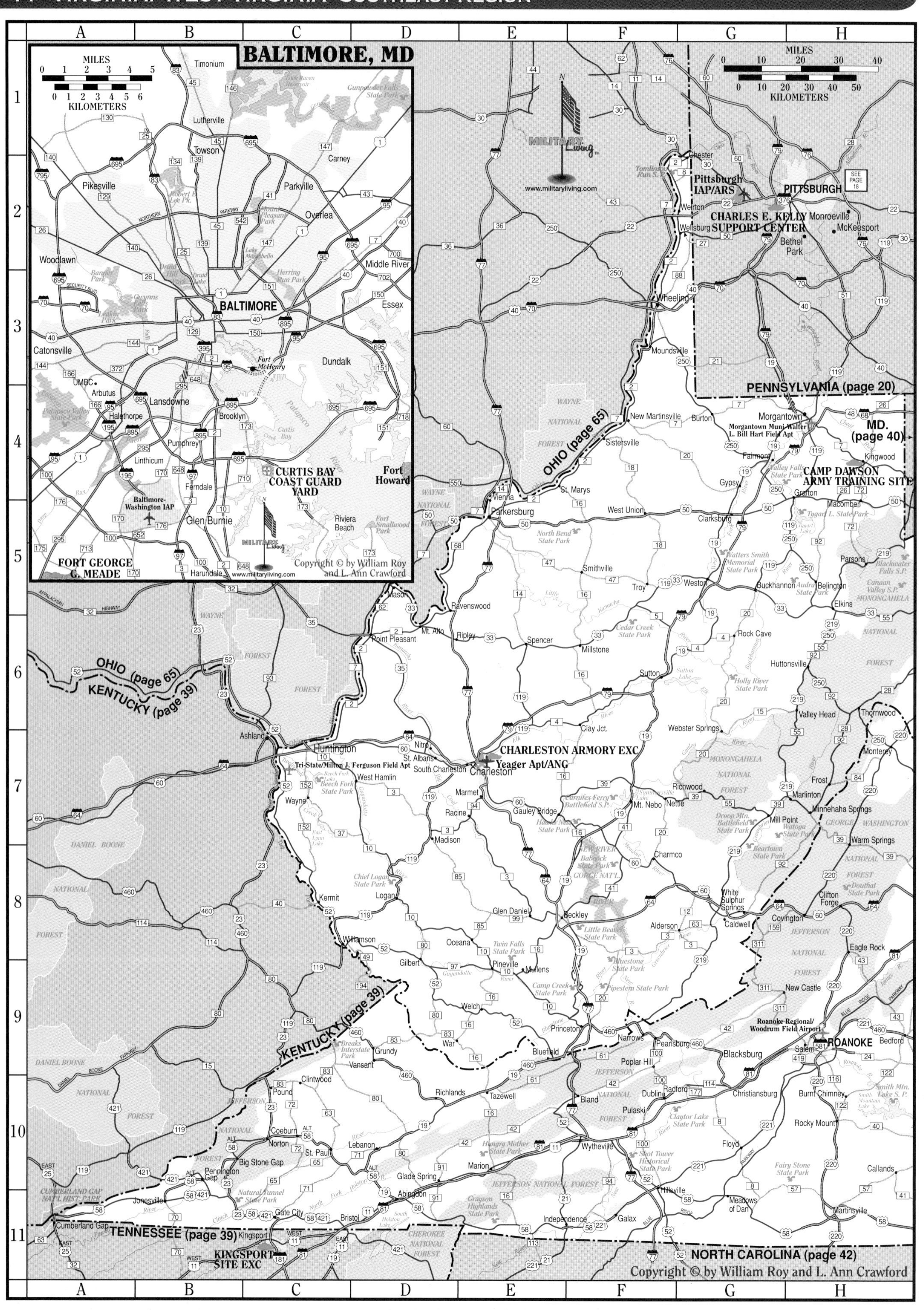
A
B
C
D
E
F
G
H
1
2
3
4
5
6
7
8
9
10
11
BALTIMORE, MD
MILES
KILOMETERS
Timonium
Lutherville
Towson
Carney
Pikesville
Parkville
Overlea
Woodlawn
Middle River
BALTIMORE
Essex
Catonsville
Dundalk
UMBC
Arbutus
Lansdowne
Halethorpe
Brooklyn
Pumphrey
Linthicum
Ferndale
CURTIS BAY COAST GUARD YARD
Fort Howard
Fort McHenry
Baltimore-Washington IAP
Glen Burnie
Riviera Beach
FORT GEORGE G. MEADE
Harundale
Copyright © by William Roy and L. Ann Crawford
www.militaryliving.com
MILITARY Living
Chester
Tomlinson Run S.P.
Pittsburgh IAP/ARS
PITTSBURGH
SEE PAGE 18
Weirton
CHARLES E. KELLY SUPPORT CENTER
Monroeville
McKeesport
Wellsburg
Bethel Park
Wheeling
Moundsville
PENNSYLVANIA (page 20)
New Martinsville
Burton
Morgantown
Morgantown Muni-Walter L. Bill Hart Field Apt
MD. (page 40)
Sistersville
Fairmont
Kingwood
OHIO (page 65)
CAMP DAWSON ARMY TRAINING SITE
Grafton
Gypsy
St. Marys
Vienna
Parkersburg
West Union
Clarksburg
Macomber
Tygart L. State Park
Parsons
Blackwater Falls S.P.
Canaan Valley S.P.
Smithville
Troy
Weston
Buckhannon
Audra State Park
Belington
Elkins
Ravenswood
Mason
Ripley
Mt. Alto
Point Pleasant
Spencer
Millstone
Cedar Creek State Park
Rock Cave
MONONGAHELA NATIONAL FOREST
WAYNE NATIONAL FOREST
Sutton
Holly River State Park
Huttonsville
Valley Head
Webster Springs
Thornwood
Monterey
Clay Jct.
Ashland
Huntington
Nitro
St. Albans
South Charleston
CHARLESTON ARMORY EXC
Yeager Apt/ANG
Charleston
Tri-State/Milton J. Ferguson Field Apt
Beech Fork State Park
West Hamlin
Wayne
Marmet
Racine
Gauley Bridge
Carnifex Ferry Battlefield S.P.
Mt. Nebo
Nettie
Richwood
Frost
Marlinton
Minnehaha Springs
Mill Point
Droop Mtn. Battlefield State Park
Watoga State Park
Madison
Hawks Nest State Park
Charmco
Warm Springs
GEORGE WASHINGTON NATIONAL FOREST
Chief Logan State Park
Logan
Kermit
NEW RIVER GORGE NAT'L RIVER
White Sulphur Springs
Caldwell
Covington
Clifton Forge
Douthat State Park
Glen Daniel
Beckley
Alderson
Little Beaver State Park
Williamson
Oceana
Twin Falls State Park
Pineville
Mullens
Gilbert
Twin Falls
Bluestone State Park
Pipestem State Park
Camp Creek State Park
JEFFERSON NATIONAL FOREST
Eagle Rock
New Castle
Welch
War
Princeton
Narrows
Pearisburg
Bluefield
KENTUCKY (page 39)
Breaks Interstate Park
Grundy
Vansant
Roanoke Regional/Woodrum Field Airport
ROANOKE
Bedford
Salem
Blacksburg
Poplar Hill
Clintwood
Pound
Richlands
Tazewell
Bland
Dublin
Radford
Christiansburg
Burnt Chimney
Smith Mtn. Lake S. P.
Pulaski
Claytor Lake State Park
Rocky Mount
DANIEL BOONE NATIONAL FOREST
Coeburn
Norton
St. Paul
Big Stone Gap
Lebanon
Hungry Mother State Park
Wytheville
Floyd
Shot Tower Historical State Park
Fairy Stone State Park
Callands
Pennington Gap
Marion
Glade Spring
Abingdon
Natural Tunnel State Park
Jonesville
Gate City
Bristol
Grayson Highlands State Park
Independence
Galax
Hillsville
Meadows of Dan
Martinsville
CUMBERLAND GAP NAT'L HIST. PARK
Cumberland Gap
TENNESSEE (page 39)
Kingsport
KINGSPORT SITE EXC
CHEROKEE NATIONAL FOREST
NORTH CAROLINA (page 42)
Copyright © by William Roy and L. Ann Crawford

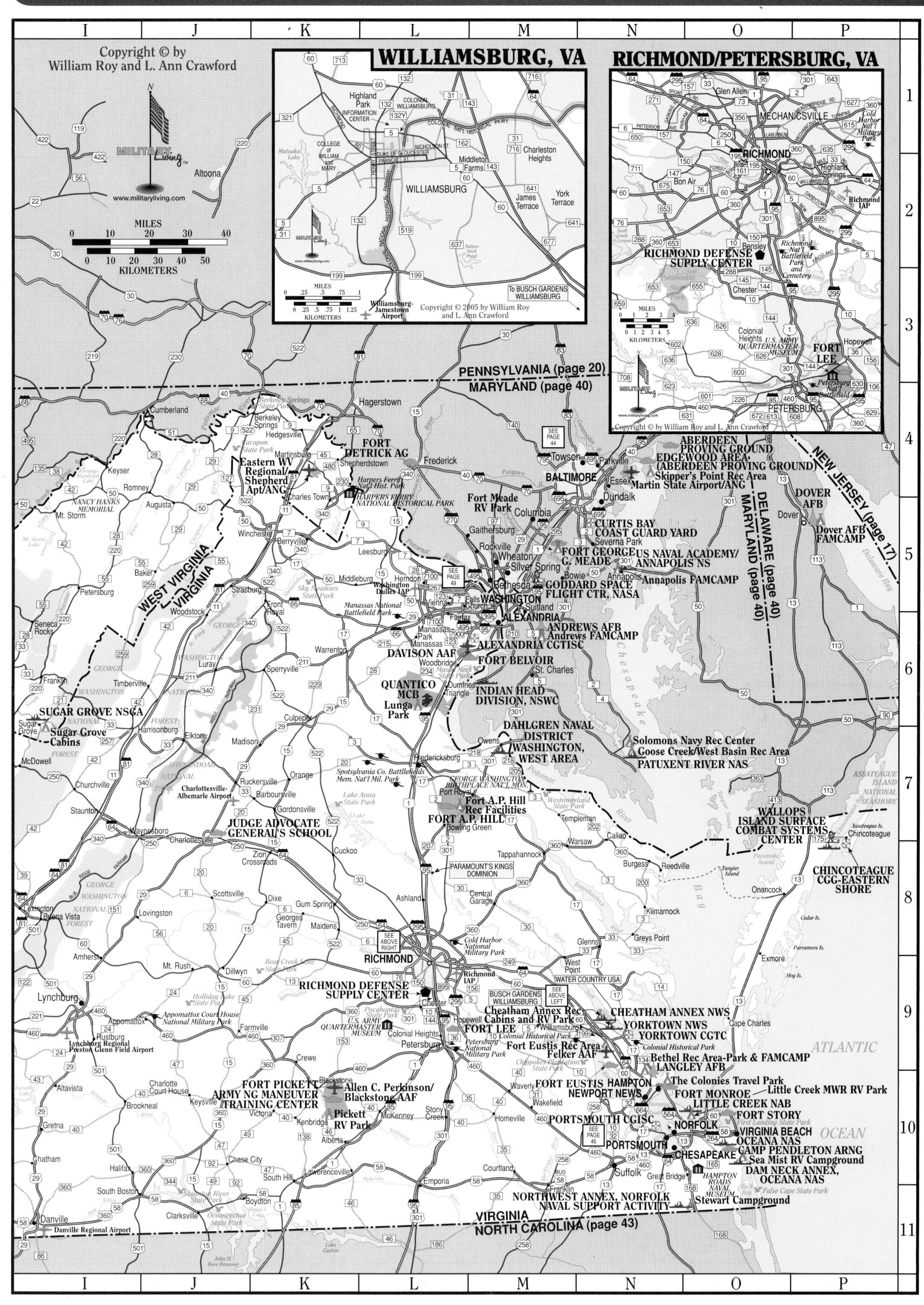
Copyright © by
William Roy and L. Ann Crawford
www.militaryliving.com
MILES
KILOMETERS
WILLIAMSBURG, VA
Highland Park
COLONIAL WILLIAMSBURG
INFORMATION CENTER
COLLEGE of WILLIAM and MARY
DUKE OF GLOUCESTER
Middleton Farms
Charleston Heights
WILLIAMSBURG
James Terrace
York Terrace
To BUSCH GARDENS WILLIAMSBURG
Williamsburg-Jamestown Airport
Copyright © 2005 by William Roy and L. Ann Crawford
RICHMOND/PETERSBURG, VA
Glen Allen
MECHANICSVILLE
Cold Harbor Nat'l Military Park
RICHMOND
Highland Springs
Bon Air
Richmond IAP
Bensley
RICHMOND DEFENSE SUPPLY CENTER
Richmond Nat'l Battlefield Park and Cemetery
Chester
Colonial Heights
U.S. ARMY QUARTERMASTER MUSEUM
FORT LEE
Hopewell
Petersburg Nat'l Battlefield
PETERSBURG
Copyright © by William Roy and L. Ann Crawford
Altoona
PENNSYLVANIA (page 20)
MARYLAND (page 40)
Cumberland
Hagerstown
Berkeley Springs
Hedgesville
Martinsburg
FORT DETRICK AG
Shepherdstown
Frederick
Eastern WV Regional/ Shepherd Apt/ANG
Harpers Ferry Nat'l Hist. Park
HARPERS FERRY NATIONAL HISTORICAL PARK
Charles Town
Keyser
Romney
NANCY HANKS MEMORIAL
Mt. Storm
Augusta
Winchester
Berryville
Leesburg
Towson
Parkville
BALTIMORE
Essex
Dundalk
ABERDEEN PROVING GROUND
EDGEWOOD AREA (ABERDEEN PROVING GROUND)
Skipper's Point Rec Area
Martin State Airport/ANG
Fort Meade RV Park
Columbia
CURTIS BAY COAST GUARD YARD
Gaithersburg
Severna Park
Rockville
FORT GEORGE G. MEADE
US NAVAL ACADEMY/ ANNAPOLIS NS
Annapolis
Annapolis FAMCAMP
Wheaton
Silver Spring
Bowie
GODDARD SPACE FLIGHT CTR, NASA
Bethesda
WASHINGTON
ALEXANDRIA
Suitland
ANDREWS AFB
Andrews FAMCAMP
ALEXANDRIA CGTISC
DOVER AFB
Dover
Dover AFB FAMCAMP
NEW JERSEY (page 17)
DELAWARE (page 40)
MARYLAND (page 40)
WEST VIRGINIA
VIRGINIA
Petersburg
Baker
Strasburg
Middleburg
Herndon
Washington Dulles IAP
Falls Church
Vienna
Fairfax
Manassas National Battlefield Park
Manassas Park
Manassas
Front Royal
Woodstock
Seneca Rocks
Warrenton
DAVISON AAF
Woodbridge
FORT BELVOIR
St. Charles
Luray
Sperryville
QUANTICO MCB
Lunga Park
Dumfries
Triangle
INDIAN HEAD DIVISION, NSWC
Franklin
Timberville
SUGAR GROVE NSGA
Sugar Grove
Sugar Grove Cabins
Harrisonburg
Elkton
Culpeper
DAHLGREN NAVAL DISTRICT WASHINGTON, WEST AREA
Owens
Solomons Navy Rec Center
Goose Creek/West Basin Rec Area
PATUXENT RIVER NAS
McDowell
Madison
Fredericksburg
Spotsylvania Co. Battlefields Mem. Nat'l Mil. Park
GEORGE WASHINGTON BIRTHPLACE NAT'L MON.
Churchville
Ruckersville
Orange
Charlottesville-Albemarle Airport
Barboursville
Gordonsville
Port Royal
Fort A.P. Hill Rec Facilities
FORT A.P. HILL
Staunton
Lake Anna State Park
Westmoreland State Park
Templeman
WALLOPS ISLAND SURFACE COMBAT SYSTEMS CENTER
Chincoteague
Waynesboro
Charlottesville
JUDGE ADVOCATE GENERAL'S SCHOOL
Bowling Green
Warsaw
Callao
Zion Crossroads
Cuckoo
Tappahannock
PARAMOUNT'S KINGS DOMINION
Burgess
Reedville
CHINCOTEAGUE CGG-EASTERN SHORE
Scottsville
Dixe
Ashland
Central Garage
Onancock
Lexington
Buena Vista
Lovingston
Gum Spring
Georges Tavern
Maidens
Kilmarnock
Cold Harbor National Military Park
Greys Point
Amherst
RICHMOND
Glenns
Exmore
Mt. Rush
Dillwyn
Richmond IAP
West Point
WATER COUNTRY USA
Lynchburg
RICHMOND DEFENSE SUPPLY CENTER
BUSCH GARDENS WILLIAMSBURG
Appomattox
Appomattox Court House National Military Park
Chester
Cheatham Annex Rec Cabins and RV Park
CHEATHAM ANNEX NWS
Farmville
Hopewell
FORT LEE
Williamsburg
YORKTOWN NWS
Cape Charles
U.S. ARMY QUARTERMASTER MUSEUM
Colonial Heights
Petersburg National Military Park
Colonial Historical Park
YORKTOWN CGTC
Rustburg
Lynchburg Regional Preston Glenn Field Airport
Petersburg
Fort Eustis Rec Area
Felker AAF
ATLANTIC
Crewe
Bethel Rec Area-Park & FAMCAMP
LANGLEY AFB
Chippokes Plantation State Park
Altavista
Charlotte Court House
FORT PICKETT ARMY NG MANEUVER TRAINING CENTER
Blackstone
Allen C. Perkinson/ Blackstone AAF
Waverly
FORT EUSTIS
HAMPTON
The Colonies Travel Park
Little Creek MWR RV Park
NEWPORT NEWS
FORT MONROE
Keysville
Victoria
Brookneal
Wakefield
LITTLE CREEK NAB
Pickett RV Park
McKenney
Stony Creek
Homeville
PORTSMOUTH CGISC
FORT STORY
Gretna
Kenbridge
NORFOLK
First Landing State Park
VIRGINIA BEACH
OCEAN
Alberta
PORTSMOUTH
OCEANA NAS
Chatham
Chase City
CAMP PENDLETON ARNG
CHESAPEAKE
Sea Mist RV Campground
Halifax
Lawrenceville
Courtland
Suffolk
DAM NECK ANNEX, OCEANA NAS
South Hill
Emporia
HAMPTON ROADS NAVAL MUSEUM
Great Bridge
South Boston
Staunton River State Park
Franklin
Boydton
NORTHWEST ANNEX, NORFOLK NAVAL SUPPORT ACTIVITY
Stewart Campground
False Cape State Park
Danville
Clarksville
Occoneechee State Park
VIRGINIA
NORTH CAROLINA (page 43)
Danville Regional Airport
Chesapeake
Bay
Delaware Bay
ASSATEAGUE ISLAND NATIONAL SEASHORE
Tangier Island
Pocomoke Sound
Cedar Is.
Parramore Is.
Hog Is.
SEE PAGE 44
SEE PAGE 49
SEE ABOVE RIGHT
SEE ABOVE LEFT
SEE PAGE 46

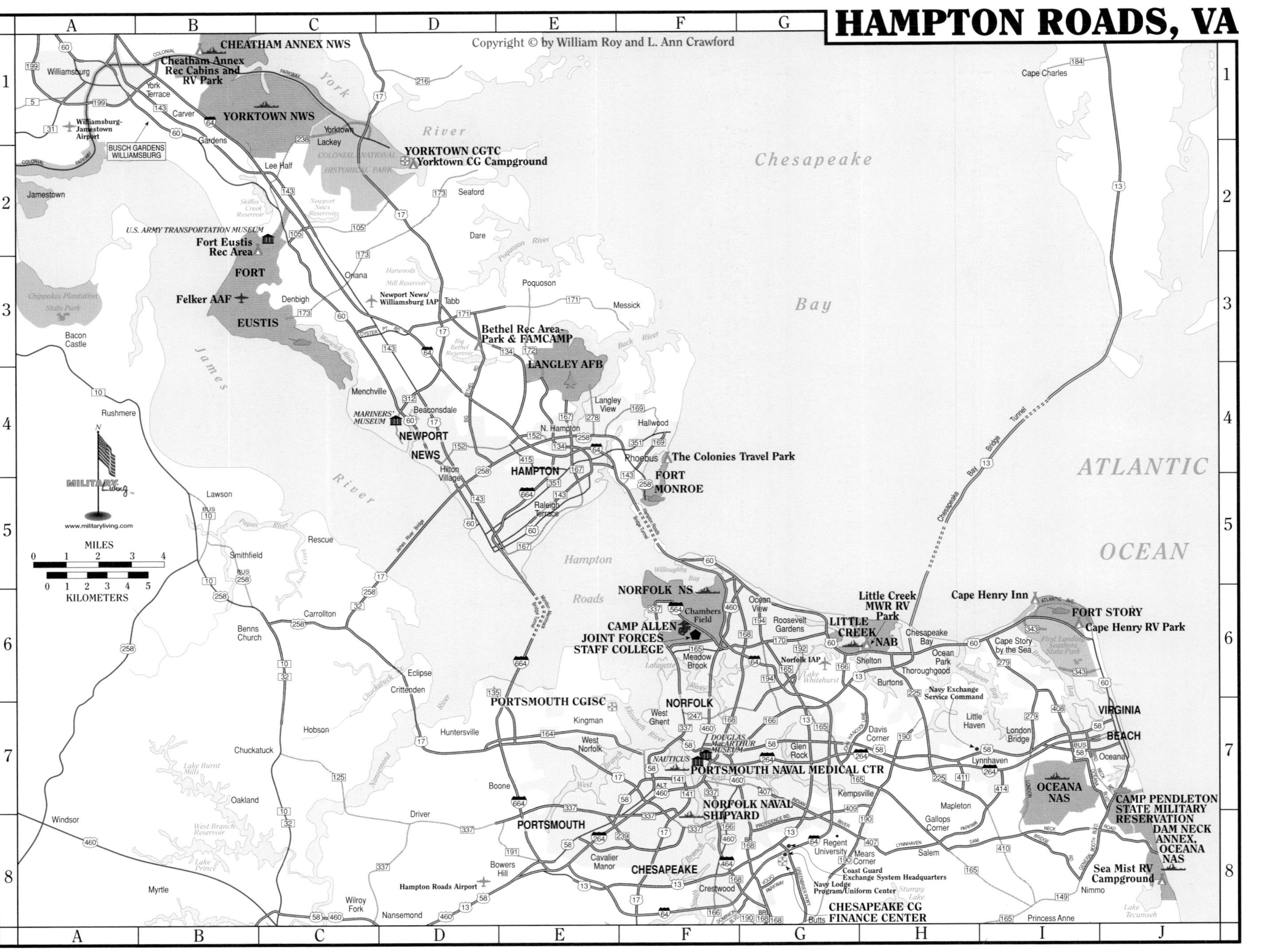
HAMPTON ROADS, VA
Copyright © by William Roy and L. Ann Crawford
ATLANTIC
OCEAN
Chesapeake
Bay
York
River
James
River
Hampton
Roads
CHEATHAM ANNEX NWS
Cheatham Annex Rec Cabins and RV Park
YORKTOWN NWS
YORKTOWN CGTC
Yorktown CG Campground
U.S. ARMY TRANSPORTATION MUSEUM
Fort Eustis Rec Area
FORT EUSTIS
Felker AAF
Bethel Rec Area-Park & FAMCAMP
LANGLEY AFB
The Colonies Travel Park
FORT MONROE
MARINERS' MUSEUM
NEWPORT NEWS
HAMPTON
Newport News/Williamsburg IAP
NORFOLK NS
Chambers Field
CAMP ALLEN
JOINT FORCES STAFF COLLEGE
NORFOLK
PORTSMOUTH CGISC
PORTSMOUTH
PORTSMOUTH NAVAL MEDICAL CTR
NORFOLK NAVAL SHIPYARD
NAUTICUS
DOUGLAS MacARTHUR MUSEUM
CHESAPEAKE
Little Creek MWR RV Park
LITTLE CREEK NAB
Norfolk IAP
Navy Exchange Service Command
Cape Henry Inn
FORT STORY
Cape Henry RV Park
VIRGINIA BEACH
OCEANA NAS
CAMP PENDLETON STATE MILITARY RESERVATION
DAM NECK ANNEX, OCEANA NAS
Sea Mist RV Campground
Regent University
Coast Guard Exchange System Headquarters
Navy Lodge Program/Uniform Center
CHESAPEAKE CG FINANCE CENTER
Hampton Roads Airport
Williamsburg-Jamestown Airport
BUSCH GARDENS WILLIAMSBURG
Chesapeake Bay Bridge Tunnel
James River Bridge
Williamsburg
Jamestown
Bacon Castle
Rushmere
Lawson
Smithfield
Benns Church
Carrollton
Rescue
Chuckatuck
Oakland
Hobson
Crittenden
Eclipse
Driver
Nansemond
Wilroy Fork
Windsor
Myrtle
Bowers Hill
Boone
Huntersville
Kingman
West Norfolk
Cavalier Manor
Crestwood
Poquoson
Dare
Seaford
Tabb
Messick
Hallwood
Langley View
Phoebus
N. Hampton
Raleigh Terrace
Hilton Village
Beaconsdale
Menchville
Denbigh
Oriana
Lee Half
Lackey
Yorktown
Carver
Gardens
York Terrace
Ocean View
Roosevelt Gardens
Meadow Brook
West Ghent
Glen Rock
Kempsville
Davis Corner
Burtons
Thoroughgood
Ocean Park
Chesapeake Bay
Shelton
Little Haven
London Bridge
Lynnhaven
Cape Story by the Sea
First Landing Seashore State Park
Oceana
Mapleton
Gallops Corner
Salem
Mears Corner
Nimmo
Princess Anne
Cape Charles
MILES
0 1 2 3 4
0 1 2 3 4 5
KILOMETERS
MILITARY Living
www.militaryliving.com

PENSACOLA, FL

ALABAMA
FLORIDA
Cottage Hill
Cantonment
Brosnahan Island
Noriegas Island
Gonzalez
Riverview
Ensley
Ferry Pass
Pace
Pea Ridge
Garden Dale
Milton
East Milton
Bagdad
Galt City
Avalon Park
Mulat
Avalon Beach
Escambia Bay
East Bay
EGLIN AIR FORCE BASE
Holley
HURLBURT FIELD
Hurlburt FAMCAMP
Navarre
Navarre Beach State Park
SAUFLEY FIELD
Bellview
Crescent Lake
Brent
Pensacola Regional Airport
CORRY STATION CENTER FOR INFORMATION DOMINANCE
Brownsville
West Pensacola
Pensacola
Myrtle Grove
Warrington
PENSACOLA NAVAL HOSPITAL
Blue Angel Naval Rec Area
Pleasant Grove
Pensacola Bay
Oriole Beach
Gulf Breeze
Villa Sabine
Pensacola Beach
U.S. MUSEUM OF NAVAL AVIATION
PENSACOLA NAS
Oak Grove RV Park & Cottages
Seaglades
Big Lagoon
Santa Rosa Island
GULF ISLANDS NATIONAL SEASHORE
Santa Rosa Sound
GULF OF MEXICO
MILES
KILOMETERS
MILITARY Living
www.militaryliving.com
Copyright © by William Roy and L. Ann Crawford

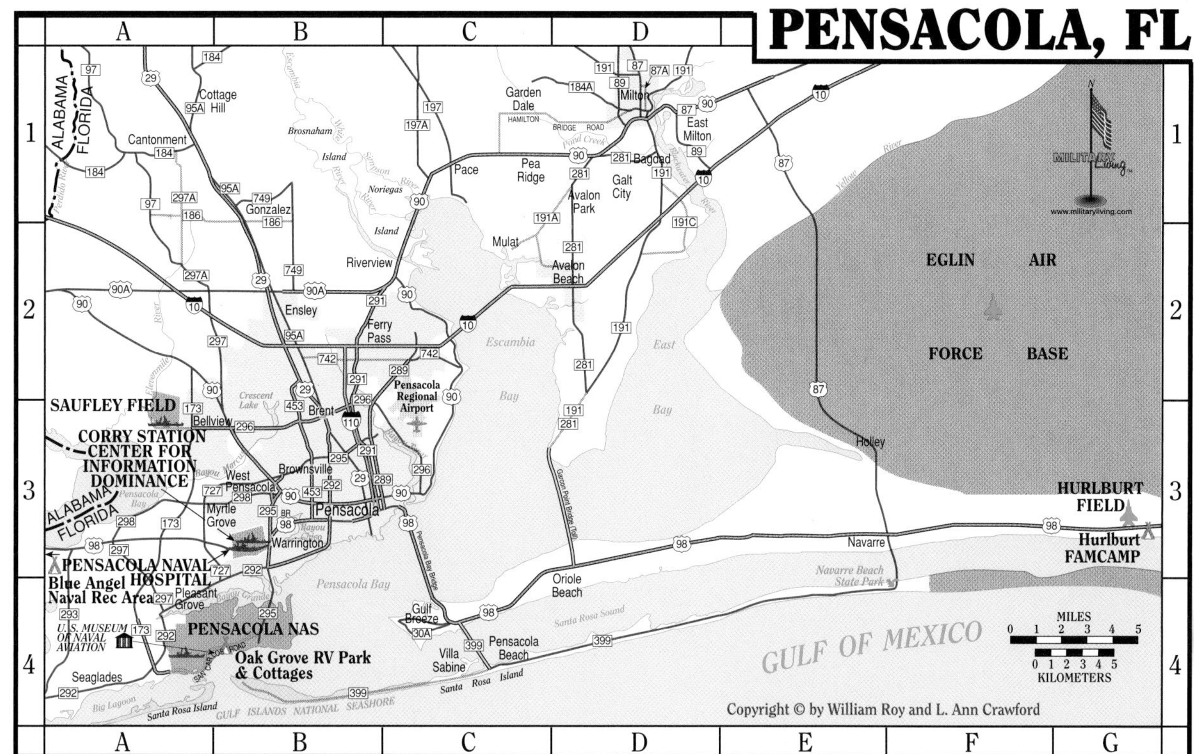

JACKSONVILLE, FL

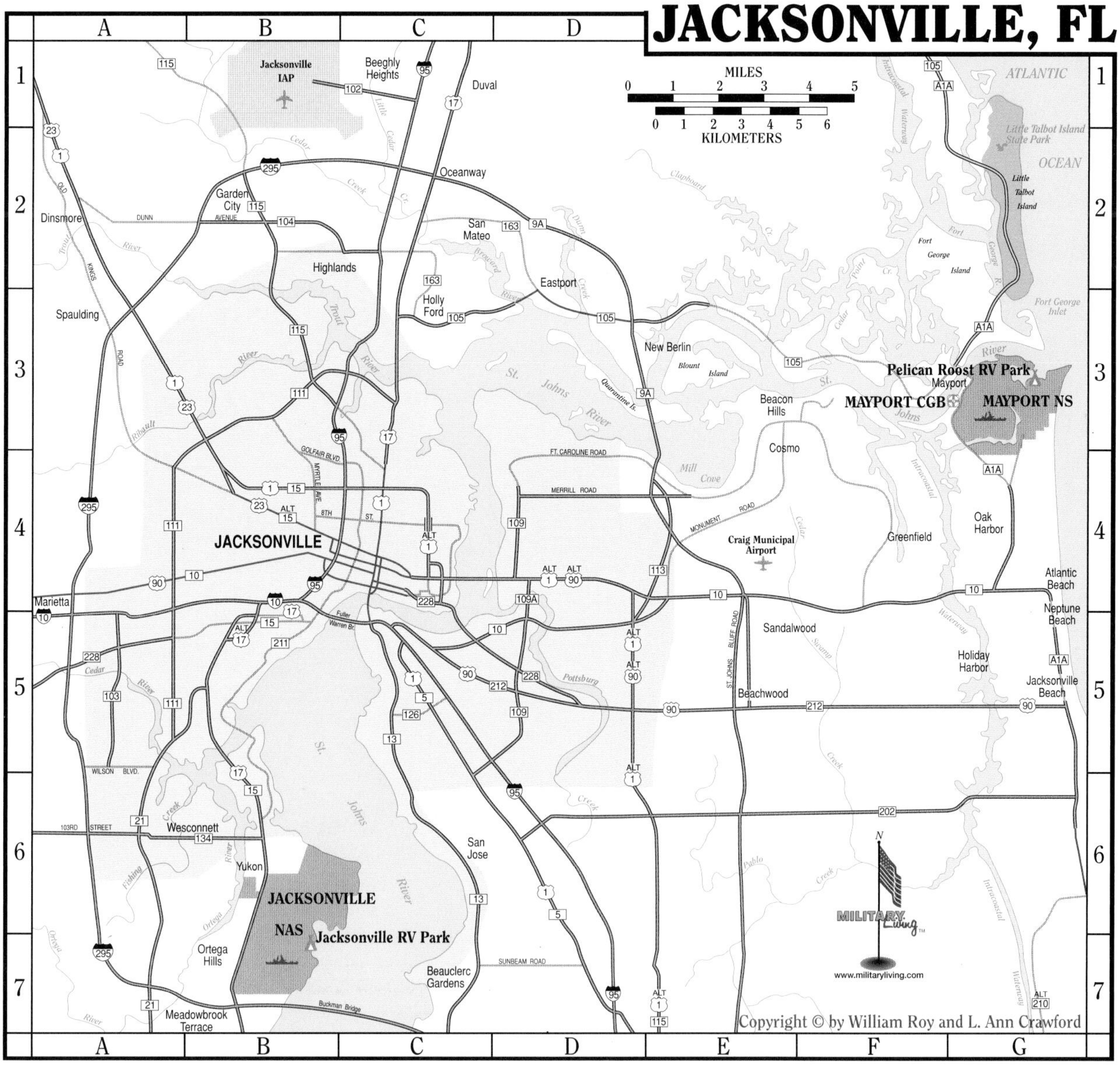

Jacksonville IAP
Beeghly Heights
Duval
Oceanway
Garden City
Dinsmore
San Mateo
Highlands
Holly Ford
Eastport
Spaulding
New Berlin
Blount Island
St. Johns River
Beacon Hills
Cosmo
Pelican Roost RV Park
Mayport
MAYPORT CGB
MAYPORT NS
Little Talbot Island State Park
ATLANTIC OCEAN
Fort George Island
JACKSONVILLE
Craig Municipal Airport
Greenfield
Oak Harbor
Atlantic Beach
Neptune Beach
Marietta
Sandalwood
Holiday Harbor
Jacksonville Beach
Beachwood
Wesconnett
Yukon
San Jose
JACKSONVILLE NAS
Jacksonville RV Park
Ortega Hills
Beauclerc Gardens
Meadowbrook Terrace
MILES
KILOMETERS
MILITARY Living
www.militaryliving.com
Copyright © by William Roy and L. Ann Crawford

MIAMI, FL

A B C D
1 2 3 4 5 6 7 8 9 10
Tamarac
Fort Lauderdale Executive Airport
Oakland Park
Lauderdale By-The-Sea
Lauderdale Lakes
Lauderhill
Wilton Manors
ATLANTIC
Sunrise
Plantation
FORT LAUDERDALE
North New River Canal
Fort Lauderdale/Hollywood IAP
Dania
South New River Canal
Davie
Cooper City
SEMINOLE INDIAN RES.
OCEAN
HOLLYWOOD
Pembroke Pines
Hallandale
Miramar
Golden Beach
North Miami Beach
Sunny Isles
Carrol City
Haulover Beach Park
MIAMI CGAS
Opa-Locka
Lake Katherine
Opa Locka Airport
North Miami
Bal Harbour
Surfside
Miami Shores
UNITED STATES SOUTHERN COMMAND
Pinewood
Normandy Isle
HIALEAH
Miami
Biscayne
Miami Springs
Bay
Beach
Miami IAP
MIAMI
MIAMI CGISC
Sweetwater
West Miami
Virginia Key
Virginia Beach Park
CORAL GABLES
Tropical Park
Olympia Heights
South Miami
Key Biscayne
Crandon Park
Cape Florida Park
Kendall Lakes
Kendall
Matheson Hammock Park
www.militaryliving.com
Richmond Heights
Chapman Field Park
Biscayne
Perrine
RICHMOND HEIGHTS CG EXC
Metro Zoo
Thompson Park
MILES
0 1 2 3
0 1 2 3 4
KILOMETERS
Cutler Ridge
BISCAYNE
Bay
Goulds
Princeton
BISCAYNE
Sands Key
NATIONAL
Naranja
NATIONAL
HOMESTEAD ARB
Leisure City
Elliott Key
PARK
PARK
Copyright © by William Roy and L. Ann Crawford

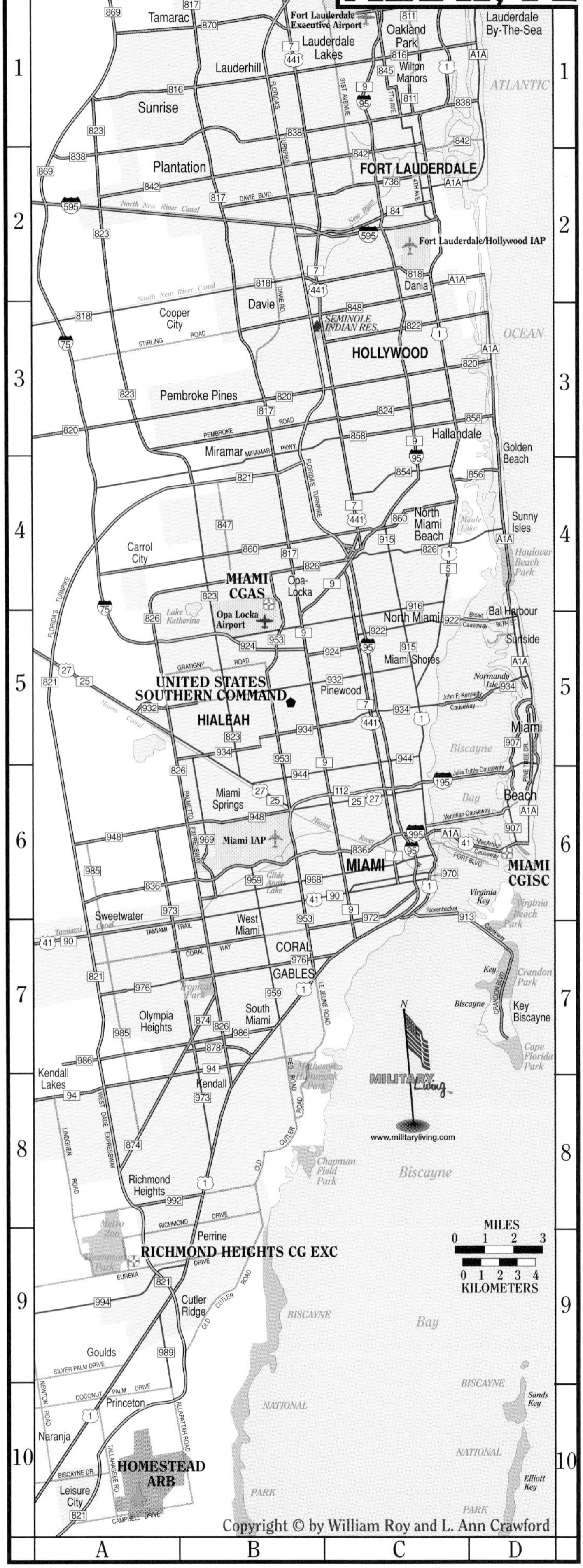

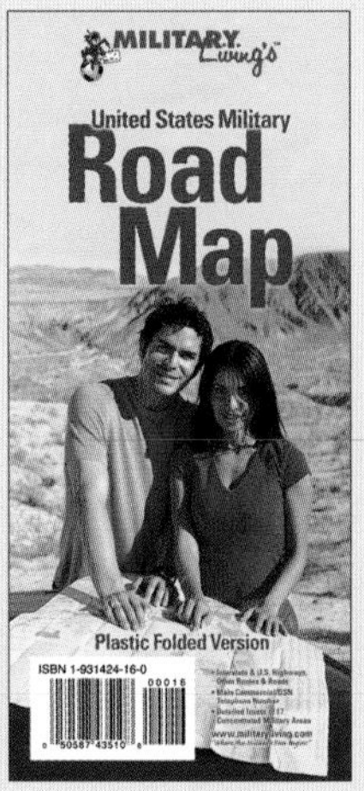

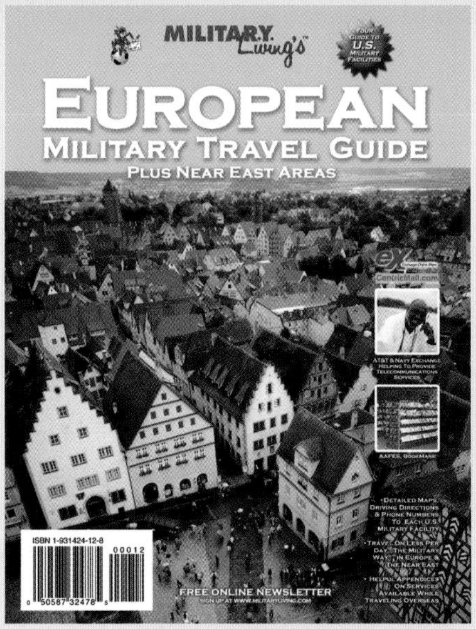

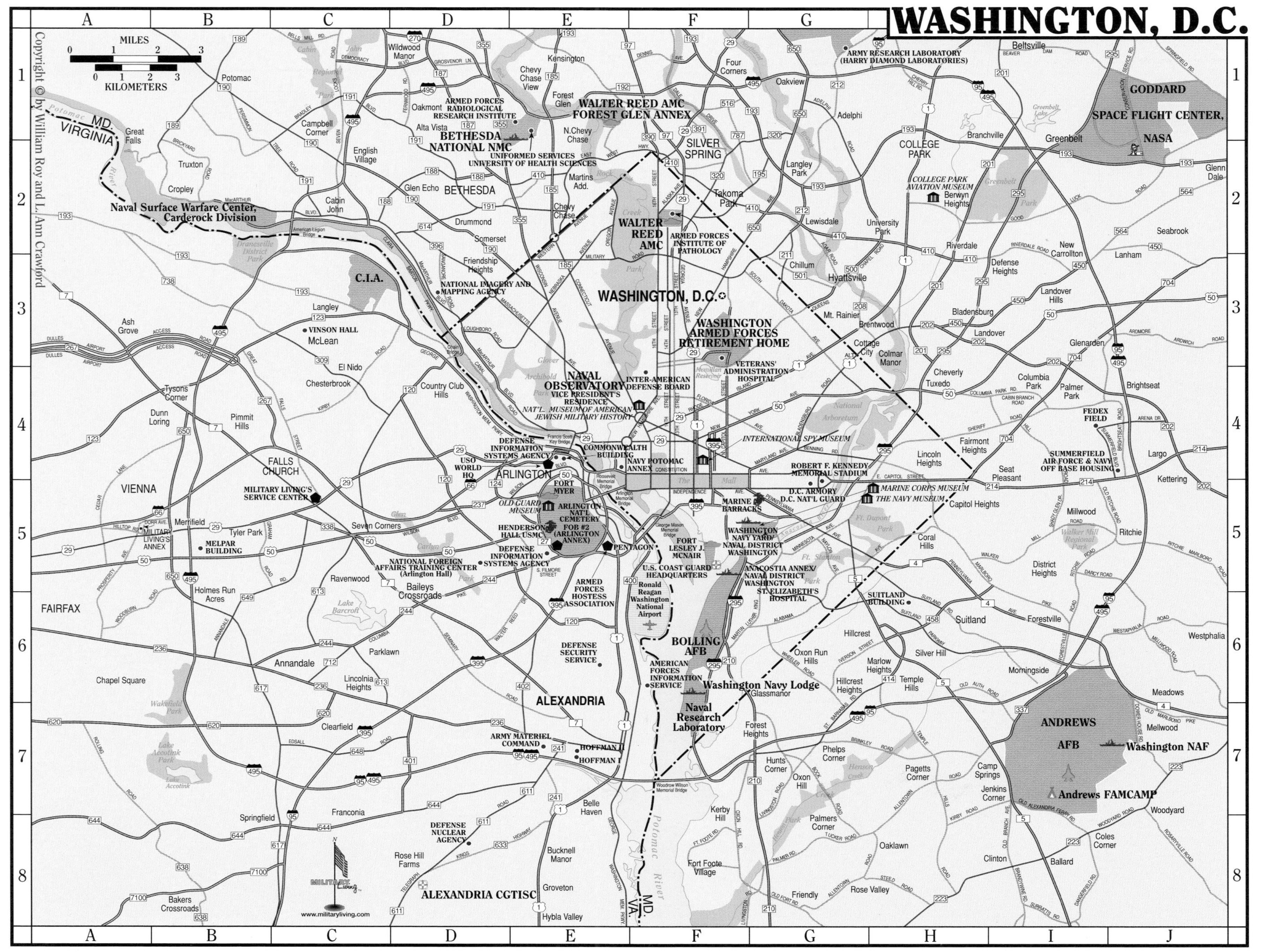
WASHINGTON, D.C.
GODDARD SPACE FLIGHT CENTER, NASA
ARMY RESEARCH LABORATORY (HARRY DIAMOND LABORATORIES)
COLLEGE PARK AVIATION MUSEUM
FEDEX FIELD
SUMMERFIELD AIR FORCE & NAVY OFF BASE HOUSING
ANDREWS AFB
Andrews FAMCAMP
Washington NAF
WALTER REED AMC FOREST GLEN ANNEX
ARMED FORCES INSTITUTE OF PATHOLOGY
WALTER REED AMC
WASHINGTON, D.C.
WASHINGTON ARMED FORCES RETIREMENT HOME
VETERANS' ADMINISTRATION HOSPITAL
INTERNATIONAL SPY MUSEUM
ROBERT F. KENNEDY MEMORIAL STADIUM
D.C. ARMORY D.C. NAT'L GUARD
MARINE CORPS MUSEUM
THE NAVY MUSEUM
MARINE BARRACKS
WASHINGTON NAVY YARD/ NAVAL DISTRICT WASHINGTON
ANACOSTIA ANNEX/ NAVAL DISTRICT WASHINGTON
ST. ELIZABETH'S HOSPITAL
SUITLAND BUILDING
BOLLING AFB
Washington Navy Lodge
Naval Research Laboratory
AMERICAN FORCES INFORMATION SERVICE
U.S. COAST GUARD HEADQUARTERS
FORT LESLEY J. MCNAIR
Ronald Reagan Washington National Airport
PENTAGON
ARMED FORCES HOSTESS ASSOCIATION
DEFENSE SECURITY SERVICE
ALEXANDRIA
HOFFMAN I
HOFFMAN II
ARMY MATERIEL COMMAND
ALEXANDRIA CGTISC
DEFENSE NUCLEAR AGENCY
INTER-AMERICAN DEFENSE BOARD
NAVAL OBSERVATORY
VICE PRESIDENT'S RESIDENCE
NAT'L. MUSEUM OF AMERICAN JEWISH MILITARY HISTORY
COMMONWEALTH BUILDING
NAVY POTOMAC ANNEX
DEFENSE INFORMATION SYSTEMS AGENCY
ARLINGTON
FORT MYER
OLD GUARD MUSEUM
ARLINGTON NAT'L CEMETERY
FOB #2 (ARLINGTON ANNEX)
HENDERSON HALL USMC
DEFENSE INFORMATION SYSTEMS AGENCY
USO WORLD HQ
NATIONAL FOREIGN AFFAIRS TRAINING CENTER (Arlington Hall)
NATIONAL IMAGERY AND MAPPING AGENCY
BETHESDA NATIONAL NMC
ARMED FORCES RADIOLOGICAL RESEARCH INSTITUTE
UNIFORMED SERVICES UNIVERSITY OF HEALTH SCIENCES
C.I.A.
VINSON HALL
FALLS CHURCH
MILITARY LIVING'S SERVICE CENTER
MELPAR BUILDING
MILITARY LIVING'S ANNEX
VIENNA
FAIRFAX
Naval Surface Warfare Center, Carderock Division
Potomac River
MD. VA.
MILES
KILOMETERS
www.militaryliving.com
Copyright © by William Roy and L. Ann Crawford

TAMPA/ST. PETERSBURG, FL

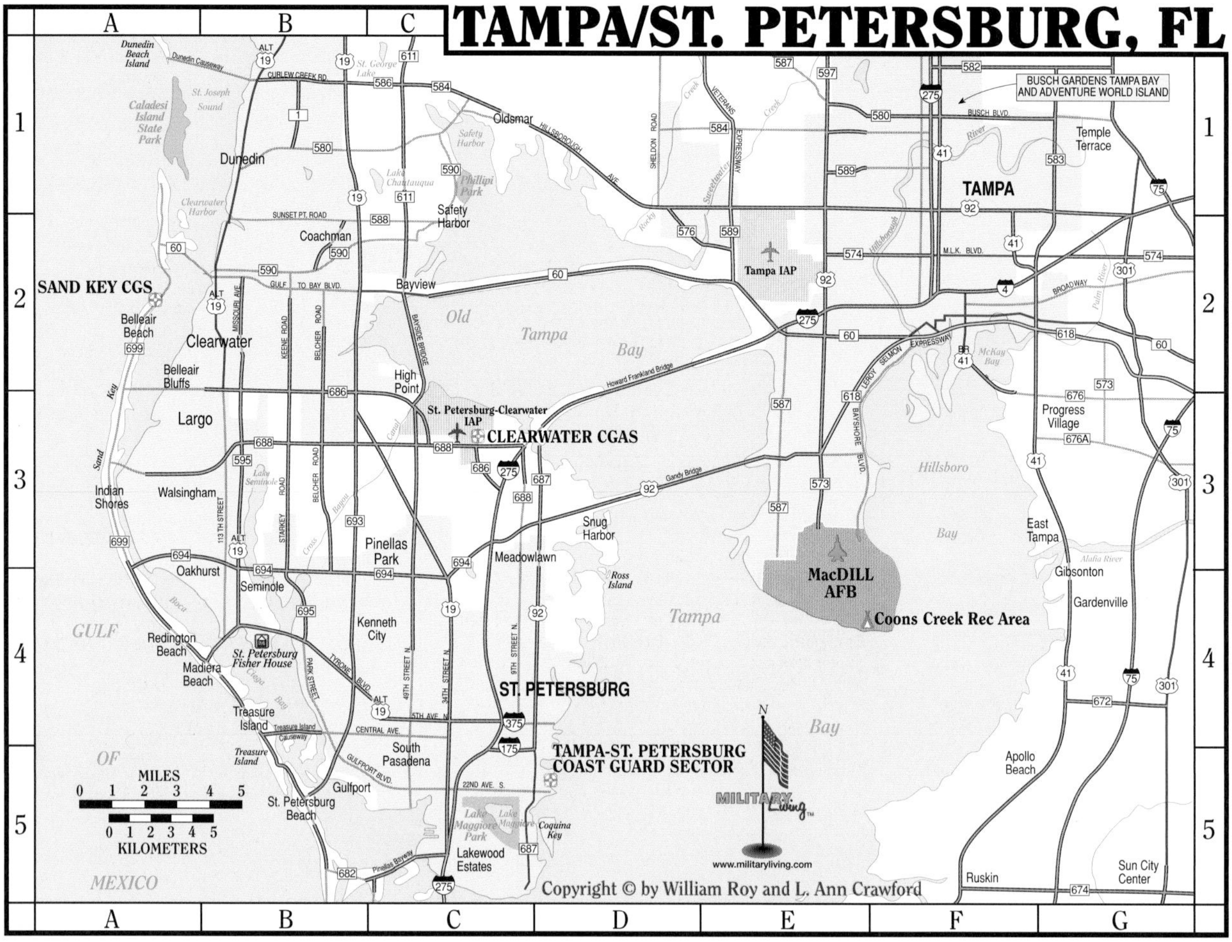

DOWNTOWN D.C.

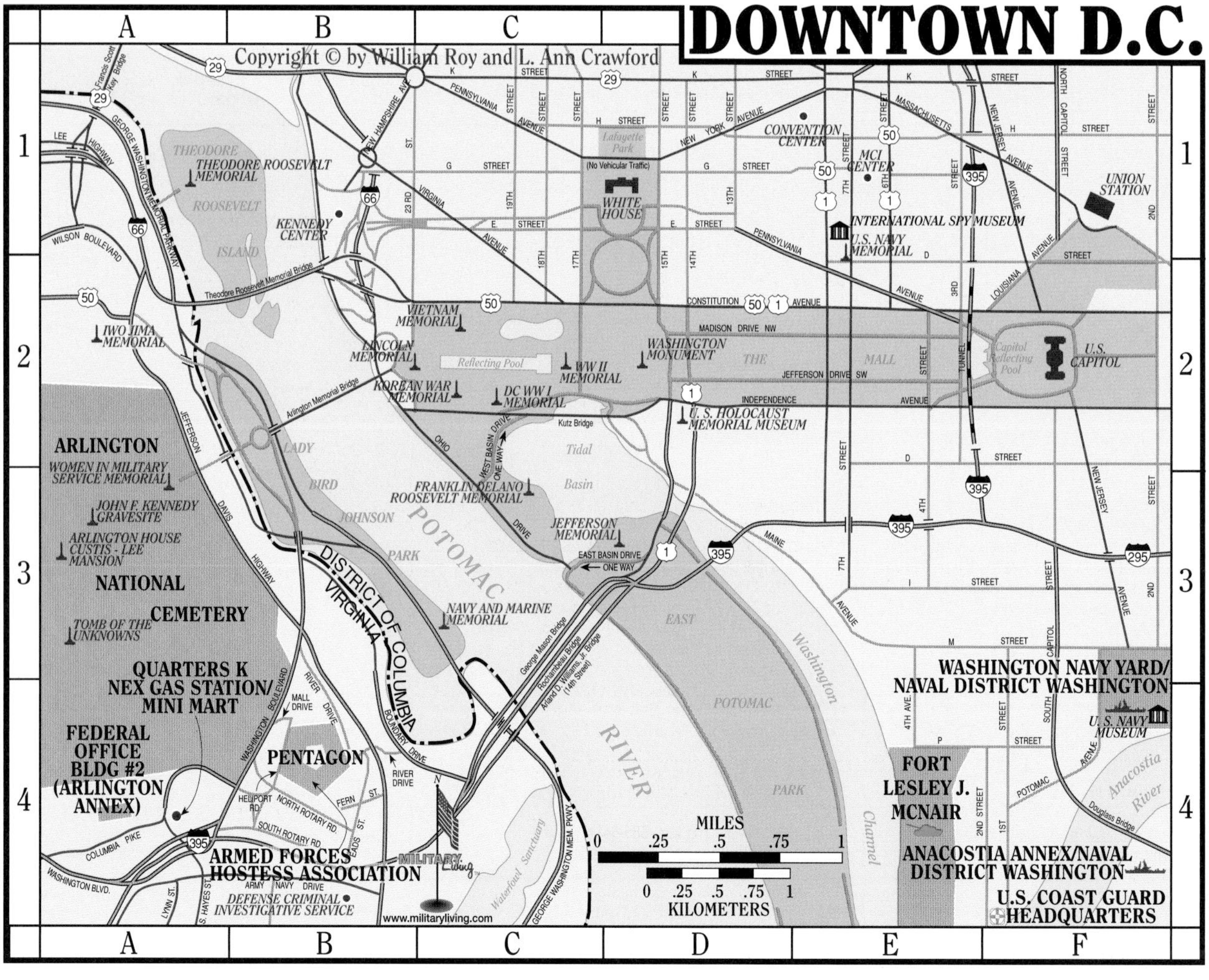

ALABAMA, pg. 34
Montgomery, pg. 34

ANNISTON ARMY DEPOT
Attn: AMSTA-AN-PA, 7 Frankford Avenue, Anniston, AL 36201-4199
C-256-235-7501, DSN-312-571-1110, Police-235-7595
e-mail:pao@anad.army.mil
WEB: www.anad.army.mil
LOCATION: From I-20 east or west, take exit 185 (Oxford) north onto US-78 west, approximately eight miles to AL-202 northeast. Take a left onto the Main Access Road, which turns into MacArthur Avenue and leads to the Depot. USMRA: AL map (F-3). NMC: Birmingham, 53 miles west.
RETAIL & DINING: Cafeteria-235-7643 Clubs-CC-235-7160
SUPPORT & FAMILY: Med-235-7521

BIRMINGHAM INTERNATIONAL AIRPORT/ AIR NATIONAL GUARD BASE
5401 East Lake Blvd, Birmingham, AL 35217-3545
C-205-714-2000, DSN-312-778-2000, Police-714-2240
e-mail:spacea@albirm.ang.af.mil
LOCATION: From east or west on I-59/I-20, take exit 128 north onto Tallapoosa Street, then north for 0.5 miles to a right on East Lake Blvd and follow the airfield fence for approximately two miles northeast to Main Gate on the right (southeast) side of street. USMRA: AL map (D-4). NMC: Birmingham, within city limits.
RECREATION & TRAVEL: SPA-714-2208/2297
RETAIL & DINING: EX-714-2348 Gas-714-2294
SUPPORT & FAMILY: Med-714-2213

DAUPHIN ISLAND COAST GUARD RECREATION FACILITY
P.O. Box 436, Dauphin Island, AL 36528-0436
C-251-861-7113, after hours C-251-441-6110, Police-861-5523
WEB: http://www.uscg.mil/mwr/Cottages/DauphinIslandRecreationComplex.htm
LOCATION: On Gulf of Mexico, approximately 40 miles south of Mobile. Take I-10 east or west to AL-163 south (exit 17); continue south approximately 25 miles to Dauphin Island. Left (east) at dead end to east end of the island. Turn right on Agassiz Street (through Dauphin Island Sea Lab property) and follow to the Coast Guard Regulation Facility. USMRA: AL map (B-11). NMC: Mobile, 25 miles north. NMI: Pascagoula NAS, approximately 32 miles northwest.
RECREATION & TRAVEL: RVC-861-7113
NOTE: *For detailed information about this off-base recreation facility, as well as on-base recreation facilities, golf courses and marinas, consult Military Living's "Military RV, Camping and Outdoor Recreation Around the World".*

FORT RUCKER
Attn: ATZQ-GSC, Bldg 115, Fort Rucker, AL 36362-5105
C-334-255-1110, DSN-312-558-1110, Police-255-2222
WEB: www-rucker.army.mil
LOCATION: From Atlanta, take I-85 south to US231 south, turn right onto AL-249 (Andrews Avenue) to gate. USMRA: AL map (F,G-8,9). NMC: Dothan, 26 miles southeast.
RECREATION & TRAVEL: Golf-598-2449 Marina-255-9520 RVC-255-2292/4305 SPA-255-8309 TML-255-2626 or 598-5216
RETAIL & DINING: Clubs-NCO-598-2491 OC-598-2426 Com-255-2212 EX-503-9044 Gas-503-9044
SUPPORT & FAMILY: Med-255-7000

GUNTER ANNEX TO MAXWELL AIR FORCE BASE
50 LeMay Plaza South
Gunter Annex to Maxwell Air Force Base, AL 36115-6112
C-334-953-1110(Maxwell AFB) or C-334-416-1110(Gunter) DSN-312-493-1110, Police-416-4250
WEB: www.maxwell.af.mil
LOCATION: From I-65 north or south, take exit 173 northeast onto AL-152 (Northern Blvd), six miles to intersection with US-231. Take south exit onto Congressman W.L. Dickinson Drive, then south 1.5 miles to Main Gate on left (southeast) side of street. From I-85 east or west, take exit 6 north onto US-231 north (Eastern Blvd). Continue north four miles to an exit south onto Congressman W.L. Dickinson Drive, then southwest 1.5 miles to Main Gate on left (south) side of street. USMRA: AL map (E,F-6). NMC: Montgomery, two miles southwest.
RECREATION & TRAVEL: TML-270-4000 or 416-5501
RETAIL & DINING: Clubs-CC-416-4967 EMC-416-4646 Com-416-3448 Dining-416-4643 EX-279-9776 Gas-272-5092
SUPPORT & FAMILY: Med-953-3368

MARSHALL SPACE FLIGHT CENTER
1 Tranquility Base, Huntsville, AL 35805-3399
C-256-837-3400, Police-722-5617
e-mail:guestservices@spacecamp.com
WEB: www.spacecamp.com
LOCATION: From I-65 north or south, take exit 340 east onto I-565. Travel about 13 miles northeast to exit 14 south onto Rideout Road for 3.7 miles to center on east side of road. USMRA: AL map (D,E-1,2). NMC: Huntsville, five miles northeast.
RETAIL & DINING: Cafeteria-721-7106 Dining-837-3400
SUPPORT & FAMILY: Med-721-7162

MAXWELL AIR FORCE BASE
HQ Air University, 55 LeMay Plaza South
Maxwell Air Force Base, AL 36112-6335
C-334-953-1110, DSN-312-493-1110, Police-953-7222
WEB: www.Maxwell.af.mil
LOCATION: Take I-85 south to I-65 north to exit 172 (Herron Street) west. Right (north) on Dickerson Street, two blocks to left (west) on Bell Street approximately one mile and follow signs to Bell Street Gate. Visitor Center on right (north) side of street. USMRA: AL map (E-6). NMC: Montgomery, 1.5 miles southeast.
RECREATION & TRAVEL: Golf-953-2209 Marina-825-6251 RVC-953-5161 RVC-953-3509/5850 SPA-953-6454/7372 TML-953-2055/2430
RETAIL & DINING: Clubs-EMC/NCO-262-8364 OC-264-6423 Com-953-7175 EX-834-5946 Gas-265-0130
SUPPORT & FAMILY: Med-953-3368

MAXWELL-GUNTER RECREATION AREA AT LAKE MARTIN
Outdoor Recreation Reservations Office 206 West Selfridge Street
Maxwell AFB, AL 36112-5959
C-334-953-3509, DSN-312-453-3509, Police (Security)-953-7222
WEB: www.au.af.mil/42abw/42svs/lakemartin.html
LOCATION: Off base. Located near Dadeville, southeast of Birmingham, northeast of Montgomery. From I-85 north of Montgomery, take exit 32, north on AL-49, 26 miles to a left onto CR-34 (Stillwaters Road), and proceed 2.5 miles to recreation area. USMRA: AL map (F-5,6). NMC: Montgomery, 60 miles southwest. NMI: Maxwell AFB, 60 miles southwest.
RECREATION & TRAVEL: RVC-953-3509 or 256-825-6251
NOTE: *For detailed information about this off-base recreation facility, as well as on-base recreation facilities, golf courses and marinas, consult Military Living's "Military RV, Camping and Outdoor Recreation Around the World".*

MOBILE COAST GUARD AVIATION TRAINING CENTER
USCG Aviation Training Center, 8501 Tanner Williams Road Mobile, AL 36608-9682.
C-251-441-6426, after hours C-251-441-6110, Police-441-6100
WEB: www.uscg.mil/hq/atcmobil/atcmobil.htm
LOCATION: From I-65, take Airport Blvd (exit 3) west 5.8 miles, right (north) on Schillinger Road for 0.7 miles, to left (west) on Tanner Williams Road, one mile. Center in on left (south). Clearly marked. USMRA: AL map (B-10). NMC: Mobile, 2.5 miles east.
RECREATION & TRAVEL: SPA-441-6861
RETAIL & DINING: Com-441-6390 Dining-441-6744 EX-441-6390 Gas-441-6326
SUPPORT & FAMILY: Med-441-6725

MOBILE COAST GUARD GROUP
South Broad Street, Brookley Complex Bldg 102
Mobile, AL 36615-1390
C-251-441-6021/6072, Emergency-441-6211
WEB: www.uscg.mil/d8/group/mobile
LOCATION: From I-10 east or west, take exit 24 south onto Broad Street, go south approximately 0.75 miles to base on left (east) side of street. USMRA: AL map (B-10). NMC: Mobile, one mile north. NMI: Pensacola NAS, Pensacola, FL.
RECREATION & TRAVEL: RVC-861-7113
RETAIL & DINING: EX-441-5091 Gas-441-5096
SUPPORT & FAMILY: Med-441-6240

REDSTONE ARSENAL
U.S. Army Aviation & Missile Command, Bldg 5300
Redstone Arsenal, AL 35898-5020
C-256-876-2151, DSN-312-746-0011, Police-876-2222
WEB: www.redstone.army.mil
LOCATION: From I-565 east or west, take exit 14 south onto Rideout Road to Gate 9. Or, from I-565 in city of Huntsville, exit south onto US-231 (Memorial Drive) for 4.5 miles to right (west) onto Martin Road to Main Gate (Gate 1). Uniformed personnel may take I-565 to US-231 (Memorial Drive) south one mile to Drake exit west. Go west on Drake, which becomes Goss Road, to Gate 8. USMRA: AL map (E-1). NMC: Huntsville, adjacent.
RECREATION & TRAVEL: Golf-883-7977/8157 RVC-876-4868/6854 SPA-876-1916 TML-876-5713/8028
RETAIL & DINING: Cafeteria-876-8894 Clubs-CC-830-2582 Com-955-6627 Dining-876-6743 EX-883-6100 Gas-881-7588
SUPPORT & FAMILY: Med-585-6414/5

DELAWARE pg. 40

BETHANY BEACH TRAINING SITE
Delaware ANG, Bethany Beach Training Site
Route 1, Bethany Beach, DE 19930-9770
C-302-854-7902, DSN-312-440-7902, Police-911
LOCATION: Located on west side of DE-1, 0.5 miles north of DE-26 and US-1 intersection in Bethany Beach. USMRA: DE/MD map (K-5). NMC: Bethany Beach, within city limits.
RECREATION & TRAVEL: RVC-854-7901/2 TML-854-7902

DOVER AIR FORCE BASE
201 Eagle Way, Dover Air Force Base, DE 19902-5201
C-302-677-3000, DSN-312-445-3000, Police-677-6666
WEB: https://public.dover.amc.af.mil
LOCATION: From Philadelphia, take I-95 south to US-13 south. Base is five miles south of Dover, on east side of DE-1 toll or US-13. Follow signs to base. Clearly marked. USMRA: DE/MD map (J-3). NMC: Dover, five miles northwest.
RECREATION & TRAVEL: Golf-677-6038/9 RVC-677-3959 SPA-677-4088 TML-677-2840/1/5983
RETAIL & DINING: Clubs-CC/OC-677-6022 EMC-677-6351 The Club-677-6024 Com-677-3915/4189 Dining-677-3925/6 EX-677-3745 Gas-677-4446
SUPPORT & FAMILY: Med-677-2858 or 888-999-5195

NEW CASTLE COUNTY AIRPORT/ AIR NATIONAL GUARD
166 Airlift Wing, 2600 Spruance Drive, Corporate Commons
New Castle, DE 19720-1615
C-302-323-3300, DSN-312-775-7300, Police-323-3440
WEB: www.delawarenationalguard.com
LOCATION: From I-95, take exit 5 to DE-141 south for one mile to intersection of DE-37 (Corporate Commons Blvd). Turn right into Corporate Commons Blvd, then left onto Spruance Drive and follow to Main Gate. USMRA: DE/MD map (I-1). NMC: Wilmington, seven miles northeast.
RECREATION & TRAVEL: SPA-323-3525
RETAIL & DINING: EX-322-5988
SUPPORT & FAMILY: Med-323-3385

DISTRICT OF COLUMBIA, pg. 49
Downtown Washington, DC pg. 50

ANACOSTIA ANNEX/ NAVAL DISTRICT WASHINGTON
1014 N Street SE, Washington Navy Yard
Washington, DC 20374-5001
C-703-545-6700, DSN-312-288-0960, Police-433-3018
WEB: www.ndw.navy.mil
LOCATION: From I-395, exit South Capitol Street, cross South Capitol Street Bridge. Entrance is on right, before Bolling AFB. USMRA: DC map (F,G-5), (F-4). NMC: Washington, DC, in southeast section of city.
RECREATION & TRAVEL: TML-433-3862
RETAIL & DINING: Clubs-CC-433-2574 All Hands-433-3041 Dining-433-2574

BOLLING AIR FORCE BASE
11 Wing PA, 20 MacDill Blvd Room 207
Bolling Air Force Base, Washington, DC 20332-5101
C-202-767-4011, DSN-312-297-4011, Police-433-3333
WEB: www.bolling.af.mil
LOCATION: Take I-95 (east portion of Capital Beltway, I-495), exit 22 to I-295 south, exit to Portland Street, and main entrance to AFB. From I-395 north, exit South Capitol Street, main entrance to AFB on right. Visitors entrance is at south gate, one mile south of Main Gate. Clearly marked. USMRA: DC map (F-6). NMC: Washington, DC, in southeast section of city.
RECREATION & TRAVEL: Marina-767-4651 TML-767-5316/5741/71
RETAIL & DINING: Cafeteria-562-4419 Clubs-563-8400 Com-767-4695 Dining-404-8510 EX-562-3000 Gas-563-6490
SUPPORT & FAMILY: Med-767-5536
Ten-digit dialing required for local calls.

FORT LESLEY J. MCNAIR
103 3rd Avenue SW, Washington, DC 20319-5058
C-703-545-6700, DSN-312-227-0101 (0700-1900 hours), Police-911
WEB: www.mdw.army.mil
LOCATION: At the confluence of Anacostia River and Washington Channel, SW. Enter on P Street, SW. Take Maine Avenue, SW, to right on Fourth Street, SW, to dead end at P Street. Left and then immediate right to the Main Gate. USMRA: DC map (F-5); Downtown DC map (E-4). NMC: Washington, DC, in southwest section of city.
RECREATION & TRAVEL: TML-696-3576/7
RETAIL & DINING: Cafeteria-202-685-3371 Clubs-CC-527-1300 OC-202-484-5800 EX-202-522-4575 Gas-202-484-5823
SUPPORT & FAMILY: Med-202-685-3092
Ten-digit dialing required for local calls.

MARINE BARRACKS
8th and I Streets, SE, Washington, DC 20390-0002
C-202-433-4073, DSN-312-288-4073

WEB: www.mbw.usmc.mil
LOCATION: At Eighth and I Streets, SE, near Washington Navy Yard. From I-95 north or Capital Beltway/I-95 south to I-295/Washington, exit to 11th Street bridge at Eighth Street. Barracks at bottom/exit. Or, from I-395 north, exit Sixth Street SE and go two blocks; turn left on Eighth Street. USMRA: DC map (F,G-5). NMC: Washington, DC, in southeast section of the city.
RETAIL & DINING: Cafeteria-544-6930 EX-433-2848
SUPPORT & FAMILY: Med-433-6224
Ten-digit dialing required for local calls.

UNITED STATES COAST GUARD HEADQUARTERS
2100 2nd Street, SW, Washington, DC 20593-0001
C-202-267-1587
WEB: www.uscg.mil
LOCATION: Next to Fort Lesley J. McNair, at confluence of Anacostia River and Washington Channel. Take I-395 to Maine Street exit. Maine Street turns into M Street. Go south on Fourth Street, SW, to dead end on P Street, SW, then left (east) on P Street, SW, to right (south) on Second Street, SW, to main entrance to USCG Hq on left (east) side of street. USMRA: DC map (F-5); Downtown DC map (F-4). NMC: Washington, DC, in the southwest section of city.
RETAIL & DINING: EX-267-2374
SUPPORT & FAMILY: Med-267-0540
Ten-digit dialing required for local calls.

WALTER REED ARMY MEDICAL CENTER
6900 Georgia Avenue, Washington, DC 20307-5001
C-202-782-3501, DSN-312-662-3501, Police-782-7511
WEB: www.wramc.amedd.army.mil
LOCATION: From I-495 (Capital Beltway), take Georgia Avenue/ Silver Spring exit south to Medical Center. To reach the Forest Glen support facilities from Georgia Avenue, go west on Georgia Avenue to left on Seminary Place to left (south) on Brookville Road to right on Steven Sitter Avenue and the Annex. USMRA: DC map (F-2). NMC: Washington, DC, in northwest section of city.
RECREATION & TRAVEL: TML-726-8700
RETAIL & DINING: EX-882-0802
SUPPORT & FAMILY: Med-782-7761
Ten-digit dialing required for local calls

WASHINGTON ARMED FORCES RETIREMENT HOME
Recreation Services, Sheridan Bldg, Room 1010
3700 North Capitol Street, NW, Washington, DC 20317-0001
C-202-730-3337 or 800-422-9988, Police-730-3111
WEB: www.afrh.gov
LOCATION: Two and a half miles north of the Capitol. Enter from North Capitol Street. Across the street from VA Hospital and Shrine of the Immaculate Conception. Take I-395 to the C Street exit. Take a left onto Louisiana Avenue, NW, and another left onto North Capitol Street. USMRA: DC map (F-3). NMC: Washington, DC, in the northwest section of city. NMI: Walter Reed Army Medical Center, 3.5 miles north.
RECREATION & TRAVEL: TML-730-3044
RETAIL & DINING: EX-291-6252
SUPPORT & FAMILY: Med-730-3284
Ten-digit dialing required for local calls.

WASHINGTON NAVY LODGE
12 Bowline Green SW, Bldg 4412, Belleview Housing Community
Washington, DC 20032-0001
C-800-NAVY-INN or 202-563-6950
WEB: www.navy-lodge.com
LOCATION: Take I-95 (east section of Capital Beltway, I-495) north or south, exit to I-295 N (exit 1) onto Overlook Avenue, right at the light. Left at next light into Bellevue Housing Community on Magazine Road. Left on Beyer Road to Navy Lodge. Located within closed base area. All visitors must log in with base police at gate. NMC: Washington, DC, within city limits.
RECREATION & TRAVEL: Navy Lodge-800-NAVY-INN or 563-6950

WASHINGTON NAVY YARD/ NAVAL DISTRICT WASHINGTON
1014 N Street SE, Washington Navy Yard
Washington, DC 20374-0001
C-703-545-6700, DSN-312-227-0101, Police-433-2411
WEB: www.ndw.navy.mil
LOCATION: Exit off I-395 north at Sixth Street SE/Navy Yard, proceed to Eighth Street, turn right on M Street, turn left into Main Gate at Ninth and M Streets, SE. USMRA: DC map (F,G-5); Downtown DC map (F-4). NMC: Washington, DC, in southeast section of city.
RECREATION & TRAVEL: TML-433-3862
RETAIL & DINING: Clubs-CC-433-3041 EX-889-7534
SUPPORT & FAMILY: Med-433-6408
Ten-digit dialing required for local calls.

FLORIDA, pg. 36-37
Jacksonville, pg. 47
Key West, pg. 37
Miami, pg. 48
Orlando, pg. 37
Pensacola, pg. 47
Tampa/St. Petersburg, pg. 50
Walt Disney World, pg. 37

BLUE ANGEL NAVAL RECREATION AREA
2100 Bronson Field Road, Pensacola, FL 32506-8470
C-850-453-2030/9435, DSN-312-922-0111, Police-452-2453
WEB: www.naspensacola.navy.mil/mwr/corry/mwrblue.htm
LOCATION: From I-10 east or west, take exit 7 south on FL-297 (Pine Forest Road) for 3.4 miles and merge with US-90 (Mobile Hwy) south. Continue one mile, then turn right onto FL-296 (Saufley Field Road) for 1.5 miles to FL-173 (Millview Road), which becomes Blue Angel Pkwy. Go south for 4.6 miles and turn right (west) on US-98. Follow for about four miles west. Turn left onto Bronson Field Road to the recreation area. Alternately, from I-10 east or west, northwest of Pensacola, take the exit towards I-110 south for nine miles to US-98 west for approximately 14 miles to left on Bronson Road and follow directions as above. USMRA: FL Panhandle map (A-6). NMC: Pensacola, eight miles east. NMI: Corry Station, eight miles northeast.
RECREATION & TRAVEL: RVC-453-2030/9435
NOTE: *For detailed information about this off-base recreation facility, as well as on-base recreation facilities, golf courses and marinas, consult Military Living's "Military RV, Camping and Outdoor Recreation Around the World".*

CAMP BLANDING JOINT TRAINING CENTER
Route 1, Box 465, Starke, FL 32091-9703
C-904-682-3462, DSN-312-822-3462, Police-682-3526
LOCATION: From I-95 north or south, exit 318 to FL-16 west for 31 miles. Follow exit signs to support activities. USMRA: FL map (G-4). NMC: Jacksonville, 30 miles north.
RECREATION & TRAVEL: RVC-682-3104 TML-682-3381
RETAIL & DINING: Clubs-CC-682-3320 NCO-682-3197 EX-682-3513
SUPPORT & FAMILY: Med-682-3106

CAPE CANAVERAL AIR FORCE STATION
Det 1, 45 MSG/CCAFS, 180 West Skid Strip Road
Patrick Air Force Base, FL 32925-2230
C-321-494-1110, DSN-312-854-1110, Police-494-2008
LOCATION: From I-95, take FL-528 east, exit toward FL-401 north to AFS. USMRA: FL map (J-7). NMC: Dna Beach, 70 miles north.
RECREATION & TRAVEL: Golf-494-7856 Marina-494-7455
RETAIL & DINING: Cafeteria-853-3271 Com-494-5841 Dining-494-4248 EX-853-4262 Gas-494-2655
SUPPORT & FAMILY: Med-494-8241

CLEARWATER COAST GUARD AIR STATION
15100 Rescue Way, Clearwater, FL 33762-2990
C-727-535-1437 (ask for extensions), Police-453-7828
WEB: www.uscg.mil/d7/units/as-clearwater
LOCATION: From I-275, take FL-60 west to FL-611 south. Follow signs to air station. USMRA: FL map (F-8); Tampa/St. Petersburg, FL, map (C-3). NMC: Tampa, 20 miles east. NMI: MacDill AFB, 18 miles east.
RECREATION & TRAVEL: SPA-535-1223
RETAIL & DINING: Cafeteria-535-1725 EX-535-1710
SUPPORT & FAMILY: Med-535-1603

CORRY STATION CENTER FOR INFORMATION DOMINANCE
640 Roberts Avenue, Pensacola, FL 32511-5138
C-850-452-6512, DSN-312-922-6512, Police-452-8888
e-mail:corry_pao@navy.mil
WEB: https://www.npdc.navy.mil/ceninfodom
LOCATION: From I-110 heading south, take Garden Street (Hwy-98) exit 1C. Continue west on Hwy-98 approximately five miles, veer right onto Chief's Way, cross New Warrington Road and proceed to Main Gate. USMRA: Florida Panhandle map (A-6). NMC: Mobile, 50 miles west. NMI: Pensacola Naval Air Station, five miles south.
RECREATION & TRAVEL: TML-452-6541/6609
RETAIL & DINING: Clubs-CC-452-6667 CPO-452-6330 EMC-452-3251 Com-452-6880 EX-453-5311 Gas-457-1228
SUPPORT & FAMILY: Med-452-6326

CORTEZ COAST GUARD STATION
4530 124th Street, Court West, Cortez, FL 34215-9999
C-941-794-1261/2, Police-794-1607
LOCATION: From I-75 south to FL-64 west (Manatee Avenue), left on 75th Street, right on Cortez Road, left on 124th Street West. Station is at end of street on right. USMRA: FL map (F-9). NMC: Tampa, 60 miles north.
RETAIL & DINING: EX-795-2805

DESTIN ARMY INFANTRY CENTER RECREATION AREA
557 Calhoun Avenue, Destin, FL 32541-1610
C-850-837-6423 or 800-642-0466, Police-651-7400
WEB: www.benningmwr.com/destin.cfm
LOCATION: Located on 15-acre site on Chotawhatchee Bay in Destin, FL. From I-10 east or west, near DeFuniak Springs, take exit 14 onto US-331 south for 26 miles to right (west) on US-98 to right (north) onto Benning Drive and a left onto Calhoun Avenue to area. USMRA: Florida Panhandle (C-6). NMC: Fort Walton Beach, 20 miles east. NMI: Eglin AFB, 17 miles north.
RECREATION & TRAVEL: RVC-837-6423 TML-800-642-0466 or 706-545-5600
NOTE: *For detailed information about this off-base recreation facility, as well as on-base recreation facilities, golf courses and marinas, consult Military Living's "Military RV, Camping and Outdoor Recreation Around the World".*

EGLIN AIR FORCE BASE
101 West D Avenue, Suite 110
Eglin Air Force Base, FL 32542-5498
C-850-882-1110, DSN-312-872-1110, Police-882-2502
WEB: www.eglin.af.mil
LOCATION: Exit 56 from I-10 onto FL-85, which leads to the Main Gate. USMRA: FL map (B,C-6); AL map (E-10); Pensacola, FL, map (E,F,G-8,9,10). NMC: Fort Walton Beach, seven miles south.
RECREATION & TRAVEL: Golf-882-2949 RVC-882-6581 SPA-882-2488 (option '0')/4757 TML-882-4534
RETAIL & DINING: Clubs-NCO-678-5127 OC-651-1010 Com-882-2677/3172 EX-651-2512 Gas-651-6741 or 729-3728
SUPPORT & FAMILY: Med-883-8600

FORT MYERS BEACH COAST GUARD STATION
719 San Carlos Drive, Fort Myers Beach, FL 33931-2221
C-239-463-5754, Police-911
LOCATION: South on I-75 exit 131, go west on Daniels Parkway, which turns into Cypress Lake Drive. Turn left on Summerlin Road, left on San Carlos Blvd, right on Main Street, left on San Carlos Drive. USMRA: FL map (G-11). NMC: Fort Myers, 15 miles north.
RETAIL & DINING: EX (off base)-437-0090

HOMESTEAD AIR RESERVE BASE
482 Fighter Wing, 29050 Coral Sea Blvd,
Homestead ARB, FL 33039-1299
C-305-224-7000, DSN-312-791-7000, Police-224-7115
WEB: http://www.afrc.af.mil/482FW/
LOCATION: Take Exit 5 (Biscayne Blvd/288th Street) off Florida Turnpike, left at bottom of ramp onto 288th Street. Road leads straight to base. Or, take exit 6 (Speedway Blvd) off Florida Turnpike, left at bottom of ramp onto 137th Avenue. At first light, take a left onto 288th Street. Road leads straight to base. USMRA: FL map (J-13,14), (A-10). NMC: Miami, 40 miles northeast.
RECREATION & TRAVEL: SPA-224-7518 TML-224-2330/7168 or 800-330-8149, ext. 7198
RETAIL & DINING: Clubs-CC-224-7485
Ten-digit dialing required for local calls.

HURLBURT FIELD
424 Cody Avenue, Bldg 90229, Hurlburt Field, FL 32544-5417
C-850-882-1110 (Eglin Base info), DSN-312-579-1110 (ask for Hurlburt), Police-884-6423
WEB: www.hurlburt.af.mil
LOCATION: Off US-98, five miles west of Fort Walton Beach, north of US-98. Take I-10 to Chase Street, which turns into Bayfront Parkway. Make a right onto US-98. Cross the bay and continue through Fort Walton to get to the Main Gate. USMRA: Florida Panhandle (B-6); Pensacola, FL (P-10). NMC: Pensacola, 35 miles west.
RECREATION & TRAVEL: Golf-881-2251 Marina-884-4097 RVC-884-4097/6939 SPA-884-3901/5781/3 TML-581-1627 or 884-6245/7115
RETAIL & DINING: Clubs-CC-884-6469 OC-884-7507 Soundside-581-3110/1 Com-881-2139 Dining-884-1276/6935 EX-581-0030 Gas-581-2224
SUPPORT & FAMILY: Med-5119/5221

JACKSONVILLE NAVAL AIR STATION
Box 102, Code N02P, Naval Air Station
Jacksonville, FL 32212-0002
C-904-542-2345/4011, DSN-312-942-2345, Police-542-2661
WEB: www.nasjax.navy.mil
LOCATION: From I-10, take exit 361 to the Roosevelt Expressway. Merge onto US-17 all the way to the main entrance. USMRA: FL map (H-3); Jacksonville, FL, map (B,C-6,7). NMC: Jacksonville, nine miles northeast. NMI: Mayport Naval Station, 46 miles northeast.
RECREATION & TRAVEL: Golf-542-3249 Marina-542-3260 RVC-542-3227 SPA-542-3825 TML-542-3138/3427/8195/6 Navy Lodge-800-NAVY-INN or 772-6000
RETAIL & DINING: Clubs-CC-542-3521 CPO/NCO-542-3461 EMC-542-3521 OC-542-3041 Com-542-3431 Dining-542-3854/8597 EX-777-7211 Gas-777-7142
SUPPORT & FAMILY: Med-542-4677

JUPITER COAST GUARD EXCHANGE

US-1, Lighthouse Park, Jupiter, FL 33458-4372
C-561-746-5402, Police-844-5030
LOCATION: From I-95, take FL-706 exit 87A to US-1 north. Take a right onto FL-707 and the first right into the station. USMRA: FL map (K-10). NMC: West Palm Beach, 15 miles south.
RETAIL & DINING: EX-746-5402

KENNEDY SPACE CENTER VISITOR COMPLEX

Delaware North Park Services Mail Code DNPS
Kennedy Space Center, FL 32899-0001
C-321-449-4444, Police-911
WEB: www.kennedyspacecenter.com
LOCATION: Traveling south (from Daytona) on I-95, take exit 215 (SR 50). Turn left (east) onto SR 50. The next intersection is SR 50 and SR 405. Turn right (east) onto SR 405 and follow signs for Kennedy Space Center. You will travel approximately 11 miles on SR 405. The KSC Visitor Complex will be on your right. Alternately, from Orlando on State Road, travel east until you reach the SR-407 and it dead ends into SR 405. Turn right (east) onto SR-405, traveling approximately nine miles, and follow the signs for Kennedy Space Center. USMRA: FL map (J-7). NMC: Orlando, 40 miles west.

KEY WEST NAVAL AIR STATION

Code 01J, P.O. Box 9001
Key West Naval Air Station, FL 33040-9001
C-305-293-2268, DSN-312-483-2268, Police-293-2531
WEB: www.naskw.navy.mil
LOCATION: Take Florida Turnpike, US-1 south to exit signs east for Key West Naval Air Station on Boca Chica Key, seven miles north of Key West. USMRA: FL map (D-10, H-16). NMC: Miami, 123 miles north.
RECREATION & TRAVEL: Marina-293-3402/4434 RVC-293-4432/3 SPA-293-2770 TML-293-4117/8 Navy Lodge-800-NAVY-INN or 292-7556
RETAIL & DINING: Clubs-CC-293-2495 CPO-293-2407 OC-293-4208 Com-293-4402 Dining-293-2435 EX-292-7200 Gas-292-7219
SUPPORT & FAMILY: Med-293-4605
Ten-digit dialing required for local calls.

LAKE PIPPIN, MAXWELL/ GUNTER RECREATION AREA

801 White Point Road, Niceville, FL 32578-3917
C-850-897-2411, Police (Eglin AFB)-882-2502
WEB: www.au.af.mil/42abw/42svs/lakepippin.html
LOCATION: From I-10 at Crestview take FL-85 south to Niceville. Take FL-20 east approximately 6.5 miles to sign for Maxwell/ Gunter Recreation Area. Mid-Bay Bridge (toll) FL-293 makes area easily accessible from both FL-20 and US-98. USMRA: Florida Panhandle (C-6). NMC: Fort Walton Beach, FL, eight miles west. NMI: Eglin AFB, FL, ten miles west.
RECREATION & TRAVEL: RVC-334-953-3509
NOTE: *For detailed information about this off-base recreation facility, as well as on-base recreation facilities, golf courses and marinas, consult Military Living's "Military RV, Camping and Outdoor Recreation Around the World".*

MACDILL AIR FORCE BASE

8208 Hangar Loop Drive, Suite 14
MacDill Air Force Base, FL 33621-5502
C-813-828-1110, DSN-312-968-1110, Police-828-3322
WEB: http://public.macdill.amc.af.mil/
LOCATION: From I-75 north or south take exit 41B to I-275 south, exit 23 at Dale Mabry Highway (US-92/573), south five miles to MacDill AFB Main Gate. USMRA: FL map (F-8); Tampa-St. Petersburg, FL, map (E,F-3,4). NMC: Tampa, five miles north.
RECREATION & TRAVEL: Golf-840-6904 Marina-828-4983 RVC-840-6919 SPA-828-2440/85 TML-831-4775/4804
RETAIL & DINING: Cafeteria-840-9005 Clubs-EMC-840-6900 NCO-828-3357 OC-837-1031 Com-828-4832 EX-840-0511 Gas-840-0448
SUPPORT & FAMILY: Med-828-2773

MARATHON RECREATION COTTAGES & RV PARK

100 MacArthur Causeway,
Miami Beach Causeway, FL 33139-5101
C-305-535-4565, Emergency-911
WEB: http://www.uscg.mil/mlclant/iscmiami/MarathonCottages.htm
LOCATION: Take US-1 onto Marathon Key. The RV park is located on the west side of US-1 at mile marker 48. USMRA: FL map (I-15). NMC: Miami, 111 miles northeast. NMI: Key West Naval Air Station on Boca Chica Key, 40 miles southwest.
RECREATION & TRAVEL: RVC-535-4565 TML-535-4565
NOTE: *For detailed information about this off-base recreation facility, as well as on-base recreation facilities, golf courses and marinas, consult Military Living's "Military RV, Camping and Outdoor Recreation Around the World".*
Ten-digit dialing required for local calls.

MAYPORT COAST GUARD GROUP

4200 Ocean Street, Atlantic Beach, FL 32233-0385
C-904-270-5401
WEB: http://www.uscg.mil/d7/units/grumayport/
LOCATION: From Jacksonville, take FL-10 (Atlantic Blvd) to FL-A1A (Mayport Road). Base is east of FL-A1A. USMRA: FL map (H-3); Jacksonville, FL, map (F-3). NMC: Jacksonville, eight miles west.
RETAIL & DINING: EX-247-8740

MAYPORT NAVAL STATION

P.O. Box 280012, Mayport Naval Station, FL 32228-0032
C-904-270-5401, DSN-312-960-5401, Police-270-5583
WEB: www.nsmayport.navy.mil
LOCATION: From the north, take I-95 South to the 9A exit. Take Atlantic Blvd and drive east until you cross the Intracoastal Waterway. After crossing the waterway, take the first exit on the right to Mayport Road. Continue for approximately five miles. From the south, take I-95 North to J. Turner Blvd. Go east to the San Pablo exit and turn left. Drive across Beach Blvd, continuing to Atlantic Blvd and turn right onto Atlantic at the light. After crossing the Intracoastal Waterway, follow the above directions. From I-10 east, continue to I-95 south, exit at HWY-90 (Beaches) until it splits into Atlantic Blvd and Beach Blvd. Take Atlantic Blvd and follow the above directions. USMRA: FL map (H-3); Jacksonville, FL, map (G-3,4). NMC: Jacksonville, ten miles west.
RECREATION & TRAVEL: Golf-270-5380 RVC-270-7808 TML-247-3964 Navy Lodge-800-NAVY-INN or 247-3964
RETAIL & DINING: Clubs-CPO-270-5432 Beach Club-270-7197 Com-249-7362 Dining-270-5373 EX-242-3240 Gas-270-5619
SUPPORT & FAMILY: Med-270-4677

MIAMI COAST GUARD AIR STATION

14750 NW 44th Court
Opa Locka Airport, Opa Locka, FL 33054-2304
C-305-953-2100, Police-953-2297
WEB: www.uscg.mil/d7/units/as-miami/
LOCATION: Take Opa-Locka Blvd exit west from I-95. Follow Opa-Locka Blvd for about four miles then turn right onto 42nd Street (LeJeune Blvd) to the Opa-Locka Airport. USMRA: FL map (J-13); Miami, FL, map (B-4). NMC: Miami, five miles south.
RECREATION & TRAVEL: SPA-953-2130
RETAIL & DINING: Clubs-CC-All Hands-953-2291 OC-953-2189 Com-953-2290 Dining-953-2187 EX-953-2290
SUPPORT & FAMILY: Med-953-2265/6
Ten-digit dialing required for local calls.

MIAMI COAST GUARD INTEGRATED SUPPORT COMMAND

100 MacArthur Causeway, Miami Beach, FL 33139-5119
C-305-535-4300, Police-535-4167
WEB: www.uscg.mil/mlclant/iscmiami
LOCATION: Take I-95 to I-359 (MacArthur Causeway) east to Terminal Isle Road, turn east. USMRA: FL map (K-13); Miami, FL, map (D-6). NMC: Miami Beach, within city limits.
RECREATION & TRAVEL: RVC-535-4565
RETAIL & DINING: Clubs-CC-All Hands-535-4366 Com-953-2115 Dining-535-4460 EX-535-4354/4410
SUPPORT & FAMILY: Med-535-4350
Ten-digit dialing required for local calls.

ORLANDO NAVY EXCHANGE

7151 Earhart Drive, Orlando, FL 32827-5051
C-407-857-3550, Police-911
WEB: www.navy-nex.com
LOCATION: From I-4 in Orlando take FL-528 (the Beeline) east until you reach the Tradeport Drive exit. Go south on Tradeport Drive for about one mile and turn right onto Earhart Drive. USMRA: FL map (H-7); Orlando, FL, map (C,D-14). NMC: Orlando, three miles from downtown. NMI: Patrick AFB, 50 miles southeast, near Cocoa Beach.
RETAIL & DINING: Com-857-3550 EX-857-3550
Ten-digit dialing required for local calls.

PANAMA CITY COAST GUARD STATION

1700 Thomas Drive, Panama City Beach, FL 32407-5898
C-850-234-4228, C-234-4228
WEB: www.uscg.mil/d8/stationpanamacity/stapc_home.htm
LOCATION: From the north, take US-331 to US-98 west, to south on Thomas Drive. Located 0.25 miles on the left to Navy Base (Coastal Systems Station). USMRA: Florida Panhandle (D-7). NMC: Panama City, adjacent. NMI: Panama City Naval Base, adjacent.
RETAIL & DINING: EX-234-2407

PANAMA CITY NAVAL SUPPORT ACTIVITY

110 Vernon Drive, Panama City, FL 32407-7018
C-850-234-4011, DSN-312-436-4011, Police-234-4332
WEB: www.ncsc.navy.mil
LOCATION: From Panama City Airport, go south on Lisenby Ave and turn right at first light onto SR-390, then go to 23rd street and turn right. Go to HWY-98 west, turn right. Go across the bridge, turn left at second light onto Thomas Drive. NASPC gate entrance is at the second light on the left. Visitors may enter through Main Gate with DoD/DHS sticker and valid military ID card. USMRA: FL map (D-7). NMC: Pensacola, eight miles north. NMI: Tyndall Air Force Base, 15 miles southeast.
RECREATION & TRAVEL: Marina-234-4402 RVC-234-4402 TML-234-4217
RETAIL & DINING: Clubs-CC-234-4375 OC-235-5502 Dining-235-5020 EX-235-2778
SUPPORT & FAMILY: Med-234-4177

PANAMA CITY NAVAL SUPPORT ACTIVITY OFF-BASE FAMILY CAMPGROUND

110 Vernon Avenue, Panama City, FL 32407-7001
C-850-234-4217, DSN-312-436-4217, Police-234-4332
LOCATION: Off base. From east or west on US-98 turn south at northwest corner of base onto FL-3031 (Thomas Drive). Go approximately 2.2 miles south on Thomas Drive to a left (east) on FL-747 (Magnolia Beach Road) to a left on Magnolia Drive approximately 0.2 miles directly to campground. Check-in on base. USMRA: Florida Panhandle map (D-7). NMC: Panama City, approximately five miles northeast.
RECREATION & TRAVEL: RVC-234-4402
NOTE: *For detailed information about this off-base recreation facility, as well as on-base recreation facilities, golf courses and marinas, consult Military Living's "Military RV, Camping and Outdoor Recreation Around the World".*

PATRICK AIR FORCE BASE

1201 Edward H. White II Street, Building 423, Rm C-129
Patrick Air Force Base, FL 32925-3237
C-321-494-1110, DSN-312-854-1110, Police-494-2008
WEB: https://www.patrick.af.mil
LOCATION: Take I-95 south to exit 191 east (Wickham Road), three miles to FL-404 (Pineda Causeway), exit to South Patrick Drive. At exit stoplight, turn left, and proceed to Patrick AFB. USMRA: FL map (J-8). NMC: Orlando, 45 miles northwest.
RECREATION & TRAVEL: Golf-494-7856 Marina-494-7456 RVC-494-4787 SPA-494-5631 TML-494-2075/5428/9/6590
RETAIL & DINING: Clubs-CC-494-7491 Com-494-5841 Dining-494-4248 EX-799-1300 Gas-494-2655
SUPPORT & FAMILY: Med-494-8241

PENSACOLA NAVAL AIR STATION

190 Radford Blvd, Pensacola Naval Air Station, FL 32508-5217
C-850-452-0111, DSN-312-922-0111, Police-452-2654
WEB: http://www.naspensacola.navy.mil/
LOCATION: Four miles south of US-98 and 12 miles south of I-10. Take Navy Blvd from US-98 or US-29 directly to the Naval Air Station. USMRA: Florida Panhandle (A-7), AL map (C,D-11). NMC: Pensacola, eight miles north.
RECREATION & TRAVEL: Golf-452-2454 Marina-452-3369/4152 RVC-452-2535 SPA-452-3311 TML-452-2755/6/3625/7782 Navy Lodge-800-NAVY-INN or 456-8676
RETAIL & DINING: Cafeteria-458-8378 Clubs-CPO-452-3251 EMC-452-3364 NCO-452-2443 OC-455-2276 Com-452-6889 Dining-452-7050 EX-458-8254 Gas-457-1229
SUPPORT & FAMILY: Med-505-7171

PENSACOLA NAVAL HOSPITAL

6000 West Highway 98, Pensacola, FL 32512-0003
C-850-505-6601, DSN-312-534-6601, Police (Security)-505-6007
WEB: http://psaweb.med.navy.mil
LOCATION: From I-10 exit south on Pine Forest Road, travel four miles to Mobile Highway, then veer left at Fairgrounds. Go three miles to New Warrington Road exit south (New Warrington becomes Navy Blvd). Take Navy Blvd to Dr. Farin Drive (US Highway 98) exit west; Hospital will be on right (northside of roadway) after two miles. USMRA: Florida Panhandle (A-6), NC, SC map (K-10). NMC: Pensacola, five miles east.
RETAIL & DINING: Dining-505-3123 EX-455-9649
SUPPORT & FAMILY: Med-505-7171

PONCE DE LEON COAST GUARD STATION

2999 North Peninsula Avenue, New Smyrna Beach, FL 32169-0370
C-386-428-9085, 428-9084/5
LOCATION: From I-95 south exit 84, or I-4 exit at FL-44 east, across two bridges, turn left at the first light onto Peninsula Avenue. USMRA: FL map (I-6). NMC: Daytona Beach, 20 miles north.
RETAIL & DINING: EX-427-2786

PORT CANAVERAL COAST GUARD STATION

9235 Grouper Road, Port Canaveral, FL 32920-4402
C-321-868-4200, Police-911
WEB: www.uscg.mil/d7/units/mso-jax/msd%20files/msd.htm
LOCATION: From I-95 north or south, exit 205, take FL-528 east. Exit onto FL-401. Make a right onto Grouper Road. USMRA: FL map (J-7). NMC: Daytona Beach, 20 miles north. NMI: Patrick AFS, 12 miles south.
RETAIL & DINING: EX-868-7769

RICHMOND HEIGHTS COAST GUARD EXCHANGE
Richmond Heights, 15298 SW 121st Avenue
Miami, FL 33177-1523
C-305-234-2479, Police-911
LOCATION: From north or south on the FL-821 (Florida Turnpike), take exit 16 west onto FL-992 (SW 152nd Street). Go west approximately 0.5 miles to SW 121st Avenue. Coast Guard Exchange is on left (south) side of SW 152nd Street. From north or south on US-1/FL-5 turn west onto FL-992 (SW 152nd Street) and drive west approximately three miles to Coast Guard Exchange on left (south) side of SW FL-992 (152nd Street). USMRA: Miami, FL map (A-9). NMC: Miami, 20 miles north.
RETAIL & DINING: EX-234-2479
Ten-digit dialing required for local calls.

SAND KEY COAST GUARD STATION
1375 Gulf Blvd, Clearwater, FL 33767-2807
C-727-596-8540
WEB: www.uscg.mil
LOCATION: From I-275 north or south, take exit 31B to FL-688. Veer right onto FL-686 (Roosevelt Blvd) all the way to Bellair Beach. Make a right onto FL-183/699 (Gulf Blvd). USMRA: FL map (E-8); Tampa/St. Petersburg, FL, map (A-2). NMC: St. Petersburg, ten miles south.
RETAIL & DINING: EX-596-8744

SAUFLEY FIELD
NETPDTC, 6490 Saufley Field Road, Pensacola, FL 32509-5237
C-850-452-1001, DSN-312-922-1628, Police-452-1628/50
LOCATION: From I-10, take exit 7 to FL-297 (Pine Forest Road) south to a right onto Longleaf Drive, which turns into Blue Angel Parkway. Take a right onto Saufley Field Road to the Main Gate. USMRA: FL map (A-6); Pensacola, FL, map (J,K-10). NMC: Pensacola, in the city.
RECREATION & TRAVEL: Golf-452-1097
RETAIL & DINING: Clubs-CMO-452-1038/1556 EX-456-3604
SUPPORT & FAMILY: Med-452-5242

SHADES OF GREEN® ON WALT DISNEY WORLD® RESORT
P.O. Box 22789, Lake Buena Vista, FL 32830-2789
C-407-824-3400 or 888-593-2242, Fax: C-407-824-3665
Police (Security)-824-1458
e-mail: reservations@shadesofgreen.org
WEB: http://www.shadesofgreen.org
LOCATION: From Orlando take I-4 to the Walt Disney World exit, follow Magic Kingdom Resort signs. Enter through Magic Kingdom toll booth, stay in far right lane following signs to resort and hotels. Once through the gate, follow the green line. At the first light turn left (Seven Seas Drive). At the three-way stop, turn right onto Floridian Way. Driveway is first road to the left, Magnolia Palm Drive. USMRA: FL map (H-7); Orlando, FL, map (A-14,15,16); Walt Disney World, FL, map (E-13). NMC: Orlando, 15 miles northeast.
RECREATION & TRAVEL: TML-824-3600 or 888-593-2242
RETAIL & DINING: Dining-824-2437
Ten-digit dialing required for local calls.

TAMPA-ST. PETERSBURG COAST GUARD SECTOR
600 8th Avenue SE, St. Petersburg, FL 33701-5099
C-727-824-7534, Police(Security)-824-7638
WEB: www.uscg.mil/d7/units/grustpete
LOCATION: Take I-275 to I-175 east and south, exit 9 to Fifth Avenue east, go three blocks, make a right onto First Street SE, which turns into Eighth Avenue and leads to the CG Group. Located adjacent to Albert Whitted Airport. USMRA: FL map (F-8); Tampa/St. Petersburg, FL, map (D-5). NMC: St. Petersburg, within city limits. NMI: MacDill AFB, 15 miles northwest.
RETAIL & DINING: Clubs-CC-824-7658 Dining-824-7651 EX-896-2816
SUPPORT & FAMILY: Med-824-7579

TYNDALL AIR FORCE BASE
445 Suwannee Road, Bldg 662, Suite 101
Tyndall Air Force Base, FL 32403-5541
C-850-283-1113, DSN-312-523-1113, Police-283-2254
WEB: www.tyndall.af.mil
LOCATION: From I-10, exit to US-231 south to US-98 east. Tyndall AFB is southeast of US-98. Clearly marked. USMRA: Florida Panhandle map (D-7). NMC: Panama City, ten miles northwest.
RECREATION & TRAVEL: Golf-286-2565 Marina-238-3199 RVC-283-2798 SPA-283-4360 TML-283-4211, ext. 3346/7/8/9
RETAIL & DINING: Clubs-EMC/NCO-283-4146 OC-286-5171 Com-283-4825 Dining-283-2239 EX-283-4110 Gas-286-5826
SUPPORT & FAMILY: Med-283-2778

UNITED STATES SOUTHERN COMMAND
3511 Northwest 91st Avenue, Miami, FL 33172-1217
C-305-437-1000 or 888-271-7955, DSN-312-567-1000
DOD Police-437-2347
WEB: www.southcom.mil
LOCATION: From I-95 north or south, take the NW 36th Street exit. Turn right onto NW 36th Street, left on NW 87th Street, right on 33rd Street, then right onto 91st Avenue. Follow signs. USMRA: Miami, FL map (B-5). NMC: Miami, within city limits.
RETAIL & DINING: EX-437-3550
SUPPORT & FAMILY: Med-437-1148
Ten-digit dialing required for local calls.

WHITING FIELD NAVAL AIR STATION
7550 USS Essex Street, Suite 206, Milton, FL 32570-6155
C-850-623-7651, DSN-312-868-7651, Police-623-7709
WEB: https://wwwcfs.cnet.navy.mil/naswf/index.cfm
LOCATION: From US-90 east exit, FL-87 north for eight miles to NAS on east side of FL-87. Take a right onto FL-87A into the station. Visitors enter through the Main Gate. USMRA: FL map (B-6). NMC: Pensacola, 30 miles southwest.
RECREATION & TRAVEL: Golf/Pro Shop-623-7348 TML-623-7605/6/7
RETAIL & DINING: Clubs-CC-623-7311 Com-623-7788 Dining-623-7311 EX-623-8066 Gas-623-8088
SUPPORT & FAMILY: Med-623-7584

GEORGIA, pg. 35
Atlanta, pg. 35

ALBANY MARINE CORPS LOGISTICS BASE
814 Radford Blvd, Albany, GA 31704-1128
C-229-639-5000, DSN-312-567-5000, Police-639-5181
WEB: www.ala.usmc.mil
LOCATION: From US-19 (Liberty Expressway), north or south in Albany, exit southwest to Sunbelt Parkway, GA-133 (Moultrie Road) to left (north) onto Mock Road to right (east) to Fleming Road. Main Gate is second gate on left. Also, from GA-82, east or west in Albany to a left on Mock Road to left on Fleming Road. Main Gate is second gate on left. USMRA: GA map (C-9). NMC: Albany, three miles west.
RECREATION & TRAVEL: TML-639-5614
RETAIL & DINING: Clubs-OC-639-5239 Com-435-1721 Dining-639-5223 EX-888-6801 Gas-436-8352
SUPPORT & FAMILY: Med-639-5976/7

ATHENS NAVAL SUPPLY CORPS SCHOOL
1425 Prince Avenue, Athens, GA 30606-2296
C-706-354-1500, DSN-312-354-1500, Police-354-7355
WEB: https://www.npdc.navy.mil
LOCATION: From Atlanta, take I-85 northeast to GA-316/US-29. Go east to Athens perimeter Loop 10. Follow loop eastbound to Prince Avenue exit. Take a left to Oglethorpe Avenue. Base is on the right. USMRA: GA map (D-5). NMC: Atlanta, 45 miles southwest.
RECREATION & TRAVEL: TML-425-2300
RETAIL & DINING: Clubs-CC-354-7381 OC-354-7230 Com-354-7371 Dining-354-7380 EX- 354-3850 Gas-354-8761
SUPPORT & FAMILY: Med-354-7320/1

ATLANTA NAVAL AIR STATION
1000 Halsey Avenue, Marietta, GA 30060-5099
C-678-655-1110, DSN-312-625-1110, Police-655-6394
LOCATION: From I-75 north or south, take exit 260. Proceed west on Windy Hill to Atlanta Road. Take right, north on Atlanta Road to George McMillian Road. Take right, east. Main Gate on left. USMRA: GA map (B-4,5). NMC: Atlanta, 15 miles southeast.
RECREATION & TRAVEL: RVC-770-974-6309 SPA-655-6359 TML-888-436-2246, ext. 9-6393
RETAIL & DINING: Clubs-CC-655-6866 Dining-655-6469 EX-428-1274 Gas-427-4400
SUPPORT & FAMILY: Med-655-5301
NOTE: *The 2005 BRAC report recommended this base for closure. As required by Federal law, the DoD has until 15 September 2007 to begin closing and realigning the bases as called for in the approved report. This process must be completed by 15 September 2011.*

CAMP FRANK D. MERRILL
1 Camp Frank D. Merrill, Dahlonega, GA 30533-9499
C-706-864-3327
LOCATION: From Atlanta, go north on GA-400/US-19 approximately 55 miles to Dahlonega. Continue north on US-19 through Dahlonega approximately 2.3 miles to a left (northwest) turn onto Camp Wahsega Road. Follow Camp Wahsega Road approximately nine miles northwest to the very end of the road at the Main Gate of Camp Frank D. Merrill. USMRA: GA map (C-3). NMC: Gainesville, 27 miles southeast.
RECREATION & TRAVEL: TML-867-3327/67/7748, ext. 130
RETAIL & DINING: Clubs-CC-All Ranks-864-3131 Com-864-3109 EX-864-3773
SUPPORT & FAMILY: Med-864-3327 ext. 800
NOTE: *For all services, use main phone number plus exention code, unless otherwise noted.*

DOBBINS AIR RESERVE BASE
94 Airlift Wing, 1430 First Street
Dobbins Air Reserve Base, GA 30069-5009
C-678-655-5055, DSN-312-625-5055, Police-655-4909
WEB: www.afrc.af.mil/22AF/94AW/default.asp
LOCATION: From Atlanta, take I-75 north to Lockheed/Dobbins Exit (exit 261 west). Merge onto Delk Road heading west which leads to the Main Gate. USMRA: GA map (B-5; F-1). NMC: Atlanta, 16 miles east. Robins AFB, 100 miles southeast.
RECREATION & TRAVEL: RVC-655-4870 SPA-655-6359 TML-655-4745 or 888-AFLODGE (235-6343)
RETAIL & DINING: Clubs-CC-625-4594 Dining-655-4975 EX-428-1274
SUPPORT & FAMILY: Med-655-5300
Ten-digit dialing required for local calls.

FORT BENNING
U.S. Army Infantry Center, Attn: PAO, 6751 Constitution Loop
Fort Benning, GA 31905-4584
C-706-545-2011, DSN-312-835-2011, Police-545-5222
WEB: www.benning.army.mil
LOCATION: From I-185, exit to US-27/280 (Victory Blvd) west. Make a left onto Fort Benning Road, which leads to the Main Gate. USMRA: GA map (B-7). NMC: Columbus, five miles northwest.
RECREATION & TRAVEL: Golf-687-1940 Marina-685-3060 RVC-545-4053/7238 or 685-3060 SPA-545-2857 TML-689-0067, ext. 1030
RETAIL & DINING: Cafeteria-687-0349 Clubs-EMC-687-1232 NCO-687-1251 OC-687-1861 Com-545-3965 EX-687-0384 Gas-687-6520
SUPPORT & FAMILY: Med-544-2273

FORT GILLEM
2309 Hood Avenue,Forest Park, GA 30297-5114
C-404-469-5000, DSN-312-797-5000, Police-464-2281/2
WEB: www.mcpherson.army.mil/Fort_Gillem.htm
LOCATION: Fort Gillem is located ten miles south of Atlanta. From north or south I-75/I-85, take I-285 east for about three miles, take I-675 south and take the first exit west (Anvil Bock Road). Drive west approximately three-fourths of a mile to the Fort Gillem Main Gate. Corner of Anvil Bock Road and HWY-42. USMRA: GA map (C-5; G,H-4). NMC: Atlanta, ten miles north.
RECREATION & TRAVEL: TML-464-2253/2980/3833
RETAIL & DINING: Clubs-CC-469-3831 Com-469-5361 EX-469-5483 Gas-366-6942
SUPPORT & FAMILY: Med-464-2778
NOTE: *The 2005 BRAC report recommended this base for closure. As required by Federal law, the DoD has until 15 September 2007 to begin closing and realigning the bases as called for in the approved report. This process must be completed by 15 September 2011. Ten-digit dialing required for local calls.*

FORT GORDON ARMY SIGNAL CENTER
U.S. Army Signal Center, Bldg 29808, Chamberlain Ave
Fort Gordon, GA 30905-5761
C-706-791-0110, DSN-312-780-1110, Police-791-4380
WEB: www.gordon.army.mil
LOCATION: From I-20 east or west, exit 183 south onto GA-47/US-221. Make a left onto US-278 which turns into US-78 and takes you to the Main Gate. USMRA: GA map (F-5,6). NMC: Augusta, 12 miles northeast.
RECREATION & TRAVEL: Golf-791-2433 Marina-541-1057 RVC-541-1057 SPA-791-5811 TML-791-2277
RETAIL & DINING: Clubs-Cafe-771-6921 Com-791-3718 Dining-Anthony's-798-1947 Burger King-793-1947/8542 Food Court-772-9742 EX-793-0233
SUPPORT & FAMILY: Med-787-7300

FORT MCPHERSON
1386 Troop Row, SW, Fort McPherson, GA 30330-1069
C-404-464-3113, DSN-312-367-3113, Police-464-2281/2
WEB: www.mcpherson.army.mil
LOCATION: Fort McPherson is on the south side of Atlanta, north of the William B. Hartsfield-Maynard H. Jackson International Airport. From north or south 1-75/ I-85, take Arthur Langford Memorial Parkway (GA-166) exit west. Drive west approximately 1.5 miles to the Fort McPherson exit and go north past MARTA station directly to Main (South) Gate. USMRA: Atlanta, GA map (G-3). NMC: Atlanta, within city limits.
RECREATION & TRAVEL: Golf-464-2178 RVC-770-974-3413 TML-464-1050/2253/3833
RETAIL & DINING: Clubs-CC-753-6991 Com-464-2264 Dining-464-2479 EX-469-5483/4 Gas-753-2114
SUPPORT & FAMILY: Med-464-2778
NOTE: *The 2005 BRAC report recommended this base for closure. As required by Federal law, the DoD has until 15 September 2007 to begin closing and realigning the bases as called for in the approved report. This process must be completed by 15 September 2011. Ten-digit dialing required for local calls.*

FORT STEWART
Attn: AFZP-GC, 3 Infantry Division & Fort Stewart
Fort Stewart, GA 31314-3421

C-912-767-1411, DSN-312-870-1411/1110, Police-767-4895
WEB: www.stewart.army.mil
LOCATION: On US-84. Accessible from US-17 or I-95. Also, GA-119/GA-144 crosses the post but may be closed occasionally. From I-95 north or south, exit 90 to GA-144 west, which leads straight to the gate. From I-16 east or west, exit 137 to GA-119 south, which leads directly to the Main Gate. USMRA: GA map (G-8). NMC: Savannah, 35 miles northeast.
RECREATION & TRAVEL: Golf-767-2370 RVC-767-2717/71 TML-767-4184/8384
RETAIL & DINING: Clubs-CC-767-2212 Com-767-1392 EX-876-2850 Gas-876-8434
SUPPORT & FAMILY: Med-435-5364/6857

GRASSY POND RECREATION AREA

Recreation Services, Grassy Pond, 5360 Grassy Pond Road
Lake Park, GA 31636-3116
C-229-559-5840, Police-333-5133
WEB: www.moody.af.mil
LOCATION: Off base. From I-75 north or south, take exit 5 west on GA-376 (Clyattville Road). Immediately watch for signs and left turn onto Loch Laurel Road and left onto Grassy Pond Drive. USMRA: GA map (D-11). NMC: Valdosta, 12 miles north. NMI: Moody AFB, 25 miles north.
RECREATION & TRAVEL: RVC-559-5840 TML-559-5840
RETAIL & DINING: Gas-257-3876
NOTE: *For detailed information about this off-base recreation facility, as well as on-base recreation facilities, golf courses and marinas, consult Military Living's "Military RV, Camping and Outdoor Recreation Around the World".*

HUNTER ARMY AIRFIELD

Garrison Command Headquarters, Attn: AFZP-GC, Bldg 1201
Hunter Army Airfield, GA 31409-5517
C-912-767-1411, DSN-312-870-1411, Police-315-6133
WEB: www.stewart.army.mil
LOCATION: From I-95 north or south exit 94 (Hwy-204/Abercorn Street). Take Hwy-204 east, turn left onto White Bluff Blvd, then left onto Stephenson Avenue, proceed to Wilson Avenue gate to installation. USMRA: GA map (H-8). NMC: Savannah, within city limits.
RECREATION & TRAVEL: Golf-315-5622 Marina-315-5974 RVC-315-5722/5974 SPA-315-5110 TML-355-1060 or 315-5834/5910
RETAIL & DINING: Clubs-Hunter-315-7923 Com-315-5007 Dining-315-2538 EX-315-8380 Gas-354-8752
SUPPORT & FAMILY: Med-315-6800

KINGS BAY NAVAL SUBMARINE BASE

1063 USS Tennessee Avenue, Kings Bay, GA 31547-2606
C-912-573-2000, DSN-312-573-2000, Police (Security)-573-2145
WEB: www.subasekb.navy.mil
LOCATION: From I-95 north or south, take exit 1 east to St. Mary's Road, which leads right into base. USMRA: GA map (G-10). NMC: Jacksonville, FL, 40 miles south.
RECREATION & TRAVEL: Golf-573-2289/8476 RVC-673-1161 or 800-818-1815 TML-573-4871/4971 Navy Lodge-800-NAVY-INN or 882-6868
RETAIL & DINING: Cafeteria-573-4643 Clubs-573-8999 Com-573-3310 EX-882-6098 Gas-573-9586
SUPPORT & FAMILY: Med-573-4242

LAKE ALLATOONA ARMY RECREATION AREA

Army Recreation Area, 40 Old Sandtown Road SE
Cartersville, GA 30121-7678
C-770-974-3413, Fax: C-770-974-1278
WEB: www.mcpherson.army.mil/recalla.htm
LOCATION: Located on 85-acre site at Lake Allatoona reservoir. From I-75 north or south of Atlanta, take exit 283 east (Emerson exit) onto Old Allatoona Road. Turn east off exit, travel 2.7 miles, turn left on Old Sandtown Road. Travel one block and bear left into park; follow signs to office. USMRA: GA map (B-4). NMC: Atlanta, 40 miles south. NMI: Dobbins ARB, 28 miles southeast.
RECREATION & TRAVEL Marina-974-3413/9420 RVC-974-3413 TML-974-3413
NOTE: *For detailed information about this off-base recreation facility, as well as on-base recreation facilities, golf courses and marinas, consult Military Living's "Military RV, Camping and Outdoor Recreation Around the World".*
Ten-digit dialing required for local calls.

MOODY AIR FORCE BASE

5113 Austin Ellipse, Suite 6
Moody Air Force Base, GA 31699-1599
C-229-257-4211, DSN-312-460-1110, Police-257-3108/3200
WEB: www.moody.af.mil
LOCATION: From Valdosta, GA go approximately ten miles north on GA-125 to South Gate (Main Gate) on right (east) side of road. (Note: North Gate is open only on limited hours/days.) Also can be reached from north or south on I-75. Take exit to GA-122 east approximately 12 miles to a right (south) turn on GA-125 for 3.5 miles south to South Gate (Main Gate) on left (east) side of road. USMRA: GA map (D,E-10). NMC: Valdosta, ten miles south.
RECREATION & TRAVEL: Golf-257-3297 RVC-559-5840 SPA-257-1776 TML-257-3893
RETAIL & DINING: Clubs-CC-257-3792 Com-257-3338 Dining-257-3032 EX-257-3431 Gas-257-3876
SUPPORT & FAMILY: Med-257-2778/3196

POINTES WEST ARMY RECREATION AREA

P.O. Box 67, Appling, GA 30802-0067
C-706-541-1057, ext.132, Police-541-1057, ext. 132
WEB: http://www.fortgordon.com/pointeswest.htm
LOCATION: Off post. From I-20 east or west, take exit 183 north on US-221 to GA-47 north to a left on Washington Road to recreation area. USMRA: GA map (F-5). NMC: Augusta, 25 miles southeast. NMI: Fort Gordon, 25 miles south.
RECREATION & TRAVEL: RVC-541-1057 TML-541-1057
NOTE: *For detailed information about this off-base recreation facility, as well as on-base recreation facilities, golf courses and marinas, consult Military Living's "Military RV, Camping and Outdoor Recreation Around the World".*

ROBINS AIR FORCE BASE

215 Page Road, Suite 106 Robins Air Force Base, GA 31098-1662
C-478-926-1110, DSN-312-468-1001/1110, Police-926-1025/2187
WEB: www.robins.af.mil
LOCATION: From Interstate 75 take exit 146 to the Georgia Highway 247 Connector (also called Watson Blvd). The road will take you directly to the base, about ten miles away from the exit. You can also exit from the north at exit 65A and take HWY-247 about 15 miles south to the base. USMRA: GA map (D-7). NMC: Macon, 15 miles northwest.
RECREATION & TRAVEL: Golf-923-7334, 19th Hole-923-1717 RVC-926-3193/4500 SPA-926-3166 TML-923-6685
RETAIL & DINING: Cafeteria-922-8635 Clubs-EMC/NCO-923-5581 OC-922-3011 Com-926-2126 Dining-926-6596 EX-923-5536 Gas-923-7292
SUPPORT & FAMILY: Med-327-7850

SAVANNAH/HILTON HEAD INTERNATIONAL AIRPORT/AIR NATIONAL GUARD

165 ANG, P.O. Box 7568, Garden City, GA 31402-7568
C-912-964-1941, DSN-312-860-1941, Police-966-8223
WEB: www.gasava.ang.af.mil
LOCATION: From I-16 (east of I-95, south of Savannah) east or west, exit 160 north onto GA-307 (Dean Forest Road), across US-80, to right onto Davidson Drive for one block, to right into gate. USMRA: GA map (H-8). NMC: Savannah, four miles southeast.
RECREATION & TRAVEL: SPA-966-8241
RETAIL & DINING: Clubs-CC-963-3345 EX-964-6842
SUPPORT & FAMILY: Med-966-8221/2

WORLD FAMOUS NAVY LAKE SITE

166 Sandtown Road, Cartersville, GA 30121-7616
C-770-974-6309, Police-919-6394
LOCATION: Off base. From I-75 north or south of Atlanta, take exit 283. Turn right on Allatoona Road, proceed 3.8 miles to marked entrance on the left. USMRA: GA map (B-4). NMC: Atlanta, 40 miles southeast. NMI: Atlanta NAS, Marietta, 20 miles southeast.
RECREATION & TRAVEL: Marina-974-6307 RVC-974-6309 TML-974-6309
NOTE: *For detailed information about this off-base recreation facility, as well as on-base recreation facilities, golf courses and marinas, consult Military Living's "Military RV, Camping and Outdoor Recreation Around the World".*
Ten-digit dialing required for local calls.

KENTUCKY, pg. 38-39
Lexington, pg. 39
Louisville, pg. 39

CAMP CARLSON ARMY RECREATIONAL AREA

9210 U.S. Route 60, Muldraugh, KY 40155-2015
C-502-624-4836, DSN-312-464-4836, Police for RV park-624-2111 Emergency-624-0911
WEB: http://www.knoxmwr.com/Rec/campCarlson.asp
LOCATION: Off post. From I-65 north or south at Elizabethtown, take exit 102, come across HWY-313 West for 11 miles. At the first light, turn right onto 31 West. Go nine miles, at light make left turn onto 60 West. Go 2.5 miles. Camp Carlson is at the bottom of the hill, on the right. USMRA: KY/TN map (H-4,5). NMC: Louisville, 30 miles north.
RECREATION & TRAVEL: RVC-624-4836
NOTE: *For detailed information about this off-base recreation facility, as well as on-base recreation facilities, golf courses and marinas, consult Military Living's "Military RV, Camping and Outdoor Recreation Around the World".*

FORT CAMPBELL

101 Airborne Division (Air Assault) & Fort Campbell
39 Normandy Blvd, Fort Campbell, KY 42223-5628
C-270-798-2151, DSN-312-635-2151, Police-798-7112
WEB: www.campbell.army.mil
LOCATION: Located in southwestern Kentucky, four miles south of the intersection of US 41A and I-24. Take I-24 exit 86 south. Gate 4 (Main Gate) is 4.4 miles ahead. Hopkinsville, KY, is 15 miles north of Fort Campbell. USMRA: KY/TN map (F-8). NMC: Nashville, TN, 50 miles southeast.
RECREATION & TRAVEL: Golf-798-1822/4906 RVC-798-2629/3126/5590 SPA-798-7146 TML-439-2229 or 798-5618
RETAIL & DINING: Clubs-CC-798-4610 Com-798-2606 EX-439-1841 Gas-439-1689
SUPPORT & FAMILY: Med-800-941-4501

FORT KNOX

U.S. Army Armor Center & Fort Knox, Attn: ATZK-PAO
Bldg 474 Spearhead Division Avenue, P.O. Box 995
Fort Knox, KY 40121-0995
C-502-624-1000, DSN-312-464-1000, Police-624-2111/2
WEB: www.knox.army.mil
LOCATION: From I-64, exit I-264 (Waterson Expressway west) to US-31 west, south to Fort Knox. Or from I-71, exit I-65 south to Gene Snyder Expressway to US-31 west then south to Fort Knox. USMRA: KY/TN map (I-4,5, N-11). NMC: Louisville, 35 miles north.
RECREATION & TRAVEL: Golf-624-2717/4218 or 888-548-5728 RVC-624-4836 SPA-624-5545/6047 TML-943-1000
RETAIL & DINING: Clubs-CC-942-0959 NCO-624-0409 Com-624-8525 Dining-Anthony's Pizza-942-7484 Burger King-942-4281 Food Court-942-4269 EX-942-0067 Gas-942-4262
SUPPORT & FAMILY: Med-624-9333

LOUISVILLE INTERNATIONAL AIRPORT/STANDIFORD FIELD/AIR GUARD STATION

123 Airlift Wing, 1101 Grade Lane, Louisville, KY 40213-2678
C-502-364-9400, DSN-312-741-9400, Police-364-9477
WEB: www.kyloui.ang.af.mil
LOCATION: From I-65 north or south, take exit 128 to Fern Valley Road heading west. Turn right onto Grade Lane, which leads to the main entrance. USMRA: KY/TN map (I-4, O-10). NMC: Louisville, within city limits.
RECREATION & TRAVEL: SPA-364-9473

MARYLAND, pg. 40
Annapolis, pg. 40
Baltimore, pg. 44

ABERDEEN PROVING GROUND

U.S. Army Garrison Aberdeen Proving Ground, Attn: AMSSB-GCO
2201 Aberdeen Blvd, Aberdeen Proving Ground, MD 21005-5001
C-410-278-5201, DSN-312-298-5201, Police-306-2222 or 436-2222
WEB: www.apg.army.mil
LOCATION: From I-95 take exit 85 to MD-22. Turn right and follow signs to US-40 west. Proceed for two miles, then right onto MD-715 east ramp to the Maryland gate and the Visitor Center. To obtain a visitor pass you must have a picture ID and auto registration cards. If approaching from Baltimore traveling on US-40 east, turn right onto MD-715 and proceed to the gate. From Edgewood area - take exit 77 to MD-24 east for two miles to the Main Gate and Visitor Center. If traveling from Baltimore on US-40 east, turn right at MD-755, then right onto MD-24 to Main Gate. USMRA: DE/MD map (H-2). NMC: Baltimore, 30 miles west.
RECREATION & TRAVEL: Golf-278-4794 or 436-2213 RVC-278-4124 TML-278-5148/9 or 436-3848
RETAIL & DINING: Clubs-OC-278-3062 or 436-4739 Com-278-3926 Dining-306-1393/8 EX-272-6828 Fast Food-Burger King-273-7464 Gas-272-1681
SUPPORT & FAMILY: Med-278-1827/5475
NOTE: *All the listed facilities are physically located on Aberdeen Proving Ground (APG), unless specified otherwise.*
Ten-digit dialing required for local calls.

ANDREWS AIR FORCE BASE

1535 Command Drive, Andrews AFB, MD 20762-7002
C-301-981-1110, DSN-312-858-1110, Police-981-2001
WEB: http://public.andrews.amc.af.mil/index.asp
LOCATION: From I-95 north (east portion of Capital Beltway, I-495), take exit 9; at the first traffic light after leaving exit ramp, turn left onto Allentown Road. At next traffic light, turn right into main gate of AFB. Also, from I-395 north, exit South Capitol Street, cross Anacostia River, bear left to Suitland Parkway east, exit at Morningside on Suitland Road east to Main Gate of AFB. From I-495 south, take exit 9; turn right at stop sign, turn right at next light onto Allentown Road; turn left into Main Gate on Suitland Road. USMRA: DE/MD map (F-4,5); VA/WV map (M-6); DC map (I,J-6,7,8). NMC: Washington, DC, ten miles northwest.
RECREATION & TRAVEL: Golf-981-2325/4401/5010 RVC-981-4109 SPA-981-1854/3526, 888-360-8700 or Wash Nav Air Fac-857-2740/4 TML-981-4614 Wash Nav Air Fac-857-2777
RETAIL & DINING: Cafeteria-568-0180 Clubs-981-5091 Com-857-7105 Dining-981-6661 EX-568-1500 Gas-735-2764
SUPPORT & FAMILY: Med-857-4052
Ten-digit dialing required for local calls.

BALTIMORE/WASHINGTON INTERNATIONAL AIRPORT

Det 1, 305 APS/TR (AMC), P.O. Box 8613
Baltimore, MD 21240-0613
C-410-918-6900, DSN-312-243-6900
Police (Security)-859-7044/5
WEB: www.bwiairport.com
LOCATION: From I-95 north or south, take the BWI exit 47 east to I-195 and airport. Also MD-295 north or south exit 2 east to I-195 and airport. USMRA: DE/MD map (F-3); VA/WV map (A,B-4,5). NMC: Baltimore, five miles north.
RECREATION & TRAVEL: SPA-918-6900 or 877-429-4262
Ten-digit dialing required for local calls.

BETHESDA NATIONAL NAVAL MEDICAL CENTER

8901 Wisconsin Avenue, Bethesda, MD 20889-5600
C-301-295-2273, DSN-312-564-0000, Police-295-1246
WEB: www.bethesda.med.navy.mil
LOCATION: From VA, take I-495 north to Wisconsin Avenue exit. Stay in left lane through two lights to NNMC entrance on left. From MD: Take I-95 south to I-495 west to Connecticut Avenue exit. Stay in center lane to light, turn left onto Connecticut Avenue. At the next light, turn right onto Jones Bridge Road, right on Wisconsin Avenue, right at next light into NNMC. USMRA: DC map (D,E-1). NMC: Washington, DC, one mile southeast.
RECREATION & TRAVEL: TML-295-5855
Navy Lodge-800-NAVY-INN or 654-1795
RETAIL & DINING: Cafeteria-295-5367 EX-295-6363
Gas-295-2665
SUPPORT & FAMILY: Med-295-4810
Ten-digit dialing required for local calls.

CURTIS BAY COAST GUARD YARD

2401 Hawkins Point Road, Baltimore, MD 21226-1797
C-410-789-1600, Police-636-3692
WEB: www.uscg.mil
LOCATION: Take I-695 east or west to exit 1. Make a right onto Quarantine Road and a right onto Hawkins Point Road to a left onto Arundel Cove Avenue and into the Coast Guard Yard. USMRA: DE/MD map (G-3); VA/WV map (C-4). NMC: Baltimore, two miles north.
RECREATION & TRAVEL: TML-636-7373
RETAIL & DINING: Clubs-CC-636-7383 Dining-636-4152
EX-636-4198
SUPPORT & FAMILY: Med-636-3144
Ten-digit dialing required for local calls.

FORT DETRICK ARMY GARRISON

810 Schreider Street, Fort Detrick, MD 21702-9214
C-301-619-8000 or C-800-256-7621, DSN-312-343-1110
Police-619-4570/7114
WEB: www.detrick.army.mil
LOCATION: From Washington, DC, take I-270 north to US-15 north. From Baltimore take I-70 west to US-15 north. From US-15 north in Frederick, exit Seventh Street to post. Clearly marked. USMRA: DE/MD map (D-2). NMC: Baltimore, 50 miles east, and Washington, DC, 50 miles southeast.
RECREATION & TRAVEL: TML-619-2154
RETAIL & DINING: Cafeteria-846-1750 Clubs-CC-619-2823/3237 Com-619-2521 Dining-619-2274 EX-619-2262
Gas-619-2262
SUPPORT & FAMILY: Med-619-7175
Ten-digit dialing required for local calls.

FORT GEORGE G. MEADE

Public Affairs, 4550 Parade Field Lane, Room 102
Fort George G. Meade, MD 20755-5025
C-301-677-6261, DSN-312-622-1110/6261, Police-677-6622
WEB: www.ftmeade.army.mil
LOCATION: From north: Take MD-295 south toward Washington to Fort Meade exit (US 175 east). Continue until it turns into Reece Road. Follow the signs on Reece Road to the Main Gate. From south: Take MD-295 Baltimore-Washington Parkway north, exit at US 175 east (Fort Meade). Follow 175 east until it turns into Reece Road. Follow the signs to the Main Gate. All visitors must go to the Vistor's Control Center. USMRA: DE/MD map (F-3); VA/WV map (A-5). NMC: Baltimore, 15 miles north.
RECREATION & TRAVEL: Golf-677-4333/5326
RVC-677-3825/6196 TML-410-674-7700
RETAIL & DINING: Clubs-CC-All Hands-677-5358 Com-677-7463 Dining-677-0864 EX-674-7170 Gas-672-1183
SUPPORT & FAMILY: Med-677-8606
NOTE: *The Lewellyn Avenue Gate will serve as the Main Gate to Fort Meade and will be open 24 hours a day while construction continues on a new Visitor Control Center. The current Visitor Control Center on Reece Road will be open from 0730-1500 hours Mon-Fri. RVs must enter through the gate at Route 32 marked "NSA Trucks."*
Ten-digit dialing required for local calls.

GODDARD SPACE FLIGHT CENTER, NASA

Visitor Center, Greenbelt, MD 20771-0001
C-301-286-8981, Police-286-8661/2
WEB: www.nasa.gov/centers/goddard/home/index.html
LOCATION: From Washington, DC, or Baltimore: take MD-295 north or south (Baltimore-Washington Parkway) to MD-193 (Greenbelt Road). Take Greenbelt Road east for about two miles. Main Gate will be on left at the first traffic light after Cipriano Road. Visitors not on NASA business should continue on to the next traffic light, turn left onto Soil Conservation Road, take next left to Visitor Center. From I-495/I-95 take exit 22A onto MD-193 (Greenbelt Road) and follow above directions. USMRA: DE/MD map (F-4); DC map (I,J-1,2). NMC: Washington, DC, ten miles.
Ten-digit dialing required for local calls.

INDIAN HEAD DIVISION, NAVAL SURFACE WARFARE CENTER

101 Strauss Avenue, Indian Head, MD 20640-1542
C-301-744-4000, DSN-312-354-4000, Police-744-4381
WEB: www.ih.navy.mil
LOCATION: Take I-495 (Capital Beltway) east, exit to MD-210 south for 25 miles to station. USMRA: DE/MD map (E-5). NMC: Washington, DC, 25 miles north.
RECREATION & TRAVEL: Golf-744-4662
RETAIL & DINING: Clubs-EMC/CPO-Globe & Anchor-744-6487 OC-Mix House-744-6487
SUPPORT & FAMILY: Med-744-4601
Ten-digit dialing required for local calls.

MARTIN STATE AIRPORT/ WARFIELD AIR NATIONAL GUARD

Bldg 1110, 2701 Eastern Blvd, Baltimore, MD 21220-2899
C-410-918-6210, DSN-312-243-6210, Police-918-6209
WEB: www.mdang.ang.af.mil
LOCATION: From I-695, exit onto MD-702 east. Take a left onto MD-150 and follow the signs to the airport. USMRA: DE/MD map (G-3). NMC: Baltimore, eight miles southwest.
RECREATION & TRAVEL: SPA-918-6551
RETAIL & DINING: Clubs-NCO-918-6592 EX-918-6443
SUPPORT & FAMILY: Med-918-6666
Ten-digit dialing required for local calls.

PATUXENT RIVER NAVAL AIR STATION

PAO Code 7.5, Bldg 409, Room 204, 22268 Cedar Point Road
Unit NASAD, Patuxent River, MD 20670-1154
C-301-342-3000, DSN-312-342-3000, Police-757-4664
WEB: www.nawcad.navy.mil
LOCATION: From I-95 (east portion of Capital Beltway, I-495), take exit 7A to Old Branch Avenue (MD-5) south. Follow MD-5 until it becomes MD-235 near Oraville, on to Lexington Park and the NAS. Main Gate is on MD-235 and Pegg Road. USMRA: DE/MD map (G-6). NMC: Washington, DC, 65 miles northwest.
RECREATION & TRAVEL: Golf-342-3597 Marina-342-3573
RVC-342-3648 SPA-342-3836/7 TML-995-3601
Navy Lodge-800-NAVY-INN or 737-2400
RETAIL & DINING: Clubs-CC-342-3200 CPO-342-5272 EMC-342-3685 OC-342-3656 Com-342-3789 Dining-342-1669 EX-342-0614 Gas-863-1258
SUPPORT & FAMILY: Med-342-1418
Ten-digit dialing required for local calls.

SOLOMONS NAVY RECREATION CENTER

P.O. Box 147, Solomons, MD 20688-0147
C-410-326-7165, Police (Security)-326-5410
WEB: www.ndw.navy.mil/mwr/nrcsolomons.html
LOCATION: In southern Maryland where the Patuxent River meets the Chesapeake Bay. From US-301, take MD-4 southeast to Solomons; or take MD-5 southeast to MD-235, then MD-4 northeast to Solomons. USMRA: DE/MD map (G-6). NMC: Washington, DC, 65 miles northwest. NMI: Patuxent River NAS, ten miles south.
RECREATION & TRAVEL: Golf-326-7165 Marinas-326-4009 RVC-326-1260 or 800-NAVY-230 (DC area) TML-326-5203/4
NOTE: *For detailed information about this, as well as other recreation facilities, golf courses and marinas, consult Military Living's "Military RV, Camping and Outdoor Recreation Around the World".*
Ten-digit dialing required for local calls.

UNITED STATES NAVAL ACADEMY/ ANNAPOLIS NAVAL STATION

121 Blake Road, Annapolis, MD 21402-5071
C-410-293-1000, DSN-312-281-1000, Police-293-3634/9300
WEB: www.usna.edu
LOCATION: The USNA and Annapolis NS are separated by the Severn River. From Washington, DC: Take US-50 east, exit 27 to MD-450 to Annapolis. Go 1.5 miles to traffic light. Proceed straight over Naval Academy Bridge to reach USNA or turn left at the light (MD-648) to go to Naval Station. From BWI Airport: Take MD-170 east to Annapolis. Turn right on Hammonds Ferry Road. Turn left on Dorsey Road, go into right lane. Take entrance ramp onto I-97 south to US-50 east. On US-50, take exit 27 to MD-450. Go 1.5 miles to first light. Cross over the Naval Academy Bridge to reach the Naval Academy or make a left at this light (MD-648) to go to the Annapolis Naval Station. USMRA: DE/MD map (C,D-6,7). NMC: Annapolis, within city limits.
RECREATION & TRAVEL: Golf-757-2022
Marinas-293-2058/3731 RVC-293-9200 TML-757-7900
Navy Lodge-800-NAVY-INN or 757-7900
RETAIL & DINING: Clubs-OC-293-2611 Com-293-9036
EX-757-0005 Gas-293-0226
SUPPORT & FAMILY: Med-293-2273
Ten-digit dialing required for local calls.

WALTER REED ARMY MEDICAL CENTER FOREST GLEN ANNEX

503 Robert Grant Avenue, Silver Spring, MD 20910-7500
C-301-319-9000, DSN-312-285-9000, Police-295-7554
WEB: www.wrair.army.mil
LOCATION: Located four miles from WRAMC. From main post, exit onto 16th Street. Go one mile north and turn left onto East West Highway. Turn right on Grubb Road, then left on Lyttonsville Road. At the stop sign, turn right on Brookville Road to Annex. From WRAMC, go north on Georgia Avenue to left on Seminary Road to left (south) on Brookville Road to right on Steven Sitter Avenue and the Annex. USMRA: DC map (E-1). NMC: Washington, DC, two miles south.
RETAIL & DINING: Com-295-7358 EX-565-0900
Gas-588-1602
Ten-digit dialing required for local calls.

MISSISSIPPI, pg. 41

COLUMBUS AIR FORCE BASE

14 FTW/PA, 555 Seventh Street, Suite 203
Columbus Air Force Base, MS 39710-1009
C-662-434-7322, DSN-312-742-1110, Police-434-7128
WEB: www.columbus.af.mil
LOCATION: From Columbus north on US-45, five miles north and west of US-45. USMRA: MS map (G-4). NMC: Columbus, ten miles south.
RECREATION & TRAVEL: Golf-434-7932 SPA-434-2862/7322 TML-434-2372/2548
RETAIL & DINING: Clubs-NCO-434-2489/7926 Com-434-7103 Dining-434-2820 EX-434-6013 Gas-434-6026
SUPPORT & FAMILY: Med-434-2273

GULFPORT ARMED FORCES RETIREMENT HOME

1800 Beach Drive, Gulfport, MS 39507-1597
C-800-332-3527, Police (Security)-897-4200
WEB: www.afrh.gov
LOCATION: From I-10, take exit 38 (Lorraine Cowan) south to Pass Road. Make a left onto Pass Road and proceed to Anniston Avenue and turn right. Continue on Anniston Avenue to the stop sign and make a left onto Beach Drive (Service Drive). The AFRH is on the left. USMRA: MS map (F-11). NMC: Gulfport, within city limits.
RETAIL & DINING: Cafeteria-897-4290 Clubs-CC-897-4035
Dining-897-4294 EX-897-4266
SUPPORT & FAMILY: Med-871-2444
NOTE: *After Hurricane Katrina, this facility closed and remaiins closed at this time. AFRH continues to work with Congress and DoD regarding the required funding.*

GULFPORT NAVAL CONSTRUCTION BATTALION CENTER

4902 Marvin Shields Blvd, Gulfport, MS 39501-5001
C-228-871-2555, DSN-312-868-2555, Police-871-2433
LOCATION: From US-90, go left on Pass Road. From I-10, take exit to US-49 south to Pass Road, continue straight ahead. Make a right onto Pass Road. USMRA: MS map (F-11). NMC: Gulfport, within city limits.
RECREATION & TRAVEL: Golf-871-2189/2494 RVC-871-5435 TML-871-2505 Navy Lodge-800-NAVY-INN or 864-3101
RETAIL & DINING: Clubs-CPO/OC-Anchors & Eagles-871-3311 EMC-Stingers-871-3153 Com-871-2039/40 Dining-871-2357 EX-864-1514 Gas-864-5527
SUPPORT & FAMILY: Med-871-2440

GULFPORT-BILOXI INTERNATIONAL AIRPORT/AIR NATIONAL GUARD

Combat Readiness Training Center, 4715 Hewes Avenue, Bldg 1
Gulfport, MS 39507-4324
C-228-214-6200, DSN-312-363-6165, Police (Security)-214-6211
WEB: www.msjack.ang.af.mil/crtc
LOCATION: Take US-49 south to Gulfport. Cross I-10, and exit east to airport. Make a left onto Airport Road, a right onto Washington Avenue and another right onto 54th Street, which turns into Hewes Avenue. USMRA: MS map (F-10,11). NMC: Gulfport, within city limits.
RETAIL & DINING: Dining-214-6156 EX-863-5746
SUPPORT & FAMILY: Med-214-6014

JACKSON-EVERS INTERNATIONAL AIRPORT/AIR NATIONAL GUARD

172 AW, 141 Military Drive, Bldg 129, Jackson, MS 39232-8881
C-601-939-3633, DSN-312-731-9210
WEB: www.msjack.ang.af.mil
LOCATION: Off I-20 east or west and US-80. From I-20, exit 52

onto MS-475. Make a right onto Old Brandon Road, and merge right onto MS-475. Make a right onto Military Drive. Clearly marked. USMRA: MS map (D-6,7). NMC: Jackson, five miles west.
RECREATION & TRAVEL: SPA-405-8761
RETAIL & DINING: EX-932-3930
SUPPORT & FAMILY: Med-405-8351

KEESLER AIR FORCE BASE
517 L Street, Room 113C, Biloxi, MS 39534-2120
C-228-377-1110, DSN-312-597-1110, Police-377-2878
WEB: www.keesler.af.mil
LOCATION: From I-10, exit 46 south on I-110. From US-90, north on White Ave to Main Gate. USMRA: MS map (F-10,11). NMC: Biloxi, within city limits.
RECREATION & TRAVEL: Golf-377-3827/32 Marinas-377-3160/86 RVC-594-0543 SPA-377-2120/4538 TML-377-2430
RETAIL & DINING: Clubs-OC-377-2439 Keesler Community Club-377-3439 Com-376-1600 Gas-432-2404
SUPPORT & FAMILY: Med-436-3546

KEESLER FAMCAMP
Outdoor Recreation, 81 SVS/SVRO, 625 Marina Drive
Keesler AFB, MS 39534-2623
C-228-594-0543, Police-377-3040
LOCATION: Off base. From I-10, take I-110 south to US-90 west approximately 5.5 miles to Beauvoir Road (before Coliseum), right 1.5 miles to Pass Road, right one mile. Right on Jim Money Road, right on Annex Road 0.25 miles. FAMCAMP is five miles west of gate 7. USMRA: MS map (F-11). NMC: Biloxi, two miles east.
RECREATION & TRAVEL: RVC-594-0543
NOTE: *For detailed information about this off-base recreation facility, as well as on-base recreation facilities, golf courses and marinas, consult Military Living's "Military RV, Camping and Outdoor Recreation Around the World".*

MERIDIAN NAVAL AIR STATION
255 Rosenbaum Avenue, Suite 201,
Meridian Naval Air Station, MS 39309-5003
C-601-679-2211, DSN-312-637-2211, Police-679-2715
WEB: https://www.cnet.navy.mil/meridian
LOCATION: Take MS-39 north from Meridian for 12 miles to four-lane access road. Turn left on John Stennis Drive for three miles to front gate. USMRA: MS map (G-6). NMC: Meridian, 15 miles southwest.
RECREATION & TRAVEL: Golf-679-2129/2526 SPA-679-2505 TML-679-2186
RETAIL & DINING: Com-679-2554 Dining-679-2634 EX-679-2665 Fast Food-679-2650 Gas-679-2664
SUPPORT & FAMILY: Med-679-2633

MERIDIAN REGIONAL AIRPORT/KEY FIELD/ AIR NATIONAL GUARD BASE
186 ARW, 6225 M Street, Meridian, MS 39307-7112
C-601-484-9000, DSN-312-778-9000, Police-484-9722
WEB: www.msmeri.ang.af.mil
LOCATION: From I-20 west, take exit 150 to US-11. Make a right onto M Street. USMRA: MS map (F,G-6,7). NMC: Meridian, within city limits.
RECREATION & TRAVEL: SPA-484-9413/9730
RETAIL & DINING: EX-485-3072
SUPPORT & FAMILY: Med-484-9206

PASCAGOULA NAVAL STATION
Bldg 34, Pascagoula, MS 39595-0001
C-228-761-2140, DSN-312-358-2140, Police (Security)-761-2020
WEB: www.cnsl.spear.navy.mil/nspascagoula/pages/nspascagoulahome.htm
LOCATION: From I-10 east, exit 69, four miles south to US-90, four miles west to Litton Road which leads to an access road to the station, three miles to the gate. USMRA: MS map (G-11). NMC: Mobile, Alabama, 30 miles east. NMI: Keesler AFB, 30 miles west.
RECREATION & TRAVEL: TML-761-2432/44
RETAIL & DINING: EX-761-5133
SUPPORT & FAMILY: Med-761-2222
NOTE: *The 2005 BRAC report recommended this base for closure. As required by Federal law, the DoD has until 15 September 2007 to begin closing and realigning the bases as called for in the approved report. This process must be completed by 15 September 2011.*

SHELBY MOBILIZATION CENTER
Bldg T900, Lee Avenue, Camp Shelby, MS 39407-5500
C-601-558-2000, DSN-312-286-2000, Police-558-2232
WEB: www.ngms.state.ms.us
LOCATION: From Hattiesburg, take US-49 south, or take US-98 east from Hattiesburg to MS-29 south, which bisects the training site. Follow signs. USMRA: MS map (F-9). NMC: Hattiesburg, ten miles north.
RECREATION & TRAVEL: RVC-558-2540
RETAIL & DINING: Clubs-NCO-558-2427, OC-558-2749 EX-558-2349
SUPPORT & FAMILY: Med-558-2805

WATERWAYS EXPERIMENT STATION
3909 Halls Ferry Road, Vicksburg, MS 39180-6199
C-601-634-2100, Police-634-3302
WEB: www.erdc.usace.army.mil
LOCATION: From I-20 take exit 1C, 1.5 miles south on Halls Ferry Road. USMRA: MS map (C-6). NMC: Vicksburg, within city limits.
RETAIL & DINING: Cafeteria-634-2560 EX-634-2136

NORTH CAROLINA, pg. 42-43
Raleigh-Durham, pg. 43
Winston-Salem/Greensboro, pg. 43

CAMP LEJEUNE MARINE CORPS BASE
Marine Corps Base, Attn: Public Affairs, P.O. Box 20004
Camp Lejeune Marine Corps Base, NC 28542-0004
C-910-451-1113, DSN-312-751-1113, Police-451-2555
WEB: www.lejeune.usmc.mil
LOCATION: Main Gate is six miles east of junction of US-17 and NC-24, off NC-24. Take US-17 to NC-24 (Johnson Blvd) southeast to the main entrance of the camp. USMRA: NC/SC map (M-5). NMC: Jacksonville, three miles northwest.
RECREATION & TRAVEL: Golf-451-5445 Marina-450-7386 or 451-8307/45 RVC-450-7473 TML-456-1070, ext. 0
RETAIL & DINING: Clubs-CPO/SNCO-451-2839 EMC-451-2872 OC-451-2465 Com-451-2172 Dining-451-1567 EX-451-5030
SUPPORT & FAMILY: Med-451-4300

CHARLOTTE/DOUGLAS INTERNATIONAL AIRPORT/AIR NATIONAL GUARD
145 Airlift Wing, 5225 Morris Field Drive
Charlotte, NC 28208-5797
C-704-391-4100, DSN-312-231-4100, Police-391-4152
WEB: www.ncchar.ang.af.mil
LOCATION: From I-77 north or south, take exit 6A/B to US-521 (Billy Graham Parkway) north to Morris Field Drive (3.5 miles), turn left. Base is on your right. From I-85, take Billy Graham Parkway; take exit 33 south to Morris Field Drive, turn right. USMRA: NC/SC map (G-4). NMC: Charlotte, three miles east.
RECREATION & TRAVEL: SPA-391-4135/8
RETAIL & DINING: Clubs-EMC-391-4426 OC-391-4427 Dining-391-4310
SUPPORT & FAMILY: Med-391-4300
Ten-digit dialing required for local calls.

CHERRY POINT MARINE CORPS AIR STATION
PSC Box 8003, Cherry Point, NC 28533-0003
C-252-466-2811, DSN-312-582-1110, Police-466-4366
WEB: www.cherrypoint.usmc.mil
LOCATION: On NC-101 between New Bern and Morehead City. US-70 connects with NC-101 at Havelock. Take US-70 to NC-101 in Havelock. Go east on NC-101 to the station. USMRA: NC/SC map (M,N-4). NMC: New Bern, 17 miles northwest.
RECREATION & TRAVEL: Golf-466-3044 Marina-466-2762 RVC-466-2172 SPA-466-2379/3232 TML-463-3061 or 466-3060
RETAIL & DINING: Cafeteria-466-5766 Clubs-OC-466-2395 SNCO-446-5555 Com-466-0800 Dining-466-4209 EX-447-7041 Gas-463-1640
SUPPORT & FAMILY: Med-466-0438

ELIZABETH CITY COAST GUARD SUPPORT CENTER
Bldg 5 Morale, Well-Being & Recreation,
Elizabeth City, NC 27909-5006
C-252-335-6000, Police-335-4321
WEB: www.uscg.mil/d5/airstation/ecity
LOCATION: Take I-64 east (in Virginia) to US-17 south to Elizabeth City, left on Halstead Blvd, three miles to Main Gate of Center; or, from I-95 north or south, exit 176 east on US-158 to Elizabeth City. USMRA: NC/SC map (O-1). NMC: Elizabeth City, within city limits. NMI: Norfolk Naval Station, VA, 50 miles north.
RECREATION & TRAVEL: RVC-335-6886 SPA-335-6333 TML-335-6397/6886
RETAIL & DINING: Cafeteria-335-6880 Clubs-CC-335-6301 OC/EMC-335-6389 Dining-335-6281 EX-335-6269 Gas-335-6187
SUPPORT & FAMILY: Med-335-6461

FORT BRAGG
XVIII Airborne Corps & Fort Bragg, Attn: AGZA-GC
Bldg I-1326, Armistead & Macomb Streets,
Fort Bragg, NC 28307-5000
C-910-396-0011, DSN-312-236-0011, Police-396-0391
WEB: www.bragg.army.mil
LOCATION: From I-95 north or south, exit 52 to NC-24 west for 15 miles. NC-24 runs through post as Bragg Blvd. From US-401 (Fayetteville Bypass) exit to All American Expressway, west five miles to Fort. USMRA: NC/SC map (I,J-4). NMC: Fayetteville, ten miles southeast.
RECREATION & TRAVEL: Golf-Ryder-436-3390 Stryker-396-3980 RVC-396-5979 TML-396-7700
RETAIL & DINING: Clubs-NCO-436-3300 OC-907-2582 Com-396-2428 or 436-2487 EX-436-2535 Gas-497-3985
SUPPORT & FAMILY: Med-432-0301

FORT FISHER AIR FORCE RECREATION AREA
118 River Front Road, Kure Beach, NC 28449-3748
C-910-458-6723, DSN-312-488-8781, Police-911
WEB: www.ftfishermilrec.com
LOCATION: Fort Fisher is located on Pleasure Island between Cape Fear River and Atlantic Ocean. On US-421, south of Wilmington, NC, go through Carolina and Kure Beaches to Fort Fisher AF Recreation Area, on the west side of US-421. USMRA: NC/SC map (L-6). NMC: Wilmington, NC, 20 miles northwest. NMI: Camp Lejeune, 65 miles northeast.
RECREATION & TRAVEL: RVC-458-6549 TML-458-6546/9
RETAIL & DINING: Dining-458-4016
NOTE: *For detailed information about this off-base recreation facility, as well as on-base recreation facilities, golf courses and marinas, consult Military Living's "Military RV, Camping and Outdoor Recreation Around the World".*

FORT MACON COAST GUARD GROUP
2301 East Fort Macon Road, Atlantic Beach, NC 28512-0237
C-252-247-4501 DSN-312-247-4598, Police-247-4598
WEB: www.uscg.mil
LOCATION: Take US-70 southeast to Atlantic Beach/Morehead City Bridge. Left at traffic light in Atlantic Beach onto NC-58 (Fort Macon Road). Proceed east to entrance at end of road on left. USMRA: NC/SC map (N-5). NMC: New Bern, 30 miles northwest.
RETAIL & DINING: Dining-240-8390 EX-247-9442
SUPPORT & FAMILY: Med-247-4551

NEW RIVER MARINE CORPS AIR STATION
PSC Box 21002, Jacksonville, NC 28545-1002
C-910-451-1113, DSN-312-751-1113, Police-449-6111
WEB: http://www.newriver.usmc.mil
LOCATION: Off US-17 north or south, two miles south of Jacksonville, on east side of US-17. Clearly marked. Visitors may enter through Main Gate if they have a DoD/DHS sticker. USMRA: NC/SC map (L,M-5). NMC: Jacksonville, two miles northeast.
RECREATION & TRAVEL: Marina-449-6578/84 RVC-449-6578 SPA-449-6316 TML-937-5024
RETAIL & DINING: Cafeteria-449-9710 Clubs-EMC-450-0589 OC-449-6409 SNCO-449-6707 Com-449-6395 Dining-449-6710 EX-449-0539 Gas-449-6092
SUPPORT & FAMILY: Med-449-6500

POPE AIR FORCE BASE
259 Maynard Street, Pope Air Force Base, NC 28308-2391
C-910-394-1110, DSN-312-424-1110, Police-394-2800
WEB: http://public.pope.amc.af.mil/
LOCATION: Take I-95, exit 46 to NC-87/24 west. Continue on NC-24 which turns into Bragg Blvd. Follow signs northwest for 15 miles to Pope AFB and Fort Bragg. Visitors can enter through Main Gate with a DoD/DHS sticker. USMRA: NC/SC map (J-4). NMC: Raleigh, 70 miles northeast; Fayetteville, 12 miles southeast.
RECREATION & TRAVEL: Golf-394-2325 SPA-394-6527/6258 TML-394-4131
RETAIL & DINING: Clubs-497-4031 Com-396-7213 Dining-394-4377 EX-436-4166 Gas-497-8181
SUPPORT & FAMILY: Med-394-4258

SEYMOUR JOHNSON AIR FORCE BASE
1510 Wright Brothers Avenue, Goldsboro, NC 27531-2468
C-919-722-1110, DSN-312-722-1110, Police-722-2737
WEB: www.seymourjohnson.af.mil
LOCATION: From US-70 Bypass east or west, take Seymour Johnson AFB exit east onto NC-1579 (Berkeley Blvd) to Main Gate. Clearly marked. USMRA: NC/SC map (L-3). NMC: Raleigh, 50 miles west.
RECREATION & TRAVEL: Golf-722-0395 RVC-722-1106 RVC-458-6549 SPA-722-4168/70 TML-722-0385
RETAIL & DINING: Clubs-EMC-722-1192 NCO-734-2993 OC-722-1340 Com-722-0319 Dining-722-1244 EX-735-8511 Gas-734-2235
SUPPORT & FAMILY: Med-722-1802

SOUTH CAROLINA, pg. 42-43
Charleston, pg. 42

BEAUFORT MARINE CORPS AIR STATION
H&HS, Bldg 596, P.O. Box 55001
Beaufort Marine Corps Air Station, SC 29904-5001
C-843-228-7100, DSN-312-335-7100, Police-228-6161
WEB: www.beaufort.usmc.mil
LOCATION: From I-95, take Beaufort exit 33 to US-21 southeast and follow signs. Sixteen miles to MCAS east of US-21. Clearly marked. USMRA: NC/SC map (G-9). NMC: Savannah, GA, 40 miles south.
RECREATION & TRAVEL: SPA-967-7005 TML-522-1663
RETAIL & DINING: Cafeteria-228-7895 Clubs-NCO-228-7534/7726 OC-228-7541/61 Com-228-2679 EX-228-7627 Gas-228-7727
SUPPORT & FAMILY: Med-228-5343

BEAUFORT NAVAL HOSPITAL
1 Pinckney Blvd, Beaufort, SC 29902-6148
C-843-228-5600, DSN-312-335-5600, Police (Security)-525-5317
WEB: http://nhbeaufort.med.navy.mil
LOCATION: From I-95 north or south, take exit 33 to US-21 South to Ribaut Road and left to Naval Hospital. USMRA: NC, SC map (G-9,10). NMC: Savannah, 25 miles south.
RETAIL & DINING: Cafeteria-228-2231 Clubs-CC-228-5424 Dining-228-2231 EX-228-5483 Gas-228-5488
SUPPORT & FAMILY: Med-228-3793/7424

CHARLESTON AIR FORCE BASE
102 East Hill Blvd, Room 223
Charleston Air Force Base, SC 29404-5154
C-843-963-1110, DSN-312-673-1110, Police-963-3600
WEB: http://public.charleston.amc.af.mil/
LOCATION: From I-26 east or west, exit 211 to West Aviation Avenue to traffic light, continue through light to second light. Make a right onto South Aviation Avenue and follow around end of runway to gate 2 (Rivers Gate). USMRA: NC/SC map (H-8). NMC: Charleston, ten miles southeast.
RECREATION & TRAVEL: Golf-963-4177 RVC-963-5270/1 SPA-963-3048/83 TML-963-3806
RETAIL & DINING: Clubs-CC-963-3920 Com-963-5695 EX-552-5000 Gas-207-0615
SUPPORT & FAMILY: Med-963-6880

CHARLESTON COAST GUARD GROUP
196 Tradd Street, Charleston, SC 29401-1899
C-843-724-7600, Police-911
WEB: www.uscg.mil/d7/units/gruchasn
LOCATION: From I-26 east, bear right onto US-17 toward Savannah. Stay in center lane, follow around to Lockwood Blvd. Follow Lockwood Blvd to Chisom Street, take right on Chisom Street to Tradd Street. Take another right on Tradd Street. Follow signs, clearly marked to CG Group. USMRA: NC/SC map (H-9). NMC: Charleston, within city limits. NMI: Charleston AFB, five miles.
RETAIL & DINING: Clubs-CC-764-7797 EX-722-8817
SUPPORT & FAMILY: Med-724-7653

CHARLESTON NAVAL WEAPONS STATION
2316 Red Bank Road, Suite 100, Goose Creek, SC 29445-8601
C-843-764-7901, DSN-312-794-7901, Police-764-7202
WEB: www.nwschs.navy.mil
LOCATION: From I-26 north or south, exit 205 south, east on US-78, to US-52 north, to SC-37 (Red Bank Road) southeast to Main Gate. USMRA: NC/SC map (H-8, C-9). NMC: Charleston, 25 miles south.
RECREATION & TRAVEL: Golf-764-7802 Marina-761-8353 or 764-7601 RVC-761-8353 TML-764-7228
RETAIL & DINING: Clubs-CC-764-7797 Com-764-2020 EX-764-7042 Gas-764-7573
SUPPORT & FAMILY: Med-764-7634

FORT JACKSON
U.S. Army Training Center & Fort Jackson Attn: PAO
Strom Thurmond Blvd, Fort Jackson, SC 29207-5060
C-803-751-7511, DSN-312-734-1110, Police-751-3113
WEB: www.jackson.army.mil
LOCATION: Exit from I-20 north of Fort, or from US-76/378 at the Main Gate. From I-20 and I-77 interchange, take exit 16 to Alpine Road. Take newly constructed Beltway south to Percival Road, right onto Percival Road to Gate 2. USMRA: NC/SC map (G-6). NMC: Columbia, 12 miles southwest.
RECREATION & TRAVEL: Golf-787-4344/4437 Marinas-751-5253 RVC-751-5253 TML-782-9802 or 800-276-6984
RETAIL & DINING: Clubs-NCO-782-2218 OC-751-4906 Com-751-5789 EX-787-1950/1 Gas-782-2076
SUPPORT & FAMILY: Med-751-4733

GEORGETOWN COAST GUARD STATION
355 Marina Drive, Georgetown, SC 29440-2412
C-800-432-2754, Police-911
WEB: www.uscg.mil
LOCATION: From US-17 north or south, turn east onto Marina Drive. USMRA: NC/SC map (I,J-7,8). NMC: Myrtle Beach, 50 miles.

MCENTIRE AIR NATIONAL GUARD STATION
1325 South Carolina Road, Eastover, SC 29044-5017
C-803-647-8301, DSN-312-583-8301, Police-647-8284
WEB: www.scang.ang.af.mil
LOCATION: On US-76/378 between Sumter and Columbia, north side of US-76/378, ten miles east of Columbia. From I-77, take the US-76 exit east to the base. USMRA: NC, SC map (G-6). NMC: Columbia, 15 miles northwest.
RECREATION & TRAVEL: SPA-647-8231
RETAIL & DINING: Clubs-647-8326 EX-782-7668
SUPPORT & FAMILY: Med-647-8296

PARRIS ISLAND MARINE CORPS RECRUIT DEPOT
Bldg 283, Blvd De France, Parris Island, SC 29905-0059
C-843-228-2111, DSN-312-832-2111, Police-228-2478
WEB: www.mcrdpi.usmc.mil
LOCATION: From I-95 north or south, exit 33 to US-17 east to US-21 south to SC-280 to SC-802 south, which leads to the Main Gate. USMRA: NC/SC map (G-10). NMC: Savannah, GA, 43 miles southwest.
RECREATION & TRAVEL: Golf-228-2240 TML-228-2627
RETAIL & DINING: Clubs-CC-228-1566 Com-228-2679 EX-228-1538 Gas-228-7351
SUPPORT & FAMILY: Med-228-3793

SHAW AIR FORCE BASE
20 Fighter Wing/PA, 517 Lance Avenue
Shaw Air Force Base, SC 29152-5041
C-803-895-1110, DSN-312-965-1110, Police-895-1073
WEB: www.shaw.af.mil
LOCATION: Off US-76/378, eight miles west of Sumter, north side of US-76/378. From I-95, take exit 135 east onto US-378/76. Clearly marked. USMRA: NC/SC map (H-6). NMC: Columbia, 35 miles west.
RECREATION & TRAVEL: Golf-895-1399 ITT/ITR-895-4774 Marina-895-0449 RVC-895-0449/50 RVC-432-7976 SPA-895-9517 TML-895-3803
RETAIL & DINING: Clubs-CC-666-3651 Com-895-1281 Dining-895-9791 EX-666-4773 Gas-666-3140
SUPPORT & FAMILY: Med-895-2273

SHORT STAY NAVY OUTDOOR RECREATION AREA
211 Short Stay Road, Moncks Corner, SC 29461-4431
C-843-743-2608, DSN-312-794-7901, Police (Security)-296-7731
WEB: www.shortstay.nwschs.navy.mil
LOCATION: Off base. On Lake Moultrie, five miles north of Moncks Corner. Take US-52 north from Charleston. Make a left onto Power House Road, a right onto Old Black Oak Road and a left onto Short Stay Road to the facility. Clearly marked. USMRA: NC/SC map (H-8). NMC: Charleston, 40 miles southeast. NMI: Charleston NWS, 25 miles southeast.
RECREATION & TRAVEL: RVC-761-8353 TML-761-8353 or 800-447-2178
NOTE: *For detailed information about this off-base recreation facility, as well as on-base recreation facilities, golf courses and marinas, consult Military Living's "Military RV, Camping and Outdoor Recreation Around the World".*

WATEREE RECREATION AREA
2030 Baron Dekalb Road, Camden, SC 29020-9405
C-803-432-7976, DSN-312-965-1110, Command Post-895-5850
LOCATION: Off base. From I-20, take exit 98 onto US-521/601 north to intersect SC-97 northwest for nine miles, then turn left for Lake Wateree access. USMRA: NC, SC map (G-5). NMC: Columbia, 35 miles southwest. NMI: Shaw AFB, 35 miles south.
RECREATION & TRAVEL: RVC-895-0449/50 TML-895-3803/4
NOTE: *For detailed information about this off-base recreation facility, as well as on-base recreation facilities, golf courses and marinas, consult Military Living's "Military RV, Camping and Outdoor Recreation Around the World".*

TENNESSEE, pg. 38-39

ARNOLD AIR FORCE BASE
100 Kindel Drive, Suite B213
Arnold Air Force Base, TN 37389-2213
C-931-454-3000, DSN-312-340-3600/5011, Police-454-5662
WEB: www.arnold.af.mil
LOCATION: From US-231 north of Huntsville, take TN-50/55 east to AEDC access highway in Tullahoma. From I-24 north or south, take AEDC exit 117, four miles south of Manchester. Clearly marked. USMRA: KY/TN map (I-10). NMC: Chattanooga, 65 miles southeast; Nashville, 65 miles northwest.
RECREATION & TRAVEL: Golf-455-5870 Marina-454-6084 RVC-454-6084 TML-454-3099
RETAIL & DINING: Cafeteria-454-5732 Clubs-CC-454-3350 Com-454-7249 Dining-454-3350 EX-454-7153
SUPPORT & FAMILY: Med-454-5351

CHATTANOOGA ARMORY EXCHANGE
1801 Holtzclaw Avenue, Chattanooga, TN 37404-4806
C-423-265-8941, Police-911
LOCATION: From I-24, take Tennessee Temple University (Fourth Avenue) exit 180, left to 23rd Street, second light to right on Holtzclaw Avenue to gate. USMRA: KY/TN map (J-11). NMC: Chattanooga, within city limits.
RETAIL & DINING: EX-265-8941

HOUSTON BARRACKS/NATIONAL GUARD
P.O. Box 41502, 3041 Sidco Drive, Nashville, TN 37204-1502
C-615-313-0662, DSN-312-683-0662, Police (Security)-313-3023
LOCATION: Take I-65 south to Armory Drive exit 79. Follow the signs to the Barracks. USMRA: KY/TN map (G-8,9; F-3). NMC: Nashville, four miles northwest.
RETAIL & DINING: EX-313-0531

KINGSPORT SITE EXCHANGE
4409 West Stone Drive, Kingsport, TN 37660-1050
C-423-247-8721, Police-911
LOCATION: From I-81 north or south, take exit 57 to I-181 north to Kingsport exit 55 west (Stone Drive). Take a left on US-11 west (Stone Drive); exchange on left. USMRA: KY/TN map (O-7). NMC: Kingsport, within city limits.
RETAIL & DINING: EX-247-8721

MCGHEE TYSON AIRPORT/ AIR NATIONAL GUARD
134 Briscoe Drive, Lewisville, TN 37777-6200
C-865-985-3200, DSN-312-266-3210, Emergency-985-4371
WEB: www.tnknox.ang.af.mil
LOCATION: Exit north or south from US-129 onto Air Base Road. There is a large national guard sign at the exit. Proceed on Air Base Road approximately two miles to Main Gate. USMRA: KY/TN map (L-9). NMC: Knoxville, ten miles northeast.
RECREATION & TRAVEL: SPA-985-4404/19
RETAIL & DINING: EX-985-3400 Gas-985-3400
SUPPORT & FAMILY: Med-985-4277

MEMPHIS INTERNATIONAL AIRPORT/ AIR NATIONAL GUARD
2815 Democrat Road, Memphis, TN 38118-1510
C-901-291-7111, DSN-312-726-7111
Police (Security)-291-7101/11
WEB: www.tnmemp.ang.af.mil
LOCATION: From I-55 north or south, exit 5A (Brooks Road) east, two miles to IAP, left on Airways, right on Democrat Road to 164 Air National Guard Base (north side of IAP), go to Aerial Port Bldg. USMRA: KY/TN map (A-11, B,C-4). NMC: Memphis, within city limits.
RECREATION & TRAVEL: SPA-291-7202
RETAIL & DINING: EX-291-7272
SUPPORT & FAMILY: Med-291-7110

MID-SOUTH NAVAL SUPPORT ACTIVITY
5722 Integrity Drive, Millington, TN 38054-5045
C-901-874-5111, DSN-312-882-5111, Police-874-5523
WEB: www.nsamidsouth.navy.mil
LOCATION: From Memphis, take US-51 north to Millington. Turn right (east) on Navy Road 205. Go approximately two miles to base entrance on south side of road. From Memphis via Covington Pike, follow Covington Pike north. After going through the traffic light at the intersection at Austin Peary, street name changes to Singleton Parkway; continue driving north-do not turn. Singleton Parkway leads straight to the south gate of the base. USMRA: KY/TN map (B-10). NMC: Memphis, 20 miles southwest.
RECREATION & TRAVEL: Golf-874-5168/7667 RVC-874-5163 TML-213-3000 Navy Inn-877-628-9466 Navy Lodge-800-NAVY-INN or 872-0121
RETAIL & DINING: Clubs-CC-874-5132 CPO/EMC-874-5442 Com-874-5125 Dining-874-5132 EX-872-0139 Gas-873-4860
SUPPORT & FAMILY: Med-874-6100

NASHVILLE INTERNATIONAL AIRPORT/ AIR NATIONAL GUARD
240 Knapp Blvd, Nashville, TN 37217-2538
C-615-399-6000, DSN-312-778-6000, Police-399-5581
WEB: www.tnnash.ang.af.mil
LOCATION: From I-40 east to exit 216B (from I-40 west to exit 216) south on Donelson Pike for two miles, right on Knapp Blvd. USMRA: KY/TN map (H-8, G-3). NMC: Nashville, within city limits.
RECREATION & TRAVEL: SPA-399-5869

SMYRNA TRAINING CENTER
Bldg 607, Fitzhugh Blvd, Smyrna, TN 37167-2040
C-615-355-3616, DSN-615-683-3778
LOCATION: From I-24 north or south, take Sam Ridley Parkway exit to airport. Follow signs to airport. Take first left after golf course onto Fitzhugh Blvd, go straight, first building on left past guard shack. USMRA: KY/TN map (H-9). NMC: Smyrna, within city limits.
RECREATION & TRAVEL: TML-355-3778
RETAIL & DINING: EX-355-3616

VIRGINIA, pg. 44-45
Hampton Roads, pg. 46
Richmond, pg. 45
Williamsburg, pg. 45

ALEXANDRIA COAST GUARD TELECOMMUNICATION AND INFORMATION SYSTEMS COMMAND
7323 Telegraph Road, Alexandria, VA 22315-3940
C-703-313-5400, C-313-5400
WEB: www.uscg.mil
LOCATION: Take I-95/I-495 to Telegraph Road exit 176B. Travel south on Telegraph Road four miles to base on left (east). USMRA: VA/WV map (M-6). NMC: Washington, DC 15 miles northeast.
RETAIL & DINING: Clubs-Anchorage Club-313-5990 EX-313-5992

SUPPORT & FAMILY: Med-313-5446
Ten-digit dialing required for local calls.

ARMED FORCES HOSTESS ASSOCIATION
6604 Army Pentagon, Room 1D110, Washington, DC 20310-6604
C-703-697-3180/6857, DSN-312-227-6857
WEB: www.army.mil/afha/main.html
LOCATION: Located in the Pentagon, on I-395 at Boundary Channel Road in Arlington, VA. From I-395 North or South of VA-244 (Columbia Pike), exit to South Parking. Paid parking is available across the street from the Pentagon City Fashion Center and requires a walk through the South Parking Lot to the Corridor Two Entrance. Parking decal is required to use Pentagon lots. Metro, bus and taxi service from Concourse. Easiest access to the the AFHA office is through the Metro Entrance and the security waiting area. Visitors with business with AFHA can call the office between 0930 and 1430 hours to ask for an escort, if necessary. USMRA: Downtown DC map (B-4). NMC: Washington, DC, adjacent.
NOTE: *Installation physically located in VA, but uses a DC mailing address. Since 11 September 2001, access to Pentagon is limited to: those with DoD badges, those working in the Pentagon, those on access list, Active Duty military with two picture IDs, Retired military with an escort, and civilians with two picture IDs and an escort.*
Ten-digit dialing required for local calls.

BETHEL RECREATION AREA-PARK & FAMCAMP
123 Saunders Road, Hampton, VA 23665-1492
C-757-766-3017/7627, DSN-312-574-1110
LOCATION: Off base. From south on I-64, take VA-134 north approximately five miles, turn left onto Big Bethel Road. Proceed about one mile (second light), turn right on Saunders Road, camp is about 0.5 miles on the right. Or, from I-64, take exit 261A to a right on Big Bethel Road. Follow Big Bethel Road for 2.5 miles and turn left onto Saunders Road. Afer about 0.5 miles, turn right into camp. USMRA: VA/WV map (N-9,10), Hampton Roads, VA map (D,E-3). NMC: Hampton, seven miles south. NMI: Langley AFB, five miles south.
RECREATION & TRAVEL: RVC-766-3017/7627
NOTE: *For detailed information about this off-base recreation facility, as well as on-base recreation facilities, golf courses and marinas, consult Military Living's "Military RV, Camping and Outdoor Recreation Around the World".*

CAMP ALLEN
1251 Yalu Street, Norfolk, VA 23515-4693
C-757-423-1187, Police-911
WEB: www.mwr-elmore.com
LOCATION: From I-64 east, take I-564. Exit at Terminal Blvd. At first light, right on Diven Street, at left fork take Fechteler Street. Go 2.5 blocks to camp on right. USMRA: Hampton Roads, VA, map (F-6). NMC: Norfolk, within city limits. NMI: Norfolk NS, two miles north.
RETAIL & DINING: Clubs-CC-423-6191 EX-423-1187 Gas-423-1539
NOTE: *Fomerly Camp Elmore.*

CAMP PENDLETON STATE MILITARY RESERVATION
P.O. Box 9, Virginia Beach, VA 23458-0009
C-757-491-5140, Police (Security)-491-5144
WEB: www.smrvabeach.homestead.com
LOCATION: Camp Pendleton is north of Dam Neck Fleet Combat Trng Ctr and south of Virginia Beach. Take exit 22 from I-264, merge right onto Birdneck Road. Follow for about four miles, then cross over General Booth Blvd. Gate is on left. USMRA: Hampton Roads, VA map (J-7). NMC: Virginia Beach, within city limits.
RECREATION & TRAVEL: TML-491-5140, ext. 20
NOTE: *For detailed information about this lodging facility, as well as other lodging facilities, consult Military Living's "Temporary Military Lodging Around the World".*

CHEATHAM ANNEX NAVAL WEAPONS STATION
108 Sanda Avenue, Williamsburg, VA 23185-8792
C-757-887-4000, DSN-312-953-4000, Police (Security)-887-4676
WEB: www.nwsy.navy.mil
LOCATION: From I-64 east or west, take exit 242B northeast to US-199 east to Main Gate of Cheatham Annex. USMRA: VA/WV map (N-9). NMC: Williamsburg, six miles west.
RECREATION & TRAVEL: Golf-887-6539 RVC-887-7418 TML-887-7224/7418
RETAIL & DINING: EX-887-3582 Gas-887-3582
SUPPORT & FAMILY: Med-887-4016

CHESAPEAKE COAST GUARD FINANCE CENTER
1430 Kristina Way, Chesapeake, VA 23326-1000
C-757-523-6700, Police-911
WEB: http://www.fincen.uscg.mil
LOCATION: From I-64 east or west, take Exit 289B (Greenbrier Parkway South). Turn right onto Eden Way, right onto Kristina Way. Finance Center is the second building on the left. USMRA: Hampton Roads, VA map (G-8). NMC: Norfolk, five miles north.
RETAIL & DINING: EX-523-6002

CHINCOTEAGUE COAST GUARD GROUP-EASTERN SHORE
3823 South Main Street, Chincoteague, VA 23336-1510
C-757-336-2874
WEB: www.uscg.mil
LOCATION: From VA-13, turn onto VA-175 and follow it over the Causeway onto Chincoteague Island. After crossing the bridge, turn right at stop light. Go about 0.33 miles and base will be on the right. USMRA: VA/WV map (P-7,8). NMC: Salisbury, MD, 50 miles north.
RETAIL & DINING: Dining-336-2820

DAHLGREN NAVAL DISTRICT WASHINGTON,WEST AREA
17320 Dahlgren Road, Dahlgren, VA 22448-5100
C-540-653-8291/2/8531, DSN-312-249-8291/2/8531 Police-653-8500
WEB: www.nswc.navy.mil
LOCATION: From I-95 in Fredericksburg, east on VA-3 to VA-206 (17 miles), left on VA-206 (Dahlgren Rd), east to Dahlgren (11 miles). From Maryland take US-301 south to VA-206, east to Main Gate of Center. USMRA: VA/WV map (M-7). NMC: Washington, DC, 38 miles north.
RECREATION & TRAVEL: Golf-663-3002 TML-653-7671/2
RETAIL & DINING: Com-653-7318 Dining-General Mess-653-8277 EX-653-2121 Fast Food-663-3301/5612
SUPPORT & FAMILY: Med-653-8241

DAM NECK ANNEX, OCEANA NAVAL AIR STATION
1912 Regulus Avenue, Virginia Beach, VA 23461-2098
C-757-444-2366/7, DSN-312-564-0000, Police-492-6302
WEB: www.nasoceana.navy.mil
LOCATION: Take I-264 east to exit 22 (Birdneck Road), turn right and follow to General Booth Blvd. Turn left and follow to Dam Neck Road. Turn left and follow to Main Gate. USMRA: VA/WV map (O-10), Hampton Roads, VA map (J-8). NMC: Virginia Beach, four miles north.
RECREATION & TRAVEL: RVC-492-6264/7545 TML-877-986-9258 Navy Lodge-800-NAVY-INN or 437-8100
RETAIL & DINING: Clubs-Beach Club-492-8354 Sea Breeze-492-7267 EX-492-7745 Gas-492-7794
SUPPORT & FAMILY: Med-314-7200

DAVISON ARMY AIRFIELD
6970 Britten Drive, Fort Belvoir, VA 22060-5133
C-703-545-6700, DSN-312-656-7225, Police-806-7682
WEB: www.belvoir.army.mil
LOCATION: From I-95 north, take exit 166 towards Belvoir/Newington. Turn right onto the Fairfax County Parkway. Take a right onto John J. Kingman Parkway, which leads to the airfield. USMRA: VA/WV map (L,M-6). NMC: Washington, DC, ten miles northeast.
RECREATION & TRAVEL: SPA-703-806-7224/7225/7682
Ten-digit dialing required for local calls.

FEDERAL OFFICE BUILDING #2 (ARLINGTON ANNEX)
Federal Office Bldg #2, Washington, DC 20371-0500
C-703-545-6700, DSN-312-227-0101, Police (Security)-602-1807
LOCATION: Physical address is 1301 Southgate Road, Arlington, VA 22214. From Columbia Pike (VA-244), exit onto Southgate Road, which leads to the entrance. USMRA: Downtown DC map (A-4). NMC: Washington, DC, one mile east.
RETAIL & DINING: EX-979-3891 Gas (at Qts K)-979-3891
SUPPORT & FAMILY: Med-614-2726
NOTE: *Installation physically located in VA, but uses a DC mailing address.*
Ten-digit dialing required for local calls.

FORT A.P. HILL
Attn: AFKA-FHA-PA, Bowling Green, VA 22427-3114
C-804-633-8710, DSN-312-578-8710, Police-633-8888
WEB: www.aphill.army.mil
LOCATION: From I-95 north or south, take Bowling Green/Fort A.P. Hill exit 126. US-17 bypass east to VA-2 south to Bowling Green, take US-301 northeast to Main Gate. Or, take exit 104 from I-95 to VA-207 north to US-301 north and to Main Gate. USMRA: VA/WV map (L,M-7). NMC: Fredericksburg, 20 miles northwest.
RECREATION & TRAVEL: RVC-633-8219 TML-633-8335
RETAIL & DINING: Clubs-CC-833-8398 Dining-633-8398 EX-633-8690
SUPPORT & FAMILY: Med-633-8339

FORT BELVOIR
Attn: ANFB-GC, 9820 Flagler, Suite 201
Fort Belvoir, VA 22060-5932
C-703-545-6700, DSN-312-227-0101, Police (Security)-806-3104
WEB: www.belvoir.army.mil
LOCATION: From Washington, DC, take I-95 south to Belvoir/Newington exit 166. Turn right, connect with the southern leg of Fairfax County Parkway. Take Parkway to the end at Richmond Highway. Turn left. At the first light, Tulley Gate is on the right. At second light, Pence Gate (main entrance) is to the right. Visitor Center is just inside Pence Gate. USMRA: VA/WV map (L,M-6). NMC: Washington, DC, ten miles northeast. NMI: Fort Myer/Pentagon, 15 miles from base.
RECREATION & TRAVEL: Golf-806-4561/5878 Marina-805-3745 TML-704-8600 or 800-295-9750
RETAIL & DINING: Clubs-CC-780-0962 OC-780-0930 Com-806-6371/6674 Dining-806-6204 EX-806-5800/1/2 Gas-North-806-5263 South-806-4581
SUPPORT & FAMILY: Med-805-0612
Ten-digit dialing required for local calls.

FORT EUSTIS
Attn: ATZF-GC, Bldg 213, Fort Eustis, VA 23604-5015
C-757-878-1212, DSN-312-878-1110/1212, Police-878-4555
WEB: www.eustis.army.mil
LOCATION: From I-64 east or west, exit 250A to VA-105, west to Fort Eustis. USMRA: VA/WV map (N-9); Hampton Roads, VA, map (B,C-2,3). NMC: Newport News, 13 miles southwest.
RECREATION & TRAVEL: Golf-878-2965 RVC-878-2610 TML-878-5807
RETAIL & DINING: Clubs-CC-878-5700 Com-878-5966 Dining-878-1917 EX-887-3564 Gas-887-0392
SUPPORT & FAMILY: Med-314-7500

FORT LEE
USACASCOM & Fort Lee, Attn: Public Affairs Office
1321 Battle Drive, Fort Lee, VA 23801-1521
C-804-765-3000, DSN-312-539-3000, Police-734-7400
WEB: www.lee.army.mil
LOCATION: From I-95 north or south, take Fort Lee/Hopewell exit 52 east, and follow VA-36 to Main Gate on right (south). USMRA: VA/WV map (L,M-9). NMC: Petersburg, three miles west.
RECREATION & TRAVEL: Golf-734-2899 TML-733-4100
RETAIL & DINING: Clubs-CC-Lee Club-734-7547 NCO- Regimental Club-734-1523 Com-765-2254 EX-861-5970 Gas-861-6621
SUPPORT & FAMILY: Med-734-9000

FORT MONROE
Attn: ATZG-CO, Bldg 77, 3 Ruckman Road
Fort Monroe, VA 23651-6000
C-757-788-2000, DSN-312-680-1110, Police-788-2238/9
WEB: www.tradoc.army.mil/monroe
LOCATION: From I-64 east or west, exit at 268 east onto VA-169 (East Mallory St/Ft. Monroe). Take left at the light onto VA-163 (South Mallory Street) for one mile. Make a right at the second light onto VA-143 (East Mellon Street). Continue approximately six miles until you cross over a small bridge prior to entering Fort Monroe. USMRA: VA/WV map (N-10); Hampton Roads, VA, map (F-5). NMC: Hampton, one mile north.
RECREATION & TRAVEL: Marinas-788-4308 RVC-788-4305 TML-788-2128
RETAIL & DINING: Clubs-CC-788-5656 EX-722-0794
SUPPORT & FAMILY: Med-314-8023
NOTE: *The 2005 BRAC report recommended this base for closure. As required by Federal law, the DoD has until 15 September 2007 to begin closing and realigning the bases as called for in the approved report. This process must be completed by 15 September 2011.*

FORT MYER
Attn: ANMY-GC, 204 Lee Avenue, Fort Myer, VA 22211-5050
C-703-545-6700, DSN-312-426-3250, Police-696-3525
WEB: www.fmmc.army.mil
LOCATION: Adjacent to Arlington National Cemetery. From VA-244 (Columbia Pike) exit onto VA-27 (Washington Blvd) to a right exit at sign for Fort Myer to the Hatfield Gate. USMRA: DC map (E-5). NMC: Washington, DC, one mile northeast.
RECREATION & TRAVEL: TML-696-3376/7
RETAIL & DINING: Clubs-CC-527-1300 OC-524-7000 Com-696-3674 EX-522-4575 Gas-522-2584
SUPPORT & FAMILY: Med-696-3447
Ten-digit dialing required for local calls.

FORT PICKETT ARMY NATIONAL GUARD MANEUVER TRAINING CENTER
Attn: VAFP-PA, Bldg 472, Military Road
Blackstone, VA 23824-9000
C-434-292-8621, DSN-312-438-8620, Police-292-8444
WEB: www.fortpickett.net
LOCATION: On US-460, one mile from Blackstone. From I-95, take I-85 South to US-460 exit. US-460 west to Business US-460 west at Blackstone, VA. Directions to Fort Pickett Main Gate are clearly marked at junction of US-460 and Business US-460 at Blackstone, VA. USMRA: VA/WV map (K-10). NMC: Petersburg, 40 miles northeast. NMI: Fort Lee, 40 miles northeast.
RECREATION & TRAVEL: RVC-298-0366 TML-292-2443
RETAIL & DINING: Clubs-CC-292-9995 Dining-292-2149 EX-292-8680
SUPPORT & FAMILY: Med-292-2210 Hospital-804-862-5000

FORT STORY

Attn: ATZF-FS, Bldg 300, Fort Story, VA 23459-5001
C-757-422-7305, DSN-312-438-7305, Police-422-7141
WEB: www.eustis.army.mil/Fort_story
LOCATION: From the south exit of US-13 (Chesapeake Bay Bridge Tunnel), east on US-60 (Atlantic Avenue) to Fort Story. Clearly marked. From I-64, take exit 282 onto US-13 north. Make a right onto US-60 east, which leads to Fort Story. From VA-44 (Norfolk-VA Beach Expressway) exit US-58, turn left, US-60 (North Atlantic Avenue) to 89th Street to Fort Story. USMRA: VA/WV map (O-10), Hampton Roads, VA map (I-6). NMC: Virginia Beach, three miles south.
RECREATION & TRAVEL: RVC-422-7601 TML-422-8818
RETAIL & DINING: Clubs-Fort Story-425-6631 EX-422-7858 MiniMall-422-7858 Gas-887-0392
SUPPORT & FAMILY: Med-422-7822/51

HENDERSON HALL USMC

1555 South Gate Road, Bldg 29, Arlington, VA 22214-0002
C-703-545-6700, DSN-312-227-0101, Police-614-2200
WEB: http://hqinet001.hqmc.usmc.mil/hh/
LOCATION: From Columbia Pike (VA-244) exit to South Orme Street (Sheraton National Hotel at corner). Go west to dead end, then left to Main Gate. Also, from VA-27 exit to Columbia Pike, at first traffic light take a right onto Southgate Road, enter gate straight ahead. USMRA: DC map (E-5). NMC: Washington, DC, one mile northeast.
RETAIL & DINING: Clubs-EMC-614-2125 EX-979-8420
SUPPORT & FAMILY: Med-614-1229
Ten-digit dialing required for local calls.

JOINT FORCES STAFF COLLEGE

Public Affairs Office Room A-101, 7800 Hampton Blvd
Norfolk, VA 23511-1702
C-757-443-6076, DSN-312-646-6000, Police-443-6085
WEB: www.jfsc.ndu.edu
LOCATION: From I-64, merge onto I-564 exit 276 toward VA-406/Naval Base/Terminal Blvd. Merge right onto Terminal Blvd. At the second light, make a right onto Hampton Blvd. College will be just ahead on the right. USMRA: Hampton Roads, VA map (F-6). NMC: Norfolk, within city limits. NMI: Norfolk Naval Station, two miles north.
RECREATION & TRAVEL: Golf-444-5572 TML-963-9600 ext. 0
RETAIL & DINING: Clubs-OC-423-4713 Com-423-3188 EX-440-2247 Gas-440-2141
SUPPORT & FAMILY: Med-314-6216

JUDGE ADVOCATE GENERAL'S SCHOOL

600 Massie Road, Charlottesville, VA 22903-1781
C-434-972-6300, DSN-312-488-6300
WEB: www.jagcnet.army.mil/tjagsa
LOCATION: On the grounds of the University of Virginia in Charlottesville. Take US-250 bypass off I-64 to the Barracks Road exit southeast. Take right at first light onto Milmont Street, first right onto Arlington Blvd, and at the three-way stop sign turn right into the parking lot. USMRA: VA/WV map (J-7). NMC: Charlottesville, within city limits.
RECREATION & TRAVEL: TML-972-6450
RETAIL & DINING: EX-972-6324

LANGLEY AIR FORCE BASE

159 Sweeney Blvd, Suite 100
Langley Air Force Base, VA 23665-2292
C-757-764-9990, DSN-312-574-1110, Police-764-5091
WEB: www.langley.af.mil
LOCATION: From I-64 east or west in Hampton, take Armistead Avenue exit 263 onto Mercury Blvd east. Make a left onto LaSalle Avenue and enter the Air Force Base. USMRA: VA/WV map (N-10). NMC: Hampton, one mile south.
RECREATION & TRAVEL: Golf-764-4547 Marina-764-7220 RVC-Park-766-3017 FAMCAMP-766-7627 SPA-764-3531/4311 TML-764-4667 or 888-AF-LODGE
RETAIL & DINING: Clubs-NCO-766-1220 OC-766-1361 Com-764-7604 Dining-764-3694 EX-766-1281 Gas-766-1286
SUPPORT & FAMILY: Med-764-6865

LITTLE CREEK NAVAL AMPHIBIOUS BASE

2600 Tarawa Court, Suite 112, Norfolk, VA 23521-3297
C-757-444-0000, DSN-312-564-0111, Police-462-4444
WEB: www.nablc.navy.mil
LOCATION: From I-64 north or south, take exit 273 to US-60 to base. From US-60 (Chesapeake Bay Bridge/Tunnel) west to base. USMRA: VA/WV map (O-10); Hampton Roads, VA, map (G,H-6). NMC: Norfolk, 11 miles southwest.
RECREATION & TRAVEL: Golf-462-8526 Marina-462-7140 RVC-462-7282 TML-462-7523 Navy Lodge 800-NAVY-INN or 464-6215
RETAIL & DINING: Clubs-CPO-462-2418 OC-462-2415 Com-464-3561/2 Galley-462-7546 EX-363-3218 Gas-363-3379
SUPPORT & FAMILY: Med-314-7429/30

MILITARY LIVING'S® SERVICE CENTER

137 North Washington Street, Suite 201
Falls Church, VA 22046-4515
C-703-237-0203, Fax: C-703-237-2233
WEB: www.militaryliving.com
LOCATION: At the corner of VA-7 and US-29. Take I-95 to I-495 west towards Tyson's Corner. Exit 47 towards Falls Church onto VA-7 east. Take VA-7 for 3.5 miles to a left onto US-29 (North Washington Street). USMRA: DC map (C-5). NMC: Washington, DC, seven miles west.

NORFOLK NAVAL SHIPYARD

Bldg 1500, Code 811, Portsmouth, VA 23709-5000
C-757-396-9085, DSN-312-386-9085, Police-396-7266
WEB: www.nnsy1.navy.mil
LOCATION: From I-264 in Portsmouth, exit 5 south on US-17 or exit 7A onto Effingham Street south to enter the Shipyard. USMRA: Hampton Roads, VA, map (F-7). NMC: Portsmouth, within city limits. NMI: Norfolk NS, seven miles north.
RECREATION & TRAVEL: TML-391-1388 or 877-986-9258
RETAIL & DINING: Cafeteria-393-4884 Clubs-CC-396-3660 Com-399-7941 Dining-396-7343 EX-391-3400 Gas-397-3511
SUPPORT & FAMILY: Med-314-6985

NORFOLK NAVAL STATION

1530 Gilbert Street, Bldg N-26, Suite 2000, Norfolk, VA 23511-2722
C-757-444-0000, DSN-312-564-0000, Police-444-2324
WEB: www.navstanorva.navy.mil
LOCATION: From I-64 east, take Naval Base exit 276 to I-564 northwest, follow signs. USMRA: Hampton Roads, VA map (F-5,6). NMC: Norfolk, within city limits.
RECREATION & TRAVEL: Golf-444-5572 Marina-444-2918 SPA-444-4118/48 TML-489-2656 or 877-986-9258 Navy Lodge-800-NAVY-INN
RETAIL & DINING: Cafeteria-423-8267 Clubs-CC-444-0773 CPO/EMC-440-5483 OC-444-0773 Com-423-8286 Galley-444-7024 EX-440-6542 Gas-440-2141/2269
SUPPORT & FAMILY: Med-314-6216/18/91
NOTE: *Must have DoD sticker and ID card to enter installation.*

NORTHWEST ANNEX, NORFOLK NAVAL SUPPORT ACTIVITY

1320 Northwest Blvd, Suite 100, Chesapeake, VA 23322-4094
C-757-421-8000, DSN-312-564-1336, Police-421-8181
WEB: www.nsa-norva.navy.mil
LOCATION: Five miles west of VA-168 at NC/VA border, turn right onto Ballahack Road and follow three miles to Main Gate (a left on Relay Road). Located between Moyock, NC, and Great Bridge, VA. USMRA: VA/WV map (N,O-11). NMC: Norfolk, 35 miles north.
RECREATION & TRAVEL: RVC-421-8264 TML-421-8282
RETAIL & DINING: Clubs-Mariner-421-8250/1 Dining-421-8276 EX-421-8254 Gas-421-8254
SUPPORT & FAMILY: Med-421-8220

OCEANA NAVAL AIR STATION

1750 Tomcat Blvd, Bldg 230, Virginia Beach, VA 23460-2191
C-757-433-2366, DSN-312-433-2366, Police-433-2224
WEB: www.nasoceana.navy.mil
LOCATION: From I-64 east or west, exit to 264 east, take the Oceana exit to Main Gate on right (Tomcat Blvd). USMRA: VA/WV map (O-10); Hampton Roads, VA, map (I-7). NMC: Virginia Beach, within city limits.
RECREATION & TRAVEL: Golf-433-2866 SPA-433-2903 TML-433-2574
RETAIL & DINING: Clubs-CPO-433-2637 EMC-433-2112 OC-428-0036 Com-428-2931 Dining-425-4200 EX-425-4200 Gas-425-4283/4
SUPPORT & FAMILY: Med-314-7000/7110

PENTAGON

OASD(PA)/PIA, 1400 Defense Pentagon, Room 3A750
Washington, DC 20301-1400
C-703-545-6700, DSN-312-227-0101, Police-697-5555
WEB: www.defenselink.mil/pubs/pentagon
LOCATION: Physically located I-395 at Boundary Channel Drive in Arlington, VA. From I-395 North or South, exit to South Parking; or, from Columbia Pike (VA-244), exit to South Parking. North Parking accessible from Boundary Channel Drive, exit from I-395 southbound or VA-110 northbound. Commercial pay parking for visitors in Haynes Street Parking Lot on north side of Army-Navy Drive. Use pedestrian tunnel under I-395 to South Parking Entrance to Pentagon. Bus, Metro, taxi no longer accessible from concourse. Follow signs to relocated access. USMRA: Downtown DC map (B-4), NMC: Washington, DC, adjacent. WARNING: Due to ongoing defense situation, force protection levels vary according to the current threat. When approaching the Pentagon, be alert to signs and prohibitions and be prepared for extremely heightened security by military, state and local police. Call ahead to your intended point of contact and ask for their instructions.
RETAIL & DINING: Gas (NEX Qtrs K)-979-3891
SUPPORT & FAMILY: Med-692-8800
NOTE: *Installation physically located in VA, but uses a DC mailing address.*
Ten-digit dialing required for local calls.

PORTSMOUTH COAST GUARD INTEGRATED SUPPORT COMMAND

4000 Coast Guard Blvd, Portsmouth, VA 23703-2199
C-757-483-8586, DSN-312-483-8532, Police-483-8586
LOCATION: From I-664 exit 9, take VA-164 east toward Portsmouth. Exit Cedar Lane, turn right. Make a left at first intersection onto West Norfolk Road. Left on Coast Guard Blvd to gate. USMRA: VA/WV map (N-10); Hampton Roads, VA, map (E-7). NMC: Norfolk, eight miles southeast.
RECREATION & TRAVEL: Marina-483-8685
RETAIL & DINING: Clubs-CC-All Hands-483-8535 Dining-483-8539 EX-483-8612/5
SUPPORT & FAMILY: Med-483-8596

PORTSMOUTH NAVAL MEDICAL CENTER

620 John Paul Jones Circle, Portsmouth, VA 23708-5100
C-757-953-5008, DSN-312-377-5008, Police-953-5225
WEB: www-nmcp.med.navy.mil
LOCATION: Off I-264 east or west in Portsmouth, take exit 7A onto Effingham Street to medical center. USMRA: Hampton Roads, VA, map (F-7). NMC: Portsmouth, within city limits.
RECREATION & TRAVEL: TML-399-5461/6889
RETAIL & DINING: Clubs-CC-953-5017 EX-397-5857/8 Snack Bar (Subway)-393-2761 or 399-5324
SUPPORT & FAMILY: Med-866-645-4584

QUANTICO MARINE CORPS BASE

Commanding General, MCB Quantico, Attn: PAO
Quantico, VA 22134-5109
C-703-784-2121, DSN-312-278-2121, Police-784-2251/2/3
WEB: www.quantico.usmc.mil
LOCATION: From I-95 north or south, take exit 150A (Quantico/Triangle) east. US-1 runs parallel to I-95 and is adjacent to the base. Directions to the base from I-95 and US-1 are clearly marked. Visitors are issued a vehicle pass and given directions to their destination. Proper identification such as a Military ID or valid state driver's license is required to enter base. USMRA: VA/WV map (L-6). NMC: Washington, DC, 36 miles north.
RECREATION & TRAVEL: Golf-784-2424/63 Marinas-784-2359/5270 RVC-784-5270 SPA-784-5487 TML-432-1341 or 784-3149
RETAIL & DINING: Clubs-EMC-784-5223/95 OC/SNCO-784-2676 TBSO-(Hawkins)-784-5238 Com-784-2233/2476 Dining-640-0965 EX-640-8800 Gas-221-4553
SUPPORT & FAMILY: Med-784-1699
Ten-digit dialing required for local calls.

RICHMOND DEFENSE SUPPLY CENTER

8000 Jefferson Davis Highway, Richmond, VA 23297-5100
C-804-279-3861, DSN-312-695-1110, Police-279-4754
WEB: www.dscr.dla.mil
LOCATION: From I-95 north or south (Richmond-Petersburg Turnpike), exit Willis Road. Make a right turn onto Jefferson Davis. Clearly marked on west side of US-1/301, Main Gate Dwight Avenue. USMRA: VA/WV map (L-9). NMC: Richmond, eight miles north. NMI: Fort Lee, ten miles.
RECREATION & TRAVEL: TML-279-1092
RETAIL & DINING: Cafeteria-279-3351/3772 Clubs-OC-279-3714 Dining-279-3351 EX-275-2654 Gas-275-1478
SUPPORT & FAMILY: Med-279-3821

WALLOPS ISLAND SURFACE COMBAT SYSTEMS CENTER

30 Battle Group Way, Wallops Island, VA 23337-2229
C-757-824-1692/1979, Police-824-2037
WEB: www.scsc.navy.mil
LOCATION: From the south, take Chesapeake Bay Bridge/Tunnel north, stay on US-13 to VA-175 (a right at T's Corner), make a left at Atlantic Road (Ocean Deli) and right at Battlegroup Way. From the north, take US-13 south, five miles over MD/VA line to VA-175, same directions as above. USMRA: VA/WV map (P-7,8). NMC: Norfolk, VA, 100 miles south.
RECREATION & TRAVEL: TML-824-2064
RETAIL & DINING: Clubs-Galley-824-1009 EX-824-5434
SUPPORT & FAMILY: Med-824-2130

YORKTOWN COAST GUARD TRAINING CENTER

Thayer Hall, Yorktown, VA 23690-5002
C-757-856-3500, DSN-312-827-3500, Police-887-7133
WEB: www.uscg.mil/tcyorktown/index.shtm
LOCATION: From I-64 east or west, exit 250B east on VA-105, follow signs to US-17. Left on US-17, then right at second light onto Cook Road. Follow this until road ends, then take a right. This will lead to the base. USMRA: VA/WV map (N-9); Hampton Roads, VA, map (D-2). NMC: Newport News, 15 miles southeast.
RECREATION & TRAVEL: RVC-856-2100 TML-856-2378
RETAIL & DINING: Clubs-EMC-856-2325 OC-856-2286 Dining-856-2728 EX-856-2153 Gas/Mini Mart-856-2156
SUPPORT & FAMILY: Med-314-6100

YORKTOWN NAVAL WEAPONS STATION

P.O. Drawer 160, Yorktown, VA 23691-0160
C-757-887-4000, DSN-312-953-4000, Police-887-4676
WEB: www.nwsy.navy.mil
LOCATION: From I-64 east, take exit 247 east, turn left. One-half mile to Gate 3 and pass office. Or from I-64 west: Take exit 247, turn right to stoplight. For pass office, turn left, 0.8 miles to Gate 3. For Station Hq: Make a left at the stoplight on VA-238 (Yorktown Road), 2.3 miles to Gate 1 on left. USMRA: VA/WV map (N-9); Hampton Roads, VA, map (B,C-1). NMC: Newport News, two miles southeast.
RECREATION & TRAVEL: Golf-887-4323 RVC-887-7418 TML-887-7621
RETAIL & DINING: Clubs-CC-887-7886 All Hands-887-4555 City Limits-887-4646 Country-887-4272 Dining-887-7140 EX-887-2307 Gas-887-2307
SUPPORT & FAMILY: Med-314-6140

USO WORLD HEADQUARTERS

2111 Wilson Blvd, Suite 1200, Arlington, VA 22201-3052
C-703-908-6400
WEB: www.uso.org
LOCATION: To find the locations of USO Centers, go to www.uso.org. USMRA: VA map, (E-4).
NOTE: *For a list of USO offices, see page 93.*
Ten-digit dialing required for local calls.

WEST VIRGINIA, pg. 44-45

CAMP DAWSON ARMY TRAINING SITE

WVARNG Training Site Command
240 Army Road, Bldg 200, Kingwood, WV 26537-1092
C-304-791-4331, DSN-312-623-4331, Police-791-4301
WEB: www.wv.ngb.army.mil
LOCATION: From I-68 east or west, take Bruceton Mills exit and go south on WV-26 towards Albright. After approximately 13 miles, turn left onto WV-26/WV-7 (Caddell-St. Joe Road). Proceed for approximately two miles and turn right into Camp Dawson Drive. USMRA: VA/WV map (H-4). NMC: Morgantown, 24 miles northwest.
RECREATION & TRAVEL: TML-791-7001
RETAIL & DINING: Clubs-CC-791-4383 Dining-791-7343 EX-791-7009
SUPPORT & FAMILY: Med-791-4314

CHARLESTON ARMORY EXCHANGE

1679 Coonskin Drive, Charleston, WV 25311-1085
C-304-346-4957, Emergency-911
LOCATION: From I-77 north or south, take exit 99 to WV-114 (Greenbrier Street) north. Veer right onto and continue on Greenbrier Street. Make a left onto Coonskin Drive, approximately 0.8 miles to Exchange on left (west) side of road. USMRA: VA/WV map (E-7). NMC: Charleston, within city limits.
RETAIL & DINING: EX-346-4957

EASTERN WEST VIRGINIA REGIONAL/ SHEPHERD AIRPORT/AIR NATIONAL GUARD

167 Airlift Wing 222 Sabre Jet Blvd, Martinsburg, WV 25401-7704
C-304-262-5100, DSN-312-242-5300, Police-262-5300
WEB: www.wvmart.ang.af.mil
LOCATION: From I-81, take exit 12 east, right to US-45 east. At the fifth traffic light, turn right onto Kelly Island Road. Follow road for approximately three miles to the base. USMRA: VA/WV map (K-4). NMC: Hagerstown, MD, 15 miles north.
RECREATION & TRAVEL: SPA-262-5250
RETAIL & DINING: Clubs-NCO-262-5298
SUPPORT & FAMILY: Med-262-5244

SUGAR GROVE NAVAL SECURITY GROUP ACTIVITY

Attn: PAO, 63 Hedrick Drive, Sugar Grove, WV 26815-5000
C-304-249-6304, DSN-312-564-7276, Police-249-6399
LOCATION: From I-81 in VA, take US-33 west from Harrisonburg, VA,
to Brandywine, WV. Turn left onto WV-21 five miles south to NSGA Sugar Grove
on the right. USMRA: VA/WV map (I-6). NMC: Harrisonburg, VA, 36 miles east.
RECREATION & TRAVEL: RVC-249-6309 TML-249-6309
RETAIL & DINING: Cafeteria-249-6537 Clubs-CC-249-6362 CPO-249-6546 EMC-249-6388 Com-249-6326 Dining-249-6362 EX-249-6355 Gas-249-6355
SUPPORT & FAMILY: Med-249-6380

YEAGER AIRPORT/AIR NATIONAL GUARD

1679 Coonskin Drive, Bldg 131, Charleston, WV 25311-1023
C-304-341-6000, DSN-312-366-6210
Police (Security)-366-6227/6301
WEB: www.wvchar.ang.af.mil
LOCATION: From I-77 north or south, take exit 99 to WV-114 (Greenbrier Street) north. Veer right onto and continue on Greenbrier Street.
Make a left onto Coonskin Drive. USMRA: VA/WV map (E-7). NMC: Charleston, four miles southwest.
RECREATION & TRAVEL: SPA-341-6185
RETAIL & DINING: EX-346-4957
SUPPORT & FAMILY: Med-341-6252

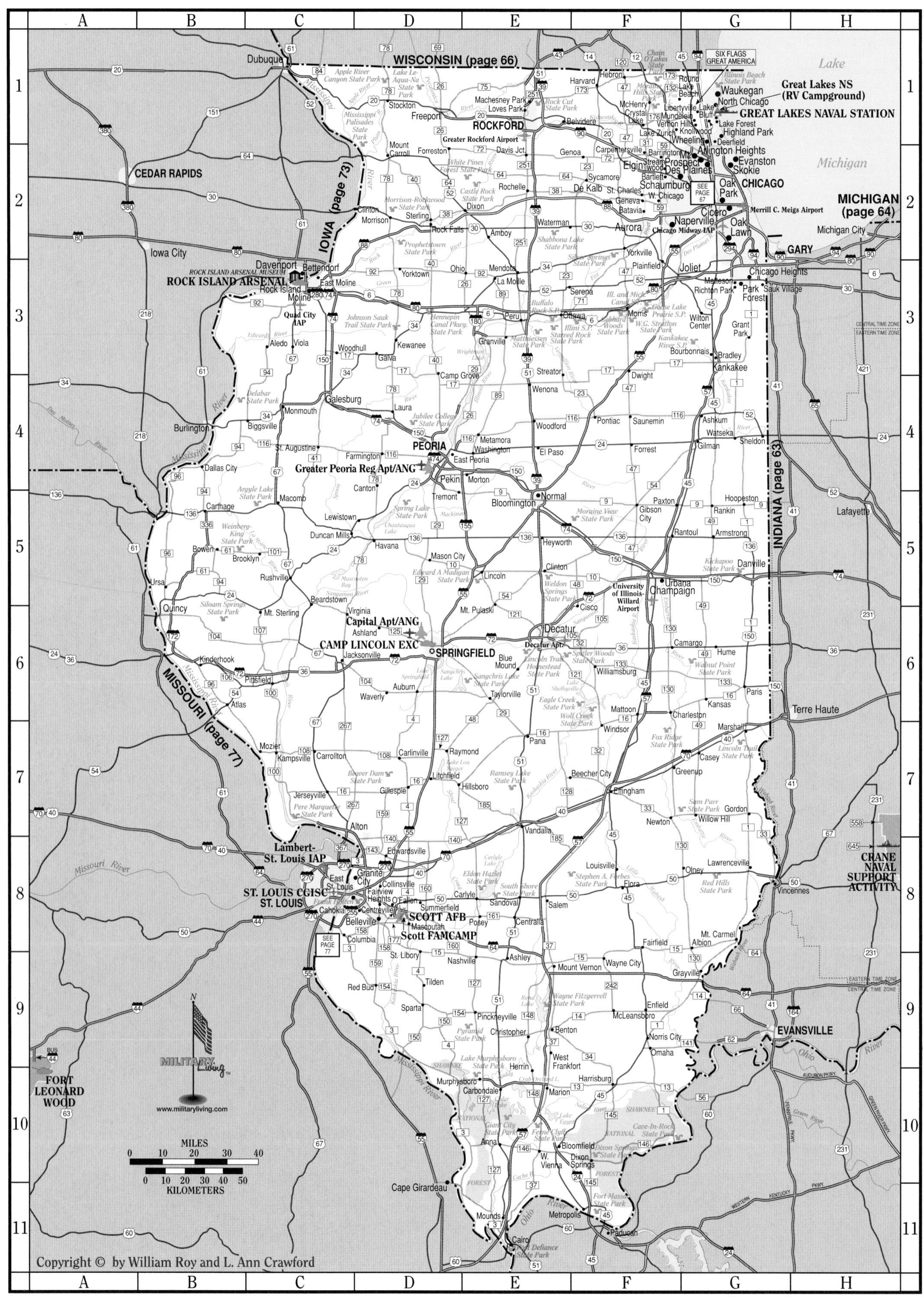
A
B
C
D
E
F
G
H
1
2
3
4
5
6
7
8
9
10
11
WISCONSIN (page 66)
IOWA (page 73)
MISSOURI (page 77)
INDIANA (page 63)
MICHIGAN (page 64)
Lake Michigan
SIX FLAGS GREAT AMERICA
Great Lakes NS (RV Campground)
GREAT LAKES NAVAL STATION
CHICAGO
Merrill C. Meigs Airport
Chicago Midway IAP
SEE PAGE 67
ROCKFORD
Greater Rockford Airport
CEDAR RAPIDS
Iowa City
Dubuque
Davenport
Bettendorf
ROCK ISLAND ARSENAL MUSEUM
ROCK ISLAND ARSENAL
Rock Island
Moline
East Moline
Quad City IAP
Galesburg
PEORIA
Greater Peoria Reg Apt/ANG
Bloomington
Normal
Champaign
Urbana
University of Illinois-Willard Airport
Decatur
Decatur Apt.
SPRINGFIELD
Capital Apt/ANG
CAMP LINCOLN EXC
Quincy
Burlington
Terre Haute
Lambert-St. Louis IAP
ST. LOUIS CGISC
ST. LOUIS
SEE PAGE 77
SCOTT AFB
Scott FAMCAMP
Belleville
Vincennes
CRANE NAVAL SUPPORT ACTIVITY
EVANSVILLE
Paducah
Cape Girardeau
Cairo
FORT LEONARD WOOD
Joliet
Aurora
Naperville
Elgin
Waukegan
North Chicago
Evanston
Skokie
Kankakee
Danville
Effingham
Mount Vernon
Carbondale
Marion
GARY
Michigan City
Lafayette
MILITARY Living
www.militaryliving.com
MILES
0 10 20 30 40
0 10 20 30 40 50
KILOMETERS

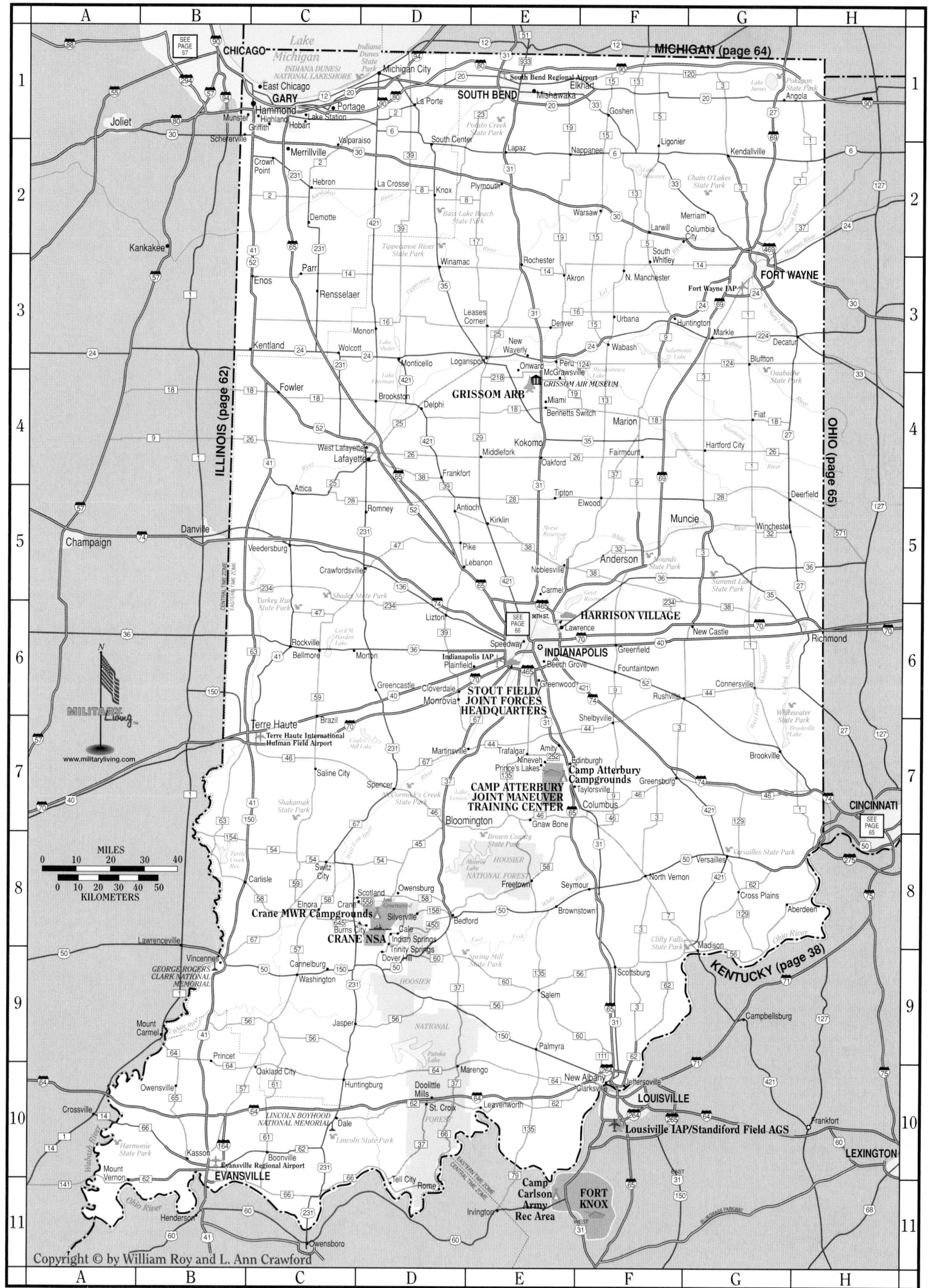
A
B
C
D
E
F
G
H
1
2
3
4
5
6
7
8
9
10
11
SEE PAGE 67
CHICAGO
Lake Michigan
Indiana Dunes State Park
INDIANA DUNES/ NATIONAL LAKESHORE
Michigan City
MICHIGAN (page 64)
South Bend Regional Airport
SOUTH BEND
Mishawaka
Elkhart
Goshen
Pokagon State Park
Lake James
Angola
East Chicago
GARY
Hammond
Portage
Munster
Highland
Lake Station
Griffith
Hobart
Joliet
Schererville
La Porte
Valparaiso
South Center
Potato Creek State Park
Lapaz
Nappanee
Ligonier
Kendallville
Merrillville
Crown Point
Hebron
La Crosse
Knox
Plymouth
Chain O'Lakes State Park
Warsaw
Merriam
Columbia City
Larwill
South Whitley
Bass Lake Beach State Park
Demotte
Kankakee
Tippecanoe River State Park
Winamac
Rochester
Akron
N. Manchester
FORT WAYNE
Fort Wayne IAP
Parr
Enos
Rensselaer
Leases Corner
Denver
Urbana
Huntington
Markle
Decatur
Monon
New Waverly
Wabash
Kentland
Wolcott
Monticello
Logansport
Onward
Peru
McGrawsville
Bluffton
Ouabache State Park
GRISSOM AIR MUSEUM
GRISSOM ARB
Miami
Bennetts Switch
Fowler
Brookston
Delphi
Marion
Fiat
ILLINOIS (page 62)
OHIO (page 65)
West Lafayette
Lafayette
Middlefork
Kokomo
Fairmount
Hartford City
Oakford
Frankfort
Attica
Tipton
Elwood
Deerfield
Romney
Antioch
Kirklin
Muncie
Winchester
Danville
Champaign
Veedersburg
Pike
Anderson
Mounds State Park
Lebanon
Noblesville
Crawfordsville
Summit Lake State Park
Carmel
Shades State Park
Turkey Run State Park
HARRISON VILLAGE
Lizton
SEE PAGE 66
56TH ST.
Lawrence
New Castle
Richmond
Rockville
Bellmore
Morton
Speedway
INDIANAPOLIS
Greenfield
Indianapolis IAP
Plainfield
Beech Grove
Fountaintown
Greencastle
Cloverdale
Greenwood
Connersville
Rushville
Monrovia
STOUT FIELD/ JOINT FORCES HEADQUARTERS
MILITARY Living
www.militaryliving.com
Terre Haute
Terre Haute International Hulman Field Airport
Brazil
Shelbyville
Whitewater State Park
Martinsville
Trafalgar
Amity
Nineveh
Prince's Lakes
Edinburgh
Camp Atterbury Campgrounds
Brookville
Saline City
Spencer
CAMP ATTERBURY JOINT MANEUVER TRAINING CENTER
Taylorsville
Greensburg
Columbus
McCormick's Creek State Park
Shakamak State Park
Bloomington
Gnaw Bone
CINCINNATI
SEE PAGE 65
MILES
KILOMETERS
Brown County State Park
Versailles State Park
Switz City
HOOSIER NATIONAL FOREST
Freetown
Versailles
Carlisle
Seymour
North Vernon
Scotland
Owensburg
Cross Plains
Elnora
Crane
Crane MWR Campgrounds
Silverville
Bedford
Brownstown
Aberdeen
Burns City
Cale
CRANE NSA
Indian Springs
Trinity Springs
Dover Hill
Clifty Falls State Park
Madison
Lawrenceville
Vincennes
Cannelburg
Washington
Spring Mill State Park
KENTUCKY (page 38)
GEORGE ROGERS CLARK NATIONAL MEMORIAL
Scottsburg
Salem
Mount Carmel
Jasper
Campbellsburg
Palmyra
Princet
Oakland City
Marengo
New Albany
Jeffersonville
Clarksville
Owensville
Huntingburg
Doolittle Mills
LOUISVILLE
Crossville
St. Croix
Leavenworth
LINCOLN BOYHOOD NATIONAL MEMORIAL
Dale
Louisville IAP/Standiford Field AGS
Frankfort
Harmonie State Park
Lincoln State Park
Kasson
Boonville
Evansville Regional Airport
LEXINGTON
Mount Vernon
EVANSVILLE
Tell City
Rome
Camp Carlson Army Rec Area
FORT KNOX
Henderson
Ohio River
Irvington
Owensboro
EASTERN TIME ZONE
CENTRAL TIME ZONE

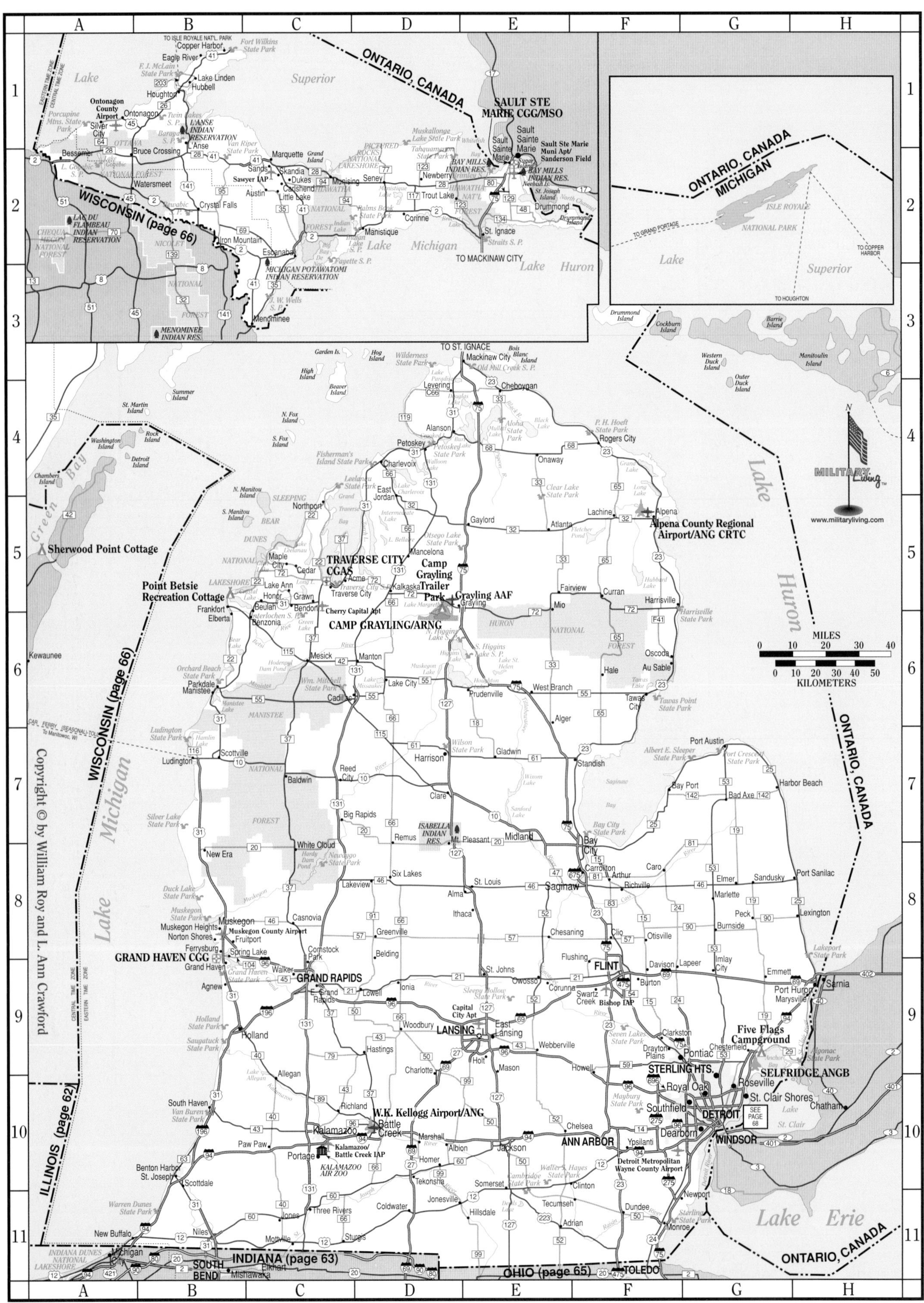

SAULT STE MARIE CGG/MSO
Sault Ste Marie Muni Apt/ Sanderson Field
ONTARIO, CANADA
WISCONSIN (page 66)
Copper Harbor
Houghton
Ontonagon County Airport
Ontonagon
Bessemer
Bruce Crossing
Watersmeet
Crystal Falls
Iron Mountain
Escanaba
Menominee
Marquette
Sawyer IAP
Munising
Seney
Newberry
Manistique
St. Ignace
TO MACKINAW CITY
MICHIGAN POTAWATOMI INDIAN RESERVATION
MENOMINEE INDIAN RES.
LAC DU FLAMBEAU INDIAN RESERVATION
BAY MILLS INDIAN RES.
ISLE ROYALE NATIONAL PARK
TO GRAND PORTAGE
TO COPPER HARBOR
TO HOUGHTON
Lake Superior
Lake Michigan
Lake Huron
Lake Erie
TO ST. IGNACE
Mackinaw City
Cheboygan
Petoskey
Charlevoix
Rogers City
Alpena
Alpena County Regional Airport/ANG CRTC
Gaylord
Sherwood Point Cottage
Point Betsie Recreation Cottage
TRAVERSE CITY CGAS
Traverse City
Cherry Capital Apt
Camp Grayling Trailer Park
Grayling AAF
CAMP GRAYLING/ARNG
Kewaunee
Manistee
Cadillac
Ludington
Oscoda
Tawas City
MILES 0 10 20 30 40
0 10 20 30 40 50 KILOMETERS
ONTARIO, CANADA
Big Rapids
Mt. Pleasant
ISABELLA INDIAN RES.
Midland
Bay City
Saginaw
Muskegon
Muskegon County Airport
GRAND HAVEN CGG
GRAND RAPIDS
Holland
Kalamazoo
Battle Creek
W.K. Kellogg Airport/ANG
Kalamazoo/ Battle Creek IAP
KALAMAZOO AIR ZOO
LANSING
Capital City Apt
FLINT
Bishop IAP
Port Huron
Five Flags Campground
SELFRIDGE ANGB
STERLING HTS.
DETROIT
SEE PAGE 68
WINDSOR
ANN ARBOR
Detroit Metropolitan Wayne County Airport
Jackson
Monroe
TOLEDO
OHIO (page 65)
INDIANA (page 63)
ILLINOIS (page 62)
SOUTH BEND
Copyright © by William Roy and L. Ann Crawford
MILITARY Living
www.militaryliving.com

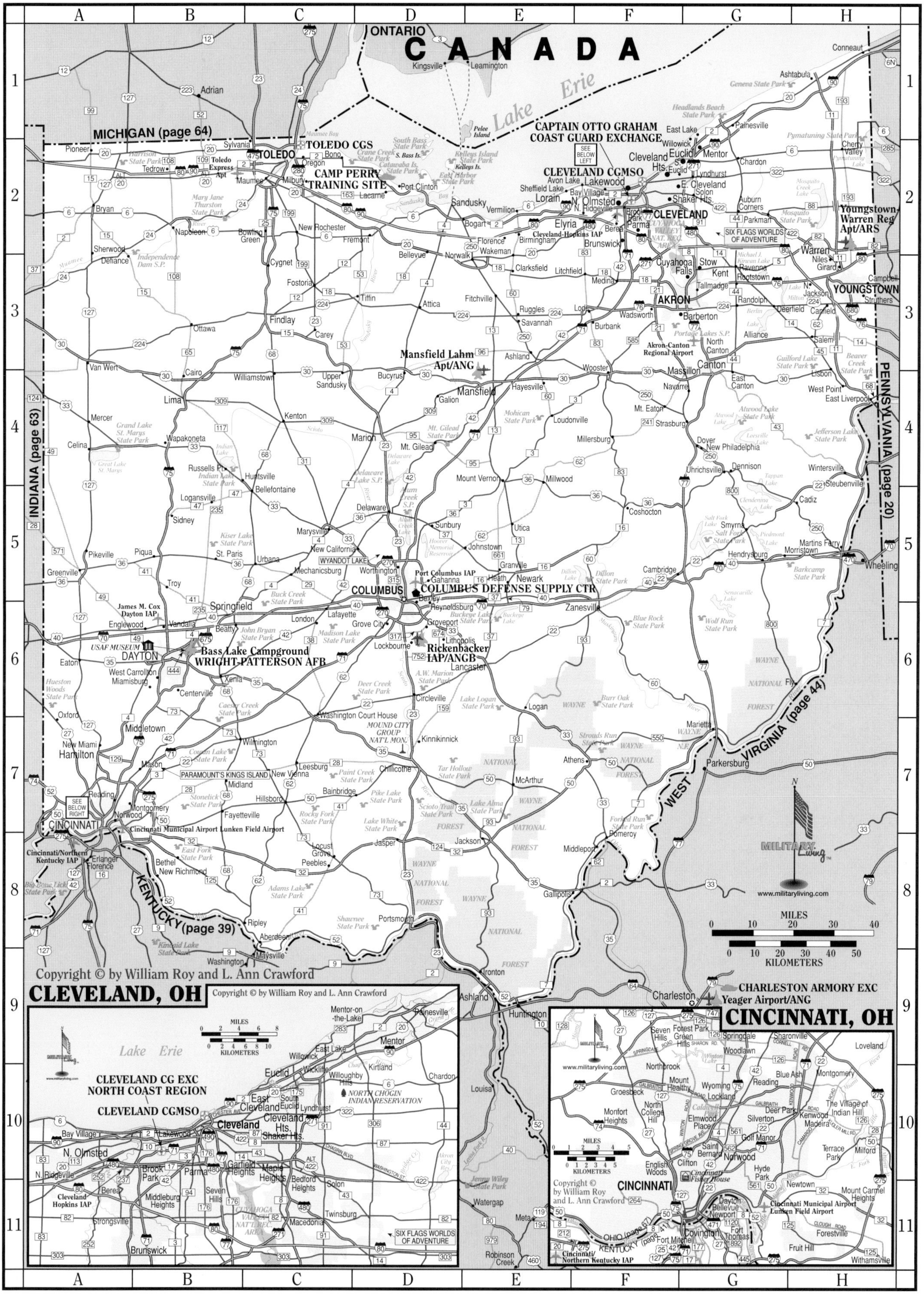

CANADA

ONTARIO

Lake Erie

MICHIGAN (page 64)

INDIANA (page 63)

PENNSYLVANIA (page 20)

WEST VIRGINIA (page 44)

KENTUCKY (page 39)

TOLEDO CGS

Toledo Express Apt

CAMP PERRY TRAINING SITE

CAPTAIN OTTO GRAHAM COAST GUARD EXCHANGE

CLEVELAND CGMSO

Cleveland-Hopkins IAP

SIX FLAGS WORLDS OF ADVENTURE

Youngstown-Warren Reg Apt/ARS

Akron-Canton Regional Airport

Mansfield Lahm Apt/ANG

Port Columbus IAP

COLUMBUS DEFENSE SUPPLY CTR

Rickenbacker IAP/ANGB

James M. Cox Dayton IAP

USAF MUSEUM

Bass Lake Campground

WRIGHT-PATTERSON AFB

PARAMOUNT'S KINGS ISLAND

WYANDOT LAKE

MOUND CITY GROUP NAT'L MON.

Cincinnati Municipal Airport Lunken Field Airport

Cincinnati/Northern Kentucky IAP

CHARLESTON ARMORY EXC

Yeager Airport/ANG

TOLEDO, Sylvania, Maumee, Oregon, Bono, Port Clinton, Sandusky, Lorain, Elyria, Lakewood, CLEVELAND, Euclid, Mentor, Painesville, Ashtabula, Conneaut, Warren, YOUNGSTOWN, AKRON, Canton, Massillon, Mansfield, Findlay, Lima, Marion, Delaware, COLUMBUS, Newark, Zanesville, Cambridge, Springfield, DAYTON, Middletown, Hamilton, CINCINNATI, Chillicothe, Lancaster, Athens, Marietta, Parkersburg, Portsmouth, Ironton, Huntington, Ashland, Charleston, Wheeling, Steubenville

www.militaryliving.com

MILES 0 10 20 30 40

0 10 20 30 40 50 KILOMETERS

CLEVELAND, OH

CLEVELAND CG EXC NORTH COAST REGION

CLEVELAND CGMSO

NORTH CHOGIN INDIAN RESERVATION

Cleveland Hopkins IAP

SIX FLAGS WORLDS OF ADVENTURE

CUYAHOGA VALLEY NAT'L REC. AREA

CINCINNATI, OH

Cincinnati Municipal Airport Lunken Field Airport

Cincinnati/ Northern Kentucky IAP

Cincinnati Fisher House

www.militaryliving.com

A B C D E F G H

1 2 3 4 5 6 7 8 9 10 11

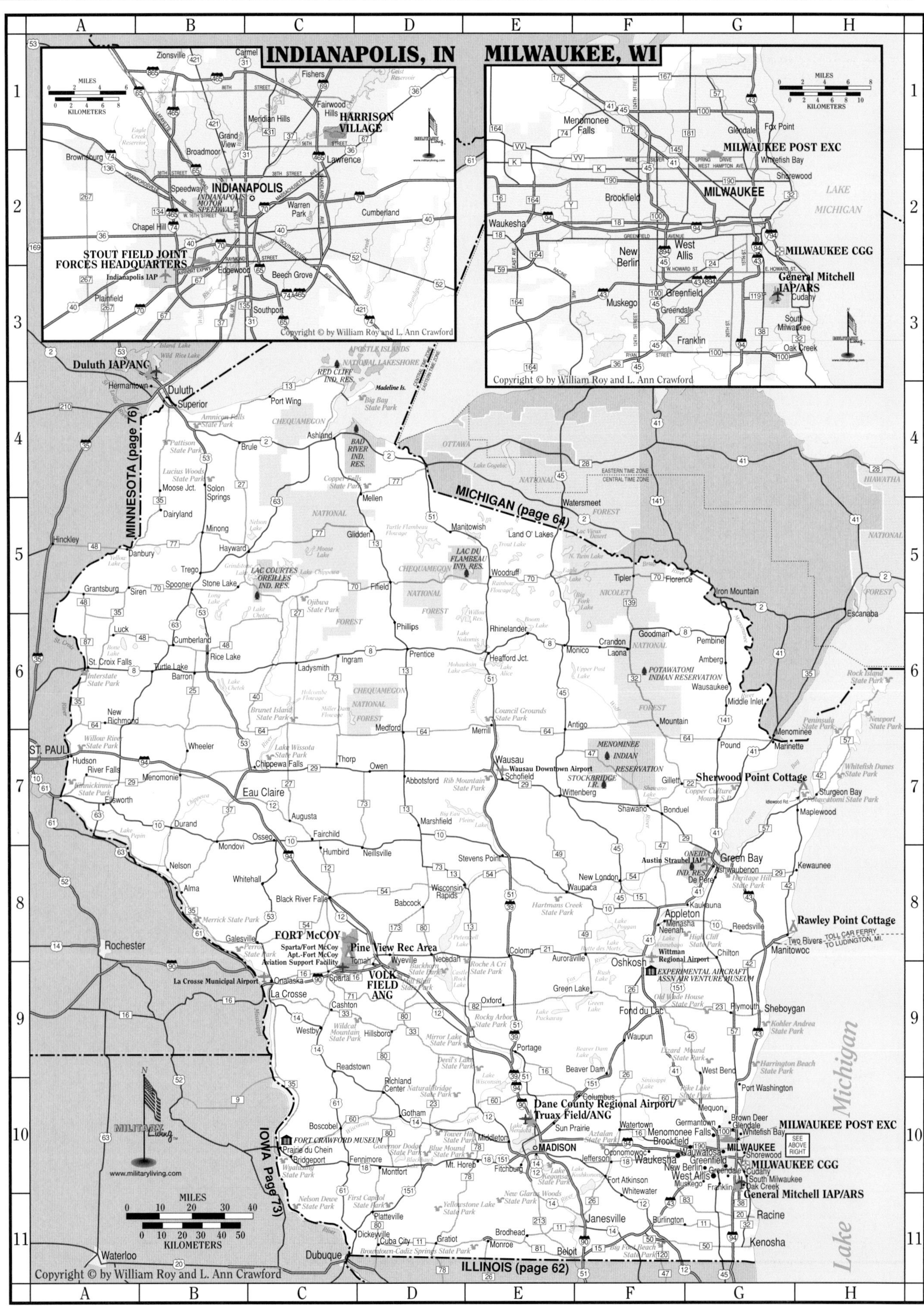

INDIANAPOLIS, IN
MILWAUKEE, WI
Zionsville
Carmel
Fishers
Geist Reservoir
Fairwood Hills
HARRISON VILLAGE
Meridian Hills
Grand View
Eagle Creek Reservoir
Broadmoor
Brownsburg
Lawrence
Speedway
INDIANAPOLIS
INDIANAPOLIS MOTOR SPEEDWAY
Warren Park
Cumberland
Chapel Hill
STOUT FIELD JOINT FORCES HEADQUARTERS
Indianapolis IAP
Edgewood
Beech Grove
Plainfield
Southport
Copyright © by William Roy and L. Ann Crawford
Menomonee Falls
Glendale
Fox Point
MILWAUKEE POST EXC
Whitefish Bay
Shorewood
Brookfield
MILWAUKEE
LAKE MICHIGAN
Waukesha
New Berlin
West Allis
MILWAUKEE CGG
General Mitchell IAP/ARS
Greenfield
Muskego
Greendale
Cudahy
South Milwaukee
Franklin
Oak Creek
Copyright © by William Roy and L. Ann Crawford
Duluth IAP/ANG
Hermantown
Duluth
Superior
APOSTLE ISLANDS NATIONAL LAKESHORE
RED CLIFF IND. RES.
Madeline Is.
Big Bay State Park
Port Wing
CHEQUAMEGON
Ashland
BAD RIVER IND. RES.
OTTAWA
MINNESOTA (page 76)
MICHIGAN (page 64)
EASTERN TIME ZONE
CENTRAL TIME ZONE
Brule
Solon Springs
Moose Jct.
Dairyland
Mellen
Watersmeet
Minong
Hayward
Glidden
Manitowish
Land O' Lakes
Hinckley
Danbury
Trego
Spooner
Stone Lake
LAC COURTES OREILLES IND. RES.
LAC DU FLAMBEAU IND. RES.
Woodruff
Tipler
Florence
Iron Mountain
Grantsburg
Siren
Fifield
NICOLET
Escanaba
Luck
Cumberland
Phillips
Rhinelander
Goodman
Pembine
Rice Lake
Crandon
Laona
Monico
Amberg
St. Croix Falls
Turtle Lake
Barron
Ladysmith
Ingram
Prentice
Hazelhurst
Heafford Jct.
POTAWATOMI INDIAN RESERVATION
Wausaukee
Rock Island State Park
Interstate State Park
New Richmond
Brunet Island State Park
Medford
Merrill
Council Grounds State Park
Antigo
Mountain
Middle Inlet
Menominee
Marinette
ST. PAUL
Hudson
River Falls
Wheeler
Lake Wissota State Park
Chippewa Falls
Thorp
Owen
Wausau
Wausau Downtown Airport
Schofield
MENOMINEE INDIAN RESERVATION
STOCKBRIDGE I.R.
Gillett
Sherwood Point Cottage
Pound
Menomonie
Eau Claire
Abbotsford
Rib Mountain State Park
Wittenberg
Shawano
Bonduel
Sturgeon Bay
Potawatomi State Park
Ellsworth
Augusta
Marshfield
Maplewood
Durand
Fairchild
Osseo
Mondovi
Humbird
Neillsville
Stevens Point
Nelson
Alma
Whitehall
Black River Falls
Babcock
Wisconsin Rapids
New London
Waupaca
Austin Straubel IAP
ONEIDA IND. RES.
Green Bay
Ashwaubenon
De Pere
Kewaunee
Kaukauna
Appleton
Menasha
Neenah
Reedsville
Rawley Point Cottage
Two Rivers
TOLL CAR FERRY TO LUDINGTON, MI.
Manitowoc
Chilton
Merrick State Park
Galesville
FORT McCOY
Sparta/Fort McCoy
Apt.-Fort McCoy
Aviation Support Facility
Pine View Rec Area
Tomah
Wyeville
Necedah
Coloma
Auroraville
Wittman Regional Airport
Oshkosh
EXPERIMENTAL AIRCRAFT ASSN AIR VENTURE MUSEUM
Rochester
La Crosse Municipal Airport
Onalaska
Sparta
VOLK FIELD ANG
La Crosse
Cashton
Oxford
Green Lake
Fond du Lac
Plymouth
Sheboygan
Kohler Andrea State Park
Westby
Hillsboro
Waupun
Readstown
Portage
Beaver Dam
West Bend
Port Washington
Richland Center
Columbus
Gotham
Dane County Regional Airport/ Truax Field/ANG
Mequon
Boscobel
Sun Prairie
Watertown
Germantown
Brown Deer
Glendale
Whitefish Bay
MILWAUKEE POST EXC
FORT CRAWFORD MUSEUM
Prairie du Chien
Bridgeport
Fennimore
Montfort
Mt. Horeb
Middleton
MADISON
Fitchburg
Jefferson
Oconomowoc
Waukesha
Menomonee Falls
Brookfield
Wauwatosa
MILWAUKEE
SEE ABOVE RIGHT
Shorewood
Greenfield
MILWAUKEE CGG
New Berlin
West Allis
Greendale
Cudahy
South Milwaukee
Muskego
Franklin
Oak Creek
General Mitchell IAP/ARS
Fort Atkinson
Whitewater
Racine
IOWA Page 73
Platteville
Dickeyville
Cuba City
Gratiot
Brodhead
Monroe
Janesville
Burlington
Beloit
Kenosha
Lake Michigan
Waterloo
Dubuque
ILLINOIS (page 62)
MILES
KILOMETERS
www.militaryliving.com
Copyright © by William Roy and L. Ann Crawford

CHICAGO, IL

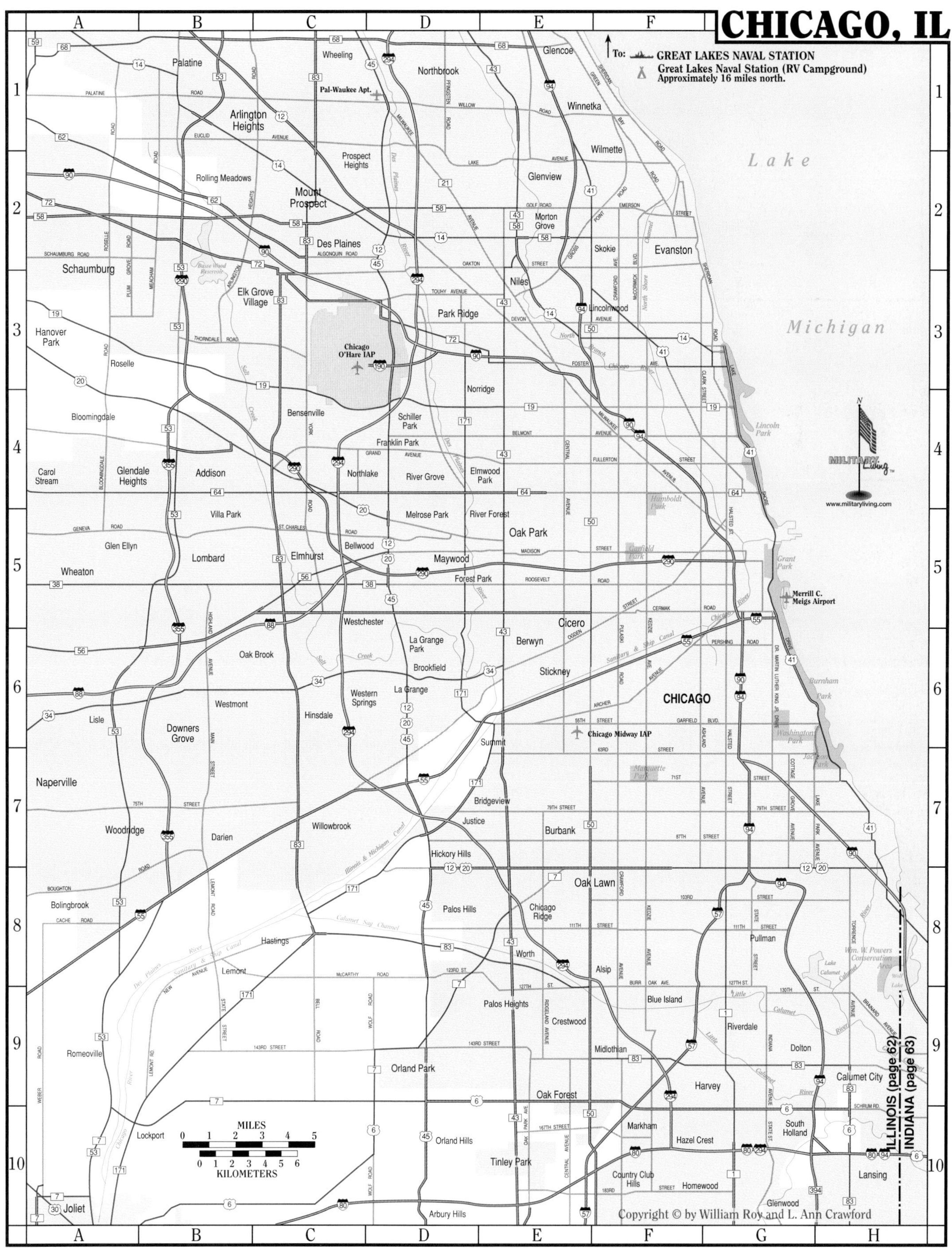

To: GREAT LAKES NAVAL STATION
Great Lakes Naval Station (RV Campground)
Approximately 16 miles north.
Lake Michigan
Palatine
Wheeling
Northbrook
Glencoe
Winnetka
Wilmette
Arlington Heights
Prospect Heights
Rolling Meadows
Mount Prospect
Glenview
Morton Grove
Des Plaines
Skokie
Evanston
Schaumburg
Elk Grove Village
Niles
Lincolnwood
Park Ridge
Hanover Park
Roselle
Chicago O'Hare IAP
Norridge
Bloomingdale
Bensenville
Schiller Park
Franklin Park
Carol Stream
Glendale Heights
Addison
Northlake
River Grove
Elmwood Park
Villa Park
Melrose Park
River Forest
Oak Park
Glen Ellyn
Lombard
Elmhurst
Bellwood
Maywood
Wheaton
Forest Park
Merrill C. Meigs Airport
Westchester
Cicero
La Grange Park
Berwyn
Oak Brook
Brookfield
Stickney
Western Springs
La Grange
CHICAGO
Lisle
Westmont
Hinsdale
Downers Grove
Chicago Midway IAP
Summit
Naperville
Bridgeview
Justice
Burbank
Woodridge
Darien
Willowbrook
Hickory Hills
Oak Lawn
Bolingbrook
Palos Hills
Chicago Ridge
Pullman
Hastings
Worth
Lemont
Alsip
Blue Island
Palos Heights
Crestwood
Riverdale
Romeoville
Midlothian
Dolton
Orland Park
Calumet City
Harvey
Oak Forest
Markham
South Holland
Lockport
Orland Hills
Hazel Crest
Tinley Park
Country Club Hills
Homewood
Lansing
Joliet
Arbury Hills
Glenwood
MILES
KILOMETERS
ILLINOIS (page 62)
INDIANA (page 63)
www.militaryliving.com
Copyright © by William Roy and L. Ann Crawford

ILLINOIS, pg. 62
Chicago, 67

CAMP LINCOLN EXCHANGE

1301 North MacArthur Blvd, Springfield, IL 62702 2317
C-217-524-1758, DSN-312-555-3500, Police-761-3511
WEB: www.il.ngb.army.mil
LOCATION: From the north, take I-55 to exit 100 (Sangamon Avenue) to a left on Fifth Street. Turn right on North Grand Avenue. Take a right onto MacArthur Blvd to the exchange. USMRA: IL map (D-6). NMC: Springfield, within city limits.
RETAIL & DINING: EX-524-1758

CAPITAL AIRPORT/AIR NATIONAL GUARD

183 Fighter Wing (ANG), 3101 J. David Jones Parkway
Springfield, IL 62707-8571
C-217-757-1200, DSN-312-892-8200, Police (Security)-757-1205
LOCATION: From I-55, exit to Sangamon Avenue, turn north on Fifth Street, approximately 0.5 miles and turn west on Browning Road. Turn right on David Jones Parkway. Follow signs to Air National Guard, which is on the west side. USMRA: IL map (D-6). NMC: Springfield, within city limits. NMI: Scott AFB, 90 miles south.
SUPPORT & FAMILY: Med-757-1221/2

GREAT LAKES NAVAL STATION

2601A Paul Jones Street, Great Lakes NTC, IL 60088-2834
C-847-688-3500, DSN-312-792-3500, Police-688-3430
WEB: www.nsgreatlakes.navy.mil
LOCATION: From I-94 north or US-41 north of Chicago, exit to IL-137 east to Sheridan Road north, turn right into the gate. Clearly marked. USMRA: IL map (G-1). NMC: Chicago, 30 miles south.
RECREATION & TRAVEL: Golf-688-4593 Marina-688-6978 RVC-688-5417 TML-688-2170/2241/3388
Navy Lodge-800-NAVY-INN or 689-1485
RETAIL & DINING: Cafeteria-578-6120 Clubs-CC-688-6946 EMC-688-4641 Com-688-2644 EX-578-6100 Gas-578-6247
SUPPORT & FAMILY: Med-688-4560
Ten-digit dialing required for local calls.

GREATER PEORIA REGIONAL AIRPORT/ AIR NATIONAL GUARD

182 Airlift Wing (ANG), 2416 South Falcon Blvd
Peoria, IL 61607-5004
C-309-633-5210, DSN-312-724-5210, Police (Security)-633-5221
WEB: www.ilpeor.ang.af.mil
LOCATION: From I-474 north or south, take exit 5 southwest to airport. Left on Airport Road to right on Smithville Road. Approximately three miles to base on right. USMRA: IL map (D-4). NMC: Peoria, seven miles northeast.
RECREATION & TRAVEL: SPA-633-5216

ROCK ISLAND ARSENAL

Attn: AMSTA-RI-CF, Rock Island, IL 61299-5001
C-309-782-6001, DSN-312-793-6001, Police-782-6116
WEB: www.ria.army.mil
LOCATION: From I-74 north in Moline, exit 2 to a right turn onto Seventh Avenue, then right onto 14th Street which turns into Rodman Avenue and follow signs to Arsenal Island, located in middle of Mississippi River. USMRA: IL map (C-3). NMC: Quad Cities of Rock Island, Moline, Davenport and Bettendorf.
RECREATION & TRAVEL: Golf-793-1601/4 TML-782-0833
RETAIL & DINING: Cafeteria-786-3445 or 793-0659 Clubs-CC-793-4337 Com-782-4614 Dining-793-4337 EX-788-4940
SUPPORT & FAMILY: Med-782-0804

SCOTT AIR FORCE BASE

101 Heritage Drive, Room 28
Scott Air Force Base, IL 62225-5001
C-618-256-1110, DSN-312-576-1110, Police-256-2223
WEB: http://public.scott.amc.af.mil/index.cfm
LOCATION: From I-64 east or west, take exit 19 east or 19A west to IL-158 south, two miles and watch for signs to AFB entry. USMRA: IL map (D-8). NMC: St. Louis, 25 miles west.
RECREATION & TRAVEL: Golf-256-2385 RVC-256-2067 SPA-256-2014/3017/4042 TML-256-1844
RETAIL & DINING: Cafeteria-256-4199 Clubs-EMC-256-1777 OC-256-1333 Com-256-2783 EX-744-9830 Gas-744-9253
SUPPORT & FAMILY: Med-256-9355

INDIANA, pg. 63
Indianapolis, pg. 66

CAMP ATTERBURY JOINT MANEUVER TRAINING CENTER

Headquarters, Camp Atterbury, P.O. Box 5000
Edinburgh, IN 46164-5000
C-812-526-1499, DSN-312-569-2499, Police-526-1109
WEB: www.campatterbury.org
LOCATION: From I-65 north or south, take exit 76 (US-31 north), left at stoplight onto IN-252 (Hospital Road), which turns into IN-800 and leads to the Main Gate. Enter post on Eggleston Street at Main Gate. USMRA: IN map (E-7). NMC: Indianapolis, 45 miles north.
RECREATION & TRAVEL: RVC-526-1128 TML-526-1128
RETAIL & DINING: Clubs-EMC/NCO-526-1141 OC-526-1143 Dining-526-1708 EX-526-1140

CRANE NAVAL SUPPORT ACTIVITY

Attn: N00164, 300 Highway 361, Crane, IN 47522-5001
C-812-854-2511, DSN-312-482-2511, Police-854-1640
WEB: www.crane.navy.mil
LOCATION: From Indianapolis, take I-465 south to IN-37 south to Bloomington, exit right on IN-45 and follow southwest. Base is approximately 2.5 miles from exit. USMRA: IN map (D-8). NMC: Bloomington, 30 miles northeast.
RECREATION & TRAVEL: Golf-854-0100 Marinas-854-1368 RVC-854-1368 TML-854-1176
RETAIL & DINING: Cafeteria-854-1519 Com-854-1297 Dining-Combined Mess-854-1501/3435 EX-854-0230 Gas-854-0234
SUPPORT & FAMILY: Med-854-1220

GRISSOM AIR RESERVE BASE

434 ARW/PA, Bldg 596, Room 200, Grissom ARB, IN 46971-5000
C-765-688-5211, DSN-312-928-2511, Police (Security)-688-2503
WEB: http://www.afrc.af.mil/434arw/
LOCATION: On US-31, 15 miles north of Kokomo and seven miles south of Peru. Turn at Grissom Aeroplex sign, proceed on Hoosier Blvd west of US-31 to Main Gate. USMRA: IN map (E-4). NMC: Indianapolis, 64 miles south.
RECREATION & TRAVEL: SPA-688-2861 TML-688-2844 or 689-8865
RETAIL & DINING: Dining-688-2414 EX-689-5270

HARRISON VILLAGE

Attn: ATZI-CDR, Indianapolis, IN 46249-5005
C-317-546-4856, Police-911
LOCATION: Take I-465 east to Fort Harrison exit 40, east on 56th Street, which leads to the fort; or, take IN-67/US-36 (Pendleton Pike) exit 42 to Post Road and north to Fort Harrison. USMRA: IN map (E-6). NMC: Indianapolis, within city limits.
RETAIL & DINING: Com-610-7210 EX-546-4856
NOTE: *Construction expected to begin soon on a new PX, scheduled for completion in 2007.*

STOUT FIELD JOINT FORCES HEADQUARTERS

2002 South Holt Road, Indianapolis, IN 46241-4839
C-317-247-3300, DSN-312-369-2300
WEB: www.inarng.org
LOCATION: From I-465 bypass northbound, exit 11 at Airport Expressway, east approximately two miles, north on Holt Road entrance. From I-70, exit on Holt Road south, approximately one mile to the entrance. USMRA: IN map (E-6). NMC: Indianapolis, within city limits.

MICHIGAN, pg. 64
Detroit, pg. 68

ALPENA COUNTY REGIONAL AIRPORT/ AIR NATIONAL GUARD COMBAT READINESS TRAINING CENTER

5884 A Street, Alpena, MI 49707-8125
C-989-354-6210, DSN-312-741-3210, Police-354-6210
WEB: www.micrtc.ang.af.mil
LOCATION: Five miles west of Alpena on MI-32, (north side of MI-32). From I-75, take exit 232 to MI-32. Continue on MI-32 until you reach the airport. USMRA: MI map (F-5). NMC: Alpena, five miles east.
RECREATION & TRAVEL: SPA-354-6226
RETAIL & DINING: EX-354-6272

CAMP GRAYLING/ARMY NATIONAL GUARD

Camp Grayling Maneuver Training Center Hq, Attn: Deputy Commander, Bldg 1117 Camp Grayling, MI 49739-0001
C-989-344-6100, DSN-312-623-3100, Fax: C-989-344-6110, Police (Security)-344-6147
WEB: www.campgrayling.com
LOCATION: Located three miles west of city of Grayling, just off I-75. Take Four Mile Road Exit, left over highway, west to Military Road, North to MI-93. Front (Main) Gate at the end of MI-93. USMRA: MI map (D-5,6). NMC: Grayling, three miles east.
RECREATION & TRAVEL: RVC-348-9033 TML-344-6208
RETAIL & DINING: Clubs-EMC/NCO-344-6244 OC-344-6246 Dining-344-6910 (Summer Only) EX-348-4781
SUPPORT & FAMILY: Med-344-6414
NOTE: *TML available for active duty only.*

DETROIT COAST GUARD GROUP

110 Mount Elliott Avenue, Detroit, MI 48207-4380
C-313-568-9525, Police-911
WEB: www.uscg.mil/d9/grudet
LOCATION: From I-94 east or west, take exit 217B to Edsel Ford Freeway. Make a right onto Mount Elliot Avenue. USMRA: Detroit, MI map (E-4). NMC: Detroit, within city limits. NMI: Selfridge ANGB, 20 miles north.
RETAIL & DINING: EX-259-6217
SUPPORT & FAMILY: Med-586-5017

GRAND HAVEN COAST GUARD GROUP

650 Harbor Drive, Grand Haven, MI 49417-1762
C-616-850-2500, Police-911
WEB: www.uscg.mil
LOCATION: From I-96 east, to US-31 south to Grand Haven, travel west on Jackson Street to the Group Office. From US-31 north, travel west on Franklin Street to Harbor Drive, turn left and follow the road to the Group Office. USMRA: MI map (B-8,9). NMC: Muskegon, 12 miles north.
RECREATION & TRAVEL: RVC-850-2510
RETAIL & DINING: EX-846-0490

POINT BETSIE RECREATION COTTAGE

Morale Officer, USCG Group, 650 Harbor Drive
Grand Haven, MI 49417-1262
C-616-850-2510, Police-911
LOCATION: Off base. About 150 miles north of Grand Rapids, take US-131 north to MI-115 west into Frankfort, go north on MI-22 for four miles to Point Betsie Road, cottage is at the end of Point Betsie Road. USMRA: MI map (B-5). NMC: Traverse City, 45 miles east. NMI: Traverse City CGAS, 45 miles east.
RECREATION & TRAVEL: RVC-850-2510 TML-850-2510
NOTE: *For detailed information about this off-base recreation facility, as well as on-base recreation facilities, golf courses and marinas, consult Military Living's "Military RV, Camping and Outdoor Recreation Around the World".*

SAULT STE. MARIE COAST GUARD GROUP/ MARINE SAFETY OFFICE

337 Water Street, Sault Ste. Marie, MI 49783-9501
C-906-635-3310, Police-911
WEB: www.uscg.mil/d9/sault/home.html
LOCATION: Take I-75 north to exit 392 (I-75 Business Spur). Turn right on Water Street; base is three blocks on left. USMRA: Mi map (E-2). NMC: Detroit, 350 miles south.
RETAIL & DINING: EX-635-3275
SUPPORT & FAMILY: Med-635-3320

SELFRIDGE AIR NATIONAL GUARD BASE

29553 George Avenue
Selfridge Air National Guard Base, MI 48045-4938
C-586-307-4011, DSN-312-273-4011, Police-307-4673
WEB: www.miself.ang.af.mil
LOCATION: Take I-94 north from Detroit to Selfridge exit 240-A, then east on M-59 to Main Gate of base. USMRA: MI map (G-9), Detroit, MI map (G-1). NMC: Detroit, 30 miles southwest.
RECREATION & TRAVEL: Golf-307-4653 Marina-307-5499 RVC-307-5499 SPA-307-5322 TML 307-4062
RETAIL & DINING: Clubs-Mulligans Golf and Dining-307-4344 Com-307-5570 EX-307-4614 Gas-307-4256
SUPPORT & FAMILY: Med-307-4022
NOTE: *The 2005 BRAC report recommended this base for closure. As required by Federal law, the DoD has until 15 September 2007 to begin closing and realigning the bases as called for in the approved report. This process must be completed by 15 September 2011.*

TRAVERSE CITY COAST GUARD AIR STATION

1175 Airport Access Road, Traverse City, MI 49650-3586
C-231-922-8300, Police-911
WEB: www.uscg.mil/d9/astc/astc.htm
LOCATION: From I-75, take exit 254 to I-75 Business/MI-72. Follow MI-72. Pick up US-31 north in Acme. From US-31 north, go south on Airport Access Road. Air Station will be on left. USMRA: MI map (C-5). NMC: Traverse City, within city limits.
RETAIL & DINING: Dining-922-8311 EX-922-8330
SUPPORT & FAMILY: Med-922-8282

W.K. KELLOGG AIRPORT/ AIR NATIONAL GUARD

110 Fighter Wing, 3545 Mustang Avenue
Battle Creek, MI 49015-5509
C-269-969-3400, DSN-312-580-3400, Police-969-3300
WEB: www.mibatt.ang.af.mil
LOCATION: From I-94 to Helmer Road (exit 95), exit north; dead end at Dickman Road, left 0.5 miles to gate. USMRA: MI map (D-10). NMC: Battle Creek, three miles northeast.
RETAIL & DINING: Clubs-CC-969-3374 EX-969-3372

OHIO, pg. 65
Cincinnati, pg. 65
Cleveland, pg. 65

CAMP PERRY TRAINING SITE

1000 Lawrence Road, Bldg 600, Port Clinton, OH, 43452-9578
C-614-336-6280, Police-911
WEB: www.cpmr-oh.org
LOCATION: On Lake Erie, just north of OH-2; six miles west of Port Clinton. USMRA: OH map (D-2). NMC: Toledo, 35 miles west. NMI: Selfridge AFB, MI, 65 miles northwest.
RECREATION & TRAVEL: TML-336-6214
RETAIL & DINING: EX-419-635-0101 (Seasonal)
Ten-digit dialing required for local calls with area code 419.

CAPTAIN OTTO GRAHAM COAST GUARD EXCHANGE

13920 West Parkway Road, Cleveland, OH 44135-4516
C-216-671-3500, Police-911
WEB: www.uscg.mil
LOCATION: From I-71 north or south, exit to 150th Street, then go one mile and turn left (west) on Puritas. At second light (0.5 mile) turn right, then take left at second driveway. USMRA: OH map (F-2). NMC: Cleveland, within city limits.
RETAIL & DINING: EX-671-3500

CLEVELAND COAST GUARD MARINE SAFETY OFFICE

1055 East Ninth Street, Cleveland, OH 44114-1092
C-216-937-0111, Emergency-937-0111 or 911
WEB: http://www.uscg.mil/d9/wwm/mso/cleveland/
LOCATION: Take I-71 north or I-90 east to OH-2 west. Exit at East Ninth Street and travel north toward Lake Erie on East Ninth Street. From I-77 north also, exit onto East Ninth Street. USMRA: OH map (B-10, F-2). NMC: Cleveland, within city limits.
RETAIL & DINING: Clubs-CG-687-1755 EX-671-3267/3500
SUPPORT & FAMILY: Med-363-2353
NOTE: *The Exchange is about a ten-minute drive from CGMSO at 13920 West Parkway Drive, C-216-671-3267/3500.*

COLUMBUS DEFENSE SUPPLY CENTER

P.O. Box 3990, Columbus, OH 43218-3990
C-614-692-3131, DSN-312-850-3131, Police-692-2111
e-mail: publicaffairs.dscc@dla.mil
WEB: www.dscc.dla.mil
LOCATION: From the East, take I-270 to exit 39 (Broad Street), Ohio Rt. 16, west to 3990 E. Broad St. From the east, take I-70 to I-670 East, to Stelzer Road exit; after Stelzer changes to James Road, turn left at Broad Street and end at 3990 E. Broad St. USMRA: OH map (D-5). NMC: Columbus, adjacent. NMI: 73 miles southwest.
RECREATION & TRAVEL: Golf-692-2075 TML-692-4758
RETAIL & DINING: Clubs-CC-231-0976 EMC/NCO/OC-239-0482 Dining-692-8736 EX-231-0976
SUPPORT & FAMILY: Med-692-2227

MANSFIELD LAHM AIRPORT/ AIR NATIONAL GUARD

179 Airlift Wing, 1947 Harrington Memorial Road
Mansfield, OH 44903-0179
C-419-520-6100, DSN-312-696-6100, Police (Security)-520-2260
WEB: www.ohionationalguard.com
LOCATION: From I-71 south or north, take US-30 west to OH-13 north, to Harrington Memorial Road for one mile. Turn left (west) on Harrington Memorial Parkway and left onto Harrington Memorial road to airport. USMRA: OH map (D,E-3,4). NMC: Mansfield, three miles south.
RECREATION & TRAVEL: SPA-520-6488
Ten digit dialing required for local calls.

RICKENBACKER INTERNATIONAL AIRPORT/ AIR NATIONAL GUARD BASE

7370 Minuteman Way, Columbus, OH 43217-1161
C-614-492-4223/4468, DSN-312-696-4223, Police-492-4321
WEB: www.ohcolu.ang.af.mil
LOCATION: From I-270 south, take Alum Creek Road exit 49 south to Rickenbacker IAP. Also accessible off US-23 south onto OH-317 east. Clearly marked. USMRA: OH map (D-6). NMC: Columbus, 13 miles northwest. NMI: Wright-Patterson AFB, 73 miles west.
RECREATION & TRAVEL: SPA-492-3143 TML-409-2660 SATO-492-3128 or 800-827-7777
RETAIL & DINING: Dining-492-3542 EX-491-4493/8424

TOLEDO COAST GUARD STATION

Bay View Park, 3900 North Summit Street
Toledo, OH , 43611-3070
C-419-729-2020/2034, Police-911
WEB: www.uscg.mil
LOCATION: From I-75 north or south, exit 209 and go east on Ottawa River Road, turn right on Summit Street, turn left on Bayview Park to Coast Guard Station. USMRA: OH map (C-2). NMC: Toledo, within city limits. NMI: Selfridge AFB, MI, 50 miles.

RETAIL & DINING: EX-729-5911
Ten-digit dialing required for local calls.

WRIGHT-PATTERSON AIR FORCE BASE

Public Affairs, 88th Air Base Wing Wright-Patterson, AFB, 5215 Thurlow Street, Wright-Patterson Air Force Base, OH 45433-1960 **C-937-257-1110,** DSN-312-787-1110, Police-257-6516
WEB: http://ascpa.public.wpafb.af.mil
LOCATION: South of I-70, off I-675 at Fairborn. From I-675, exit 18 to OH-844 into the AFB. Also accessible from OH-4 north or south. AFB clearly marked. USMRA: OH map (B-6). NMC: Dayton, ten miles southwest.
RECREATION & TRAVEL: Golf-257-4130/7961 RVC-257-2579 SPA-257-7741 TML-257 3451/3810 or 879-5921 or 888-AF-LODGE
RETAIL & DINING: Clubs-CC-257-9762 Com-257-7420 Dining-257-7151 EX-879-5730 Gas-252-8934 or 878-7260
SUPPORT & FAMILY: Med-257-2969

YOUNGSTOWN-WARREN REGIONAL AIRPORT/ AIR RESERVE STATION

Attn: 910 AW/PA, 3976 King Graves Road, Unit 12
Vienna, OH 44473-5912
C-330-609-1000 or 800-278-7046 (press 2, then 1000)
DSN-312-346-1000, Police-609-1277
WEB: http://www.afrc.af.mil/910aw/
LOCATION: From OH-11 north or south, exit to King Graves Road and turn right. Air Reserve Station is 0.5 miles on the right. Base is clearly marked. USMRA: OH map (H-2). NMC: Youngstown, three miles south.
RECREATION & TRAVEL: TML-609-1268
RETAIL & DINING: Clubs-CC-609-1295/1423 EX-609-1395
SUPPORT & FAMILY: Med-609-1233
Ten-digit dialing required for local calls.

WISCONSIN, pg. 66
Milwaukee, pg. 66

DANE COUNTY REGIONAL AIRPORT/ TRUAX FIELD/AIR NATIONAL GUARD

115 Fighter Wing~3110 Mitchell Street, Bldg 500
Madison, WI 53704-2591
C-608-245-4300, DSN-312-724-8300, Police-245-4560
e-mail: pa@wimadi.ang.af.mil
WEB: http://www.wimadi.ang.af.mil
LOCATION: From I-90/94, take exit 135 South on US-151 for 1.5 miles. Go north on Hwy 51 for 0.5 miles. Take a left onto Anderson Street, a right onto Wright Street and a left onto Mitchell Street. USMRA: WI map (E-10). NMC: Madison, within city limits.
RETAIL & DINING: Clubs-CC-249-6201 EX-249-5229
SUPPORT & FAMILY: Med-245-4567

FORT MCCOY

Attn: AFRC-FM-CO, 100 East Headquarters Road
Fort McCoy, WI 54656-5263
C-608-388-2222, DSN-312-280-1110, Police-388-2266
WEB: www.mccoy.army.mil
LOCATION: From I-90/94, exit 143 west to WI-21 west to fort. Main Gate is on north side of WI-21. USMRA: WI map (C-8). NMC: La Crosse, 35 miles west.
RECREATION & TRAVEL: RVC-388-3517 SPA-388-5641 TML-388-2107
RETAIL & DINING: Cafeteria-269-4865 Clubs-CC-388-2065 Com-388-3542 Dining-388-4182 EX-388-4134 Gas-269-5364
SUPPORT & FAMILY: Med-388-3128
NOTE: *Visitors must stop at Main Gate to obtain a pass.*

GENERAL MITCHELL INTERNATIONAL AIRPORT/AIR RESERVE STATION

300 East College Avenue, Milwaukee, WI 53207-6299
C-414-482-5000 or 877-412-0126 (AFRC), DSN-741-5000
e-mail: 440aw.pa@generalmitchell.af.mil, Police-482-5375
WEB: www.afrc.af.mil/440aw/Homepage.htm
LOCATION: From I-94/43 north or south, take exit 318 east to WI-119 east and to the airport. Right onto Howell Avenue. Left on College Avenue to base entrance. USMRA: WI map (G-3; G-10). NMC: Milwaukee, within city limits.
RECREATION & TRAVEL: SPA-944-8732
RETAIL & DINING: Clubs-CC-482-5711 Dining-482-5701 EX-744-8028
SUPPORT & FAMILY: Med-482-6009
NOTE: *Main Gate is closed for approximately six months. Enter through the West Gate, located on Howell Avenue. The 2005 BRAC report recommended this base for closure. As required by Federal law, the DoD has until 15 September 2007 to begin closing and realigning the bases as called for in the approved report. This process must be completed by 15 September 2011.*

MILWAUKEE COAST GUARD GROUP

2420 South Lincoln Memorial Drive, Milwaukee, WI 53207-1997
C-414-747-7100, C-747-7100 or 911
WEB: www.uscg.mil/d9/grumil/
LOCATION: Take I-94 north or south to Milwaukee to exit 310, east on I-794. Proceed over Hoan Bridge on I-794, take left at stop sign and travel for a quarter mile to the office. USMRA: WI map (G-2; G-10). NMC: Milwaukee, three miles north. NMI: Great Lakes Naval Training Station, 60 miles south.
RECREATION & TRAVEL: RVC-747-7185
RETAIL & DINING: Dining-747-7118 EX-747-1466
SUPPORT & FAMILY: Med-747-7111
NOTE: *Gate is not manned due to automated gate. Military personnel can call from the box and request entry. Base OOD will meet person to verify.*

MILWAUKEE POST EXCHANGE

4828 West Silver Spring Drive, Bldg 304
Milwaukee, WI 53218-3440
C-414-438-6219, Police-911
LOCATION: From I-43, exit 78 west on Silver Spring Drive, proceed approximately five miles to exchange. USMRA: WI map (G-2; G-10). NMC: Milwaukee, within city limits.
RETAIL & DINING: EX-438-6219

RAWLEY POINT COTTAGE

Commander, Group Milwaukee USCG
2420 South Lincoln Memorial Drive. Milwaukee, WI 53207-1997
C-414-747-7100, Emergency-911
LOCATION: Off base. From I-43 north or south near Two Rivers, take exit 52, north on WI-42 into the city. Right on 17th Street, cross drawbridge, right on East Street, four blocks to Two Rivers CG Station at 13 East Street. Cottage is located five miles north of CG Station. Directions to cottage will be sent when reservations are made. USMRA: Wi map (G-8). NMC: Manitowoc, ten miles south.
RECREATION & TRAVEL: RVC-747-7185
NOTE: *For detailed information about this off-base recreation facility, as well as on-base recreation facilities, golf courses and marinas, consult Military Living's "Military RV, Camping and Outdoor Recreation Around the World".*

SHERWOOD POINT COTTAGE

Coast Guard Group Morale Fund
2420 South Lincoln Memorial Drive, Milwaukee, WI 53207-1997
C-414-747-7185, Emergency-911
LOCATION: Off base. Take I-43 to exit 185 onto WI-54/WI-57 north to Sturgeon Bay. Continue on WI-57 north to a left turn onto Duluth Street, then a left onto CR-C. Make a right onto CR-M, a right towards Potawatomi State Park. Turn left just before a log cabin tavern. This is the access road to the Coast Guard lighthouse. Approximately nine miles from Elm and CR-M. USMRA: WI map (H-7). NMC: Green Bay, 45 miles southwest. NMI: Fort McCoy, 190 miles southwest.
RECREATION & TRAVEL: RVC-747-7185
NOTE: *For detailed information about this off-base recreation facility, as well as on-base recreation facilities, golf courses and marinas, consult Military Living's "Military RV, Camping and Outdoor Recreation Around the World".*

VOLK FIELD AIR NATIONAL GUARD

Camp Douglas, WI 54618-5001
C-608-427-1210, DSN-312-871-1210, Police-427-1236
WEB: www.volkfield.ang.af.mil
LOCATION: From Madison, take I-90/94 west, 85 miles to Camp Douglas exit northeast. From Lacrosse, take I-90 east to I-94 east to Camp Douglas exit (55 miles). USMRA: WI map (D-8,9). NMC: La Crosse, 55 miles west. NMI: Fort McCoy, 25 miles northwest.
RECREATION & TRAVEL: SPA-427-1205
RETAIL & DINING: Clubs-CC-427-1276 EX-427-1274

TRAVEL ON LESS PER DAY... THE MILITARY WAY™

AND $AVE AT EVERY MILITARY INSTALLATION ENROUTE!

*Q103Z

*K705Y Paper

*T618A Plastic

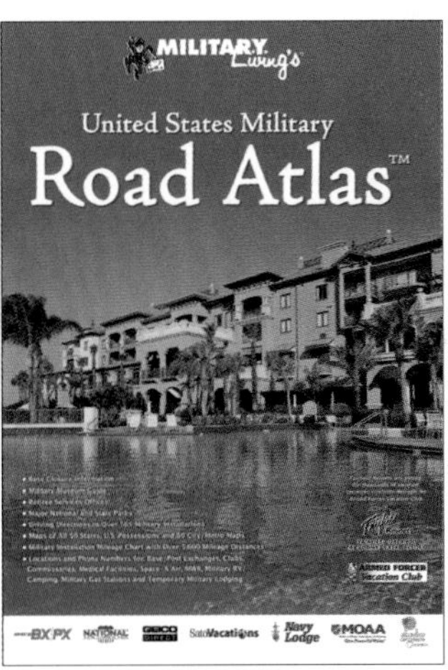

*I830P

New Edition Coming 2006 Call for Item #

*T517P

New Edition Coming 2006 Call for Item #

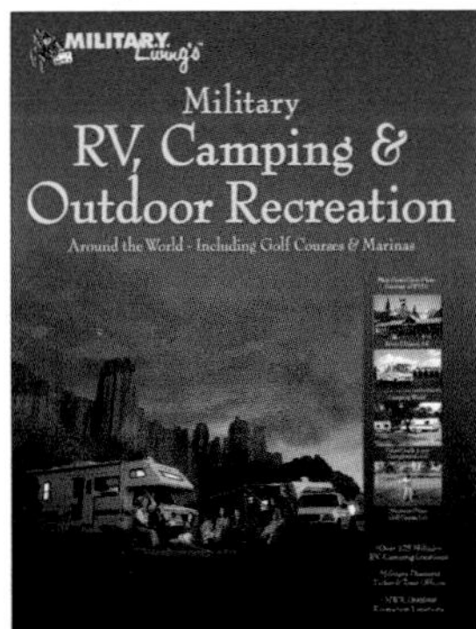

*T060F

MILITARY PUBLICATIONS Living™

AVAILABLE AT YOUR LOCAL EXCHANGE
WWW.AAFES.COM OR BY CALLING AAFES AT

When ordering, provide the item number (*) shown above.

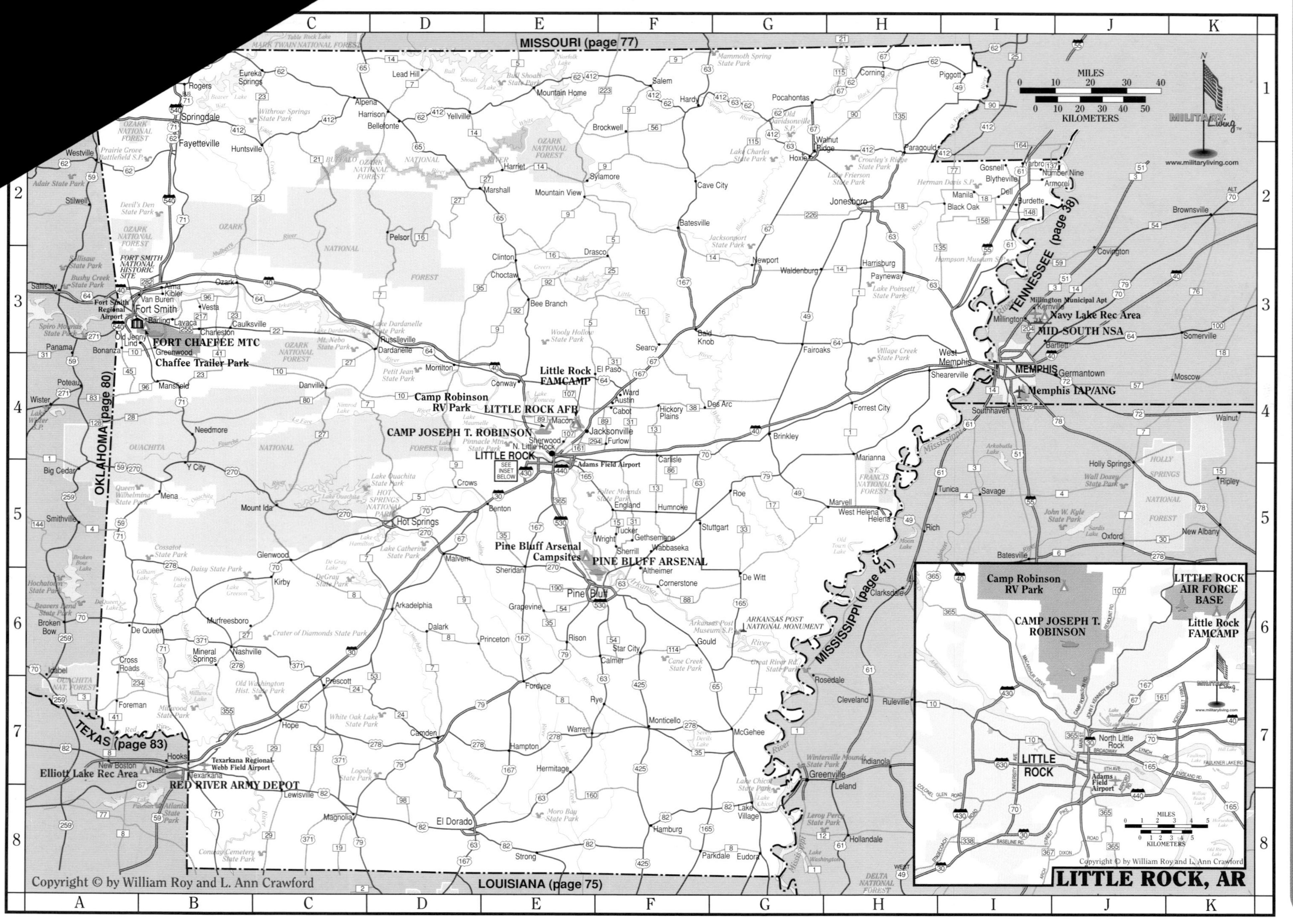

MISSOURI (page 77)
TENNESSEE (page 38)
MISSISSIPPI (page 41)
LOUISIANA (page 75)
TEXAS (page 83)
OKLAHOMA (page 80)
MILES
KILOMETERS
www.militaryliving.com
MEMPHIS
Millington Municipal Apt
Navy Lake Rec Area
MID SOUTH NSA
Memphis IAP/ANG
LITTLE ROCK
SEE INSET BELOW
Little Rock FAMCAMP
LITTLE ROCK AFB
Camp Robinson RV Park
CAMP JOSEPH T. ROBINSON
Adams Field Airport
PINE BLUFF ARSENAL
Pine Bluff Arsenal Campsites
FORT CHAFFEE MTC
Chaffee Trailer Park
Fort Smith Regional Airport
RED RIVER ARMY DEPOT
Texarkana Regional-Webb Field Airport
Elliott Lake Rec Area
LITTLE ROCK AIR FORCE BASE
LITTLE ROCK, AR
Copyright © by William Roy and L. Ann Crawford

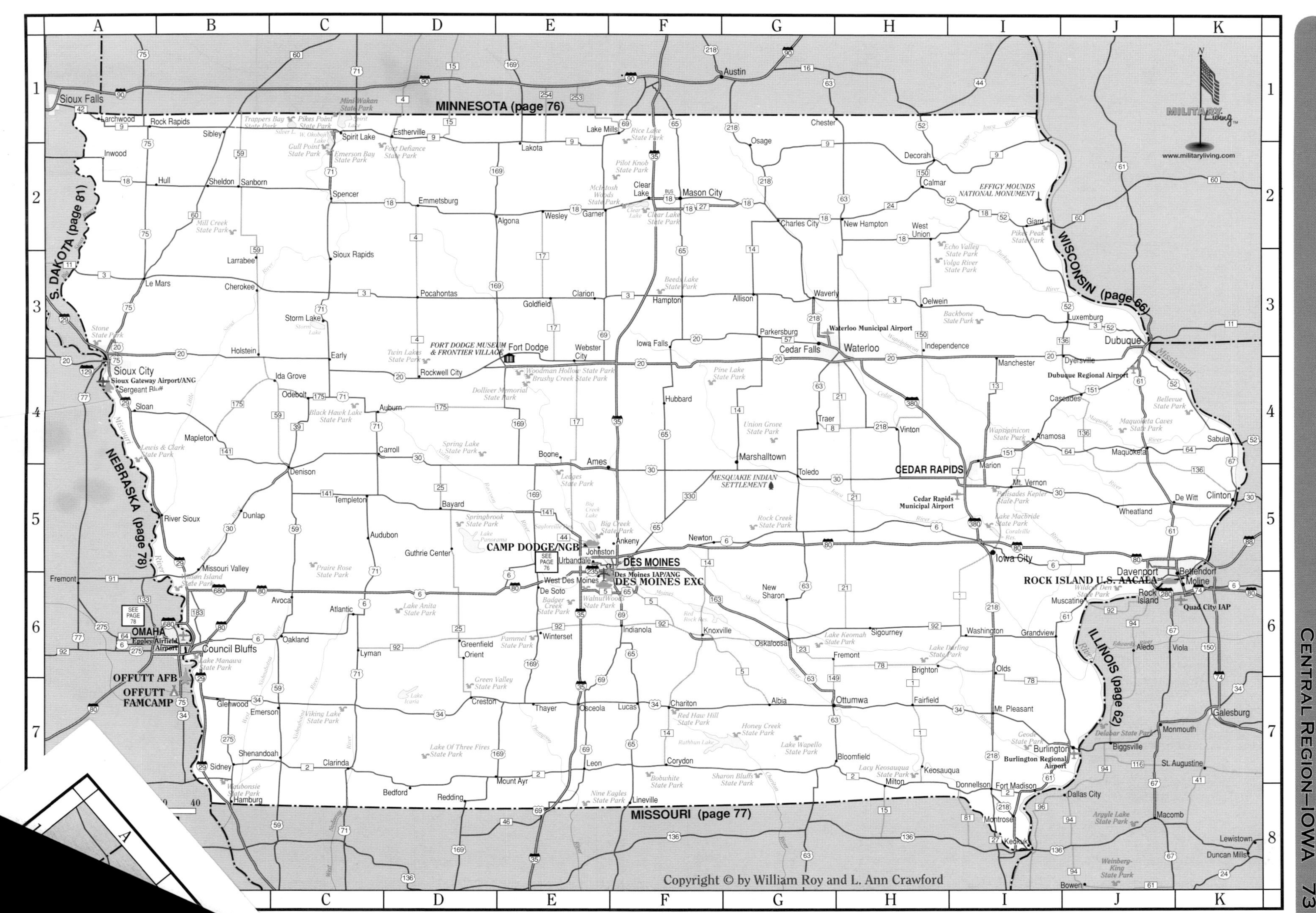
MINNESOTA (page 76)
WISCONSIN (page 66)
ILLINOIS (page 62)
MISSOURI (page 77)
NEBRASKA (page 78)
S. DAKOTA (page 81)
www.militaryliving.com
DES MOINES
Des Moines IAP/ANG
DES MOINES EXC
CAMP DODGE/NGB
SEE PAGE 76
CEDAR RAPIDS
Cedar Rapids Municipal Airport
ROCK ISLAND U.S. AACALA
Quad City IAP
OFFUTT AFB
OFFUTT FAMCAMP
OMAHA
Eppley Airfield Airport
SEE PAGE 78
Sioux City
Sioux Gateway Airport/ANG
Waterloo Municipal Airport
Dubuque Regional Airport
Burlington Regional Airport
FORT DODGE MUSEUM & FRONTIER VILLAGE
EFFIGY MOUNDS NATIONAL MONUMENT
MESQUAKIE INDIAN SETTLEMENT
Iowa City
Davenport
Council Bluffs
Ames
Mason City
Cedar Falls
Waterloo
Dubuque
Clinton
Burlington
Ottumwa
Fort Dodge
Marshalltown
Copyright © by William Roy and L. Ann Crawford

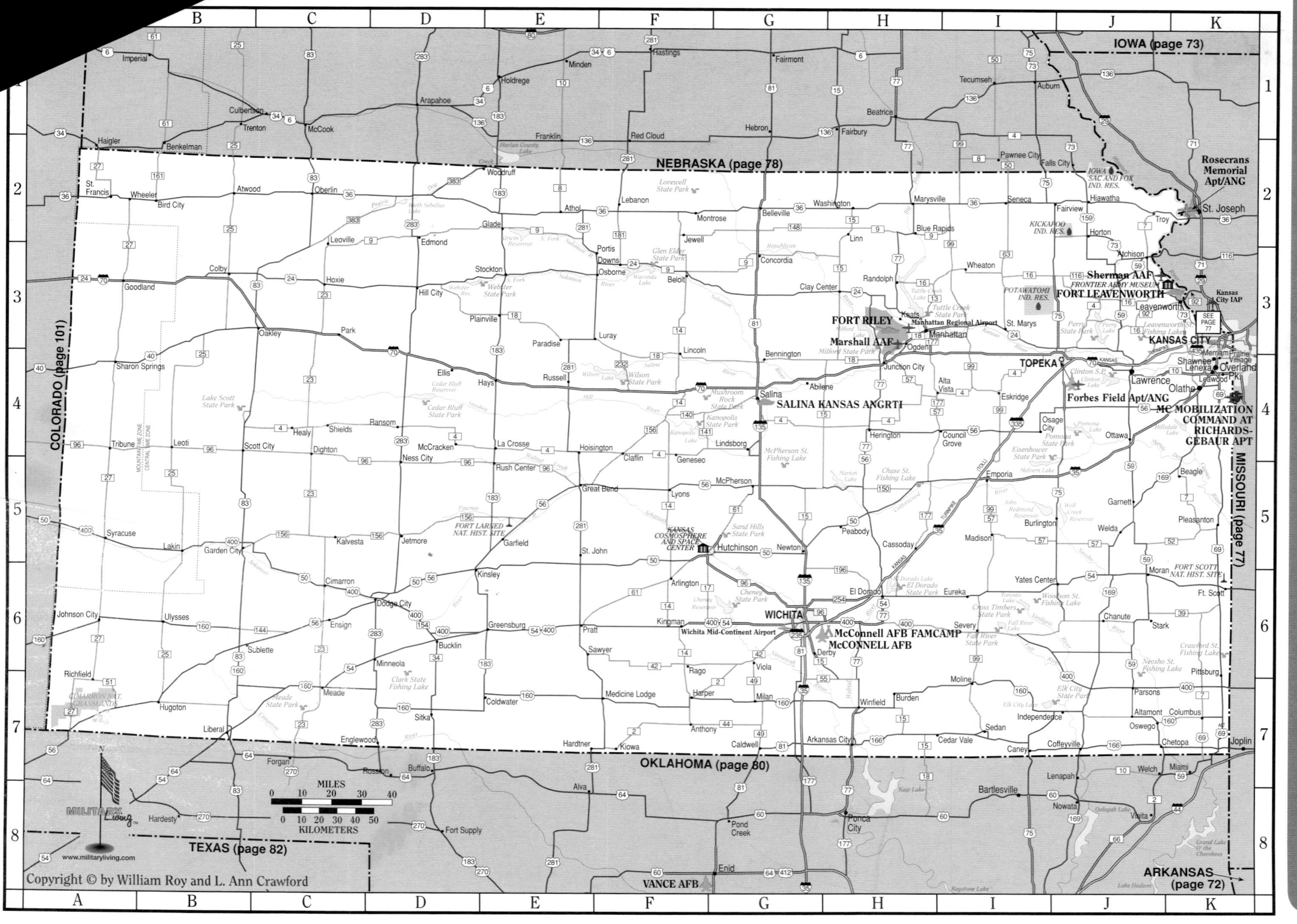

MISSOURI (page 77)
IOWA (page 73)
NEBRASKA (page 78)
COLORADO (page 101)
OKLAHOMA (page 80)
TEXAS (page 82)
ARKANSAS (page 72)
Rosecrans Memorial Apt/ANG
St. Joseph
Kansas City IAP
SEE PAGE 77
KANSAS CITY
MC MOBILIZATION COMMAND AT RICHARDS-GEBAUR APT
Sherman AAF
FRONTIER ARMY MUSEUM
FORT LEAVENWORTH
Leavenworth
Lawrence
Olathe
Forbes Field Apt/ANG
TOPEKA
Manhattan Regional Airport
Manhattan
FORT RILEY
Marshall AAF
Junction City
SALINA KANSAS ANGRTI
Salina
Abilene
Emporia
Hutchinson
WICHITA
McConnell AFB FAMCAMP
McCONNELL AFB
Wichita Mid-Continent Airport
El Dorado
Newton
McPherson
Great Bend
Hays
Russell
Dodge City
Garden City
Liberal
Goodland
Colby
Oakley
Pittsburg
Parsons
Chanute
Coffeyville
Independence
Arkansas City
Winfield
Pratt
Kingman
Medicine Lodge
FORT LARNED NAT. HIST. SITE
FORT SCOTT NAT. HIST. SITE
KANSAS COSMOSPHERE AND SPACE CENTER
POTAWATOMI IND. RES.
KICKAPOO IND. RES.
IOWA SAC AND FOX IND. RES.
VANCE AFB
Enid
Ponca City
Bartlesville
MOUNTAIN TIME ZONE
CENTRAL TIME ZONE
MILES
KILOMETERS
www.militaryliving.com
Copyright © by William Roy and L. Ann Crawford

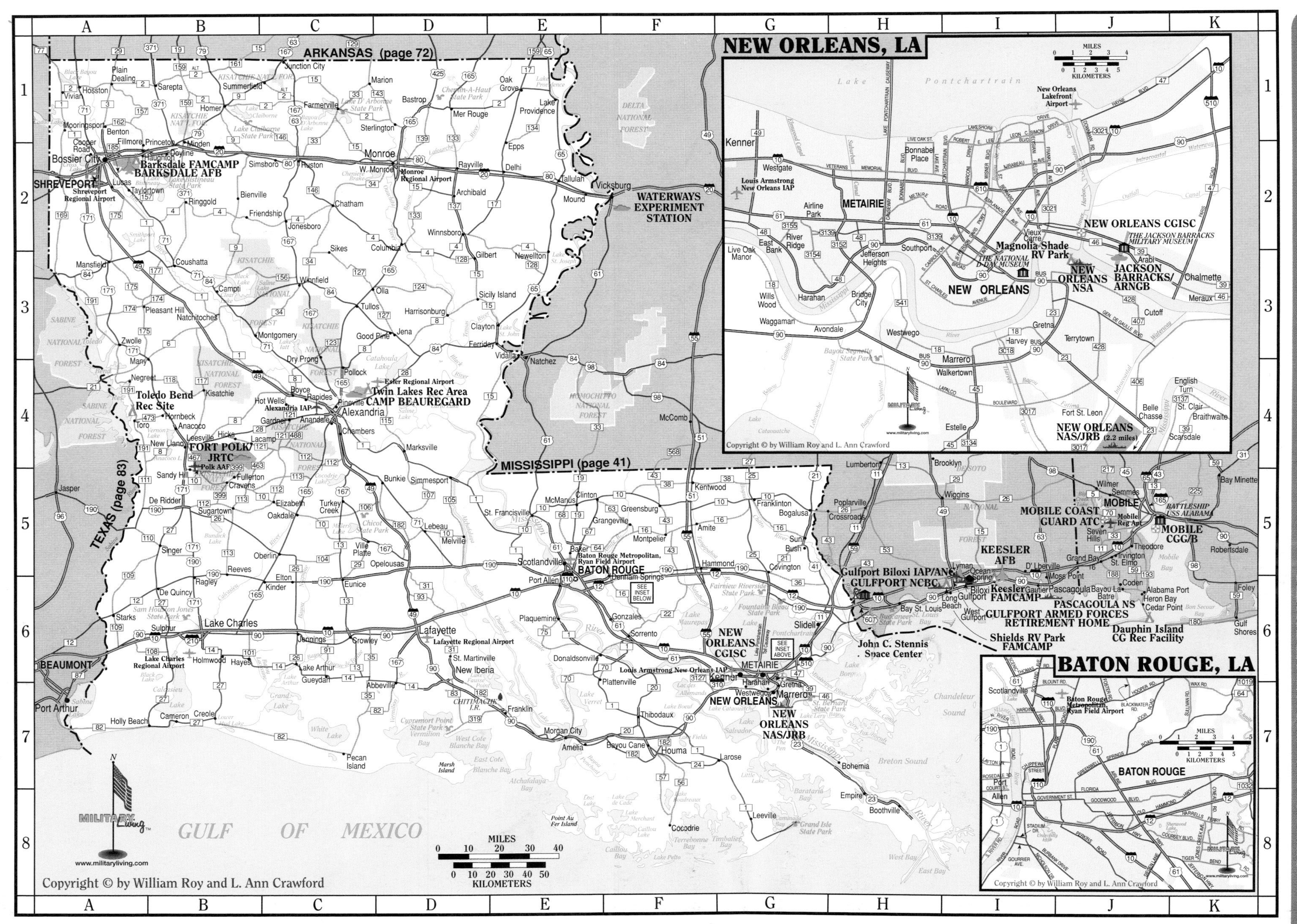
NEW ORLEANS, LA
BATON ROUGE, LA
ARKANSAS (page 72)
MISSISSIPPI (page 41)
TEXAS (page 83)
GULF OF MEXICO
Barksdale FAMCAMP
BARKSDALE AFB
FORT POLK/JRTC
CAMP BEAUREGARD
Twin Lakes Rec Area
Toledo Bend Rec Site
WATERWAYS EXPERIMENT STATION
NEW ORLEANS CGISC
NEW ORLEANS NAS/JRB
JACKSON BARRACKS/ARNGB
NEW ORLEANS NSA
Magnolia Shade RV Park
KEESLER AFB
Keesler FAMCAMP
Gulfport Biloxi IAP/ANG
GULFPORT NCBC
GULFPORT ARMED FORCES RETIREMENT HOME
PASCAGOULA NS
Shields RV Park FAMCAMP
Dauphin Island CG Rec Facility
MOBILE COAST GUARD ATC
MOBILE CGG/B
John C. Stennis Space Center
MILES
KILOMETERS
www.militaryliving.com
Copyright © by William Roy and L. Ann Crawford

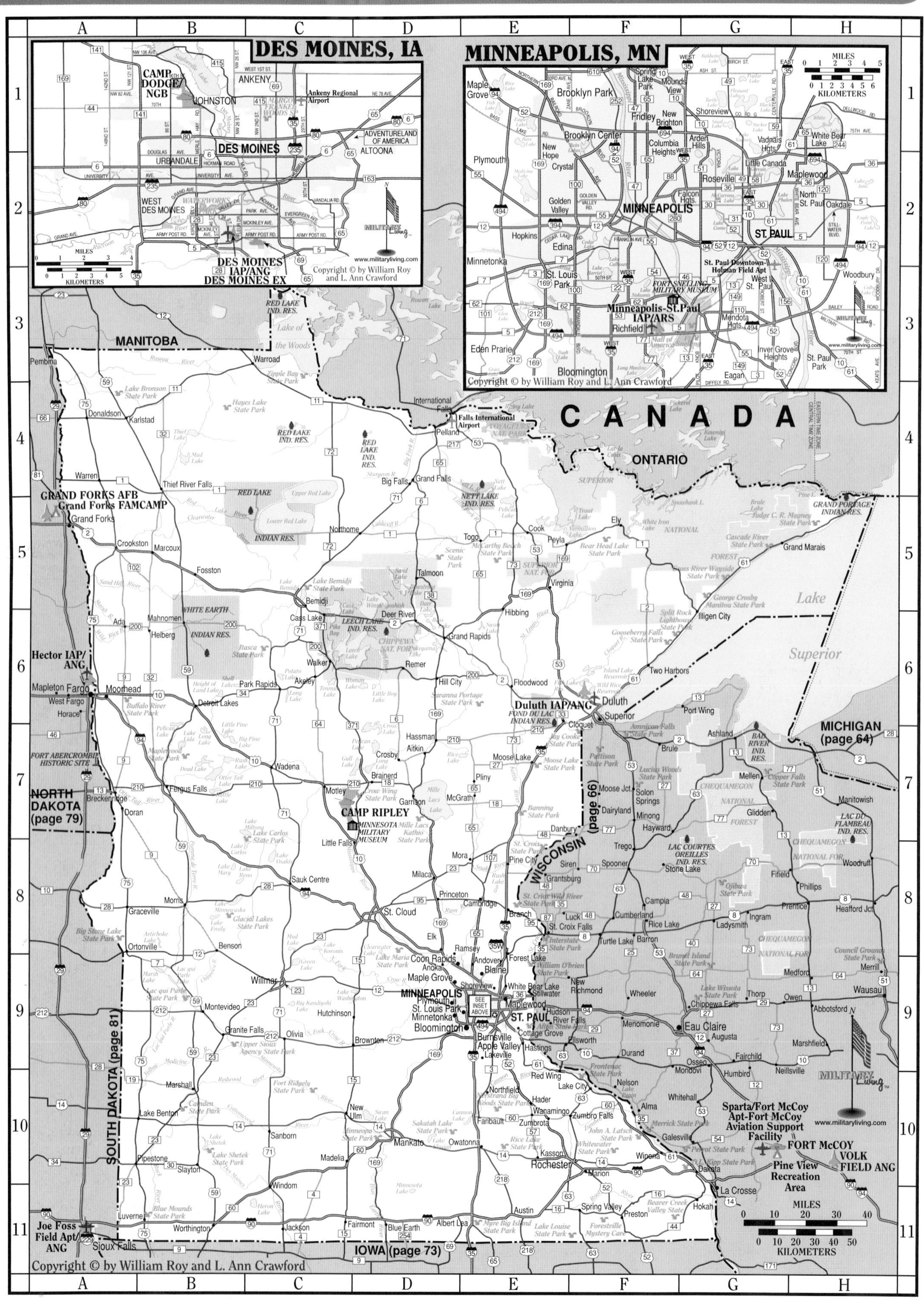

DES MOINES, IA
MINNEAPOLIS, MN
CAMP DODGE/ NGB
JOHNSTON
ANKENY
Ankeny Regional Airport
DES MOINES
URBANDALE
WEST DES MOINES
ALTOONA
ADVENTURELAND OF AMERICA
DES MOINES IAP/ANG
DES MOINES EX
Copyright © by William Roy and L. Ann Crawford
www.militaryliving.com
Brooklyn Park
Maple Grove
Fridley
New Brighton
Brooklyn Center
Shoreview
White Bear Lake
Vadnais Hgts
Plymouth
New Hope
Crystal
Columbia Heights
Arden Hills
Little Canada
Maplewood
Roseville
Golden Valley
MINNEAPOLIS
Falcon Hgts.
North St. Paul
Oakdale
Hopkins
Edina
ST. PAUL
Minnetonka
St. Louis Park
St. Paul Downtown-Holman Field Apt
West St. Paul
Woodbury
FORT SNELLING MILITARY MUSEUM
Minneapolis-St.Paul IAP/ARS
Richfield
Mendota Hgts.
Eden Prarie
Bloomington
Inver Grove Heights
St. Paul Park
Eagan
Copyright © by William Roy and L. Ann Crawford
MANITOBA
CANADA
ONTARIO
RED LAKE IND. RES.
Lake of the Woods
Warroad
International Falls
Falls International Airport
Pembina
Donaldson
Karlstad
Warren
Thief River Falls
GRAND FORKS AFB
Grand Forks FAMCAMP
Grand Forks
Crookston
Marcoux
Fosston
Big Falls
Grand Falls
Northome
Togo
Cook
Ely
Grand Marais
GRAND PORTAGE INDIAN RES.
Bemidji
Cass Lake
Deer River
Grand Rapids
Hibbing
Virginia
Illigen City
Two Harbors
Lake Superior
Ada
Mahnomen
Helberg
WHITE EARTH INDIAN RES.
LEECH LAKE IND. RES.
Hector IAP/ ANG
Mapleton Fargo
Moorhead
West Fargo
Horace
Detroit Lakes
Park Rapids
Walker
Akeley
Remer
Hill City
Floodwood
Duluth IAP/ANG
Duluth
Superior
Cloquet
FOND DU LAC INDIAN RES.
Port Wing
Ashland
MICHIGAN (page 64)
Hassman
Aitkin
Crosby
Brainerd
Wadena
Fergus Falls
Breckenridge
Doran
NORTH DAKOTA (page 79)
FORT ABERCROMBIE HISTORIC SITE
Moose Lake
Pliny
McGrath
Motley
CAMP RIPLEY
MINNESOTA MILITARY MUSEUM
Garrison
Little Falls
Moose Jct.
Solon Springs
Dairyland
Minong
Hayward
Mellen
Manitowish
Glidden
Danbury
WISCONSIN (page 66)
Mora
Pine City
Siren
Grantsburg
Spooner
Trego
Stone Lake
LAC COURTES OREILLES IND. RES.
Fifield
Phillips
Woodruff
Sauk Centre
Milaca
Princeton
Cambridge
Morris
Graceville
St. Cloud
Elk
Branch
Luck
St. Croix Falls
Cumberland
Rice Lake
Ladysmith
Ingram
Prentice
Heafford Jct
Ortonville
Benson
Ramsey
Coon Rapids
Anoka
Andover
Blaine
Forest Lake
Turtle Lake
Barron
Medford
Merrill
Willmar
Maple Grove
Shoreview
White Bear Lake
Stillwater
New Richmond
Wheeler
Chippewa Falls
Thorp
Owen
Wausau
Abbotsford
Montevideo
MINNEAPOLIS
Plymouth
St. Louis Park
Minnetonka
Bloomington
Maplewood
ST. PAUL
Hudson
River Falls
Menomonie
Eau Claire
Augusta
Hutchinson
Granite Falls
Olivia
Brownton
Burnsville
Apple Valley
Lakeville
Cottage Grove
Hastings
Ellsworth
Durand
Mondovi
Osseo
Fairchild
Neillsville
Marshfield
Marshall
Northfield
Red Wing
Lake City
Nelson
Alma
Humbird
Whitehall
SOUTH DAKOTA (page 81)
Lake Benton
Sanborn
New Ulm
Faribault
Hader
Wanamingo
Zumbro Falls
Zumbrota
Galesville
Sparta/Fort McCoy Apt-Fort McCoy Aviation Support Facility
FORT McCOY
VOLK FIELD ANG
Pipestone
Slayton
Madelia
Mankato
Owatonna
Kasson
Rochester
Winona
Marion
Dakota
Pine View Recreation Area
La Crosse
Windom
Austin
Spring Valley
Preston
Hokah
Luverne
Joe Foss Field Apt/ ANG
Sioux Falls
Worthington
Jackson
Fairmont
Blue Earth
Albert Lea
IOWA (page 73)
Copyright © by William Roy and L. Ann Crawford

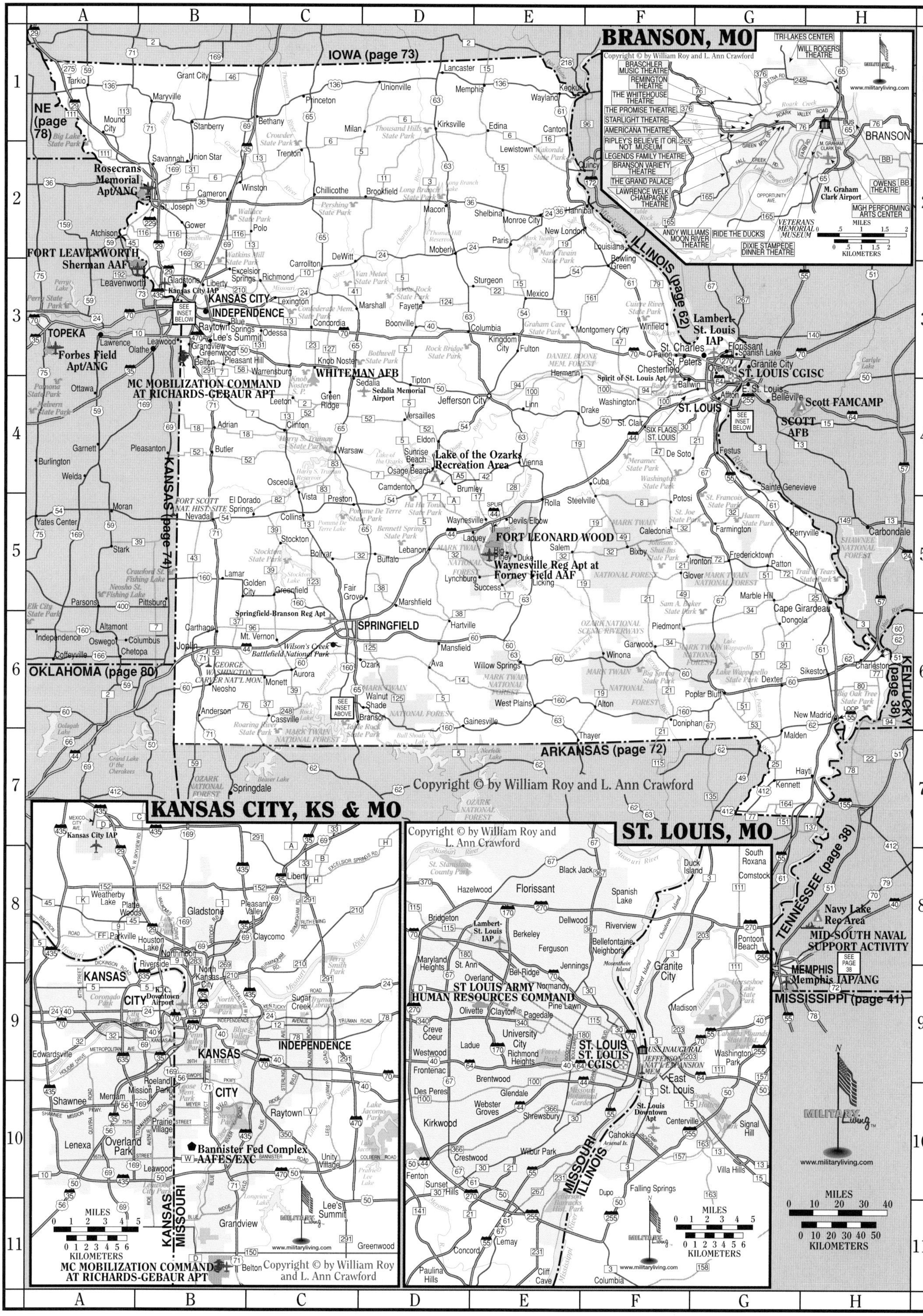

A B C D E F G H

1 2 3 4 5 6 7 8 9 10 11

IOWA (page 73)

NE (page 78)

Tarkio, Mound City, Maryville, Grant City, Stanberry, Bethany, Princeton, Unionville, Lancaster, Memphis, Kirksville, Edina, Wayland, Keokuk, Canton, Lewistown, Milan, Thousand Hills State Park, Crowder State Park, Trenton, Savannah, Union Star, Big Lake State Park

Rosecrans Memorial Apt/ANG

St. Joseph, Cameron, Winston, Chillicothe, Brookfield, Long Branch State Park, Macon, Shelbina, Monroe City, Hannibal, Quincy, Wallace State Park, Pershing State Park, Polo, Gower, Atchison

FORT LEAVENWORTH Sherman AAF

Leavenworth, Watkins Mill State Park, Excelsior Springs, Richmond, Carrollton, DeWitt, Thomas Hill Reservoir, Moberly, Paris, Mark Twain Lake, New London, Louisiana, Bowling Green, Mark Twain State Park, Gladstone, Liberty, Kansas City IAP

KANSAS CITY

INDEPENDENCE

Lexington, Van Meter State Park, Arrow Rock State Park, Marshall, Fayette, Sturgeon, Mexico, Cuivre River State Park, Winfield, Lambert-St. Louis IAP, Florissant, Spanish Lake

TOPEKA

Forbes Field Apt/ANG

Lawrence, Olathe, Leawood, Raytown, Blue Springs, Lee's Summit, Odessa, Concordia, Confederate Mem. State Park, Boonville, Columbia, Kingdom City, Fulton, Graham Cave State Park, Montgomery City, O'Fallon, St. Charles, St. Peters, Chesterfield, Granite City, Grandview, Greenwood, Belton, Pleasant Hill, Warrensburg, Knob Noster, Bothwell State Park, Rock Bridge State Park, Daniel Boone Mem. Forest, Hermann, Spirit of St. Louis Apt, Overland, Ballwin, Affton

WHITEMAN AFB

MC MOBILIZATION COMMAND AT RICHARDS-GEBAUR APT

ST. LOUIS CGISC

Ottawa, Pomona State Park, Melvern State Park, Sedalia, Sedalia Memorial Airport, Tipton, Green Ridge, Leeton, Jefferson City, Linn, Drake, Washington, St. Clair, E. St. Louis, Belleville, Scott FAMCAMP

ST. LOUIS

SCOTT AFB

Garnett, Pleasanton, Adrian, Butler, Clinton, Versailles, Eldon, Harry S. Truman State Park, Warsaw, Sunrise Beach, Osage Beach, Six Flags St. Louis, De Soto, Festus, Burlington, Welda

Lake of the Ozarks Recreation Area

Meramec State Park, Washington State Park, Vienna, Cuba, Osceola, Camdenton, Brumley, Sainte Genevieve, Ha Ha Tonka State Park, Rolla, Steelville, Potosi, St. Francois State Park, Moran, Fort Scott Nat. Hist. Site, El Dorado Springs, Nevada, Preston, Pomme De Terre State Park, Collins, Vista, Stockton, Bennett Spring State Park, Waynesville, Devils Elbow, Mark Twain, St. Joe State Park, Caledonia, Farmington, Hawn State Park, Perryville, Carbondale, Yates Center

KANSAS (page 74)

FORT LEONARD WOOD

Waynesville Reg Apt at Forney Field AAF

Laquey, Big Piney, Duke, Lynchburg, Success, Licking, Salem, Bixby, Johnson's Shut-Ins State Park, Ironton, Fredericktown, Patton, Trail of Tears State Park, Glover, Mark Twain National Forest, Shawnee National Forest, Stark, Stockton State Park, Bolivar, Buffalo, Lebanon, Lamar, Golden City, Greenfield, Fair Grove, Marshfield, Crawford St. Fishing Lake, Neosho St. Fishing Lake, Parsons, Pittsburg, Elk City State Park, Sam A. Baker State Park, Marble Hill, Cape Girardeau, Dongola

Springfield-Branson Reg Apt

SPRINGFIELD

Carthage, Mt. Vernon, Hartville, Piedmont, Ozark National Scenic Riverways, Altamont, Oswego, Columbus, Chetopa, Independence, Coffeyville, Joplin, Wilson's Creek Battlefield National Park, Mansfield, Garwood, Winona, Lake Wappapello, George Washington Carver Nat'l Mon., Aurora, Ozark, Ava, Willow Springs, Wappapello State Park, Sikeston, Charleston, Neosho, Monett, Poplar Bluff, Dexter, Big Oak Tree State Park, Big Spring State Park

OKLAHOMA (page 80)

KENTUCKY (page 38)

Anderson, Cassville, Table Rock Lake, Walnut Shade, Branson, Table Rock State Park, Roaring River State Park, Gainesville, West Plains, Alton, Doniphan, Thayer, New Madrid, Malden, Oologah Lake, Grand Lake O' the Cherokees, Bull Shoals Lake, Norfolk Lake

SEE INSET BELOW

SEE INSET ABOVE

ARKANSAS (page 72)

Ozark National Forest, Springdale, Beaver Lake, Hayti, Kennett

Copyright © by William Roy and L. Ann Crawford

BRANSON, MO

Copyright © by William Roy and L. Ann Crawford

TRI-LAKES CENTER, WILL ROGERS THEATRE, BRASCHLER MUSIC THEATRE, REMINGTON THEATRE, THE WHITEHOUSE THEATRE, THE PROMISE THEATRE, STARLIGHT THEATRE, AMERICANA THEATRE, RIPLEY'S BELIEVE IT OR NOT MUSEUM, LEGENDS FAMILY THEATRE, BRANSON VARIETY THEATRE, THE GRAND PALACE, LAWRENCE WELK CHAMPAGNE THEATRE, ANDY WILLIAMS MOON RIVER THEATRE, RIDE THE DUCKS, VETERANS MEMORIAL MUSEUM, DIXIE STAMPEDE DINNER THEATRE, OWENS THEATRE, MGH PERFORMING ARTS CENTER

BRANSON

M. Graham Clark Airport

Roark Creek, Roark Valley Road, Gretna Rd, Green Mtn. Dr., Fall Creek Rd., Opportunity Ave., Lake Taneycomo

MILES 0 .5 1 1.5 2

KILOMETERS 0 .5 1 1.5 2

www.militaryliving.com

ILLINOIS (page 62)

KANSAS CITY, KS & MO

Kansas City IAP, Mexico City Ave., Weatherby Lake, Platte Woods, Parkville, Houston Lake, Northmoor, Riverside, Gladstone, Pleasant Valley, Liberty, Claycomo, North Kansas City, K.C. Downtown Airport, Sugar Creek, Truman Library

KANSAS CITY

INDEPENDENCE

Edwardsville, Shawnee, Merriam, Mission, Roeland Park, Prairie Village, Overland Park, Lenexa, Leawood, Raytown, Unity Village, Lake Jacomo, Lee's Summit, Grandview, Greenwood, Belton

Bannister Fed Complex AAFES/EXC

MC MOBILIZATION COMMAND AT RICHARDS-GEBAUR APT

KANSAS / MISSOURI

MILES 0 1 2 3 4 5

KILOMETERS 0 1 2 3 4 5 6

www.militaryliving.com

Copyright © by William Roy and L. Ann Crawford

ST. LOUIS, MO

Copyright © by William Roy and L. Ann Crawford

St. Stanislaus County Park, Black Jack, Duck Island, South Roxana, Comstock, Hazelwood, Florissant, Spanish Lake, Bridgeton, Lambert-St. Louis IAP, Berkeley, Dellwood, Riverview, Bellefontaine Neighbors, Ferguson, Jennings, Pontoon Beach, Maryland Heights, St. Ann, Overland, Bel-Ridge, Normandy, Granite City, Madison

ST LOUIS ARMY HUMAN RESOURCES COMMAND

Olivette, Clayton, Pagedale, Pine Lawn, Creve Coeur, Ladue, University City, Richmond Heights, Westwood, Frontenac, Des Peres, Brentwood, Glendale, Webster Groves, Shrewsbury, Kirkwood, Crestwood, Fenton, Sunset Hills, Concord, Lemay, Paulina Hills, Cliff Cave, Columbia, Falling Springs, Dupo, Cahokia, Centerville, East St. Louis, Washington Park, Signal Hill, Villa Hills

ST. LOUIS CGISC

USS Inaugural, Jefferson Nat'l Expansion Mem., St. Louis Downtown Apt

MISSOURI / ILLINOIS

MILES 0 1 2 3 4 5

KILOMETERS 0 1 2 3 4 5 6

www.militaryliving.com

TENNESSEE (page 38)

Navy Lake Rec Area

MID-SOUTH NAVAL SUPPORT ACTIVITY

MEMPHIS

Memphis IAP/ANG

SEE PAGE 38

MISSISSIPPI (page 41)

www.militaryliving.com

MILES 0 10 20 30 40

KILOMETERS 0 10 20 30 40 50

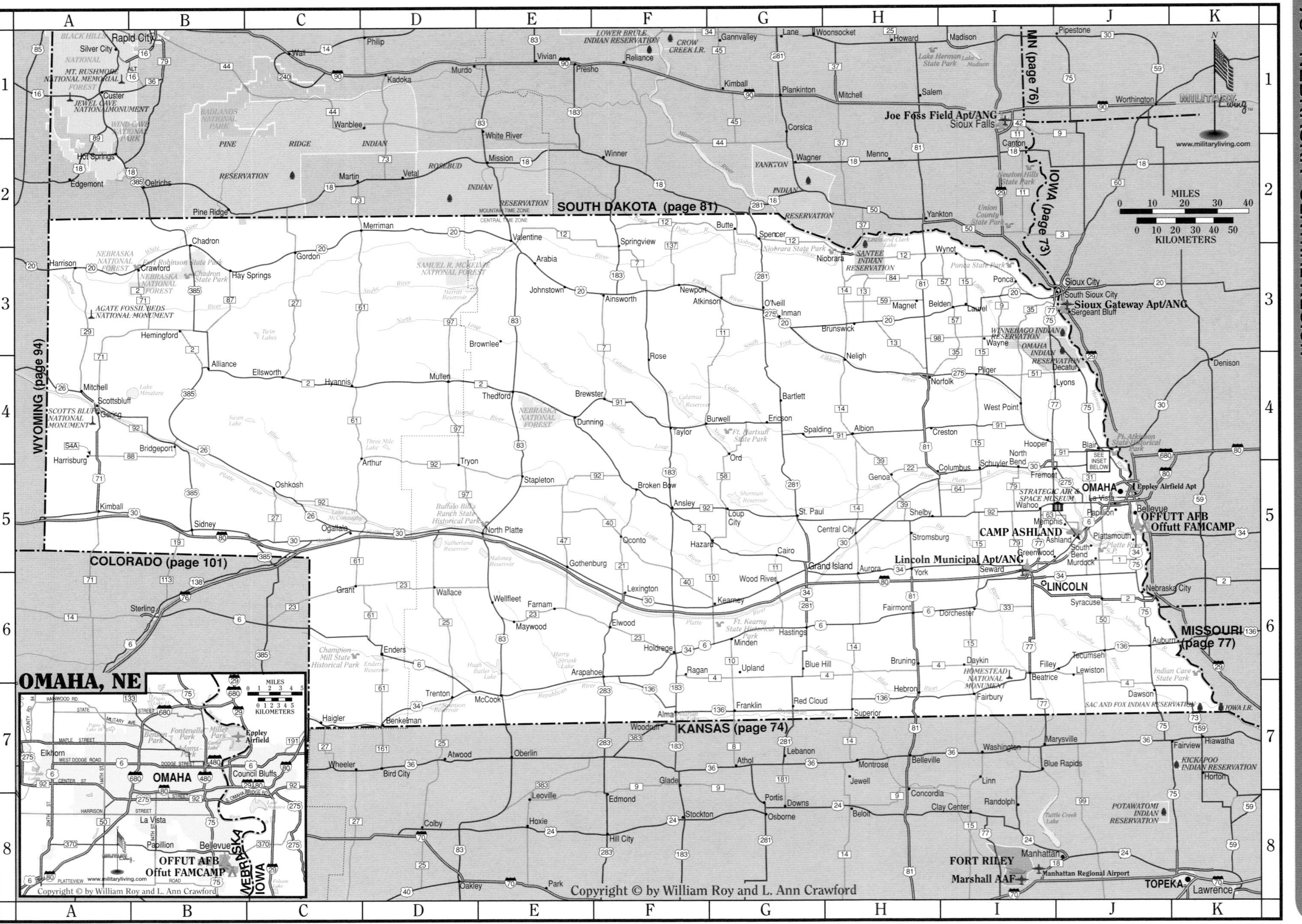

MILES
KILOMETERS
www.militaryliving.com
MN (page 76)
IOWA (page 73)
SOUTH DAKOTA (page 81)
MISSOURI (page 77)
KANSAS (page 74)
COLORADO (page 101)
WYOMING (page 94)
Joe Foss Field Apt/ANG
Sioux Falls
Sioux Gateway Apt/ANG
Sioux City
OMAHA
OFFUTT AFB
Offutt FAMCAMP
Eppley Airfield Apt
CAMP ASHLAND
LINCOLN
Lincoln Municipal Apt/ANG
STRATEGIC AIR & SPACE MUSEUM
FORT RILEY
Marshall AAF
Manhattan Regional Airport
TOPEKA
Valentine
North Platte
Grand Island
Kearney
Scottsbluff
Norfolk
Columbus
Hastings
McCook
Rapid City
OMAHA, NE
Council Bluffs
Bellevue
La Vista
Papillion
NEBRASKA
IOWA
Copyright © by William Roy and L. Ann Crawford

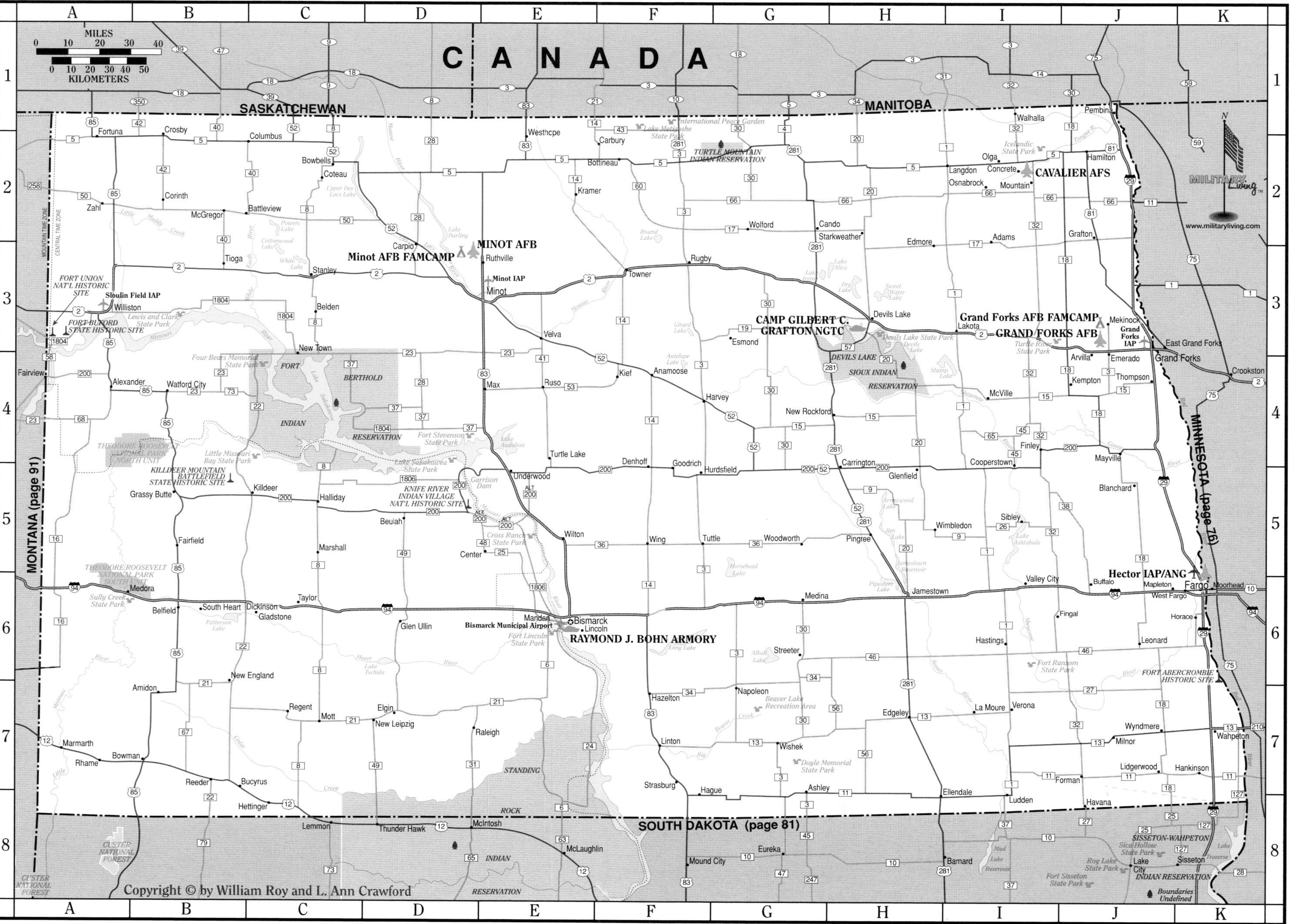

CANADA
SASKATCHEWAN
MANITOBA
MINNESOTA (page 76)
SOUTH DAKOTA (page 81)
MONTANA (page 91)
MILES
KILOMETERS
www.militaryliving.com
CAVALIER AFS
Grand Forks AFB FAMCAMP
GRAND FORKS AFB
Grand Forks IAP
CAMP GILBERT C. GRAFTON NGTC
MINOT AFB
Minot AFB FAMCAMP
Minot IAP
Hector IAP/ANG
RAYMOND J. BOHN ARMORY
Bismarck Municipal Airport
Sloulin Field IAP
TURTLE MOUNTAIN INDIAN RESERVATION
DEVILS LAKE SIOUX INDIAN RESERVATION
FORT BERTHOLD INDIAN RESERVATION
STANDING ROCK INDIAN RESERVATION
SISSETON-WAHPETON INDIAN RESERVATION
FORT UNION NAT'L HISTORIC SITE
FORT BUFORD STATE HISTORIC SITE
KNIFE RIVER INDIAN VILLAGE NAT'L HISTORIC SITE
KILLDEER MOUNTAIN BATTLEFIELD STATE HISTORIC SITE
FORT ABERCROMBIE HISTORIC SITE
THEODORE ROOSEVELT NATIONAL PARK SOUTH UNIT
THEODORE ROOSEVELT NATIONAL PARK NORTH UNIT
CUSTER NATIONAL FOREST
CENTRAL TIME ZONE
MOUNTAIN TIME ZONE
Pembina
Grand Forks
East Grand Forks
Crookston
Fargo
Moorhead
West Fargo
Jamestown
Valley City
Devils Lake
Minot
Bismarck
Mandan
Lincoln
Williston
Dickinson
Wahpeton
Langdon
Rugby
Carrington
Bottineau
Medora
Copyright © by William Roy and L. Ann Crawford

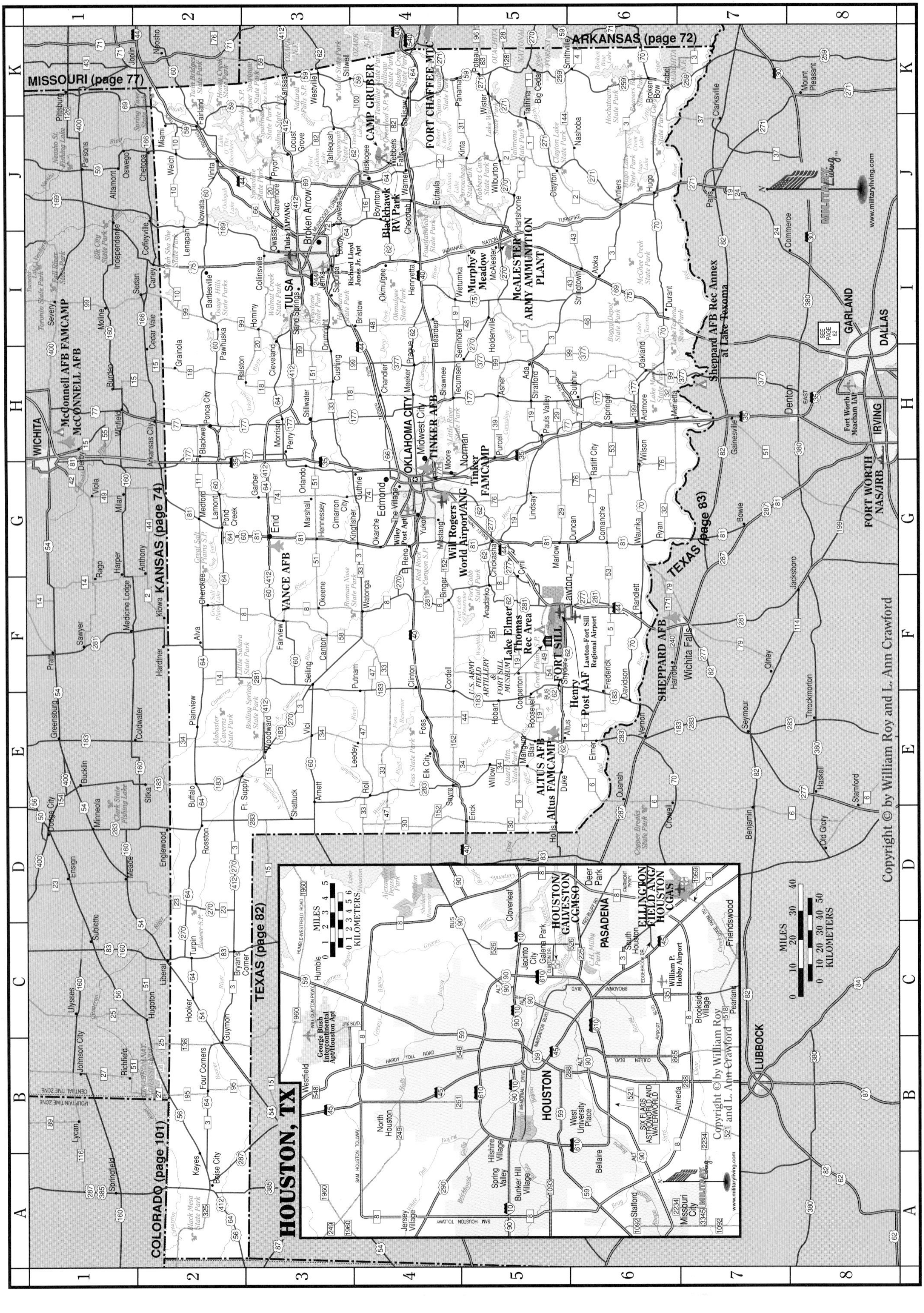

HOUSTON, TX

MISSOURI (page 77)

ARKANSAS (page 72)

KANSAS (page 74)

COLORADO (page 101)

TEXAS (page 82)

TEXAS (page 83)

www.militaryliving.com

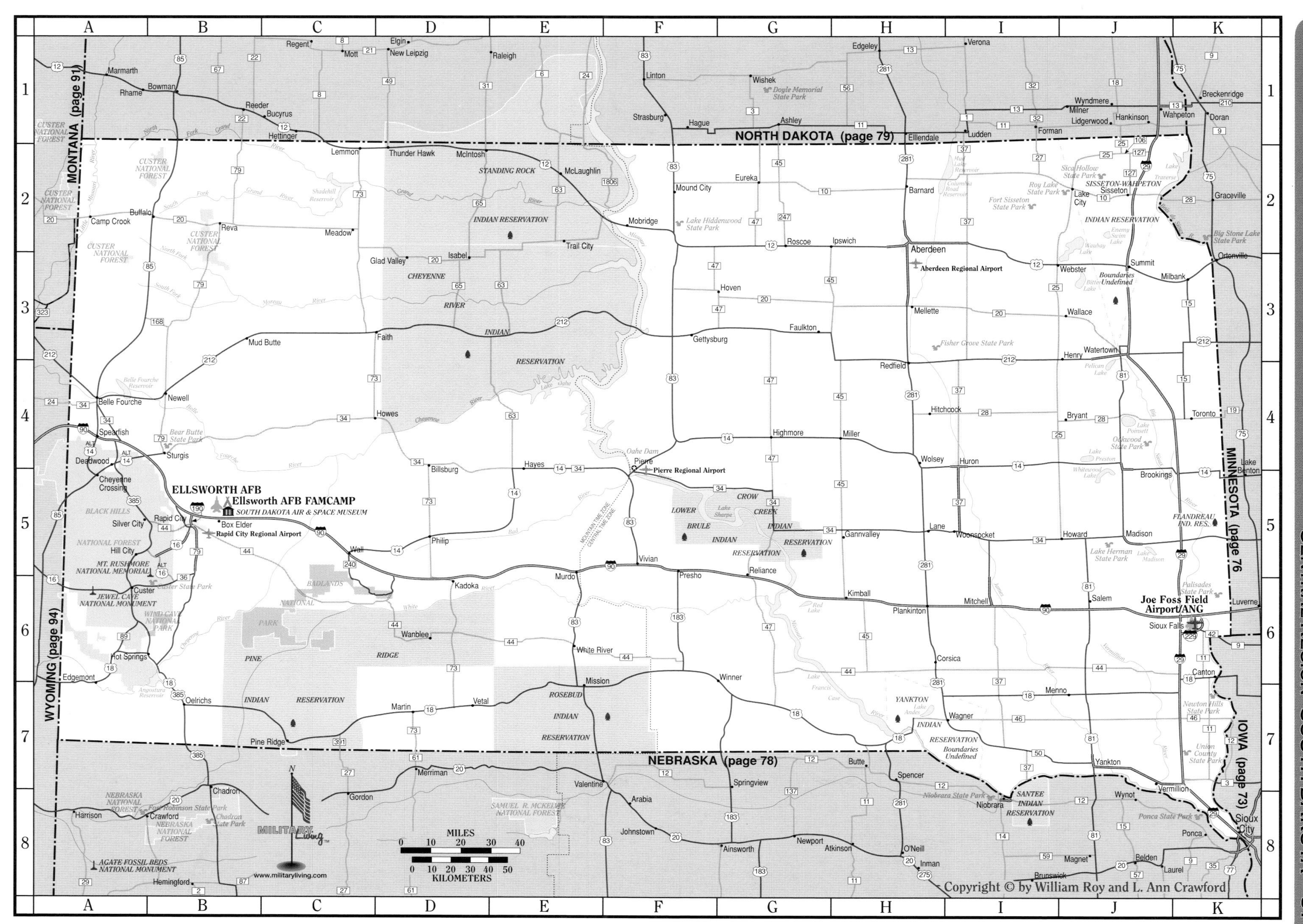
NORTH DAKOTA (page 79)
MINNESOTA (page 76)
IOWA (page 73)
NEBRASKA (page 78)
WYOMING (page 94)
MONTANA (page 91)
ELLSWORTH AFB
Ellsworth AFB FAMCAMP
SOUTH DAKOTA AIR & SPACE MUSEUM
Rapid City Regional Airport
Pierre Regional Airport
Aberdeen Regional Airport
Joe Foss Field Airport/ANG
Sioux Falls
Pierre
Aberdeen
Rapid City
Watertown
Brookings
Mitchell
Huron
Yankton
Mobridge
Sturgis
Spearfish
Deadwood
Box Elder
STANDING ROCK INDIAN RESERVATION
CHEYENNE RIVER INDIAN RESERVATION
CROW CREEK INDIAN RESERVATION
LOWER BRULE INDIAN RESERVATION
ROSEBUD INDIAN RESERVATION
PINE RIDGE INDIAN RESERVATION
YANKTON INDIAN RESERVATION
BADLANDS NATIONAL PARK
BLACK HILLS NATIONAL FOREST
MT. RUSHMORE NATIONAL MEMORIAL
JEWEL CAVE NATIONAL MONUMENT
WIND CAVE NATIONAL PARK
CUSTER NATIONAL FOREST
MILES
KILOMETERS
MILITARY Living
www.militaryliving.com
Copyright © by William Roy and L. Ann Crawford

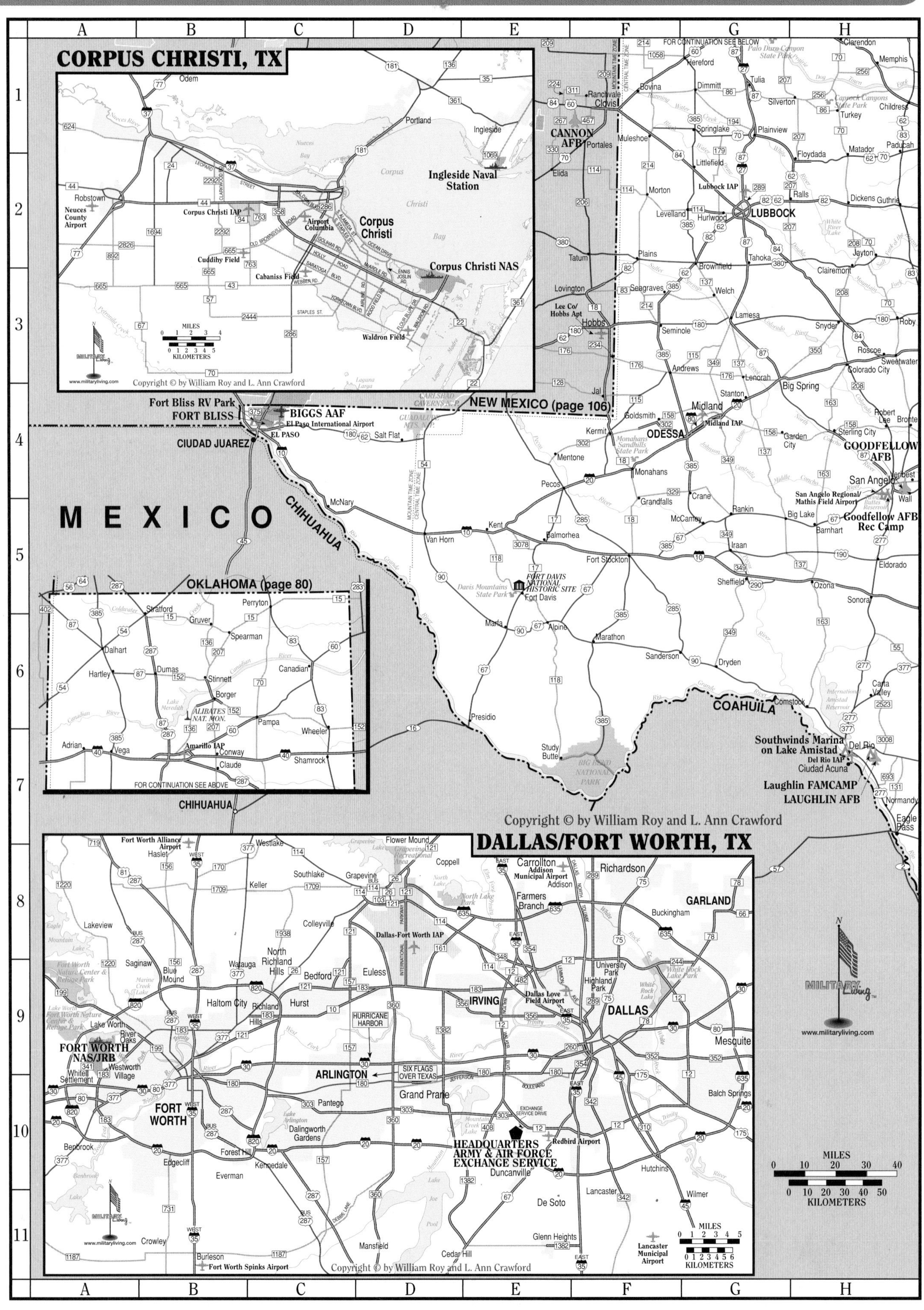
CORPUS CHRISTI, TX
Ingleside Naval Station
Corpus Christi
Corpus Christi IAP
Corpus Christi NAS
Cuddihy Field
Cabaniss Field
Waldron Field
Neuces County Airport
Robstown
Portland
Ingleside
Odem
Copyright © by William Roy and L. Ann Crawford
Fort Bliss RV Park
FORT BLISS
BIGGS AAF
El Paso International Airport
EL PASO
CIUDAD JUAREZ
NEW MEXICO (page 106)
CANNON AFB
Clovis
Portales
Lubbock IAP
LUBBOCK
Lee Co/ Hobbs Apt
Hobbs
Midland
Midland IAP
ODESSA
GOODFELLOW AFB
San Angelo
San Angelo Regional/ Mathis Field Airport
Goodfellow AFB Rec Camp
MEXICO
CHIHUAHUA
COAHUILA
FORT DAVIS NATIONAL HISTORIC SITE
BIG BEND NATIONAL PARK
Southwinds Marina on Lake Amistad
Del Rio
Del Rio IAP
Ciudad Acuna
Laughlin FAMCAMP
LAUGHLIN AFB
Eagle Pass
OKLAHOMA (page 80)
Amarillo IAP
ALIBATES NAT. MON.
FOR CONTINUATION SEE ABOVE
FOR CONTINUATION SEE BELOW
Copyright © by William Roy and L. Ann Crawford
DALLAS/FORT WORTH, TX
Fort Worth Alliance Airport
Dallas-Fort Worth IAP
Addison Municipal Airport
Dallas Love Field Airport
FORT WORTH NAS/JRB
FORT WORTH
ARLINGTON
IRVING
DALLAS
GARLAND
Mesquite
HURRICANE HARBOR
SIX FLAGS OVER TEXAS
HEADQUARTERS ARMY & AIR FORCE EXCHANGE SERVICE
Redbird Airport
Lancaster Municipal Airport
Fort Worth Spinks Airport
Copyright © by William Roy and L. Ann Crawford
www.militaryliving.com
MILES 0 10 20 30 40
KILOMETERS 0 10 20 30 40 50

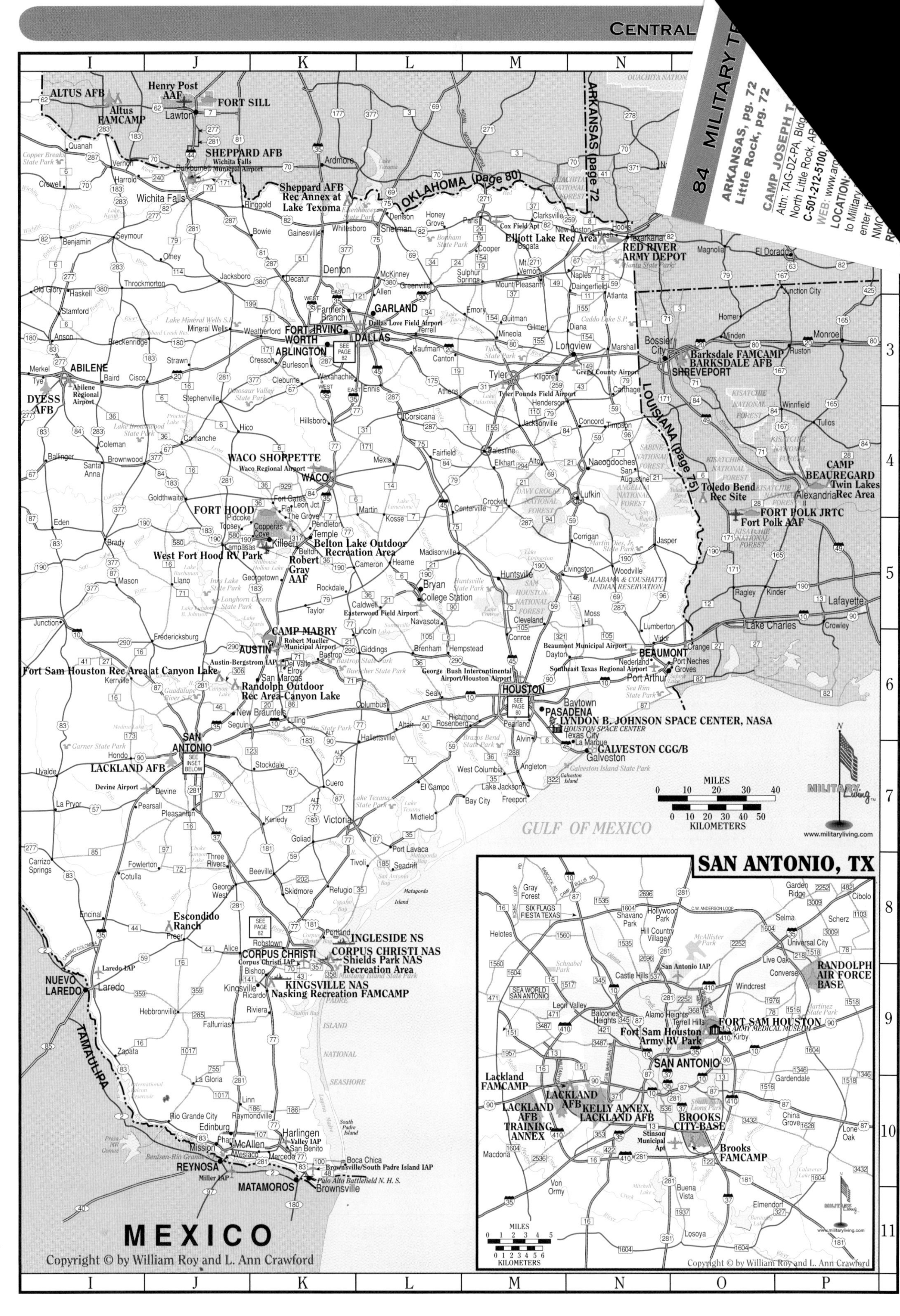
I J K L M N O P
ALTUS AFB
Altus FAMCAMP
Henry Post AAF
FORT SILL
Lawton
SHEPPARD AFB
Wichita Falls Municipal Airport
Wichita Falls
Sheppard AFB Rec Annex at Lake Texoma
ARKANSAS (page 72)
OKLAHOMA (page 80)
Ardmore
Denison
Sherman
Gainesville
Denton
Paris
Cox Field Apt
Elliott Lake Rec Area
Texarkana
RED RIVER ARMY DEPOT
Magnolia
El Dorado
Junction City
McKinney
GARLAND
Dallas Love Field Airport
FORT WORTH
IRVING
DALLAS
ARLINGTON
SEE PAGE 82
Mineral Wells
Weatherford
Terrell
Kaufman
Longview
Marshall
Bossier City
Barksdale FAMCAMP
BARKSDALE AFB
SHREVEPORT
Minden
Monroe
Ruston
ABILENE
Abilene Regional Airport
DYESS AFB
Tyler
Tyler Pounds Field Airport
Gregg County Airport
Henderson
Carthage
LOUISIANA (page 75)
Winnfield
Tullos
Corsicana
Waxahachie
Hillsboro
Jacksonville
Palestine
Nacogdoches
Lufkin
WACO SHOPPETTE
Waco Regional Airport
WACO
CAMP BEAUREGARD
Twin Lakes Rec Area
Alexandria
Toledo Bend Rec Site
FORT HOOD
Fort Gates
Copperas Cove
Killeen
Temple
Belton Lake Outdoor Recreation Area
West Fort Hood RV Park
Robert Gray AAF
FORT POLK JRTC
Fort Polk AAF
Huntsville
Livingston
ALABAMA & COUSHATTA INDIAN RESERVATION
Jasper
Bryan
College Station
Easterwood Field Airport
Lafayette
Lake Charles
CAMP MABRY
Robert Mueller Municipal Airport
AUSTIN
Austin-Bergstrom IAP
Fort Sam Houston Rec Area at Canyon Lake
Randolph Outdoor Rec Area-Canyon Lake
San Marcos
New Braunfels
Beaumont Municipal Airport
BEAUMONT
Southeast Texas Regional Airport
Port Arthur
George Bush Intercontinental Airport/Houston Airport
HOUSTON
SEE PAGE 80
PASADENA
Baytown
LYNDON B. JOHNSON SPACE CENTER, NASA
HOUSTON SPACE CENTER
Texas City
GALVESTON CGG/B
Galveston
SAN ANTONIO
SEE INSET BELOW
LACKLAND AFB
Devine Airport
Victoria
GULF OF MEXICO
MILES 0 10 20 30 40
0 10 20 30 40 50 KILOMETERS
www.militaryliving.com
Escondido Ranch
Laredo IAP
NUEVO LAREDO
Laredo
CORPUS CHRISTI
Corpus Christi IAP
INGLESIDE NS
CORPUS CHRISTI NAS
Shields Park NAS Recreation Area
KINGSVILLE NAS
Nasking Recreation FAMCAMP
PADRE ISLAND NATIONAL SEASHORE
TAMAULIPA
Harlingen
Valley IAP
McAllen
REYNOSA
Miller IAP
MATAMOROS
Brownsville/South Padre Island IAP
Palo Alto Battlefield N.H.S.
Brownsville
MEXICO
Copyright © by William Roy and L. Ann Crawford
SAN ANTONIO, TX
SIX FLAGS FIESTA TEXAS
SEA WORLD SAN ANTONIO
San Antonio IAP
RANDOLPH AIR FORCE BASE
FORT SAM HOUSTON
U.S. ARMY MEDICAL MUSEUM
Fort Sam Houston Army RV Park
Lackland FAMCAMP
LACKLAND AFB
KELLY ANNEX, LACKLAND AFB
LACKLAND AFB TRAINING ANNEX
BROOKS CITY-BASE
Stinson Municipal Apt
Brooks FAMCAMP
MILES 0 1 2 3 4 5
0 1 2 3 4 5 6 KILOMETERS
Copyright © by William Roy and L. Ann Crawford
3 4 5 6 7 8 9 10 11

ROBINSON

6000
72199-9600
DSN-312-962-5100, Police-212-5282
uard.org
From east or west on I-40, take Burns Park exit 150 Drive, then follow signs to camp (two miles). Visitors can rough Main Gate. ID is required. USMRA: AR map (D-7). : North Little Rock, one mile south.
ECREATION & TRAVEL: Golf-791-8592 RVC-212-5274 or 888-366-3205 TML-212-5274/5
RETAIL & DINING: Cafeteria-212-4596 Clubs-CC-758-8468 All Ranks-758-5076 EX-753-9017
SUPPORT & FAMILY: Med-212-5262

FORT CHAFFEE MANEUVER TRAINING CENTER

1370 Fort Smith Blvd, Fort Chaffee, AR 72905-1370
C-479-484-3170, DSN-312-962-3998, Police-484-2666
WEB: http://www.5tharmy.army.mil/2_393/default.htm
LOCATION: From I-40, take the I-540 exit 7 southwest in Fort Smith. From I-540, exit 8 onto AR-22 southeast (Rogers Avenue); continue through the town of Barling to Fort Chaffee, one mile east of Barling. USMRA: AR map (B-3). NMC: Fort Smith, six miles northwest.
RECREATION & TRAVEL: Golf-478-6971 RVC-484-2252/2917 TML-484-2252/2917
RETAIL & DINING: EX-478-6131

LITTLE ROCK AIR FORCE BASE

314 AW/PA, 1250 Thomas Avenue, Suite 160
Little Rock Air Force Base, AR 72099-4940
C-501-987-1110, DSN-312-731-1110, Police-987-3221
WEB: www.littlerock.af.mil
LOCATION: From I-40, take exit 155 north on US-67/167 to Jacksonville, then take exit 11 west to Vandenberg Blvd. Follow signs to Main Gate west of US-67/167. USMRA: AR map (E-4). NMC: Little Rock, 18 miles southwest.
RECREATION & TRAVEL: Golf-987-6825 RVC-987-3365 SPA-987-3342/93 TML-987-6753
RETAIL & DINING: Clubs-CC-987-5555 EMC-987-3760 OC-987-1111 Com-987-3203 Dining-987-1141 EX-988-1150/80 Gas-987-2301
SUPPORT & FAMILY: Med-987-8811

PINE BLUFF ARSENAL

Attn: AMSSB-CO, 10020 Kambrich Circle
Pine Bluff Arsenal, AR 71602-9500
C-870-540-3000, DSN-312-966-3000, Police-540-3505
WEB: www.pba.army.mil
LOCATION: Southeast of Little Rock, take US-65 south to exit 32, then east on AR-256 to Main Gate. Off US-65 northwest of Pine Bluff, take AR-256. Cross AR-365 into Main Gate. USMRA: AR map (E,F-6). NMC: Pine Bluff, eight miles southeast. NMI: Little Rock Air Force Base, 50 miles north.
RECREATION & TRAVEL: Golf-540-3028/3788 RVC-540-3778/9 TML-540-3008
RETAIL & DINING: Com-540-3474 EX-540-3474
SUPPORT & FAMILY: Med-540-3409

IOWA, pg. 73
Des Moines, pg. 76

CAMP DODGE/NATIONAL GUARD BASE

7105 Northwest 70th Avenue, Johnston, IA 50131-1824
C-515-252-4000, DSN-312-431-4000, Police (Security)-240-4538
WEB: www.iowanationalguard.com
LOCATION: From I-35/80 east or west, take Merle Hay Road/ Camp Dodge exit 131 north on IA-401 (Merle Hay Road) to Northwest Beaver Drive, left to Camp Dodge. Clearly marked. USMRA: IA map (E-5); MN map (B-1). NMC: Des Moines, eight miles southeast.
RECREATION & TRAVEL: TML-252-4238 or 800-294-6607 ext 4010
RETAIL & DINING: EX-252-4382
SUPPORT & FAMILY: Med-252-4317
NOTE: *These facilities are not manned by full-time personnel; call Public Affairs at 252-4582 for information.*

DES MOINES EXCHANGE

Bldg 106, 217 East Army Post Road
Des Moines, IA 50315-5842
C-515-287-7671, Police-256-8223
LOCATION: From I-235, take US-69 exit south to Army Post Road. Make a right onto Army Post Road and another right onto Union Street. USMRA: IA map (E,F-6); MN map (C-2). NMC: Des Moines, within city limits.
RETAIL & DINING: EX-287-7671

DES MOINES INTERNATIONAL AIRPORT/ AIR NATIONAL GUARD

132 Fighter Wing, 3100 McKinley Avenue
Des Moines, IA 50321-2720
C-515-256-8210, DSN-312-256-8210, Police-256-8223
LOCATION: From I-235, take 42nd Street exit onto 42nd Street. Make a left onto Grand Avenue, a right onto Fleur Drive and another right onto McKinley Avenue. USMRA: IA map (E,F-5,6), MN map (B-2). NMC: Des Moines, within city limits.
RETAIL & DINING: EX-256-8550 (annex of Des Moines EX)

SIOUX GATEWAY AIRPORT/ AIR NATIONAL GUARD

185 Air Refueling Wing, 2920 Headquarters Avenue
Sioux City, IA 51111-1300
C-712-233-0200, DSN-585-0200, Police-233-0780
WEB: www.flysiouxgateway.com
LOCATION: From I-29 north or south to Sergeant Bluff airport exit (exit 141), west toward airport exit to F-16 airplane, south to gate. USMRA: IA map (A-4). NMC: Sioux City, ten miles north.
RETAIL & DINING: EX-233-0759
SUPPORT & FAMILY: Med-233-0510

KANSAS, pg. 74
Kansas City, pg. 77

FORBES FIELD AIRPORT/ AIR NATIONAL GUARD

Forbes Field Air National Guard Base
5920 Southwest Coyote Drive, Topeka, KS 66619-1429
C-785-861-4210, DSN-312-720-4295, Police-861-4593
LOCATION: From I-70 east or west, take exit 361A to Alternate US-75 south. Main Gate is located at second stoplight on US-75. Base is east of US-75 south. USMRA: KS map (J-4). NMC: Topeka, within city limits.
RECREATION & TRAVEL: SPA-861-4558
RETAIL & DINING: EX-861-4962
SUPPORT & FAMILY: Med-861-4522

FORT LEAVENWORTH

USACAC & Fort Leavenworth, Attn: ATZL-GC
600 Thomas Avenue, Fort Leavenworth, KS 66027-1417
C-913-684-4021, DSN-312-552-4201, Police-684-2111
WEB: http://garrison.leavenworth.army.mil
LOCATION: From I-70 east or west, exit 223 to US-73 north to Leavenworth. Make a left onto Metropolitan Avenue and take this road to the Main Gate. From I-29 north or south, exit 19, KS-92 west to Leavenworth. Fort is adjacent to city of Leavenworth. Main Gate on US-73 (Metropolitan Avenue). USMRA: KS map (K-3). NMC: Kansas City, 30 miles southeast.
RECREATION & TRAVEL: Golf-684-3994 SPA-684-6041 TML-684-4091
RETAIL & DINING: Cafeteria-651-6573 Clubs-CC-684-2287 Com-684-4907 EX-651-7270 Gas-651-6541
SUPPORT & FAMILY: Med-684-6250

FORT RILEY

24 Infantry Division (Mech) & Fort Riley
Attn: AFZN-GC, Bldg 500, Fort Riley, KS 66442-5007
C-785-239-3911, DSN-312-856-3911, Police-239-6767
WEB: www.riley.army.mil
LOCATION: Near Junction City. From east or west on I-70, take exit 301 northwest onto Henry Drive directly to the base, or take exit 296 at Junction City north onto Washington Street. Continue north through Junction City across Republican River to post. Follow signs. USMRA: KS map (H-3). NMC: Topeka, 50 miles east.
RECREATION & TRAVEL: Golf-239-5412 TML-239-2830
RETAIL & DINING: Cafeteria-239-5322 Com-239-6621 EX-784-4439 Gas-784-2493
SUPPORT & FAMILY: Med-239-3627

MCCONNELL AIR FORCE BASE

57837 Coffeyville Street, Suite 240
McConnell Air Force Base, KS 67221-3504
C-316-759-6100, DSN-312-743-1110, Police-759-3976
WEB: http://public.mcconnell.amc.af.mil
LOCATION: Take I-35 north or south to Wichita, exit at US-54/400 (Kellogg Street) west to Rock Road, south to McConnell AFB, west of Rock Road. USMRA: KS map (G,H-6). NMC: Wichita, six miles northwest.
RECREATION & TRAVEL: Golf-759-4039 RVC-759-6999 SPA-759-5169 TML-759-6999 or 888-AF-LODGE
RETAIL & DINING: Cafeteria-759-6114 Clubs-EMC-759-6183 OC-759-6182 Com-759-5627 Dining-759-6185 EX-685-0231 Fast Food-759-4272 Gas-685-0231
SUPPORT & FAMILY: Med-691-6300

SALINA KANSAS ARMY NATIONAL GUARD REGIONAL TRAINING INSTITUTE

Nickell Hall, 2930 Scanlan Avenue, Salina, KS 67401-8129
C-785-822-3296, Police-911
WEB: http://www.ks.ngb.army.mil/rti
LOCATION: From I-135 take exit 89, Schilling Road, and turn right. Continue approximately one mile through three traffic lights, then turn right. Entrance to Nickell Hall is on the left. This post has no gates. USMRA: KS map (G-4). NMC: Salina, within city limits. NMI: Fort Riley, 60 miles east.
RETAIL & DINING: Dining-822-3296
SUPPORT & FAMILY: Med-822-6611

LOUISIANA, pg. 75
Baton Rouge, pg. 75
New Orleans, pg. 75

BARKSDALE AIR FORCE BASE

2 Bomb Wing, 109 Barksdale Blvd West, Suite 209
Barksdale Air Force Base, LA 71110-2164
C-318-456-1110, DSN-312-781-1110, Police-456-2551
WEB: www.barksdale.af.mil
LOCATION: From I-20 east or west, take Airline Drive exit 22, go south to Old Minden Road (0.25 miles), left on Old Minden Road (one block), then right on North Gate Drive (one mile) to North Gate of AFB. USMRA: LA map (A-2). NMC: Shreveport, one mile west.
Co-located with Bossier City and Shreveport.
RECREATION & TRAVEL: Golf-456-2263 RVC-456-2679 SPA-456-8814/5 TML-456-3091
RETAIL & DINING: Clubs-EMC-456-8328/8179 OC-456-4926 Com-456-8263 Dining-456-8367 EX-746-2554 Gas-746-5662
SUPPORT & FAMILY: Med-456-6555

CAMP BEAUREGARD

Training Site, Detachment 1 HQ STARC
409 F Stree, Pineville, LA 71360-3737
C-318-641-5600, DSN-312-435-5600, Police-641-5666
LOCATION: West off US-165, seven miles south of Pollock to Beauregard Drive, which leads to the Main Gate. USMRA: LA map (C-4). NMC: Alexandria, five miles southwest.
RECREATION & TRAVEL: RVC-641-5669 TML-641-5669
RETAIL & DINING: Clubs-EMC-640-8219 OC-641-8277 EX-641-9661

FORT POLK/JOINT READINESS TRAINING CENTER

Attn: AFZX-PO, 7073 Radio Road, Bldg 411
Fort Polk, LA 71459-5342
C-337-531-2911, DSN-312-863-1110, Police-531-2677
WEB: www.jrtc-polk.army.mil
LOCATION: Off US-171 north or south, nine miles south of Leesville. East of US-171 south. From I-10, take exit 33 to US-171 north. Make a right onto LA-10 (Pitkin Highway), which leads straight to the entrance. USMRA: LA map (B-4). NMC: Alexandria, 60 miles southwest.
RECREATION & TRAVEL: Golf-531-4661 Marina-888-718-9088 RVC-565-3084 SPA-531-4831 TML-531-9000
RETAIL & DINING: Clubs-CC-531-4440/4652 Com-531-6132 EX-537-1001 Gas-537-8269
SUPPORT & FAMILY: Med-531-3118/9

JACKSON BARRACKS/ ARMY NATIONAL GUARD BASE

Louisiana National Guard Base, Jackson Barracks
Bldg 35, Room 213, New Orleans, LA 70146-0330
C-504-271-6262, DSN-312-485-8309, Police-278-8460
LOCATION: From Baton Rouge, take I-10 east to exit 236, I-10/610 east to exit 2 onto North Claiborne Street. Go straight over overpass, then cross drawbridge. Entrance to Jackson Barracks is about two miles past drawbridge. Claiborne Avenue will go through Jackson Barracks. USMRA: LA map (J-3). NMC: New Orleans, within city limits.
RECREATION & TRAVEL: TML-278-8364
RETAIL & DINING: Clubs-CC-278-8490 (Only open drill weekends) EX-278-8245

NEW ORLEANS COAST GUARD INTEGRATED SUPPORT COMMAND

P.O. Box 751064, New Orleans, LA 70175-1064
C-504-942-3032 Police(Security)-678-2622
WEB: http://www.uscg.mil/iscneworleans

LOCATION: From NOLA Internatial Airport (MSY), merge onto I-610 E via exit 230 on the left, toward Slidell. Take the Franklin Ave exit 4. Turn right onto Franklin Ave. Make a U-turn onto Franklin Ave. Turn right onto N. Robertson St./LA-39 S. Turn right onto Poland Avenue, left onto Urquhart St. End at ISC New Orleans. USMRA: LA map (G-6; J-2). NMC: New Orleans, within city limits. NMI: New Orleans NAS, less than one mile south.
RETAIL & DINING: EX-846-5911
SUPPORT & FAMILY: Med-678-7989

NEW ORLEANS NAVAL AIR STATION/ JOINT RESERVE BASE

400 Russell Avenue, Bldg 46, New Orleans, LA 70143-5012
C-504-678-3253, DSN-312-678-3253, Police-678-3827
WEB: https://navyregionsouth.cnatra.navy.mil/nasno/index.html
LOCATION: From I-10 take Westbank exit onto RT-90 across the Greater New Orleans Bridge. Take Lafayette Street exit. Make a left turn onto Belle Chasse Highway. Follow to Main Gate (about 15 minutes). Visitors can enter through Main Gate with ID. USMRA: LA map (G-7; J-4). NMI: New Orleans NSA, 20 miles northwest. NMC: New Orleans, ten miles north.
RECREATION & TRAVEL: Golf-678-3453 RVC-678-3448 SPA-678-3101 TML-678-3840
RETAIL & DINING: Clubs-CC-678-3844 EX-678-3510 Gas-678-3506
SUPPORT & FAMILY: Med-678-3660

NEW ORLEANS NAVAL SUPPORT ACTIVITY

2300 General Meyer Avenue, New Orleans, LA 70142-5007
C-504-678-5011, DSN-312-678-5011, Police-678-2570
LOCATION: On the west bank of the Mississippi River. From I-10 east, take Crescent City Connection Bridge to the west bank. Take General DeGaulle east exit after passing over bridge and turn left at Shirley Drive, which leads to NSA. USMRA: LA map (J-3). NMC: New Orleans, within city limits.
RECREATION & TRAVEL: RVC-678-9014 TML-678-2220 Navy Lodge-800-NAVY-INN or 366-3266
RETAIL & DINING: Clubs-CC-678-2218 Com-678-9453 EX-678-2702 Gas-678-2747
SUPPORT & FAMILY: Med-678-2480

TOLEDO BEND RECREATION SITE

1310 Army Recreation Road, Florien, LA 71429-5000
C-888-718-9088 DSN-312-863-1110, Police-531-6825
WEB: http://www.fortpolkmwr.com/id52.html
LOCATION: Off post. Take US-171 north from Leesville, west at Hornbeck onto LA-392. Proceed 0.5 miles, then turn right onto LA-473. Continue for seven miles, turn left onto LA-191 and continue for a few miles to Recreation Site on right (west) side at Army RV Park sign. USMRA: LA map (A-4). NMC: Alexandria, 60 miles northeast. NMI: Fort Polk, 45 miles southeast.
RECREATION & TRAVEL: RVC-565-4235 or 888-718-9088
NOTE: *For detailed information about this off-base recreation facility, as well as on-base recreation facilities, golf courses and marinas, consult Military Living's "Military RV, Camping and Outdoor Recreation Around the World".*

TWIN LAKES RECREATION AREA

301 F Street, Camp Beauregard, LA 71360-3737
C-318-641-5399, DSN-312-435-5600, Police-641-5666
WEB: http://cbbilletin.com/eform
LOCATION: Seven miles from Camp Beauregard. Take US-165 to LA-116 east and follow four miles to the recreation area. USMRA: LA map (C-4). NMC: Alexandria, six miles south.
RECREATION & TRAVEL: RVC-641-5669
NOTE: *For detailed information about this off-base recreation facility, as well as on-base recreation facilities, golf courses and marinas, consult Military Living's "Military RV, Camping and Outdoor Recreation Around the World".*

MINNESOTA, pg. 76
Minneapolis/St. Paul, pg. 76

CAMP RIPLEY

15000 Highway 115, Little Falls, MN 56345-4173
C-320-632-7000, DSN-312-871-7000, Police-632-7375/7665
WEB: www.dma.state.mn.us/cpripley/index.htm
LOCATION: West of MN-371, 23 miles south of Brainerd, west of Mille Lacs Lake, in central Minnesota. Take US-10 to Little Falls. Exit off US-10 to MN-371. Make a left onto MN-115, then a right onto Bettenburg Avenue and Main Gate. USMRA: MN map (C,D-7). NMC: Little Falls, seven miles south.
RECREATION & TRAVEL: TML-632-7378
RETAIL & DINING: Clubs-CC-632-7255 OC-632-7239 EX-632-7382

DULUTH INTERNATIONAL AIRPORT/ AIR NATIONAL GUARD

4680 Viper Street, Duluth, MN 55811-6031
C-218-788-7210, DSN-312-825-7210, Police (Security)-788-7442
LOCATION: From I-35, turn left onto Midway Road Drive ten miles and turn right onto W. Arrowhead Road Drive five miles and turn left onto Haines Road USMRA: MN map (F-6). NMC: Duluth, within city limits.
RETAIL & DINING: EX-727-8365
SUPPORT & FAMILY: Med-788-7225

MINNEAPOLIS-ST. PAUL INTERNATIONAL AIRPORT/AIR RESERVE STATION

760 Military Highway, Minneapolis, MN 55450-2100
C-612-713-1110, DSN-312-783-1110, Police-713-1102
WEB: www.afrc.af.mil/934aw/
LOCATION: From I-35 west or MN-55 south to crosstown MN-62, exit at 34th Avenue and entrance. Or take I-494 east to exit 1A on MN-5 and entrance west to airport. USMRA: Minneapolis, MN map (F-3). NMC: Minneapolis-St Paul, within city limits.
RECREATION & TRAVEL: RVC-Veterans on the Lake Resort-800-777-7538 SPA-713-2461/74 TML-713-9440
RETAIL & DINING: Clubs-NCO-713-1655 OC-713-3678 EX-726-9023

MISSOURI, pg. 77
Branson, pg. 77
Kansas City, pg. 77
St. Louis, pg. 77

FORT LEONARD WOOD

Attn: ATZT-PAO, 203 Illinois Avenue, Suite 8
Fort Leonard Wood, MO 65473-8936
C-573-596-0131, DSN-312-581-0131, Police-596-6141
WEB: www.wood.army.mil
LOCATION: Take exit 161 two miles south of I-44. Take a left onto Missouri Avenue, which leads to the front gate (adjacent to St. Robert and Waynesville) at Fort Leonard Wood exit. USMRA: MO map (E-5). NMC: Springfield, 85 miles southwest.
RECREATION & TRAVEL Golf-329-4770 LORA Marina-346-5640/73 RVC-346-5640 SPA-596-0165 TML-800-677-8356
RETAIL & DINING: Cafeteria-329-3601 Clubs-CC-329-2455/6533 EMC-329-2455 OC-329-6500 Davis Club-329-6080 Com-596-0689 Dining-596-9843 EX-329-2200 Gas-329-3373
SUPPORT & FAMILY: Med-329-8600

LAKE OF THE OZARKS RECREATION AREA

797 Olney Circle, Linn Creek, MO 65052-9731
C-573-346-5640, DSN-312-581-0131, Police-346-3693
WEB: www.fortleonardwoodmwr.com
LOCATION: Located on Grand Glaize Arm of the Lake of the Ozarks in the center of a State Wildlife Refuge. From I-70, take exit 128A at Columbia south onto US-63 towards Jefferson City. Then take US-54 south across Lake of the Ozarks; left at CR-A for six miles to Freedom, left onto McCubbins Drive. Continue north to point where McCubbins Drive bears right. Continue straight ahead onto Olney Drive to northwest end of peninsula directly to recreation area. Or from I-44, take exit 150 to MO-7 north approximately 9.3 miles to Richland. On west side of Richland, turn right onto CR-A. Continue on CR-A northwest approximately 19.8 miles to Freedom. Turn right on McCubbins Drive and follow instructions above to recreation area. USMRA: MO map (D-4). NMC: Jefferson City, 40 miles northeast.
RECREATION & TRAVEL: Marina-346-5640 RVC-346-5640 TML-346-5640
NOTE: *For detailed information about this off-base recreation facility, as well as on-base recreation facilities, golf courses and marinas, consult Military Living's "Military RV, Camping and Outdoor Recreation Around the World".*

MARINE CORPS MOBILIZATION COMMAND AT RICHARDS-GEBAUR AIRPORT

15424 Andrews Road. Kansas City, MO 64147-1219
C-816-843-3395, DSN-312-894-3395, Police-911
WEB: http://mobcom.mfr.usmc.mil/MOBCOM.asp
LOCATION: From I-470, take US-71 south to 155th Street exit west, then take a left onto Andrews Road. Between Grandview and Belton. USMRA: MO map (B-3); KS/MO map (B-11). NMC: Kansas City, 17 miles north.
RECREATION & TRAVEL: TML-843-3850/1/2
RETAIL & DINING: Clubs-EMC-318-8130 NCO-318-8130 OC-318-8130 EX-331-2019

ROSECRANS MEMORIAL AIRPORT/ AIR NATIONAL GUARD

705 Memorial Drive, St. Joseph, MO 64503-9307
C-816-236-3300, DSN-312-956-3001/3300, Police-236-3394
WEB: http://aw139.ang.af.mil
LOCATION: From US-36 east or west, take exit 70 west of I-229 on MO-238. Straight 1.5 miles to airport entrance. USMRA: MO map (B-2). NMC: St. Joseph, four miles southeast. NMI: Fort Leavenworth, KS, 28 miles south.
RECREATION & TRAVEL: SPA-236-3225/60
RETAIL & DINING: Cafeteria-236-3263

ST. LOUIS ARMY HUMAN RESOURCES COMMAND

1 Reserve Way. St Louis, MO 63132-5299
C-314-592-0707, DSN-312-892-0100, Police (Security)-592-0255
WEB: https://www.hrc.army.mil
LOCATION: From I-170 west, take Page exit and turn right. At the sign for Federal Records Center take left. USMRA: St. Louis, MO map (E-9). NMC: St. Louis, within city limits. NMI: Scott Air Force Base, IL, 30 miles east.
RETAIL & DINING: Cafeteria-538-4349

ST. LOUIS COAST GUARD INTEGRATED SUPPORT COMMAND

U.S. Coast Guard Integrated Support Command
1222 Spruce Street, Room 2102 B, St Louis, MO 63103-2832
C-314-539-3900, Police-539-3900, ext. 2277/9
WEB: www.uscg.mil
LOCATION: From I-64 west, take exit 40A north (towards Busch Stadium) onto South Seventh Street, then right on Spruce Street to SLGISC. From I-64 east, take exit 39C on left, north (toward Busch Stadium) onto 11th Street, then turn left onto Spruce Street to CGISC. USMRA: MO map (G-3,4); St. Louis, MO map (F-9). NMC: St. Louis, within city limits.
SUPPORT & FAMILY: Med-539-3900, ext. 2312

WHITEMAN AIR FORCE BASE

509 Spirit Blvd, Suite 111
Whiteman Air Force Base, MO 65305-5097
C-660-687-1110, DSN-312-975-1110, Police-687-3700
WEB: www.whiteman.af.mil
LOCATION: From I-70, exit 49 south to US-13 south to US-50 east for ten miles. Take MO-23 south leading to base. USMRA: MO map (C-3,4). NMC: Kansas City, 60 miles west.
RECREATION & TRAVEL: Golf-687-5572 SPA-687-3101 TML-687-1844
RETAIL & DINING: Clubs-CC-563-2273 Com-687-5655 Dining-686-5469 EX-563-3001/3 Gas-563-5445
SUPPORT & FAMILY: Med-687-2188

NEBRASKA, pg. 78
Omaha, pg. 78

CAMP ASHLAND

220 County Road 'A', Building 508, Ashland, NE 68003-9801
C-402-309-7616, DSN-312-279-7616, Police-911
WEB: www.neguard.com/unit/rti/
LOCATION: From I-80 north or south, take exit 432 onto NE-31, north 0.25 miles to US-6. Go west four miles to road signs indicating Nebraska National Guard Camp (Camp Ashland). USMRA: NE map (J-5). NMC: Omaha, 20 miles east.
RECREATION & TRAVEL: TML-309-7616

LINCOLN MUNICIPAL AIRPORT/ AIR NATIONAL GUARD

155 Air Refueling Wing, 2420 West Butler Avenue
Lincoln, NE 68524-1897
C-402-309-1110, DSN-312-279-1110, Police-309-1563
WEB: www.neguard.com
LOCATION: Adjacent to Lincoln Municipal Airport, right on I-80. From I-80 east or west, take exit 399 onto West Adams Street. Make a left onto West Butler Avenue. USMRA: NE map (I-5,6). NMC: Lincoln, two miles southeast.
RECREATION & TRAVEL: SPA-309-1248
RETAIL & DINING: EX-474-3454

OFFUTT AIR FORCE BASE

906 SAC Blvd, Suite 1, Offutt Air Force Base, NE 68113-3206.
C-402-294-1110, DSN-312-271-1110, Police-294-6110
WEB: www.offutt.af.mil
LOCATION: From I-80 east or west, exit 452 to US-75 south to AFB exit, 6.5 miles south of I-80/US-75 interchange, on east side of US-75. USMRA: NE map (J-5). NMC: Omaha, eight miles north.
RECREATION & TRAVEL: Golf-292-1680 or 294-3362 RVC-294-2108 SPA-294-8510/1 TML-291-9000 or 294-3671
RETAIL & DINING: Cafeteria-291-9596 Clubs-EMC-292-6785 NCO/OC-292-1600 Com-294-5920/6783 Dining-294-

3980 EX-291-9100 Fast Food-292-6769 Gas-291-8743
SUPPORT & FAMILY: Med-293-6500

OFFUTT FAMCAMP
Outdoor Recreation, FAMCAMP, 55 SVS/SVRO
109 Grant Circle, Suite 301,Offutt AFB, NE 68113-2084
C-402-294-2108, DSN-312-271-2108, Police-294-6110
LOCATION: Off base. From I-80 in Omaha, take exit 452 onto US-75 to Bellevue. East on NE-370 (Mission Avenue), through town, right on Hancock Street for 1.5 miles, left to Base Lake and FAMCAMP. USMRA: NE map (J-5). NMC: Omaha, eight miles north. NMI: Offutt AFB, two miles west.
RECREATION & TRAVEL: RVC-294-2108
NOTE: *For detailed information about this off-base recreation facility, as well as on-base recreation facilities, golf courses and marinas, consult Military Living's "Military RV, Camping and Outdoor Recreation Around the World".*

NORTH DAKOTA, pg. 79

CAMP GILBERT C. GRAFTON NATIONAL GUARD TRAINING CENTER
4417 Highway 20, Devils Lake, ND 58301-9000
C-701-662-0200, DSN-312-422-0200, Police-662-0291
WEB: www.guard.bismarck.nd.us
LOCATION: From the intersection of US-2 (east or west) and ND-20 in Devils Lake, turn south. Drive approximately five miles south. Main Gate will be on the west (right hand) side of the highway. USMRA: ND map (H-3). NMC: Devils Lake, five miles north.
RECREATION & TRAVEL: Bowling-662-8411 TML-662-0239
RETAIL & DINING: Clubs-CC-662-0221 Dining-662-0419 Snack Bar-662-0285 (Lunch only Mon-Fri)
SUPPORT & FAMILY: Med-662-5323

CAVALIER AIR FORCE STATION
830 Patrol Road, #260, Cavalier AFS, ND 58220-9350
C-701-993-3292, DSN-312-330-3292, Police-993-3365
LOCATION: Traveling north or south on I-29, take ND-5 west, Cavalier exit. Go west 18 miles to town of Cavalier, continuing west through town on ND-5 another 16 miles to site, on left (south) side of road. There is a sign for the air station on the left hand side of the road. USMRA: ND map (I-2). NMC: Grand Forks, 75 miles south.
RETAIL & DINING: EX-993-3224 Snack Bar-993-3228

GRAND FORKS AIR FORCE BASE
319 ARW/PA, 375 Steen Blvd, Bldg 313, Room 102
Grand Forks Air Force Base, ND 58205-6015
C-701-747-3000, DSN-312-362-1110, Police-747-5351
WEB: http://public.grandforks.amc.af.mil/
LOCATION: From I-29 north or south, take US-2 west exit for 14 miles to Grand Forks, County Road B-3 (Emeraldo/Air Base) north one mile to AFB on west (left) side of road. USMRA: ND map (J-3). NMC: Grand Forks, 13 miles east.
RECREATION & TRAVEL: Golf-747-4279 RVC-747-3688 SPA-747-7105 TML-747-7200
RETAIL & DINING: Clubs-EMC-747-3392 OC-594-5576 or 747-3131 Com-747-3083 Dining-747-3210 EX-594-5542 Fast Food-594-4663/8581 Gas-594-5684
SUPPORT & FAMILY: Med-594-3000

HECTOR INTERNATIONAL AIRPORT/ AIR NATIONAL GUARD
119 Fighter Wing, 1400 28th Avenue North, Fargo, ND 58102-1031 **C-701-451-2112,** DSN-312-362-8112, Police-451-2288
WEB: www.HappyHooligans.com
LOCATION: From I-29 north or south to exit 67/19th Avenue, exit east to University Drive North to Hector Field on left. The base is located at the intersection of University Drive and 28th Avenue North. USMRA: ND map (K-5,6). NMC: Fargo, within city limits.
RETAIL & DINING: EX-451-2184

MINOT AIR FORCE BASE
201 Summit Drive, Unit 4, Minot Air Force Base, ND 58705-5037
C-701-723-1110, DSN-312-4531110, Police-723-3096
WEB: www.minot.af.mil
LOCATION: On US-83 north or south,13 miles north of Minot. USMRA: ND map (D-3). NMC: Minot,13 miles south.
RECREATION & TRAVEL: Golf-723-3164 RVC-723-3648 SPA-723-1854 TML-723-6161
RETAIL & DINING: Clubs-EMC-R.Rockers-727-7625 OC-Jimmy Doolittle-723-3731 Com-723-4559 Dining-723-2359 EX-727-4717 Gas-727-4876
SUPPORT & FAMILY: Med-723-5633

RAYMOND J. BOHN ARMORY
North Dakota Army National Guard, P.O. Box 5511
4200 East Divide Avenue, Bismarck, ND 58506-5511
C-701-333-2000, DSN-312-373-2000, Police-911
WEB: www.guard.bismarck.nd.us
LOCATION: From I-94 east or west, take exit 161 (Centennial Road). Take first left onto East Divide Avenue. USMRA: ND map (E-6.) NMC: Bismarck, two miles north.
RETAIL & DINING: EX-333-3277

OKLAHOMA, pg.80

ALTUS AIR FORCE BASE
97 AMW/PA, 100 Inez Blvd, Suite 2
Altus Air Force Base, OK 73523-5047
C-580-482-8100, DSN-312-866-1110
e-mail: 97AMW.PA@altus.af.mil, Police-481-7444
WEB: www.altus.af.mil
LOCATION: From Lawton or Duke on Hwy 62, turn north on Veterans Drive (towards car dealership on right). Approximately two miles down the road the Altus AFB main gate will be on your right. Take the right fork in the road. From Vernon, TX, on Hwy 283, drive into town and turn right onto Flacon Road. Drive about four miles; leads straight to AFB's main gate. USMRA: OK map (E-5). NMC: Lawton, 56 miles east.
RECREATION & TRAVEL: Golf-481-7207 RVC-481-6704 SPA-481-6428 TML-481-7356
RETAIL & DINING: Clubs-CC-481-6600 OC-481-6224 Com-481-5810 Dining-481-7781 EX-482-7441/8733 Gas-481-7095
SUPPORT & FAMILY: Med-481-5235/5302

CAMP GRUBER
P.O. Box 29, Bldg 154, Braggs, OK 74423-0029
C-918-549-6001, Police-549-6021
WEB: www.omd.state.ok.us/CGTS
LOCATION: From I-40 east or west, exit north at Webber Falls (exit 287) onto US-62. Take US-62 east to Gore. From US-64, exit onto OK-10 north to Braggs. First entrance to camp after passing through Braggs. Or, from north, take OK-62 east out of Muskogee, take OK-10 south to Braggs and Camp Gruber. USMRA: OK map (J-4). NMC: Muskogee, 15 miles north.

FORT SILL
U.S. Army Field Artillery Center
Attn: ATZR-CS, Bldg 455, Fort Sill, OK 73503-5001
C-580-442-8111, DSN-312-639-7090, Police-442-2103
WEB: http://sill-www.army.mil
LOCATION: From Lawton, take I-44 north to Key Gate exit. Clearly marked. USMRA: OK map (F-5.) NMC: Lawton, on the north border.
RECREATION & TRAVEL: Golf-353-0411 or 442-3875 RVC-442-5541 TML-442-5000 or 877-902-3607
RETAIL & DINING: Clubs-EMC-355-3201 or 442-3060 OC-355-9112 or 442-5300 Com-442-3601 Dining-442-5431 EX-351-0504 Gas-357-0786
SUPPORT & FAMILY: Med-458-2000

LAKE ELMER THOMAS RECREATION AREA
MWR, 7463 Deer Creek Canyon Road, Fort Sill, OK 73503-0307
C-580-442-5541/5854, Police-442-2103
WEB: www.sillmwr.com/letra.htm
LOCATION: Off post. Take I-44 north or south to OK-49 (Medicine Park) exit 45 west. Follow signs to LETRA. USMRA: OK map (F-5). NMC: Wichita Falls, TX, 64 miles southwest. NMI: Fort Sill, 12 miles southwest.
RECREATION & TRAVEL: RVC-442-5541/5854
NOTE: *For detailed information about this off-base recreation facility, as well as on-base recreation facilities, golf courses and marinas, consult Military Living's "Military RV, Camping and Outdoor Recreation Around the World".*

MCALESTER ARMY AMMUNITION PLANT
Attn: SMAMC-CA, 1 C Tree Road, Bldg 659-A
McAlester, OK 74501-9002
C-918-420-6591, DSN-312-956-6591, Police-420-6642
e-mail: pa@mcaap.army.mil
WEB: www.mcaapmwr.com/
LOCATION: Off Indian Nation Turnpike, west of US-69. From Indian Nation Turnpike, take exit 5 to US-69 south, right onto C Tree Road and into the plant. USMRA: OK map (I-5). NMC: Tulsa, 90 miles north.
RECREATION & TRAVEL: RVC-420-7484 TML-420-7484
RETAIL & DINING: Cafeteria-420-6669 Clubs-CC-420-7529 Dining-420-6669 EX-420-6388
SUPPORT & FAMILY: Med-420-7496

TINKER AIR FORCE BASE
3001 Staff Drive, Suite 1AG78A
Tinker Air Force Base, OK 73145-3010
C-405-732-7321, DSN-312-884-1110, Police-734-3737
WEB: www-ext.tinker.af.mil
LOCATION: Southeast Oklahoma City, off I-40. Use Tinker gate exit 157A to a left onto Southeast 29th Street and a right onto South Air Depot Blvd. Clearly marked. USMRA: OK map (G-4). NMC: Oklahoma City, 12 miles northwest.
RECREATION & TRAVEL: RVC-734-2289/2847 SPA-739-4339 TML-734-2822
RETAIL & DINING: Cafeteria-734-3884 Clubs-Tinker-734-3418 Com-734-5965 Dining-734-2918 EX-734-3035 Gas-734-3040
SUPPORT & FAMILY: Med-734-2778

TULSA INTERNATIONAL AIRPORT/ AIR NATIONAL GUARD
4200 North 93rd East Avenue, Bldg 313, Tulsa, OK, 4115-1699
C-918-833-7321, DSN-312-894-7370, Police-833-7321
WEB: www.oktuls.ang.af.mil
LOCATION: From I-44 east or west, get on I-244. Take exit 13B towards US-169 (Mingo Valley Expressway) and proceed north. Exit onto East 36th Street North. Keep right on the ramp. Turn right onto North Mingo Road (North 97th East Ave). Make a left onto 42nd Street North then a right onto 93rd East Avenue and follow signs to the base. USMRA: OK map (I-3). NMC: Tulsa, within city limits.
RETAIL & DINING: EX-833-7771

VANCE AIR FORCE BASE
246 Brown Parkway, Vance Air Force Base, OK 73705-5712
C-580-213-5000, DSN-312-448-7110, Police-213-7415
WEB: https://www.vance.af.mil/
LOCATION: Off of US-81 south of Enid (on west side of US-81). Clearly marked. USMRA: OK map (G-3). NMC: Oklahoma City, 90 miles southeast.
RECREATION & TRAVEL: TML-213-7358
RETAIL & DINING: Clubs-CC-213-7595 Com-213-7788 EX-237-6765 Gas-237-7445
SUPPORT & FAMILY: Med-237-7416

WILL ROGERS WORLD AIRPORT/ AIR NATIONAL GUARD
137 Airlift Wing (ANG), 5624 Air Guard Drive
Oklahoma City, OK 73179-1090
C-405-686-5210, DSN-312-720-5210, Police-686-5301
LOCATION: From I-40 east or west, exit 144 south to MacArthur Blvd south. Take Airport Road exit. Exit onto Meridian Drive. Veer right onto Southwest 54th Street. Make a left onto Air Guard Drive. USMRA: OK map (G-4). NMC: Oklahoma City, seven miles northeast.
RECREATION & TRAVEL: SPA-686-5550
RETAIL & DINING: Clubs-NCO-686-5279 Dining-686-5276
SUPPORT & FAMILY: Med-686-5245

SOUTH DAKOTA, pg. 81

ELLSWORTH AIR FORCE BASE
1958 Scott Drive, Suite 1
Ellsworth Air Force Base, SD 57706-4710
C-605-385-1000, DSN-312-675-1110 Police-385-4001
e-mail: 28bw.pa@ellsworth.af.mil
WEB: www.ellsworth.af.mil
LOCATION: Two miles north of I-90. Seven miles east of Rapid City. From I-90, take exit 67B north approximately two miles to gate. Clearly marked. USMRA: SD map (B-5). NMC: Rapid City, seven miles west.
RECREATION & TRAVEL: Golf-923-4999 RVC-385-2997 SPA-385-1180 TML-385-2844
RETAIL & DINING: Cafeteria-923-1623 Clubs-CC-385-1764 OC-385-2427 Com-385-4364 Dining-385-1625 EX-923-4774 Fast Food-Burger King-923-1925 Gas-923-1489
SUPPORT & FAMILY: Med-385-3662

JOE FOSS FIELD AIRPORT/ AIR NATIONAL GUARD
114 Fighter Wing, 1201 West Algonquin Street
Sioux Falls, SD 57104-0264
C-605-988-5700, DSN-312-798-7700
WEB: www.sdsiou.ang.af.mil
LOCATION: From I-90 east or west, merge off onto exit 399. Turn left onto Cliff Avenue and right onto SD-38 Alternate (East 60th Street North). Turn left onto Minnesota Avenue and right onto Algonquin Street to Main Gate. USMRA: SD map (K-6). NMC: Sioux Falls, within city limits.
RETAIL & DINING: Dining-988-5712 EX-988-5772
SUPPORT & FAMILY: Med-988-5860

TEXAS, pg. 82-83
Corpus Christi, pg. 82
Dallas/Ft. Worth, pg. 82
Houston, pg. 80
San Antonio, pg. 83

BIGGS ARMY AIRFIELD
11210 CSM East Slewitzke Street
Biggs Army Airfield, TX 79916-1467
C-915-568-2121, DSN-312-978-2121, Police-568-2115
e-mail: pao@bliss.army.mil
WEB: www.bliss.army.mil
LOCATION: From I-10, take exit 25 (Airport Road) north. Airport Road will turn to the west. After first traffic light, look for gradual right turn before second traffic light. Heading north on Airport Road, pass three traffic lights (not counting military crossing). Entrance to Biggs AAF is on right. Or from US-54 southbound, take Fred Wilson Drive exit. At first traffic light, turn left (east) and continue to fifth traffic light, turn left into Biggs AAF. USMRA: TX Map (C-4). NMC: El Paso, within city limits.
RECREATION & TRAVEL: Golf-562-1273/2066 SPA-568-8088/97 TML-565-7777 or 568-0106
RETAIL & DINING: Clubs-EMC/NCO-562-5969 CPO-568-2738 OC-568-7013 Com-568-6084 Dining-568-9719 EX-562-7200 Fast Food-562-3005 Gas-566-8371
SUPPORT & FAMILY: Med-568-3088

BROOKS CITY-BASE
311th HSW/PA, 2510 Kennedy Circle, Bldg 150, Room 140
Brooks City-Base, TX 78235-5115
C-210-536-1110, DSN-312-240-1110, Police-536-2851
WEB: www.brooks.af.mil
LOCATION: At the intersection of I-37 (north or south) and Loop 13 (Military Drive), take exit 135. Drive west on Military Drive. Turn left on S. Presa. Turn right on Henderson Court. USMRA: San Antonio, TX map (O-10). NMC: San Antonio, five miles northwest.
RECREATION & TRAVEL: Golf-536-2636 RVC-536-2881 TML-536-1844 or 888-AF-LODGE
RETAIL & DINING: Clubs-CC-536-4158 Brooks-536-3782 Sidney's-536-2077 EX-533-9254 Gas-532-2191
SUPPORT & FAMILY: Med-536-1847
NOTE: *The 2005 BRAC report recommended this base for closure. As required by Federal law, the DoD has until 15 September 2007 to begin closing and realigning the bases as called for in the approved report. This process must be completed by 15 September 2011.*

CAMP MABRY
2210 West 35th Street, Austin, TX 78763-5218
C-512-782-5001, DSN-312-954-5001, Police-782-5004
e-mail: paotx@tx.ngb.army.mil
WEB: www.agd.state.tx.us
LOCATION: From Dallas, take I-35 to Austin exit 237A right (38th Street exit). Turn onto 35th Street going west. Cross over Loop 1; installation is on the right. USMRA: TX map (K-6). NMC: Austin, within city limits.
RECREATION & TRAVEL: TML-782-5500
RETAIL & DINING: Cafeteria-782-6720 Clubs-CC-Bay Club-961-2541 EX-782-5120

CORPUS CHRISTI NAVAL AIR STATION
11001 D Street, Suite 143
Corpus Christi Naval Air Station, TX 78419-5021
C-361-961-2811, DSN-312-861-1110, Police-961-2282
e-mail: nascc-pao@nrst.navy.mil
WEB: https://nascc.cnatra.navy.mil/
LOCATION: From San Antonio, take I-37 southeast to exit 4A, TX-358 southeast (South Pedro Island Drive). Exit northeast for 12 miles. Watch out for NAS-SEACAD. USMRA: Corpus Christi, TX map (D-3), TX map (K-8,9). NMC: Corpus Christi, ten miles west.
RECREATION & TRAVEL: Golf-961-3250 Marina-961-1293/4/5 RVC-961-1293/4/5 SPA-961-2505 TML-937-6361 or 961-2388/9 Navy Lodge-800 NAVY-INN or 939-6630
RETAIL & DINING: Com-961-2544 EX-961-2166 Gas-937-7237
SUPPORT & FAMILY: Med-961-2994

DYESS AIR FORCE BASE
466 Fifth Street, Dyess Air Force Base, TX 79607-1240
C-325-696-3113, DSN-312-461-3113, Police (Security)-696-2131
e-mail: 7bwpa@dyess.af.mil
WEB: www.dyess.af.mil
LOCATION: From I-20 West exit San Angelo/Ballinger, exit South 7th Street. Turn right onto South 7th Street. Continue west on 7th, turn left onto Arnold Blvd. Turn right at the next stop light. USMRA: TX map (I-3). NMC: Abilene, 11 miles east.
RECREATION & TRAVEL: Golf-696-4384 SPA-696-3333/4505 TML-696-2681
RETAIL & DINING: Cafeteria-692-7470 Clubs-CC-696-2405 NCO-696-4311 OC-696-2405 Com-696-4802 Dining-696-2421 EX-692-8996 Gas-692-6721
SUPPORT & FAMILY: Med-696-4677
NOTE: *Visitors to Dyess AFB must have a DoD vehicle sticker and a valid military ID (active or retired).*

ELLINGTON FIELD AIR NATIONAL GUARD/ HOUSTON COAST GUARD AIR STATION
147 Fighter Wing, 14657 Sneider Street, Houston, TX 77034-5586
C-281-929-2110, DSN-312-454-2110, Police-929-2041
LOCATION: From I-45 south from Houston, take exit 31 to Ellington Field. Take Dixie Farm Road-1959, then proceed 2.5 miles east of I-45 to base. USMRA: Houston Map (D-6). NMC: Houston, 19 miles northwest.
RECREATION & TRAVEL: SPA-929-2141/2/3
RETAIL & DINING: EX-484-5892
Ten digit dialing required for local calls.

ESCONDIDO RANCH
Attn: Reservations, P.O. Box 1810, Freer, TX 78357-1810
C-830-373-4419
LOCATION: Off base. Located 23 miles northwest of Freer. Take TX-44, turn right onto CR-401 to the ranch. There is a brown sign that marks the ranch. USMRA: TX map (J-8). NMC: Corpus Christi, 80 miles east. NMC: Kingsville NEX, 90 miles southeast.
RECREATION & TRAVEL: RVC-373-4419
NOTE: *For detailed information about this off-base recreation facility, as well as on-base recreation facilities, golf courses and marinas, consult Military Living's "Military RV, Camping and Outdoor Recreation Around the World".*

FORT BLISS
U.S. Army Air Defense Artillery Center & School
1733 Pleasonton Road, Bldg 15, Fort Bliss, TX 79916-6816.
C-915-568-2121, DSN-312-978-0831/2121, Police-568-2115
WEB: https://www.bliss.army.mil
LOCATION: Take I-10 east or west to exit 23A onto US-54 north, then take exit for Fort Bliss/Casey Road. USMRA: TX map (C-4). NMC: El Paso, within city limits.
RECREATION & TRAVEL: Golf-562-1273/2066 RVC-568-0106/4693 SPA-568-8088/97 TML-565-7777
RETAIL & DINING: Clubs-CC-562-3503 NCO-568-9330 OC-568-7013 Com-568-6084 Dining-568-9719 EX-562-7200 Gas-566-8371
SUPPORT & FAMILY: Med-568-3088

FORT HOOD
Hq III Corps & Fort Hood, Attn: PAO
Bldg 1001, Rm. W105, Fort Hood, TX 76544-5056
C-254-287-1110, DSN-312-737-1110, Police-287-5019 or 288-1062
WEB: www.hood.army.mil/fthood/
LOCATION: From I-35 North or South, exit to US-190 West, go 12 miles through Killeen. Main Gate is clearly marked. Visitors go to Main Gate Visitors Control Center. USMRA: TX map (K-4). NMC: Killeen, adjacent.
RECREATION & TRAVEL: Golf-287-1535/6921 Marina-287-2249/6073 RVC-287-2523/8303, 286-6705 or 288-9926 SPA-288-9200 TML-532-5157/8233
RETAIL & DINING: Cafeteria-288-5703/7959 Clubs-EMC-287-6737 OC-532-5329 Com-287-6648/8025 EX-532-7200/8100 Gas-532-2155/5499
SUPPORT & FAMILY: Med-288-8000

FORT SAM HOUSTON
Attn: AFZG-CO, 1212 Stanley Road, Bldg 124
Fort Sam Houston, TX 78234-7654
C-210-221-1211, DSN-312-471-1110/1211, Police- 221-2222
WEB: www.cs.amedd.army.mil
LOCATION: Accessible from I-410 or I-35. From I-35 North or South, take exit 159A North on New Braunfels Avenue to gate. USMRA: San Antonio, TX map (O-9). NMC: San Antonio, within city limits.
RECREATION & TRAVEL: Golf-222-9386 Marina-830-964-3318 or 888-882-9878 RVC-964-3318 RVC-221-5502 TML-357-2705
RETAIL & DINING: Clubs-NCO/OC-224-2721 Com-221-4676 Dining-221-3021 EX-225-5566 Gas-221-3865
SUPPORT & FAMILY: Med-916-6141

FORT SAM HOUSTON RECREATION AREA AT CANYON LAKE
698 Jacobs Creek Park Road, New Braunfels, TX 78133-3535
C-830-226-5357, DSN-312-471-1110/1211, Police-911
WEB: www.FortSamHoustonMWR.com/rfd/canyonlake
LOCATION: Off base. Take I-35 to Canyon Lake, exit 191 West. Turn west onto FR-306, and drive approximately 16 miles to Canyon City. Continue another 1.5 miles past the blinking light in Canyon City to Jacobs Creek Park Road. Turn left, and the recreation area will be on the right. USMRA: TX map (J-6). NMC: San Antonio, 48 miles south. NMI: Fort Sam Houston, 20 miles.
RECREATION & TRAVEL: RVC-226-5357 or 888-882-9878 TML-357-2705 or 888-882-9878
NOTE: *For detailed information about this off-base recreation facility, as well as on-base recreation facilities, golf courses and marinas, consult Military Living's "Military RV, Camping and Outdoor Recreation Around the World".*

FORT WORTH NAVAL AIR STATION/ JOINT RESERVE BASE
Commanding Officer, NAS/JRB
1510 Chennault Avenue, Fort Worth, TX 76127-1053
C-817-782-5000, DSN-312-739-5000, Police-782-5200
LOCATION: On TX-183. From Fort Worth, west on I-30, exit at 7-B north on TX-183, 1.5 miles to gate on left/north of TX-183. USMRA: Dallas/Fort Worth, TX map (A-9). NMC: Fort Worth, seven miles east.
RECREATION & TRAVEL: Marina-782-6375 SPA-782-6071/6288/6289 TML-782-5392/3 Navy Lodge-800-NAVY-INN or 569-1700
RETAIL & DINING: Dining-782-7383 EX-738-1943 Fast Food-Burger King-569-0468 Food Court-738-4916 Gas-989-2852
SUPPORT & FAMILY: Med-782-5897
Ten-digit dialing required for local calls.

GALVESTON COAST GUARD GROUP
P.O. Box 1912, End of Ferry Road, Galveston, TX 77553-1912.
C-409-766-5620/1, Police-911
WEB: www.uscg.mil/d8/groups/grugalv/
LOCATION: Take I-45 South to Island, changes to Broadway, at the seawall make a left onto TX-87, which turns into Ferry Road and leads to the base. Clearly marked. USMRA: TX map (N-7). NMC: Galveston, three miles south.
RETAIL & DINING: Dining-766-5663 EX-766-5673
SUPPORT & FAMILY: Med-766-5661

GOODFELLOW AIR FORCE BASE
17 TRW/PA, 184 Fort Lancaster Avenue
Goodfellow Air Force Base, TX 76904-4304
C-325-654-1110, DSN-312-477-1110, Police-654-3504
WEB: www.goodfellow.af.mil
LOCATION: Goodfellow is located on the southeastern corner of San Angelo, Texas. Major routes leading to San Angelo are U.S. Highway 277, which runs north to south, and U.S. Highway 87, which runs northwest to southwest. Goodfellow has two major gates: the South Gate on FM 1223 (or Chadbourne Street) and the North Gate on Paint Rock Road. Traffic signs on the major roads and highways will point the direction to the base. USMRA: TX map (H-4). NMC: San Angelo, two miles southeast.
RECREATION & TRAVEL: RVC-944-1012 TML-654-3332/3686
RETAIL & DINING: Clubs-CC-654-5327 Goodfellow-654-5327 Com-653-2441 Dining-654-3153 EX-654-3361 Gas-655-5780
SUPPORT & FAMILY: Med-654-4353
NOTE: *The entrance to the Visitor Control Center is located at the South Gate, off of FM 1223/Chadbourne Street.*

GOODFELLOW AIR FORCE BASE RECREATION CAMP
1950 South Concho Drive, San Angelo, TX 76904-7912.
C-325-944-1012, DSN-312-477-1110, Police-657-4498 or 911
LOCATION: Off base. From US-67 at San Angelo. Just south of San Angelo US-67 turns into Loop-306, exit to RR-584 (Knickerbocker Road) and proceed south for three miles. Turn left on South Concho (left turn is shortly after crossing Lake Nasworthy). The campground is on the left and marked by a sign. USMRA: TX map (H-4). NMC: San Angelo, ten miles north. NMI: Goodfellow AFB, ten miles northeast.
RECREATION & TRAVEL: Marina-944-1012 RVC-944-1012
NOTE: *For detailed information about this off-base recreation facility, as well as on-base recreation facilities, golf courses and marinas, consult Military Living's "Military RV, Camping and Outdoor Recreation Around the World".*

HEADQUARTERS ARMY & AIR FORCE EXCHANGE SERVICE
3911 South Walton Walker Blvd, Dallas, TX 75236-1598
C-214-312-2011, DSN-312-967-2011, Police-911
WEB: www.aafes.com
LOCATION: Take I-35 south to exit 423 to US-67. Exit west at

Loop 12, west to Walton Walker Blvd; enter at Exchange Service Drive. AAFES headquarters located at 3911. USMRA: Dallas/Fort Worth, TX map (E-10). NMC: Dallas, within city limits.
RETAIL & DINING: EX-312-2011
Ten-digit dialing required for local calls.

HOUSTON SPACE CENTER
1601 NASA Road 1, Houston, TX 77058-3145
C-281-244-2100, Police-911
WEB: www.spacecenter.org
LOCATION: Follow signs on I-45 south from Houston, then take exit 35 onto East NASA Road, which leads east to Center. Clearly marked. USMRA: TX map (M-6). NMC: Houston, 20 miles north. Show ID for military discount.
SUPPORT & FAMILY: Visitor Center-244-2100
NOTE: *Official Visitors Center of NASA's Johnson Space Center, which is the home of astronaut training and Mission Control.*
Ten-digit dialing required for local calls.

HOUSTON/GALVESTON COAST GUARD MARINE SAFETY OFFICE
9640 Clinton Drive, Houston, TX 77029-4328
C-713-671-5100
WEB: www.uscg.mil/msohoustongalveston
LOCATION: From I-610 north, take Clinton Drive exit east, make left at light and get in the right lane; go 0.5 miles, turn right at Gate 8. USMRA: Houston, TX map (C-5). NMC: Houston, within city limits. NMI: Ellington Field ANG Base, 15 miles south.
RETAIL & DINING: Dining-672-1980 EX-678-4573
Ten-digit dialing required for local calls.

INGLESIDE NAVAL STATION
1455 Ticonderoga Road, Suite W210, Ingleside, TX 78362-5009
C-361-776-4551, DSN-312-776-4200, Police-776-4238
WEB: https://www.nsi.navy.mil/
LOCATION: I-37 south to exit 1A. Follow US-181 northeast to FR-1069 east and Naval Station. USMRA: TX map (K-8). NMC: Corpus Christi, 19 miles south.
RECREATION & TRAVEL: Marina-758-0350 TML-776-4420
RETAIL & DINING: Dining-776-4424 EX-776-4100
SUPPORT & FAMILY: Med-776-4580
NOTE: *The 2005 BRAC report recommended this base for closure. As required by Federal law, the DoD has until 15 September 2007 to begin closing and realigning the bases as called for in the approved report. This process must be completed by 15 September 2011.*

KELLY ANNEX, LACKLAND AIR FORCE BASE
1701 Kenley Avenue, Suite 102
Lackland Air Force Base, TX 78236-5103
C-210-925-1110, DSN-312-945-1110, Police (Security)-671-2018
WEB: www.lackland.af.mil
LOCATION: I-10, I-35, I-37 and I-410 all intersect with US-90 in southwest San Antonio. From US-90, take either the Gen. Hudnell or Gen. McMullen exit and go south to AFB. USMRA: San Antonio, TX map (N-10). NMC: San Antonio, seven miles northeast.
RECREATION & TRAVEL: SPA-925-8714/5 TML-925-1844/8279
RETAIL & DINING: Clubs-NCO-925-8354 OC-925-8254

KINGSVILLE NAVAL AIR STATION
554 McCain Street, Suite 309, Kingsville, TX 78363-5054
C-361-516-6333, DSN-312-876-6333, Police-516-6217
e-mail: nask.pao@nrs.navy.mil
WEB: https://www.nask.navy.mil/
LOCATION: Off US-77 north or south, exit to TX-425 southeast to Main Gate. USMRA: TX map (K-9). NMC: Corpus Christi, 50 miles northeast.
RECREATION & TRAVEL: RVC-830-373-4419 RVC-516-6191/6443 SPA-516-6108 TML-516-6321/6581
RETAIL & DINING: Clubs-CPO/EMC/OC-516-6121 Com-516-6241 EX-516-6361 Gas-516-6106
SUPPORT & FAMILY: Med-516-6238/6305

LACKLAND AIR FORCE BASE
1701 Kenly Avenue, Suite 102
Lackland Air Force Base, TX 78236-5103
C-210-671-1110, DSN-312-473-1110, Police-671-2018
e-mail: publicaf@lackland.af.mil
WEB: www.lackland.af.mil
LOCATION: Located in the southwestern quadrant of the city. Take either I-10 or I-35 to US-90 south. Loop 13 (Military Drive) bisects Lackland AFB. USMRA: TX map (J-7). NMC: San Antonio, six miles northeast.
RECREATION & TRAVEL: Golf-671-3466 or 977-5100 RVC-671-5179 TML-671-2556/3622/4277
RETAIL & DINING: Clubs-NCO/OC-645-7034 Com-671-1110 Dining-670-1666 or 671-3784 EX-674-6465 Gas-674-8094
SUPPORT & FAMILY: Med-292-7100

LAUGHLIN AIR FORCE BASE
47 FTW/PA, 561 Liberty Drive, Suite 3
Laughlin Air Force Base, TX 78843-5230
C-830-298-3511, DSN-312-732-1110, Police-298-5100
WEB: www.laughlin.af.mil
LOCATION: Take US-90 west from San Antonio for 150 miles to Liberty Drive, which leads to the base; or take I-10 east or west to US-277 south and make a left onto TX-317, which leads to the base. The AFB is clearly marked off US-90. USMRA: TX map (H-7). NMC: Del Rio, six miles northwest.
RECREATION & TRAVEL: Golf-298-5451 Marina-775-7800 RVC-775-7800 RVC-298-5830 SPA-298-5308/9 TML-298-5731
RETAIL & DINING: Clubs-EMC-298-5346 OC-298-5134 Com-298-5821 Dining-298-5295 EX-298-3627 Gas-298-3867
SUPPORT & FAMILY: Med-298-3578

RANDOLPH AIR FORCE BASE
1 Washington Circle, Suite 4
Randolph Air Force Base, TX 78150-4562
C-210-652-1110, DSN-312-487-1110, Police-652-5700
e-mail: publicaffairs@randolph.af.mil
WEB: www.randolph.af.mil
LOCATION: From I-35 north or south, take exit 172 south on TX-1604 to AFB; or, I-10 exit 587 north on TX-1604 to AFB. USMRA: San Antonio, TX map (P-9). NMC: San Antonio, five miles southwest.
RECREATION & TRAVEL: Golf-652-4570 RVC-800-280-3466 SPA-652-3725/5287 TML-652-1844
RETAIL & DINING: Clubs-EMC/NCO-658-3557 OC-658-7445 Com-652-6547 Dining-652-5665 EX-658-7471 Gas-658-1515
SUPPORT & FAMILY: Med-652-4373

RANDOLPH OUTDOOR RECREATION AREA-CANYON LAKE
781 Jacobs Creek Park Road, Canyon Lake, TX 78133-3569
C-800-280-3466 or 210-652-1110, DSN-312-487-1110 Police-652-5510
WEB: www.servicesatrandolph.com
LOCATION: Off base. From I-35 north from San Antonio, through New Braunfels to Canyon Lake exit. Turn left on FR-306, follow for 16 miles to Canyon City. Go another 1.5 miles past the blinking traffic light to Jacobs Creek Park Road, turn left. Clearly marked. Must have military ID to enter base. USMRA: TX map (J-6). NMC: San Antonio, 48 miles south. NMI: Randolph AFB, 43 miles southeast.
RECREATION & TRAVEL: Marina-830-964-3804 RVC-800-280-3466

RED RIVER ARMY DEPOT
100 Main Drive, Texarkana, TX 75507-0001
C-903-334-2141, DSN-312-829-2141, Police-334-3151
WEB: www.redriver.army.mil
LOCATION: From east or west on I-30, take Red River Army Depot exit 206 off of I-30 and turn left at the traffic light on US-82. Watch for signs to the base. USMRA: TX map (N-2). NMC: Dallas, 170 miles southwest.
RECREATION & TRAVEL: RVC-334-2254/2688 TML-334-2254/2688
RETAIL & DINING: EX-832-2687
SUPPORT & FAMILY: Med-334-2155
Ten-digit dialing required for local calls.

SHEPPARD AIR FORCE BASE
82 TRW/PA, 419 G Avenue, Suite 3
Sheppard Air Force Base, TX 76311-2943
C-940-676-2511/2732, DSN-312-736-2511, Police-676-6302
WEB: www.sheppard.af.mil
LOCATION: Take US-281 north from Wichita Falls, exit to TX-325 which leads to Main Gate. Clearly marked. USMRA: TX map (J-2). NMC: Wichita Falls, five miles southwest.
RECREATION & TRAVEL: Golf-676-6369 RVC-523-4613 SPA-676-2511 TML-855-7370
RETAIL & DINING: Clubs-EMC-676-2083 NCO-676-6427 OC-676-6460 Com-676-7269 Dining-676-2080 EX-855-4151 Gas-855-4341
SUPPORT & FAMILY: Med-676-1847

SHEPPARD AIR FORCE BASE RECREATION ANNEX AT LAKE TEXOMA
1030 Sheppard AFB Road, Whitesboro, TX 76311-9999
C-903-523-4613, DSN-312-736-2511, Police-903-893-4388
WEB: www.sheppard.af.mil/82svs/lake_texoma.htm
LOCATION: Located approximately 120 miles east of base at Wichita Falls, near the Texas/Oklahoma line. From US-82 east of Gainesville, take US-377 north approximately 11 miles (past Gordonville exit) to FR-901 and turn left. Just prior to this exit is a green SAFB Annex sign. Go two miles; turn right at SAFB Annex sign. Follow signs approximately five miles to recreation annex. Recreation area is located on Texas side of Lake Texoma. USMRA: TX map (K-2). NMC: Dallas, 95 miles south.
RECREATION & TRAVEL: Marina-523-4613 RVC-523-4613 TML-523-4613
NOTE: *For detailed information about this off-base recreation facility, as well as on-base recreation facilities, golf courses and marinas, consult Military Living's "Military RV, Camping and Outdoor Recreation Around the World".*
Ten-digit dialing required for local calls for area code 903.

SOUTHWINDS MARINA ON LAKE AMISTAD
HCR #3, Box 3J, Del Rio, TX 78840-9804
C-830-775-7800, DSN-312-732-1110, Police-911
LOCATION: Off base. From US-90 north of Del Rio, take Spur 349 (Amistad Dam Road) to recreation area. USMRA: TX map (H-7). NMC: Del Rio, 12 miles southeast. NMI: Laughlin AFB, 22.5 miles southeast.
RECREATION & TRAVEL: RVC-775-7800
NOTE: *For detailed information about this off-base recreation facility, as well as on-base recreation facilities, golf courses and marinas, consult Military Living's "Military RV, Camping and Outdoor Recreation Around the World".*

WACO SHOPPETTE
1801 Exchange Parkway, Waco, TX 76712-6908
C-254-666-8309, Police-911
LOCATION: In Waco, exit TX-6 west to Bagby Avenue, to AAFES Distribution Center. USMRA: TX map (K-4). NMC: Waco, within city limits.
RETAIL & DINING: EX-666-8309/8466

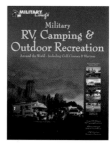

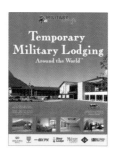

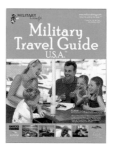

Visit our NEW 20,500 Square Foot Facility - NOW OPEN!

"They Shall Not Be Forgotten"

A memorial to generations of American men and women who have honorably served our nation, during peacetime and war, so that all Americans might enjoy the freedoms we have today.

- Eighty-five 8'x7' Display Cases
- "USO" Reception Area
- Veterans Wall of Honor (Tiles Honoring Veterans)
- Gift Shop
- Laurence Mark Library
- POW/MIA Remembrance Setting
- Stan Price Viewing Room
- 30'x60' U.S. American Flag from USS Abraham Lincoln
- Displays from Revolutionary War to Present - **Weapons, Uniforms, Equipment, Medal, Letters, Photographs, Memorabilia**

Summer Hours: (June-Sept) Tue-Sat 10 A.M. - 5 P.M., SUN 1 P.M. - 5 P.M.
Winter Hours: (Oct-May) Tue-Sat 10 A.M. - 5 P.M., Closed Sunday
Admission: Adults - $5.00, Students $3.00, Under Six - Free

For Information Call (360) 740-8875
100 S.W. Veterans Way • Chehalis, WA 98532
www.veteransmuseum.org E-mail: vmm@quik.com

Museum within 100-mile radius of Mt. St. Helens, ocean beaches, Seattle & Portland

Order Military Living's R&R Travel News®

for 3, 5 or 7 years and get one of our maps, travel guides or atlases

MILITARY Living's

R&R Travel News®

HIGHLIGHTS

Our military travelers visit . . .

- Timbuktu, Mali, Part II
- Hawaii, Guam, Yokota & Singapore
- Slovenia and Hungary
- Retiree Living in Korea
- PLUS Tag Along with Ann

A worldwide travel newsletter published ... ©2006 Military Living Publications www.militaryliving.com

STAN & DEE INK'S SPACE-A ADVENTURE

TO HAWAII, GUAM, YOKOTA & SINGAPORE

. . . AND NEXT ISSUE, ON TO AUSTRALIA!

TUESDAY, NOV. 29, 2005- Dee and I (Stan) are off again this morning. We were going to fly our small plane to Jacksonville, FL, but the weather did not cooperate. We are now driving to Interlachen, FL. Dee's brother, Guy, is taking us to Jacksonville Naval Air Station and bringing the car back to his house until we return. We expect to catch a Navy 737 Space-A flight tomorrow morning from Jacksonville to Kaneohe Bay Marine Corps Base, HI which begins this trip that we hope will get us to Australia. We hope to make it all the way on Space-A flights.

We checked on our flight at the terminal, then Guy dropped us at the Navy Lodge. We walked a bit, exploring the woods and a walkway along St. John's Bay, and then had dinner at a sports bar at the golf club.

WEDNESDAY, NOVEMBER 30- We called about 0600 and a Duty Driver took us to the terminal. Nice service. ***Editor's Note: This service is usually only offered to duty passengers, so don't expect it!*** We checked in and took a bus to the plane by 0800. We were airborne before 0900 in a 72-seat Navy C-40 plane. It is configured to be a half-cargo plane. The seats were spaced so that we had lots of leg room. There were only 25 passengers. It was five and a half hours to North Island NAS, San Diego. We stayed for about one and a half hours for refueling. The flight to Kaneohe took six hours. We picked up snacks at the terminal, including a cheeseburger that we heated in the plane's microwave. The pilot had to do a "go around" when landing, reversing the end of the runway.

We got to Kaneohe about 1600 local time (2100 EST). Enterprise Rent-A-Car was waiting for us to go to their office for a car that I had reserved. By

Stan & Dee Ink with Ted and Sandy Finnerty

Continued on page 10

WHERE IN THE WORLD DO YOU WANT TO RETIRE?

In this issue, we have a feature by Jack Terwiel, the director of Osan AB Retiree office. Jack gives us a heads up on what it is like to retire to South Korea.

With Jack's feature in mind, I selected one of our favorite places for possible retirement. We currently live in the Washington, DC area. The place that we keep going to for R&R is Virginia Beach, VA, which is in the area called Hampton Roads. If we love to go there to have a bit of relaxation, surely we would love to live in that area.

Virginia Beach has miles of oceanfront and even more waterfront property located on lakes, rivers and the Chesapeake Bay, Back Bay, Broad Bay, Lynnhaven Bay and others. It also has the intracoastal waterway which avid boaters find to be ideal.

Continued on page 2

See page 16 to nd out about our new
Militar Space-A Air Travel Map and Pocket Director™

Our subscribers travel on less per day . . . the military way!™ 1 R&R Travel News® Report 207 Mar-Apr 2006 Volume 36, No. 2

R&R Travel News® is published 6 times per year by Military Living Publications

ABSOLUTELY FREE!

3 Years Standard Mail $56 First Class $84

Choose your **FREE** Map below:
United States Military Road Map™—Paper ($11.20) or Plastic ($13.70*)
Military Space-A Air Travel Map & Pocket Directory™—Plastic ($17.20*)

5 Years Standard Mail $84 First Class $134

Choose you **FREE** Travel Guide below:
European Military Travel Guide™ ($26.75*)
Military RV, Camping & Outdoor Recreation Around the World™ ($21.30*)
Military Travel Guide U.S.A.™ ($19.05)
Temporary Military Lodging Around the World™ ($23.75*)

7 Years Standard Mail $106 First Class $181

Choose your **FREE** Atlas below:
United States Military Road Atlas™ ($27.55*)
United States Military Road Atlas, Compact Edition™ (Spiral Binding)

* Military Living Mail Order Value ** Offer expires 12/31/2006. After this date visit our website at www.militaryliving.com for 2007 special offers.

CALL (703) 237-0203 Ext 1 and place your order today!

We accept Visa, Mastercard, American Express and Discover. Sorry, no billing.

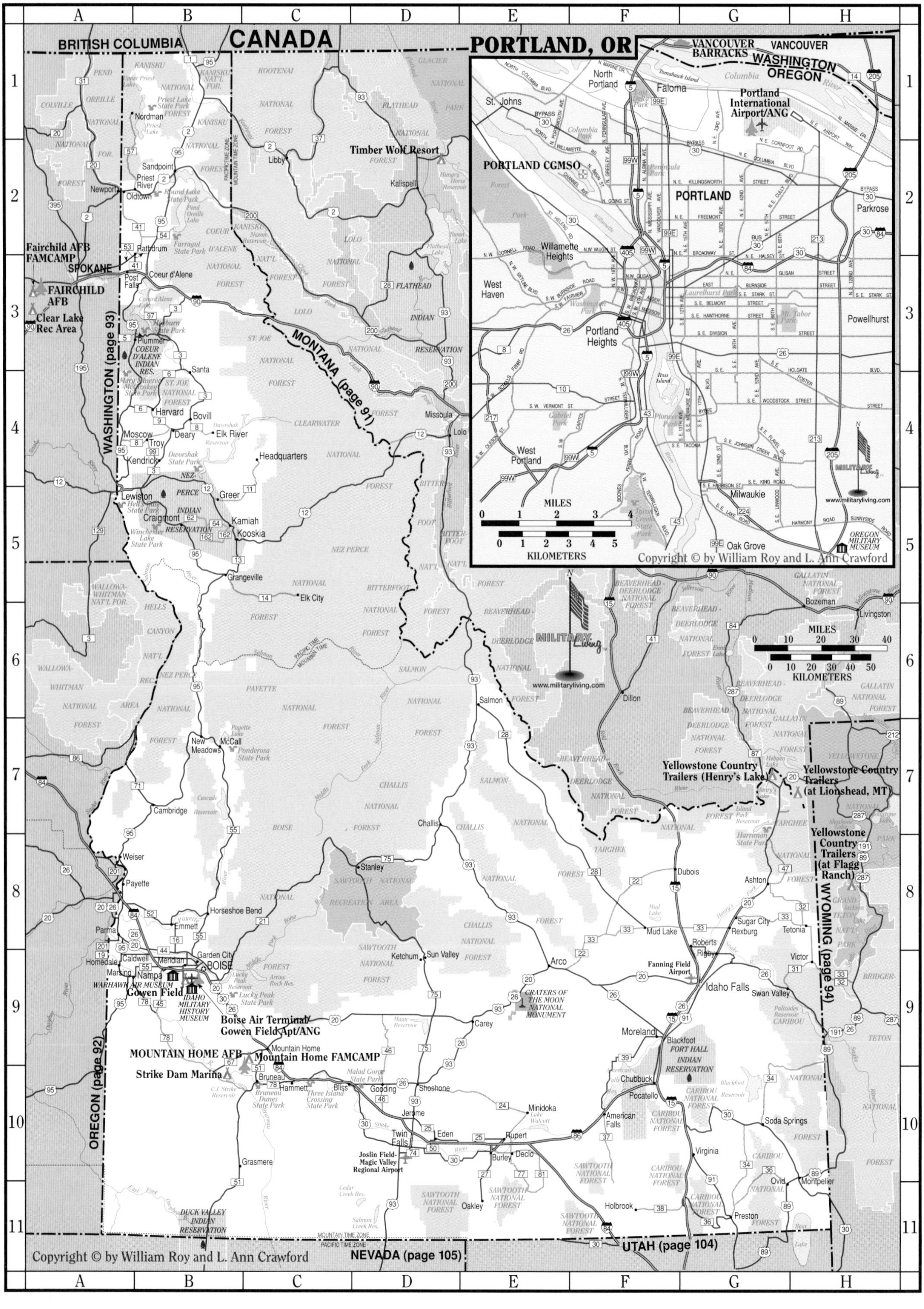

BRITISH COLUMBIA

CANADA

PORTLAND, OR

VANCOUVER BARRACKS

VANCOUVER

WASHINGTON

OREGON

North Portland

Faloma

St. Johns

Portland International Airport/ANG

PORTLAND CGMSO

PORTLAND

Parkrose

Willamette Heights

West Haven

Portland Heights

Powellhurst

West Portland

Milwaukie

Oak Grove

OREGON MILITARY MUSEUM

MILES 0 1 2 3 4

0 1 2 3 4 5 KILOMETERS

www.militaryliving.com

Fairchild AFB FAMCAMP

SPOKANE

FAIRCHILD AFB

Clear Lake Rec Area

Timber Wolf Resort

Kalispell

Libby

Sandpoint

Priest River

Newport

Oldtown

Rathdrum

Coeur d'Alene

Post Falls

Plummer

Santa

Harvard

Bovill

Moscow

Troy

Deary

Elk River

Kendrick

Headquarters

Lewiston

Greer

Craigmont

Kamiah

Kooskia

Grangeville

Elk City

Missoula

Lolo

Bozeman

Livingston

Dillon

Salmon

New Meadows

McCall

Cambridge

Challis

Weiser

Payette

Stanley

Horseshoe Bend

Emmett

Parma

Homedale

Caldwell

Meridian

Garden City

BOISE

Marsing

Nampa

WARHAWK AIR MUSEUM

Gowen Field

IDAHO MILITARY HISTORY MUSEUM

Boise Air Terminal/Gowen Field Apt/ANG

MOUNTAIN HOME AFB

Mountain Home

Mountain Home FAMCAMP

Strike Dam Marina

Bruneau

Hammett

Bliss

Gooding

Shoshone

Ketchum

Sun Valley

Arco

Carey

CRATERS OF THE MOON NATIONAL MONUMENT

Minidoka

Jerome

Twin Falls

Eden

Rupert

Burley

Declo

Joslin Field-Magic Valley Regional Airport

Oakley

Grasmere

DUCK VALLEY INDIAN RESERVATION

Dubois

Mud Lake

Roberts

Rigby

Fanning Field Airport

Idaho Falls

Swan Valley

Ashton

Sugar City

Rexburg

Tetonia

Victor

Moreland

Blackfoot

FORT HALL INDIAN RESERVATION

Chubbuck

Pocatello

American Falls

Soda Springs

Virginia

Holbrook

Ovid

Montpelier

Preston

Yellowstone Country Trailers (Henry's Lake)

Yellowstone Country Trailers (at Lionshead, MT)

Yellowstone Country Trailers (at Flagg Ranch)

MILES 0 10 20 30 40

0 10 20 30 40 50 KILOMETERS

WASHINGTON (page 93)

MONTANA (page 91)

WYOMING (page 94)

OREGON (page 92)

NEVADA (page 105)

UTAH (page 104)

PACIFIC TIME ZONE / MOUNTAIN TIME ZONE

Copyright © by William Roy and L. Ann Crawford

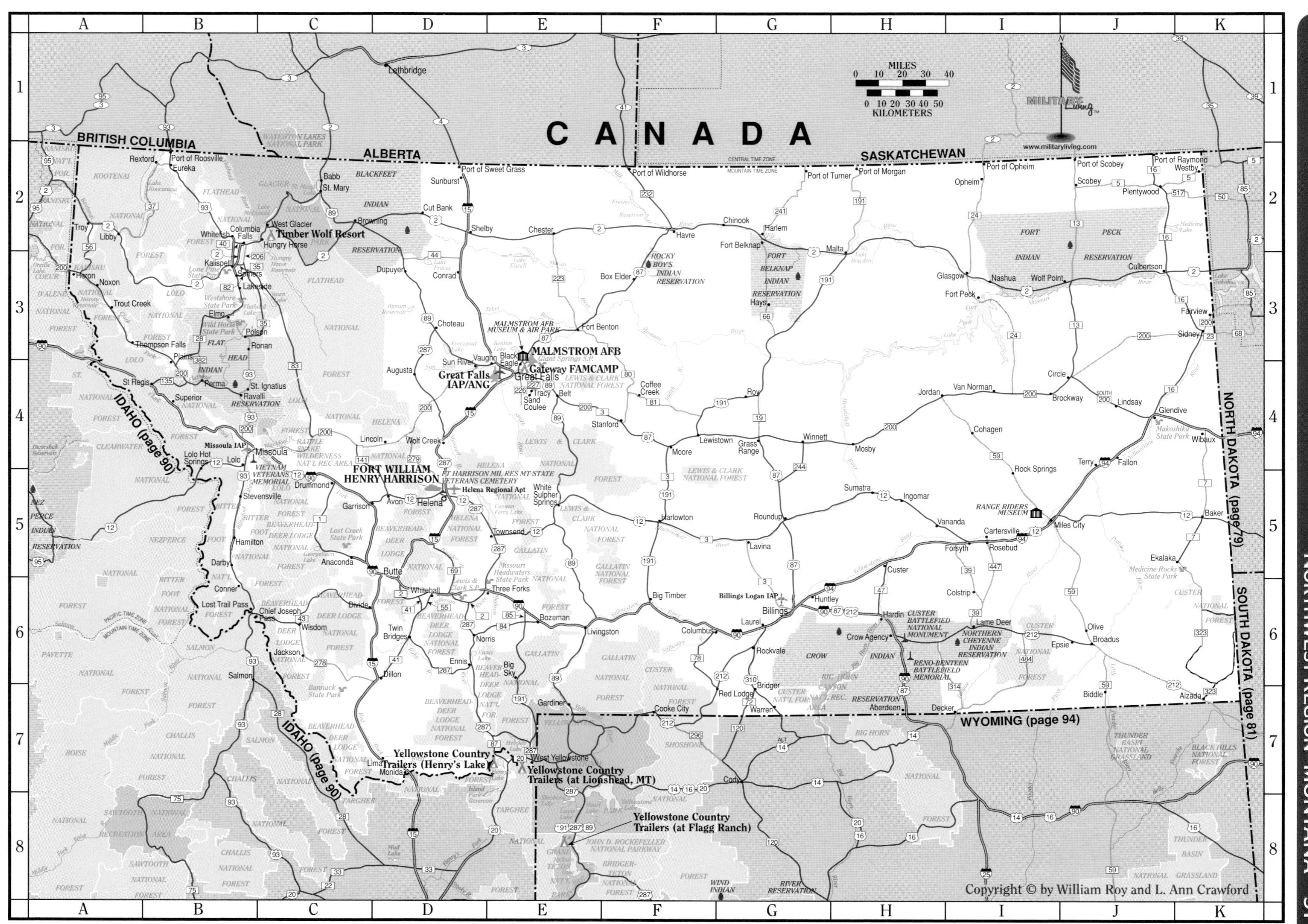
CANADA
BRITISH COLUMBIA
ALBERTA
SASKATCHEWAN
NORTH DAKOTA (page 79)
SOUTH DAKOTA (page 81)
WYOMING (page 94)
IDAHO (page 90)
IDAHO (page 90)
MILES
KILOMETERS
www.militaryliving.com
MALMSTROM AFB
Gateway FAMCAMP
Great Falls IAP/ANG
MALMSTROM AFB MUSEUM & AIR PARK
FORT WILLIAM HENRY HARRISON
FT HARRISON MIL RES MT STATE VETERANS CEMETERY
Helena Regional Apt
Timber Wolf Resort
Yellowstone Country Trailers (Henry's Lake)
Yellowstone Country Trailers (at Lionshead, MT)
Yellowstone Country Trailers (at Flagg Ranch)
Billings Logan IAP
Missoula IAP
RANGE RIDERS MUSEUM
CUSTER BATTLEFIELD NATIONAL MONUMENT
RENO-BENTEEN BATTLEFIELD MEMORIAL
Lethbridge
Kalispell
Missoula
Helena
Butte
Bozeman
Great Falls
Billings
Havre
Glasgow
Miles City
Glendive
Lewistown
Livingston
Copyright © by William Roy and L. Ann Crawford

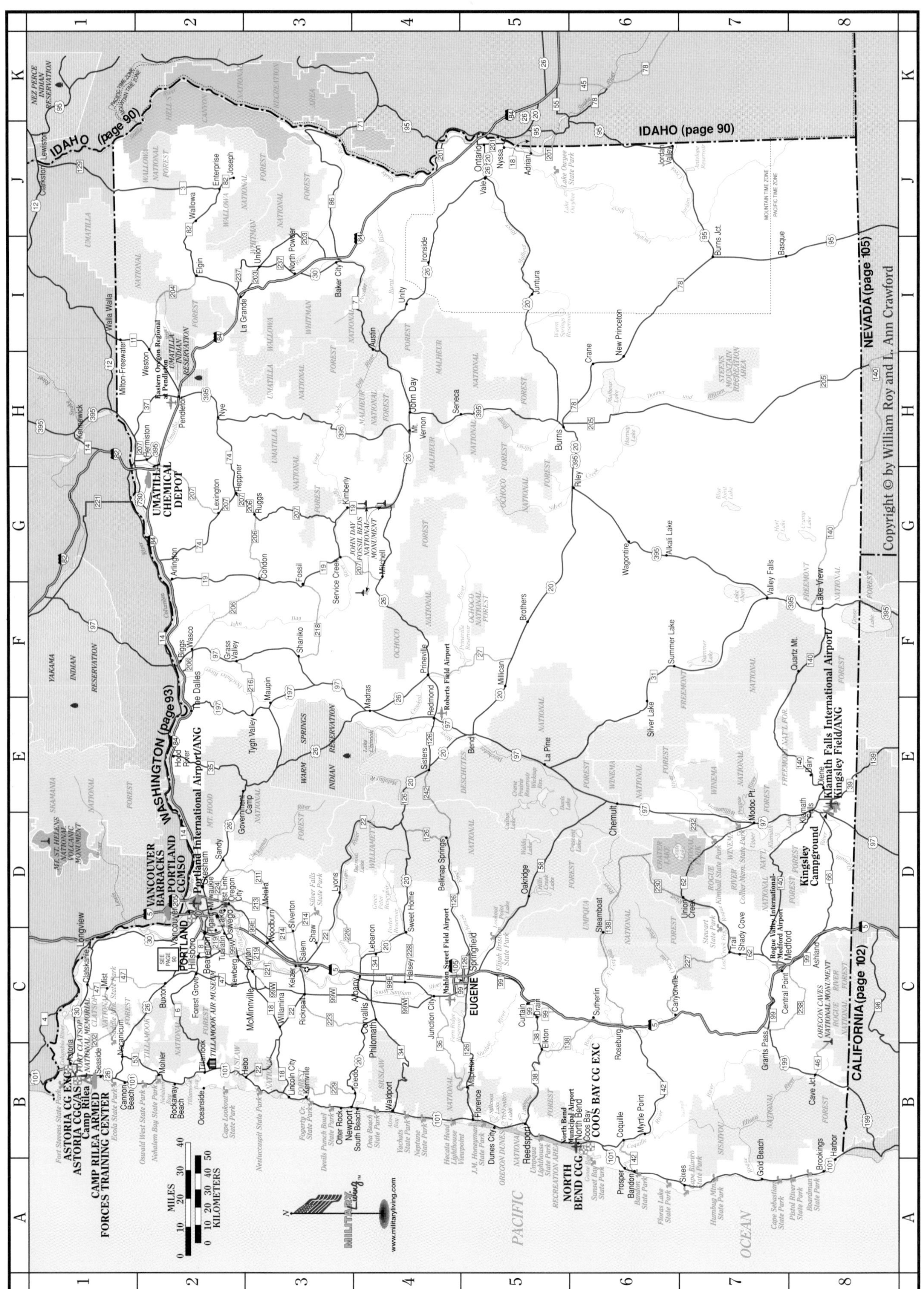
ASTORIA CG EXC
ASTORIA CGG/AS
Camp Rilea
CAMP RILEA ARMED FORCES TRAINING CENTER
VANCOUVER BARRACKS
PORTLAND CGMSO
Portland International Airport/ANG
UMATILLA CHEMICAL DEPOT
Eastern Oregon Regional at Pendleton
Roberts Field Airport
Mahlon Sweet Field Airport
EUGENE
PORTLAND
NORTH BEND CGG
COOS BAY CG EXC
North Bend Municipal Airport
Rogue Valley International-Medford Airport
Kingsley Campground
Klamath Falls International Airport/Kingsley Field/ANG
WASHINGTON (page 93)
IDAHO (page 90)
NEVADA (page 105)
CALIFORNIA (page 102)
SEE PAGE 90
PACIFIC
OCEAN
MILES 0 10 20 30 40
KILOMETERS 0 10 20 30 40 50
www.militaryliving.com
Copyright © by William Roy and L. Ann Crawford

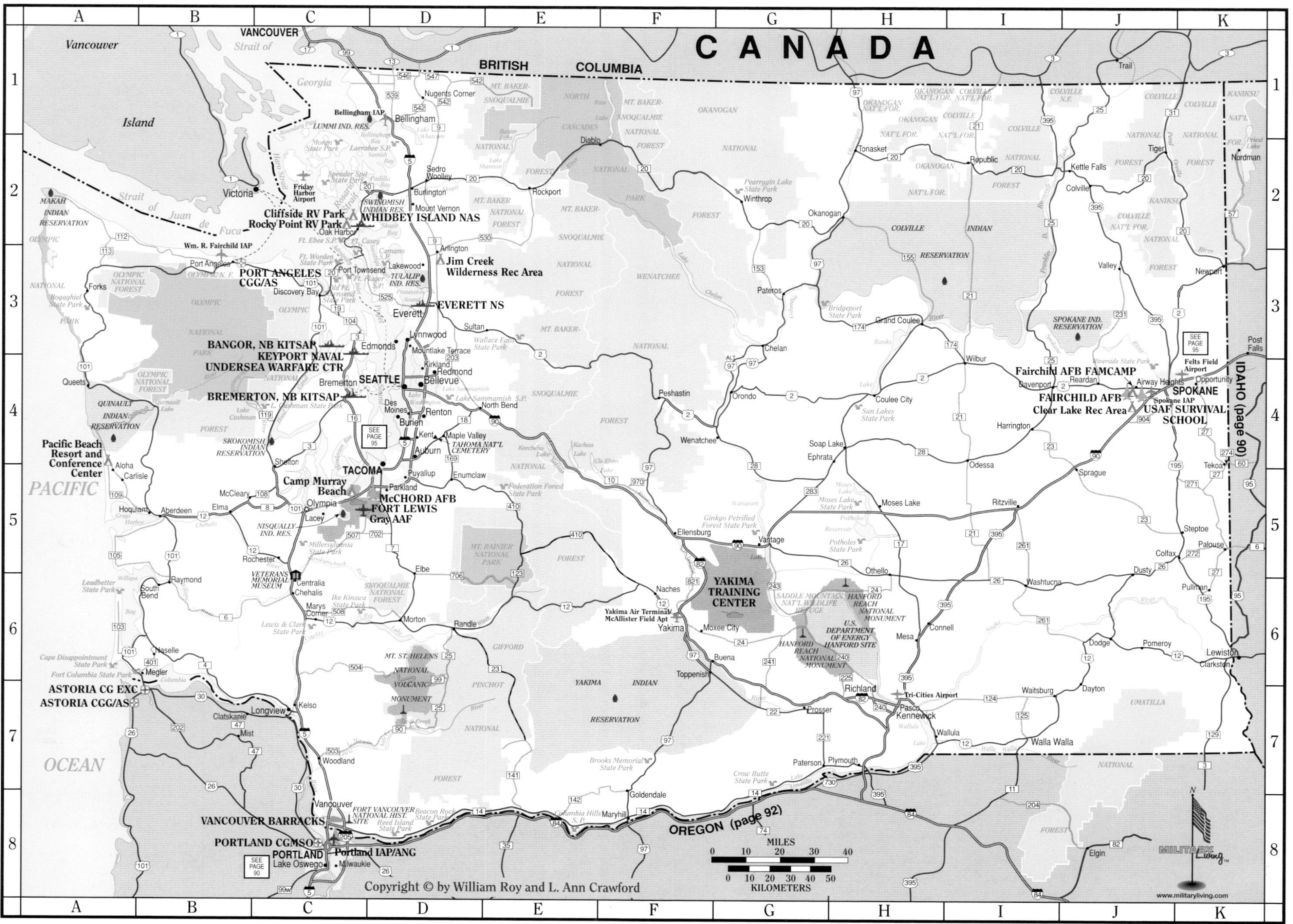
CANADA
BRITISH COLUMBIA
IDAHO (page 90)
OREGON (page 92)
PACIFIC
OCEAN
Vancouver Island
Strait of Juan de Fuca
Strait of Georgia
VANCOUVER
Victoria
SEATTLE
TACOMA
SPOKANE
Fairchild AFB FAMCAMP
FAIRCHILD AFB
Clear Lake Rec Area
USAF SURVIVAL SCHOOL
Spokane IAP
Felts Field Airport
EVERETT NS
Jim Creek Wilderness Rec Area
WHIDBEY ISLAND NAS
Cliffside RV Park
Rocky Point RV Park
Friday Harbor Airport
Bellingham IAP
Wm. R. Fairchild IAP
PORT ANGELES CGG/AS
BANGOR, NB KITSAP
KEYPORT NAVAL UNDERSEA WARFARE CTR
BREMERTON, NB KITSAP
Camp Murray Beach
McCHORD AFB
FORT LEWIS
Gray AAF
Pacific Beach Resort and Conference Center
ASTORIA CG EXC
ASTORIA CGG/AS
VANCOUVER BARRACKS
PORTLAND CGMSO
PORTLAND
Portland IAP/ANG
YAKIMA TRAINING CENTER
Yakima Air Terminal McAllister Field Apt
Tri-Cities Airport
HANFORD REACH NATIONAL MONUMENT
U.S. DEPARTMENT OF ENERGY HANFORD SITE
YAKIMA INDIAN RESERVATION
COLVILLE INDIAN RESERVATION
SPOKANE IND. RESERVATION
MT. RAINIER NATIONAL PARK
MT. ST. HELENS NATIONAL VOLCANIC MONUMENT
VETERANS MEMORIAL MUSEUM
TAHOMA NAT'L CEMETERY
SEE PAGE 95
SEE PAGE 90
MILES
KILOMETERS
Copyright © by William Roy and L. Ann Crawford
www.militaryliving.com

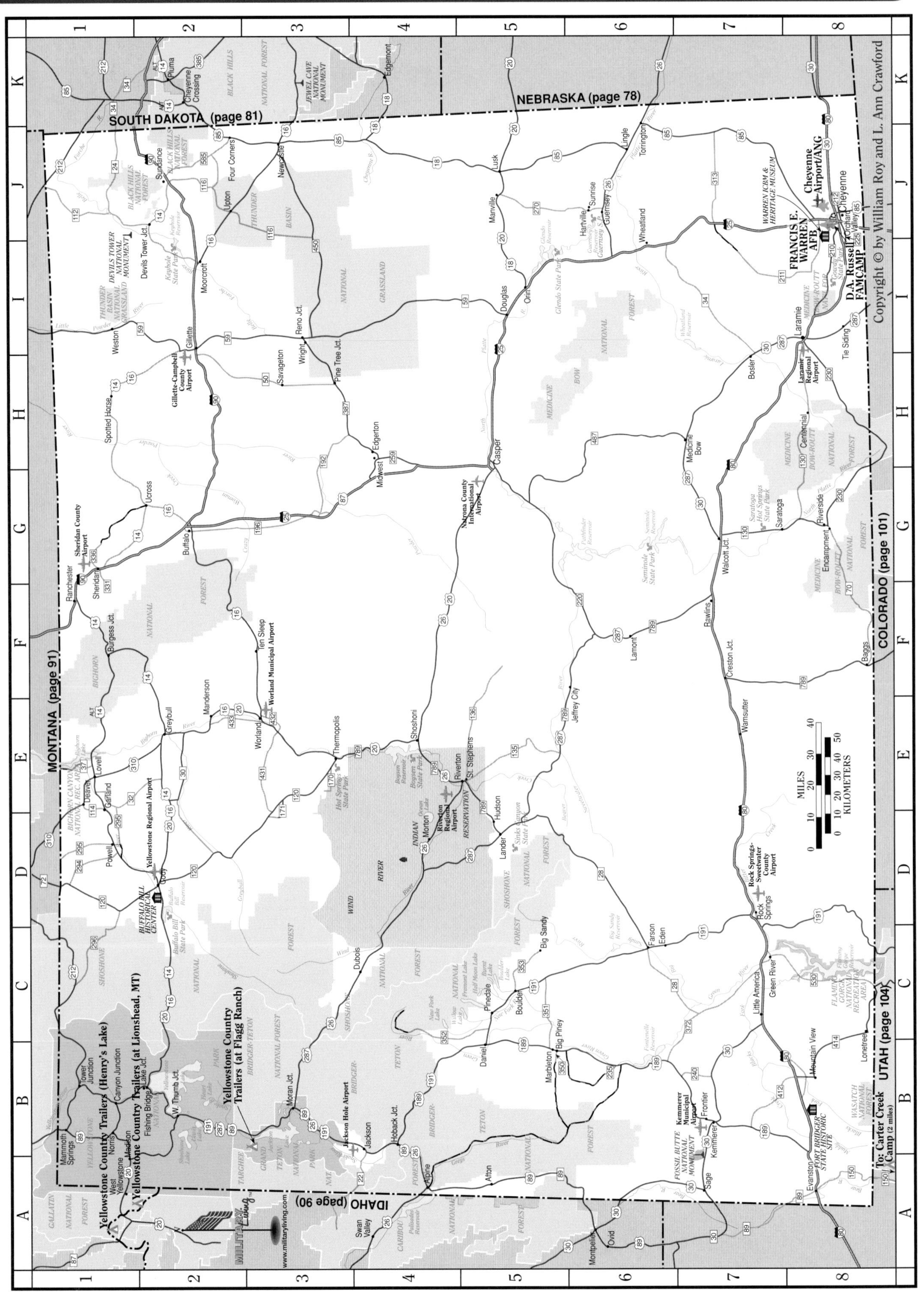
MONTANA (page 91)
SOUTH DAKOTA (page 81)
NEBRASKA (page 78)
COLORADO (page 101)
UTAH (page 104)
IDAHO (page 90)
Yellowstone Country Trailers (Henry's Lake)
Yellowstone Country Trailers (at Lionshead, MT)
Yellowstone Country Trailers (at Flagg Ranch)
To: Carter Creek Camp (2 miles)
FRANCIS E. WARREN AFB
Cheyenne Airport/ANG
WARREN ICBM & HERITAGE MUSEUM
D.A. Russell FAMCAMP
BUFFALO BILL HISTORICAL CENTER
Yellowstone Regional Airport
Sheridan County Airport
Gillette-Campbell County Airport
Natrona County International Airport
Worland Municipal Airport
Riverton Regional Airport
Jackson Hole Airport
Kemmerer Municipal Airport
Rock Springs-Sweetwater County Airport
Laramie Regional Airport
DEVILS TOWER NATIONAL MONUMENT
FOSSIL BUTTE NATIONAL MONUMENT
FORT BRIDGER STATE HISTORIC SITE
FLAMING GORGE NATIONAL RECREATION AREA
BIGHORN CANYON NATIONAL REC. AREA
WIND RIVER INDIAN RESERVATION
MILES 0 10 20 30 40
KILOMETERS 0 10 20 30 40 50
www.militaryliving.com
Copyright © by William Roy and L. Ann Crawford

SEATTLE/TACOMA, WA

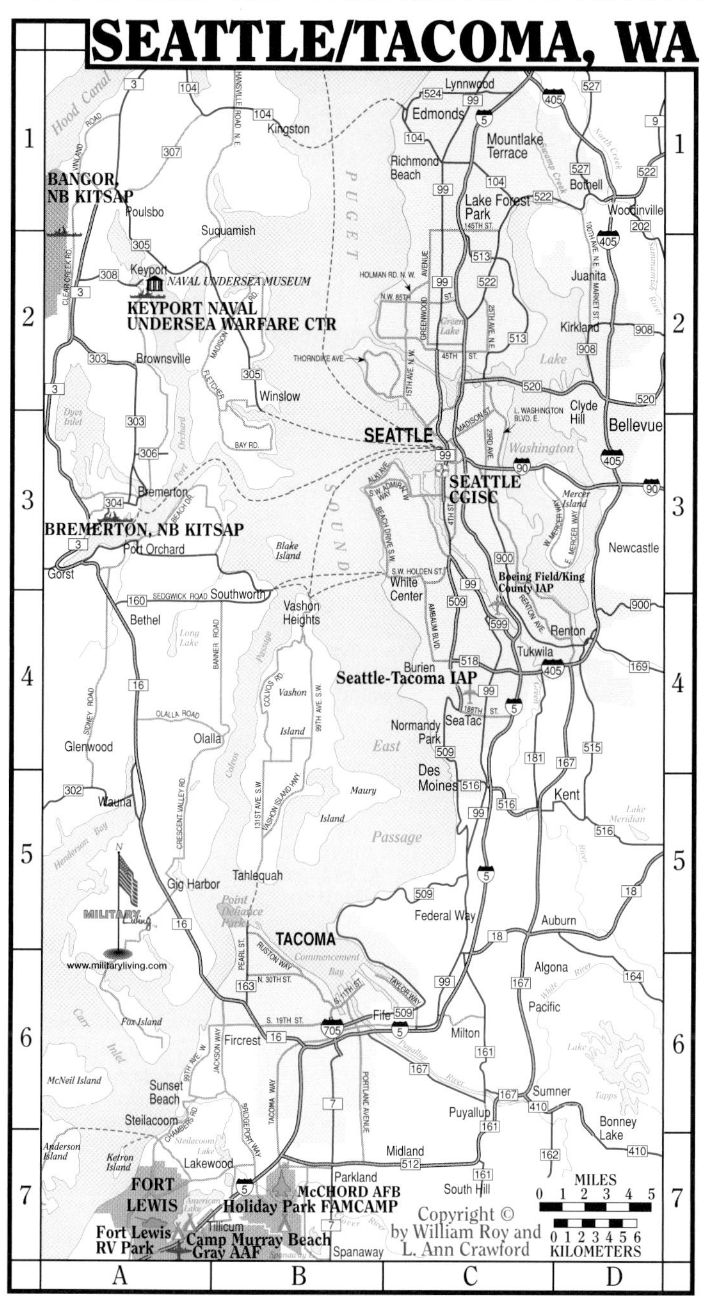

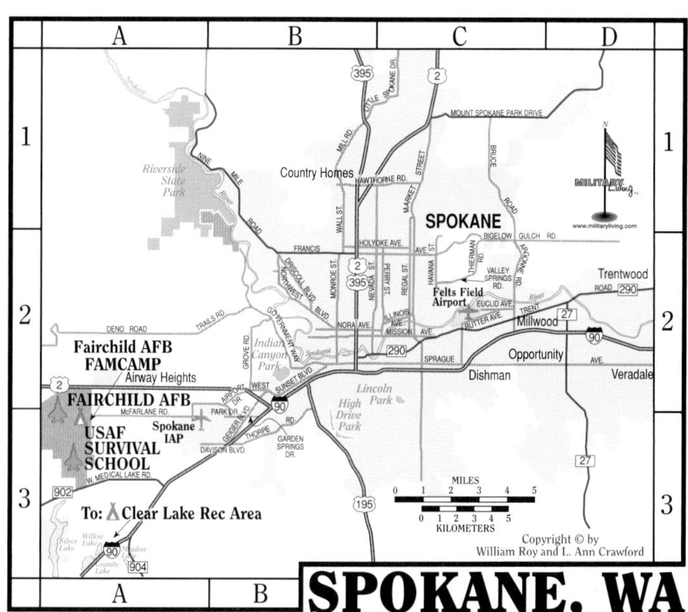

SPOKANE, WA

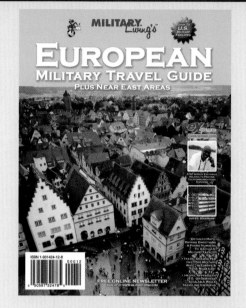

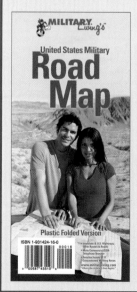

IDAHO, PG. 90

BOISE AIR TERMINAL/GOWEN FIELD AIRPORT/AIR NATIONAL GUARD

4474 S. DeHavilland Street, Boise, ID 83705-8103
C-208-422-5226, DSN-312-422-5322, Police-422-5366
e-mail: pa.124wg@idbois.and.af.mil
WEB: www.idaho.ang.af.mil
LOCATION: From I-84 east or west, take Orchard Street exit (exit 52 south). Turn left and remain on Gowen Road as it goes behind the airport. Watch for 'Gowen Field' sign near tanks. Turn left into Main Gate. USMRA: ID map (B-9). NMC: Boise, five miles north.
RECREATION & TRAVEL: RVC-422-4451 SPA-422-5989 or 888-252-3285 TML-422-4451
RETAIL & DINING: Clubs-NCO-422-5674 OC-422-5667/8 EX-422-5676 Snack Bar-422-5674
SUPPORT & FAMILY: Med-422-5369

MOUNTAIN HOME AIR FORCE BASE

366 Gunfighter Avenue, Suite 152
Mountain Home Air Force Base, ID 83648-5258
C-208-828-1110, DSN-312-728-1110, Police-828-2256
e-mail: pa.news@mountainhome.af.mil
WEB: www.mountainhome.af.mil
LOCATION: From Boise, take I-84 southeast, 39 miles to Mountain Home, exit 95 west, follow road through town to ID-67 west (Airbase Road), ten miles to Main Gate on left. USMRA: ID map (B,C-9,10). NMC: Boise, 50 miles northwest.
RECREATION & TRAVEL: Golf-828-6151/6559 RVC-828-6333 SPA-828-4841 TML-828-5152/5200
RETAIL & DINING: Clubs-CC-828-2105 Com-828-2286 Dining-828-6420 EX-832-4353 Gas-832-4660
SUPPORT & FAMILY: Med-828-1560

STRIKE DAM MARINA

Attn: Strike Dam Marina, Bldg 2800, 366 SVS/SVRM
Mountain Home AFB, ID 83648-5125
C-208-828-6333, DSN-312-728-1110, Police-828-2256
LOCATION: Off base. From I-84 at Mountain Home, exit 95 west, follow road through Mountain Home to ID-67 (Air Base Road), continue past AFB for approximately 20 miles to the C.J. Strike Reservoir on the Snake River south of ID-67. USMRA: ID map (B-10). NMC: Boise, 60 miles north. NMI: Mountain Home AFB, 20 miles northeast.
RECREATION & TRAVEL: Marina-834-2723 (Open Memorial Day through Labor Day) RVC-828-6333
NOTE: *For detailed information about this off-base recreation facility, as well as on-base recreation facilities, golf courses and marinas, consult Military Living's "Military RV, Camping and Outdoor Recreation Around the World".*

YELLOWSTONE COUNTRY TRAILERS

SVS/SVRO Outdoor Recreation 655 Pine Street, Bldg 2800
Mountain Home AFB, ID 83648-5237
C-208-828-2111, DSN-312-728-1110
LOCATION: Off base. One trailer at Henry's Lake is located about five miles off US-20 on the north side of the lake. Four trailers at Lionshead are just off US-20, about eight miles from the west entrance of Yellowstone. Eight other trailers are located two miles south of Yellowstone's south entrance between Yellowstone and Grand Tetons National Parks. Directions, instructions and keys will be provided at the time of booking. USMRA: ID map (G,H-7). NMC: Idaho Falls, 80 miles south. NMI: Malmstrom AFB, 254 miles north.
RECREATION & TRAVEL: RVC-828-6333 TML-828-6333
NOTE: *For detailed information about this off-base recreation facility, as well as on-base recreation facilities, golf courses and marinas, consult Military Living's "Military RV, Camping and Outdoor Recreation Around the World".*

MONTANA, PG. 91

FORT WILLIAM HENRY HARRISON

P.O. Box 4789, Bldg 1011 Helena, MT 59604-4789
C-406-324-3355, DSN-312-324-3355, Police-911
LOCATION: Take I-15 north or south toward Helena. Take the Cedar Street exit, and turn right onto Cedar Street. Turn right onto N Harris Street. Follow signs for Camp Stan Stevens/Fort Harrison to front gate. USMRA: MT map (D-5). NMC: Helena, two miles east.
RETAIL & DINING: Clubs-NCO-324-3355 Dining-324-3355 EX-443-0837

GREAT FALLS INTERNATIONAL AIRPORT/ AIR NATIONAL GUARD

120 Fighter Wing, 2800 Airport Avenue B
Great Falls, MT 59404-5570
C-406-727-4650, DSN-312-791-0286, Police-791-0276
WEB: www.mtgrea.ang.af.mil
LOCATION: From I-15, exit 277 to Airport Drive. Make a left onto Airport Avenue B. USMRA: MT map (E-4). NMC: Great Falls, one mile. NMI: Malmstom AFB, 10 miles northeast.
RECREATION & TRAVEL: SPA-731-4622
RETAIL & DINING: Dining-791-0165 EX-791-0299
SUPPORT & FAMILY: Med-791-0288

MALMSTROM AIR FORCE BASE

341 Space Wing, 21, 77th Street North
Malmstrom Air Force Base, MT 59402-7538
C-406-731-1110, DSN-312-632-1110, Police-731-3895
WEB: www.malmstrom.af.mil
LOCATION: From I-15, take Tenth Avenue South, exit 278 to Malmstrom AFB. From the east, take Malmstrom exit off US-87/89. Clearly marked. USMRA: MT map (E-3). NMC: Great Falls, one mile west.
RECREATION & TRAVEL: RVC-387-9653 or 731-3262/4202 TML-727-8600 or 731-3394
RETAIL & DINING: Clubs-Malmstrom-761-6430 Com-452-6473 Dining-731-2003 EX-761-8004 Gas-761-3333
SUPPORT & FAMILY: Med-731-1911

TIMBER WOLF RESORT

9105 Highway 2 East, P. O. Box 190800
Hungry Horse, MT 59919-0800
C-406-387-9653 or 877-846-9653, Police-911
WEB: www.timberwolfresort.com
LOCATION: Off base. From I-15 north to Conrad, take MT-44 west past Valier to US-89 north to Browning. From Browning, take US-2 to Hungry Horse. Resort is at corner of US-2 and Hungry Horse Dam Road. USMRA: MT map (C-2). NMC: Kalispell, 20 miles west.
RECREATION & TRAVEL: RVC-731-3263 TML-387-9653
NOTE: *For detailed information about this off-base recreation facility, as well as on-base recreation facilities, golf courses and marinas, consult Military Living's "Military RV, Camping and Outdoor Recreation Around the World".*

OREGON, PG. 92
Portland, PG. 90

ASTORIA COAST GUARD EXCHANGE

1240 West Marine Drive, Astoria, OR 97103-5612
C-503-325-0108
WEB: www.uscg.mil
LOCATION: From US-101/OR-202 junction, head southeast on OR-202 (West Marine Drive) approximately 1.5 miles. Exchange is the first right-hand turn, clearly visible. USMRA: OR map (B-1).
RETAIL & DINING: EX-325-0108

ASTORIA COAST GUARD GROUP/ AIR STATION

2185 Southeast Airport Road, 12th Place
Warrenton, OR 97146-9693
C-503-861-6220
WEB: www.uscg.mil
LOCATION: Take OR-30 from Portland west to Astoria. Go through Astoria and across the Young River Bridge. Follow signs, plainly marked. USMRA: OR map (B-1). NMC: Portland, 100 miles east.
RETAIL & DINING: Com-325-0108 EX-325-0108, ext. 13 Gas-325-0108
SUPPORT & FAMILY: Med-861-6240

CAMP RILEA ARMED FORCES TRAINING CENTER

33168 Patriot Way, Warrenton, OR 97146-9711
C-503-861-4000, DSN-312-355-4000, Police-861-2755
LOCATION: From Portland, take US-26 northwest to Oregon Coast and US-101 (approximately 75 miles), then proceed north on US-101 for 20 miles. Turn left onto Patriot Way. Camp located between Seaside and Astoria. USMRA: OR map (B-1). NMC: Astoria, five miles north. NMI: Fort Lewis, WA, 144 miles north.
RECREATION & TRAVEL: RVC-861-4018 TML-861-4042/52
RETAIL & DINING: EX-861-3623

COOS BAY COAST GUARD EXCHANGE

1684 Ocean Blvd, Coos Bay, OR 97420-1143
C-541-756-9223
WEB: www.uscg.mil
LOCATION: From US-101, turn west onto Commercial, which turns into Ocean Blvd. USMRA: OR map (B-6). NMC: Eugene, 85 miles northeast.
RETAIL & DINING: EX-756-5285

KLAMATH FALLS INTERNATIONAL AIRPORT/KINGSLEY FIELD/ AIR NATIONAL GUARD

211 Arnold Avenue, Suite 11, Klamath Falls, OR 97603-1925
C-541-885-6350, DSN-312-830-6350, Police-885-6663
LOCATION: Take I-5 to exit 30 to OR-62. Take a right onto OR-140 for 5.5 miles to Southside Bypass. Go east approximately 4.5 miles to the airport. USMRA: OR map (D,E-8). NMC: Medford, 80 miles west.
RECREATION & TRAVEL: RVC-885-6150 SPA-885-6686 TML-885-6365
RETAIL & DINING: Clubs-CC-885-6484 EX-885-6371
SUPPORT & FAMILY: Med-885-6312

NORTH BEND COAST GUARD GROUP

2000 Connecticut Avenue, North Bend, OR 97459-2399
C-541-756-9210/20
WEB: www.uscg.mil/d13/units/grunbend/group
LOCATION: Take US-101 north, turn west on Virginia Avenue for one mile, then turn right on Connecticut Avenue. Follow signs for Coast Guard Air Station. USMRA: OR map (A,B-6). NMC: Eugene, 80 miles northeast.
RECREATION & TRAVEL: TML-756-9201
RETAIL & DINING: EX-888-5285
SUPPORT & FAMILY: Med-756-9234

PORTLAND COAST GUARD MARINE SAFETY OFFICE

6767 North Basin Avenue, Portland, OR 97217-3929
C-503-240-9310
WEB: www.uscg.mil/d13/units/msoportland
LOCATION: From airport, take I-205 south exit to I-84 west, and then I-5 north to exit 303 (Killingsworth/Swan Island) onto North Greeley Avenue. Make a left onto North Going Street and right onto North Basin Avenue to the USCG and Reserve Center. USMRA: OR map (D-2); Portland, OR map (F-2); WA map (C-8). NMC: Portland, within city limits.
RETAIL & DINING: Dining-240-9354 EX-286-3510
SUPPORT & FAMILY: Med-240-9343
Ten-digit dialing required for local calls.

PORTLAND INTERNATIONAL AIRPORT/ AIR NATIONAL GUARD

6801 Northeast Cornfoot Road, Portland, OR 97218-2797
C-503-335-4000, DSN-312-638-4000, Police-335-4221
WEB: www.orport.ang.af.mil
LOCATION: Go south on I-205 to Northeast Airport Way exit, west on Northeast Airport Way to Alderwood, south on Alderwood to Northeast Cornfoot Road. Co-located with Portland International Airport. USMRA: OR map (D-2), Portland, OR map (G-1), WA map (C-8). NMC: Portland, within city limits.
RECREATION & TRAVEL: SPA-335-4390/4421
RETAIL & DINING: Clubs-CC-335-5151 EX-249-0997
SUPPORT & FAMILY: Med-335-4756
Ten-digit dialing required for local calls.

UMATILLA CHEMICAL DEPOT

Building 1, Hermiston, OR 97838-9544
C-541-564-5312, Police-564-5240
LOCATION: Take I-84 east from Portland or west from Pendleton, to exit 177 and follow signs to the base. Take I-82 south from Tri-Cities, WA, to I-84 and exit 177. Follow signs to the base. USMRA: OR map (G-2). NMC: Hermiston, seven miles east.
RECREATION & TRAVEL: RVC-564-5312
SUPPORT & FAMILY Med-564-5215
NOTE: *The 2005 BRAC report recommended this base for closure. As required by Federal law, the DoD has until 15 September 2007 to begin closing and realigning the bases as called for in the approved report. This process must be completed by 15 September 2011.*

WASHINGTON, PG. 93
Seattle/Tacoma, PG. 95
Spokane, PG. 95

BANGOR NAVAL BASE KITSAP

1100 Hunley Road, Silverdale, WA 98315-1199
C-360-396-6111, DSN-312-744-6111, Police-396-6555
WEB: www.nbk.navy.mil
LOCATION: From Seattle-Tacoma Airport, take I-5 south to Tacoma. Take exit 132 (Bremerton exit) from I-5. Follow WA-16 west to WA-3 at Gorst. Take WA-3 north approximately 12 miles to the Naval Submarine Base Bangor exit; the exit will be to the right and then crosses back over the highway. USMRA: Seattle/Tacoma, WA map (A-1,2). NMC: Silverdale, two miles south.
RECREATION & TRAVEL: TML-396-4034 DV/VIP-396-6581 Navy Lodge-800-NAVY-INN or 779-9100

RETAIL & DINING: Cafeteria-396-4296 Clubs-CC-353-5977 Com-396-6025 Dining-396-6891 EX-697-8716 Gas-697-8711
SUPPORT & FAMILY: Med-315-4391

BREMERTON NAVAL BASE KITSAP

120 South Dewey Street, Bremerton, WA 98314-5020
C-360-476-3711, DSN-312-476-3711, Police-476-3393
WEB: www.nbk.navy.mil
LOCATION: From Seattle-Tacoma Airport follow signs for I-5 south; after taking I-5 south exit, go approximately 30 miles to exit 132, WA-16, Bremerton and Gig Harbor. Follow WA-16 approximately 34 miles to WA-3N, take WA-3N to Kitsap Way exit. Go right at stop sign, right onto Naval Avenue to 24-hour gate. One-hour ferry ride from Seattle. USMRA: WA map (C-4), Seattle/Tacoma, WA map (A-3). NMC: Bremerton, within city limits.
RECREATION & TRAVEL: TML-475-3030/5 or 476-1791/2455/97 or 800-576-9327
RETAIL & DINING: Cafeteria-476-5756 Clubs-CC-535-5977 Com-405-1971 Dining-476-6136 EX-478-5570
SUPPORT & FAMILY: Med-479-6552

CAMP MURRAY BEACH

P.O. Box 92055, Lakewood, WA 98492-0055
C-253-584-5411, Police-512-8939 (Security)
LOCATION: From I-5 south of Tacoma, take exit 122 west across railroad tracks, left through Camp Murray gate and follow signs to beach. USMRA: WA map (C-5). NMC: Tacoma, ten miles north.
RECREATION & TRAVEL: RVC-512-7610, 584-5411 or 800-588-6420
NOTE: *For detailed information about this, as well as other recreation facilities, golf courses and marinas, consult Military Living's "Military RV, Camping and Outdoor Recreation Around the World".*

CLEAR LAKE RECREATION AREA

S 14824 Clear Lake Road, Cheney, WA 99004-9276
C-509-299-5129 or 247-2511 Emergency-911
WEB: public.fairchild.amc.af.mil/~services/info_mgt/Clear%20Lake.htm
LOCATION: Off base. From I-90 east or west, take exit 264 north onto WA-902 (Salnave Road), then take a right on Clear Lake Road for 0.5 miles. Turn left onto an unnamed road and travel for 0.7 miles and turn left into the campground. USMRA: WA map (J-4). NMC: Spokane, 12 miles northeast. NMI: Fairchild AFB, 7.5 miles north.
RECREATION & TRAVEL: RVC-299-5129 SPA-585-6409 TML-299-5129
NOTE: *For detailed information about this off-base recreation facility, as well as on-base recreation facilities, golf courses and marinas, consult Military Living's "Military RV, Camping and Outdoor Recreation Around the World".*

EVERETT NAVAL STATION

2000 West Marine View Drive. Everett, WA 98207-5001
C-425-304-3000, DSN-312-727-3000, Police-304-3136
WEB: www.everett.navy.mil
LOCATION: Take I-5 north, exit 193 to Pacific Avenue. Turn right onto West Marine View Drive, base is on the left. To Smokey Point Navy Support Complex (13910 45th Avenue NE, Marysville, WA 98271-7855), which is located about 11 miles north of the main base. Take I-5 north, then take exit 202, and turn right. Turn left on State Street/Smokey Point Blvd. Turn right onto 136th Street. Turn left on 45th to Family Support Complex. USMRA: WA map (D-3). NMC: Seattle, 25 miles south.
RECREATION & TRAVEL: Marina-304-3918 RVC-276-4414 TML-304-3111/4860 Navy Lodge-800-NAVY-INN or 360-653-6390
RETAIL & DINING: Com-304-3411 Dining-304-3169 EX-Fleet-304-4455 Smokey Point-304-4940
SUPPORT & FAMILY: Med-304-4062

FAIRCHILD AIR FORCE BASE

1 East Bong Street, Suite 103
Fairchild Air Force Base, WA 99011-9433
C-509-247-1212, DSN-312-657-1110/1212, Police-247-5493
WEB: http://public.fairchild.amc.af.mil/index.html
LOCATION: Take US-2 exit from I-90 west of Spokane. Follow US-2 through Airway Heights, then after two miles turn left to Main Gate and visitors' control center. USMRA: WA map (J-4). NMC: Spokane, 18 miles east.
RECREATION & TRAVEL Golf-247-5973 RVC-299-5129 RVC-247-2511/5366 SPA-247-3406 TML-247-5519
RETAIL & DINING: Clubs-EMC/NCO/OC-244-3622 Com-244-5591 Dining-247-5348/5553 EX-244-2832 Fast Food-244-2680/88 Gas-244-5095
SUPPORT & FAMILY: Med-247-5551

FORT LEWIS

Attn: AFZH-GCMS 1, I Corps & Fort Lewis
Fort Lewis, WA 98433-9500
C-253-967-1110, DSN-312-357-1110, Police-967-3107
WEB: www.lewis.army.mil
LOCATION: On I-5 north or south, exit 120 in Puget Sound area, 14 miles northeast of Olympia, 12 miles southwest of Tacoma. Clearly marked. USMRA: WA map (C-5), Seattle/Tacoma, WA map (A,B-7). NMC: Tacoma, 12 miles north. NMI: McChord Air Force Base, 14 miles south.
RECREATION & TRAVEL: Golf-967-6522 Marina-967-2510 RVC-967-5415 SPA-967-5998/6628 TML-967-2815/5051/6754
RETAIL & DINING: Clubs-American Lake-964-2555 Club North-964-0144 Madigan Cafe-964-4054 Russell Landing-966-0400 Com-966-8453 EX-964-3161 Fast Food-Burger King-964-8998 Gas- 964-5459
SUPPORT & FAMILY: Med-964-7136

JIM CREEK WILDERNESS RECREATION AREA

21027 Jim Creek Road, Arlington, WA 98223-8599
C-425-304-5315/5363,C-888-463-6697 (WA only), DSN-312-727-5315/5363, Police-304-5314
WEB: www.navylifepnw.com/site/67/jim-creek.aspx
LOCATION: Take I-5 to exit 208, east on SR-530 through Arlington towards Darrington for 7.5 miles. Turn right on Jim Creek Road half a mile past mile marker 25 (266th St. NE). You will pass the Trafton Store and Gas Station on your left just before coming to Jim Creek Road on the right. Follow Jim Creek Road approximately seven miles to the front gate of Naval Radio Station Jim Creek. USMRA: WA map (D-3). NMC: Arlington, 14 miles west. NMI: Everett NS, 35 miles south.
RECREATION & TRAVEL: RVC-304-5315/63
NOTE: *For detailed information about this off-base recreation facility, as well as on-base recreation facilities, golf courses and marinas, consult Military Living's "Military RV, Camping and Outdoor Recreation Around the World".*

KEYPORT NAVAL UNDERSEA WARFARE CENTER

610 Dowell Street, Keyport, WA 98345-7610
C-360-396-5111, DSN-744-0111, Police (Security)-396-2822 Emergency-396-6211
WEB: www-keyport.kpt.nuwc.navy.mil
LOCATION: Approximately ten miles north of Bremerton on WA-3, exit east to WA-308. Base clearly marked. USMRA: WA map (C-3,4). NMC: Bremerton, ten miles south.

MCCHORD AIR FORCE BASE

62 Airlift Wing 100 Main Street
McChord Air Force Base, WA 98438-1109
C-253-982-1110, DSN-312-382-1110, Police-982-5624
WEB: http://public.mcchord.amc.af.mil
LOCATION: From I-5 north or south, take exit 125 east onto Bridgeport Bay. One mile to Main Gate. Clearly marked. USMRA: WA map (D-5), Seattle/Tacoma, WA map (B-7). NMC: Tacoma, nine miles north.
RECREATION & TRAVEL: Golf-982-4927 RVC-982-5488 SPA-982-7259/60 TML-982-3591
RETAIL & DINING: Clubs-CC-982-2795 Com-982-3285 Dining-982-3287 EX-582-9451 Gas-589-4807
SUPPORT & FAMILY: Med-982-5776

PACIFIC BEACH RESORT AND CONFERENCE CENTER

P.O. Box O, 108 First Street, Pacific Beach, WA 98571-1700
C-888-463-6697 or C-360-276-4414, Police-911
e-mail: reservations@pacbeach.everett.navy.mil
WEB: www.navylifepnw.com
LOCATION: From I-5 at Olympia, take exit 104 (Aberdeen/Port Angeles). Go west on WA-8 and US-12 through Aberdeen to Hoquiam, then follow US-101 north for approximately four miles to sign indicating Ocean Beaches. Turn left and continue on Ocean Beach Road through Copalis Crossing, Carlisle and Aloha to the Pacific Beach. Follow Main Street to entrance to Pacific Beach Resort and Conference Center. Watch for signs to office. USMRA: WA map (A-4,5). NMC: Aberdeen, 25 miles southeast. NMI: Fort Lewis, 115 miles northeast.
RECREATION & TRAVEL: RVC-276-4414 or 888-463-6697 TML-276-4414 or 888-463-6697
RETAIL & DINING: Dining-276-8199
NOTE: *For detailed information about this off-base recreation facility, as well as on-base recreation facilities, golf courses and marinas, consult Military Living's "Military RV, Camping and Outdoor Recreation Around the World".*

PORT ANGELES COAST GUARD GROUP/ AIR STATION

Commander U.S. Coast Guard Group
Ediz Hook Road, Port Angeles, WA 98362-0159
C-360-417-5840, Police-417-5840 or 911
WEB: www.uscg.mil/d13/units/grupangeles/default/htm
LOCATION: Take I-5 to exit 179 onto 220th Street. Make a right onto WA-99 and a left onto 212th Street, which turns into Main Street and leads to the Edmonds Ferry Station. Take the ferry to Kingston. In Kingston, take WA-104 across the Hood Canal Bridge to US-101 north into Port Angeles. The air station is on the north side of US-101. USMRA: WA map (B-3). NMI: Kitsap Naval Base Bremerton, 50 miles southeast.
RETAIL & DINING: EX-417-5960
SUPPORT & FAMILY: Med-417-5895

ROCKY POINT RV PARK

Gallery Golf Course, 3065 North Cowpens Road, Bldg 130
Whidbey Island Naval Air Station, Oak Harbor, WA 98278-1900
C-360-257-2211, DSN-312-820-2211, Police-257-3122
LOCATION: From I-5 north or south, exit 230 west to WA-20. Turn onto Ault Field Road, follow to Clover Valley Road (do not bear right on Ault Field Road). Continue straight on Clover Valley, bear left at Golf Course Road. Sign in at the Pro Shop at the Gallery Golf Course. USMRA: WA map (C-2). NMC: Seattle, 60 miles southeast.
RECREATION & TRAVEL: Golf-257-2178 RVC-257-2178
NOTE: *For detailed information about this off-base recreation facility, as well as on-base recreation facilities, golf courses and marinas, consult Military Living's "Military RV, Camping and Outdoor Recreation Around the World".*

SEATTLE COAST GUARD INTEGRATED SUPPORT COMMAND

1519 Alaskan Way, South, Seattle, WA 98134-1192
C-206-217-6400, Police-217-6990
WEB: www.uscg.mil/mlcpac/iscseattle
LOCATION: From I-5 north or south, take exit 164 (Fourth Avenue South, Kingdome) and stay right. At the light take right onto Fourth Avenue South, then take next right onto Royal Brougham Way. (SAFECO will be on your left.) Follow to the end, take left onto Alaskan Way South. Pier 36 will be on the right. Or, from the east, take I-90 west until it ends. Follow signs for SAFECO field, then follow above directions. USMRA: Seattle/Tacoma, WA map (C-3). NMC: Seattle, within city limits.
RETAIL & DINING: Cafeteria-217-6416 Dining-217-6417 EX-587-0307
SUPPORT & FAMILY: Med-217-6430

UNITED STATES AIR FORCE SURVIVAL SCHOOL

336 TRG/CCE, 811 West Los Angeles Avenue, Suite 101
Fairchild AFB, WA 99011-8648
C-509-247-1212 DSN-312-657-1110/1212
Police-247-1110 or 911
WEB: public.fairchild.amc.af.mil/336trg/main
LOCATION: From US-2 west of Fairchild AFB, take first left after Rambo Road through Main Gate and visitors center. USMRA: WA map (J-4). NMC: Spokane, 15 miles west.
RECREATION & TRAVEL: TML-244-3028
RETAIL & DINING: Dining-247-5553 EX-244-9615

VANCOUVER BARRACKS

Bldg 752, Hathaway Road, Vancouver, WA 98661-3826
C-360-906-5800
LOCATION: Take I-5 north or south, exit 1C east on Mill Plain Blvd. Follow signs to Fort Vancouver and Officers' Row (first right after exit). USMRA: WA map (C-8). NMC: Vancouver, within city limits.
RETAIL & DINING: EX-695-8749

WHIDBEY ISLAND NAVAL AIR STATION

3730 North Charles Porter Avenue, Building 385, Room 219
Oak Harbor, WA 98278-4909
C-360-257-2211, DSN-312-820-2211I; Fax C-360-257-3972
Police-257-3122, e-mail: whdb_naswi_pao@navy.mi
e-mail: whdb_naswi_pao@navy.mil
WEB: www.naswi.navy.mil
LOCATION: From I-5 north or south, take exit 230, turn left onto WA-20 and proceed toward Oak Harbor. Make a right onto Ault Field Road; at the second traffic light, turn right on Langley Blvd and proceed to Main Gate. All commercial vehicles must proceed to Charles Porter Gate off Ault Field Road, right at first traffic light. USMRA: WA map (C,D-2). NMC: Seattle, 80 miles southeast.
RECREATION & TRAVEL: Golf-257-2178 Marina-257-3355 RVC-257-2178 RVC-257-2434 SPA-257-2604 TML-257-2529 Navy Lodge-800-NAVY-INN or 675-0633

RETAIL & DINING: Clubs-CPO-257-2891 OC-257-2852 Com-257-3310/8 Dining-257-2852/92 EX-257-0600 Gas- 257-2829
SUPPORT & FAMILY: Med-257-9500
NOTE: *Visitor's Gate entrance: Only those with DoD/DHS stickers can pass through any of the gates. Other visitors must visit the Pass & Decal office at Langley Gate.*

YAKIMA TRAINING CENTER

Bldg T-201, Yakima, WA 98901-9399
C-509-577-3205, DSN-312-638-3205, Police (Security)-225-8225
WEB: www.lewis.army.mil/yakima
LOCATION: Take I-82 west from Yakima. Take exit 26 to Yakima Training Center. Turn east at stop sign. USMRA: WA map (F,G-5,6). NMC: Yakima, six miles.
RETAIL & DINING: Clubs-CC-577-3415 EX-452-7356 or 577-3416

WYOMING, PG.94

CHEYENNE AIRPORT/AIR NATIONAL GUARD

217 Dell Range Blvd, Cheyenne, WY 82009-4799
C-307-772-6110 or 800-832-1959, DSN-312-388-6132 Police(Security)-307-772-6309
WEB: www.wychey.ang.af.mil
LOCATION: From I-25 north or south, exit on Central Avenue exit 12 east to airport. Turn onto Yellowstone Road to first light. Turn onto Dell Range Blvd, first right into guard base. USMRA: WY map (J-8). NMC: Cheyenne, one mile south.
RECREATION & TRAVEL: SPA-307-772-6347

FRANCIS E. WARREN AIR FORCE BASE

5305 Randall Avenue, Bldg 250, Room 201
Francis E. Warren Air Force Base, WY 82005-2266
C-307-773-1110, DSN-312-481-1110, Police-773-3501
e-mail: 90sw.pa@warren.af.mil
WEB: www.warren.af.mil
LOCATION: Off I-25, exit 11 west on Randall Avenue. Main Gate two miles north of I-80. Clearly marked. USMRA: WY map (I,J-8). NMC: Cheyenne, adjacent.
RECREATION & TRAVEL: Golf-773-3556 RVC-773-2988/3874 TML-773-1844
RETAIL & DINING: Clubs-CC-773-3024/48 Com-773-2427 Dining-778-3838 EX-638-1593 Fast Food-773-2399 Gas-634-7298
SUPPORT & FAMILY: Med-773-2277
NOTE: *Visitor's Gate: Gate 1 hosts Visitors Center, Gate 2 requires DoD sticker and identification--only open 6 a.m. to 6 p.m. Mon through Fri.*

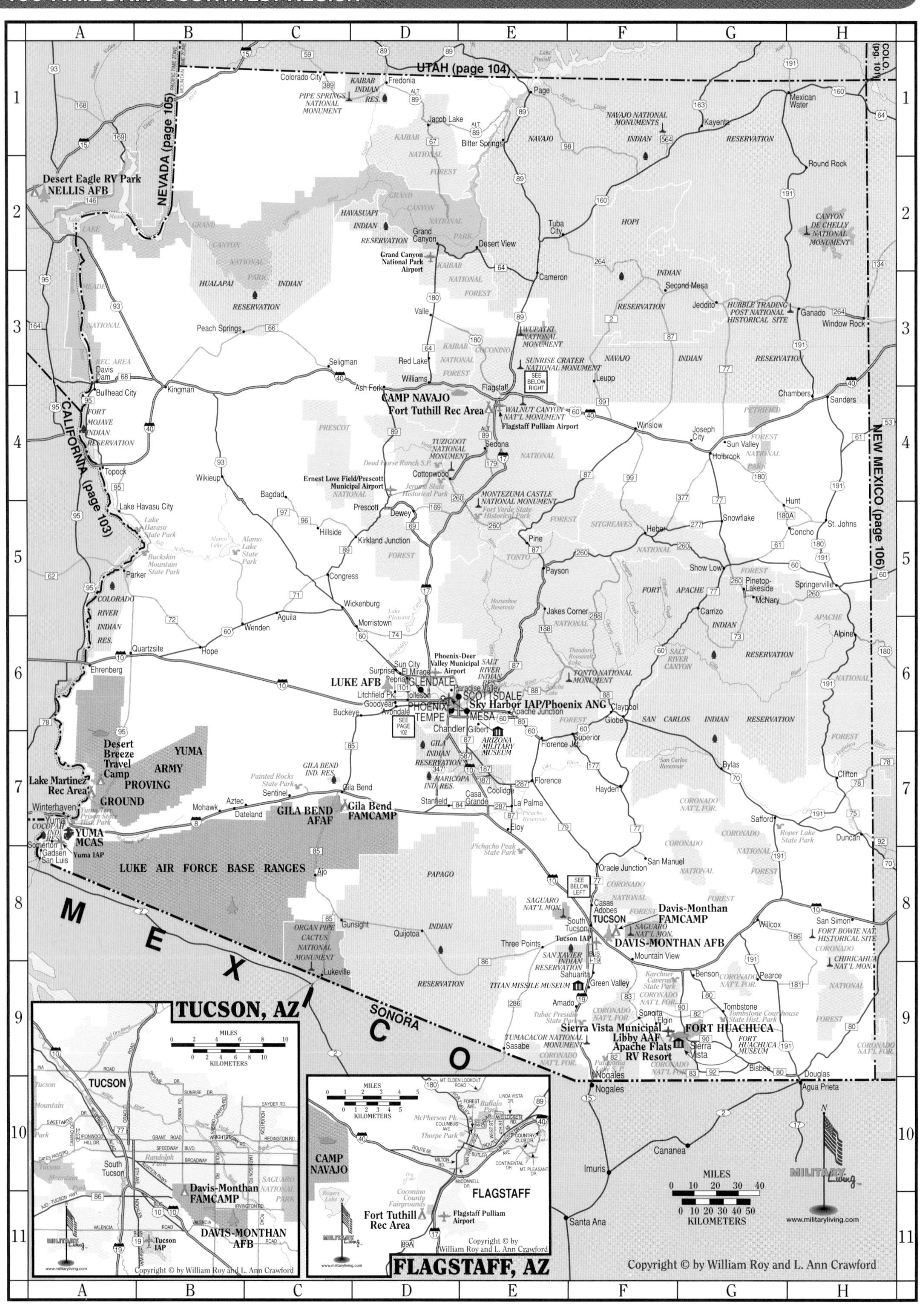
UTAH (page 104)
NEVADA (page 105)
CALIFORNIA (page 103)
NEW MEXICO (page 106)
COLO. (pg. 101)
MEXICO
SONORA
Desert Eagle RV Park
NELLIS AFB
Colorado City
Fredonia
KAIBAB INDIAN RES.
PIPE SPRINGS NATIONAL MONUMENT
Page
Jacob Lake
Bitter Springs
KAIBAB NATIONAL FOREST
NAVAJO NATIONAL MONUMENTS
Kayenta
Mexican Water
NAVAJO INDIAN RESERVATION
Round Rock
HAVASUPAI INDIAN RESERVATION
Grand Canyon
GRAND CANYON NATIONAL PARK
Desert View
Grand Canyon National Park Airport
Tuba City
HOPI
Cameron
CANYON DE CHELLY NATIONAL MONUMENT
HUALAPAI INDIAN RESERVATION
Second Mesa
Jeddito
HUBBLE TRADING POST NATIONAL HISTORICAL SITE
Ganado
Window Rock
Valle
Peach Springs
WUPATKI NATIONAL MONUMENT
SUNRISE CRATER NATIONAL MONUMENT
Seligman
Red Lake
Williams
Leupp
Davis Dam
Bullhead City
Kingman
Ash Fork
Flagstaff
SEE BELOW RIGHT
CAMP NAVAJO
Fort Tuthill Rec Area
WALNUT CANYON NAT'L MONUMENT
Flagstaff Pulliam Airport
Chambers
Sanders
FORT MOJAVE INDIAN RESERVATION
PRESCOTT
TUZIGOOT NATIONAL MONUMENT
Sedona
Winslow
Joseph City
Holbrook
Sun Valley
PETRIFIED FOREST NATIONAL PARK
Topock
Wikieup
Dead Horse Ranch S.P.
Cottonwood
Ernest Love Field/Prescott Municipal Airport
Jerome State Historical Park
MONTEZUMA CASTLE NATIONAL MONUMENT
Fort Verde State Historical Park
Lake Havasu City
Bagdad
Prescott
Dewey
Hunt
St. Johns
Lake Havasu State Park
Hillside
Kirkland Junction
SITGREAVES
Heber
Snowflake
Concho
Alamo Lake State Park
Buckskin Mountain State Park
Pine
TONTO
Show Low
Parker
Congress
Payson
FORT APACHE
Pinetop-Lakeside
McNary
Springerville
COLORADO RIVER INDIAN RES.
Wickenburg
Jakes Corner
Carrizo
Morristown
Aguila
Wenden
Alpine
Quartzsite
Hope
SALT RIVER CANYON
Ehrenberg
Sun City
Surprise
El Mirage
Peoria
Phoenix-Deer Valley Municipal Airport
SALT RIVER INDIAN RES.
TONTO NATIONAL MONUMENT
LUKE AFB
GLENDALE
Litchfield Pk.
Tolleson
SCOTTSDALE
Paradise Valley
Goodyear
Avondale
PHOENIX
TEMPE
MESA
Sky Harbor IAP/Phoenix ANG
Apache Junction
Claypool
Globe
SAN CARLOS INDIAN RESERVATION
Buckeye
SEE PAGE 102
Chandler
Gilbert
ARIZONA MILITARY MUSEUM
Superior
Florence Jct.
Desert Breeze Travel Camp
YUMA ARMY PROVING GROUND
GILA INDIAN RESERVATION
GILA BEND IND. RES.
San Carlos Reservoir
Bylas
Clifton
Lake Martinez Rec Area
Painted Rocks State Park
Sentinel
Gila Bend
MARICOPA IND. RES.
Florence
Hayden
Winterhaven
Yuma
Mohawk
Aztec
Dateland
GILA BEND AFAF
Gila Bend FAMCAMP
Stanfield
Casa Grande
Coolidge
La Palma
Eloy
Safford
YUMA MCAS
Somerton
Gadsen
San Luis
Yuma IAP
COCOPAH IND. RES.
LUKE AIR FORCE BASE RANGES
Ajo
PAPAGO
Pichacho Peak State Park
San Manuel
Oracle Junction
Duncan
SEE BELOW LEFT
SAGUARO NAT'L MON.
Casas Adobes
TUCSON
Davis-Monthan FAMCAMP
South Tucson
Tucson IAP
DAVIS-MONTHAN AFB
ORGAN PIPE CACTUS NATIONAL MONUMENT
Gunsight
Quijotoa
INDIAN RESERVATION
Three Points
Willcox
San Simon
FORT BOWIE NAT. HISTORICAL SITE
Mountain View
SAN XAVIER INDIAN RESERVATION
Lukeville
Sahuarita
TITAN MISSILE MUSEUM
Green Valley
Benson
Pearce
CHIRICAHUA NAT'L MON.
Karchner Caverns State Park
Amado
Sonoita
Elgin
Tombstone
Tombstone Courthouse State Hist. Park
Tubac Presidio State Park
Sierra Vista Municipal
Libby AAF
Apache Flats RV Resort
FORT HUACHUCA
Sierra Vista
FORT HUACHUCA MUSEUM
TUMACACOR NATIONAL MONUMENT
Sasabe
Patagonia Lake S.P.
Nogales
Bisbee
Douglas
Agua Prieta
Cananea
Imuris
Santa Ana
MILES
KILOMETERS
www.militaryliving.com
Copyright © by William Roy and L. Ann Crawford
TUCSON, AZ
Tucson Mountain Park
South Tucson
Davis-Monthan FAMCAMP
DAVIS-MONTHAN AFB
Tucson IAP
SAGUARO NATIONAL PARK
Copyright © by William Roy and L. Ann Crawford
FLAGSTAFF, AZ
CAMP NAVAJO
FLAGSTAFF
Fort Tuthill Rec Area
Flagstaff Pulliam Airport
Buffalo Park
McPherson Pk.
Thorpe Park
Coconino County Fairgrounds
Copyright © by William Roy and L. Ann Crawford

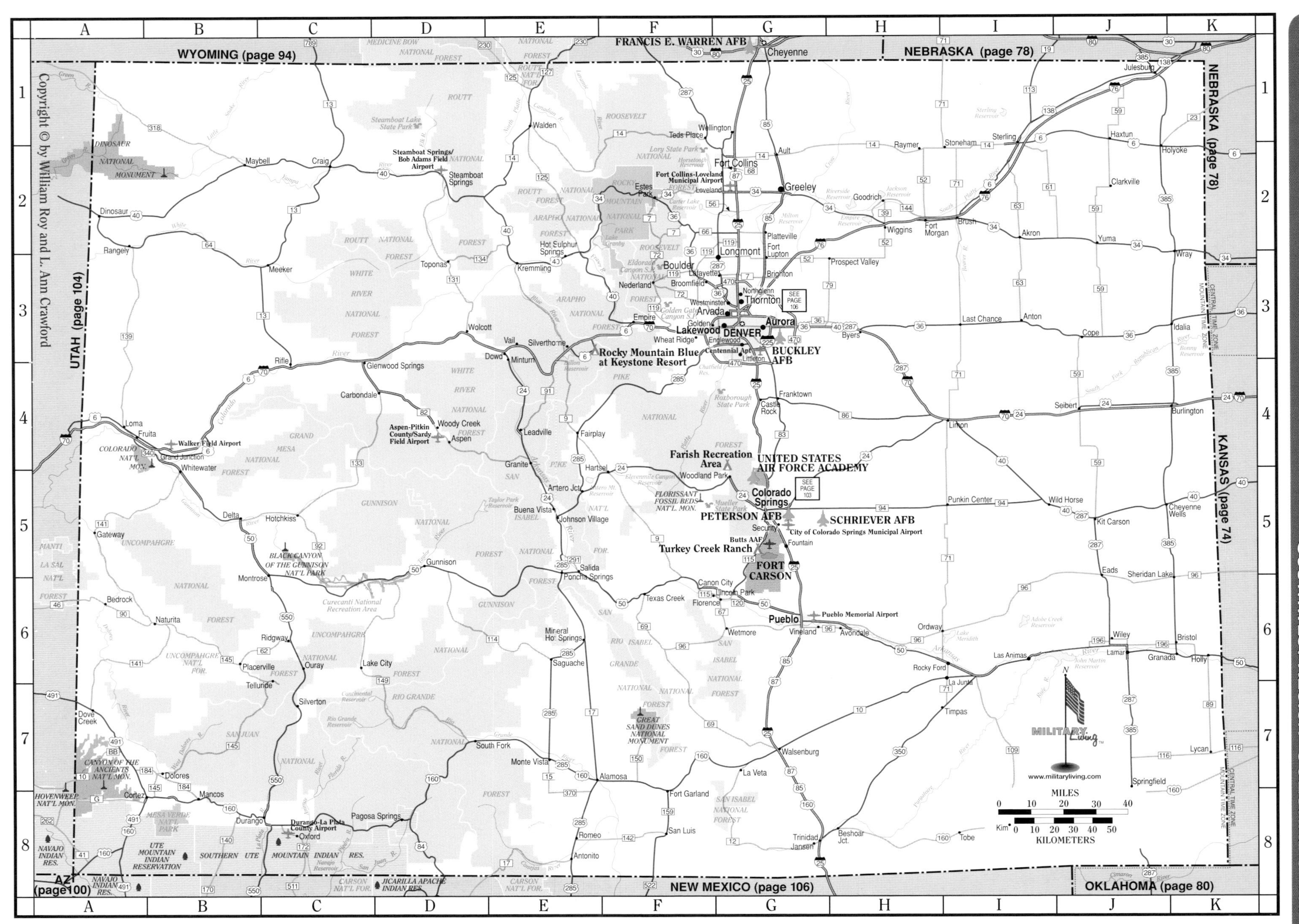
WYOMING (page 94)
FRANCIS E. WARREN AFB
NEBRASKA (page 78)
UTAH (page 104)
KANSAS (page 74)
NEW MEXICO (page 106)
OKLAHOMA (page 80)
AZ (page100)
CENTRAL TIME ZONE
MOUNTAIN TIME ZONE
Copyright © by William Roy and L. Ann Crawford
Cheyenne
Julesburg
Holyoke
Haxtun
Clarkville
Sterling
Stoneham
Raymer
Ault
Wellington
Teds Place
Fort Collins
Fort Collins-Loveland Municipal Airport
Loveland
Estes Park
Greeley
Goodrich
Wiggins
Fort Morgan
Brush
Akron
Yuma
Wray
Platteville
Fort Lupton
Longmont
Boulder
Lafayette
Broomfield
Nederland
Brighton
Prospect Valley
Northglenn
Thornton
Westminster
Arvada
Golden
Empire
Lakewood
DENVER
Aurora
Wheat Ridge
Englewood
Centennial Apt
Littleton
BUCKLEY AFB
SEE PAGE 106
Byers
Last Chance
Anton
Cope
Idalia
Franktown
Castle Rock
Limon
Seibert
Burlington
Rocky Mountain Blue at Keystone Resort
Farish Recreation Area
UNITED STATES AIR FORCE ACADEMY
Woodland Park
Colorado Springs
SEE PAGE 103
PETERSON AFB
SCHRIEVER AFB
Security
City of Colorado Springs Municipal Airport
Fountain
Butts AAF
Turkey Creek Ranch
FORT CARSON
Punkin Center
Wild Horse
Kit Carson
Cheyenne Wells
Eads
Sheridan Lake
Canon City
Lincoln Park
Florence
Pueblo
Pueblo Memorial Airport
Vineland
Avondale
Wetmore
Ordway
Rocky Ford
La Junta
Las Animas
Wiley
Lamar
Granada
Holly
Bristol
Timpas
Walsenburg
La Veta
Trinidad
Jansen
Beshoar Jct.
Tobe
Springfield
Lycan
Fort Garland
San Luis
Alamosa
Monte Vista
South Fork
Romeo
Antonito
Saguache
Mineral Hot Springs
Salida
Poncha Springs
Texas Creek
Buena Vista
Johnson Village
Artero Jct
Hartsel
Fairplay
Leadville
Granite
Gunnison
Montrose
Delta
Hotchkiss
Ridgway
Ouray
Placerville
Telluride
Silverton
Lake City
Pagosa Springs
Durango
Durango-La Plata County Airport
Oxford
Mancos
Cortez
Dolores
Dove Creek
Naturita
Bedrock
Gateway
Grand Junction
Whitewater
Walker Field Airport
Fruita
Loma
Rifle
Glenwood Springs
Carbondale
Woody Creek
Aspen
Aspen-Pitkin County/Sardy Field Airport
Vail
Dowd
Minturn
Silverthorne
Wolcott
Meeker
Rangely
Dinosaur
Maybell
Craig
Toponas
Steamboat Springs
Steamboat Springs/ Bob Adams Field Airport
Kremmling
Hot Sulphur Springs
Walden
DINOSAUR NATIONAL MONUMENT
COLORADO NAT'L MON.
BLACK CANYON OF THE GUNNISON NAT'L PARK
Curecanti National Recreation Area
GREAT SAND DUNES NATIONAL MONUMENT
FLORISSANT FOSSIL BEDS NAT'L MON.
CANYON OF THE ANCIENTS NAT'L MON.
HOVENWEEP NAT'L MON.
MESA VERDE NAT'L PARK
UTE MOUNTAIN INDIAN RESERVATION
SOUTHERN UTE MOUNTAIN INDIAN RES.
NAVAJO INDIAN RES.
JICARILLA APACHE INDIAN RES.
www.militaryliving.com
MILES
KILOMETERS

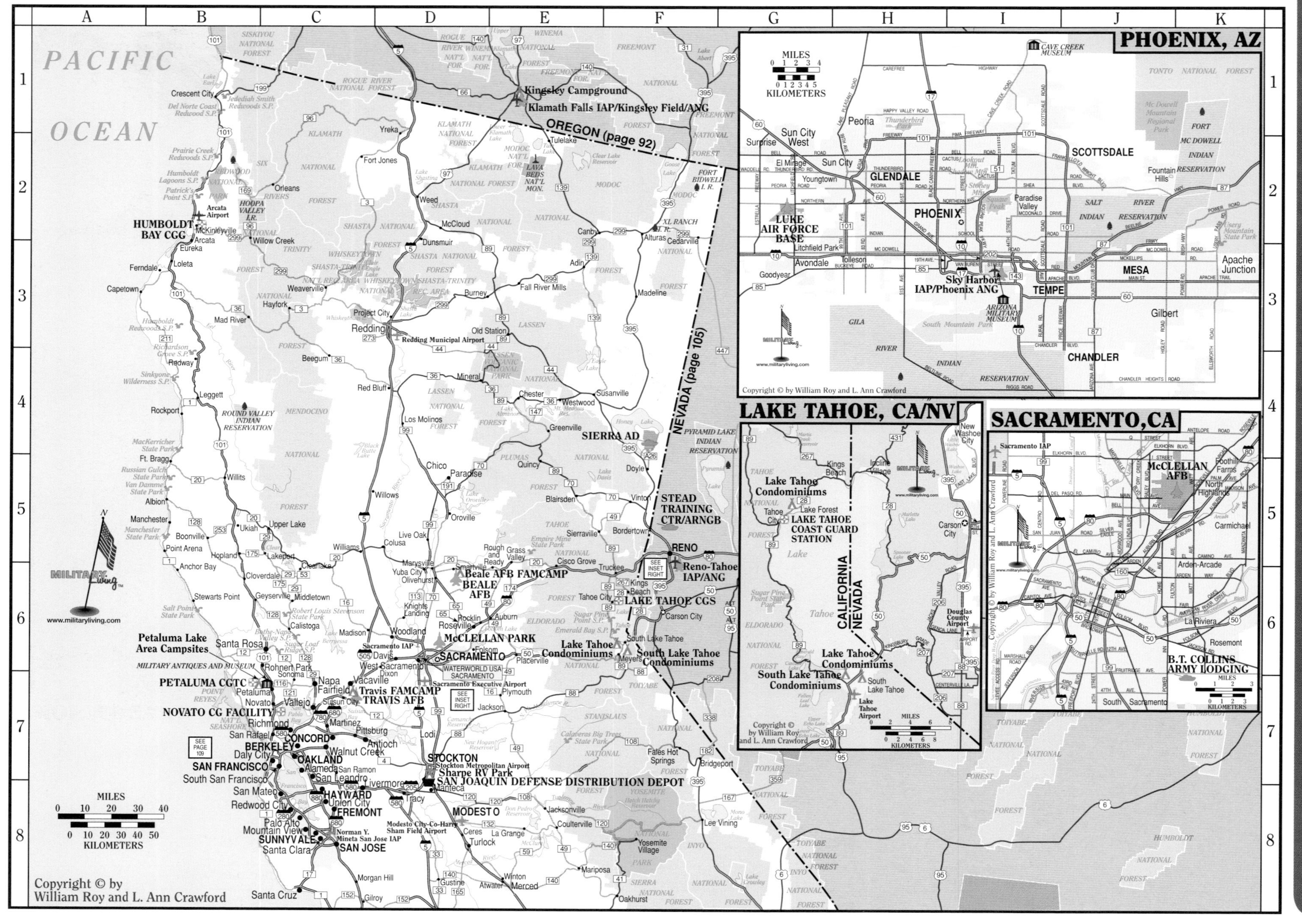

PACIFIC OCEAN
OREGON (page 92)
NEVADA (page 105)
Kingsley Campground
Klamath Falls IAP/Kingsley Field/ANG
HUMBOLDT BAY CGG
Arcata Airport
SIERRA AD
STEAD TRAINING CTR/ARNGB
RENO
Reno-Tahoe IAP/ANG
LAKE TAHOE CGS
Lake Tahoe Condominiums
South Lake Tahoe Condominiums
Beale AFB FAMCAMP
BEALE AFB
McCLELLAN PARK
SACRAMENTO
Sacramento IAP
Sacramento Executive Airport
Redding Municipal Airport
Petaluma Lake Area Campsites
MILITARY ANTIQUES AND MUSEUM
PETALUMA CGTC
NOVATO CG FACILITY
Travis FAMCAMP
TRAVIS AFB
STOCKTON
Stockton Metropolitan Airport
Sharpe RV Park
SAN JOAQUIN DEFENSE DISTRIBUTION DEPOT
MODESTO
Modesto City-Co-Harry Sham Field Airport
SAN FRANCISCO
OAKLAND
BERKELEY
CONCORD
HAYWARD
FREMONT
SUNNYVALE
SAN JOSE
Norman Y. Mineta San Jose IAP
SEE PAGE 109
SEE INSET RIGHT
MILES
KILOMETERS
www.militaryliving.com
Copyright © by William Roy and L. Ann Crawford
PHOENIX, AZ
SCOTTSDALE
GLENDALE
PHOENIX
MESA
TEMPE
CHANDLER
Gilbert
Apache Junction
Fountain Hills
Paradise Valley
Peoria
Sun City
Sun City West
Surprise
El Mirage
Youngtown
Litchfield Park
Avondale
Tolleson
Goodyear
LUKE AIR FORCE BASE
Sky Harbor IAP/Phoenix ANG
CAVE CREEK MUSEUM
ARIZONA MILITARY MUSEUM
SALT RIVER INDIAN RESERVATION
FORT MC DOWELL INDIAN RESERVATION
GILA RIVER INDIAN RESERVATION
Copyright © by William Roy and L. Ann Crawford
LAKE TAHOE, CA/NV
CALIFORNIA
NEVADA
Lake Tahoe Condominiums
LAKE TAHOE COAST GUARD STATION
South Lake Tahoe Condominiums
Lake Tahoe Airport
Douglas County Airport
Carson City
Incline Village
Kings Beach
Tahoe City
South Lake Tahoe
Copyright © by William Roy and L. Ann Crawford
SACRAMENTO, CA
McCLELLAN AFB
B.T. COLLINS ARMY LODGING
Sacramento IAP
Foothill Farms
North Highlands
Carmichael
Arden-Arcade
La Riviera
Rosemont
South Sacramento
Copyright © by William Roy and L. Ann Crawford

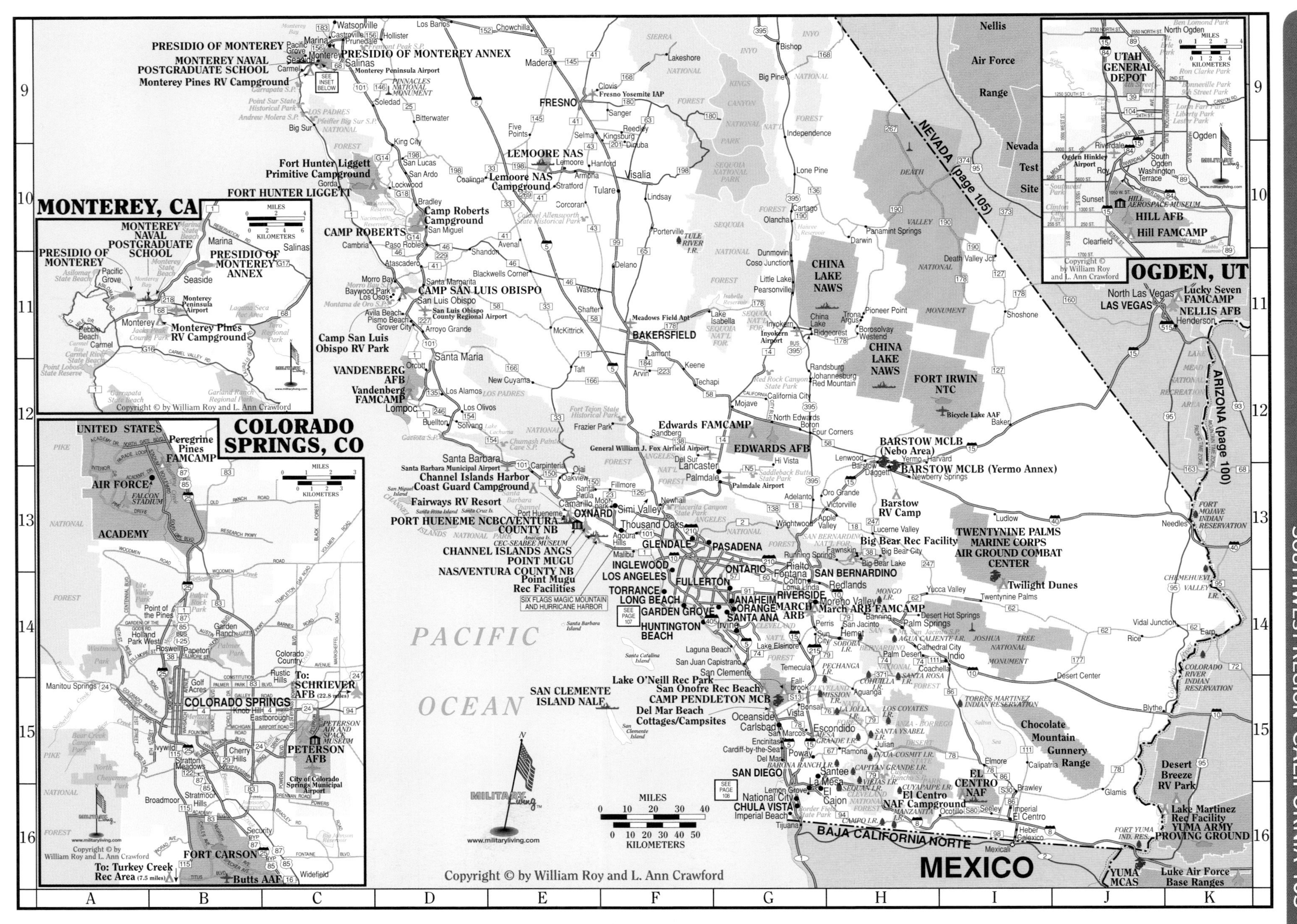

PRESIDIO OF MONTEREY
MONTEREY NAVAL POSTGRADUATE SCHOOL
Monterey Pines RV Campground
PRESIDIO OF MONTEREY ANNEX
MONTEREY, CA
Fort Hunter Liggett Primitive Campground
FORT HUNTER LIGGETT
CAMP ROBERTS
Camp Roberts Campground
CAMP SAN LUIS OBISPO
Camp San Luis Obispo RV Park
VANDENBERG AFB
Vandenberg FAMCAMP
LEMOORE NAS
Lemoore NAS Campground
FRESNO
BAKERSFIELD
COLORADO SPRINGS, CO
UNITED STATES AIR FORCE ACADEMY
Peregrine Pines FAMCAMP
To: SCHRIEVER AFB (22.8 miles)
PETERSON AFB
FORT CARSON
Butts AAF
To: Turkey Creek Rec Area (7.5 miles)
Channel Islands Harbor Coast Guard Campground
Fairways RV Resort
PORT HUENEME NCBC/VENTURA COUNTY NB
CHANNEL ISLANDS ANGS
POINT MUGU
NAS/VENTURA COUNTY NB Point Mugu Rec Facilities
SIX FLAGS MAGIC MOUNTAIN AND HURRICANE HARBOR
SEE PAGE 107
PACIFIC
OCEAN
SAN CLEMENTE ISLAND NALF
Lake O'Neill Rec Park
San Onofre Rec Beach
CAMP PENDLETON MCB
Del Mar Beach Cottages/Campsites
SAN DIEGO
SEE PAGE 108
Edwards FAMCAMP
EDWARDS AFB
CHINA LAKE NAWS
FORT IRWIN NTC
BARSTOW MCLB (Nebo Area)
BARSTOW MCLB (Yermo Annex)
Barstow RV Camp
Big Bear Rec Facility
MARCH ARB
March ARB FAMCAMP
TWENTYNINE PALMS MARINE CORPS AIR GROUND COMBAT CENTER
Twilight Dunes
Chocolate Mountain Gunnery Range
EL CENTRO NAF
El Centro NAF Campground
Desert Breeze RV Park
Lake Martinez Rec Facility
YUMA ARMY PROVING GROUND
YUMA MCAS
Luke Air Force Base Ranges
BAJA CALIFORNIA NORTE
MEXICO
NEVADA (page 105)
ARIZONA (page 100)
Nellis Air Force Range
Nevada Test Site
LAS VEGAS
Lucky Seven FAMCAMP
NELLIS AFB
OGDEN, UT
UTAH GENERAL DEPOT
HILL AFB
Hill FAMCAMP
Copyright © by William Roy and L. Ann Crawford
MILES
KILOMETERS
www.militaryliving.com
Copyright © by William Roy and L. Ann Crawford

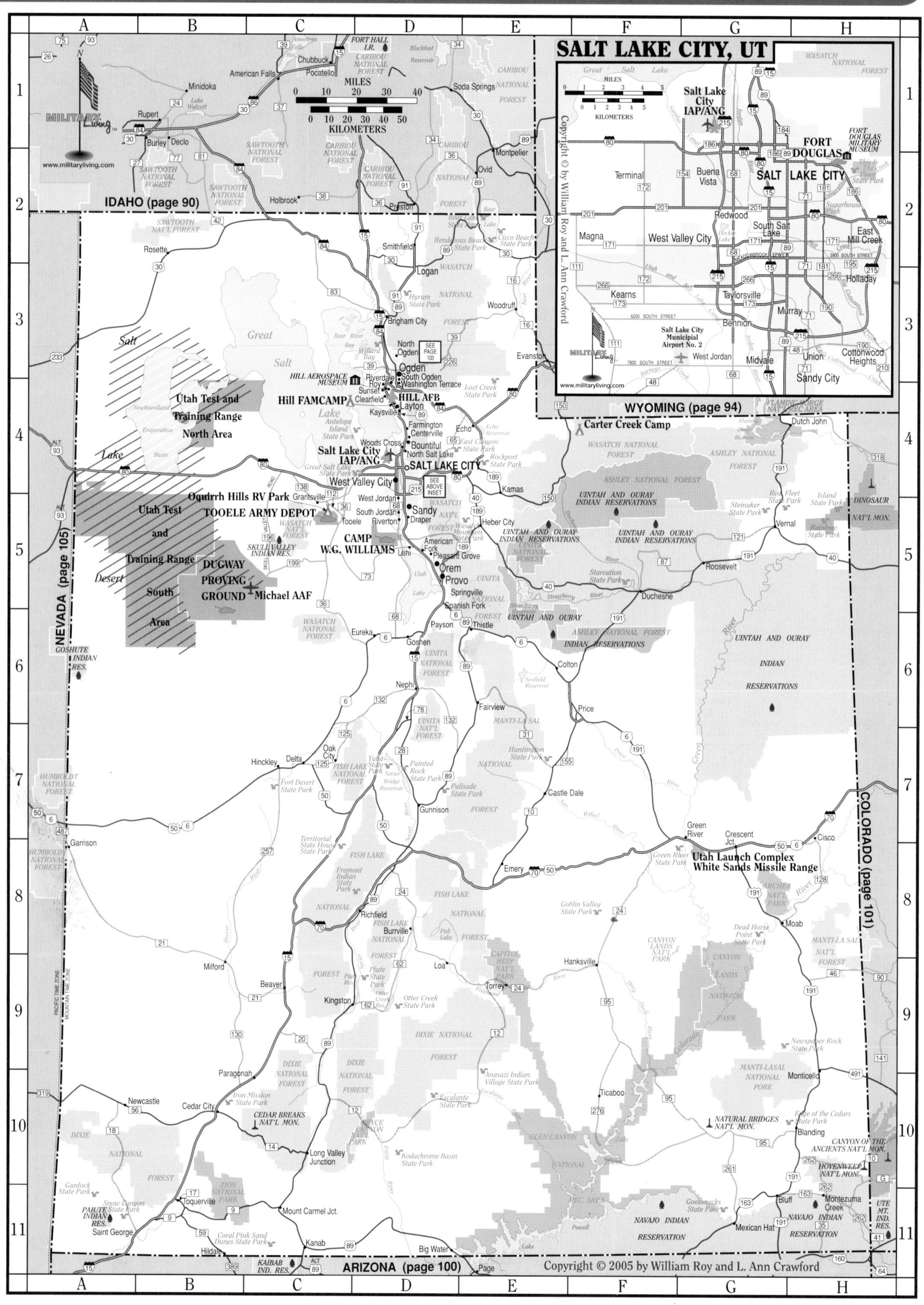
SALT LAKE CITY, UT
Salt Lake City IAP/ANG
FORT DOUGLAS
FORT DOUGLAS MILITARY MUSEUM
SALT LAKE CITY
IDAHO (page 90)
WYOMING (page 94)
NEVADA (page 105)
COLORADO (page 101)
ARIZONA (page 100)
MILES
KILOMETERS
Utah Test and Training Range North Area
Utah Test and Training Range South Area
Hill FAMCAMP
HILL AFB
HILL AEROSPACE MUSEUM
Salt Lake City IAP/ANG
Oquirrh Hills RV Park
TOOELE ARMY DEPOT
CAMP W.G. WILLIAMS
DUGWAY PROVING GROUND
Michael AAF
Carter Creek Camp
Utah Launch Complex White Sands Missile Range
Great Salt Lake
Great Salt Lake Desert
www.militaryliving.com
Copyright © by William Roy and L. Ann Crawford
Copyright © 2005 by William Roy and L. Ann Crawford

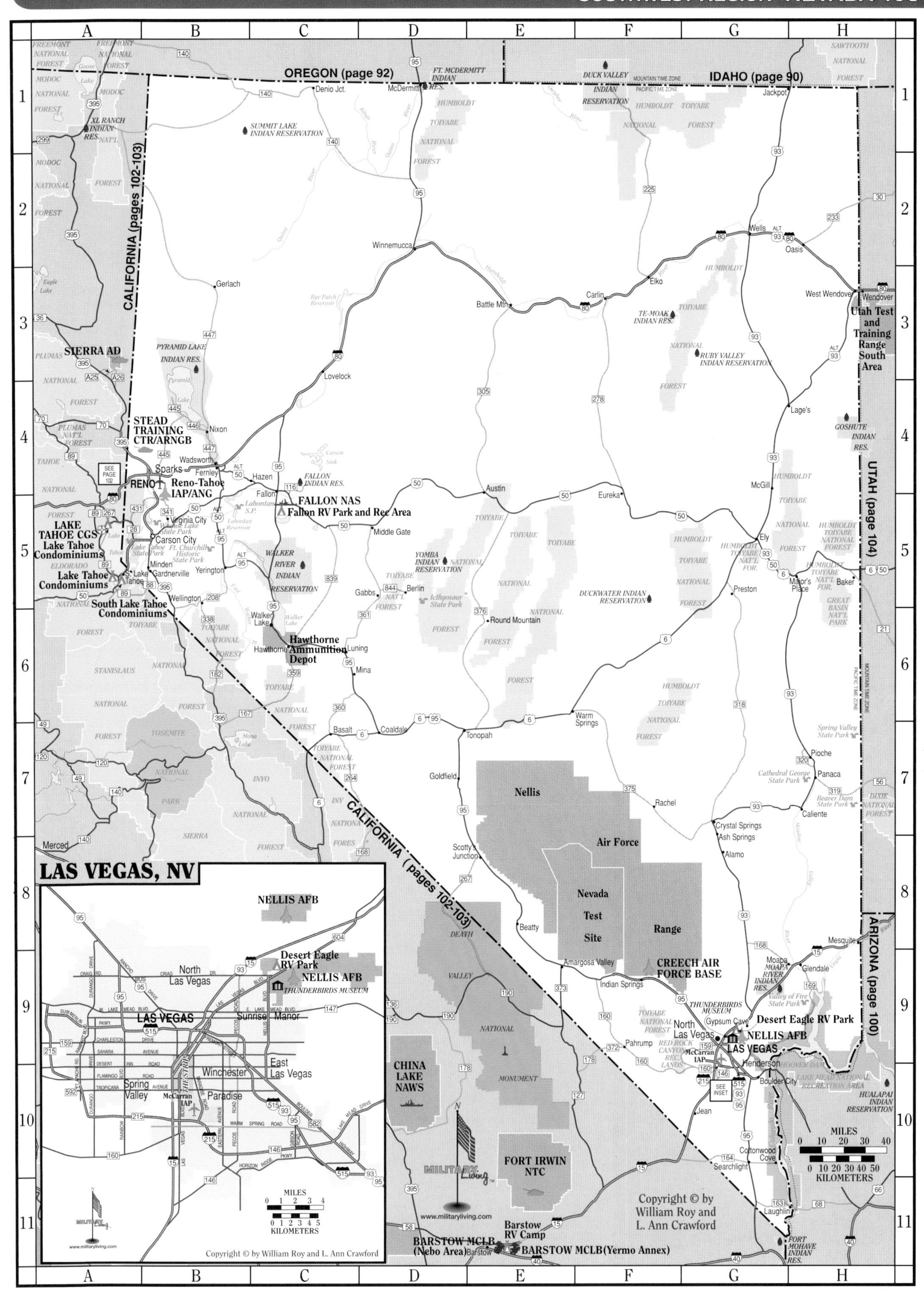
OREGON (page 92)
IDAHO (page 90)
CALIFORNIA (pages 102-103)
UTAH (page 104)
ARIZONA (page 100)
Denio Jct.
McDermitt
Jackpot
Winnemucca
Wells
Oasis
Elko
Carlin
Battle Mtn
West Wendover
Wendover
Utah Test and Training Range South Area
Gerlach
Lovelock
SIERRA AD
STEAD TRAINING CTR/ARNGB
Nixon
Wadsworth
Sparks
Fernley
Hazen
RENO
Reno-Tahoe IAP/ANG
Fallon
FALLON NAS
Fallon RV Park and Rec Area
Austin
Eureka
McGill
Ely
Lage's
LAKE TAHOE CGS
Lake Tahoe Condominiums
Virginia City
Carson City
Minden
Gardnerville
Yerington
Lake Tahoe Condominiums
South Lake Tahoe Condominiums
Wellington
Middle Gate
Gabbs
Berlin
Walker Lake
Hawthorne
Hawthorne Ammunition Depot
Luning
Mina
Round Mountain
Preston
Major's Place
Baker
Basalt
Coaldale
Tonopah
Warm Springs
Goldfield
Pioche
Panaca
Caliente
Rachel
Nellis Air Force
Nevada Test Site
Range
Crystal Springs
Ash Springs
Alamo
Scotty's Junction
Beatty
Amargosa Valley
Indian Springs
CREECH AIR FORCE BASE
Mesquite
Glendale
Pahrump
North Las Vegas
NELLIS AFB
LAS VEGAS
Desert Eagle RV Park
Henderson
Boulder City
Jean
Searchlight
Cottonwood Cove
Laughlin
CHINA LAKE NAWS
FORT IRWIN NTC
Barstow RV Camp
BARSTOW MCLB (Nebo Area)
BARSTOW MCLB(Yermo Annex)
Copyright © by William Roy and L. Ann Crawford
www.militaryliving.com
LAS VEGAS, NV
NELLIS AFB
Desert Eagle RV Park
THUNDERBIRDS MUSEUM
North Las Vegas
LAS VEGAS
Sunrise Manor
Winchester
East Las Vegas
Spring Valley
Paradise
McCarran IAP
Copyright © by William Roy and L. Ann Crawford

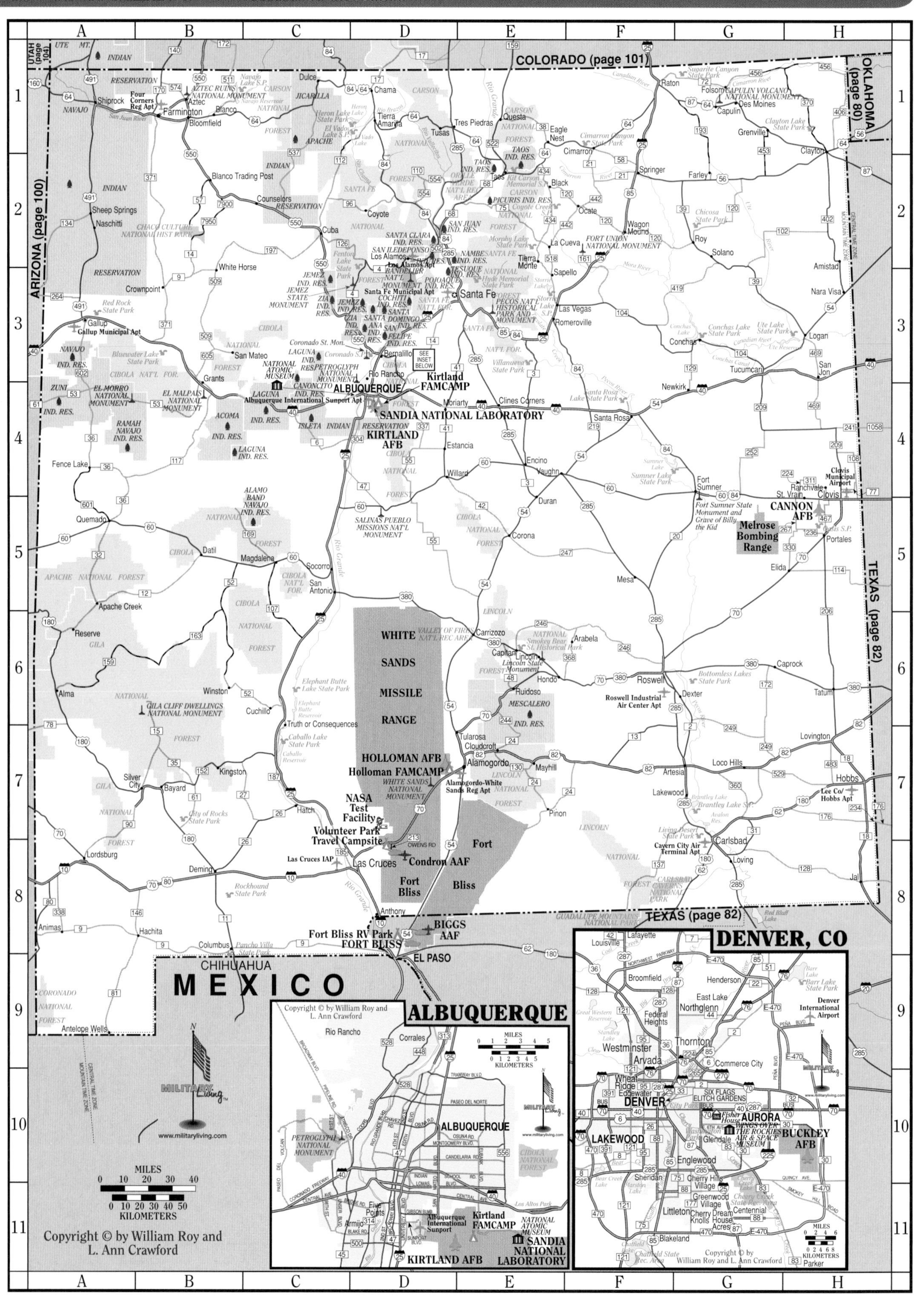
COLORADO (page 101)
OKLAHOMA (page 80)
ARIZONA (page 100)
TEXAS (page 82)
UTAH (page 104)
MEXICO
CHIHUAHUA
Santa Fe
ALBUQUERQUE
Kirtland FAMCAMP
SANDIA NATIONAL LABORATORY
KIRTLAND AFB
WHITE SANDS MISSILE RANGE
HOLLOMAN AFB
Holloman FAMCAMP
NASA Test Facility
Volunteer Park Travel Campsite
Condron AAF
Fort Bliss
Fort Bliss RV Park
FORT BLISS
BIGGS AAF
EL PASO
CANNON AFB
Melrose Bombing Range
Las Cruces
Roswell
Carlsbad
Gallup
Farmington
Las Vegas
Clovis
Hobbs
Alamogordo
Deming
Lordsburg
Silver City
Socorro
Tucumcari
Raton
Clayton
ALBUQUERQUE
Copyright © by William Roy and L. Ann Crawford
DENVER, CO
DENVER
AURORA
BUCKLEY AFB
LAKEWOOD
Denver International Airport
Copyright © by William Roy and L. Ann Crawford
MILES 0 10 20 30 40
0 10 20 30 40 50 KILOMETERS
www.militaryliving.com
Copyright © by William Roy and L. Ann Crawford

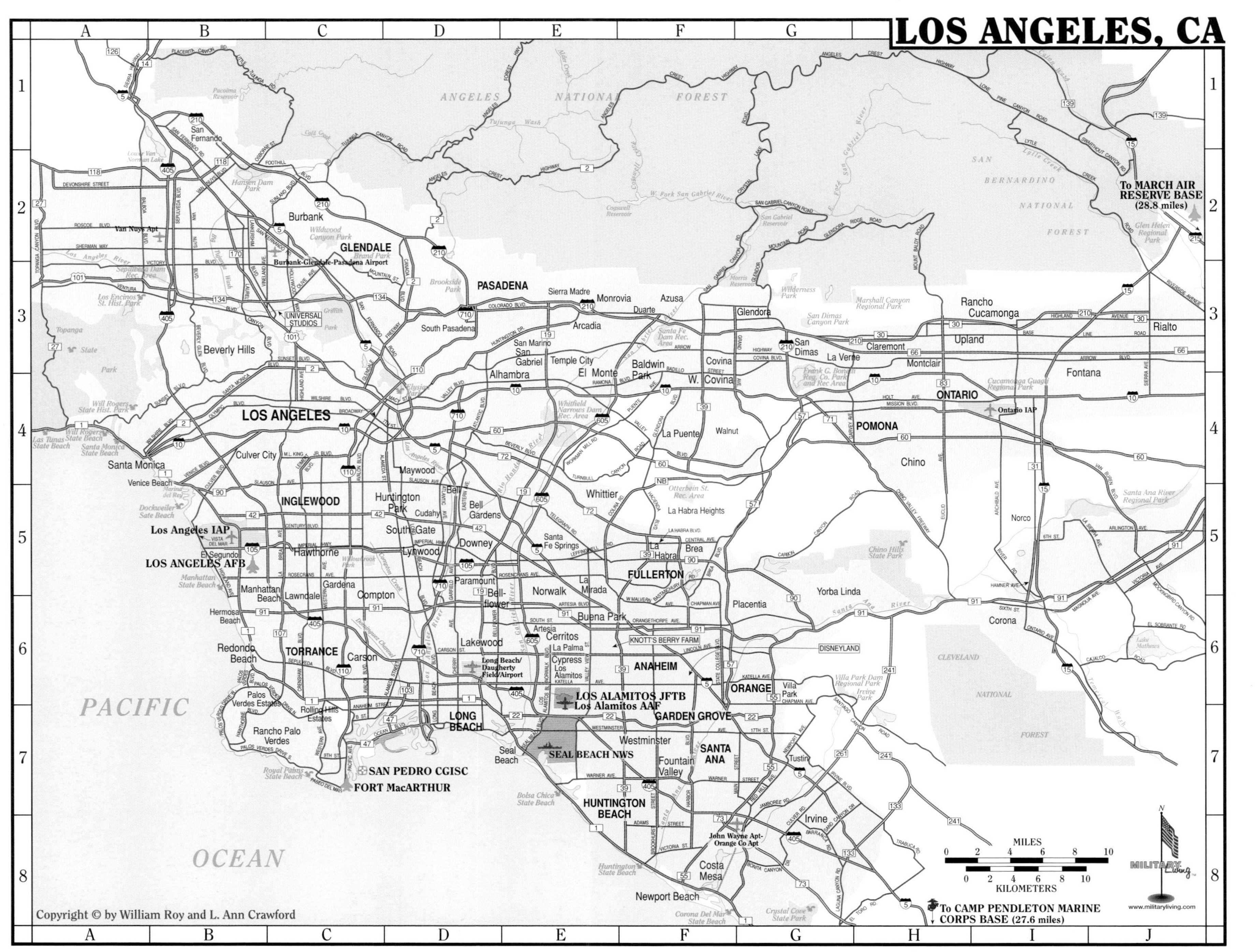
LOS ANGELES, CA
To MARCH AIR RESERVE BASE (28.8 miles)
To CAMP PENDLETON MARINE CORPS BASE (27.6 miles)
MILES
KILOMETERS
PACIFIC
OCEAN
LOS ANGELES
PASADENA
GLENDALE
INGLEWOOD
TORRANCE
LONG BEACH
FULLERTON
ANAHEIM
ORANGE
GARDEN GROVE
SANTA ANA
HUNTINGTON BEACH
ONTARIO
POMONA
LOS ANGELES AFB
Los Angeles IAP
LOS ALAMITOS JFTB
Los Alamitos AAF
SEAL BEACH NWS
SAN PEDRO CGISC
FORT MacARTHUR
Ontario IAP
www.militaryliving.com
Copyright © by William Roy and L. Ann Crawford

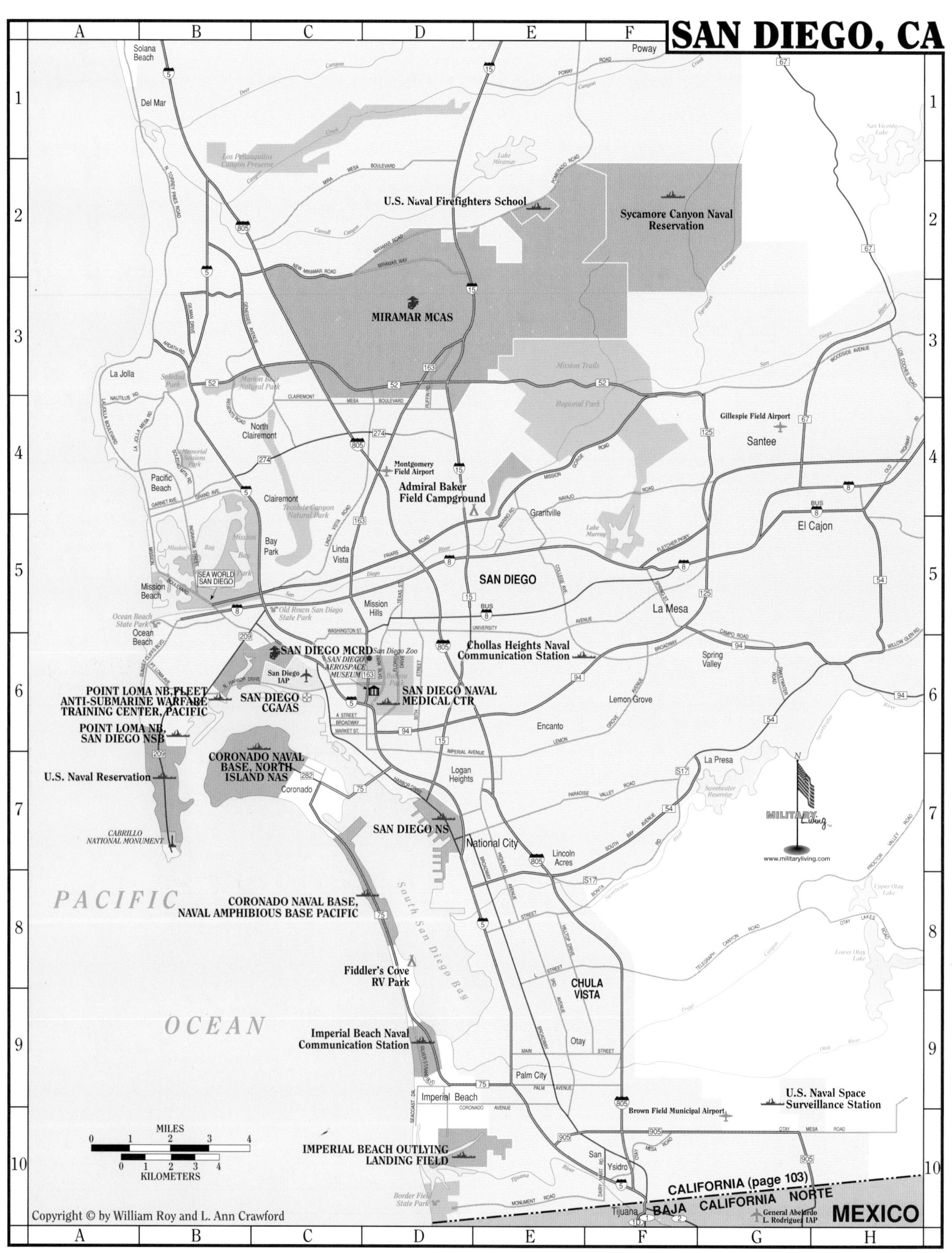

SAN DIEGO, CA
U.S. Naval Firefighters School
Sycamore Canyon Naval Reservation
MIRAMAR MCAS
Montgomery Field Airport
Admiral Baker Field Campground
Gillespie Field Airport
SAN DIEGO MCRD
San Diego IAP
SAN DIEGO AEROSPACE MUSEUM
San Diego Zoo
Chollas Heights Naval Communication Station
POINT LOMA NB, FLEET ANTI-SUBMARINE WARFARE TRAINING CENTER, PACIFIC
SAN DIEGO CGA/AS
SAN DIEGO NAVAL MEDICAL CTR
POINT LOMA NB, SAN DIEGO NSB
CORONADO NAVAL BASE, NORTH ISLAND NAS
U.S. Naval Reservation
CABRILLO NATIONAL MONUMENT
SAN DIEGO NS
CORONADO NAVAL BASE, NAVAL AMPHIBIOUS BASE PACIFIC
Fiddler's Cove RV Park
Imperial Beach Naval Communication Station
IMPERIAL BEACH OUTLYING LANDING FIELD
Brown Field Municipal Airport
U.S. Naval Space Surveillance Station
General Abelardo L. Rodriguez IAP
SEA WORLD SAN DIEGO
Old Rown San Diego State Park
Los Peñasquitos Canyon Preserve
Marion Bear Natural Park
Tecolote Canyon Natural Park
Mission Trails Regional Park
Border Field State Park
Ocean Beach State Park
Solana Beach
Del Mar
Poway
La Jolla
North Clairemont
Clairemont
Pacific Beach
Bay Park
Linda Vista
Mission Beach
Ocean Beach
Mission Hills
Grantville
SAN DIEGO
Santee
El Cajon
La Mesa
Spring Valley
Lemon Grove
Encanto
Logan Heights
Coronado
La Presa
National City
Lincoln Acres
CHULA VISTA
Otay
Palm City
Imperial Beach
San Ysidro
Tijuana
PACIFIC OCEAN
South San Diego Bay
CALIFORNIA (page 103)
BAJA CALIFORNIA NORTE
MEXICO
MILITARY Living
www.militaryliving.com
MILES
0 1 2 3 4
KILOMETERS
0 1 2 3 4
Copyright © by William Roy and L. Ann Crawford
A B C D E F G H
1 2 3 4 5 6 7 8 9 10

SAN FRANCISCO, CA

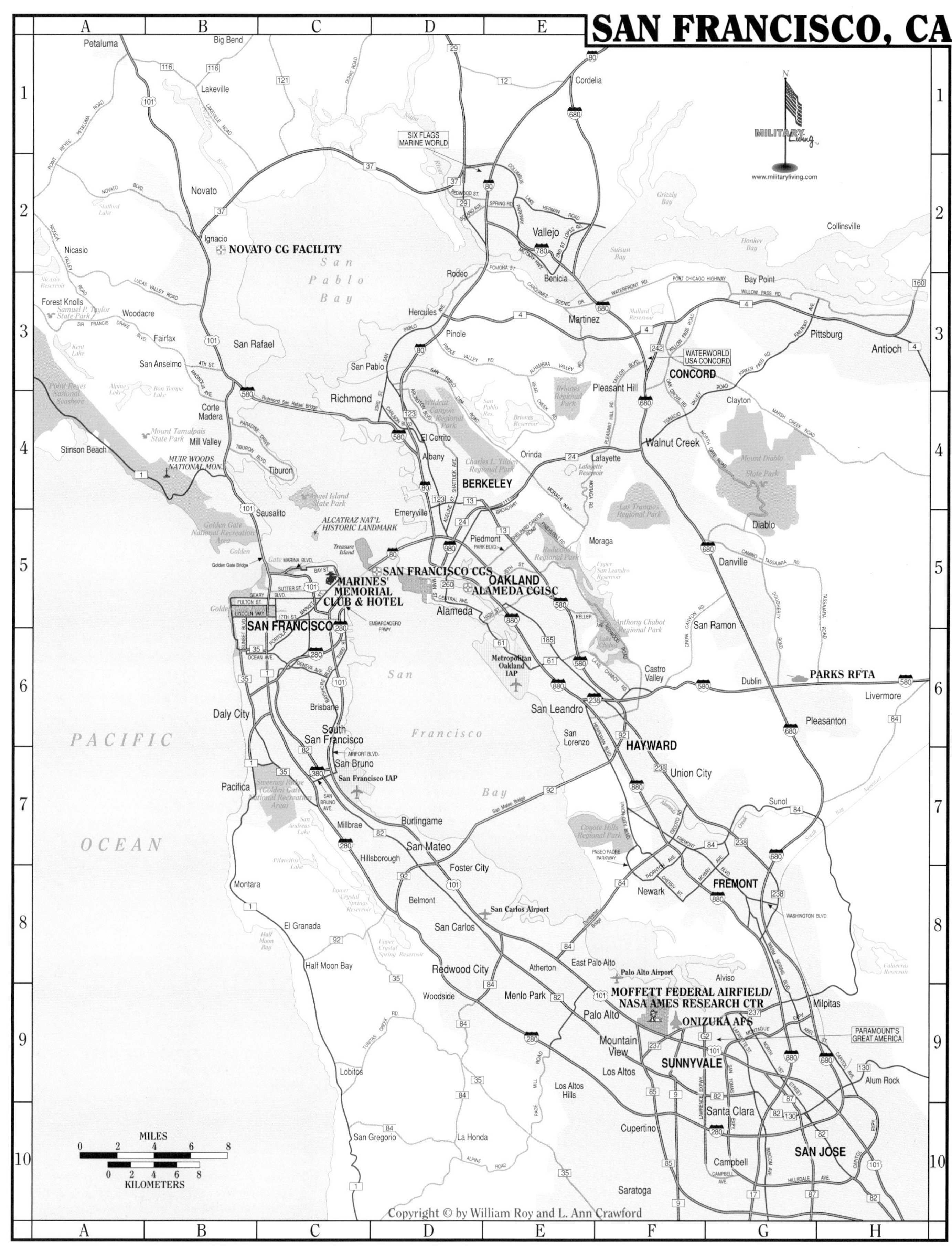

ARIZONA, pg. 100
Flagstaff, pg. 100
Phoenix, pg. 102
Tucson, pg. 100

CAMP NAVAJO

#1 Hughes Avenue, P.O. Box 16123,Bellemont, AZ 86015-6123
C-928-773-3238, DSN-312-853-3238, Police (Security)-773-3298
WEB: www.campnavajo.com
LOCATION: From I-40 and I-17 intersection at Flagstaff, go west on I-40 approximately ten miles and get off at exit 185. Follow the signs for approximately one mile to the Visitors Center and Security Operations Bldg. USMRA: AZ map (D,E-4). NMC: Flagstaff, ten miles east.
RECREATION & TRAVEL: TML-773-3238
RETAIL & DINING: Clubs-Post Club-773-3289

DAVIS-MONTHAN AIR FORCE BASE

355 Wing, Hq 12 Air Force, 5275 East Granite Street
Davis-Monthan Air Force Base, AZ 85707-3010
C-520-228-3900, DSN-312-228-1110/3900, Police-228-3200
WEB: www.dm.af.mil
LOCATION: From the east on I-10, exit 270 north onto Kolb Road, north six miles to Golf Links Road, left (west) to Craycroft Road, left (south) to Main Gate. From the west on I-10, exit 264A onto Irvington Road. Make a left onto Alvernon Way (Alvernon Way turns into Golf Links Road at intersection with Ajo Way). Make a right onto Craycroft Road and follow to the Main Gate. USMRA: AZ map (F-8). NMC: Tucson, within city limits.
RECREATION & TRAVEL: Golf-228-3734 RVC-747-9144 SPA-228-2322 TML-228-3230/3309
RETAIL & DINING: Cafeteria-228-3072 Clubs-EMC/NCO-228-3100 OC-228-3301 Com-228-3116 EX-748-7887 Gas-745-3866
SUPPORT & FAMILY: Med-228-266

FORT HUACHUCA

USAIC & Fort Huachuca, Attn:ATZS-CDR
Fort Huachuca, AZ 85613-6000
C-520-538-7111, DSN-312-879-7111, Police-533-2181 or 911
WEB: http://huachuca-www.army.mil
LOCATION: From I-10, take exit 302 south onto AZ-90 south approximately 28 miles to Sierra Vista. Main Gate to fort on right (west) side of road. USMRA: AZ map (F,G-9). NMC: Tucson, 75 miles northwest. NMI: Davis-Monthan AFB, 75 miles northwest.
RECREATION & TRAVEL: Golf-533-7092 RVC-533-1335 SPA-538-2860 TML-533-2222
RETAIL & DINING: Clubs-CC-533-7322 EMC-Ozone-533-0861 NCO-La Hacienda-533-3802 O/CIV-Lakeside-533-2194 Time Out-533-3837 Com-533-5540 Dining-533-6393 EX-458-7830 Gas-459-4022
SUPPORT & FAMILY: Med-533-9026

FORT TUTHILL RECREATION AREA

HC 39, Box 5, Flagstaff, AZ 86001-8701
C-623-856-3401 or 800-552-6268, DSN-312-896-3401
Police-774-5228
WEB: www.forttuthill.com
LOCATION: Located at an elevation of 7,000 feet at the base of the San Francisco peaks. Four miles south of Flagstaff. Exit 337 off I-17. Enter Fort Tuthill County Park, then follow the signs to Luke AFB Recreation Area. Check-in at main lodge (large grey building). USMRA: AZ map (E-4). NMC: Flagstaff, four miles north. NMI: Camp Navajo 16 miles northwest.
RECREATION & TRAVEL: RVC-928-774-8893 or 800-552-6268
TML-928-774-8893 or 800-552-6268
NOTE: *For detailed information about this off-base recreation facility, as well as on-base recreation facilities, golf courses and marinas, consult Military Living's "Military RV, Camping and Outdoor Recreation Around the World".*

GILA BEND AIR FORCE AUXILIARY FIELD

3096 First Street
Gila Bend Air Force Auxiliary Field, AZ 85337-5000
C-928-683-6169, Police-683-6220
LOCATION: From I-10, 34 miles west of Phoenix, take exit 112 (Yuma/Gila Bend); south on AZ-85 through Gila Bend; right (west) at Gila Bend AFAF/Ajo sign, approximately 3.5 miles to the AFAF. Also take I-8 east or west, exit 115 north to left (west) at Gila Bend AFAF/Ajo sign and 3.5 miles to base. USMRA: AZ map (C-7). NMC: Phoenix, 69 miles northeast.
RECREATION & TRAVEL: ITT/ITR-None. See Luke AFB listing.
RVC-683-6211/38 TML-683-2911

LAKE MARTINEZ RECREATIONAL AREA

MCCS Box 9119, MCAS Yuma, AZ 85369-9119
C-928-269-2011 or 783-3422, DSN-312-269-2011
Police-Sheriff-783-4427 PMO-269-2361
WEB: www.yuma.usmc-mccs.org
LOCATION: Off base. Located on the Colorado River 38 miles north of Yuma. From I-8, east or west, exit 2 to north on US-95 for 20 miles to left onto Martinez Lake Road. Turn right onto Red Cloud Mine Road. There will be a sign for the recreation facility. Continue following the signs. USMRA: AZ map (A-7). NMC: Yuma, 38 miles south. NMI: Yuma Army Proving Ground 15 miles north.
RECREATION & TRAVEL: RVC-269-2011/2262 or 783-3422
NOTE: *For detailed information about this off-base recreation facility, as well as on-base recreation facilities, golf courses and marinas, consult Military Living's "Military RV, Camping and Outdoor Recreation Around the World".*

LUKE AIR FORCE BASE

7131 North Litchfield Road, Luke Air Force Base, AZ 85309-1501
C-623-856-1110/7411, DSN-312-896-1110, Police-856-6347
WEB: www.luke.af.mil
LOCATION: From Phoenix, west on I-10 to Litchfield Road, exit 128, north on Litchfield Road approximately five miles. Also, from Phoenix, north on I-17 to Glendale Avenue, exit 205 west on Glendale Avenue to intersection of Glendale Avenue and Litchfield Road approximately ten miles. From Loop 101 (Aqua Fria Highway), exit on Glendale Avenue and turn west; travel five miles west to Litchfield Road; turn right (north) to the next light at Thunderbird Street and turn left to the Main Gate. USMRA: AZ map (D-6), Phoenix, AZ map (G-2). NMC: Phoenix, 15 miles east.
RECREATION & TRAVEL: Golf-535-8355 RVC-800-552-6268 SPA-856-6105/6941 TML-856-3941 or 935-2641
RETAIL & DINING: Cafeteria-856-6396 Clubs-EMC-856-7136 NCO-935-2610 OC-856-6446 Com-935-3821 EX-935-1263 Gas-935-4953/5599
SUPPORT & FAMILY: Med-856-2273

SKY HARBOR INTERNATIONAL AIRPORT/ PHOENIX AIR NATIONAL GUARD

161 Air Refueling Wing (ANG), 3200 East Old Tower Road
Phoenix, AZ 85034-7263
C-602-302-9000, DSN-312-853-9000
Police (Security)-302-9133
WEB: www.azphoe.ang.af.mil
LOCATION: From I-10 in Phoenix, take the 24th Street exit 150B; go north 0.25 miles, turn east on Old Tower Road; follow Old Tower Road to front gate. USMRA: AZ map (D,E-6); Phoenix, AZ map (I-3). NMC: Phoenix, five miles west. NMI: Luke AFB, 30 miles west.
RECREATION & TRAVEL: SPA-302-9162

YUMA ARMY PROVING GROUND

Attn: CSTE-DTC-YP-PA, 301 C Street
Yuma Army Proving Ground, AZ 85365-9100
C-928-328-2151, DSN-312-899-2151, Police-328-2720
WEB: www.yuma.army.mil
LOCATION: Northeast of I-8, turn right (north) on US-95 which bisects the post. Southwest of I-10 turn left (south) on US-95. USMRA: AZ map (A-6,7; B-7). NMC: Yuma, 27 miles southwest.
RECREATION & TRAVEL: RVC-328-3989 TML-328-2129
RETAIL & DINING: Clubs-CC-328-2097 Com-328-2240 EX-328-2252 Gas-343-1365
SUPPORT & FAMILY: Med-328-2502

YUMA MARINE CORPS AIR STATION

Box 99100, Third Street
Yuma Marine Corps Air Station, AZ 85369-9113
C-928-269-2011, DSN-312-269-2011, Police-269-2205/2361
WEB: www.yuma.usmc.mil
LOCATION: From I-8 east or west, take exit 3 onto Avenue 3E south for one mile to base on right, adjacent to Yuma IAP. USMRA: AZ map (A-7). NMC: Yuma, within city limits.
RECREATION & TRAVEL: RVC-269-2262 SPA-269-2729 TML-269-2262
RETAIL & DINING: Cafeteria-269-5183 Clubs-CC-269-2171/2406/2711 Com-269-2245 Dining-269-2448 EX-269-2747 Gas-269-2110
SUPPORT & FAMILY: Med-269-2772

CALIFORNIA, pg. 102-103
Lake Tahoe, pg. 102
Los Angeles, pg. 107
Monterey, pg. 103
Sacramento, pg. 102
San Diego, pg. 108
San Francisco, pg. 109

ADMIRAL BAKER FIELD CAMPGROUND

c/o Navy Golf Course, Friar's Road and Santo Road
San Diego, CA 92120-2325
C-619-556-5525, DSN-312-532-4111
Police for campground-556-5555
LOCATION: Off base. From north or south on I-15 approximately one mile north of intersection with I-8, exit east onto Friars Road for approximately 0.5 miles to left (north) on Santo Road and an immediate right (northeast) onto Admiral Baker Road. USMRA: San Diego, CA map (D,E-4,5). NMC: San Diego, four miles southwest. NMI: San Diego NS, ten miles south.
RECREATION & TRAVEL: RVC-556-5525
NOTE: *For detailed information about this off-base recreation facility, as well as on-base recreation facilities, golf courses and marinas, consult Military Living's "Military RV, Camping and Outdoor Recreation Around the World".*

ALAMEDA COAST GUARD INTEGRATED SUPPORT COMMAND

Coast Guard Island, Bldg 16, Alameda, CA 94501-5100
C-510-437-3035, Police-437-3151
WEB: www.uscg.mil/mlcpac/iscalameda
LOCATION: From the north on I-880, exit at 16th Street/Embarcadero; left (south) on Embarcadero approximately 0.3 miles to right (west) on Dennison Street. Follow signs to causeway and island. Signs posted. From the south on I-880, exit on 23rd Street north. Make left U-turn at first left, cross overpass onto southbound 23rd Street, then first right through the light, follow signs around to causeway and island. USMRA: San Francisco, CA map (D-5). NMC: Oakland, one mile northwest.
RECREATION & TRAVEL: TML-437-3541/78
RETAIL & DINING: Dining-437-3303 EX-437-3165 Gas-437-3165
SUPPORT & FAMILY: Med-437-3581/2

BARSTOW MARINE CORPS LOGISTICS BASE

Command Headquarters, Box 110100
Barstow Marine Corps Logistics Base, CA 92311-5001
C-760-577-6211 or 800-THE-USMC (843-8762)
DSN-312-282-6961, Police-577-6669
WEB: https://www.bam.usmc.mil
LOCATION: From Ontario International Airport take Interstate 10 east toward San Bernardino. Merge onto Interstate 15 north toward Barstow/Las Vegas for about 80 miles. From Barstow, take Interstate 40 for two miles until you reach the installation. If coming from the east, Barstow is the second to the last stop on Interstate 40. USMRA: CA map (H-12,13). NMC: Los Angeles, 120 miles southwest. NMI: Fort Irwin NTC, 40 miles northeast.
RECREATION & TRAVEL: Golf-577-6431 RVC-577-6418 TML-577-6418
RETAIL & DINING: Clubs-EMC/NCO-577-6495 OC/SNCO-577-6432 Com-577-6404 Dining-577-6428 EX-256-8974 Gas-256-8974
SUPPORT & FAMILY: Med-577-6491

BEALE AIR FORCE BASE

5900 C Street, Beale Air Force Base, CA 95903-1211
C-530-634-3000, DSN-312-368-1110, Police-634-2131
WEB: www.beale.af.mil
LOCATION: From CA-70 north or south, take Feather River Blvd exit east (south of Marysville), follow to North Beale Road and take a right (east). Follow signs to Beale, continuing for seven miles to Main Gate. USMRA: CA map (D-6). NMC: Sacramento, 35 miles southwest.
RECREATION & TRAVEL: Golf-634-2124 RVC-634-2054/3382 SPA-634-9167/8793 TML-634-2953/4
RETAIL & DINING: Cafeteria-634-2537 Clubs-CC-Reece Point-788-0286 Com-634-2422 EX-634-2987 Gas-788-0214/5
SUPPORT & FAMILY: Med-634-2941

BIG BEAR RECREATION FACILITY

P.O. Box 1664, Big Bear Lake, CA 92315-1664
C-858-577-4126/41 DSN-312-267-1011
WEB: http://www.mccsmiramar.com/bigbear/bigbear.html
LOCATION: Off base. Located at Big Bear Lake. From I-10 at Redlands, take CA-30 north to CA-330. Go north on CA-330 to CA-18 at Running Springs. Take CA-18 east to Big Bear Lake. At the Big Bear Dam, turn right. This is still CA-18, but is also called Big Bear Blvd. Take Big Bear Blvd past the village and turn right on Moonridge Road. Turn right on Elm Street, then right onto Switzerland Drive, then take an immediate left. Facility is approximately 0.25 miles down the dirt road. Note: Don't be tempted to take a shortcut through Snow Summit Ski Area, as the road is gated during winter months. USMRA: CA map (H-13). NMC: San Bernardino, 40 miles southwest. NMI: March ARB, approximately 50 miles southwest.
RECREATION & TRAVEL: RVC-577-4126/41
TML-577-4126/41

CAMP PENDLETON MARINE CORPS BASE

P.O. Box 555019, Camp Pendleton, CA 92055-5019
C-760-725-4111, DSN-312-365-4111, Police-911
WEB: www.cpp.usmc.mil
LOCATION: From north or south of Oceanside, take I-5 which is adjacent to Camp Pendleton along the Pacific Ocean. From I-5 north or south, take the 'Camp Pendleton' off-ramp from I-5 at Oceanside to Vandegraft Blvd. USMRA: CA map (G-15). NMC: Oceanside, adjacent to base southwest.
RECREATION & TRAVEL: Golf-725-4756 Marina-725-2820/5135/7245 RVC-725-2134/4241 or 725-7935 (campsites) or 725-7629 (cottages) TML-430-4702 Ward Lodge-725-5304
RETAIL & DINING: Clubs-CC-725-4481/5331 EMC-725-4896 OC-725-2828/6571 Com-725-4012 EX-725-6233 Gas-725-2391/6387
SUPPORT & FAMILY: Med-725-1288

CAMP ROBERTS

California Army National Guard, Maneuver Training Center (Heavy), Headquarters, Bldg 109, Camp Roberts, CA 93451-5000
C-805-238-3100, DSN-312-949-8210, Police-238-8190
WEB: www.calguard.ca.gov/cprbts
LOCATION: On US-101, halfway between Los Angeles and San Francisco, 13 miles north of Paso Robles, exit 24 toward East Garrison. USMRA: CA map (D-10). NMC: Paso Robles, 13 miles north.
RECREATION & TRAVEL: RVC-238-8312 TML-238-8312
RETAIL & DINING: Clubs-CC-Consolidated Mess-238-8237 EX-238-8195

CAMP SAN LUIS OBISPO

San Joaquin Avenue, Bldg 738, P.O. Box 4360
San Luis Obispo, CA 93403-4360
C-805-594-6510, DSN-312-630-6510, Police (Security)-594-6665
LOCATION: From US-101 north or south to San Luis Obispo, then northwest on CA-1 (Pacific Coast Highway) for approximately five miles toward Morro Bay to Camp San Luis Obispo on southwest side of Hwy CA-1. USMRA: CA map (D-11). NMC: San Luis Obispo, five miles southeast.
RECREATION & TRAVEL: RVC-594-6500 TML-594-6500
RETAIL & DINING: Clubs-NCO/OC-541-6168 Dining-782-6873 EX-541-3284

CHANNEL ISLANDS AIR NATIONAL GUARD STATION

146 Airlift Wing, 100 Mulcahey Drive
Port Hueneme, CA 93041-4000
C-805-986-8000, DSN-312-893-7000, Police (Security)-986-7449
WEB: www.146aw.ca.ang.af.mil
LOCATION: From US-101 north or south to Camarillo, go south on South Las Posas Road to East Port Hueneme Road past CA-1, then left (southeast) on Navalair Road. ANG Station entrance is on right side of road. USMRA:CA map (E-13). NMC: Oxnard, 3.5 miles northwest. NMI: Point Mugu NAS/Ventura County NB, adjacent.
RECREATION & TRAVEL: RVC-984-7705 SPA-986-7577
NOTE: *Open Tues-Fri.*

CHANNEL ISLANDS HARBOR COAST GUARD CAMPGROUND

11 Coast Guard District, 4202 South Victoria Avenue
Oxnard, CA 93035-8399
C-805-984-7705, Police-385-7600 or 986-6530
WEB: http://www.uscg.mil/mwr/cottages/ChannelIslandsHarbor-Campground.htm
LOCATION: Off base. Across from Coast Guard Station, behind the Coast Guard recruiting office. From US-101, exit south on Victoria Blvd. Continue past Channel Islands Blvd. Entrance to camp will be on the left side. USMRA: CA map (E-13). NMC: Los Angeles, 60 miles southeast. NMI: Port Hueneme Naval Facilities Expeditionary Logistics Center.
RECREATION & TRAVEL: RVC-984-7705
NOTE: *For detailed information about this recreation facility, as well as other recreation facilities, golf courses and marinas, consult Military Living's "Military RV, Camping and Outdoor Recreation Around the World".*

CHINA LAKE NAVAL AIR WEAPONS STATION

1 Administration Circle, Bldg 00001, China Lake, CA 93555-6100
C-760-939-9011, DSN-312-437-9011, Police-939-3323
LOCATION: From north or south on US-395 or CA-14, go east on CA-178 to Ridgecrest to the Main Gate. USMRA: CA map (G,H-10,11,12) NMC: Los Angeles, 150 miles south.
RECREATION & TRAVEL: Golf-939-2990 SPA-939-5301/8 TML-939-2383/3146
RETAIL & DINING: Clubs-CC-939-3166 Com-939-3138 Dining-939-8660 EX-446-6707 Gas-446-5044
SUPPORT & FAMILY: Med-939-8000

CORONADO NAVAL BASE, NAVAL AMPHIBIOUS BASE PACIFIC

Bldg 678, McCain Blvd, P.O. Box 357033
North Island Naval Air Station, CA 92135-7138
C-619-437-1011, DSN-312-524-1011, Police-437-3432
WEB: www.nbc.navy.mil
LOCATION: From San Diego, take I-5 south to CA-75 across Coronado-San Diego Bay Bridge. Left on Orange Avenue (which becomes Silver Strand Blvd) for 2.2 miles. Pass Hotel del Coronado and watch for signs to base. Left turn at fourth light after hotel. USMRA: San Diego, CA map (C,D-7,8). NMC: San Diego, five miles north. NMI: Coronado NB, North Island NAS, three miles northwest.
RECREATION & TRAVEL: Marina-522-8680 RVC-522-8680/1 TML-437-3860
RETAIL & DINING: Clubs-EMC-437-3171 Coronado-437-2181/2637 Dining-437-2160 Restaurant-437-3040 EX-522-7403 Gas-522-7415
SUPPORT & FAMILY: Med-437-3047/8

CORONADO NAVAL BASE, NORTH ISLAND NAVAL AIR STATION

Bldg 678, McCain Blvd, P.O. Box 357033
North Island Naval Air Station, CA 92135-7138
C-619-545-1011, DSN-312-524-1011, Police-545-6122
WEB: www.nbc.navy.mil
LOCATION: From San Diego, take I-5 north or south to CA-75 across Coronado-San Diego Bay Bridge to CA-282 northwest directly to Main Gate. Also, take CA-75 north from Imperial Beach to downtown Coronado, then left on CA-282 directly to Main Gate. Adjacent to Coronado. USMRA: San Diego, CA map (B,C-6,7). NMC: San Diego: four miles northeast.
RECREATION & TRAVEL: Golf-545-9659 SPA-545-9567 TML-545-9551 Navy Lodge-800-NAVY-INN, 545-6490 or 435-0191
RETAIL & DINING: Cafeteria-522-7267 Clubs-CC-545-9084 Com-545-6566 EX-522-7222 Gas-522-7282
SUPPORT & FAMILY: Med-545-4264/4266/9473
NOTE: *Shares PAO with Coronado.*

EDWARDS AIR FORCE BASE

AFFTC/PA, 1 South Rosamond Blvd
Edwards Air Force Base, CA 93523-1225
C-661-277-1110, DSN-312-527-1110, Police-277-3340
WEB: www.edwards.af.mil
LOCATION: From north or south on CA-14, to Rosamond (11 miles north of Lancaster). Exit east onto Rosamond Blvd, then east approximately 16 miles to Edwards AFB. Also, from east or west on CA-58, exit at Mojave south onto CA-14, then approximately 12 miles south to Rosamond, then east on Rosamond Avenue approximately 16 miles to the base. USMRA: CA map (G-12). NMC: Los Angeles, 90 miles southwest.
RECREATION & TRAVEL: Golf-275-7888 RVC-275-7368 TML-275-7666
RETAIL & DINING: Cafeteria-275-2233 Clubs-Muroc-275-2582 Stripes-275-2582 Com-277-4589 Dining-275-8733 EX-258-1078 Gas-258-5091
SUPPORT & FAMILY: Med-277-7118

EL CENTRO NAVAL AIR FACILITY

Naval Air Facility Command, El Centro, CA 92243-5001
C-760-339-2220, DSN-312-658-2220, Police-339-2585
WEB: www.nafec.navy.mil
LOCATION: From east or west on I-8, two miles west of El Centro, to CR-S30 (Forrester Road) exit, north 1.5 miles to CR-S80 (Evan Hewes Highway) left for four miles, right on Bennet Road to Main Gate. USMRA: CA map (I-16). NMC: El Centro, seven miles east.
RECREATION & TRAVEL: RVC-339-2486 SPA-339-2426 TML-339-2266/2935 Navy Lodge-800-NAVY-INN or 339-2342
RETAIL & DINING: Clubs-CC-339-2330 Com-337-5253 or 339-2558 EX-339-2342 Gas-339-2670
SUPPORT & FAMILY: Med-339-2674

FIDDLER'S COVE RV PARK

c/o NASNI MWR Dept Code 92, Box 357081
San Diego, CA 92135-7081
C-619-522-8681, DSN-312-735-8680 Fax: 619-522-7969
Police for RV park-437-3432
LOCATION: Off base. From north or south on I-5 in San Diego, take San Diego-Coronado Bay Bridge (CA-75) exit; cross bridge and go left on Orange Avenue, which becomes Silver Strand. Continue south on CA-75 past Amphibious Base gate for approximately 1.5 miles. RV Park is next to Naval Amphibious Base Marina (Navy Yacht Club) and Aquatic Sports Center. USMRA: San Diego, CA map (D-8). NMC: San Diego, 6.5 miles northeast. NMI: Coronado NB, NAB Pacific, 1.5 miles north.
RECREATION & TRAVEL: RVC-522-8680/1
NOTE: *For detailed information about this off-base recreation facility, as well as on-base recreation facilities, golf courses and marinas, consult Military Living's "Military RV, Camping and Outdoor Recreation Around the World".*

FORT HUNTER LIGGETT

U.S. Army Garrison, Bldg 178, Attn: AFRC-FMH-PAO
P.O. Box 7000, Jolon, CA 93928-7000
C-831-386-3000, DSN-312-686-2291, Police-386-2613
WEB: www.liggett.army.mil
LOCATION: From US-101 north or south, exit approximately one mile southwest of King City onto G-14 (Jolon Road), then south approximately 19 miles to Main Gate. USMRA: CA map (C,D-10). NMC: King City, approximately 20 miles north.
RECREATION & TRAVEL: RVC-386-2605/12 TML-386-2511
RETAIL & DINING: Clubs-CPO-386-2900 Com-386-2190 EX-385-4585 Gas-385-6032

FORT IRWIN NATIONAL TRAINING CENTER

Attn: AFZJ-GC, Inner Loop Road, Bldg 983
Fort Irwin National Training Center, CA 92310-5090
C-760-380-1111, DSN-312-470-1111, Police-380-3474/4444
WEB: www.irwin.army.mil
LOCATION: From I-15 north or south, take the Irwin Road exit (north to Barstow). Watch for signs. USMRA: CA map (H,I-12). NMC: San Bernardino, 70 miles southwest.
RECREATION & TRAVEL: Golf-380-3434 TML-386-4040
RETAIL & DINING: Clubs-CC-Leaders/Reggie's-380-3293 Outer Limits-380-8646 Com-380-3560 EX-386-2060 Gas-386-2417
SUPPORT & FAMILY: Med-380-3777

FORT MACARTHUR

2400 South Pacific Avenue, Bldg 37, San Pedro, CA 90731-2960
C-310-363-1110, DSN-312-833-1110, Police (Security)-363-8385
WEB: www.losangeles.af.mil
LOCATION: From I-110 (Harbor Freeway), go south toward San Pedro. Keep left to Gaffney Street, continue south approximately 1.5 miles to 19th Street, then left to Pacific Avenue and right to Main Gate on left side of street. USMRA: Los Angeles, CA map (C-7). NMC: Los Angeles, within city limits. NMI: Los Angeles AFB, 20 miles north.
RECREATION & TRAVEL: TML-363-8296
RETAIL & DINING: Gas-313-1878
SUPPORT & FAMILY: Med-363-0037

HUMBOLDT BAY COAST GUARD GROUP

1001 Lycoming Avenue, McKinleyville, CA 95519-9308
C-707-839-6103
WEB: www.uscg.mil/d11/humboldt/siteunits/units.htm
LOCATION: From Eureka, take US-101 north approximately 14 miles to Airport Road exit east. Go east on Airport Road to first left onto Coast Guard Road, then left at 'T.' Follow road to Main Gate. USMRA: CA map (B-2). NMC: Eureka, 15 miles south.
RETAIL & DINING: Cafeteria-839-6171
SUPPORT & FAMILY: Med-839-6175

IMPERIAL BEACH OUTLYING LANDING FIELD

1498 13th Street, Imperial Beach, CA 91932-3798
C-619-437-1011, DSN-312-524-1011, Police-524-2037
LOCATION: From San Diego, take I-5 south to Palm Avenue exit. Go west on Palm Avenue approximately one mile, then left (south) on 13th Street to base. Watch for signs. USMRA: San Diego, CA map (D,E-10). NMC: San Diego, nine miles north.
RETAIL & DINING: Com-437-9478 EX-424-2910 Gas-575-8451

LAKE TAHOE COAST GUARD STATION

P.O. Box 882, 2500 Lake Forest Road
Tahoe City, CA 96145-0882
C-530-583-4433
WEB: www.uscg.mil
LOCATION: From I-80 east or west to Truckee, exit onto CA-89 south. Go 12 miles south to Tahoe City. At intersection with CA-28 (to Kings Beach), continue straight through stoplight onto CA-28 northeast approximately 1.5 miles. Turn right on Lake Forest Road and right at entrance. USMRA: CA map (F-6). NMC: Reno, NV, 45 miles northeast. NMI: Reno/Tahoe IAP/ANG, NV, 40 miles northeast.
RECREATION & TRAVEL: TML-583-4433/7438
NOTE: *For detailed information about this recreation facility, as well as other recreation facilities, golf courses and marinas, consult Military Living's "Military RV, Camping and Outdoor Recreation Around the World".*

LAKE TAHOE CONDOMINIUMS

USISC Alameda MWR, Bldg 16, Coast Guard Island
Alameda, CA 94501-5100
C-530-583-7438
WEB: www.uscg.mil/mlcpac/iscalameda
LOCATION: Off base. Two condos, located at Lake Tahoe. To Lake Forest Glen (North Shore Condo): Take I-80 to CA-89 (to Tahoe City). CA-89 becomes CA-28 (North Lake Blvd). Go through Tahoe City, turn right on Lake Forest Road. Turn left on Bristlecone. To Tahoe Keys (South Shore Condo): Take I-80 to US-50 toward Placerville to South Shore Lake Tahoe. Follow US-50 toward Nevada state line. Turn left on Tahoe Keys Blvd. USMRA: CA map (F-6). NMC: Carson City NV, 30 miles southeast. NMI: Reno/Tahoe IAP/ANG, NV, 20 miles northeast.
RECREATION & TRAVEL: RVC-437-3541 TML-437-3578
NOTE: *For detailed information about this off-base recreation facility, as well as on-base recreation facilities, golf courses and marinas, consult Military Living's "Military RV, Camping and Outdoor Recreation Around the World".*

LEMOORE NAVAL AIR STATION

700 Avenger Avenue, Lemoore Naval Air Station, CA 93246-5001
C-559-998-0100, DSN-312-949-1110, Police-998-4811
WEB: www.lemoore.navy.mil
LOCATION: From north or south on I-5, exit onto CA-198 east for approximately 24 miles to Main Gate on left side of highway. From north or south on CA-99, exit onto CA-198 west for approximately 27 miles to Main Gate on right side of CA-198. USMRA: CA map (E-10). NMC: Fresno, 40 miles north.
RECREATION & TRAVEL: RVC-997-7000 SPA-998-1680/1 TML-997-7000/1 Navy Lodge-800-NAVY-INN or 998-5791
RETAIL & DINING: Clubs-CPO-998-4858 EMC-Tailgates-998-8919 OC-998-4857 Com-998-4827 Dining-998-4810 EX-998-4722 Fast Food-998-3734 Gas-998-4731
SUPPORT & FAMILY: Med-998-4481

LOS ALAMITOS JOINT FORCES TRAINING BASE

Bldg 15, Post Hq, Los Alamitos, CA 90720-5165
C-562-795-2090, DSN-312-972-2090, Police-795-2100
LOCATION: From I-405 (San Diego Freeway) north or south, take exit to I-605 (San Gabriel River Freeway) north approximately 1.5 miles to exit east onto East Katella Avenue, then east 1.7 miles to right on Lexington Drive and proceed to Main Gate. Clearly marked. USMRA: Los Angeles, CA map (E-6,7). NMC: Los Angeles, 15 miles northwest.
RECREATION & TRAVEL: Golf-430-9913 SPA-795-2571 TML-795-2124
RETAIL & DINING: EX-430-1076

LOS ANGELES AIR FORCE BASE

2420 Vela Way, SMC/PA, Suite 1467
El Segundo, CA 90245-1467
C-310-653-1110, DSN-310-633-1110, Police-363-2123
WEB: www.losangeles.af.mil
LOCATION: From I-405 (San Diego Freeway) north or south, take El Segundo Blvd exit. Base is on both sides of street. USMRA: Los Angeles, CA map (B-5). NMC: Los Angeles, ten miles northeast.
RETAIL & DINING: Clubs-CC-363-2230 Com-536-2913 EX-725-9912
SUPPORT & FAMILY: Med-363-0037/5029

MARCH AIR RESERVE BASE

452 AMW/PA, 2145 Graeber Street, Suite 211
March Air Reserve Base, CA 92518-1671
C-951-655-1110, DSN-312-447-1110
WEB: http://www.afrc.af.mil/march/
LOCATION: From north or south on I-215/CA-215 use March ARB exit east onto Cactus Avenue. Continue east approximately 1.5 miles to traffic light at Main Gate on right side of road. USMRA: CA map (G-14). NMC: Riverside, nine miles northwest.
RECREATION & TRAVEL: Golf-697-6690 RVC-655-2816 SPA-655-2397 TML-655-5241
RETAIL & DINING: Clubs-CC-653-2121 Com-655-3967 EX-655-3111

MARINES' MEMORIAL CLUB & HOTEL

609 Sutter Street, San Francisco, CA 94102-1022
C-415-673-6672, Reservations:C-800-5-MARINE (562-7463), Police-911
WEB: www.marineclub.com
LOCATION: From East Bay take I-80 and cross the San Francisco/Oakland Bay Bridge. Take first exit from Bridge onto Fremont Street, cross Market Street, take first left on Pine Street to Mason Street, take left on Mason and then an immediate right on Sutter Street. Marines' Memorial Club & Hotel located on corner of Sutter and Mason. USMRA: San Francisco, CA map (C-5). NMC: San Francisco, within city limits.
RECREATION & TRAVEL: Dining-671-6672 TML-673-6672
NOTE: *This base also has a library, museum and theater, for detailed information about this off-base recreation facility, as well as on-base recreation facilities, golf courses and marinas, consult Military Living's "Military RV, Camping and Outdoor Recreation Around the World".*

MCCLELLAN PARK

5443 Dudley Blvd, Bldg 911, McClellan Park, CA 95652-1128
C-916-920-0537, Police (Security)-546-8165
LOCATION: From west on I-80, take exit onto Watt Avenue north for approximately 1.25 miles. Main Gate and visitor's gate are on left side of street. From northeast on I-80, take exit onto Madison Avenue west for approximately 1.25 miles to intersection with Watt Avenue, then right to Main Gate and visitor's gate on left side of street. Clearly marked. USMRA: CA map (D-6). NMC: Sacramento, nine miles southwest.
RECREATION & TRAVEL: SPA-Sacramento CG Air Station C-643-7659
RETAIL & DINING: Com-925-8541 EX-920-0537 Gas-922-8860

MIRAMAR MARINE CORPS AIR STATION

Commanding Officer, Headquarters & Headquarters Squadron
Attn: PAO, P.O. Box 452013, San Diego, CA 92145-2013
C-858-577-1011, DSN-312-267-1011, Police-577-4068
WEB: www.miramar.usmc.mil
LOCATION: From I-15 north of San Diego, take Miramar Way exit west which leads directly to the Main Gate. USMRA: San Diego, CA map (C,D,E,F-2,3). NMC: San Diego, ten miles southwest.
RECREATION & TRAVEL: Golf-577-4155 RVC-577-4126/41 SPA-577-4283/4/5 TML-577-4233/5 Navy Lodge-800-NAVY-INN or 271-7111
RETAIL & DINING: Cafeteria-577-1380 Clubs-EMC-577-4820/8 OC-577-4808 SNCO-577-4799 Com-577-4523 Dining-577-1382 EX-695-7288 Gas-695-7287
SUPPORT & FAMILY: Med-577-4656

MOFFETT FEDERAL AIRFIELD/ NASA AMES RESEARCH CENTER

P.O. Box 0128, Moffett Federal Airfield, CA 94035-0128
C-650-604-5000, DSN-312-359-5000, Police-604-5461
WEB: www.arc.nasa.gov
LOCATION: On north side of US-101 (Bayshore Freeway), 35 miles south of San Francisco. Take Moffett Federal Airfield exit north onto Clark Road. Turn right onto Moffett Blvd which leads to Main Gate. USMRA: San Francisco, CA map (F-9). NMC: San Jose, seven miles south, San Francisco, 35 miles north.
RECREATION & TRAVEL: Golf-603-8026 TML-603-7101 Navy Lodge-800-NAVY-INN or 962-1542
RETAIL & DINING: Cafeteria-604-5969 Com-603-9976 EX-603-9927

MONTEREY NAVAL POSTGRADUATE SCHOOL

1 University Circle, Monterey, CA 93943-5029
C-831-656-2441, DSN-312-756-2441, Police-656-2556
WEB: www.nps.edu
LOCATION: Take CA-1 south to central Monterey exit, right (west) at light onto Aguajito Road. Take first right (right fork) (east) onto Tenth Street, turn left (north) at stop sign onto Sloat Avenue, and right at Ninth Street gate. From north on CA-1, use Aguajito Road exit to Mark Thomas Drive north, to left (north) on Sloat Avenue, right (east) at Ninth Street gate. USMRA: CA map (C-9). NMC: Monterey, within city limits.
RECREATION & TRAVEL: Golf-656-2167 Marina-656-3118 RVC-656-7563 TML-656-2060/9 Navy Lodge-800-NAVY-INN or 372-6133
RETAIL & DINING: Clubs-CC-656-2170 OC-656-2170 Com-242-7671 Dining-656-2170 EX-373-7277 Gas-373-7271
SUPPORT & FAMILY: Med-625-4900

MONTEREY PINES RV CAMPGROUND

MWR Department Naval Postgraduate School
1 University Circle, P.O. Box 8688, Monterey, CA 93943-5001
C-831-656-7563, DSN-312-878-7563
LOCATION: Off base. From north or south on CA-1, in Monterey, exit at Casa Verde Way and turn east at the stop sign. Proceed straight east through the traffic light at Fremont Street and turn right (south) on Fairgrounds Road. At the next light, turn left (east) on Garden Road, make an immediate left (north) at entrance to the Monterey Fairgrounds/Navy Golf Course. Please note that this is a gated installation. USMRA: CA map (C-9). NMC: Monterey, 0.5 miles north.
RECREATION & TRAVEL: RVC-656-7563
NOTE: *For detailed information about this off-base recreation facility, as well as on-base recreation facilities, golf courses and marinas, consult Military Living's "Military RV, Camping and Outdoor Recreation Around the World".*

NOVATO COAST GUARD FACILITY

227 South Oakwood Drive #7, Novato, CA 94949-6516
C-415-506-3130
WEB: www.uscg.mil/mlcpac/iscalameda/divisions/housing/novato.html
LOCATION: Southbound on US-101 take exit onto Bel Marin Keyes Blvd/Hamilton Field. Circle up and over US-101 on the overpass. Stay in the right lane and make a right at the stop light into Nave Drive. Then, turn left at the light, onto Hamilton Parkway Drive. At the intersection with San Pablo (a dead end), make a right. Enter the circle intersection and take the fourth right off the circle, which is South Oakwood Drive and proceed to the first long building on the right. From US-101 north, take the Hamilton Field exit. At the third light, make a right onto Hamilton Parkway Drive and follow directions as above. USMRA: CA map (C-7). NMC: San Francisco, 25 miles south. NMI: Petaluma CGTC, 21 miles northwest.
RECREATION & TRAVEL TML-506-3130
RETAIL & DINING: EX-883-3006

ONIZUKA AIR FORCE STATION

1080 Lockheed Martin Way, Box 129, Sunnyvale, CA 94089-1235
C-408-752-3000, DSN-312-561-3000, Police-752-3200
WEB: www.onizuka.af.mil
LOCATION: On northeast side of US-101 (Bayshore Freeway) and north on CA-237, exit on Mathilda Avenue to Lockheed Martin Way, to Main Gate. USMRA: San Francisco, CA map (F-9). NMC: San Jose, seven miles south, San Francisco, 37 miles north.
RECREATION & TRAVEL: Golf-650-603-8026
RETAIL & DINING: Com-650-603-9981 EX-650-603-9902 Snack Bar/Fast Food-752-3218 Gas-650-603-9940
NOTE: *Onizuka is a closed installation, meaning visitors must be sponsored by someone on base. The 2005 BRAC report recommended this base for closure. As required by Federal law, the DoD has until 15 September 2007 to begin closing and realigning the bases as called for in the approved report. This process must be completed by 15 September 2011.*

PARKS RESERVE FORCES TRAINING AREA

Bldg 790, Dublin, CA 94568-5201
C-925-875-4600, Police-875-4720
WEB: www.usarc.army.mil/parksrfta
LOCATION: East Bay area, east of Dublin. From east or west on I-580, exit north onto Dougherty Road (0.8 miles east of I-680 interchange). Go right on Dublin Blvd. Entrance is on left side of Dublin Blvd, clearly marked. USMRA: San Francisco, CA map (G-6). NMC: San Francisco, 30 miles west.
RECREATION & TRAVEL: TML-803-5326
RETAIL & DINING: Clubs-CC-803-0570 Dining-875-4207 EX-829-7780

PETALUMA COAST GUARD TRAINING CENTER

599 Tomales Road, Petaluma, CA 94952-5002
C-707-765-7153, Police-765-7215
WEB: www.uscg.mil/hq/tcpet
LOCATION: From north or south on US-101, exit at Petaluma onto East Washington Street southwest through city of Petaluma; Washington Street becomes Bodega Avenue. Continue west following signs to Coast Guard Training Center approximately 11 miles. Turn left (southwest) onto Tomales Road. A flashing amber light marks the Main Gate. Between 0600 and 0900 hours, enter the training center by taking a left on Spring Hill Road, off of Bodega Avenue. Training center is on right-hand side. USMRA: CA map (B,C-7). NMC: San Francisco, approximately 58 miles south.
RECREATION & TRAVEL: RVC-765-7348 TML-765-7248
RETAIL & DINING: Cafeteria-765-7168 Clubs-CC-765-7247 EX-765-7256 Snack Bar/Fast Food-765-7247 Gas-765-7254
SUPPORT & FAMILY: Med-765-7200

POINT LOMA NAVAL BASE, FLEET ANTI-SUBMARINE WARFARE TRAINING CENTER, PACIFIC

32444 Echo Lane, Bldg 17C, San Diego, CA 92106-3521
C-619-524-1011, DSN-312-524-1011, Police-524-2030
WEB: www.fasw.navy.mil
LOCATION: From I-5 or I-8, take Rosecrans Street exit, follow southwest on Rosecrans Street for three miles to Nimitz Drive. Left on Nimitz Drive to Harbor Drive. Left on Harbor Drive to next light, right into Gate 1 (front gate). Watch for signs. USMRA: San Diego, CA map (B-6). NMC: San Diego, ten miles east.
RECREATION & TRAVEL: TML-524-5382
RETAIL & DINING: Cafeteria-221-2054 Clubs-Admiral Kidd-524-0280/6287 Cafe-524-1260 EX-221-1073 Gas-221-1049

POINT LOMA NAVAL BASE, SAN DIEGO NAVAL SUBMARINE BASE
140 Sylvester Road, San Diego, CA 92106-3521
C-619-553-1011, DSN-312-524-1011, Police-553-9870
LOCATION: From I-8 or I-5, take CA-209 (Rosecrans Street) exit, follow Rosecrans Street for 5.5 miles to front gate. USMRA: San Diego, CA map (B-6). NMC: San Diego, five miles southeast.
RECREATION & TRAVEL: TML-553-9381
RETAIL & DINING: Clubs-CC-Harbor Inn -553-9247 CPO-553-7597 EMC-553-7519 OC-553-9384 Ocean View-221-1541 EX-221-1099 Gas-221-1095

POINT MUGU NAVAL AIR STATION/ VENTURA COUNTY NAVAL BASE
Naval Station Ventura County, 521 9th Street
Bldg 1, Room 117, Point Mugu, CA 93042-5001
C-805-989-1704, DSN-312-351-1110, Police-989-7097
WEB: www.nbvc.navy.mil
LOCATION: Eight miles south of Oxnard and 40 miles north of Santa Monica on CA-1 (Pacific Coast Highway). From north or south on CA-1, take exit at Los Posas Road south onto Pacific Road directly to Gate 3 (Los Posas Gate). Take Frontage Road parallel to CA-1 northwest to Gate 1 and Main Gate or take exit onto Wood Road southwest to Frontage Road and all three gates will be on southwest (right) side of road. USMRA: CA map (E,F-13). NMC: Oxnard, eight miles north.
RECREATION & TRAVEL: Golf-989-7109 RVC-989-8407 SPA-986-7577 TML-989-8251/87
RETAIL & DINING: Cafeteria-989-8898 Clubs-CPO-989-8570 EM-989-7747 OC-989-8849 Dining-Mugu's Pizza-989-7747 The Point-989-7571 EX-989-8896 Gas-488-0161
SUPPORT & FAMILY: Med-989-8815
NOTE: *Formerly Point Mugu Naval Air Warfare Center, Weapons Division.*

PORT HUENEME NAVAL FACILITIES EXPEDITIONARY LOGISTICS CENTER/ VENTURA COUNTY NAVAL BASE
Naval Station Ventura County, 1000 23rd Avenue
Port Hueneme, CA 93043-4301
C-805-982-4711, DSN-312-551-4711, Police-982-4591
WEB: http://www.nbvc.navy.mil/
LOCATION: From east or west on US-101 (Ventura Freeway), exit onto Wagon Wheel Road north to Ventura Road for approximately six miles to right on Pleasant Valley Road directly to Main Gate. USMRA: CA map (E-13). NMC: Oxnard, within city limits.
RECREATION & TRAVEL: Golf-982-2620 RVC-982-6123, ext. 0 TML-982-6025/6778 Navy Lodge-800-NAVY-INN or 985-2624/7
RETAIL & DINING: Clubs-EMC-982-2872 OC-982-2757 Com-982-6854 EX-982-6800 Gas-982-4770
SUPPORT & FAMILY: Med-982-6301

PRESIDIO OF MONTEREY
Defense Language Institute Foreign Language Center
Presidio of Monterey, CA 93944-5006
C-831-242-5104/5555, DSN-312-768-5104/5555
Police-242-7851
WEB: www.monterey.army.mil or www.pom-odr.com
LOCATION: From north or south on CA-1 in Monterey, exit to Del Monte Blvd and go west approximately two miles onto Lighthouse Avenue. Merge right onto Foam Avenue, turn left onto Reeside Avenue, then left on Lighthouse Avenue and right on Private Bolio Road. USMRA: CA map (C-9). NMC: Monterey, within city limits.
RECREATION & TRAVEL: Golf-899-2351 RVC-242-5506/6133 TML-645-1199 or 888-719-8886
RETAIL & DINING: Dining-242-5008/5384 EX-899-2336 Gas-372-0702
SUPPORT & FAMILY: Med-242-5332

PRESIDIO OF MONTEREY ANNEX
Defense Language Institute, Foreign Language Center
Presidio of Monterey, CA 93944-5006
C-831-242-5104/5555, DSN-312-768-5104/5555
Police-242-7851
WEB: http://pom-www.army.mil
LOCATION: From north or south on CA-1, use Fort Ord exit east directly to Main Gate of post. USMRA: CA map (C-9). NMC: Seaside, three miles south of former Fort Ord.
RETAIL & DINING: Com-242-7671 EX-899-2336 Gas-394-8219

SACRAMENTO B.T. COLLINS ARMY LODGING
8300 Santa Cruz Street, Bldg 650, Sacramento, CA 85828-0909
C-916-381-1258, FAX: 916-381-0341, Police-911
LOCATION: Off of I-5 and 99. Take Fruitridge all the way down to Florin Perkins Road to Main Gate. Directions from Main Gate: Drive through the Main Gate and make the first right. Drive straight, then make the first left into the parking lot, which is behind the lodging facility. NMC: Sacramento, within city limits. NMI: Sacramento Coast Guard Air Station, ten miles northwest. USMRA: CA map (D-6).
RECREATION & TRAVEL: TML-381-1258

SAN CLEMENTE ISLAND NAVAL AUXILIARY LANDING FIELD
P.O. Box 357054, San Diego, CA 92135-7054
C-619-545-1011, DSN-312-524-9214, Police-524-9214
LOCATION: This is a closed island accessible by air or boat only. Visitors must be sponsored by military stationed on the island. USMRA: CA map (E,F-15). NMC: Los Angeles, 50 miles east.
RECREATION & TRAVEL: TML-524-9202
RETAIL & DINING: Clubs-CC-524-9227

SAN DIEGO COAST GUARD SECTOR
2710 North Harbor Drive, San Diego, CA 92101-1079
C-619-278-7031/2 or 800-854-9834, Police (Security)-278-6031/2
WEB: www.uscg.mil/d11/sandiego
LOCATION: From south on I-5, take exit south onto North Hawthorn Street which becomes North Kettner Road. Continue southeast on North Kettner Road. turn right on West Laurel Street, which runs into North Harbor Drive. Main entrance is on left side of road. From north on I-5, exit west onto West Hawthorn Street, continue southwest for one mile to right on North Harbor Drive for one mile to gate on left side of road. USMRA: San Diego, CA map (C-6). NMC: San Diego, within city limits.
RETAIL & DINING: Galley-683-6327 EX-683-6325
SUPPORT & FAMILY: Med-278-7131

SAN DIEGO MARINE CORPS RECRUIT DEPOT
1600 Henderson Avenue, Suite 120, San Diego, CA 92140-5093
C-619-524-1011, DSN-312-524-1011, Police-524-4202
WEB: www.mcrdsd.usmc.mil
LOCATION: Adjacent to San Diego International Airport, on the west side of I-5. From north or south on I-5, use Old Town Avenue exit south to Hancock Street, then southeast one block to Witherby Street, then southwest directly to Main Gate and follow signs. USMRA: San Diego, CA map (C-6). NMC: San Diego, two miles southeast.
RECREATION & TRAVEL Marina-524-5269 TML-524-4401
RETAIL & DINING: Clubs-CC-524-6878 NCO-524-4448 Dining-524-6878 EX-297-2500 Gas-221-1049
SUPPORT & FAMILY: Med-524-1565

SAN DIEGO NAVAL MEDICAL CENTER
34800 Bob Wilson Drive, San Diego, CA 92134-1098
C-619-532-6400, DSN-312-522-6400
WEB: www.nmcsd.med.navy.mil
LOCATION: From north or south on I-5, exit northeast onto Pershing Drive north for approximately 0.3 miles, then left (west) on Florida Canyon Drive to entrance on left (west) side of road. USMRA: San Diego map (D-6). NMC: San Diego, within city limits.
RECREATION & TRAVEL: TML-532-6282/9055
RETAIL & DINING: EX-525-1502
SUPPORT & FAMILY: Med-532-8275

SAN DIEGO NAVAL STATION
3455 Senn Road, Room 108, San Diego, CA 92136-5084
C-619-556-1011, DSN-312-532-4111, Police-556-1527
WEB: www.navstasd.navy.mil
LOCATION: From north or south on I-5, seven miles south of San Diego, take 28th Street exit south to Main Street. Station is at 28th and Main Streets. Continue southwest on 28th Street and south to Main Gate at 32nd Street. USMRA: San Diego, CA map (D-7). NMC: San Diego, within city limits.
RECREATION & TRAVEL: Golf-556-5520/7502 RVC-520-6858 or 556-5525 TML-556-8672/3/4 Navy Lodge-800-NAVY-INN or 234-6142
RETAIL & DINING: Cafeteria-556-0446 Clubs-CPO-556-7050
EMC-556-1918 OC-556-7948/3113 Com-556-7199 Dining-556-5502 EX-544-2100 Gas-544-2289
SUPPORT & FAMILY: Med-556-6302

SAN FRANCISCO COAST GUARD STATION
Yerba Buena Island, San Francisco, CA 94130-9309
C-415-399-3455, Police (Security)-399-3478
WEB: www.uscg.mil/d11/
LOCATION: On Yerba Buena Island, just south of where the east span of the San Francisco-Oakland Bay Bridge crosses the island. From I-80 east or west, take Treasure Island exit. Follow signs. USMRA: San Francisco, CA map (C-5). NMC: San Francisco, one mile west.
RETAIL & DINING: Dining-399-3461

SAN JOAQUIN DEFENSE DISTRIBUTION DEPOT
25600 S. Chrisman Road, Tracy, CA 95296-0002
C-209-839-4000, Police-982-2560
WEB: http://www.ddc.dla.mil/Sites/ddjc.asp
LOCATION: Take CA-120 toward Manteca. Merge onto I-5 south toward San Fansisco/Los Angeles, and take the exit toward Tracy. Stay straight to go onto W 11th Street/I-205 BR west, and turn left onto S Chrisman Road to main gate. USMRA: CA map (D-7). NMC: Stockton, seven miles north.
RECREATION & TRAVEL: RVC-639-1016
RETAIL & DINING: EX-234-3781

SAN PEDRO COAST GUARD INTEGRATED SUPPORT COMMAND
Commanding Officer, 1001 South Seaside Avenue
San Pedro, CA 90731-0208
C-310-732-7400, Police (Security)-345-8501
WEB: http://www.uscg.mil/mlcpac/iscspedro/
LOCATION: On southwest end of Terminal Island. From San Pedro, go east on CA-47 across Vincent Thomas Bridge to south on South Ferry Street to right (west) on East Terminal Way which becomes South Seaside Avenue. Follow Coast Guard and Federal Corrections signs south to end of South Seaside Avenue. Or, from Long Beach, go west on Ocean Blvd to south on South Ferry Street and follow above directions. USMRA: Los Angeles, CA map (C-7). NMC: Long Beach, six miles northeast.
RECREATION & TRAVEL TML-732-7444/6
RETAIL & DINING: Dining-732-7540 EX-732-7555
SUPPORT & FAMILY: Med-732-7500

SEAL BEACH NAVAL WEAPONS STATION
800 Seal Beach Blvd, Seal Beach, CA 90740-5607
C-562-626-7011, DSN-312-873-7011, Police (Security)-626-7299
WEB: www.sbeach.navy.mil
LOCATION: From east or west on I-405 exit onto Seal Beach Blvd heading south. Continue south approximately one mile. Turn left on Westminster Avenue. The Main Gate and Pass & ID office are located at the corner of Seal Beach Blvd and Forrestal Avenue. USMRA: Los Angeles, CA map (E-7). NMC: Long Beach, adjacent.
RECREATION & TRAVEL: Golf-430-9913 RVC-626-7106
RETAIL & DINING: Clubs-CC-All Hands-626-7105 CDO-626-7229 Dining-626-7105
SUPPORT & FAMILY: Med-626-7322

SIERRA ARMY DEPOT
74 C Street, Herlong, CA 96113-5166
C-530-827-2111, DSN-312-855-4910, Police-827-4345
WEB: www.sierra.army.mil
LOCATION: Fifty-five miles northwest of Reno, NV, northeast of US-395. Northbound on US-395 from Reno, turn right (north) on CA-A26 (Garnier Road). When traveling south on US-395, turn left (northeast) on CA-25 (Herlong Access Road). Watch for signs. USMRA: CA map (F-4). NMC: Reno, NV, 55 miles southeast.
RECREATION & TRAVEL: TML-827-4154/4544
RETAIL & DINING: Snack Bar-827-4442
SUPPORT & FAMILY: Med-827-4575

SOUTH LAKE TAHOE RECREATIONAL HOUSING
242 Fort Marina Place, Suite 1, 228 Lewis Hall
Presidio of Monterey, CA 93944-5006
C-831-242-5506/6133, DSN-312-768-5506/6133
WEB: www.pom-odr.com
LOCATION: Off post. Located at Lake Tahoe. Specific directions will be furnished when reservation is made. USMRA: CA map (F-6). NMC: Carson City, NV, 30 miles southeast.
RECREATION & TRAVEL: RVC-242-5506/6133 TML-242-5091/5506/6133
NOTE: *For detailed information about this off-base recreation facility, as well as on-base recreation facilities, golf courses and marinas, consult Military Living's books "Temporary Military Lodging Around the World" or "Military RV, Camping and Outdoor Recreation Around the World".*

TRAVIS AIR FORCE BASE
60 AMW/PA, 400 Brennan Circle, Bldg 51
Travis Air Force Base, CA 94535-2712
C-707-424-1110, DSN-312-837-1110, Police-424-3293
WEB: http://public.travis.amc.af.mil/public/index.asp
LOCATION: Halfway between San Francisco and Sacramento, off I-80. From north or south on I-80, take Airbase Parkway exit east at Fairfield directly to Main Gate. Clearly marked. USMRA: CA map (C-7). NMC: San Francisco, 45 miles southwest.
RECREATION & TRAVEL: Golf-424-5797 or 448-7186 Marina-332-2319 or 877-792-6060 RVC-424-3583 SPA-424-5703/4 TML-424-8000 or 437-0700
RETAIL & DINING: Clubs-CC-424-1977 Com-437-4004/9211

Dining-424-0906/2155 EX-437-4633 Fast Food-Burger King-437-6444 Food Court-437-4490 Godfather's-437-3663 Gas-437-5849
SUPPORT & FAMILY: Med- Hospital-423-7300

TWENTYNINE PALMS MARINE CORPS AIR GROUND COMBAT CENTER

P.O. Box 788101, Twentynine Palms, CA 92278-8101
C-760-830-6000, DSN-312-230-6000, Police-830-6800
WEB: www.29palms.usmc.mil
LOCATION: East or west on I-10 to CA-62 (exit to Twentynine Palms/Yucca Valley). Take CA-62 (29 Palms Highway) east approximately 46 miles to town of Twentynine Palms. Once in town, take Adobe Road north (left) to Main Gate of base, approximately five miles. USMRA: CA map (I-13,14). NMC: Palm Springs, 60 miles northwest.
RECREATION & TRAVEL: Golf-830-6132 RVC-830-6583 TML-830-7375
RETAIL & DINING: Clubs-NCO-830-6608 OC-830-6610 SNCO-830-5081 Com-830-7572 EX-830-6163 Gas-830-6693
SUPPORT & FAMILY: Hospital-830-2190

VANDENBERG AIR FORCE BASE

30 SW/PA, 747 Nebraska Avenue, Suite A 103, Bldg 10577
Vandenberg Air Force Base, CA 93437-6267
C-805-606-1110, DSN-312-276-1110, Police-606-3911
WEB: www.vandenberg.af.mil
LOCATION: From the north on US-101, exit westbound at Santa Maria onto Clark Avenue, then go west approximately 2.3 miles to left (south) on CA-135 which merges into CA-1. Continue southbound on CA-1 directly to Main Gate. From the south, take US-101 north to Buelton. Exit northwest onto CA-246. Just before Lompoc, bear right on Purisima Road which runs into CA-1. Follow CA-1 northwest to the Main Gate on left. USMRA: CA map (D-12). NMC: Santa Barbara, 55 miles southeast.
RECREATION & TRAVEL: Golf-734-1333 RVC-606-0960/8579 SPA-606-7742 TML-734-1111, ext. 2802
RETAIL & DINING: Cafeteria-606-3330 Clubs-CC-606-3330 Com-605-8812 Dining-606-7540 EX-734-5521 Gas-734-2185
SUPPORT & FAMILY: Med-606-3011/3875
NOTE: *Base tours are available the second and fourth Wednesday of each month, mission permitting. Reservations required at least two weeks in advance. For information, call C-805-606-3595.*

COLORADO, pg. 101
Colorado Springs, pg. 103
Denver, pg. 106

BUCKLEY AIR FORCE BASE

460 Air Base Wing, 18401 E A-Basin Avenue, Stop 88
Aurora, CO 80011-9524
C-720-847-9011, DSN-312-847-9011, Police-847-9930
WEB: www.buckley.af.mil
LOCATION: From north or south on I-225, take exit 9 east onto CO-30 (East Sixth Avenue) 2.5 miles east to Main Gate on right side of road. Clearly marked. USMRA: CO map (G-3), Denver, CO map (G,H-10). NMC: Denver, 21 miles west.
RECREATION & TRAVEL: SPA-847-9650
RETAIL & DINING: Clubs-CC-677-9840 Com-847-7100 Dining-847-9642 EX-859-9628 Gas-859-0754
SUPPORT & FAMILY: Med-677-6458 or 847-6474
Ten-digit dialing required for local calls.

FARISH RECREATION AREA

P.O. Box 146, Woodland Park, CO 80866-0146
C-719-687-9098, DSN-312-333-1110, Police-911
WEB: http://atlas.usafa.af.mil/svk/orc/farish.htm
LOCATION: From north or south on I-25 at Colorado Springs, take exit 141 onto US-24 west for 18 miles to Woodland Park. At second stoplight turn right (north) onto CR-22 (Baldwin Street) which changes to Rampart Range Road. Follow road through four stop signs. Road forks just past water treatment facility; keep left and follow Farish signs. Approximately 0.2 miles after road changes from asphalt to dirt, turn right onto Forest Service Road 312. USMRA: CO map (G-4,5). NMC: Colorado Springs, 30 miles southeast. NMI: U.S. Air Force Academy, 35 miles east; Peterson AFB and Fort Carson, 30 miles southeast.
RECREATION & TRAVEL: RVC-687-9098 TML-333-4910
NOTE: *For detailed information about this off-base recreation facility, as well as on-base recreation facilities, golf courses and marinas, consult Military Living's "Military RV, Camping and Outdoor Recreation Around the World".*

FORT CARSON

Attn: Commanding General, 7th ID & Fort Carson, Bldg 1430
Fort Carson, CO 80913-5098
C-719-526-5811, DSN-312-691-5811, Police-526-2333
WEB: www.carson.army.mil
LOCATION: From north or south on I-25, take exit 135 west onto CO-83 (Academy Blvd) for two miles then left (south) on CO-115 for two miles to Main Gate on left (east) side of road. Clearly marked. USMRA: CO map (G-5,6). NMC: Colorado Springs, six miles north.
RECREATION & TRAVEL: Golf-526-4122 RVC-526-3905 SPA-526-7111 TML-526-4832
RETAIL & DINING: Clubs-NCO-556-4194 OC-576-4181 Com-526-2560 Dining-556-4180 EX-576-4141 Gas-597-0360
SUPPORT & FAMILY: Med-526-7000
NOTE: *Space-A flights fly from Butts Army Airfield, which is run by Fort Carson. Consult Military Living's "Military Space-A Travel Guide" for more details.*

PETERSON AIR FORCE BASE

21 Space Wing, 775 Loring Avenue, Suite 219
Peterson Air Force Base, CO 80914-1294
C-719-556-7321, DSN-312-834-7321, Police-556-4805
WEB: www.peterson.af.mil
LOCATION: Off US-24 (Platte Avenue) east of Colorado Springs. Eastbound from Colorado Springs on US-24, keep right onto CO-94 turn right (south) on Peterson Blvd directly to Main Gate. From westbound on US-24, take exit south onto CO-94 then west to south (right) on Peterson Blvd directly to Main Gate. Clearly marked. USMRA:CO map (G-5); Colorado Springs, CO map (C-15,16). NMC: Colorado Springs, six miles west.
RECREATION & TRAVEL: Golf-556-7414 SPA-556-1638/4521 TML-556-7851
RETAIL & DINING: Clubs-NCO-556-4194 OC-576-4181 Com-556-4247 Dining-556-4180 EX-596-7270 Gas-597-0360
SUPPORT & FAMILY: Med-556-2273

ROCKY MOUNTAIN BLUE AT KEYSTONE RESORT

Keystone Resort, Hwy 6, Box 38, Keystone, CO 80435-8473
C-866-768-2583, DSN-312-333-1110, Police-970-668-8600
WEB: www.rockymountainblue.com
LOCATION: From I-70 east or west, take exit 205, Silverthorne/Dillon exit. At the end of the exit ramp, turn left to go to US-6. Follow US-6 around Lake Dillon, for about six miles and turn right at the Keystone traffic light. Take the next immediate right. The parking lot will be on the left. USMRA: CO map (E,F-3). NMC: Denver, 60 miles southwest. NMI: Buckley AFB, 90 miles southwest.
RECREATION & TRAVEL: TML-866-768-2583
NOTE: *Open to all branches of service and DoD ID card holders. For detailed information about this off-base recreation facility, as well as on-base recreation facilities, golf courses and marinas, consult Military Living's "Military RV, Camping and Outdoor Recreation Around the World".*

SCHRIEVER AIR FORCE BASE

210 Falcon Parkway, Suite 2102
Schriever Air Force Base, CO 80912-3024
C-719-567-1110, DSN-312-560-1110, Police-567-5642
WEB: www.schriever.af.mil
LOCATION: From Colorado Springs, go east on US-24 to intersection with CO-94. Keep right and continue east on CO-94 approximately nine miles beyondintersection to a right turn on Enoch Road. Facility is located on east side of Enoch Road. USMRA: CO map (G,H-5). NMC Colorado Springs, 10 miles west.
RETAIL & DINING: Dining-567-2216 Gas-567-3915
SUPPORT & FAMILY: Med-567-4455
NOTE: *This is a closed-security base.*

TURKEY CREEK RANCH

15300 Turkey Creek Lane, Fort Carson, CO 80913-4850
C-719-526-3905, DSN-312-691-5811, Police-526-2333
WEB: http://www.ftcarsonmwr.com/recreationFacilities/turkey_creek/turkey_creek_ranch.html
LOCATION: Off base. From CO-115, south of Colorado Springs, turn east onto Turkey Creek Lane. Follow straight to entrance. USMRA: CO map (G-5). NMC: Colorado Springs, 17 miles north. NMI: Fort Carson, adjacent.
RECREATION & TRAVEL: RVC-526-3905
NOTE: *For detailed information about this off-base recreation facility, as well as on-base recreation facilities, golf courses and marinas, consult Military Living's "Military RV, Camping and Outdoor Recreation Around the World".*

UNITED STATES AIR FORCE ACADEMY

2304 Cadet Drive, Suite 318
United States Air Force Academy, CO 80840-5001
C-719-333-1110, DSN-312-333-1110, Police-333-2000
WEB: www.usaf.af.mil
LOCATION: West of I-25, north of Colorado Springs. From I-25 north or south, use exit 150B northwest onto Southgate Blvd which leads to main visitors entrance. Or, take exit 150A west onto Northgate Blvd on the left side of the road. Clearly marked. USMRA: CO map (F-4,5); Colorado Springs, CO, map (A,B-12,13). NMC: Colorado Springs, eight miles.
RECREATION & TRAVEL: Golf-333-4735 RVC-333-4356/4980 RVC-687-9098 TML-333-4910 or 888-AF-LODGE(235-6343)
RETAIL & DINING: Clubs-EMC-333-4377 OC-333-4253 Com-333-3610 Dining-Airmen's Dining Hall-333-4730 EX-472-0861 Gas-472-0395
SUPPORT & FAMILY: Med-333-5000

NEVADA, pg. 105
Lake Tahoe, pg. 102
Las Vegas, pg. 105

CREECH AIR FORCE BASE

1st Street, Indian Springs, NV 89018-5000
C-702-652-1110, DSN-312-682-1110, Police-652-0556
WEB: www.nellis.af.mil
LOCATION: Off US-95, 47 miles northwest of Nellis Air Force Base. On the north side of US-95, take Indian Springs exit north. USMRA: NV map (F-9). NMC: Las Vegas, 45 miles southeast.
RECREATION & TRAVEL: TML-652-0401
RETAIL & DINING: EX-652-0125
SUPPORT & FAMILY: Med-652-0286

DESERT EAGLE RV PARK

4907 FAMCAMP Drive, Las Vegas, NV 89115-1917
C-702-643-3060, DSN-312-682-1110, Police-652-2311
WEB: www.nellis.af.mil/information/famcamp.htm
LOCATION: Off base. From I-15 north of Las Vegas, exit 48 east on Craig Road west to NV-604 (Las Vegas Blvd North), left onto Range Road (directly across from Nellis North Gate). Also from US-93/95 (Boulder Highway) in Las Vegas, go north on Nellis Blvd approximately eight miles, continue north on NV-604 (Las Vegas Blvd North). From both routes, continue to North Gate, turn left onto Range Road directly across from gate. USMRA: NV map (G-9). NMC: Las Vegas, eight miles southwest.
RECREATION & TRAVEL: RVC-643-3060
NOTE: *For detailed information about this off-base recreation facility, as well as on-base recreation facilities, golf courses and marinas, consult Military Living's "Military RV, Camping and Outdoor Recreation Around the World".*

FALLON NAVAL AIR STATION

4755 Pasture Road, Fallon Naval Air Station, NV 89496-0001
C-775-426-5161, DSN-312-890-2110, Police-426-2853
WEB: www.fallon.navy.mil
LOCATION: From Reno, take I-80 east or west to Fernley (exit 48). Go to stop light and turn left onto Alternate US-50 to Fallon. Once through Fallon, turn right on US-95 south (Taylor Street). After approximately three miles, turn left on Union Street, follow road to the end. Turn right on Pasture Road, Main Gate is on the right. USMRA: NV map (C-5). NMC: Reno, 72 miles west.
RECREATION & TRAVEL: Driving Range-426-2598 SPA-426-3415 TML-426-2589 or 428-3003/4 Navy Lodge-800-NAVY-INN or 426-2818
RETAIL & DINING Clubs-CPO-426-2483 EMC-426-2445 OC-426-2625 Com-426-3420 Dining-426-2520 EX-426-2400 Gas-426-2853
SUPPORT & FAMILY: Med-426-3110

NELLIS AIR FORCE BASE

4370 North Washington Blvd
Nellis Air Force Base, NV 89191-7078
C-702-652-1110, DSN-312-682-1110, Police-652-3211
WEB: www.nellis.af.mil
LOCATION: Off I-15. Also accessible from US-93/95. Exit 48 east on Craig Road to north on Las Vegas Blvd to Main Gate on right. Clearly marked. USMRA: NV map (G-9). NMC: Las Vegas, eight miles southwest.
RECREATION & TRAVEL: Golf-652-2602 SPA-652-2562 TML-652-2711
RETAIL & DINING: Clubs-CC-652-5014 EMC/NCO-652-9733 OC-644-2582 Com-652-4563 Dining-652-6744 EX-643-3526 Fast Food-644-8516 Gas-643-1686
SUPPORT & FAMILY: Med-653-2343

RENO/TAHOE INTERNATIONAL AIRPORT/ AIR NATIONAL GUARD
1776 National Guard Way, Reno, NV 89502-4415
C-775-788-4500, DSN-312-830-4500, Police-328-6470
WEB: www.nv.ngb.mil
LOCATION: From I-80, exit 15 on US-395 south, to Reno-Tahoe International Airport Exit. Veer right towards National Guard Way. Front gate will be on the left. Co-located with the IAP. USMRA: NV map (B-4,5). NMC: Reno, within city limits.
RECREATION & TRAVEL: SPA-788-4709
RETAIL & DINING: Clubs-CC-788-4570
SUPPORT & FAMILY: Med-786-7200

STEAD TRAINING CENTER/ ARMY NATIONAL GUARD BASE
4600 Alpha Avenue, Reno, NV 89506-1276
C-775-677-5213 or 800-797-8323, DSN-312-530-5213
Police (Security)-972-2761
WEB: www.nv.ngb.army.mil/Army/Units/421stRTI
LOCATION: From I-80, exit to NV-395 to Stead exit 15 to Stead Blvd. Make a left onto Mount Anderson Street and a right onto Alpha Avenue to the Main Gate. USMRA: NV map (B-4). NMC: Reno, ten miles south. NMI: Fallon NAS, 60 miles east.
RECREATION & TRAVEL: TML-677-5213

NEW MEXICO, pg. 106
Albuquerque, pg. 106

CANNON AIR FORCE BASE
100 South DL Ingram Blvd, Suite 204
Cannon Air Force Base, NM 88103-5219
C-505-784-3311, DSN-312-681-1110, Police-784-4111
WEB: www.cannon.af.mil
LOCATION: From Clovis, near the Texas border,west on US-60/84 for seven miles to AFB south of US-60/84. From NM-467 north or south, enter the Portales gate. USMRA: NM map (H-5). NMC: Clovis, seven miles east.
RECREATION & TRAVEL: Golf-784-2800 SPA-784-2978 TML-784-2918/9
RETAIL & DINING: Clubs-CC-Landing Club-784-2853 End-zone-784-2448 Com-784-4331 Dining-Pecos Trail-784-2420 EX-784-2141 Gas-784-5766
SUPPORT & FAMILY: Med-784-4033
NOTE: *The 2005 BRAC report recommended this base for closure. As required by Federal law, the DoD has until 15 September 2007 to begin closing and realigning the bases as called for in the approved report. This process must be completed by 15 September 2011.*

HOLLOMAN AIR FORCE BASE
490 First Street, Suite 2800
Holloman Air Force Base, NM 88330-8287
C-505-572-1110, DSN-312-572-1110, Police-572-7171
WEB: www.holloman.af.mil
LOCATION: Exit US-70, eight miles southwest of Alamogordo. Route to AFB north of US-70 is clearly marked. USMRA: NM map (D-7). NMC: Las Cruces, 50 miles southwest.
RECREATION & TRAVEL: Golf-572-3574 SPA-572-5411 TML-572-3311/7160
RETAIL & DINING: Cafeteria-572-5859 Clubs-NCO-572-3226 OC-572-3611 Com-572-5127 EX-479-6164 Snack Bar-572-6657 Gas-479-2201
SUPPORT & FAMILY: Med-572-2778

KIRTLAND AIR FORCE BASE
377 Air Base Wing, 2000 Wyoming Blvd SE
Kirtland Air Force Base, NM 87117-5606
C-505-846-0011, DSN-312-246-0011, Police-846-7913
WEB: www.kirtland.af.mil
LOCATION: From I-40 east or west, take exit 65 onto Wyoming Blvd, travel south for two miles to Wyoming gate to AFB. USMRA: NM map (D-4). NMC: Albuquerque, one mile northwest.
RECREATION & TRAVEL: Golf-846-1169/1574 RVC-846-0337 SPA-846-7000 TML-846-9652/3
RETAIL & DINING: Clubs-CPO-265-6791 NCO-846-1467 OC-846-5165 Com-846-9588 Dining-846-8048 EX-846-9642 Gas-265-7552/9093
SUPPORT & FAMILY: Med-846-3730

WHITE SANDS MISSILE RANGE
Bldg 1782, Headquarters Avenue
White Sands Missile Range, NM 88002-5047
C-505-678-2121, DSN-312-258-2121, Police-678-1234
WEB: www.wsmr.ararmy.mil
LOCATION: From I-25 north or south at Las Cruces, NM, take exit 6 onto US-70 northeast. Go approximately 19 miles northeast to a right turn on NM-213 (Owen Road), go south approximately four miles to Main Gate. From Alamogordo, follow US-70 southeast approximately 44 miles to a left turn onto NM-213 (Owen Road), then go south approximately four miles to Main Gate. USMRA: NM map (D-6,7,8). NMC: El Paso, TX, 40 miles south.
RECREATION & TRAVEL: Golf-678-1759 RVC-678-1713 TML-678-4559
RETAIL & DINING: Cafeteria-678-2081 Com-678-2313 EX-678-2072 Gas-678-4877
SUPPORT & FAMILY: Med-678-5411

UTAH, pg. 104
Ogden, pg. 103
Salt Lake City, pg. 104

CAMP W.G. WILLIAMS
17800 South Camp Williams Road, Riverton, UT 84065-4999
C-801-253-5400, DSN-312-766-5400, Police-253-5455
WEB: www.ut.ngb.army.mil/campwilliams
LOCATION: From I-15, take exit 294 (Draper/Riverton UT-71). Turn left at UT-68, drive approximately seven miles, and Camp Williams is on the left. USMRA: UT map (D-5). NMC: Salt Lake City, 25 miles north.
RECREATION & TRAVEL: TML-253-5410
RETAIL & DINING: Cafeteria-253-5506 Clubs-NCO-253-5730
OC-254-5466 Dining-253-5656 EX-253-5729
SUPPORT & FAMILY: Med-253-5723

CARTER CREEK CAMP
Outdoor Recreation, Bldg 805, Hill AFB, UT 84056-5720
C-801-777-9666, DSN-312-777-9666, Police-911
WEB: www.hill.af.mil/services
LOCATION: Off base. From I-80 near Evanston, WY, take WY/UT-150 south 30 miles to the Bear River Service Station. Turn left at 'Mill Creek RS-7'. Proceed approximately four miles to camp on the right side of the road. USMRA: UT map (E,F-4). NMC: Salt Lake City, 105 miles southwest. NMI: Hill AFB, 55 miles west.
RECREATION & TRAVEL: RVC-777-2225/9666
NOTE: *For detailed information about this off-base recreation facility, as well as on-base recreation facilities, golf courses and marinas, consult Military Living's "Military RV, Camping and Outdoor Recreation Around the World".*

DUGWAY PROVING GROUND
Attn: CSTE-DTC-DP-PA, Bldg 4142, Dugway, UT 84022-1083
C-435-831-2151, DSN-312-789-2151, Police-831-2929
LOCATION: Isolated, but can be reached from I-80. Take exit 77 south, UT-196, Skull Valley Road for 40 miles south to Dugway and entrance to Proving Ground. USMRA: UT map (B,C-5,6). NMC: Salt Lake City, 80 miles northeast.
RECREATION & TRAVEL: Golf-831-2305 TML-831-2333
RETAIL & DINING: Clubs-CC-831-2901 Com-831-2164 Dining-831-2901 EX-831-4773 Gas-831-4773
SUPPORT & FAMILY: Med-831-2222
NOTE: *When calling from Salt Lake City the prefix is 522 instead of 831 and the area code is 801 instead of 435.*

FORT DOUGLAS
96 Regional Readiness Command. Bldg 100
Soldiers Circle SADAFRC, Fort Douglas, UT 84113-5007
C-801-656-3300, Police-656-3365
WEB: http://www.fortdouglas.org
LOCATION: On northeastern edge of Salt Lake City. From east or west on I-80 or from the south on I-215, exit northbound onto UT-186 (Foothill Drive) for approximately 3.7 miles to a right (north) turn onto UT-282 (Wasatch Drive) to Fort Douglas. Turn right (north) onto Pollock Road for entrance on left (northwest) side of road, or keep left on Wasatch Drive to Hempstead Road and entrance to museum on right. Watch for signs. USMRA: Salt Lake City, UT map. (H-1,2). NMC: Salt Lake City, UT, within city limits.
RETAIL & DINING: EX-736-4400/1/2/3

HILL AIR FORCE BASE
7981 Georgia Street, Hill Air Force Base, UT 84056-5824
C-801-777-1110, DSN-312-777-1110, Police-777-3056
WEB: www.hill.af.mil
LOCATION: Adjacent to I-15 between Ogden and Salt Lake City. From I-15, take exit 334, go north to UT-232 to south gate on South Gate Drive; or exit 338 to west gate. USMRA: UT map (D-4). NMC: Ogden, eight miles north. NMI: Salt Lake City IAP/ANG, 30 miles north.
RECREATION & TRAVEL: Golf-777-3272 RVC-777-2225/9666 RVC-777-3250 SPA-777-2887/3088 TML-777-1844
RETAIL & DINING: Clubs-CC-Club Hill-777-2309/3166 Com-777-2300 Dining-777-3428/8161 EX-773-1207 Gas-773-3600
SUPPORT & FAMILY: Med-728-2600

SALT LAKE CITY INTERNATIONAL AIRPORT/AIR NATIONAL GUARD
151 Air Refueling Wing, 765 North 2200 West
Salt Lake City, UT 84116-2999
C-801-245-2200, DSN-312-245-2200, Police-245-2327
WEB: www.utsalt.ang.af.mil/151
LOCATION: From I-215 north or south take exit 25, go west one block, turn right on McDonnell Douglas Way. ANG is on the immediate left. USMRA: UT map (D-4; G-1). NMC: Salt Lake City, five miles southeast. NMI: Hill AFB, 30 miles south.
RECREATION & TRAVEL: SPA-245-2274/2415
RETAIL & DINING: EX-355-1923
SUPPORT & FAMILY: Med-245-2337

TOOELE ARMY DEPOT
Attn: SJMTE-CO, Bldg 1, Tooele, UT 84074-5008
C-435-833-2211, DSN-312-790-2211, Police-833-2559
WEB: www.tead.army.mil
LOCATION: From west I-80, exit 99 south, to UT-36 south for about 15 miles to main entrance on right side of UT-36. USMRA: UT map (C-5). NMC: Salt Lake City, 40 miles northeast.
RECREATION & TRAVEL: RVC-833-3301 TML-833-2056
RETAIL & DINING: Clubs-CC-833-5555 CPAC-833-2412
SUPPORT & FAMILY: Med-833-2572

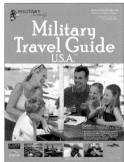

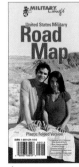

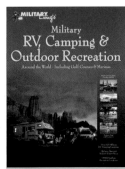

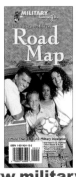

Subscribe to R&R Travel News®

and travel on less per day . . . the military way!™

MILITARY

R&R Travel News

HIGHLIGHTS

Ann & Roy Visit Honolulu, HI

Tag Along with Ann

Oak Grove Park is Back!

Features

Be among the first to know about new military travel opportunities! R&R Travel News® is a six-time yearly, by-subscription, 16 page military travel newsletter. Read about fellow military travelers' trips in the U.S. and abroad. Our R&R subscribers are circling the globe flying SPACE-A on military aircraft, staying in military lodging, taking trips and tours with ITT/ITR travel offices and having fun at military RV/camping and outdoor recreation areas. Together, these subscribers have a powerful clearinghouse of information by sharing their travel finds with each other via Military Living's R&R Travel News®.

How to Subscribe

For Subscription rates and information and any current special gift offers, visit our website at www.militaryliving.com. You may also call us at (703) 237-0203 Ext. 1 and subscribe using your Visa, Mastercard, American Express or Discover.

FREE GIFT WITH 3, 5, OR 7 YEAR SUBSCRIPTION TO R&R TRAVEL NEWS®!

3 YEAR SUBSCRIPTION STANDARD MAIL $56.00 FIRST CLASS $84.00

Receive one of the following FREE:

United States Military Road MapTM - Paper (A $11.20 Value)
United States Military Road MapTM - Plastic (A $13.70 Value)
Military Space-A Air Travel Map & Pocket Directory™ - Plastic (A $17.20 Value)

5 YEAR SUBSCRIPTION STANDARD MAIL $84.00 FIRST CLASS $134.00

Receive one of the following FREE:

European Military Travel GuideTM (A $26.75 Value)
Military RV, Camping & Outdoor Recreation Around the World™ (A $21.30 Value)
Military Travel GuideTM (A $19.05 Value)
Temporary Military Lodging Around the WorldTM (A $23.75 Value)

7 YEAR SUBSCRIPTION STANDARD MAIL $106.00 FIRST CLASS $181.00

Receive a FREE:

United States Military Road AtlasTM (A $27.55 Value)

Excerpted from the May/June 2006 Issue

Ann & Roy Visit Honolulu, HI

HONOLULU, HI - There is a lot of excitment here in Hawaii regarding the arrival of the fourth new C-17 Globemaster III out of a total of eight to be assigned here by the end of the year. Hickam is the first base outside of the continental U.S. to permanently host the C-17. This is also the first time since the Vietnam War that Hickam AFB has had this kind of mission. Their new name is the 15th Airlift Wing, and they will jointly operate and maintain the aircraft with the Air National Guard's 154th Wing. The aircraft, maintenance, support and leadership teams are a mix of active duty and Air National Guard Airmen.

LESSON LEARNED—The Hale Koa, where we stayed, has such a superb location on Waikiki and so many dining and recreational opportunities, that we did not need to rent a car during our short visit. Later, when we decided to visit Hickam AFB and the Air Passenger Terminal, we took a taxi which was $35 plus tip.

After leaving the air terminal, we took a base shuttle bus going to the PX/BX. While there, we learned of a local bus that stopped across the street in the housing area. Lo and behold, the fare for us as seniors was only one dollar each to get us back to Waikiki. It was two dollars for others. We enjoyed the ride and met several interesting people who provided more tips on seeing Hawaii for a song. To learn about "the bus" and its many routes, visit www.thebus.org In future issues, we will give you more info on our visit to Hawaii.

SPACE-A AIR TRAVEL—HICKAM AFB, HI

Prior to visiting the air passenger terminal, I called their Space-A information line and found flights going to Kadena, Okinawa, Japan; Guam; North Island NAS, CA; Fairchild AFB, WA and the General Mitchell IAP/ARS, Milwaukee, WI. The recording did not indicate the kind of aircraft to be used.

For security reasons, the best place to obtain up-to-date flight info is at the air passsenger terminal itself. I found more information posted there.

For possible Space-A air opportunities, call C-808-449-1515. The fax number is C-808-448-1503. E-mail address: spacea@hickam.af.mil.

Thousands of military families agree—there's no place like Hawaii, and especially the Hale Koa Hotel. For more information on the Hale Koa, see their listing on page 123 under Fort Derussy, Hale Koa Armed Forces Recreation Area. Photos courtesy of Hale Koa Hotel.

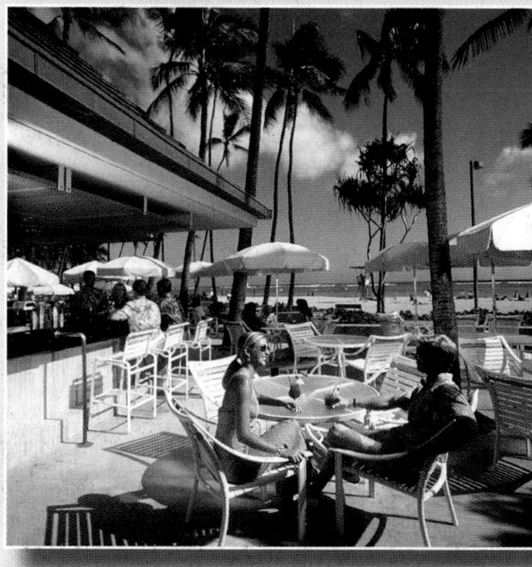

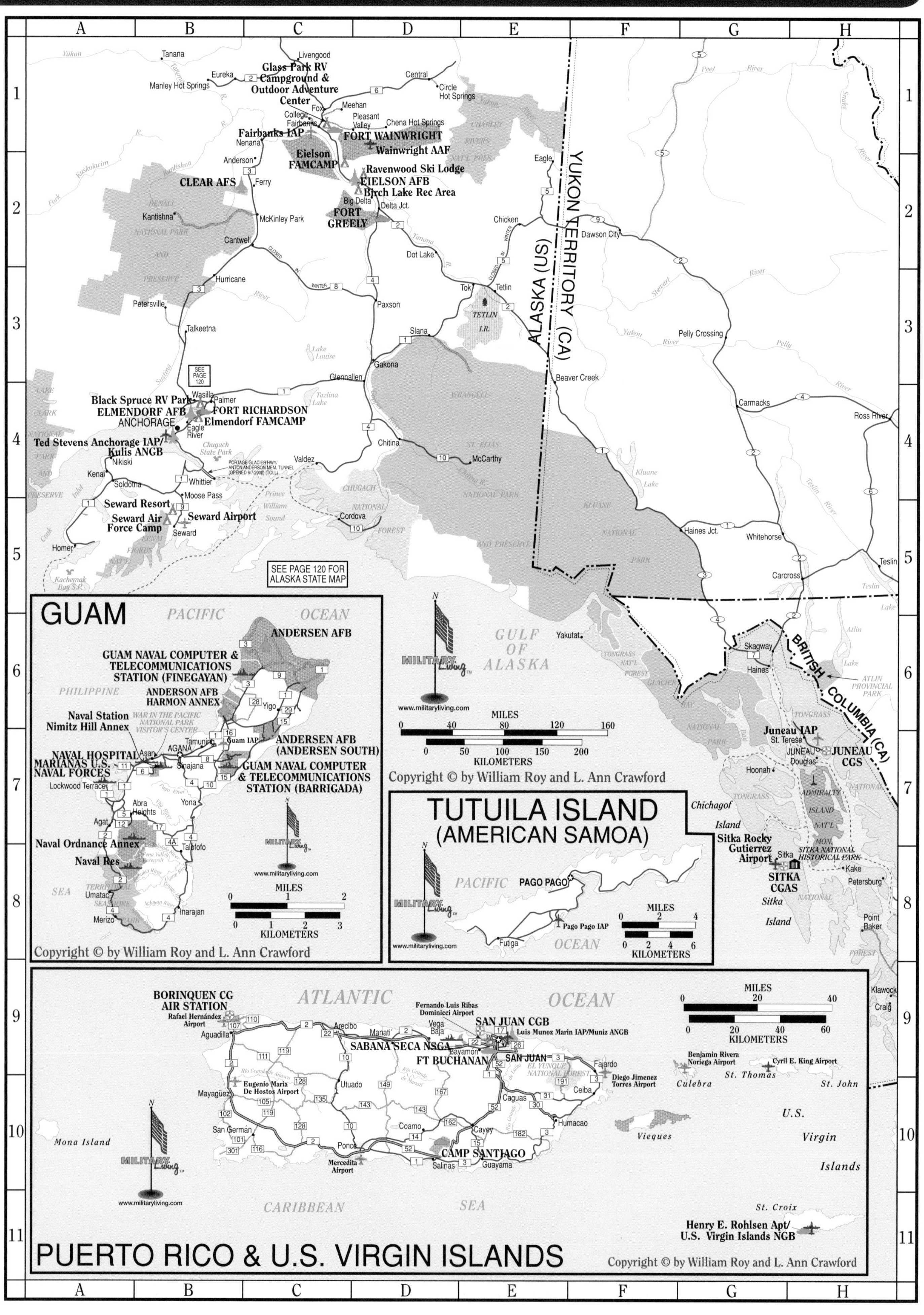

GUAM
TUTUILA ISLAND (AMERICAN SAMOA)
PUERTO RICO & U.S. VIRGIN ISLANDS
SEE PAGE 120 FOR ALASKA STATE MAP
Fairbanks IAP
FORT WAINWRIGHT
Wainwright AAF
Eielson FAMCAMP
EIELSON AFB
Ravenwood Ski Lodge
Birch Lake Rec Area
FORT GREELY
CLEAR AFS
Glass Park RV Campground & Outdoor Adventure Center
Black Spruce RV Park
ELMENDORF AFB
FORT RICHARDSON
Elmendorf FAMCAMP
ANCHORAGE
Ted Stevens Anchorage IAP/ Kulis ANGB
Seward Resort
Seward Air Force Camp
Seward Airport
ALASKA (US)
YUKON TERRITORY (CA)
BRITISH COLUMBIA (CA)
GULF OF ALASKA
Juneau IAP
JUNEAU CGS
Sitka Rocky Gutierrez Airport
SITKA CGAS
ANDERSEN AFB
GUAM NAVAL COMPUTER & TELECOMMUNICATIONS STATION (FINEGAYAN)
ANDERSON AFB HARMON ANNEX
Naval Station Nimitz Hill Annex
NAVAL HOSPITAL
MARIANAS U.S. NAVAL FORCES
ANDERSEN AFB (ANDERSEN SOUTH)
GUAM NAVAL COMPUTER & TELECOMMUNICATIONS STATION (BARRIGADA)
Naval Ordnance Annex
Naval Res
PAGO PAGO
Pago Pago IAP
BORINQUEN CG AIR STATION
Rafael Hernández Airport
Fernando Luis Ribas Dominicci Airport
SAN JUAN CGB
Luis Munoz Marin IAP/Muniz ANGB
SABANA SECA NSGA
FT BUCHANAN
SAN JUAN
Eugenio Maria De Hostos Airport
Diego Jimenez Torres Airport
Benjamin Rivera Noriega Airport
Cyril E. King Airport
CAMP SANTIAGO
Mercedita Airport
Henry E. Rohlsen Apt/ U.S. Virgin Islands NGB
U.S. Virgin Islands
www.militaryliving.com

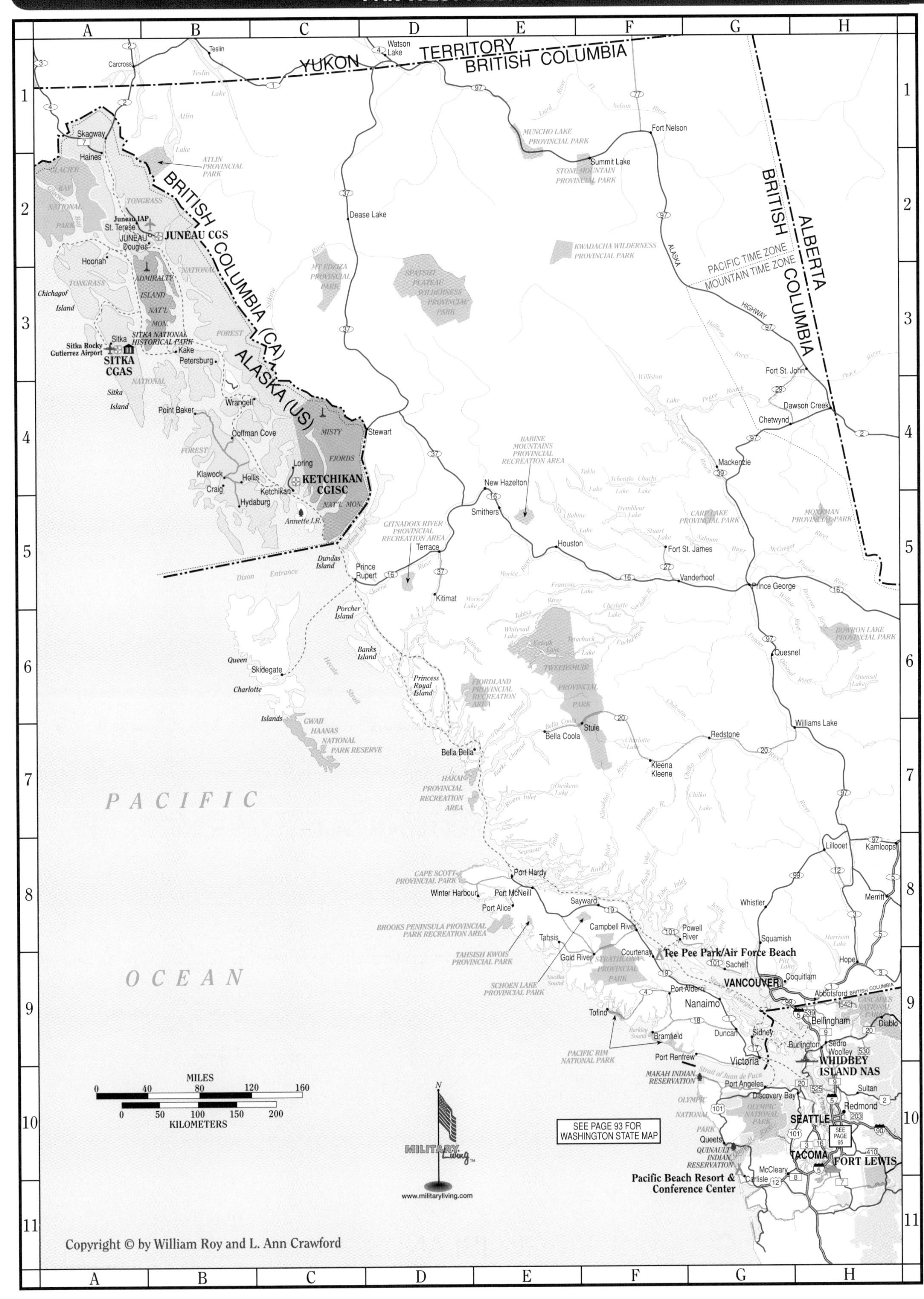
YUKON TERRITORY
BRITISH COLUMBIA
ALBERTA
ALASKA (US)
BRITISH COLUMBIA (CA)
PACIFIC TIME ZONE
MOUNTAIN TIME ZONE
PACIFIC OCEAN
Teslin
Carcross
Watson Lake
Skagway
Haines
Atlin
ATLIN PROVINCIAL PARK
GLACIER BAY NATIONAL PARK
TONGRASS NATIONAL FOREST
Juneau IAP
St. Terese
JUNEAU
Douglas
JUNEAU CGS
Hoonah
ADMIRALTY ISLAND NAT'L MON.
Chichagof Island
Sitka
SITKA NATIONAL HISTORICAL PARK
Sitka Rocky Gutierrez Airport
SITKA CGAS
Kake
Petersburg
Sitka Island
Wrangell
Point Baker
Coffman Cove
MISTY FJORDS NAT'L MON.
Stewart
Loring
Klawock
Hollis
Craig
Ketchikan
KETCHIKAN CGISC
Hydaburg
Annette I.R.
Dease Lake
MT EDZIZA PROVINCIAL PARK
SPATSIZI PLATEAU WILDERNESS PROVINCIAL PARK
MUNCHO LAKE PROVINCIAL PARK
Fort Nelson
Summit Lake
STONE MOUNTAIN PROVINCIAL PARK
KWADACHA WILDERNESS PROVINCIAL PARK
ALASKA HIGHWAY
Fort St. John
Dawson Creek
Chetwynd
Mackenzie
BABINE MOUNTAINS PROVINCIAL RECREATION AREA
New Hazelton
Smithers
GITNADOIX RIVER PROVINCIAL RECREATION AREA
Terrace
Dundas Island
Prince Rupert
Dixon Entrance
Kitimat
Houston
Fort St. James
Vanderhoof
Prince George
CARP LAKE PROVINCIAL PARK
MONKMAN PROVINCIAL PARK
BOWRON LAKE PROVINCIAL PARK
Porcher Island
Banks Island
Queen Charlotte Islands
Skidegate
Hecate Strait
GWAII HAANAS NATIONAL PARK RESERVE
Princess Royal Island
FIORDLAND PROVINCIAL RECREATION AREA
TWEEDSMUIR PROVINCIAL PARK
Quesnel
Williams Lake
Bella Bella
Bella Coola
Stuie
Redstone
Kleena Kleene
HAKAI PROVINCIAL RECREATION AREA
Lillooet
Kamloops
CAPE SCOTT PROVINCIAL PARK
Port Hardy
Winter Harbour
Port McNeill
Port Alice
Sayward
Whistler
Merritt
BROOKS PENINSULA PROVINCIAL PARK RECREATION AREA
TAHSISH KWOIS PROVINCIAL PARK
Tahsis
Campbell River
Powell River
Squamish
Gold River
Courtenay
Tee Pee Park/Air Force Beach
Sechelt
STRATHCONA PROVINCIAL PARK
SCHOEN LAKE PROVINCIAL PARK
Hope
VANCOUVER
Coquitlam
Port Alberni
Nanaimo
Abbotsford
Tofino
Bellingham
Diablo
Bamfield
Duncan
Sidney
PACIFIC RIM NATIONAL PARK
Port Renfrew
Burlington
Sedro Woolley
Victoria
WHIDBEY ISLAND NAS
MAKAH INDIAN RESERVATION
Strait of Juan de Fuca
Port Angeles
Discovery Bay
Sultan
OLYMPIC NATIONAL PARK
Redmond
SEATTLE
Queets
QUINAULT INDIAN RESERVATION
TACOMA
FORT LEWIS
Pacific Beach Resort & Conference Center
McCleary
Carlisle
SEE PAGE 95
SEE PAGE 93 FOR WASHINGTON STATE MAP
MILES 0 40 80 120 160
KILOMETERS 0 50 100 150 200
MILITARY Living
www.militaryliving.com
Copyright © by William Roy and L. Ann Crawford

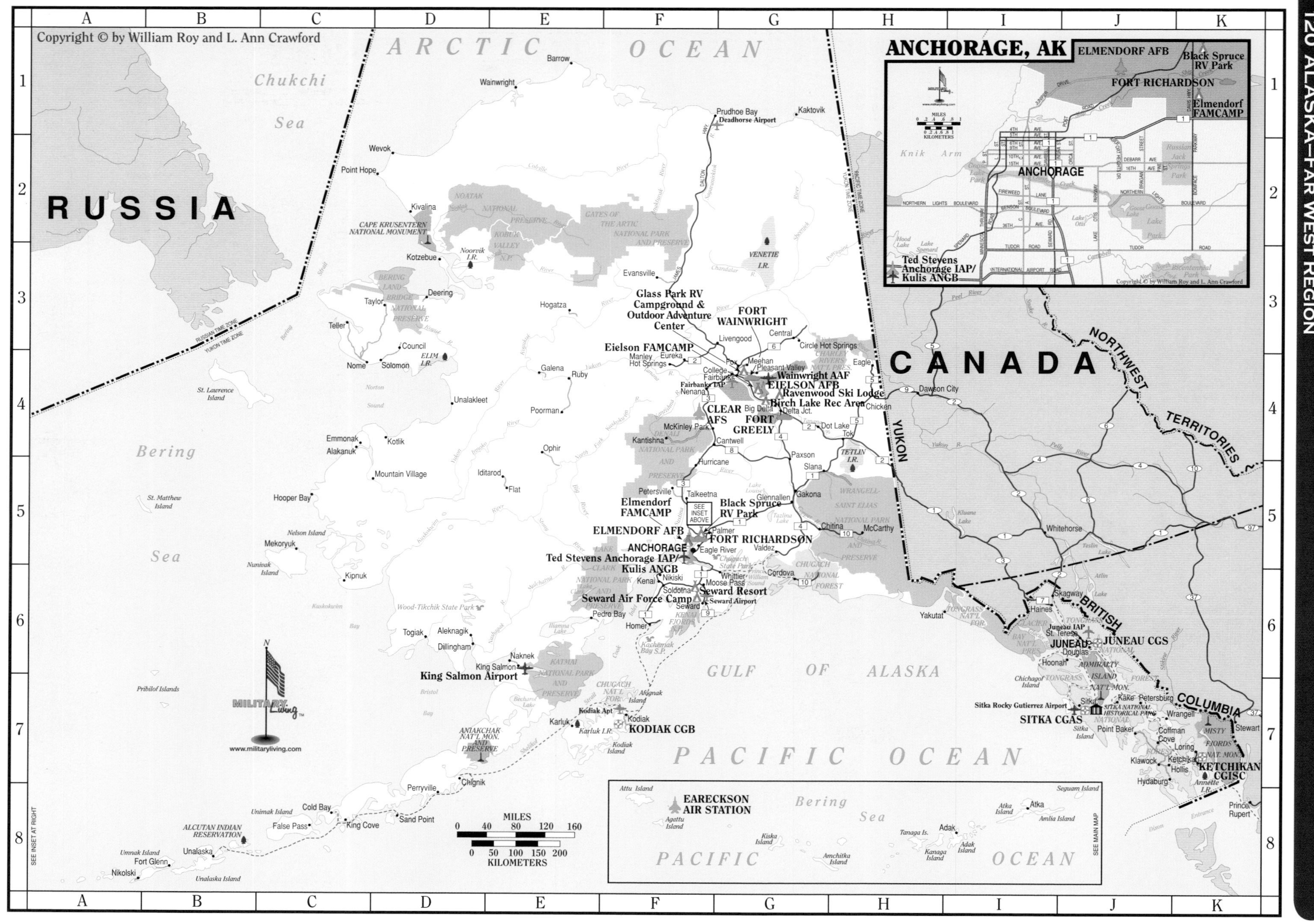
Copyright © by William Roy and L. Ann Crawford
ARCTIC OCEAN
Chukchi Sea
RUSSIA
Bering Sea
CANADA
YUKON
NORTHWEST TERRITORIES
BRITISH COLUMBIA
GULF OF ALASKA
PACIFIC OCEAN
ANCHORAGE, AK
ELMENDORF AFB
Black Spruce RV Park
FORT RICHARDSON
Elmendorf FAMCAMP
ANCHORAGE
Ted Stevens Anchorage IAP/ Kulis ANGB
Glass Park RV Campground & Outdoor Adventure Center
FORT WAINWRIGHT
Eielson FAMCAMP
Wainwright AAF
EIELSON AFB
Ravenwood Ski Lodge
Birch Lake Rec Area
CLEAR AFS
FORT GREELY
Elmendorf FAMCAMP
Black Spruce RV Park
ELMENDORF AFB
ANCHORAGE
FORT RICHARDSON
Ted Stevens Anchorage IAP/ Kulis ANGB
Seward Air Force Camp
Seward Resort
Seward Airport
King Salmon Airport
KODIAK CGB
JUNEAU CGS
Sitka Rocky Gutierrez Airport
SITKA CGAS
KETCHIKAN CGISC
EARECKSON AIR STATION
Barrow
Wainwright
Prudhoe Bay
Deadhorse Airport
Kaktovik
Point Hope
Kotzebue
Nome
Fairbanks
Valdez
Cordova
Homer
Kodiak
Juneau
Sitka
Dawson City
Whitehorse
MILES
KILOMETERS
SEE INSET AT RIGHT
SEE MAIN MAP
www.militaryliving.com

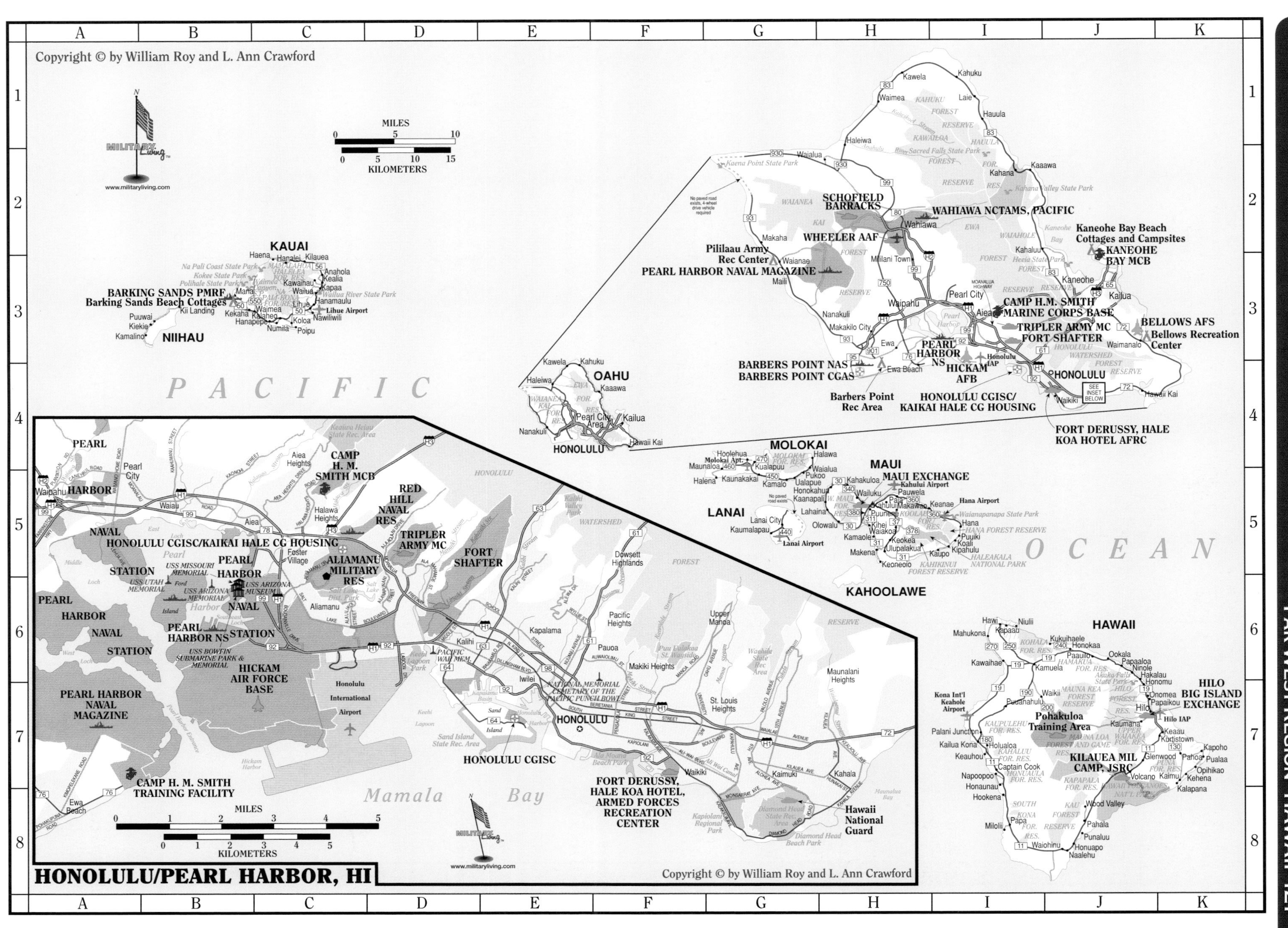

Copyright © by William Roy and L. Ann Crawford
MILES
KILOMETERS
www.militaryliving.com
KAUAI
BARKING SANDS PMRF
Barking Sands Beach Cottages
NIIHAU
Lihue Airport
PACIFIC
OAHU
HONOLULU
SCHOFIELD BARRACKS
WAHIAWA NCTAMS, PACIFIC
WHEELER AAF
Pililaau Army Rec Center
PEARL HARBOR NAVAL MAGAZINE
Kaneohe Bay Beach Cottages and Campsites
KANEOHE BAY MCB
CAMP H.M. SMITH
MARINE CORPS BASE
TRIPLER ARMY MC
FORT SHAFTER
BELLOWS AFS
Bellows Recreation Center
PEARL HARBOR NS
HICKAM AFB
BARBERS POINT NAS
BARBERS POINT CGAS
Barbers Point Rec Area
HONOLULU CGISC/
KAIKAI HALE CG HOUSING
FORT DERUSSY, HALE KOA HOTEL AFRC
MOLOKAI
MAUI
MAUI EXCHANGE
Kahului Airport
Hana Airport
LANAI
Lanai Airport
KAHOOLAWE
OCEAN
HAWAII
Kona Int'l Keahole Airport
Pohakuloa Training Area
KILAUEA MIL CAMP, JSRC
HILO BIG ISLAND EXCHANGE
Hilo IAP
PEARL HARBOR
CAMP H. M. SMITH MCB
RED HILL NAVAL RES
TRIPLER ARMY MC
FORT SHAFTER
NAVAL STATION
HONOLULU CGISC/KAIKAI HALE CG HOUSING
ALIAMANU MILITARY RES
USS MISSOURI MEMORIAL
USS UTAH MEMORIAL
USS ARIZONA MEMORIAL
USS ARIZONA MUSEUM
PEARL HARBOR NS
NAVAL STATION
USS BOWFIN SUBMARINE PARK & MEMORIAL
HICKAM AIR FORCE BASE
PEARL HARBOR NAVAL MAGAZINE
Honolulu International Airport
NATIONAL MEMORIAL CEMETARY OF THE PACIFIC PUNCH BOWL
HONOLULU
HONOLULU CGISC
PACIFIC WAR MEM.
Sand Island State Rec. Area
CAMP H. M. SMITH TRAINING FACILITY
Mamala Bay
FORT DERUSSY, HALE KOA HOTEL, ARMED FORCES RECREATION CENTER
Hawaii National Guard
Diamond Head Beach Park
Kapiolani Regional Park
HONOLULU/PEARL HARBOR, HI
Copyright © by William Roy and L. Ann Crawford

ALASKA, PG. 120

Anchorage, PG. 120

BIRCH LAKE RECREATION AREA

354 SVS/SVRO, 354 Broadway Street, U-6
Eielson AFB, AK 99702-1875
C-907-377-1317, DSN-317-377-1110
WEB: www.eielsonservices.com
LOCATION: Off base. On southwest side of AK-2 (Richardson Highway) at mile post 305, 38 miles south of Eielson AFB. Turn southwest at Recreation Area sign; one mile to entrance. Check-in at Boat Shop. USMRA: AK map (G-4). NMC: Fairbanks, 64 miles north. NMI: Eielson AFB, 38 miles north.
RECREATION & TRAVEL: RVC-488-6161
NOTE: *For detailed information about this off-base recreation facility, as well as on-base recreation facilities, golf courses and marinas, consult Military Living's "Military RV, Camping and Outdoor Recreation Around the World".*

CLEAR AIR FORCE STATION

13 SWS, P.O. Box 40013,Clear Air Force Station, AK 99704-0013
C-907-585-6409, DSN-317-585-6110, Police-585-6313
WEB: www.clear.af.mil
LOCATION: From Fairbanks, 80 miles southwest on AK-3 (Fairbanks/Anchorage Highway). Located on east side of highway. USMRA: AK map (F,G-4). NMC: Fairbanks: 80 miles northeast.
RETAIL & DINING: Clubs-NCO/O-585-6536
Polar Bar-585-6536 EX-585-6409
SUPPORT & FAMILY: Med-585-6414

EIELSON AIR FORCE BASE

354 Broadway Avenue, Unit 15A
Eielson Air Force Base, AK 99702-1895
C-907-377-1110, DSN-317-377-1110, Police-377-5130
WEB: www.eielson.af.mil
LOCATION: On east side of AK-2 (Richardson
Highway) at mile post 341. AFB is clearly marked. USMRA: AK map (G-4). NMC: Fairbanks, 26 miles northwest.
RECREATION & TRAVEL: RVC-488-6161
RVC-377-1232 SPA-377-1250/1854 TML-377-1844
RETAIL & DINING: Clubs-NCO-377-2635 OC-377-2051
Com-377-5134 Dining-377-2563 EX-377-4154 Gas-377-1218
SUPPORT & FAMILY: Med-377-1847/2259

ELMENDORF AIR FORCE BASE

3 Wing/PA,10480 22nd Street, Suite 120
Elmendorf Air Force Base, AK 99506-2400
C-907-552-1110, DSN-317-552-1110, Police-552-3421
WEB: www.elmendorf.af.mil
LOCATION: Off AK-1 (Glenn Highway) adjacent to north Anchorage. Take Boniface Parkway exit. Take either Elmendorf Access Road or North Post Road to the base. The base is adjacent to Fort Richardson. USMRA: AK map (F-5; J-1). NMC: Anchorage, two miles southeast.
RECREATION & TRAVEL: Golf-552-2773/3821
RVC-552-5526 RVC-552-2023 SPA-552-4616/8588
TML-552-2454, ext. 1118 or 552-5526
RETAIL & DINING: Cafeteria-753-2280/6146
Clubs-EMC-753-5190 NCO-753-5205
OC-753-3131 Com-580-4425 Dining-552-2528
EX-753-6275 Gas-753-7120
SUPPORT & FAMILY: Med-552-2778

FORT GREELY

Box 507, Delta Junction, AK 99737-0507
C-907-873-7301, DSN-317-873-7301
WEB: http://www.usarak.army.mil/greely
LOCATION: West of AK-4 six miles south of junction of AK-2 and AK-4. Five miles south of Delta Junction. USMRA: AK map (G-4). NMC: Fairbanks, 105 miles northwest.
RETAIL & DINING: Com-873-4404 Gas-869-3200

FORT RICHARDSON

600 Richardson Drive, #5900, Fort Richardson, AK 99505-5900
C-907-384-1110, DSN-317-384-1110, Police-384-0823
WEB: www.usarak.army.mil
LOCATION: Main Gate is on Glenn Highway, eight miles south of Eagle River. USMRA: AK map (F-5, J,K-1). NMC: Anchorage, eight miles southwest.
RECREATION & TRAVEL: Golf-428-0056 RVC-Otter Lake Lodge-384-1476 or Seward Resort-224-2654/2659/5559 RVC-384-7740 TML-224-2654/2659/5559 or 384-5660
RETAIL & DINING: Clubs-Down Under-384-7619
Dining-384-1704 EX-753-4420 Gas-428-1248
SUPPORT & FAMILY: Med-384-6677

FORT WAINWRIGHT

1060 Gaffney Road #3402, Fort Wainwright, AK 99703-3402
C-907-353-1110, DSN-317-353-1110, Police-353-7535
WEB: www.wainwright.army.mil
LOCATION: From Fairbanks, take AK-3 (Airport Way) east which changes to Gaffney Road and leads to the Main Gate of the post. USMRA: AK map (G-4). NMC: Fairbanks, adjacent.
RECREATION & TRAVEL: Golf-353-6223 RVC-353-6349/6350 SPA-353-6514/7212 TML-353-3800
RETAIL & DINING: Clubs-Last Frontier Club-353-7755 Com-353-7805 EX-356-1345 Gas-353-1263
SUPPORT & FAMILY: Med-353-5172 or 463-2140

JUNEAU COAST GUARD STATION

709 West 9th Street, Juneau, AK 99802-1807
C-907-463-2000
WEB: www.uscg.mil/d17
LOCATION: Accessible by air or boat. From ferry, right (southeast) on AK-7 (Eagan Drive) 13 miles to east onto West 10th Street. Make a right onto Glacier Avenue and a left onto West Ninth Street. Clearly marked. USMRA: AK map (J-6). NMC: Juneau, within city limits.
RETAIL & DINING: Clubs-CC-463-2370
EMC-463-2370 Dining-463-2370
SUPPORT & FAMILY: Med-463-2140

KETCHIKAN COAST GUARD INTEGRATED SUPPORT COMMAND

1300 Stedman Street, Ketchikan, AK 99901-6698
C-907-228-0211
WEB: www.uscg.mil/d17/iscketch/ketchpages
LOCATION: Accessible only via AK-7, also known as North and South Tongass. Located three miles south of the ferry terminals on AK-7. USMRA: AK map (K-7). NMC: Ketchikan, within city limits.
RETAIL & DINING: Cafeteria-228-0258
Clubs-CC-All Hands-228-0254 CPO/EMC-228-0230
EX-225-4528
SUPPORT & FAMILY: Med-228-0320

KODIAK COAST GUARD BASE

P.O. Box 190094, Kodiak, AK 99619-0094
C-907-487-5700, Police-487-5266, ext. 010
WEB: www.uscgalaska.com
LOCATION: From Kodiak City, take Chiniak Highway southwest for seven miles. Base is on left (southeast) side. USMRA: AK map (F-7). NMC: Kodiak, seven miles northeast.
RECREATION & TRAVEL: Golf-486-5323/9793
SPA-487-5149 TML-487-5446
RETAIL & DINING: Cafeteria-487-5710 Clubs- CC-487-5109
Com-487-5204 Dining-487-5235 EX-487-5370
Gas-487-5107
SUPPORT & FAMILY: Med-487-5757

SEWARD AIR FORCE CAMP

P.O. Box 915
Seward, AK 99664-0915
C-907-552-5526 or 907-224-5425, DSN-317-552-1110
WEB: www.elmendorfservices.com
LOCATION: Off base. From Anchorage, south on AK-1 to AK-9 south to mile post 2.1 of the Seward Highway. Camp is on right (west) side of AK-9 on Reurrection Bay. Follow signs. USMRA: AK map (F-6). NMC: Anchorage, 124 miles north. NMI: Anchorage IAP/Kulis ANGB, 135 miles north.
RECREATION & TRAVEL: RVC-552-2454
TML-552-2454
NOTE: *Formerly Seward Recreation Camp. For detailed information about this off-base recreation facility, as well as on-base recreation facilities, golf courses and marinas, consult Military Living's "Military RV, Camping and Outdoor Recreation Around the World".*

SEWARD RESORT

2305 Dimond Blvd, Seward, AK 99664-0329
C-907-224-2654/59/5559 or 800-770-1858, DSN-317-384-1110
WEB: http://www.sewardresort.com
LOCATION: Off post, 125 miles south of Anchorage. Take AK-1 (Seward Highway) south to AK-9. Continue south to Seward. Make a right onto Hemlock Street, then make a left onto Dimond Blvd. Resort is on the right. USMRA: AK map (F-6). NMC: Anchorage, 125 miles north. NMI: Fort Richardson, 140 miles north.
RECREATION & TRAVEL: RVC-224-2654/2659/5559
TML-224-2654/2659/5559
RETAIL & DINING: Clubs-CC-224-5559
Shoppette-224-7127
NOTE: *For detailed information about this off-base recreation facility, as well as on-base recreation facilities, golf courses and marinas, consult Military Living's "Military RV, Camping and Outdoor Recreation Around the World".*

SITKA COAST GUARD AIR STATION

611 Airport Road, Sitka, AK 99835-6500
C-907-966-5435
WEB: http://www.uscg.mil/d17/
LOCATION: Located at end of Airport Road on Japonski Island, five miles north of airport terminal. From the ferry station, take Halibut Point Highway for about six miles. Make a right onto Harbor Drive which turns into Airport Road. USMRA: AK map (J-7). NMC: Juneau, 90 miles by air or ferry.
RECREATION & TRAVEL: SPA-966-0580/5542
RETAIL & DINING: Cafeteria-966-5440
Clubs-CC-Eagles Nest-966-5516
SUPPORT & FAMILY: Med-966-5430

TED STEVENS ANCHORAGE INTERNATIONAL AIRPORT/KULIS AIR NATIONAL GUARD BASE

5005 Raspberry Road, Anchorage, AK 99502-1992
C-907-249-1176, DSN-317-626-1176, Police-249-1271
WEB: www.akanch.ang.af.mil
LOCATION: From downtown Anchorage, go south on Minnesota Thruway to right (west) on International Airport Road to left (south) on Jewel Lake Road, turn right onto Raspberry Road. Main Gate is approximately one mile on right (north) side of road. USMRA: AK map (F-5; H-3). NMC: Anchorage, within city limits.
RECREATION & TRAVEL: SPA-249-1000/1475
RETAIL & DINING: Cafeteria-249-1103 Clubs-NCO/PA-428-6030 or 249-1131
SUPPORT & FAMILY: Med-249-1415
NOTE: *The 2005 BRAC report recommended this base for closure. As required by Federal law, the DoD has until 15 September 2007 to begin closing and realigning the bases as called for in the approved report. This process must be completed by 15 September 2011.*

AMERICAN SAMOA, PG. 118

PAGO PAGO INTERNATIONAL AIRPORT

Pago Pago International Airport, P.O. Box 50018280
Pago Pago, American Samoa 96799-9999
C-011-684-699-4262, Police-699-9101
LOCATION: On the south coast of the Island of Tutuila in American Samoa. Approximately 2,630 miles southwest of Honolulu, HI, and 2,660 miles northeast of Christchurch, NZ. USMRA: AK/WA map (E-8). NMC: Village of Utulei, main U.S. Government offices, nine miles from IAP.
RECREATION & TRAVEL: SPA-011-684-699-4262
RETAIL & DINING: EX-699-2269

GUAM, PG. 118

ANDERSEN AIR FORCE BASE

36 ABW/PA, Unit 14003, Box 25,APO, AP 96543-4003
C-671-366-1110, DSN-315-366-1110, Police- 366-2913 or 911
WEB: www.andersen.af.mil
LOCATION: On the north end of the island, accessible from Marine Drive, which extends the entire length of the island of Guam. USMRA: AK/WA map (C-6,7). NMC: Agana, 15 miles south.
RECREATION & TRAVEL: Golf-362-4653 RVC-366-5204
SPA-366-5135/5165 TML-362-2804/4444
RETAIL & DINING: Cafeteria-362-3247 Clubs-CC-366-6166 or 653-9810/1 Com-366-5159 Dining-366-2195 EX-653-1141 Gas-653-4677
SUPPORT & FAMILY: Med-366-2978/6082

GUAM NAVAL COMPUTER & TELECOMMUNICATIONS STATION

Attn: PA, PSC 488, Box 101, FPO, AP 96540-1099
C-671-355-1110, DSN-315-355-1110, Police-355-5261/6
WEB: www.guam.navy.mil or https://www.nctsguam.navy.mil
LOCATION: From GU-10A, take a right (east) onto GU-1 (Marine Drive). Follow GU-1 to GU-3. Go west on GU-3. Clearly marked. USMRA: AK/WA map (B,C-7). NMC: Agana, three miles southwest.

RECREATION & TRAVEL: Golf-344-5838 Marina-564-1846 TML-355-5793
RETAIL & DINING: Dining-355-2321/43 EX-655-2315
SUPPORT & FAMILY: Med-355-4804

MARIANAS U.S. NAVAL FORCES

Bldg 100, Johnson Road, PSC 455, Box 152, FPO, AP 96540-1000
C-671-355-1110, DSN-315-355-1110, Police (Security)-339-2989
WEB: www.guam.navy.mil
LOCATION: South on Marine Drive on west side of island, clearly marked. USMRA: AK/WA map (A-7). NMC: Agana, ten miles north.
RECREATION & TRAVEL: Golf-344-5838 Marina-564-1846 RVC-564-1826 TML-339-5259
RETAIL & DINING: Cafeteria-564-3124 Clubs-CPO-564-1833/4 Com-339-5177 Dining-564-4124 EX-564-3178
SUPPORT & FAMILY: Med-344-9202

NAVAL HOSPITAL

PSC 490, Box 7607, Bldg 100, Farenholt Avenue
FPO, AP 96538-1600
C-671-344-9340, DSN-315-344-9525
WEB: www.usnhguam.med.navy.mil
LOCATION: From GU-10A, turn west onto GU-1 (Marine Drive), follow road to GU-4. Go around rotunda and go south on GU-4. Turn right at third traffic light, go to next traffic light and turn left. Go uphill. Gate to Naval Hospital is on right. USMRA: AK/WA map (B-7). NMI: Andersen AFB, 16 miles northeast.
SUPPORT & FAMILY: Med-344-9679

HAWAII, PG. 121

Honolulu, PG. 121

ALIAMANU MILITARY RESERVATION

1875 Aliamanu Drive, Honolulu, HI 96818-1405
C-808-449-7110, DSN-315-449-1110/7110
WEB: www.hawaii.navy.mil
LOCATION: From Honolulu, take HI-78 northwest to exit 2 (Red Hill) and make a right onto Aliamanu Drive into the reservation. From Ewa, take exit 2 (Red Hill) and make a right to enter reservation. Make a left onto Aliamanu Drive after guard shack. USMRA: HI map (C-6). NMC: Honolulu, eight miles southeast.
RETAIL & DINING: EX-833-6997 Gas-833-6997

BARBERS POINT COAST GUARD AIR STATION

1 Coral Sea Road, Kapolei, HI 96707-3693
C-808-682-2771
LOCATION: From airport, take H-1 west toward Waianae; take the Makakilo exit, left at a light (south) onto Fort Barrette Road, then left on Roosevelt Avenue. Take right on Coral Sea Road to CGAS. USMRA: HI map (H-4). NMC: Honolulu 25 miles east.
RETAIL & DINING: Clubs-CG-Hideaway-682-2731 EX-682-3074
SUPPORT & FAMILY: Med-682-2673

BARBERS POINT NAVAL AIR STATION

517 Russell Avenue, Suite 110, Pearl Harbor, HI 96860-4884
C-808-449-7110, DSN-315-449-1110/7110, Police-471-5141
LOCATION: Take H-1 west (toward Waianae) to Barbers Point NAS/Makakilo/Kadolei exit. Turn left (south) at light on off-ramp, go south on Fort Barrette Road for a mile to Main Gate. USMRA: HI map (H-4). NMC: Honolulu, 15 miles east. NMI: Pearl Harbor NS, 12 miles east.
RECREATION & TRAVEL: Golf-682-1911 RVC-682-2019
RETAIL & DINING: Com-682-7214 Snack Bar-682-1906 Gas-682-3074
SUPPORT & FAMILY: Med-684-2673/4300

BARKING SANDS PACIFIC MISSILE RANGE FACILITY

P.O. Box 128, Kekaha, Kauai, HI 96752-0128
C-808-335-4254/5, DSN-315-471-6255, Police-335-4523/5
WEB: www.pmrf.navy.mil
LOCATION: Located at mile 30 of HWY 50 (4 miles west of Kekaha). Vehicle pass and ID required. USMRA: HI map (B-3). NMC: Lihue, 30 miles east.
RECREATION & TRAVEL: RVC-335-4752 SPA-335-4310 TML-335-4383
RETAIL & DINING: Cafeteria-335-4163 Clubs-CC-335-4368 Dining-335-4249 EX-335-4300 Gas-335-4347
SUPPORT & FAMILY: Med-335-4203

BELLOWS AIR FORCE STATION

220 Tinker Road, Waimanalo, HI 96795-1010
C-808-259-8080, Police-259-4204
WEB: www.bellowsafs.com
LOCATION: On the eastern shore of Oahu. From Honolulu, take H-1 east to exit 21A HI-61 (Pali Highway), go north. Take a right onto HI-72 (Kalanianaole) south to AFS. Off HI-72 to Main Gate, then left on Hughes Road to registration on right. Clearly marked. USMRA: HI map (J-3). NMC: Kaneohe, nine miles northwest
RECREATION & TRAVEL: Golf-259-8080 RVC-259-4121/8080 or 800-437-2607 TML-259-8080 or 800-437-2607
RETAIL & DINING: EX-259-4138 Snack Bar-259-4210 Gas-259-5913

CAMP H.M. SMITH MARINE CORPS BASE

P.O. Box 64124, Bldg 1B, Camp H.M. Smith, HI 96861-5001
C-808-449-7110, DSN-315-449-1110/7110, Police-477-7114
LOCATION: Off H-1 west in Halawa Heights. Take Halawa Heights Road to Elrod Road to Main Gate on right (east). Clearly marked. USMRA: HI map (C-5; I-3), (C-1). NMC: Honolulu, ten miles southeast. NMI: Pearl Harbor Naval Station, five miles southwest.
RETAIL & DINING: Clubs-CC-484-9322 EX-254-3890 Gas-484-9321
SUPPORT & FAMILY: Med-477-3773

FORT DERUSSY, HALE KOA HOTEL ARMED FORCES RECREATION CENTER

2055 Kalia Road, Honolulu, HI 96815-1998
C-800-367-6027, DSN-315-438-6739 from CONUS (0800-1600 hours daily HI time except Sunday and Federal holidays). Fax: C-808-HALE-FAX (425-3329), DSN-315-839-2336
WEB: www.halekoa.com
LOCATION: From H-1, take the Punahou Street Exit. Take a right on Punahou Street. Take a right on Beretania Street. Take a left onto Kalakaua Avenue. Take a right onto Ala Moana Blvd, then take a left on Kalia Road. USMRA: HI map (I,J-4; F-7). NMC: Honolulu, within city limits.
RECREATION & TRAVEL: TML-808-955-0555
RETAIL & DINING: Dining-808-955-0555, ext. 546 (or ask for dining) EX-955-0060
SUPPORT & FAMILY: Med-808-955-0555
NOTE: *For further info on recreation/activities, call hotel operator at 808-955-0555.*

FORT SHAFTER

Attn: Public Affairs, Bldg T-100, Honolulu, HI 96858-5100
C-808-449-7110, DSN-315-449-1110/7110, Police-438-7114
WEB: www.usarpac.army.mil
LOCATION: Take H-1 east or west, exit at Fort Shafter on middle street to Main Gate. Clearly marked. USMRA: HI map (I-3; D,E-5). NMC: Honolulu, two miles east.
RECREATION & TRAVEL: Golf-438-9587 RVC-696-4158 TML-438-1685
RETAIL & DINING: Clubs-CC-438-1974 Com-438-1367 EX-438-9217 Gas-848-0404
SUPPORT & FAMILY: Med-433-8850

HICKAM AIR FORCE BASE

800 Scott Circle, Hickam Air Force Base, HI 96853-5328
C-808-449-7110, DSN-315-449-1110/7110, Police-449-2200
WEB: www2.hickam.af.mil
LOCATION: Adjacent to the Honolulu International Airport. Accessible from H-1 exit 15 to Nimitz Highway south. Exit the Nimitz Highway to O'Malley Blvd. Exit right onto Vandenberg Blvd which leads to the Main Gate. Clearly marked. USMRA: HI map (B,C-6,7; I-3,4). NMC: Honolulu, six miles east.
RECREATION & TRAVEL: Golf-449-2047/6490/8048 Marina-449-5215 RVC-449-5215 SPA-449-1515 TML-448-5400
RETAIL & DINING: Clubs-NCO-449-1292 OC-449-1592/4608 Com-449-7692 Dining-449-1666 EX-423-1304 Gas-422-5822
SUPPORT & FAMILY: Med-448-6110

HILO BIG ISLAND EXCHANGE

1300 Kekuanaoa Street, Bldg 505, Hilo, HI 96720-4568
C-808-935-3449
LOCATION: Located in the Hilo International Airport. From HI-11, make a right onto Kekuanaoa Street. USMRA: HI map (K-7). NMC: Hilo, within city limits.
RETAIL & DINING: EX-935-3449

HONOLULU COAST GUARD INTEGRATED SUPPORT COMMAND/KAIKAI HALE COAST GUARD HOUSING

400 Sand Island Access Road, Honolulu, HI 96819-4398
C-808-842-2970
WEB: www.uscg.mil/mlcpac/ischon
LOCATION: Take HI-92 (Nimitz Highway) east or west and exit at HI-64 south to Sand Island Access Road east to base. USMRA: HI map (I-4; C-5). NMC: Honolulu, within city limits.
RETAIL & DINING: Clubs-CC-842-2962 Dining-842-2960 EX-832-2564 Gas-833-2565

KANEOHE BAY MARINE CORPS BASE

Fourth Street, Bldg 216, Base Hq, P.O. Box 63002
Kaneohe Bay, HI 96863-3002
C-808-449-7110, DSN-315-449-1110/7110, Police-257-2123
WEB: www.mcbh.usmc.mil
LOCATION: At the end of HI-3 on the Windward (east) side of Oahu. From Honolulu IAP: Take HI-1 west to H-3 interchange. Take HI-3 east to Kaneohe, continue to Main Gate. Off Mokapu Blvd and Kaneohe Bay Drive. Clearly marked. USMRA: HI map (J-2,3). NMC: Honolulu, 14 miles southwest.
RECREATION & TRAVEL: Golf-254-1745/2107 Marina-254-7666/7 RVC-Campsites-254-7666/7 Cottages-254-2806 SPA-257-1604 TML-The Lodge at Kaneohe Bay-254-2716/2806 BOQ/BEQ-257-2409
RETAIL & DINING: Clubs-EMC-254-7660 NCO/SNCO-254-5592 OC-254-7649 Com-257-1452/63 Dining-257-1004 EX-254-3890 Gas-254-2775
SUPPORT & FAMILY: Med-257-2145

KILAUEA MILITARY CAMP, JOINT SERVICES RECREATION CENTER

Crater Rim Drive,Hawaii Volcanoes National Park, HI 96718-0216
C-808-967-8333/4
WEB: www.kmc-volcano.com
LOCATION: On island of Hawaii, 216 air miles southeast of Honolulu, 32 miles southwest off HI-11 from Hilo International Airport. Scheduled bus transportation to camp: reservations required 48 hours prior. Hilo to Kilauea Military Camp (KMC), take HI-11 into Hawaii Volcanoes National Park (28 mile marker). Enter park to reach military camp. USMRA: HI map (J-7,8). NMC: Hilo, 32 miles northeast.
RECREATION & TRAVEL: Golf-967-7331 RVC-967-8333 TML-967-8333
RETAIL & DINING: Cafeteria-967-8356 EX-Country Store-967-4364 Gas-967-8362

MAUI EXCHANGE

1686 Kaahumanu Avenue, Wailuku, HI 96793-2579
C-808-244-3006
LOCATION: Off HI-30 in the northwest section of Maui Island. Traveling on HI-30 north, make a right onto HI-32, which is Kaahumanu Avenue. USMRA: HI map (H-5). NMC: Wailuku, within city limits.
RETAIL & DINING: EX-244-3006

PEARL HARBOR NAVAL MAGAZINE

562 G Avenue, Ewa Beach, HI 96706-3381
C-808-474-4341 or C-808-449-7110, Police-668-7114
WEB: www.hawaii.navy.mil
LOCATION: Follow H-1 west to Fort Weaver Road south. Turn left at intersection of Fort Weaver and North Road. Follow North Road to intersection of Iroquois Drive, then turn right. Pearl Harbor Naval Magazine West Loch Branch gate is on left. USMRA: HI map (A-7). NMC: Honolulu, 20 miles southeast. NMI: Pearl Harbor Naval Base, four miles northeast.
RECREATION & TRAVEL: TML-474-7908
RETAIL & DINING: Clubs-Koa-499-2539 Dining-474-7846 EX-423-3344

PEARL HARBOR NAVAL STATION

Commander Navy Region Hawaii, 517 Russell Avenue, Suite 110
Pearl Harbor, HI 96860-4884
C-808-449-7110 or 808-474-4341, DSN-315-449-1110/7110, Police-474-1238
WEB: www.hawaii.navy.mil
LOCATION: From Honolulu IAP, take H-1 west. Follow signs for Pearl Harbor/Hickam AFB. Take exit 15 north on Kamehameha Highway to Makalapa Gate on North Road. USMRA: HI map (B-6). NMC: Honolulu, five miles east.
RECREATION & TRAVEL: Golf-471-0142 Marina-473-0279 TML-421-6113 Navy Lodge-800-NAVY-INN or 440-2290
RETAIL & DINING: Clubs-CPO-473-1583 EMC-Club Pearl-

473-0841 Beeman-473-2582 Com-471-8402 Dining-473-1815 EX-423-3344 Gas-423-3229
SUPPORT & FAMILY: Med-473-1880/4410

PILILAAU ARMY RECREATION CENTER

85-010 Army Street, Waianae, HI 96792-2435
C-808-696-4158 or 800-333-4158 (from mainland) and 800-847-6771 (from outer islands), Police-696-2811
WEB: www.mwrarmyhawaii.com/lodging/waianaelg.asp
LOCATION: On the west coast of Oahu. Take HI-1 west to HI-93 north (Farrington Highway) to Waianae. Look for the Aloha gas station on your left (west); turn left at Army Street. USMRA: HI map (G-2). NMC: Honolulu, 35 miles southeast. NMI: Schofield Barracks, 20 miles northeast.
RECREATION & TRAVEL: RVC-696-4158 (see numbers above for calls from other islands or mainland) TML-696-4158
RETAIL & DINING: Clubs-Beach Club-696-4778 Dining-696-4778 Shoppette-696-2886
NOTE: *For detailed information about this off-base recreation facility, as well as on-base recreation facilities, golf courses and marinas, consult Military Living's "Military RV, Camping and Outdoor Recreation Around the World".*

SCHOFIELD BARRACKS

25 Infantry Division (Light) & U.S. Army, Hawaii
Bldg 580, Room 229, Schofield Barracks, HI 96857-6000
C-808-449-7110, DSN-315-449-1110/7110, Police-655-0911
WEB: www.25idl.army.mil
LOCATION: Off H-2 or HI-99, west on HI-750 to gates, in the center of the island of Oahu. Clearly marked. USMRA: HI map (H-2). NMC: Honolulu, 20 miles southeast.
RECREATION & TRAVEL: Golf-Leilehua Course-655-4653 TML-624-9640/50 or 800-490-9638
RETAIL & DINING: Clubs-NCO-655-2251 Sports Dome-624-2230 Com-655-5066 Dining-624-5600 EX-622-1773 Gas-624-9857
SUPPORT & FAMILY: Med-433-2778

TRIPLER ARMY MEDICAL CENTER

1 Jarrett White Road, Tripler Army Medical Center, HI 96859-5000
C-808-433-6661/2, DSN-315-433-6662
WEB: www.tamc.amedd.army.mil
LOCATION: Take H-1 west to HI-78. Take exit 3 to HI-7310 (Jarret White Road), which leads to the medical center. USMRA: HI map (D-5; I-3). NMC: Honolulu, three miles southeast.
RECREATION & TRAVEL: TML-839-2336, ext. 0
RETAIL & DINING: Cafeteria-433-6067 Dining-433-5330 EX-833-1267
SUPPORT & FAMILY: Med-433-6661

WAHIAWA NAVAL COMPUTER AND TELECOMMUNICATIONS AREA MASTER STATION, PACIFIC [NCTAMS PAC]

500 Center Street, Wahiawa, HI 96786-3050
C-808-653-5385/8450, DSN-315-453-5385, Police-653-0234
WEB: www.nctamspac.navy.mil
LOCATION: Take HI-1 west aproximately seven miles to H-2 north interchange. Take HI-2 to Wahiawa exit, proceed through town of Wahiawa; cross the trestle bridge. At next traffic light, take a right onto Whitmore Avenue (turns into Center Street), continue four miles straight ahead to Main Gate. USMRA: HI map (H-2). NMC: Honolulu, 20 miles southeast.
RETAIL & DINING: EX-622-0424 Gas-622-0424
SUPPORT & FAMILY: Med-653-5340

WHEELER ARMY AIRFIELD

25 ID, Bldg 580, Room 229, Schofield Barracks, HI 96857-6000
C-808-449-7110, DSN-315-449-1110/7110, Police-655-7114
WEB: www.25idl.army.mil
LOCATION: Off HI-2 or HI-99 in the center of the island of Oahu. Adjacent to and south of Schofield Barracks. Kunra Gate from HI-750. Take HI-2 to HI-99. Exit onto HI-750. Follow the signs to the Main Gate. USMRA: HI map (H-2). NMC: Honolulu, 20 miles southeast.
RETAIL & DINING: Dining-656-0337/8022 Exhange-624-9818

PACIFIC ISLANDS (NO MAPS)

KWAJALEIN ATOLL, U.S. ARMY

USAKA Commander, Attn: Public Affairs, P.O. Box 26
APO, AP 96555-2526
C-805-355-1098, DSN-315-254-1098, Police (Security)-355-4445/9
LOCATION: Republic of the Marshall Islands. NMC: Honolulu, HI, 2300 air miles NE. NMI: Hickam AFB, HI, 2300 air miles NE.
RECREATION & TRAVEL: Golf-355-3768 Marina-355-3643 SPA-355-2169 or 808-449-1515 TML-355-3477/85
RETAIL & DINING: Cafeteria-355-3425 Clubs-CC-355-4339 Com-355-3607 Dining-355-3425 EX-355-2143
SUPPORT & FAMILY: Med-355-2224

WAKE ISLAND AIRFIELD

Chugach Support Services, Inc., Terminal Bldg
Wake Island, WK 96898-5000
C-808-424-2101, DSN-315-424-2101, Police-424-2381
LOCATION: A U.S. island in the Mid-Pacific, 2300 air miles west of Hawaii. NMC: Honolulu, 2300 air miles southeast. NMI: Kwajalein Atoll, 650 miles south.
RECREATION & TRAVEL: SPA-424-2210 TML-424-2210/2797
RETAIL & DINING: Cafeteria-424-2210, ext. 486 Clubs-CC-424-2310 Dining-424-2486 EX-424-2210, ext. 310 Gas-424-2242
SUPPORT & FAMILY: Med-424-2455
NOTE: *Wake Island is a USAF installation in caretaker status. Space-A travelers require prior coordination and approval from the Wake Island Site Manager.*

PUERTO RICO, PG. 118

BORINQUEN COAST GUARD AIR STATION

240 Guard Road, Aguadilla, PR 00603-1304
C-787-890-8400, Police-890-8472
WEB: www.uscg.mil/d7/units/as-borinquen
LOCATION: At the old Ramie Air Force Base, north of Aguadilla. Take PR-22/2 West from San Juan or North from Mayaguez to PR-110 North of CGAS. Main Gate is at the end of Wing Road, just past Fifth Street. USMRA: AK/WA map (B-9). NMC: San Juan, 65 miles east.
RECREATION & TRAVEL: Golf-890-1196/2987 SPA-890-8400, ext. 8124 TML-890-8492
RETAIL & DINING: Clubs-CPO-8499 CG/EMC/NCO-890-8490 EX-890-0435
SUPPORT & FAMILY: Med-890-8477
Ten-digit dialing required for local calls.

CAMP SANTIAGO

P.O. Box 1166, Salinas, PR 00751-1166
C-787-824-7400
LOCATION: I-52 from San Juan to south area of Puerto Rico. Camp Santiago is at the town of Salinas, west of the exit of I-52. USMRA: AK/WA map (D-10). NMC: Ponce, 25 miles.
RETAIL & DINING: Clubs-EMC-824-7662 OC-824-7521 EX-824-4270
Ten-digit dialing required for local calls.

FORT BUCHANAN

Attn: SOF B-PO, Fort Buchanan, PR 00934-5065
C-787-707-3400, DSN-313-740-3400, Police-707-3337
WEB: www.buchanan.army.mil
LOCATION: From the main terminal of Luis Muñoz Marin IAP, follow Avenida Salvador y Caro (the exit road) until it becomes PR-17. Continue directly across PR-26 staying on PR-17 southwest across the Teodoro Moscoso Bridge. Stay on PR-17 and bear right (west) on PR-17 (Avenida Jesus Pinero) approximately 2.5 miles to a right (north) onto PR-18 (Expresso Las Americas). Take the first exit (Norte). Take the lane farthest left. You will be driving into PR-22 (De Diego Expressway). Stay to the left until you see signs for Fort Buchanan and exit to your left. Stay in the right lane and turn right into the Main Gate. USMRA: AK/WA map (E-9). NMC: San Juan, six miles southwest.
RECREATION & TRAVEL: Golf-707-3852/3980 TML-792-7977
RETAIL & DINING: Clubs-CC-707-3758 EX-792-8989 Gas-792-4297
SUPPORT & FAMILY: Med-277-2050
Ten-digit dialing required for local calls.

LUIS MUÑOZ MARIN INTERNATIONAL AIRPORT/MUÑIZ AIR NATIONAL GUARD BASE

156 Airlift Wing/198 Airlift Squadron ANG
200 Jose A. Santana Avenue, San Juan, PR 00979-1502
C-787-253-5100, DSN-740-9100/9629
WEB: http://www.prsanj.ang.af.mil/
LOCATION: Leaving main terminal of airport, follow signs for town of Carolina on Highway 26 east. Pass two exits on right and watch for sign for Base Muñiz/Cargo Area. Go straight under the bridge/overpass to base. Follow signs toward Air National Guard/Cargo Area. Base Main Gate is the first entrance on the right. About 5-10 minutes from airport main terminal building. Visitors may enter with DoD/DHS sticker and proper DoD ID. USMRA: AK/WA map (E-9). NMC: San Juan, five miles west; Carolina, five miles east. NMI: Fort Buchanan, six miles west.
RECREATION & TRAVEL: SPA-253-7417/99
RETAIL & DINING: EX-253-5103/26
Ten-digit dialing required for local calls.

SAN JUAN COAST GUARD BASE

5 La Puntilla Street, San Juan, PR 00901-1800
C-787-729-6800, Police-729-1128
WEB: http://www.uscg.mil/d7/sector/sanjuan/index.html
LOCATION: From Luis Muñoz Marin IAP, take Road 26 (Baldorioty DeCastro Avenue), toward San Juan, pass Condado Lagoon until merging into Muñoz Rivera Avenue. Bear right to Old San Juan City and CGB gate. Road 25 (Ponce De Leon Avenue) and/or Road 35 (Fernandez Juncos) will also lead to the base. Base San Juan is located at the end of La Puntilla Street behind the Customs Federal Building. Visitors must have military sticker or ID and/or driver's license. If no sticker, Main Gate will provide a one-day vehicle pass. USMRA: AK/WA map (E-9). NMC: San Juan, within city limits. NMI: Ft. Buchanan.
RETAIL & DINING: Cafeteria-289-8676 Dining-729-2377 EX-289-8665/7
SUPPORT & FAMILY: Med-729-2305

U.S. VIRGIN ISLANDS, PG. 118

CYRIL E. KING AIRPORT

Alliance Aviation, P.O. Box 308654
Charlotte Amalie, St. Thomas, VI 00803-1707
C-340-774-5100
LOCATION: From Jackson Drive, follow signs to airport. Alliance Aviation (SPA) is located at the north ramp of the airport. USMRA: AK/WA map (G-9), NMC: Charlotte Amalie, across island.
RECREATION & TRAVEL: SPA-Alliance Aviation-777-4646

HENRY E. ROHLSEN AIRPORT/U.S. VIRGIN ISLANDS NATIONAL GUARD BASE

Army Aviation Operating Facility, VI National Guard, P.O. Box 2270 Kingshill, St. Croix, VI 00851-2270
C-340-712-7890, DSN-727-7890
LOCATION: On the south central coast of the island of St. Croix. USMRA: AK/WA map (H-11). NMC: Christiansted, Virgin Islands, eight miles northeast.
RECREATION & TRAVEL: SPA-712-0589 or 778-1012
RETAIL & DINING: EX-773-6570

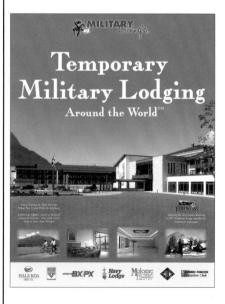

Call Telephone Number 511 in the United States for Traveler Information

The 511 number provides vital information, which saves lives, time and money. On 21 July 2000 the Federal Communications Commission (FCC) designated "511" as the single traffic information telephone number to be made available to states and local jurisdictions across the country. Information provided to this number is collected via state and local government Intelligent Transportation Systems (ITS). This information can be obtained by drivers and shippers by telephone or cell phone using one easy-to-remember number—511. To-date over twenty-five states and regions have implemented the telephone number with many more states initiating the program this year.

Listed below is the Department of Transportation for each state. If 511 is listed, then the service is now active in part or all of the state. We have also included telephone numbers and websites that each state has provided for information regarding road condition, construction and weather.

Alabama
Department of Transportation
(334) 242-6356
www.dot.state.al.us

Alaska
Department of Transportation and Public Facilities
511
(866) 282-7577 (outside AK)
(907) 269-0450
511.alaska.gov

Arizona
Department of Transportation
511
(888) 411-7623
www.az511.com

Arkansas
State Highway and Transportation Department
(501) 569-2227
(800) 245-1672
(501) 569-2374
www.arkansashighways.com

California
Department of Transportation
511 (San Francisco Bay Area)
(800) 427-7623 (in CA)
(916) 445-7623
www.dot.ca.gov

Colorado
Department of Transportation
(877) 315-7623 (in CO)
(303) 639-1111
www.cotrip.org

Connecticut
Department of Transportation
(800) 443-6817 (in CT)
(860) 594-3020
www.ct.gov/dot

Delaware
Department of Transportation
(800) 652-5600 (in DE)
(302) 760-2080
www.deldot.net

District of Columbia
Department of Transportation
(202) 673-6813
www.ddot.dc.gov

Florida
Department of Transportation
511 (State-wide by the end of 2005)
(866) 374-3368
www.dot.state.fl.us

Georgia
Department of Transportation
(888) 635-8287
(404) 635-8000
www.dot.state.ga.us

Hawaii
Department of Transportation
(808) 587-2160
www.hawaii.gov/dot

Idaho
Transportation Department
(888) 432-7623 (in ID)
(208) 334-8000
www.itd.idaho.gov

Illinois
Department of Transportation
(800) 452-4368
(312) 368-4636
(217) 782-7820
www.dot.state.il.us
www.illinoisroads.info

Indiana
Department of Transportation
(800) 261-7623
www.in.gov/dot

Iowa
Department of Transportation
511
(800) 288-1047
www.dot.state.ia.us

Kansas
Department of Transportation
511
(866) 511-5368
www.ksdot.org

Kentucky
Transportation Cabinet
511
(866) 737-3767
www.511.ky.gov

Louisiana
Department of Transportation and Development
511 (in development)
(225) 379-1232
www.dotd.state.la.us

Maine
Department of Transportation
511
(866) 282-7578
www.511maine.gov

Maryland
CHART (joint program between department of transportation and state police)
(800) 327-3125
(800) 541-9595
www.chart.state.md.us

Massachusetts
Executive Office of Transportation and Highway Department
(617) 374-1234 (SmarTraveler, Greater Boston only)
www.masspike.com

Michigan
Department of Transportation
(800) 381-8477
(888) 305-7283 (for West and Southwest Michigan)
(800) 641-6368 (Detroit)
www.michigan.gov/mdot

Minnesota
Department of Transportation
511
(800) 542-0220
www.dot.state.mn.us

Mississippi
Department of Transportation
(601) 987-1211
(601) 359-7301
www.mdot.state.ms.us

Missouri
Department of Transportation
(800) 222-6400 (in MO)
www.modot.state.mo.us

Montana
Department of Transportation
511
(800) 226-7623
www.mdt.mt.gov

Nebraska
Department of Roads
511
(800) 906-9069
www.dor.state.ne.us

Nevada
Department of Transportation
(877) 687-6237
www.nevadadot.com

New Hampshire
Department of Transportation
511
(866) 282-7579
www.511nh.com

New Jersey
Department of Transportation and Turnpike Authority
(732) 247-0900, then 2 (turnpike)
(800) 336-5875 (turnpike)
(732) 727-5929 (Garden State Parkway)
www.state.nj.us/njcommuter
www.state.nj.us/turnpike

New Mexico
Department of Transportation
(800) 432-4269
www.nmshtd.state.nm.us

New York
State Thruway Authority and Department of Transportation
(800) 847-8929 (thruway)
(518) 457-6195
www.thruway.state.ny.us (thruway)
www.dot.state.ny.us (all other roads)

North Carolina
Department of Transportation
511
(877) 368-4968
www.ncsmartlink.org
www.ncdot.org

North Dakota
Department of Transportation
511
(866) 696-3511
www.state.nd.us/dot

Ohio
Department of Transportation and Turnpike Commission
(888) 264-7623 (in OH)
(614) 644-7031
(440) 234-2030 (turnpike)
(888) 876-7453 (turnpike)
www.buckeyetraffic.org
www.ohioturnpike.org

Oklahoma
Department of Transportation
(405) 425-2385
www.okladot.state.ok.us

Oregon
Department of Transportation
511
(800) 977-6368 (in OR)
(503) 588-2941
www.tripcheck.com

Pennsylvania
Department of Transportation
(888) 783-6783 (in PA)
(717)783-5186
(215) 567-5678 (SmarTraveler, Camden/Philadelphia area)
www.dot.state.pa.us

Rhode Island
Department of Transportation
511
www.dot.state.ri.us

South Carolina
Department of Transportation
www.dot.state.sc.us

South Dakota
Department of Transportation
511
(866) 697-3511
(605) 367-5707
www.sddot.com

Tennessee
Department of Transportation
(800) 342-3258
(800) 858-6349
www.tdot.state.tn.us

Texas
Department of Transportation
(800) 452-9292
www.dot.state.tx.us

Utah
Department of Transportation and Commuter Link
511
(866) 511-8824
(800) 492-2400
www.dot.state.ut.us
www.commuterlink.utah.gov

Vermont
Agency of Transportation
511
(800) 429-7623
www.aot.state.vt.us/travelinfo.htm
www.511vt.org

Virginia
Department of Transportation
511
(800) 578-4111
www.511virginia.org

Washington
Department of Transportation
511
(800) 695-7623
www.wsdot.wa.gov

West Virginia
Department of Transportation
(877) 982-7623
www.wvdot.com

Wisconsin
Department of Transportation
(800) 762-3947
www.dot.state.wi.us

Wyoming
Department of Transportation
(888) 996-7623 (in WY)
(307) 772-0824
www.dot.state.wy.us

Alabama Bureau of Tourism & Travel
800-252-2262
www.touralabama.org

Alaska Travel Industry Association
907-929-2200
www.travelalaska.com

Arizona Office of Tourism
866-275-5816
www.arizonaguide.com

Arkansas Department of Parks & Tourism
800-828-8974
800-628-8725
www.arkansas.com

California Travel & Tourism Commission
916-444-4429
800-862-2543
www.gocalif.ca.gov

Colorado Tourism Office
800-265-6723
www.colorado.com

Connecticut Tourism
888-288-4748
www.tourism.state.ct.us

Delaware Tourism Office
866-284-7483
www.visitdelaware.net

District of Columbia Convention & Tourism Corporation
800-422-8644
202-789-7000
www.washington.org

Visit Florida
888-735-2872
www.flausa.com

Georgia Office of Tourism
800-847-4842
www.georgia.org/tourism

Hawaii Visitors & Convention Bureau
800-464-2924
www.gohawaii.com

Idaho Tourism
800-847-4843
www.visitid.org

Illinois Bureau of Tourism
800-2CONNECT
800-406-6418
www.enjoyillinois.com

Indiana Tourism Division
888-365-6946
www.enjoyindiana.com

Louisiana Office of Tourism
225-342-8100
www.louisianatravel.com

Maine Office of Tourism
888-624-6345
www.visitmaine.com

Maryland Office of Tourism
800-634-7386
866-639-3526
www.mdisfun.org

Massachusetts Office of Travel & Tourism
800-227-6277
617-973-8500
www.massvacation.com

Travel Michigan
888-784-7328
800-644-2489
www.michigan.org

Minnesota Office of Tourism
800-657-3700
651-296-5029
www.exploreminnesota.com

Mississippi Division of Tourism
800-927-6378
866-733-6477
www.visitmississippi.org

Missouri Division of Tourism
800-810-5500
800-519-2100
573-751-4133
www.missouritourism.org

Travel Montana
800-847-4868
406-841-2870
www.visitmt.com

Nebraska Division of Travel & Tourism
877-NEBRASKA
800-228-4307
402-471-3796
www.visitnebraska.org

Nevada Commission on Tourism
800-638-2328
www.travelnevada.com

New Hampshire Division of Travel & Tourism Development
800-386-4664
www.visitnh.com

New Jersey Office of Travel & Tourism
800-847-4865
609-777-0885
www.visitnj.org

New Mexico Department of Tourism
800-733-6396 Ext. 0643
www.newmexico.org

New York State Tourism
800-225-5697
518-474-4116
www.iloveny.com

North Carolina Division of Tourism
800-847-4862
919-733-8372
www.visitnc.com

North Dakota Tourism Division
800-435-5663
701-328-2525
www.ndtourism.com

Ohio Division of Travel & Tourism
800-282-5393
614-466-8844
www.discoverohio.com

Oklahoma Tourism & Recreation Department
800-652-6552
405-230-8400
www.travelok.com

Oregon Tourism Commission
800-547-7842
www.traveloregon.com

Pennsylvania Center for Travel & Marketing
800-847-4872
www.visitpa.com

Rhode Island Tourism Division
800-556-2484
www.visitrhodeisland.com

South Carolina Department of Parks, Recreation & Tourism
888-727-6453
803-734-1700
www.discoversouthcarolina.com

South Dakota Department of Tourism
800-732-5682
605-773-3301
605-578-7702
www.travelsd.com

Tennessee Department of Tourist Development
800-462-8366
615-741-2159
www.tnvacation.com

Texas Tourism Division
800-888-8839
www.traveltex.com

Utah Travel Council
800-200-1160
800-882-4386
801-538-1030
www.utah.com

Vermont Department of Tourism and Marketing
800-837-6668
802-828-3676
www.travel-vermont.com

Virginia Tourism Corporation
800-321-3244
800-847-4882
804-786-4484
www.virginia.org

Washington State Tourism
800-544-1800
877-260-2731
www.experiencewashington.com

West Virginia Division of Tourism
800-225-5982
www.wvtourism.com

Wisconsin Department of Tourism
800-432-8747
www.travelwisconsin.com

Wyoming Travel & Tourism
800-225-5996
www.wyomingtourism.org

U.S. Possessions

American Samoa Office of Tourism
684-699-9411
www.amsamoa.com/tourism

Guam Visitors Bureau
671-646-5278/9
www.visitguam.org

Puerto Rico Tourism
787-721-2400
www.gotopuertorico.com

U.S. Virgin Islands Tourism Office
www.usvitourism.vi

GENERAL REFERENCE

ICON KEY - FACILITIES & SERVICE BRANCHES

- Bank/CU
- Bowling
- Cafeteria/Dining/Clubs (designated as CC, EMC, OC)
- RVC (On Base)
- RVC (Off Base)
- Car Rental
- CDO/OOD/Q Deck/SDO
- Chapel
- Class VI/Package Store
- Commissary
- Convenience Store/Shoppette
- Dental Clinic
- Exchange
- Fast Food/Snack Bar
- Fitness Center/Gym
- Gas Station
- Golf
- ITT/ITR
- Library
- Marina
- Medical Facilities
- MCSS (Military Clothing Store)
- MWR/Services
- Outdoor Recreation
- SPA-Space Available Air Travel
- TML-Temporary Military Lodging
- Travel Office
- Visitor Center
- Air Force
- Airport
- Army
- Coast Guard
- DoD or Commercial Facility
- Marine Corps
- Merchant Marines
- NASA
- Navy
- Recreation Area

GENERAL ABBREVIATIONS USED IN THIS ATLAS

This list contains general abbreviations used in this atlas. Commonly understood abbreviations and standard abbreviations found in addresses have not been included in an effort to save space.

A

AAF-Army Airfield
AAFES-Army & Air Force Exchange Service
AB-Air Base
AD-Active Duty/Army Depot
AF-Air Force
AFAF-Air Force Auxiliary Field
AFB-Air Force Base
AFRC-Armed Forces Recreational Center
AFS-Air Force Station
AG-Army Garrison
AGS-Air Guard Station
AMC-Air Mobility Command/Army Medical Center
ANG-Air National Guard
ANGB-Air National Guard Base
AP-Army Pacific
APG-Army Proving Ground
APO-Army Post Office
Apt-Airport
ARB-Air Reserve Base
ARC-Army Reserve Center
ARNGTS-Army Reserve National Guard Training Site
ARS-Air Reserve Station
AS-Air Station
ATC-Aviation Training Center
Attn-Attention
AW-Airlift Wing

B

BEQ-Bachelor Enlisted Quarters
Bldg-Building
BN-Battalion
BNOQ-Bachelor Noncommisioned Officers' Quarters
BOQ-Bachelor Officers' Quarters
BRAC-Base Realignment and Closure
BX-Base Exchange

C

C-Commercial telephone number
CC-Consolidated/Combined Club
Com-Commissary
CDO-Command Duty Officer
CG-Coast Guard
CGA-Coast Guard Activities
CGAS-Coast Guard Air Station
CGB-Coast Guard Base
CGG-Coast Guard Group
CGISC-Coast Guard Integrated Support Command
CGMSO-Coast Guard Marine Safety Office
CGS-Coast Guard Station
CGTC-Coast Guard Training Center
Civ-Civilian
Class VI-Alcoholic Beverages
Conv-Convenience Store
CONUS-Continental United States
CPOC-Chief Petty Officers' Club
CTR-Center
CRTC-Combat Readiness Training Center
CU-Credit Union

D

DDC-Defense Distribution Center
DDD-Defense Distribution Depot
Dir-Directions
DoD-Department of Defense
DSN-Defense Switched Network

E

E-Enlisted
E-mail-Electronic Mail
EMC-Enlisted Members' Club
EXC-Exchange
Ext-Extension

F

FCTC-Fleet Combat Training Center
FPO-Fleet Post Office
FW-Fighter Wing

G

Gym-Gymnasium

H

HRC-Human Resources Command
Hq-Headquarters
HWY-Highway

I

IAP-International Airport
ITR-Information, Ticketing and Registration
ITT-Information, Tickets and Tours

J

JAG-Judge Advocate General
JRB-Joint Reserve Base
JRTC-Joint Reserve Training Center

L

L-Locator

M

MC-Marine Corps
MCAS-Marine Corps Air Station
MCB-Marine Corps Base
MCLB-Marine Corps Logistics Base
MCRD-Marine Corps Recruit Depot
MCSS-Military Clothing Sales Store
Med-Medical
Mil-Military
MSO-Marine Safety Office
MTC-Maneuver Training Center
MWR-Morale, Welfare and Recreation

N

NAB-Naval Air Base or Naval Amphibious Base
NAES-Naval Air Engineering Station
NAF-Naval Air Facility
NAS-Naval Air Station
NAWS-Naval Air Weapons Station
NB-Naval Base
NCBC-Naval Construction Battalion Center
NCOC-Noncommissioned Officers' Club
NCTAMS-Naval Computer & Telecommunications Area Master Station
NCTS-Naval Computer & Telecommunications Station
NDW-Naval District Washington
NEX-Navy Exchange
NG-National Guard
NGTS-National Guard Training Site
NL-Navy Lodge
NMC-Nearest Major City or Naval Medical Center
NMI-Nearest Military Installation
NS-Naval Station
NSA-Naval Support Activity
NSCS-Naval Supply Corps School
NSGA-Naval Security Group Activity
NSS-Naval Security Station or Naval Support Station
NSWC-Naval Surface Warfare Center
NSY-Naval Shipyard
NTC-Naval Training Center
NTTC-Naval Technical Training Center
NUWC-Naval Undersea Warfare Center
NWS-Naval Weapons Station

O

O-Officer
OC-Officers' Club
OCONUS-Outside Continental United States
ODD-Officer of the Day/Deck
OOD-Officer of the Day

P

P-Police
PA-Public Affairs
PAO-Public Affairs Officer
pg-Page
PG-Proving Ground
Pkg-Package
PMRF-Pacific Missile Range Facility
PX-Post Exchange

Q

Q-Deck-Quarterdeck

R

Rec-Recreation
RSO-Retirement Services Offices
RVC-Recreational Vehicle, Camping & Rec Area

S

SATO-Scheduled Airline Ticket Office
SC-Supply Center
SDO-Staff Duty Officer
SNCOC-Senior Noncommisioned Officers' Club
SPA-Space-Available Air Travel
SSC-Soldier Systems Center
St/Ste-Saint
Sta-Station
Svcs-Services

T

TML-Temporary Military Lodging

U

U.S.-United States
USA-United States Army
USAF-United States Air Force
USCG-United States Coast Guard
USMC-United States Marine Corps
USMRA-United States Military Road Atlas
USN-United States Navy
USNA-United States Naval Academy
USO-United Service Organizations
USS-United States Ship

Sample Listing

NAME OF INSTALLATION → **FORT BELVOIR**
Mailing Address → Attn: ANFB-GC, 9820 Flagler, Suite 201
Fort Belvoir, VA 22060-5932
C-703-545-6700, DSN-312-227-0101, Police (Security)-806-3104
Worldwide WEB address → WEB: www.belvoir.army.mil
LOCATION: From Washington, DC, take I-95 south to Belvoir/Newington exit 166. Turn right, connect with the southern leg of Fairfax County Parkway. Take Parkway to the end at Richmond Highway. Turn left. At the first light, Tulley Gate is on the right. At second light, Pence Gate (main entrance) is to the right. Visitor Center is just inside Pence Gate. USMRA: VA/WV map (L,M-6). NMC: Washington, DC, ten miles northeast. NMI: Fort Myer/Pentagon, 15 miles from base.
RECREATION & TRAVEL: Golf-806-4561/5878 Marina-805-3745 TML-704-8600 or 800-295-9750
RETAIL & DINING: Clubs-CC-780-0962 OC-780-0930 Com-806-6371/6674 Dining-806-6204 EX-806-5800/1/2 Gas-North-806-5263 South-806-4581
SUPPORT & FAMILY: Med-805-0612
Ten-digit dialing required for local calls.

Commercial telephone number, Defense Switched Network (312 area code used only when calling from OCONUS), police/ security phone number.

LOCATION: Includes driving directions, United States Military Road Atlas map coordinates, nearest major city, and nearest military installation.

RECREATION & TRAVEL, RETAIL & DINING, SUPPORT & FAMILY Lists installation support activities and phone numbers. See abbreviation and icon lists above for further explanation.

Sponsor Index

AK Eielson AFB 907-377-2285/3192
AK Elmendorf AFB 907-552-2499
AK Fort Richardson 907-384-3500
AK Fort Wainwright 907-353-2102
AL Fort Rucker 334-255-9241
AL Maxwell AFB 334-953-6725
AL Redstone Arsenal 256-876-2022
AR Fort Chaffee MTC 479-782-3421
AR Little Rock AFB 501-987-6095
AZ Davis-Monthan AFB 520-228-4387/5100
AZ Fort Huachuca 520-533-5733
AZ Luke AFB 623-856-3923/6827
AZ Yuma MCAS 928-269-5616
CA Barstow MCLB 760-577-6755
CA Beale AFB 530-634-2157
CA Camp Pendleton MCB 760-725-9791
CA China Lake NAWS 760-939-0978
CA Coronado NB, NAB Pacific 619-437-2780
CA Edwards AFB 661-277-4931
CA Lemoore NAS 559-998-4042
CA Los Angeles AFB 310-363-0183
CA March ARB 909-655-4077
CA Miramar MCAS 858-577-4806
CA Monterey Naval Postgraduate School 831-656-3699
CA Port Hueneme 805-982-1023
CA San Diego MCRD 619-524-5301
CA San Diego NMC 619-556-8987
CA Seal Beach NWS 562-626-7152
CA Travis AFB 707-424-3904
CA Twentynine Palms MCAGCC 760-830-7550
CA Vandenberg AFB 805-606-5474
CO Buckley AFB 303-677-6693/6694
CO Fort Carson 719-526-8470
CO Peterson AFB 719-556-7153
CT New London NSB 860-694-3284
DC Anacostia Annex/NDW 202-433-6150
DC Bolling AFB 202-767-5244
DC Walter Reed AMC 202-782-3353
DE Dover AFB 302-677-4612
FL Eglin AFB 850-882-5916
FL Homestead ARB 305-224-7580
FL Hurlburt Field 850-884-5443
FL Jacksonville NAS 904-542-5783
FL MacDill AFB 813-828-4555
FL Mayport NS 904-270-5783
FL Orlando 407-646-4204
FL Patrick AFB 321-494-5464
FL Pensacola NAS 850-452-5990
FL Tyndall AFB 850-283-2737
FL Whiting Field NAS 850-623-7177
GA Athens NSCS 706-354-7335
GA Atlanta NAS 678-655-6735
GA Fort Benning 706-545-2715
GA Fort Gordon/U.S. Army Signal Ctr 706-791-2654
GA Fort McPherson 404-464-3219
GA Fort Stewart 912-767-5013
GA Kings Bay NSB 912-573-4517/4509
GA Moody AFB 229-257-3209
GA Robins AFB 478-926-2019
GU Andersen AFB 671-366-4590
HI Barking Sands PMRF 808-335-4493/4
HI Camp H.M. Smith MCB 808-477-8372
HI Hickam AFB 808-449-0658
HI Kaneohe Bay MCB 808-257-7790
HI Pearl Harbor NS 808-473-3345
HI Schofield Barracks 808-655-1514
IA Camp Dodge/NGB 515-252-4413
ID Boise Air Terminal/Gowen Field Apt/ANG 208-422-5817
ID Mountain Home AFB 208-828-4878
IL Great Lakes NTC 847-688-5434
IL Scott AFB 618-256-5092
IN Crane NSA 812-854-1222
KS Fort Leavenworth 913-684-2425
KS Fort Riley 785-239-3667
KS McConnell AFB 316-759-3829/3830
KY Fort Campbell 270-798-3310
KY Fort Knox 502-624-1765
LA Barksdale AFB 318-456-4480
LA Fort Polk/JRTC 337-531-4515
LA New Orleans NAS/JRB 504-678-2134
LA New Orleans NSA 504-678-2134
MA Hanscom AFB 781-377-2476
MA Otis ANGB/Cape Cod CGAS 508-968-6572
MA Westover ARB 413-557-3918
MD Aberdeen PG 410-278-4331/2649
MD Andrews AFB 301-981-2726/2180
MD Bethesda National NMC 301-295-4120
MD Fort Detrick Army Garrison 301-619-3340/2191
MD Fort Meade 301-677-9600/2
MD Patuxent River NAS 301-342-4911
MD U.S. Naval Academy/Annapolis NS 410-293-2641
ME Bangor IAP/ANG 207-990-7387
ME Brunswick NAS 207-921-2609
MI Selfridge ANGB 586-307-5580
MN Minneapolis 612-726-9391x303
MO Fort Leonard Wood 573-596-0947
MO Kansas City 816-843-3652
MO St. Louis 314-263-6443
MO Whiteman AFB 660-687-6457
MS Columbus AFB 662-434-2599
MS Gulfport Armed Forces Retirement Home 228-897-4026
MS Gulfport NCBC 228-871-2581x35
MS Keesler AFB 228-377-3871
MS U.S. Naval Home 228-897-4026
MT Malmstrom AFB 406-731-4751
NC Camp Lejeune MCB 910-451-5927
NC Cherry Point MCAS 252-466-4401
NC Fort Bragg 910-396-5304
NC New River MCAS 910-449-6110
NC Pope AFB 910-394-1950
NC Seymour Johnson AFB 919-722-1119
ND Grand Forks AFB 701-747-4899
ND Minot AFB 701-723-3440
ND Raymond J. Bohn Armory 701-333-068/9
NE Lincoln 402-470-2136
NE Offutt AFB 402-294-7693
NH Portsmouth 207-438-1868
NJ Earle NWS 732-866-2115
NJ Fort Dix Army Garrison 609-562-2666
NJ Fort Monmouth 732-532-4673
NJ Lakehurst NAES 732-323-5099
NJ McGuire AFB 609-754-2459
NM Cannon AFB 505-784-4932
NM Holloman AFB 505-572-3140
NM Kirtland AFB 505-846-1536
NV Fallon NAS 775-426-3333
NV Nellis AFB 702-652-8712
NY Fort Drum 315-772-6434
NY Fort Hamilton 718-630-4552
NY Niagara Falls IAP/ARS 716-236-2389
NY U.S. Military Academy, West Point 845-938-4217
NY Saratoga Springs NSU 518-583-2900x202
NY Watervliet Arsenal 518-266-5810
OH Columbus DSC 614-692-4165
OH Wright-Patterson AFB 937-257-3221
OH Youngstown-Warren Reg Apt/ARS 330-609-1196
OK Altus AFB 580-481-5671
OK Fort Sill 580-442-5963/4009
OK Tinker AFB 405-739-7388
OK Vance AFB 580-213-6330
OR Central Point 541-857-4988
OR Eugene 541-686-9266
OR Klamath Falls IAP/Kingsley Field/ANG 541-885-6122
OR Portland IAP/ANG 503-335-4945
PA Carlisle Barracks 717-245-4501
PA Charles E. Kelly Support Facility 724-693-2477
PA Fort Indiantown Gap Military Reservation 717-861-8901
PA Philadelphia Defense Supply Ctr 215-737-7300
PA Pittsburgh IAP/ARS 412-474-8558
PA Tobyhanna Army Depot 570-895-7834/7019
PA Willow Grove NAS/JRB 215-443-6033
PR Fort Buchanan 787-707-3877
PR Luis Munoz Marin IAP/ANG 787-253-7568
RI Newport NS 401-841-4089/2283
SC Beaufort Naval Hospital 843-228-2905
SC Charleston AFB 843-963-2228
SC Charleston NWS 843-764-7480x16
SC Fort Jackson 803-751-6715
SC Parris Island MCRD 843-228-3473
SC Shaw AFB 803-895-1612
SD Ellsworth AFB 605-385-5050
TN Arnold AFB 931-454-4574
TN Mid-South NSA 901-874-5195
TX Brooks City-Base 210-536-2116
TX Camp Mabry 512-782-5090
TX Corpus Christi NAS 361-961-3113
TX Dyess AFB 325-696-4980/1484
TX Fort Bliss 915-568-5204
TX Fort Hood 254-287-5210
TX Fort Sam Houston 210-221-0835
TX Fort Worth NAS/JRB 817-782-5661
TX Goodfellow AFB 325-654-5388
TX Houston 713-795-4109
TX Ingleside NS 361-776-4551
TX Kingsville NAS 361-516-6333
TX Lackland AFB 210-671-2728
TX Laughlin AFB 830-298-4393
TX Randolph AFB 210-652-6880
TX San Antonio 210-225-2997x119
TX Sheppard AFB 940-676-5088
UT Hill AFB 801-777-5735
UT Tooele Army Depot 435-833-2249
VA Dahlgren NDW, West 540-653-1839
VA Fort Belvoir 703-805-2675
VA Fort Eustis 757-878-2953
VA Fort Lee 804-734-6980
VA Fort Monroe 757-788-2093
VA Fort Myer 703-696-5948
VA Henderson Hall USMC 703-614-6828/7337
VA Langley AFB 757-764-7386
VA Little Creek NAB 757-462-7763
VA Norfolk Naval Shipyard 757-396-4484
VA Norfolk NS 757-322-9113 or 800-372-5463
VA Portsmouth NMC 757-953-7689
VA Quantico MCB 703-784-3351
WA Bangor, NB Kitsap 360-396-4115
WA Bremerton, NB Kitsap 360-476-5113
WA Everett NS 425-304-3775
WA Fairchild AFB 509-247-5359
WA Fort Lewis 253-966-5882
WA McChord AFB 253-982-3214
WA Whidbey Island NAS 360-257-8054
WI Dane County Regional APT/ Truax Field/ANG 608-242-3115
WI Fort McCoy 608-388-3716
WI General Mitchell IAP/ARS 414-482-5207
WI Milwaukee CGG 414-744-9766
WY Francis E. Warren AFB 307-773-2309

Francis E. Warren AFB, WY	1173	6993	1652	1311	1265	1273	2047	110	1834	1133	1587	1772	961	1733	2780	302	1527	743	1733	3230	1729	1681	1017	1215	1209	1735	926	927	1262	563	1046	747	1768	2664	858		1000	1932
Great Lakes NS, IL	2153	7988	733	541	2174	2043	1122	1027	971	2102	668	941	1730	814	3355	886	812	1474	849	2477	813	756	1127	2160	364	849	453	292	970	656	1246	903	960	3239	1008	1000		1004
Hanscom AFB, MA	3101	8920	421	1075	3127	2996	159	1976	733	3019	382	936	2595	362	4265	1866	1161	2339	747	2594	265	320	1885	3109	967	551	1298	1282	1640	1538	2004	1748	1043	4149	1777	1932	1004	
**Hickam AFB, HI	2400	3784	5243	4749	3142	3240	5641	3500	5316	2848	5178	5141	3274	5324	2788	3826	4874	3538	5194	6532	5323	5275	4119	2554	4794	5291	4384	4483	4429	4131	4101	3997	5099	3147	4091	3596	4591	5523
Hill AFB, UT	760	6576	2081	1740	840	848	2488	540	2263	739	2016	2201	811	2162	2631	644	1956	915	2162	3659	2154	2106	1383	821	1638	2164	1335	1321	1649	980	1358	1152	2197	2515	1247	434	1429	2361
Jacksonville NAS, FL	2801	8525	734	506	3067	3011	1297	1752	474	2387	838	261	1918	830	4382	1815	283	1629	424	1456	888	1160	1090	2644	723	604	881	1319	781	1257	1094	1204	114	4266	1041	1795	1041	1151
Keesler AFB, MS	2338	8093	1029	502	2691	2691	1718	1456	916	1941	1091	653	1481	1123	4119	1507	332	1167	786	1875	1325	1497	651	2195	657	911	561	1121	300	927	620	772	506	4003	616	1464	937	1440
Key West NAS, FL	3274	8973	1223	986	3542	3478	1785	2225	963	2835	1327	750	2386	1319	4870	2303	750	2094	913	1250	1397	1669	1558	3092	1203	1093	1348	1807	1234	1724	1539	1652	603	4746	1489	2282	1521	1640
Kirtland AFB, NM	1087	6867	1878	1281	1487	1495	2344	457	1848	811	1834	1673	432	1971	3278	832	1406	272	1726	3064	1981	2000	673	1055	1332	1823	915	1296	1026	678	735	529	1633	3162	623	531	1330	2210
Little Rock AFB, AR	1968	7762	1007	410	2298	2276	1577	966	977	1719	1033	802	1259	1100	3704	1092	539	979	855	2242	1166	1256	472	1900	486	952	316	831	279	522	607	430	798	3588	365	1057	664	1413
Los Angeles AFB, CA	377	6169	2677	2080	1059	1162	3118	1052	2644	86	2633	2472	500	2770	2967	1351	2149	791	2525	3789	2775	2750	1369	260	2131	2622	1714	2008	1769	1473	1354	1328	2367	2854	1363	1124	2069	3001
Malmstrom AFB, MT	1197	6977	2074	1878	819	688	2242	789	2253	1292	2009	2282	1364	2155	2096	549	2094	1427	2190	3799	2095	1924	1602	1307	1705	2190	1493	1144	1923	1148	1730	1431	2335	1980	1614	684	1355	2308
Maxwell AFB, AL	2460	8174	796	280	2710	2654	1349	1432	642	2041	858	447	1581	890	4082	1470	99	1292	553	1781	953	1202	752	2295	438	678	524	1034	489	900	859	853	317	3966	687	1450	756	1207
McChord AFB, WA	768	6578	2742	2495	186	61	2969	1359	2980	1179	2677	2950	1530	2818	1869	1166	2711	1743	2858	4414	2822	2651	2122	934	2373	2858	2080	1812	2412	1801	2186	1976	2914	1783	2074	1253	2023	2976
Mid-South NSA, TN	2107	7892	887	290	2384	2348	1439	1105	857	1836	913	686	1379	980	3776	1144	423	1099	735	2126	1030	1120	608	2040	337	832	218	736	416	594	747	560	682	3660	520	1124	563	1293
Minn-St. Paul IAP/ARS, MN	2040	7780	1111	919	1783	1651	1511	914	1360	1946	1046	1319	1617	1192	2963	564	1190	1361	1227	2855	1191	1123	1087	2002	742	1227	597	111	1097	555	1206	863	1338	2847	963	827	392	1382
Minot AFB, ND	1622	7469	1623	1431	1357	1240	1807	807	1847	1708	1558	1831	1643	1704	2480	442	1702	1425	1739	3367	1689	1474	1414	1776	1254	1739	1107	623	1560	769	1510	1160	1888	2365	1249	682	904	1813
Mountain Home AFB, ID	692	6510	2346	2005	586	594	2717	812	2534	913	2281	2466	1030	2427	2382	887	2221	1189	2427	3926	2411	2363	1553	843	1903	2429	1620	1474	1923	1245	1632	1422	2462	2266	1504	699	1682	2626
Nellis AFB, NV	574	6355	2429	1856	1091	1186	2828	856	2414	356	2364	2248	418	2510	2974	1062	1981	709	2301	3639	2518	2470	1237	503	1885	2398	1490	1719	1493	1220	1272	1104	2174	2858	1181	832	1777	2709
New Orleans NAS/JRB, LA	2283	8043	1116	548	2641	2649	1668	1400	968	1888	1142	755	1420	1209	4136	1577	434	1106	888	1977	1264	1459	590	2145	703	1013	584	1147	260	960	570	722	608	4026	559	1403	980	1522
New York CGS, NY	2918	8739	225	879	2983	2852	343	1796	537	2823	186	740	2399	166	4164	1685	965	2143	551	2398	69	316	1689	2907	771	355	1102	1101	1444	1342	1808	1552	847	4048	1581	1751	823	197
Newport NS, RI	3083	8907	402	1056	3151	3020	213	1957	714	3000	363	917	2576	343	4316	1853	1142	2320	728	2575	246	371	1866	3079	948	532	1279	1269	1621	1519	1985	1729	1024	4200	1758	1919	991	54
Norfolk Naval Station, VA	2968	8752	188	668	3058	2941	688	1755	202	2696	309	425	2259	198	4253	1775	693	1979	246	2087	285	605	1457	2780	669	89	1029	1190	1201	1275	1584	1420	533	4137	1380	1798	912	542
Offutt AFB, NE	1667	7489	1154	833	1761	1700	1552	541	1357	1603	1089	1294	1257	1235	3135	516	1049	1001	1235	2758	1234	1186	797	1781	731	1237	418	447	848	202	916	529	1252	3019	632	501	502	1434
Orlando Navy EX, FL	2898	8608	864	621	3169	3113	1427	1846	604	2470	968	391	2009	960	4497	1925	385	1717	554	1337	1026	1298	1181	2727	838	734	983	1434	864	1359	1174	1287	244	4381	1124	1905	1156	1281
Parris Is. MCRD, SC	2760	8536	576	465	2972	2974	1139	1689	298	2427	680	85	1980	672	4322	1710	309	1683	266	1633	711	983	1144	2684	680	446	862	1189	878	1226	1202	1204	76	4206	1081	1776	981	993
Pease ANGB, NH	3156	8968	492	1146	3121	2990	78	2031	803	3042	453	1007	2664	433	4259	1914	1232	2408	818	2665	335	371	1955	3140	1038	622	1366	1330	1711	1600	2075	1817	1111	4143	1847	1980	1057	84
Pensacola NAS, FL	2451	8182	971	455	2780	2776	1528	1568	770	2044	1033	557	1578	1065	4204	1583	272	1286	720	1779	1122	1371	750	2301	613	853	646	1169	438	1022	748	861	410	4088	698	1544	931	1382
Pentagon, VA	2825	8632	15	654	2885	2754	571	1669	343	2672	125	514	2235	108	4066	1587	736	1955	325	2172	172	446	1464	2756	628	129	979	1003	1219	1219	1583	1396	618	3950	1356	1644	725	425
Quantico MCB, VA	2855	8659	37	650	2912	2781	600	1698	315	2668	152	486	2210	137	4093	1623	717	1935	297	2144	144	471	1444	2798	624	101	984	1030	1199	1230	1579	1392	590	3977	1331	1617	752	454
San Diego NS, CA	502	6282	2675	2078	1177	1276	3153	1105	2626	38	2643	2428	422	2768	3083	1401	2101	740	2523	3759	2785	2800	1321	378	2141	2620	1724	2061	1653	1482	1306	1317	2319	2967	1318	1171	2119	3019
Scott AFB, IL	2078	7929	852	372	2207	2151	1304	864	937	1879	787	833	1455	933	3541	967	643	1199	815	2308	932	968	832	1963	270	817	158	476	702	403	951	608	791	3425	713	947	333	1163
Selfridge ANGB, MI	2424	8249	559	633	2485	2354	844	1297	863	2361	494	888	1975	640	3623	1195	881	1719	743	2517	637	475	1363	2421	420	675	697	611	1157	899	1484	1148	964	3507	1251	1261	333	687
Travis AFB, CA	51	5857	2786	2360	685	783	3184	1234	2927	471	2721	2752	870	2867	2591	1369	2485	1161	2805	4143	2866	2818	1742	213	2337	2869	1995	2026	2040	1674	1724	1608	2710	2475	1702	1139	2134	3066
U.S Air Force Academy, CO	1325	7106	1692	1232	1393	1401	2133	61	1797	1103	1627	1693	804	1773	2932	454	1431	586	1673	3134	1772	1767	835	1181	1130	1677	800	1026	1055	467	904	620	1651	2816	717	152	1083	2003
U.S. CG Academy, CT	3030	8852	347	1001	3100	2965	244	1904	659	2949	308	862	2521	288	4277	1798	1087	2265	673	2520	191	333	1811	3028	893	477	1224	1218	1566	1464	1930	1674	969	4161	1703	1864	936	85
U.S Military Academy, West Point, NY	2924	8755	276	924	2999	2868	332	1798	588	2862	231	791	2438	217	4180	1701	1016	2182	602	2449	120	264	1734	2927	810	406	1140	1117	1489	1379	1853	1591	898	4064	1626	1767	839	186
U.S. Naval Academy/ Annapolis NS, MD	2849	8655	31	693	2908	2777	556	1692	375	2711	113	546	2274	70	4089	1610	775	1994	357	2204	153	429	1503	2795	667	161	1002	1026	1258	1242	1622	1435	653	3973	1395	1667	748	404
Wright-Patterson AFB, OH	2526	8212	488	405	2481	2350	941	1199	674	2225	423	688	1801	569	3662	1183	653	1545	552	2305	568	605	1143	2309	192	554	504	599	931	744	1262	954	748	3546	1035	1224	321	799
Yuma MCAS, AZ	670	6436	2490	1893	1317	1415	2974	1092	2441	219	2459	2243	246	2583	3223	1377	1916	564	2338	3574	2609	2628	1145	533	1957	2435	1546	2686	1477	1306	1121	1132	2153	3107	1133	1081	1963	2835

* Does not include mileage for ferry travel involved.
** Includes air miles. Flights from San Francisco, Miami and Elmendorf AFB, Alaska.
*** The above mileage has been compiled using Departments of the Army, Navy and Air Force Transportation and Travel Official Tabels of Distances, and Military Living data. Distances are computed over shortest, hard surfaced, all weather State, Federal and Interstate highways and are measured from a designed "center point" of a city town, or front entrance to a military installation. Distances may vary due to temporary closing of a highway for construction, seasonal snow, or high water.

	Alameda CGISC, CA	**Andersen AFB, GU	Andrews AFB, MD	Arnold AFB, TN	Astoria CGG/AS, OR	Bangor NB Kitsap, WA	Brunswick NAS, ME	Buckley AFB, CO	Camp Lejeune MCB, NC	Camp Pendleton MCB, CA	Carlisle Barracks, PA	Charleston AFB, SC
Alameda CGISC, CA		5950	2959	2370	718	814	3233	1278	2971	455	2767	2782
Andersen AFB, GU**	5950		8640	8146	6539	6637	9038	6760	8713	6245	8575	8538
Andrews AFB, MD	2959	8640		669	2893	2762	567	1682	348	2687	126	519
Arnold AFB, TN	2370	8146	669		2571	2515	1121	1222	618	2090	695	467
Astoria CGG/AS, OR	718	6539	2893	2571		160	3120	1362	3115	1140	2828	3032
Bangor NB Kitsap, WA	814	6637	2762	2515	160		2989	1357	3000	1238	2697	2970
Brunswick NAS, ME	3233	9038	567	1121	3120	2989		2108	879	3152	528	1082
Buckley AFB, CO	1278	6760	1682	1222	1362	1357	2108		1799	1068	1611	1690
Camp Lejeune MCB, NC	2971	8713	348	618	3115	3000	879	1799		2657	463	233
Camp Pendleton MCB, CA	455	6245	2687	2090	1140	1238	3152	1068	2657		2643	2460
Carlisle Barracks, PA	2767	8575	126	695	2828	2697	528	1611	463	2643		623
Charleston AFB, SC	2782	8538	519	467	3032	2970	1082	1690	233	2460	623	
Davis-Monthan AFB, AZ	864	6644	2250	1653	1491	1589	2742	894	2237	460	2219	2003
Dover AFB, DE	2934	8721	100	762	2974	2843	508	1778	389	2780	161	612
Elmendorf AFB, AK*	3077	4583	4074	3882	1906	1877	4257	3236	4312	3046	4009	4282
Ellsworth AFB, SD	1471	7223	1695	1331	1317	1186	1983	424	1832	1386	1530	1070
Fort Benning, GA	2548	8271	750	277	2787	2731	1307	1505	585	2133	812	377
Fort Bliss, TX	1179	6935	1970	1373	1755	1763	2484	722	1948	778	1963	1714
Fort Bragg, NC	2856	8591	330	494	2993	2878	893	1697	151	2535	445	209
Fort Buchanan, PR**	3830	9729	2177	1942	4490	4434	2740	2860	1917	3829	2281	1704
Fort Dix AG, NJ	2915	8721	170	828	2973	2842	422	1759	532	2747	151	685
Fort Drum, NY	2888	8672	442	990	2802	2803	384	1762	804	2762	349	957
Fort Hood, TX	1762	7516	1479	882	2134	2142	2031	1016	1409	1365	1505	1175
Fort Hunter Liggett, CA	200	5951	2891	2294	895	973	3210	1239	2861	341	2727	2686
Fort Knox, KY	2345	8191	643	223	2469	2393	1113	1168	726	2141	591	640
Fort Lee, VA	2904	8688	134	604	2995	2878	697	1691	218	2632	249	389
Fort Leonard Wood, MO	1999	7781	987	521	2156	3000	1436	847	1003	1722	922	962
Fort McCoy, WI	2104	7880	1011	819	1963	1832	1400	978	1249	2044	946	1219
Fort Polk/JRTC, LA	2132	7826	1234	666	2424	2432	1786	1177	1109	1753	1260	911
Fort Riley, KS	1744	7528	1227	767	1813	1821	1670	473	1311	1483	1162	1228
Fort Sam Houston, TX	1727	7498	1598	1001	2198	2206	2150	1126	1486	1338	1624	1273
Fort Sill, OK	1603	7394	874	814	1988	1996	1887	748	1381	1338	1372	1206
Fort Stewart, GA	2736	8496	623	425	2990	2934	1216	1676	293	2351	730	153
Fort Wainwright, AK*	2962	4947	3958	3766	1790	1751	4142	3122	4196	2930	3893	4166
Fort Worth NAS/JRB, TX	1773	7488	1371	774	2086	2094	1923	860	1312	1350	1397	1114
Francis E. Warren AFB, WY	1173	6993	1652	1311	1265	1273	2047	110	1834	1133	1587	1772
Great Lakes NS, IL	2153	7988	733	541	2174	2043	1122	1027	971	2102	668	941
Hanscom AFB, MA	3101	8920	421	1075	3127	2996	159	1976	733	3019	382	936

	Davis-Monthan AFB, AZ	Dover AFB, DE	*Elmendorf AFB, AK	Ellsworth AFB, SD	Fort Benning, GA	Fort Bliss, TX	Fort Bragg, NC	**Fort Buchanan, PR	Fort Dix AG, NJ	Fort Drum, NY	Fort Hood, TX	Fort Hunter Liggett, CA
Alameda CGISC, CA	864	2934	3077	1471	2548	1179	2856	3830	2915	2888	1762	200
Andersen AFB, GU**	6644	8721	4583	7223	8271	6935	8591	9729	8721	8672	7516	5951
Andrews AFB, MD	2250	100	4074	1695	750	1970	330	2177	170	442	1479	2891
Arnold AFB, TN	1653	762	3882	1331	277	1373	494	1942	828	990	882	2294
Astoria CGG/AS, OR	1491	2974	1906	1317	2787	1755	2993	4490	2973	2802	2134	895
Bangor NB Kitsap, WA	1589	2843	1877	1186	2731	1763	2878	4434	2842	2803	2142	973
Brunswick NAS, ME	2742	508	4257	1983	1307	2484	893	2740	422	384	2031	3210
Buckley AFB, CO	894	1778	3236	424	1505	722	1697	2860	1759	1762	1016	1239
Camp Lejeune MCB, NC	2237	389	4312	1832	585	1948	151	1917	532	804	1409	2861
Camp Pendleton MCB, CA	460	2780	3046	1386	2133	778	2535	3829	2747	2762	1365	341
Carlisle Barracks, PA	2219	161	4009	1530	812	1963	445	2281	151	349	1505	2727
Charleston AFB, SC	2003	612	4282	1070	377	1714	209	1704	685	957	1175	2686
Davis-Monthan AFB, AZ		2343	3392	1262	1676	318	2098	3334	2374	2404	871	741
Dover AFB, DE	2343		4155	1685	844	2063	426	2273	111	418	1572	2859
Elmendorf AFB, AK*	3392	4155		2645	4153	3523	4190	5818	4154	3940	3757	2801
Ellsworth AFB, SD	1262	1685	2645		1547	1044	1711	3250	1674	1617	1207	1445
Fort Benning, GA	1676	844	4153	1547		1387	499	1708	910	1159	848	2390
Fort Bliss, TX	318	2063	3523	1044	1387		1818	3042	2108	2142	585	1032
Fort Bragg, NC	2098	426	4190	1711	499	1818		1867	496	768	1279	2739
Fort Buchanan, PR**	3334	2273	5818	3250	1708	3042	1867		2343	2615	2506	4048
Fort Dix AG, NJ	2374	111	4154	1674	910	2108	496	2343		361	1638	2872
Fort Drum, NY	2404	418	3940	1617	1159	2142	768	2615	361		1728	2844
Fort Hood, TX	871	1572	3757	1207	848	585	1279	2506	1638	1728		1613
Fort Hunter Liggett, CA	741	2859	2801	1445	2390	1032	2739	4048	2872	2844	1613	
Fort Knox, KY	1717	733	3705	1266	494	452	604	2159	136	777	961	2345
Fort Lee, VA	2195	230	4190	1711	632	1915	200	2047	300	572	1404	2836
Fort Leonard Wood, MO	1300	1068	3528	776	699	1045	965	2402	1067	1101	678	1929
Fort McCoy, WI	1696	1092	3074	664	1090	1490	1127	2755	1091	1034	1154	2102
Fort Polk/JRTC, LA	1371	1327	3960	1597	584	942	1015	2182	1393	1516	403	1945
Fort Riley, KS	1074	1308	3299	601	977	820	1210	2680	1307	1324	629	1569
Fort Sam Houston, TX	881	1691	3918	1248	952	567	1398	2495	1757	1847	153	1585
Fort Sill, OK	892	1504	3522	923	943	612	1259	2608	1517	1551	303	1593
Fort Stewart, GA	1964	722	4301	1718	238	1618	316	1577	792	1064	1079	2621
Fort Wainwright, AK*	3276	4039	364	2529	4037	3407	4074	5702	4038	3824	3641	2685
Fort Worth NAS/JRB, TX	901	1464	3639	1039	787	600	1218	2430	1516	1626	147	1607
Francis E. Warren AFB, WY	961	1733	2780	302	1527	743	1733	3230	1729	1681	1017	1215
Great Lakes NS, IL	1730	814	3355	886	812	1474	849	2477	813	756	1127	2160
Hanscom AFB, MA	2595	362	4265	1866	1161	2339	747	2594	265	320	1885	3109

	Fort Knox, KY	Fort Lee, VA	Fort Leonard Wood, MO	Fort McCoy, WI	Fort Polk/JRTC, LA	Fort Riley, KS	Fort Sam Houston, TX	Fort Sill, OK	Fort Stewart, GA	*Fort Wainwright, AK	Fort Worth NAS/JRB, TX
Alameda CGISC, CA	2345	2904	1999	2104	2132	1744	1727	1603	2736	2962	1773
Andersen AFB, GU**	8191	8688	7781	7880	7826	7528	7498	7394	8496	4947	7488
Andrews AFB, MD	643	134	987	1011	1234	1227	1598	874	623	3958	1371
Arnold AFB, TN	223	604	521	819	666	767	1001	814	425	3766	774
Astoria CGG/AS, OR	2469	2995	2156	1963	2424	1813	2198	1988	2990	1790	2086
Bangor NB Kitsap, WA	2393	2878	3000	1832	2432	1821	2206	1996	2934	1751	2094
Brunswick NAS, ME	1113	697	1436	1400	1786	1670	2150	1887	1216	4142	1923
Buckley AFB, CO	1168	1691	847	978	1177	473	1126	748	1676	3122	860
Camp Lejeune MCB, NC	726	218	1003	1249	1109	1311	1486	1381	293	4196	1312
Camp Pendleton MCB, CA	2141	2632	1722	2044	1753	1483	1338	1338	2351	2930	1350
Carlisle Barracks, PA	591	249	922	946	1260	1162	1624	1372	730	3893	1397
Charleston AFB, SC	640	389	962	1219	911	1228	1273	1206	153	4166	1114
Davis-Monthan AFB, AZ	1717	2195	1300	1696	1371	1074	881	892	1964	3276	901
Dover AFB, DE	733	230	1068	1092	1327	1308	1691	1504	722	4039	1464
Elmendorf AFB, AK*	3705	4190	3528	3074	3960	3299	3918	3522	4301	364	3639
Ellsworth AFB, SD	1266	1711	776	664	1597	601	1248	923	1718	2529	1039
Fort Benning, GA	494	632	699	1090	584	977	952	943	238	4037	787
Fort Bliss, TX	1452	1915	1045	1440	942	820	567	612	1618	3407	600
Fort Bragg, NC	604	200	965	1127	1015	1210	1398	1259	316	4074	1218
Fort Buchanan, PR**	2159	2047	2402	2755	2182	2680	2495	2608	1577	5702	2430
Fort Dix AG, NJ	736	300	1067	1091	1393	1307	1757	1517	792	4038	1516
Fort Drum, NY	777	572	1101	1034	1516	1324	1847	1551	1064	3824	1626
Fort Hood, TX	961	1404	678	1154	403	629	153	303	1079	3641	147
Fort Hunter Liggett, CA	2345	2836	1929	2102	1945	1569	1585	1593	2621	2685	1607
Fort Knox, KY		606	420	642	749	665	1080	870	642	3589	853
Fort Lee, VA	606		967	1127	1140	1212	1523	1356	496	4074	1316
Fort Leonard Wood, MO	420	967		591	625	346	797	454	920	3412	558
Fort McCoy, WI	642	1127	591		1137	622	1273	930	1238	2958	1035
Fort Polk/JRTC, LA	749	1140	625	1137		741	415	505	809	3844	500
Fort Riley, KS	665	1212	346	622	741		748	361	1186	3183	469
Fort Sam Houston, TX	1080	1523	797	1273	415	748		400	1122	3710	264
Fort Sill, OK	870	1356	454	930	505	361	400		1164	3411	167
Fort Stewart, GA	642	496	920	1238	809	1186	1122	1164		4185	1005
Fort Wainwright, AK*	3589	4074	3412	2958	3844	3183	3710	3411	4185		3523
Fort Worth NAS/JRB, TX	853	1316	558	1035	500	469	264	167	1005	3523	
Francis E. Warren AFB, WY	1209	1735	926	927	1262	563	1046	747	1768	2864	858
Great Lakes NS, IL	364	849	453	292	970	656	1246	903	960	3239	1008
Hanscom AFB, MA	967	551	1298	1282	1640	1538	2004	1748	1043	4149	1777

3596	434	1795	1464	2282	531	1057	1124	684	1450	1253	1124	827	682	699	832	1403	1751	1919	1798	501	1905	1776	1980	1544	1644	1617	1171	947	1261	1139	152	1864	1767	1667	1224	1081	Francis E. Warren AFB, WY
4591	1429	1041	937	1521	1330	664	2069	1355	756	2023	563	392	904	1682	1777	980	823	991	912	502	1156	981	1057	931	725	752	2119	333	333	2134	1083	936	839	748	321	1963	Great Lakes NS, IL
5523	2361	1151	1440	1640	2210	1413	3001	2308	1207	2976	1293	1382	1813	2626	2709	1522	197	54	542	1434	1281	993	84	1382	425	454	3019	1163	687	3066	2003	85	186	404	799	2835	Hanscom AFB, MA
	3179	5128	4696	5576	3470	4365	2772	3577	4777	3181	4495	4383	4072	3113	2965	4646	5342	5519	5355	4092	5211	5139	5571	4785	5235	5262	2885	4532	4852	2460	3709	5455	5358	5258	4815	3039	Hickam AFB, HI
3179		2224	1851	2711	647	1467	730	553	1879	828	1553	1221	1001	274	438	1790	2180	2348	2227	930	2334	2215	2409	1931	2073	701	777	1376	1690	722	562	2293	2196	2096	1653	753	Hill AFB, UT
5128	2224		430	502	1660	801	2400	2315	355	2991	703	1430	1902	2481	2218	576	955	1132	644	1329	143	190	1210	378	729	2096	2355	872	1072	2739	1711	1077	1006	761	867	2170	Jacksonville NAS, FL
4696	1851	430		927	1228	441	1954	2054	239	2671	380	1211	1668	2125	1803	91	1244	1421	972	1009	550	626	1511	119	1015	995	1903	672	1067	2307	1322	1366	1295	1054	839	1727	Keesler AFB, MS
5576	2711	502	927		2108	1286	2848	2782	822	3458	1170	1910	2382	2953	2674	1021	1444	1621	1133	1796	383	681	1710	823	1218	1190	2803	1352	1561	3187	2178	1566	1495	1250	1350	2618	Key West NAS, FL
3470	647	1660	1228	2108		897	801	1200	1309	1475	1027	1217	1213	921	577	1178	2014	2191	1887	857	1743	1671	2275	1317	1863	1859	811	1070	1575	1081	374	2140	2053	1902	1416	631	Kirtland AFB, NM
4365	1467	801	441	1286	897		1696	1639	462	2256	136	811	1253	1732	1472	453	1217	1394	1016	594	917	806	1484	517	992	972	1681	396	877	1976	930	1339	1262	1031	668	1505	Little Rock AFB, AR
2772	730	2400	1954	2848	801	1696		1283	2054	1103	1806	1911	1699	898	292	1893	2813	2988	2686	1570	2482	2445	3049	2051	2662	2642	124	1869	2330	395	1090	2933	2836	2701	2215	284	Los Angeles AFB, CA
3577	553	2315	2054	2782	1200	1639	1283		2017	668	1691	963	564	597	991	2064	2164	2332	2253	1063	2472	2266	2302	2130	2066	2037	1330	1514	1666	1120	836	2277	2180	2089	1662	1306	Malmstrom AFB, MT
4777	1879	355	239	822	1309	462	2054	2017		2634	326	1134	1631	2144	1884	330	1011	1188	739	972	456	395	1278	172	782	762	2003	583	848	2388	1354	1133	1062	821	620	1827	Maxwell AFB, AL
3181	828	2991	2671	3458	1475	2256	1103	668	2634		2328	1631	1220	574	1130	2629	2832	3000	2921	1680	3093	2954	2970	2756	2734	2761	1216	2131	2334	724	1381	2945	2848	2757	2330	1356	McChord AFB, WA
4495	1553	703	380	1170	1027	136	1806	1691	326	2328		847	1311	1823	1593	426	1097	1274	896	666	805	684	1363	468	872	868	1824	298	745	2106	1048	1219	1137	911	519	1639	Mid-South NSA, TN
4383	1221	1430	1211	1910	1217	811	1911	963	1134	1631	847		512	1434	1619	1226	1201	1369	1290	380	1530	1298	1430	1251	1103	1131	1958	578	711	1926	926	1314	1217	1126	699	1844	Minn-St. Paul IAP/ARS, MN
4072	1001	1902	1668	2382	1213	1253	1699	564	1631	1220	1311	512		1062	1407	1680	1713	1864	1802	684	2042	1857	1807	1744	1615	1643	1746	1090	1171	1615	834	1826	1729	1638	1211	1722	Minot AFB, ND
3113	274	2481	2125	2953	921	1732	898	597	2144	574	1823	1434	1062		612	2064	2445	2613	2492	1195	2599	2384	2674	2205	2338	2361	951	1641	1955	656	827	2558	2461	2361	1918	927	Mountain Home AFB, ID
2965	438	2218	1803	2674	577	1472	292	991	1884	1130	1593	1619	1407	612		1742	2528	2696	2462	1278	2314	2252	2757	1883	2421	2444	339	1623	2038	569	798	2641	2544	2444	1964	315	Nellis AFB, NV
4646	1790	576	91	1021	1178	453	1893	2064	330	2629	426	1226	1680	2064	1742		1326	1503	1074	1032	656	684	1592	230	1101	1097	1856	712	1111	2257	1272	1448	1371	1140	885	1671	New Orleans NAS/JRB, LA
5342	2180	955	1244	1444	2014	1217	2813	2164	1011	2832	1097	1201	1713	2445	2528	1326		178	346	1253	1085	797	268	1186	229	258	2823	967	624	2885	1807	123	55	209	603	2639	New York CGS, NY
5510	2348	1132	1421	1621	2191	1394	2988	2332	1188	3000	1274	1369	1864	2613	2696	1503	178		523	1421	1262	974	138	1363	406	435	3000	1144	738	3053	1984	55	188	385	780	2816	Newport NS, RI
5355	2227	644	972	1133	1887	1016	2686	2253	739	2921	896	1290	1802	2492	2462	1074	346	523		1300	774	486	613	914	192	164	2684	880	738	2932	1740	468	397	209	617	2499	Norfolk Naval Station, VA
4092	930	1329	1009	1796	857	594	1570	1063	972	1680	666	380	684	1195	1278	1032	1253	1421	1300		1431	1292	1482	1094	1146	1173	1620	469	763	1635	584	1366	1269	1169	726	1490	Offutt AFB, NE
5211	2334	143	550	383	1743	917	2482	2472	456	3098	805	1530	2042	2599	2314	656	1085	1262	774	1431		320	1351	458	859	831	2438	987	1202	2822	1813	1207	1136	891	985	2253	Orlando Navy EX, FL
5139	2215	190	626	681	1671	806	2445	2266	395	2954	684	1298	1857	2384	2252	684	797	974	486	1292	320		1063	486	571	543	2395	831	876	2750	1691	923	848	603	728	2210	Parris Is. MCRD, SC
5571	2409	1210	1511	1710	2275	1484	3049	2302	1278	2970	1363	1430	1807	2674	2757	1592	268	138	613	1482	1351	1063		1444	496	516	3080	1234	735	3114	2063	169	257	475	870	2904	Pease ANGB, NH
4785	1931	378	119	823	1317	517	2051	2130	172	2756	468	1251	1744	2205	1883	230	1186	1363	914	1094	458	486	1444		957	938	2012	705	1021	2396	1411	1308	1237	996	795	1827	Pensacola NAS, FL
5235	2073	729	1015	1218	1863	992	2662	2066	782	2734	872	1103	1615	2338	2421	1101	229	406	192	1146	859	571	496	957		32	2657	839	551	2778	1684	351	280	39	480	2475	Pentagon, VA
5262	2096	701	995	1190	1859	972	2642	2039	762	2761	868	1131	1643	2361	2444	1097	258	435	164	1173	831	543	516	938	32		2656	835	576	2805	1695	380	309	68	507	2471	Quantico MCB, VA
2885	777	2360	1903	2803	811	1681	124	1330	2003	1216	1824	1958	1746	951	339	1856	2823	3000	2684	1620	2438	2395	3080	2012	2651	2656		1879	2378	508	1103	2945	2862	2699	2225	187	San Diego NS, CA
4532	1376	872	672	1352	1070	396	1869	1514	583	2131	298	578	1090	1641	1623	712	967	1144	880	469	987	831	1234	705	839	835	1879		570	2075	868	1089	1006	867	371	1695	Scott AFB, IL
4852	1690	1072	1067	1561	1575	877	2330	1666	848	2334	745	711	1171	1955	2038	1111	624	738	738	763	1202	876	735	1021	551	576	2378	570		2395	1344	743	598	574	238	2205	Selfridge ANGB, MI
2460	722	2739	2307	3187	1081	1976	395	1120	2388	724	2106	1926	1615	656	569	2257	2885	3053	2932	1635	2822	2750	3114	2396	2778	2805	508	2075	2395		1252	3002	2901	2801	2358	662	Travis AFB, CA
3709	562	1711	1322	2178	374	930	1090	836	1354	1381	1048	926	834	827	798	1272	1807	1984	1740	584	1813	1691	2063	1411	1684	1695	1103	868	1344	1252		1929	1844	1707	1209	932	U.S. Air Force Academy, CO
5455	2293	1077	1366	1566	2140	1339	2933	2277	1133	2945	1219	1314	1826	2558	2641	1448	123	55	468	1366	1207	923	169	1308	351	380	2945	1089	743	3002	1929		133	330	725	2761	U.S. CG Academy, CT
5358	2196	1006	1295	1495	2053	1262	2836	2180	1062	2848	1137	1217	1729	2461	2544	1371	55	188	397	1269	1136	848	257	1237	280	309	2862	1006	598	2901	1844	133		259	642	2678	U.S. Military Academy, West Point, NY
5258	2096	761	1054	1250	1902	1031	2701	2089	821	2757	911	1126	1638	2361	2444	1140	209	385	209	1169	891	603	475	996	39	68	2699	867	574	2801	1707	330	259		503	2514	U.S. Naval Academy/ Annapolis NS, MD
4815	1653	867	839	1350	1416	668	2215	1662	620	2330	519	699	1211	1918	1964	885	603	780	617	726	985	728	870	795	480	507	2225	371	238	2358	1209	725	642	503		2041	Wright-Patterson AFB, OH
3039	753	2170	1727	2618	631	1505	284	1306	1827	1356	1639	1844	1722	927	315	1671	2639	2816	2499	1490	2253	2210	2904	1827	2475	2471	187	1695	2205	662	932	2761	2678	2514	2041		Yuma MCAS, AZ

	Hickam AFB, HI**	Hill AFB, UT	Jacksonville NAS, FL	Keesler AFB, MS	Key West NAS, FL	Kirtland AFB, NM	Little Rock AFB, AZ,	Los Angeles AFB, CA	Malmstrom AFB, MT	Maxwell AFB, AL	McChord AFB, WA	Mid-South NSA, TN	Minn-St. Paul IAP/ARS, MN	Minot AFB, ND	Mountain Home AFB, ID	Nellis AFB, NV	New Orleans NAS/JRB, LA	New York CGA, NY	Newport NSA, RI	Norfolk Naval Station, VA	Offutt AFB, NE	Orlando Navy EX, FL	Parris Is. MCRD, SC	Pease ANGB, NH	Pensacola NAS, FL	Pentagon, VA	Quantico MCB, VA	San Diego NS, CA	Scott AFB, IL	Selfridge ANGB, MI	Travis AFB, CA	U.S. Air Force Academy, CO	U.S. CG Academy,	U.S. Military Academy, West Point, NY	U.S. Naval Academy/ Annapolis NS, MD	Wright-Patterson AFB, OH	Yuma MCAS, AZ
Alameda CGISC, CA	2400	760	2801	2338	3274	1087	1968	377	1197	2460	768	2107	2040	1622	692	574	2283	2918	3083	2968	1667	2898	2760	3156	2451	2825	2855	502	2078	2424	51	1325	3030	2924	2849	2526	670
Andersen AFB, GU**	3784	6576	8525	8093	8973	6867	7762	6169	6977	8174	6578	7892	7780	7469	6510	6355	8043	8739	8907	8752	7489	8608	8536	8968	8182	8632	8659	6282	7929	8249	5857	7106	8852	8755	8655	8212	6436
Andrews AFB, MD	5243	2081	734	1029	1223	1878	1007	2677	2074	796	2742	887	1111	1623	2346	2429	1116	225	402	188	1154	864	576	492	971	15	37	2675	852	559	2786	1692	347	276	31	488	2490
Arnold AFB, TN	4749	1740	506	502	986	1281	410	2080	1878	280	2495	290	919	1431	2005	1856	548	879	1056	668	833	621	465	1146	455	654	650	2078	372	633	2360	1232	1001	924	693	405	1893
Astoria CGG/AS, OR	3142	840	3067	2691	3542	1487	2298	1059	819	2710	186	2384	1783	1357	586	1091	2641	2983	3151	3058	1761	3169	2972	3121	2780	2885	2912	1177	2207	2485	685	1393	3100	2999	2908	2481	1317
Bangor NB Kitsap, WA	3240	848	3011	2691	3478	1495	2276	1162	688	2654	61	2348	1651	1240	594	1186	2649	2852	3020	2941	1700	3113	2974	2990	2776	2754	2781	1276	2151	2354	783	1401	2965	2868	2777	2350	1415
Brunswick NAS, ME	5641	2488	1297	1718	1785	2344	1577	3118	2242	1349	2969	1439	1511	1807	2717	2828	1668	343	213	688	1552	1427	1139	78	1528	571	600	3153	1304	844	3184	2133	244	332	556	941	2974
Buckley AFB, CO	3500	540	1752	1456	2225	457	966	1052	789	1432	1359	1105	914	807	812	856	1400	1796	1957	1755	541	1846	1689	2031	1568	1669	1698	1105	864	1297	1234	61	1904	1798	1692	1199	1092
Camp Lejeune MCB, NC	5316	2263	474	916	963	1848	977	2644	2253	642	2980	857	1360	1847	2534	2414	968	537	714	202	1357	604	298	803	770	343	315	2626	937	863	2927	1797	659	588	375	674	2441
Camp Pendleton MCB, CA	5848	739	2387	1941	2835	811	1719	86	1292	2041	1179	1836	1946	1708	913	356	1888	2823	3000	2696	1603	2470	2427	3042	2044	2672	2668	38	1879	2361	471	1103	2940	2862	2711	2225	219
Carlisle Barracks, PA	5178	2016	838	1091	1327	1834	1033	2633	2009	858	2677	913	1046	1558	2281	2364	1142	186	363	309	1089	968	680	453	1033	125	152	2643	787	494	2721	1627	308	231	113	423	2459
Charleston AFB, SC	5141	2201	261	653	750	1673	802	2472	2282	447	2950	686	1319	1831	2466	2248	755	740	917	425	1294	391	85	1007	557	514	486	2428	833	888	2752	1693	862	791	546	688	2243
Davis-Monthan AFB, AZ	3274	811	1918	1481	2386	432	1259	500	1364	1581	1530	1379	1617	1643	1030	418	1420	2399	2576	2259	1257	2009	1980	2664	1578	2235	2210	422	1455	1975	870	804	2521	2438	2274	1801	246
Dover AFB, DE	5324	2162	830	1123	1319	1971	1100	2770	2155	890	2818	980	1192	1704	2427	2510	1209	166	343	198	1235	960	672	433	1065	108	137	2768	933	640	2867	1773	288	217	70	569	2583
Elmendorf AFB, AK*	2783	2631	4382	4119	4870	3278	3704	2967	2096	4082	1869	3776	2963	2480	2382	2974	4136	4164	4316	4253	3135	4497	4322	4259	4204	4066	4093	3083	3541	3623	2591	2932	4277	4180	4089	3662	3223
Ellsworth AFB, SD	3826	644	1815	1507	2303	832	1092	1351	549	1470	1166	1144	564	442	887	1062	1577	1685	1853	1774	516	1925	1710	1914	1583	1587	1623	1401	967	1195	1369	454	1798	1701	1610	1183	1377
Fort Benning, GA	4874	1956	283	332	750	1406	539	2149	2094	99	2711	423	1190	1702	2221	1981	434	965	1142	693	1049	385	309	1232	272	736	717	2101	643	881	2485	1431	1087	1016	775	653	1916
Fort Bliss, TX	3538	915	1629	1167	2094	272	979	791	1427	1292	1743	1099	1361	1425	1189	709	1106	2143	2320	1979	1001	1717	1683	2408	1286	1955	1935	740	1199	1719	1161	586	2265	2182	1994	1545	564
Fort Bragg, NC	5194	2162	424	786	913	1726	855	2525	2190	553	2858	735	1227	1739	2422	2301	888	551	728	246	1235	554	266	818	720	325	297	2523	815	743	2805	1675	673	602	357	552	2338
Fort Buchanan, PR**	6532	3659	1456	1875	1250	3064	2242	3789	3799	1781	4414	2126	2855	3367	3926	3639	1977	2398	2575	2087	2758	1337	1633	2665	1779	2172	2144	3759	2308	2517	4143	3134	2520	2449	2204	2305	3574
Fort Dix AG, NJ	5323	2154	888	1325	1397	1981	1166	2775	2095	953	2822	1030	1191	1689	2411	2518	1264	69	246	285	1234	1026	711	335	1122	172	144	2785	932	637	2866	1772	191	120	153	568	2609
Fort Drum, NY	5275	2106	1160	1497	1669	2000	1256	2750	1924	1202	2651	1120	1123	1474	2363	2470	1459	316	371	605	1186	1298	983	371	1371	446	471	2800	968	475	2818	1767	333	264	429	605	2628
Fort Hood, TX	4119	1383	1090	651	1558	673	472	1369	1602	752	2122	608	1087	1414	1553	1237	590	1689	1866	1457	797	1181	1144	1955	750	1464	1444	1321	832	1363	1742	835	1811	1734	1503	1143	1145
Fort Hunter Liggett, CA	2554	821	2644	2196	3092	1055	1900	260	1307	2295	934	2040	2002	1776	843	503	2145	2907	3079	2780	1781	2727	2684	3140	2301	2756	2798	378	1963	2421	213	1181	3028	2927	2795	2309	533
Fort Knox, KY	4794	1638	723	657	1203	1332	486	2131	1705	438	2373	337	742	1254	1903	1885	703	771	948	669	731	838	680	1038	613	628	624	2141	270	420	2337	1130	893	810	667	192	1957
Fort Lee, VA	5291	2164	604	911	1093	1823	952	2622	2190	678	2858	832	1227	1739	2429	2398	1013	355	532	89	1237	734	446	622	853	129	101	2620	817	675	2869	1677	477	406	161	554	2435
Fort Leonard Wood, MO	4384	1355	881	561	1348	915	316	1714	1493	524	2080	218	597	1107	1620	1490	584	1102	1279	1029	418	983	862	1366	646	979	984	1724	158	697	1995	800	1224	1140	1002	504	1546
Fort McCoy, WI	4483	1321	1319	1121	1807	1296	831	2008	1144	1034	1812	736	111	623	1474	1719	1147	1101	1269	1190	447	1434	1189	1330	1169	1003	1030	2061	476	611	2026	1026	1218	1117	1026	599	2686
Fort Polk/JRTC, LA	4429	1649	781	300	1234	1026	279	1769	1923	489	2412	416	1097	1560	1923	1493	260	1444	1621	1201	848	864	878	1711	438	1219	1199	1653	702	1157	2040	1055	1566	1489	1258	931	1477
Fort Riley, KS	4131	980	1257	927	1724	678	522	1473	1148	900	1801	594	555	769	1245	1220	960	1342	1519	1275	202	1359	1226	1600	1022	1219	1230	1482	403	899	1674	467	1464	1379	1242	744	1306
Fort Sam Houston, TX	4101	1358	1094	620	1539	735	607	1354	1730	859	2186	747	1206	1510	1632	1272	570	1808	1985	1584	916	1174	1202	2075	748	1583	1579	1306	951	1484	1724	904	1930	1853	1622	1262	1121
Fort Sill, OK	3997	1152	1204	772	1652	529	430	1328	1431	853	1976	560	863	1160	1422	1104	722	1552	1729	1420	529	1287	1204	1817	861	1396	1392	1317	608	1148	1608	620	1674	1591	1435	954	1132
Fort Stewart, GA	5099	2197	114	506	603	1633	798	2367	2335	317	2914	682	1338	1888	2462	2174	608	847	1024	533	1252	244	76	1111	410	618	590	2319	791	964	2710	1651	969	898	653	748	2153
Fort Wainwright, AK*	3147	2515	4266	4003	4746	3162	3588	2854	1980	3966	1783	3660	2847	2365	2266	2858	4026	4048	4200	4137	3019	4381	4206	4143	4088	3950	3977	2967	3425	3507	2475	2816	4161	4064	3973	3546	3107
Fort Worth NAS/JRB, TX	4091	1247	1041	616	1489	623	365	1363	1614	687	2074	520	963	1249	1504	1181	559	1581	1758	1380	632	1124	1081	1847	698	1356	1331	1318	713	1251	1702	717	1703	1626	1395	1035	1133

Alabama (pg. 36)
Anniston Army Depot ... 256-235-7160
Fort Rucker ... 334-255-2997/9517
Gunter Annex to Maxwell AFB ... 334-416-4646
Maxwell Air Force Base ... 334-953-6351
Redstone Arsenal ... 256-876-4531

Alaska (pg. 126)
Eielson Air Force Base ... 907-377-2722
Elmendorf Air Force Base ... 907-552-2378

Arizona (pg. 108)
Fort Huachuca ... 520-533-2404
Luke Air Force Base ... 623-856-6000
Yuma Army Proving Ground ... 928-328-2530
Yuma Marine Corps Air Station ... 928-269-2278

Arkansas (pg. 76)
Little Rock Air Force Base ... 501-987-6921

California (pg. 110-111)
Barstow Marine Corps Logistics Base ... 760-577-6541
Beale Air Force Base ... 530-634-4882
Camp Pendleton Marine Corps Base 760-725-5805/64
China Lake Naval Air Weapons Station ... 760-939-8644
Coronado NB, NAB Pacific ... 619-437-3018
Coronado NB, North Island NAS ... 619-545-9576
Edwards Air Force Base ... 661-275-8747
El Centro Naval Air Facility ... 760-339-2575
Lemoore Naval Air Station ... 559-997-7000
Los Angeles Air Force Base ... 310-363-2190
March Air Reserve Base ... 951-655-4123
Miramar Marine Corps Air Station ... 858-577-4126
Monterey Naval Postgraduate School ... 831-656-3223
Point Loma NB, Fleet Anti-Submarine Warfare Training Center, Pacific ... 619-524-0568
Point Loma NB, San Diego NSB ... 619-553-7550
Point Mugu NAS/Ventura County NB ... 805-989-7628
Recording ... 805-989-8349
Port Hueneme Naval Facilities Expeditionary Logistics Center/Ventura County NB ... 805-982-4284
Presidio of Monterey ... 831-242-5377
San Diego Marine Corps Recruit Depot ... 619-524-6772
San Diego Naval Station ... 619-556-2180/7498
San Joaquin Defense Distribution Depot ... 209-839-4358
Seal Beach Naval Weapons Station ... 562-626-7555
Sierra Army Depot ... 530-827-4655
Travis Air Force Base ... 707-424-0969
Twentynine Palms Marine Corps Air Ground Combat Center ... 760-830-6873
Vandenberg Air Force Base ... 805-606-7976

Colorado (pg. 109)
Buckley Air Force Base ... 720-847-6853
Fort Carson ... 719-526-5366
Peterson Air Force Base ... 719-556-1760
Rocky Mountain Blue at Keystone Resort ... 719-333-7367
Schriever Air Force Base ... 719-567-6050
United States Air Force Academy ... 719-333-3241
Sports Tickets ... 719-472-1895

Connecticut (pg. 16-17)
New London Naval Submarine Base ... 860-694-3238
United States Coast Guard Academy ... 860-444-8154

Delaware (pg. 42)
Dover Air Force Base ... 302-677-3955

District of Columbia (pg. 51-52)
Anacostia Annex/Naval District Washington ... 202-433-2068
Bolling Air Force Base ... 202-767-6211
Marine Barracks ... 202-433-2112/2338
Walter Reed Army Medical Center ... 202-782-0600
Washington Navy Yard/ Naval District Washington ... 202-433-2068/6666

Florida (pg. 38-39)
Cape Canaveral Air Force Station ... 321-494-5158
Corry Station Center for Information Dominance ... 850-452-6354
Eglin Air Force Base ... 850-882-5930
Hurlburt Field ... 850-884-7848
Jacksonville Naval Air Station ... 904-542-3318
Key West Naval Air Station ... 305-293-4173
MacDill Air Force Base ... 813-828-1860/2478
Mayport Naval Station ... 904-270-5145
Miami CGISC ... 305-535-4565
Orlando Navy Exchange ... 407-855-0116
Panama City Naval Support Activity ... 850-234-4374
Patrick Air Force Base ... 321-494-5158
Pensacola Naval Air Station ... 850-452-6354
Tyndall Air Force Base ... 850-283-2499
Whiting Field Naval Air Station ... 850-623-7313

Georgia (pg. 37)
Albany Marine Corps Logistics Base ... 229-639-8177
Atlanta Naval Air Station ... 678-655-6502
Dobbins Air Reserve Base ... 678-655-6502
Fort Gillem ... 404-464-3097/4392
Fort McPherson ... 404-464-3097/4392
Hunter Army Airfield ... 912-315-9295
Kings Bay Naval Submarine Base ... 912-573-2289
Moody Air Force Base ... 229-257-3280
Robins Air Force Base ... 478-926-2945

Hawaii (pg. 129)
Barbers Point Naval Air Station ... 808-682-2019
Barking Sands Pacific Missile Range Facility ... 808-335-4195
Bellows Air Force Station ... 808-259-8080
Camp H.M. Smith MCB ... 808-477-5143
Fort Shafter ... 808-438-1985
Honolulu CGISC/Kaikai Hale CG Housing ... 808-842-2963, ext. 2413
Kaneohe Bay Marine Corps Base ... 808-254-7562
Kilauea Military Camp, Joint Services Rec Ctr ... 808-967-8333 or from Oahu 438-6707
Pearl Harbor Naval Station ... 808-473-1190
Pililaau Army Recreation Center ... 808-655-9971
Schofield Barracks ... 808-655-9971
Tripler Army Medical Center ... 808-438-1985

Illinois (pg. 64)
Great Lakes Naval Station ... 847-688-3537
Rock Island Arsenal ... 309-782-5890

Indiana (pg. 65)
Crane Naval Support Activity ... 812-854-6059

Iowa (pg. 77)
Camp Dodge/National Guard Base ... 515-270-2445

Kansas (pg. 78)
Fort Leavenworth ... 913-684-3373
Fort Riley ... 785-239-5614
McConnell Air Force Base ... 316-759-6007

Kentucky (pg. 40-41)
Fort Campbell ... 270-798-7436
Fort Knox ... 502-624-1081/5030

Louisiana (pg. 79)
Barksdale Air Force Base ... 318-456-1866
New Orleans NAS/Joint Reserve Base ... 504-678-3695
New Orleans NSA (only open on Friday) ... 504-678-3508

Maine (pg. 18)
Brunswick Naval Air Station ... 207-921-2555

Maryland (pg. 42)
Aberdeen Proving Ground ... 410-278-4011
Andrews Air Force Base ... 301-981-4413
Bethesda National Naval Medical Center ... 301-295-0434
Fort George G. Meade ... 301-677-7354
Indian Head Division, NSWC ... 301-744-4850
Patuxent River Naval Air Station ... 301-342-3648
United States Naval Academy/Annapolis NS ... 410-293-9200

Massachusetts (pg. 16-17)
Hanscom Air Force Base ... 781-377-3262

Minnesota (pg. 80)
Minneapolis-St. Paul IAP/ARS ... 612-713-1496

Mississippi (pg. 43)
Columbus Air Force Base ... 662-434-7858
Gulfport NCBC ... 228-871-2231
Keesler Air Force Base ... 228-377-3818
Meridian Naval Air Station ... 601-679-3773
Pascagoula Naval Station ... 228-761-2432

Missouri (pg. 81)
Fort Leonard Wood ... 573-329-8587
Whiteman Air Force Base ... 660-687-5643

Nevada (pg. 113)
Fallon Naval Air Station ... 775-426-2865
Nellis Air Force Base ... 702-652-2192

New Hampshire (pg. 23)
Portsmouth Naval Shipyard ... 207-438-2713

New Jersey (pg. 19)
Cape May CGTC ... 609-898-6922/69
Earle Naval Weapons Station ... 732-866-2167
Fort Dix Army Garrison ... 609-724-3737
Fort Monmouth ... 732-389-0449
Lakehurst NAES ... 732-323-1362
McGuire Air Force Base ... 609-754-4271/6032
Picatinny Arsenal ... 973-724-4186

New Mexico (pg. 114)
Cannon Air Force Base ... 505-784-1275
Kirtland Air Force Base ... 505-846-2924
White Sands Missile Range ... 505-678-4134

New York (pg. 20-21)
Fort Drum ... 315-772-8222/3
New York CGS ... 718-354-4407
Niagara Falls IAP/ARS ... 716-236-3367
Saratoga Springs Naval Support Unit ... 518-885-5138
Stewart IAP/ANG ... 845-563-2007
United States Military Academy, West Point ... 845-938-3601

North Carolina (pg. 44-45)
Camp Lejeune MCB ... 910-451-5380
Cherry Point MCAS ... 252-463-1680 or 466-2197
Fort Bragg ... 910-396-8687
New River MCAS ... 910-449-6715
Pope Air Force Base ... 910-394-4478

Ohio (pg. 67)
Columbus Defense Supply Center ... 614-692-1111
Wright-Patterson Air Force Base ... 937-257-7670

Oklahoma (pg. 84)
Altus Air Force Base ... 580-481-7416
Fort Sill ... 580-442-6211
McAlester Army Ammunition Plant ... 918-420-6504
Tinker Air Force Base ... 405-734-3791
Vance Air Force Base ... 580-213-6268

Pennsylvania (pg. 22)
Carlisle Barracks ... 717-245-3309/4048
Philadelphia Defense Supply Center ... 215-697-9092
Susquehanna Defense Distribution Center ... 717-770-7670
Tobyhanna Army Depot ... 570-895-7584
Willow Grove NAS/Joint Reserve Base ... 215-443-6082

Rhode Island (pg. 16-17)
Carr Point Recreation Facilities ... 401-841-3116
Newport Naval Station ... 401-841-3116

South Carolina (pg. 44-45)
Beaufort MCAS ... 843-228-6375/6377/7340
Beaufort Naval Hospital ... 843-228-5424
Charleston NWS ... 843-764-7601
Fort Jackson ... 803-751-6219
Parris Island MCRD ... 843-228-7340
Shaw Air Force Base ... 803-895-4774

Tennessee (pg. 40-41)
Arnold Air Force Base ... 931-454-3128
Mid-South Naval Support Activity ... 901-874-5455

Texas (pg. 86-87)
Biggs Army Airfield ... 915-568-7506
Corpus Christi Naval Air Station ... 361-961-2267
Dyess Air Force Base ... 325-696-5207
Fort Bliss ... 915-568-7506
Fort Hood ... 254-287-7310
Fort Sam Houston ... 210-224-2721
Fort Worth NAS/JRB ... 817-782-6121
Goodfellow Air Force Base ... 325-654-5249
Ingleside Naval Station ... 361-776-4227
Kelly Annex, Lackland AFB ... 210-925-1151
Kingsville Naval Air Station ... 361-516-6449
Lackland Air Force Base ... 210-671-3133
Randolph Air Force Base ... 210-652-2301
Sheppard Air Force Base ... 940-676-2302

Utah (pg. 112)
Dugway Proving Ground ... 435-831-2318
Hill Air Force Base ... 801-777-3525
Tooele Army Depot ... 435-833-3100/29

Virginia (pg. 46-47)
Cheatham Annex NWS ... 757-887-7418
Dahlgren Naval District Washington, West Area ... 540-653-8785
Fort Belvoir ... 703-805-3714/5/6
Fort Eustis ... 757-878-3694
Fort Monroe ... 757-764-7176
Fort Story ... 757-422-7472
Henderson Hall USMC ... 703-979-4011
Langley Air Force Base ... 757-764-5890/7176
Little Creek Naval Amphibious Base ... 757-462-7793
Norfolk Naval Shipyard ... 757-396-1776
Norfolk Naval Station ... 757-445-6663
Oceana Naval Air Station ... 757-433-3301
Pentagon ... 703-697-3816
Portsmouth Naval Medical Center ... 757-953-5439
Quantico Marine Corps Base ... 703-630-2881
Yorktown Coast Guard Training Center ... 757-877-4609
Yorktown Naval Weapons Station ... 757-887-4609

Washington (pg. 101)
Bangor Naval Base Kitsap ... 360-535-5918
Bremerton Naval Base Kitsap ... 360-476-3178
Everett Naval Station ... 425-304-3167
Fairchild Air Force Base ... 509-247-5649
Fort Lewis ... 253-967-2050
McChord Air Force Base ... 253-982-2206
Whidbey Island Naval Air Station ... 360-257-2432

West Virginia (pg. 46-47)
Sugar Grove Naval Security Group Activity ... 304-249-6321

Wisconsin (pg. 68)
Fort McCoy ... 608-388-3213

Wyoming (pg. 102)
Francis E. Warren Air Force Base ... 307-773-2988

U.S. Possessions (pg. 126)

Puerto Rico
Fort Buchanan ... 787-707-7620

Wesier (A-8)

ILLINOIS (pg. 62)

Albion (G-8)
Aledo (C-3)
Alton (C,D-7)
Amboy (E-2)
Anna (E-10)
Arlington Heights (G-2)
Armstrong (G-5)
Ashkum (G-4)
Ashland (D-6)
Ashley (E-9)
Atlas (B-6)
Auburn (D-6)
Aurora (F-2)
Barrington (F-2)
Bartlett (F-2)
Batavia (F-2)
Beardstown (C-5)
Beecher City (F-7)
Belleville (D-8)
Belvidere (E-1)
Benton (E-9)
Biggsville (B,C-4)
Bloomfield (E-10)
Bloomington (E-5)
Blue Mound (E-6)
Bourbonnais (G-3)
Bowen (B-5)
Bradley (G-3)
Brooklyn (C-5)
Cahokia (C-8)
Cairo (E-11)
Camargo (F-6)
Camp Grove (D-3)
Canton (D-4)
Carbondale (E-10)
Carlinville (D-7)
Carlyle (E-8)
Carpentersville (F-2)
Carrollton (C-7)
Carthage (B-5)
Casey (G-7)
Centralia (E-8)
Centreville (D-8)
Champaign (F-5)
Charleston (F-6)
Chicago (F,G-1,2)
Chicago Heights (G-3)
Christopher (E-9)
Cicero (G-2)
Cisco (F-5)
Clinton (E-5)
Collinsville (D-8)
Columbia (C-8)
Crystal Lake (F-1)
Dallas City (B-4)
Danville (G-5)
Davis Junction (E-2)
De Kalb (F-2)
Decatur (E-6)
Deerfield (G-1)
Des Plaines (G-2)
Dixon (E-2)
Dixon Springs (F-10)
Duncan Mills (D-5)
Dwight (F-3)
East Moline (C-3)
East Peoria (D-4)
East St. Louis (D-8)
Edwardsville (D-8)
Effingham (F-7)
El Paso (E-4)
Elgin (F-2)
Enfield (F-9)
Evanston (G-2)
Fairfield (F-8)
Fairview Heights (D-8)
Farmington (D-4)
Flora (F-8)
Forrest (F-4)
Forreston (D-2)
Freeport (D-1)
Galesburg (C-4)
Galva (D-3)
Geneva (F-2)
Genoa (F-2)
Gibson City (F-5)
Gillespie (D-7)
Gilman (G-4)
Gordon (G-7)
Granite City (D-8)
Grant Park (G-3)
Granville (E-3)
Grayville (G-9)
Greenup (F-7)
Harrisburg (F-10)
Harvard (F-1)
Havana (D-5)
Hebron (F-1)
Herrin (E-10)
Heyworth (E-5)
Highland Park (G-1)
Hillsboro (D-7)
Hoopeston (G-5)
Hume (G-6)
Jacksonville (C-6)
Jerseyville (C-7)
Joliet (F,G-3)
Kampsville (C-7)
Kankakee (G-3,4)
Kansas (G-6)
Kewanee (D-3)
Kinderhook (B-6)
Knollwood (G-1)
La Moille (E-3)
Lake Bluff (G-1)
Lake Forest (G-1)
Lake Zurich (G-1)
Laura (D-4)
Lawrenceville (G-8)
Lewistown (D-5)
Libertyville (G-1)
Lincoln (E-5)
Litchfield (D-7)
Louisville (F-8)
Loves Park (E-1)
Machesney Park (E-1)
Macomb (C-5)
Marion (E-10)
Marshall (G-7)
Mascoutah (D-8)
Mason City (D-5)
Matteson (G-3)
Mattoon (F-6)
McHenry (F-1)
McLeansboro (F-9)
Mendota (E-3)
Metamora (E-4)
Metropolis (F-11)
Moline (C-3)
Monmouth (C-4)
Morris (F-3)
Morrison (D-2)
Morton (E-4)
Mounds (E-11)
Mount Carmel (G-8)
Mount Carroll (D-2)
Mount Prospect (G-2)
Mount Pulaski (E-5)
Mount Sterling (C-6)
Mount Vernon (E-9)
Mozier (C-7)
Mundelein (G-1)
Murphysboro (E-10)
Naperville (F-2)
Nashville (E-9)
Newton (F-7)
Normal (E-4)
Norris City (F-9)
North Chicago (G-1)
Oak Lawn (G-2)
Oak Park (G-2)
Ohio (E-3)
Olney (G-8)
Omaha (F-9)
Ottawa (E-3)
O'Fallon (D-8)
Pana (E-7)
Paris (G-6)
Park Forest (G-3)
Paxton (F-5)
Pekin (D-4)
Peoria (D-4)
Peru (E-3)
Pinckneyville (E-9)
Pittsfield (C-6)
Plainfield (F-3)
Pontiac (F-4)
Posey (E-8)
Quincy (B-6)
Rankin (G-5)
Rantoul (F-5)
Raymond (D-7)
Red Bud (D-9)
Richton Park (G-3)
Rochelle (E-2)
Rock Falls (D-2)
Rock Island (C-3)
Rockford (E-1)
Round Lake Beach (F-1)
Rushville (C-5)
Salem (E-8)
Sandoval (E-8)
Sauk Village (G-3)
Saunemin (F-4)
Schaumburg (F-2)
Serena (E-3)
Sheldon (G-4)
Skokie (G-2)
Sparta (D-9)
Springfield (D-6)
St. Augustine (C-4)
St. Charles (F-2)
St. Libory (D-8,9)
Sterling (D-2)
Stockton (D-1)
Streamwood (F-2)
Streator (E-4)
Summerfield (D-8)
Sycamore (F-2)
Taylorville (E-6)
Tilden (D-9)
Tremont (D-5)
Urbana (F-5)
Ursa (B-5)
Vandalia (E-7)
Vernon Hills (G-1)
Viola (C-3)
Virginia (C-6)
Washington (E-4)
Waterman (E-2)
Watseka (G-4)
Waukegan (G-1)
Waverly (D-6)
Wayne City (F-9)
Wenona (E-4)
West Chicago (F-2)
West Frankfort (E-9)
West Vienna (E-10)
Wheeling (G-1)
Williamsburg (F-6)
Willow Hill (G-7)
Wilton Center (G-3)
Windsor (F-7)
Woodford (E-4)
Woodhull (C-3)
Yorktown (D-3)
Yorkville (F-2)

Chicago (pg. 67)

Addison (B-4)
Alsip (F-8)
Arbury Hills (D-10)
Arlington Heights (B,C-1)
Bellwood (C,D-5)
Bensenville (C-4)
Berwyn (E-6)
Bloomingdale (A-4)
Blue Island (F-9)
Bridgeview (D,E-7)
Brookfield (D-6)
Burbank (E-7)
Calumet City (H-9)
Carol Stream (A-4)
Chicago Ridge (E-8)
Cicero (E-5)
Country Club Hills (F-10)
Crestwood (E-9)
Darien (B-7)
Des Plaines (C-2)
Dolton (G-9)
Downers Grove (B-6)
Elk Grove Village (B,C-3)
Elmhurst (C-5)
Elmwood Park (D,E-4)
Evanston (F-2)
Forest Park (D,E-5)
Franklin Park (D-4)
Glen Ellyn (A-5)
Glencoe (E-1)
Glendale Heights (A,B-4)
Glenview (E-2)
Glenwood (G-10)
Hanover Park (A-3)
Harvey (F,G-9)
Hastings (C-8)
Hazel Crest (F,G-10)
Hickory Hills (D-7)
Hinsdale (C-6)
Homewood (F,G-10)
Joliet (A-10)
Justice (D,E-7)
La Grange (D-6)
La Grange Park (D-6)
Lansing (H-10)
Lemont (B-8)
Lincolnwood (E,F-3)
Lisle (A-6)
Lockport (A,B-10)
Lombard (B-5)
Markham (F-10)
Maywood (D-5)
Melrose Park (D-5)
Midlothian (F-9)
Morton Grove (E-2)
Mount Prospect (C-2)
Naperville (A-7)
Niles (E-3)
Norridge (D,E-3,4)
Northbrook (D-1)
Northlake (C,D-4)
Oak Brook (B,C-6)
Oak Forest (E-9)
Oak Lawn (E,F-8)
Oak Park (E-5)
Orland Park (D-9)
Palatine (B-1)
Palos Heights (E-9)
Palos Hills (D-8)
Park Ridge (D-3)
Prospect Heights (C,D-2)
Pullman (G-8)
River Forest (D,E-5)
River Grove (D-4)
Riverdale (G-9)
Rolling Meadows (B-2)
Romeoville (A-9)
Roselle (A-3)
Schaumburg (A-2,3)
Schiller Park (D-4)
Skokie (F-2)
South Holland (G-10)
Stickney (E-6)
Summit (E-6)
Tinley Park (E-10)
Villa Park (B-5)
Westchester (C,D-5)
Western Springs (C,D-6)
Westmont (B-6)
Wheaton (A-5)
Wheeling (C-1)
Willobrook (C-7)
Wilmette (F-1,2)
Woodridge (A,B-7)
Worth (E-8)

INDIANA (pg. 63)

Aberdeen (G-8)
Akron (E-3)
Amity (E-7)
Anderson (F-5)
Angola (G-1)
Antioch (D-5)
Attica (C-5)
Bedford (D-8)
Beech Grove (E-6)
Bellmore (C-6)
Bennetts Switch (E-4)
Bloomington (D-7)
Bluffton (G-3)
Boonville (C-10)
Brazil (C-6)
Brookston (D-3,4)
Brookville (G-7)
Brownstown (E-8)
Burns City (D-8)
Cale (D-8)
Cannelburg (C-9)
Carlisle (C-8)
Carmel (E-5)
Clarksville (F-10)
Cloverdale (D-6)
Columbus (E,F-7)
Columbia City (F-2)
Connersville (G-6)
Crane (D-8)
Crawfordsville (D-5)
Cross Plains (G-8)
Crown Point (C-2)
Dale (C-10)
Decatur (G-3)
Deerfield (G-5)
Delphi (D-4)
Demotte (C-2)
Denver (E-3)
Doolittle Mills (D-10)
Dover Hill (D-9)
East Chicago (C-1)
Edinburgh (E-7)
Elkhart (E,F-1)
Elnora (C-8)
Elwood (F-5)
Enos (C-3)
Evansville (B-10,11)
Fairmount (F-4)
Fiat (G-4)
Fort Wayne (G-2,3)
Fountaintown (F-6)
Fowler (C-4)
Frankfort (D-4)
Freetown (E-8)
Gary (C-1)
Gnaw Bone (E-7)
Goshen (F-1)
Greencastle (D-6)
Greenfield (F-6)
Greensburg (F-7)
Greenwood (E-6)
Griffith (C-1)
Hammond (C-1)
Hartford City (G-4)
Hebron (C-2)
Highland (C-1)
Hobart (C-1)
Huntingburg (C-10)
Huntington (F-3)
Indian Springs (D-8)
Indianapolis (E-6)
Jasper (D-9)
Jeffersonville (C-9)
Kasson (B-10)
Kendallville (G-2)
Kentland (B,C-3)
Kirklin (E-5)
Knox (D-2)
Kokomo (E-4)
La Crosse (D-2)
La Porte (D-1)
Lafayette (D-4)
Lake Station (C-1)
Lapaz (E-2)
Larwill (F-2)
Lawrence (E-6)
Leases Corner (E-3)
Leavenworth (E-10)
Lebanon (D,E-5)
Ligonier (F-2)
Lizton (D-6)
Logansport (E-3)
Madison (G-8,9)
Marengo (D-10)
Marion (F-4)
Markle (G-3)
Martinsville (E-7)
McGrawsville (E-4)
Merriam (G-2)
Merrillville (C-2)
Miami (E-4)
Michigan City (D-1)
Middlefork (E-4)
Mishawaka (E-1)
Monon (D-3)
Monrovia (D-6)
Monticello (D-3)
Morton (D-6)
Mount Vernon (A-11)
Muncie (F,G-5)
Munster (C-1)
Nappanee (E-2)
New Albany (F-9)
New Castle (G-6)
New Waverly (E-3)
Nineveh (E-7)
Noblesville (E-5)
North Manchester (F-3)
North Vernon (F-8)
Oakford (E-4)
Oakland City (C-10)
Onward (E-4)
Owensburg (D-8)
Owensville (B-10)
Palmyra (E-9)
Parr (C-3)
Peru (E-3)
Pike (D-5)
Plainfield (E-6)
Plymouth (E-2)
Portage (C-1)
Prince's Lakes (E-7)
Princeton (B-9)
Rensselaer (C-3)
Richmond (H-6)
Rochester (E-3)
Rockville (C-6)
Rome (D-11)
Romney (D-5)
Rushville (F,G-6)
Salem (E-9)
Saline City (C-7)
Schererville (C-1)
Scotland (D-8)
Scottsburg (F-9)
Seymour (F-8)
Shelbyville (F-7)
Silverville (D-8)
South Bend (E-1)
South Center (D-1,2)
South Whitley (E-3)
Speedway (E-6)
Spencer (D-7)
St. Croix (D-10)
Switz City (C-8)
Taylorsville (F-7)
Tell City (D-10,11)
Terre Haute (C-7)
Tipton (E-5)
Trafalgar (E-7)
Trinity Springs (D-8)
Urbana (F-3)
Valparaiso (C-2)
Veedersburg (C-5)
Versailles (G-8)
Vincennes (B-9)
Wabash (F-3)
Warsaw (F-2)
Washington (C-9)
West Lafayette (D-4)
Winamac (D-3)
Winchester (G-5)
Wolcott (C-3)

Indianapolis (pg. 66)

Beech Grove (C-3)
Broadmoor (B-2)
Brownsburg (A-2)
Carmel (C-1)
Chapel Hill (B-2)
Edgewood (B-3)
Fairwood Hills (C-1)
Fishers (C-1)
Grandview (B-1)
Lawrence (C-2)
Meridian Hills (C-1)
Plainfield (A-3)
Speedway (B-2)
Southport (C-3)

IOWA (pg. 73)

Albia (G-7)
Algona (E-2)
Allison (G-3)
Ames (E,F-4,5)
Anamosa (I-4)
Ankeny (F-5)
Atlantic (C-6)
Auburn (C-4)
Audubon (C-5)
Avoca (C-6)
Bayard (D-5)
Bedford (D-8)
Bettendorf (K-6)
Bloomfield (G,H-7)
Boone (E-4)
Brighton (H-6)
Burlington (J-7)
Calmar (H-2)
Carroll (C-4)
Cascades (J-4)
Cedar Falls (G-3)
Cedar Rapids (I-4,5)
Chariton (F-7)
Charles City (G-2)
Cherokee (B-3)
Chester (H-1)
Clarinda (C-7)
Clarion (E-3)
Clear Lake (F-2)
Clinton (K-5)
Corydon (F-7)
Council Bluffs (B-6)
Creston (D-7)
Davenport (J,K-5,6)
De Soto (E-6)
De Witt (K-5)
Decorah (H-2)
Denison (C-5)
Des Moines (F-5,6)
Donnellson (I-8)
Dubuque (J-3,4)
Dunlap (B-5)
Dyersville (J-3,4)
Early (C-4)
Emerson (C-7)
Emmetsburg (D-2)
Estherville (D-1)
Fairfield (H-7)
Fort Dodge (E-3)
Fort Madison (I-8)
Fremont (G-6)
Garner (E-2)
Giard (I-2)
Glenwood (B-7)
Goldfield (E-3)
Grandview (I-6)
Greenfield (D-6)
Guthrie Center (D-5)
Hamburg (B-8)
Hampton (F-3)
Holstein (B-3)
Hubbard (F-4)
Hull (A,B-2)
Ida Grove (C-4)
Independence (H-3)
Indianola (F-6)
Inwood (A-2)
Iowa City (I-5)
Iowa Falls (F-3)
Johnston (E-5)
Keokuk (I-8)
Keosauqua (H-7)
Knoxville (F-6)
Lake Mills (F-1)
Lakota (E-2)
Larchwood (A-1)
Larrabee (B-3)
Le Mars (A-3)
Leon (E-7)
Lineville (F-8)
Lucas (F-7)
Luxemburg (J-3)
Lyman (C-6)
Manchester (I-4)
Mapleton (B-4)
Maquoketa (J-4)
Marion (I-4)
Marshalltown (G-4)
Mason City (F-2)
Milton (H-8)
Missouri Valley (B-5)
Montrose (I-8)
Mount Ayr (D,E-7)
Mount Vernon (I-5)
Mt. Pleasant (I-7)
Muscatine (J-6)
New Hampton (H-2)
New Sharon (G-6)
Newton (F-5)
Oakland (C-6)
Odebolt (C-4)
Oelwien (H-3)
Olds (I-6)
Orient (D-6)
Osage (G-2)
Osceola (E-7)
Oskaloosa (G-6)
Ottumwa (G,H-7)
Parkersburg (G-3)
Pocahontas (D-3)
Redding (D-8)
River Sioux (B-5)
Rock Rapids (A-1)
Rockwell City (D-4)
Sabula (K-4)
Sanborn (B-2)
Sergeant Bluff (A-4)
Sheldon (B-2)
Shenendoah (C-7)
Sibley (B-1)
Sidney (B-7)
Sigourney (H-6)
Sioux City (A-3,4)
Sioux Rapids (C-3)
Sloan (A-4)
Spencer (C-2)
Spirit Lake (C-1)
Storm Lake (C-3)
Templeton (C-5)
Thayer (E-7)
Toledo (G-5)
Traer (G-4)
Urbandale (E-5)
Vinton (H-4)
Washington (I-6)
Waterloo (G,H-3,4)
Waverly (G-3)
Webster City (E-4)
Wesley (E-2)
West Des Moines (E-6)
West Union (H-2)
Wheatland (J-5)
Winterset (E-6)

Des Moines (pg. 76)

Ankeny (C-1)
West Des Moines (B-2)
Urbandale (B-2)

KANSAS (pg. 74)

Abilene (G-4)
Alta Vista (H,I-4)
Altamont (J-7)
Anthony (F-7)
Arkansas City (H-7)
Arlington (F-6)
Atchison (J-3)
Athol (E-2)
Atwood (B-2)
Beagle (K-5)
Belleville (G-2)
Beloit (F-3)
Bennington (G-4)
Bird City (B-2)
Blue Rapids (H-2)
Bucklin (D-6)
Burden (H-7)
Burlington (J-5)
Caldwell (G-7)
Caney (I-7)
Cassoday (H-5)
Cedar Vale (H,I-7)
Chanute (J-6)
Chetopa (J-7)
Cimarron (C-6)
Claflin (F-4)
Clay Center (H-3)
Coffeyville (J-7)
Colby (B-3)
Coldwater (E-7)
Columbus (K-7)
Concordia (G-3)
Council Grove (I-4)
Derby (G-6)
Dighton (C-4)
Dodge City (D-6)
Downs (F-3)
Edmond (D-2)
El Dorado (H-6)
Ellis (D-4)
Emporia (I-5)
Englewood (D-7)
Ensign (C-6)
Eskridge (I-4)
Eureka (I-6)
Fairview (I,J-2)
Fort Scott (K-6)
Garden City (B-5)
Garfield (E-5)
Garnett (J-5)
Geneseo (F-4)
Glade (E-2)
Goodland (A-3)
Great Bend (E-5)
Greensburg (D-6)
Hardtner (E-7)
Harper (F-7)
Hays (E-4)
Healy (C-4)
Herington (H-4)
Hiawatha (J-2)
Hill City (D-3)
Hoisington (E-4)
Horton (J-2)
Hoxie (C-3)
Hugoton (B-7)
Hutchinson (F,G-5)
Independence (I-7)
Jetmore (D-5)
Jewell (F-2)
Johnson City (A-6)
Junction City (H-4)
Kalvesta (C-5)
Kansas City (K-3,4)
Keats (H-3)
Kingman (F-6)
Kinsley (D-6)
Kiowa (F-7)
La Crosse (E-4)
Lakin (B-5)
Lawrence (J-4)
Leavenworth (K-3)
Leawood (K-4)
Lebanon (F-2)
Lenexa (K-4)
Leoti (B-4)
Leoville (C-3)
Liberal (B-7)
Lincoln (F-4)
Lindsborg (G-4)
Linn (H-2)
Luray (F-3)
Lyons (F-5)
Madison (I-5)
Manhattan (H-3)
Marysville (H-2)
McCracken (D-4)
McPherson (G-5)
Meade (C-7)
Medicine Lodge (F-7)
Merriam (K-4)
Milan (G-7)
Minneola (D-6)
Moline (I-7)
Montrose (F-2)
Moran (J-6)
Ness City (D-5)
Newton (G-5)
Oakley (C-3)
Oberlin (C-2)
Ogden (H-3)
Olathe (K-4)
Osage City (I-4)
Osborne (F-3)
Oswego (J-7)
Ottawa (J-4)
Overland Park (K-4)
Paradise (E-3)
Park (C-3)
Parsons (J-7)
Peabody (H-5)
Pittsburg (K-6)
Plainville (E-3)
Pleasanton (K-5)
Portis (F-3)
Prairie Village (K-4)
Pratt (E-6)
Rago (F-6)
Randolph (H-3)
Ransom (D-4)
Richfield (A-7)
Rush Center (E-5)
Russell (E-4)
Salina (G-4)
Sawyer (E-6)
Scott City (B-4)
Sedan (I-7)
Seneca (I-2)
Severy (I-6)
Sharon Springs (A-4)
Shawnee (K-4)
Shields (C-4)
Sitka (D-7)
St. Francis (A-2)
St. John (E-5)
St. Marys (I-3)
Stark (J-6)
Stockton (E-3)
Sublette (B-6)
Syracuse (A-5)
Topeka (J-4)
Tribune (A-4)
Troy (J-2)
Ulysses (B-6)
Viola (G-6)
Washington (H-2)
Welda (J-5)
Wheaton (I-3)
Wheeler (A-2)
Wichita (G,H-6)
Winfield (H-7)
Woodruff (D-2)
Yates Center (J-6)

KENTUCKY (pg. 38-39)

Aberdeen (G,H-6)
Arlington (C-7)
Ashland (N-3)
Aurora (E-7)
Bardstown Junction (I-4)
Bardstown (I-5)
Bardwell (C-7)
Beattyville (L,M-5)
Beaumont (I-7)
Bedford (I,J-3)
Belmont (I-4,5)
Bennettstown (F-7)
Big Creek (M-6)
Bowling Green (H-7)
Bronston (K-6)
Cadiz (E-7)
Campbellsburg (J-3)
Campbellsville (J-6)
Caneyville (H-6)
Cannonsburg (N-3)
Canton (E-7)
Carr Creek (N-6)
Cartwright (J-7)
Cave City (I-6)
Cawood (N-7)
Central City (G-5)
Clifty (G-7)
Columbia (J-6)
Corbin (L-6,7)
Covington (K-2)
Cumberland (N-6)
Cynthiana (K-3)
Danville (K-5)
Eddyville (E-6)
Edmonton (I-6)
Elizabethtown (I-5)
Elk Creek (I-4)
Elkton (G-7)
Erlanger (K-2)
Flemingsburg (L-3)
Florence (K-2)
Fordsville (G-5)
Frankfort (J-4)
Franklin (H-7)
Freedom (J-7)
Fulton (C,D-8)
Georgetown (K-4)
Glasgow (I-6)
Graefenburg (J-4)
Grayson (N-3)
Guthrie (G-7)
Hardin (E-7)
Hardinsburg (H-5)
Harned (H-5)
Harrodsburg (J-5)
Hartford (G-5)
Hawesville (G-5)
Hazard (N-6)
Heidrick (L-7)
Henderson (F-5)
Hima (L,M-6)
Hodgenville (I-5)
Hopkinsville (F-7)
Horse Cave (I-6)
Hyden (M-6)
Index (M-4)
Irvine (L-5)
Irvington (H-4)
Island (G-6)
Jeffersontown (I-4)
Jenkins (O-6)
La Fayette (F-7)
Lake City (E-7)
Lawrenceburg (J-4)
Lebanon (J-5)
Lebanon Junction (I-5)
Leitchfield (H-5)
Lewisport (G-5)
Lexington (K-4)
Livingston (L-6)
London (L-6)
Lone Oak (D-7)
Long Ridge (J-3)
Long View (I-5)
Louisa (N,O-4)
Louisville (I-4)
Madisonville (F-6)
Marion (E-6)
Mayfield (D-7)
Maysville (L-3)
McKee (L-5)
Meta (O-5)
Middlesborough (M-7)
Monticello (K-7)
Morehead (M-4)
Morganfield (E-5)
Mortons Gap (F-6)
Mount Sterling (L-4)
Mount Vernon (K-6)
Munfordville (I-6)
Murray (D-7)
New Castle (J-3)
Newport (K-2)
Nicholasville (K-4)
Okolona (I-4)
Owensboro (G-5)
Owingsville (L-4)
Paducah (D-6)
Paintsville (N,O-4,5)
Paris (K-4)
Perryville (J-5)
Pine Knot (K-7)
Pineville (M-7)
Pleasure Ridge (I-4)
Prestonsburg (N-5)
Princeton (E-6)
Providence (E,F-6)
Quicksand (M-5)
Radcliff (I-5)
Richmond (K-5)
Roaring Spring (F-7)
Robinson Creek (O-5)
Russell Springs (J-6)
Russellville (G-7)
Salyersville (N-5)
Shelbyville (J-4)
Shepherdsville (I-4)
Shively (I-4)
Short Creek (H-5)
Smiths Grove (H-6)
Somerset (K-6)
South Williamson (O-5)
Springfield (J-5)
St. Matthews (I-4)
Stanford (K-5)
Sullivan (E-5)
Tinsley (M-7)
Tri City (D-7)
Valley Station (I-4)
Vancleve (M-5)
Washington (L-3)
Water Valley (D-7)
Watergap (N-5)
West Point (H-4)
West Liberty (M-4)
Whitesburg (N-6)
Williamsburg (L-7)
Williamstown (K-3)
Winchester (L-4)

Lexington (pg. 39)

Lexington (O-1,2)

Louisville (pg. 39)

Ballardsville (P-9)
Belmont (O-11)
Clarksville (O-10)
Crestwood (P-10)
Douglas Hills (O,P-10)
Highview (O-10)
Hillview (O-10)
Jeffersontown (O,P-10)
Jeffersonville (O-10)
La Grange (P-9)
Lebanon Junction (O-11)
New Albany (O-10)
Okolona (O-10)
Pleasure Ridge Park (N-10)
Prospect (O-9)
Radcliff (N-11)
Shepardsville (O-11)
Shivley (O-10)
St. Matthews (O-10)
Valley Station (N-10)
West Point (N-11)

LOUISIANA (pg. 75)

Abbeville (D-7)
Alexandria (C-4)
Amelia (E-7)
Amite (F-5)
Anacoco (B-4)
Anandale (C-4)
Archibald (D-2)
Baker (E-5)
Bastrop (D-1)
Baton Rouge (E-5,6)
Bayou Cane (F-7)
Benton (A-1)
Bienville (B-2)
Bogalusa (G-5)
Bohemia (H-7)
Boothville (H-8)
Bossier City (A-2)
Boyce (C-4)
Bunkie (D-5)
Bush (G-5)
Cameron (B-7)
Campti (B-3)
Chambers (C-4)
Chatham (C-2)
Clayton (E-3)
Clinton (E-5)
Cocodrie (F-8)
Columbia (D-2)
Cooper Road (A-2)
Coushatta (B-3)
Covington (G-5)
Cravens (B-5)
Creole (B-7)
Crowley (C-6)
De Quincy (B-6)
De Ridder (B-5)
Delhi (E-2)
Denham Springs (F-6)
Donaldsonville (E-6)
Doyline (B-2)
Dry Prong (C-3)
Elizabeth (C-5)
Elton (C-6)
Empire (H-8)
Epps (E-2)
Eunice (C-6)
Farmerville (C-1)
Ferriday (E-3)
Fillmore (A-2)
Franklin (E-7)
Franklinton (G-5)
Friendship (B-2)
Fullerton (B-5)
Gardner (C-4)
Gilbert (D-3)
Gonzales (F-6)
Good Pine (D-3)
Grangeville (F-5)
Greensburg (F-5)
Gretna (G-7)
Gueydan (C-6)
Hammond (F-5)
Harahan (G-7)
Harrisonburg (D-3)
Haughton (A-2)
Hayes (B-6)
Hicks (B-4)
Holly Beach (B-7)
Holmwood (B-6)
Homer (B-1)
Hornbeck (B-4)
Hosston (A-1)
Hot Wells (C-4)
Houma (F-7)
Jena (D-3)
Jennings (C-6)
Jonesboro (C-2)
Junction City (C-1)
Kenner (G-6)
Kentwood (F-5)
Kinder (C-6)
Kisatchie (B-4)
Lacamp (B-4)
Lafayette (D-6)
Lake Arthur (C-6)
Lake Charles (B-6)
Lake Providence (E-1)
Larose (G-7)
Lebeau (D-5)
Leesville (B-4)
Leeville (G-8)
Lucas (A-2)
Mansfield (A-3)
Many (B-3,4)
Marion (C-1)
Marksville (D-4)
Marrero (G-7)
McManus (E-5)
Melville (D-5)
Mer Rouge (D-1)
Metairie (G-6)
Minden (B-2)
Monroe (D-2)
Montgomery (B-3)
Montpelier (F-5)
Mooringsport (A-1)
Morgan City (E-7)
Mound (E-2)
Natchitoches (B-3)
Negreet (A-4)
New Iberia (D-6)
New Llano (B-4)
New Orleans (G-6,7)
Newellton (E-3)
Oak Grove (E-1)
Oakdale (C-5)
Oberlin (C-5)
Olla (C-3)
Opelousas (D-5)
Pecan Island (C-7)
Pineville (C-4)
Plain Dealing (A-1)
Plaquemine (E-6)
Plattenville (E-6,7)
Pleasant Hill (A-3)
Pollock (C-4)
Port Allen (E-6)
Princeton (A-2)
Ragley (B-6)
Rapides (C-4)
Rayville (D-2)
Reeves (B-5)
Ringgold (B-2)
Ruston (C-2)
Sandy Hill (B-4,5)
Sarepta (B-1)
Scotlandville (E-5)
Shreveport (A-2)
Sicily Island (D-3)
Sikes (C-2,3)
Simmesport (D-5)
Simmsboro (CColo-2)
Singer (B-5)
Slidell (G-6)
Sorrento (F-6)
St. Francisville (E-5)
St. Martinville (D-6)
Starks (A-6)
Sterlington (D-1)
Sugartown (B-5)
Sulphur (B-6)
Summerfield (C-1)
Sun (G-5)
Tallulah (E-2)
Taylortown (A-2)
Thibodaux (F-7)
Toro (A-4)
Tullos (C-3)
Turkey Creek (C-5)
Vidalia (E-3)
Ville Platte (C-5)
Vivian (A-1)
West Monroe (D-2)
Westwego (G-7)
Winnfield (C-3)
Winnsboro (D-2)
Zwolle (A-3)

Baton Rouge (pg. 75)

Baton Rouge (J-7)
Port Allen (I-7,8)
Scotlandville (I-7)

New Orleans (pg. 75)

Airline Park (G-2)
Arabi (J-3)
Avondale (G,H-3)
Belle Chasse (J-4)
Bonnebel Place (H-2)
Braithwaite (K-4)
Bridge City (H-3)
Chalmette (K-3)
Cutoff (J-3)
East Bank (G-2)
English Turn (K-4)
Estelle (I-4)
Fort St. Leon (J-4)
Gretna (I,J-3)
Harahan (G-3)
Harvey (I-3)
Jefferson Heights (H-3)
Kenner (G-1,2)
Live Oak Manor (G-2,3)
Marrero (H,I-3,4)
Meraux (K-3)
Metairie (H-2)
River Ridge (G-2)
Scarsdale (K-4)
Southport (H-2)
St. Clair (K-4)
Terrytown (J-3)
Vieux Carre (I-2)
Waggaman (G-3)
Walkertown (H,I-4)
Westgate (G-2)
Westwego (H-3)
Wills Wood (G-3)

MAINE (pg. 16)

Abbot Village (D-6)
Amherst (F-7)
Ashland (F-3)
Auburn (B-9)
Augusta (C-8)
Aurora (F-7)
Bangor (E-7)
Bar Harbor (F-8)
Baring (G-6)
Bath (C-9)
Belfast (E-8)
Bethel (A-8)
Biddeford (B-10)
Bingham (C-6)
Blue Hill Falls (E-8)
Brewer (E-7)
Bridgewater (F,G-3)
Bridgton (B-9)
Brunswick (C-9)
Camden (D-8,9)
Caribou (F-2)
Cherryfield (F-8)
Christmas Cove (D-9)
Clifton (E-7)
Corea (F-8)
Cornish (A-9)
Crawford (G-6)
Cutler (H-7)
Danforth (G-5)
Dickey (D-1,2)
Dover-Foxcroft (D-6)
East Holden (E-7)
East Machias (G-7)
East Waterboro (B-10)
Eddington (E-7)
Ellsworth (F-8)
Farmington (C-7)
Fort Kent (E-1)
Freeport (C-9)
Friendship (D-9)
Fryeburg (A-9)
Gardiner (C-8)
Georgetown (C-9)
Gouldsboro (F-8)
Hallowell (C-8)
Haynesville (F-5)
Houlton (G-4)
Jackman (B-5)
Jacksonville (G-7)
Jonesport (G-8)
Kennebunkport (B-11)
Kingfield (C-7)
Kittery (A-11)
Knowles Corners (F-4)
Lewiston (B-9)
Limerick (A-10)
Limestone (G-2)
Lincoln (E-6)
Lisbon Falls (C-9)
Machias (G-7)
Machiesport (G-7)
Macwahoc (F-5)
Madawaska (F-1)
Mariaville (F-7)
Medway (E-5)
Millinocket (E-5)
Milo (E-6)
New Sweden (F-2)
Newport (D-7)
Newry (A-8)
North Haven (E-9)
North Turner (B-8)
Oakfield (F-4)
Ocean Point (C,D-9)
Old Town (E-7)
Oqunquit (B-11)
Oquossoc (A-7)
Orland (E-8)
Orono (E-7)
Patten (E,F-4)
Pemaquid Point (D-9)
Phillips (B-7)
Port Clyde (D-9)
Portland (B-10)
Presque Isle (F-3)
Prospect Harbor (F-8)
Rockland (D-9)
Rockwood (C-5)
Roque Bluffs (G-7)
Rumford (B-8)
Saco (B-10)
Sanford (A-10)
Sherman (F-4)
Skowhegan (C-7)
Smyrna Mills (F-4)
Solon (C-7)
South Paris (B-8)
South Portland (B-10)
Springfield (F-6)
Starboard (G-7)
Stockton Springs (E-8)
Stonington (E-9)
Stratton (B-6)
Topsfield (G-6)
Topsham (C-9)
Unity (D-7)
Van Buren (F-1)
Vinalhaven (E-9)
Waldoboro (D-9)
Waterville (E-8)
Wesley (G-7)
West Enfield (E-6)
West Newfield (A-10)
Westbrook (B-10)
Wilton (B-7)
Winter Harbor (F-8)
Winthrop (C-8)
Wiscasset (C-9)
Woolwich (C-9)
York Beach (B-11)

MARYLAND (pg. 40)

Aberdeen (H-2)
Aikin (H-2)
Allens Fresh (F-6)
Andersontown (I-5)
Annapolis (G-4)
Arnold (G-4)
Ashton (F-3)
Baltimore (F,G-2,3)
Beaver Dam (J-7)
Bel Air (G-2)
Beltsville (F-4)
Benedict (F-6)
Benson (G-2)
Berlin (J-6)
Bethesda (E-4)
Black Horse (G-2)
Bloomington (B-3)
Boonsboro (D-2)
Bowie (F-4)
Braddock Heights (D-2)
Bridgetown (I-4)
Bryans Road (E-5)
Burtonsville (F-4)
Bush River (H-2)
Butler (F-2)
California (G-6)
Cambridge (H-5)
Cascade (D-1)
Catonsville (F-3)
Cavetown (D-1)
Centreville (H-4)
Ceresville (E-2)
Chaptico (F-6)
Chesapeake Beach (G-5)
Chesapeake City (I-2)
Chestertown (H-3)
Chewsville (D-1)
Church Creek (H-6)
Church Hill (H-3)
Churchville (H-2)
Claiborne (H-4)
Clarksville (F-3)
Clear Spring (C-1)
Clinton (F-5)
Cockeysville (G-2)
College Park (F-4)
Columbia (F-3)
Conowingo (H-1)
Cooksville (F-3)
Cranberry (F-2)
Crisfield (I-7)
Cumberland (A-1)
Damascus (E-3)
Dawsonville (E-3)
Denton (I-4)
Doncaster (E-6)
Drum Point (G-6)
Dublin (H-1)
Dundalk (G-3)
Easton (H-5)
Eden (I-6)
Edgewood (H-2)
Eldersburg (F-3)
Elkton (I-2)
Emmitsburg (E-1)
Essex (G-3)
Etchison (E-3)
Fair Hill (I-1)
Federalsburg (I-5)
Fenby (F-2)
Forestville (F-4)
Frederick (D-2)
Friendsville (A-3)
Frostburg (B-3)
Fruitland (I-6)
Gaithersburg (E-3)
Galena (I-3)
Glen Burnie (G-3)
Goldsboro (I-4)
Gorman (A-4)
Great Mills (G-7)
Greenbelt (F-4)
Hagerstown (D-1)
Halethorpe (F-3)
Hall (F-4)
Hancock (B-1)
Helen (F-6)
Hampstead (F-2)
Hereford (G-2)
Hermanville (G-7)
Hillcrest Heights (F-4)
Honga (H-6)
Hudson (H-5)
Hughesville (F-5,6)
Hyattstown (E-3)
Hyattsville (F-4)
Indian Head (E-5)
Indian Springs (C-1)
Jones (K-6)
Joppatowne (G-2)
Keysers Ridge (B-3)
Kitzmiller (B-4)
Lakesville (H-6)
LaPlata (F-5)
Lappans (D-2)
Largo (F-4)
Laurel (F-3)
Leonardtown (G-6)
Lewistown (D-2)
Libertytown (E-2)
Lutherville (G-2)
Lyons Creek (G-5)
Madison (H-6)
Magnolia (G-2)
Manchester (F-1)
Marbury (E-5)
Mardela Springs (I-6)
Marshall Hall (E-5)
Mason Springs (E-5)
McCoole (B-3)
McDaniel (H-4)
McHenry (A-3)
Mexico (F-2)
Middle River (G-3)
Millersville (G-4)
Millington (I-3)
Monrovia (E-2)
Montgomery Village (E-3)
Mount Airy (E-2)
Nanticoke (H-6)
New Carrollton (F-4)
Newcomb (H-5)
Norrisville (G-1)
Oakland (A-4)
Ocean City (K-6)
Oldtown (A-2)
Olney (E-3)
Overlea (G-2)
Owings (G-5)
Park Hall (G-7)
Parkville (G-2)
Pen Mar (D-1)
Perry Hall (G-2)
Perryman (H-2)
Pikesville (F-2)
Pittsville (J-6)
Pocomoke City (J-7)
Point Lookout (G-7)
Point of Rocks (D-3)
Pomonkey (E-5)
Potomac Heights (E-5)
Pratt (A-1)
Prince Fredrick (G-5)
Princess Anne (I-7)
Queenstown (H-4)
Randallstown (F-2)
Redhouse (A-4)
Reisterstown (F-2)
Ridge (G-7)
Rison (E-5)
Riverside (E-6)
Rock Hall (H-3)
Rockville (E-3)
Salisbury (I,J-6)
Savage (F-3)
Severn (F-3)
Severna Park (G-3)
Sharpsburg (D-2)
Sharptown (I-5)
Silver Spring (F-4)
Snow Hill (J-7)
Solomons (G-6)
Spring Gap (A-2)
St. Charles (F-5)
St. Martin (J-6)
St. Marys City (G-7)
Sudlersville (I-3)
Suitland (F-4)
Sunderland (G-5)
Sunshine (E-3)
Sykesville (F-2)
Taneytown (E-1)
Taylors Island (H-6)
Taylorsville (E-2)
Thayerville (A-3)
Thurmont (E-2)
Tilghman (G-5)
Timonium (G-2)
Town Creek (G-6)
Towson (G-2)
Tuscarora (D-3)
Unicorn (I-3)
Upper Marlboro (F-4)
Vale Summit (B-3)
Vienna (I-6)
Waldorf (F-5)
Warwick (I-2)
Waterloo (F-3)
Waterview (I-6)
Wenona (H,I-7)
West Friendship (F-3)
Westernport (B-3)
Westminster (F-2)
Westover (I-7)
Weverton (D-3)
Wheaton (E-4)
White Plains (F-5)
Willards (J-6)
Williamsport (C-2)
Woodsboro (E-2)
Wye Mills (H-4)
Yellow Springs (D-2)

Annapolis (pg. 40)

Bestgate (A-6)
Bywater Estates (A-7,8)
Carrs Manor (C-8)
Dorsey Heights (A-7)
Forest Villa (B-7)
Greenbriar Gardens (B-7)
Harness Creek Park (B-8)
Harness Woods (C-8)
Heritage (B-7)
Lincoln Heights (A-6)
Lindamoor on the Severn (B-6)
Loretta Heights (A-6)
Parole (A-6,7)
Pendennis Mount (C-6)
Truxton Heights (B-7)
Victor Haven (C-8)
Wardour Bluffs (C-6)
Weens Creek (B-6)

Baltimore (pg. 44)

Arbutus (A-4)
Brooklyn (B,C-4)
Carney (C-2)
Catonsville (A-3)
Dundalk (C-3)
Essex (D-3)
Ferndale (B-4)
Glen Burnie (B-5)
Halethorpe (A,B-4)
Harundale (B-5)
Lansdowne (B-4)
Linthicum (B-4)
Lutherville (B-1)
Middle River (D-2)
Overlea (C-2)
Parkville (C-2)
Pikesville (A-2)
Pumphrey (B-4)
Riviera Beach (C-5)
Timonium (B-1)
Towson (B-1)
Woodlawn (A-2)

MASSACHUSETTS (pg. 14-15)

Abington (L-5)
Acton (J-3)
Adams (D-2)
Amherst (F-3)
Andover (K-2)
Arlington (K-3)
Attleboro (J-5)
Auburn (H-4)
Ayer (I-2)
Barnstable (N-7)
Barre (G,H-3)
Bedford (J-3)
Belchertown (F-4)
Bellingham (J-5)
Belmont (K-3)
Beverly (L-2)
Boston (K-3,4)
Braintree (K-4)
Bridgewater (L-5)
Brockton (K,L-5)
Brookline (K-4)
Burlington (K-3)
Cambridge (K-3)
Cedarville (M-6)
Charlemont (D,E-2)
Chelmsford (J-2)
Chelsea (K-3)
Cherry Valley (H-4)
Chicopee (F-4,5)
Clinton (I-3)
Cochesett (K-5)
Cohasset (L-4)
Concord (J-3)
Cummington (D-3)
Dalton (C-3)
Danvers (L-2)
Dedham (K-4)
Douglas (I-5)
East Hampton (E-4)
East Longmeadow (F-5)
East Princeton (H-3)
Everett (K-3)
Fairhaven (L-7)
Fall River (K-7)
Fitchburg (H-2)
Forestdale (M-7)
Foxboro (K-5)
Framingham (J-4)
Franklin (J-5)
Gardner (H-2)
Georgetown (K-2)
Gloucester (M-2)
Goshen (E-3)
Grafton (I-4)
Great Barrington (C-4)
Green Harbor (M-5)
Greenbush (L-4)
Greenfield (F-2)
Groton (I-2)
Halifax (L-5)
Hartsville (C-4)
Harvard (I-3)
Hatchville (M-7)
Hathorne (K-2)
Haverhill (K-1)
Holbrook (K-4)
Holliston (J-4)
Holyoke (E,F-4)
Humarock (M-4)
Huntington (E-4)
Hyannis (N-7)
Ipswich (L-2)
Island Creek (M-5)
Kingston (L-5)
Lancaster (I-3)
Lawrence (K-2)
Leominster (I-3)
Lexington (K-3)
Littleton Common (J-2)
Longmeadow (F-5)
Lowell (J-2)
Ludlow (F-4)
Lunenburg (I-2)
Lynn (L-3)
Malden (K-3)
Mansfield (K-5)
Marblehead (L-3)
Marlborough (I-3)
Marshfield (M-5)
Mashpee (M,N-7)
Medfield (J-4)
Medford (K-3)
Melrose (K-3)
Merrimac (K-1)
Middleboro (L-6)
Milford (I,J-4,5)
Millbury (I-4)
Millers Falls (F-2)
Milton (K-4)
Nantucket (O-9)
Natick (J-4)
Needham (K-4)
New Bedford (L-7)
New Boston (D-5)
Newburyport (L-1)
Newton (J,K-3)
North Adams (D-2)
North Amherst (F-3)
North Attleboro (J-5)
North Carver (L-5,6)
North Dartmouth (L-7)
North Hanover (L-4,5)
North Lexington (K-3)
North Oxford (H-4)
Northampton (E,F-4)
Northfield (F-2)
Norwood (K-4)
Oak Bluffs (M-8)
Orange (G-2)
Orleans (O-6)
Otis (D-4)
Palmer (G-4)
Paxton (H-4)
Peabody (L-2)
Phillipston Four Corners (G-2)
Pittsfield (C-3)
Plymouth (M-5)
Princeton (H-3)
Provincetown (O-5)
Quincy (K-4)
Randolph (K-4)
Reading (K-2,3)
Rehoboth (J,K-6)
Revere (K-3)
Rockland (L-4)
Rockport (M-2)
Rowley (L-2)
Sagamore (M-6)
Salem (L-3)
Salisbury Beach (L-1)
Saugus (K-3)
Savoy (D-2)
Shelburne Falls (E-2)
Shrewsbury (I-4)
Somerville (K-3)
South Dartmouth (L-7)
South Deerfield (F-3)
South Egremont (C-4)
South Hadley Falls (F-4)
South Hadley (F-4)
South Hingham (L-4)
South Yarmouth (O-7)
Southbridge (H-5)
Southwick (E-5)
Spencer (H-4)
Springfield (F-5)
Still River (I-3)
Stoneham (K-3)
Stoughton (K-5)
Stow (I-3)
Sturbridge (H-5)
Swampscott (L-3)
Taunton (K-6)
Townsend (I-2)
Truro (O-5)
Uxbridge (I-5)
Vineyard Haven (M-8)
Wakeby (M,N-7)
Wakefield (K-3)
Waltham (J-3)
Ware (G-4)
Wareham (L,M-6)
Watertown (K-3)
Wayland (J-3)
Webster (H-5)
Wellesley (J-4)
Wellfleet (O-5)
West Gloucester (L-2)
West Medway (J-4)
West Orange (G-2)
West Springfield (E,F-5)
Westborough (I-4)
Westfield (E-5)
Weymouth (L-4)
Williamstown (C-2)
Wilmington (K-2,3)
Winchendon (H-2)
Winchester (K-3)
Windsor (D-3)
Winthrop (K-3)
Woburn (K-3)
Woods Hole (M-7)
Worcester (H,I-4)

Boston (pg. 22)

Aberdeen (D-5)
Arlington (C-3)
Ashmont (E-7)
Auburndale (A,B-5)
Bedford (A-1)
Belmont (C-4)
Blue Hills (D-8)
Braintree (F,G-9)
Brookline (C,D-6)
Burlington (B-1)
Cambridge (D,E-5)
Canton (C,D-10)
Chelsea (F-4)
Chestnut Hill (C-6)
Dedham (C-8)
East Boston (F-4)
East Lexington (B,C-3)
Everett (E,F-3,4)
Forest Hills (D-7)
Greenlodge (C,D-8)
Grove Hall (E-6)
Highland (C-7)
Holbrook (F,G-10)
Hull (H-6)
Jamaica Plain (D-6)
Lexington (B-2)
Lincoln (A-3)
Lower Mills (E-7)
Lynn (G,H-2)
Malden (E-3)
Medford (E-3)
Medford Hillside (D-3)
Melrose (E-2)
Melrose Highlands (E-2)
Milton (E-8)
Milton Center (D,E-7)
Nahant (H-3)
Needham (A,B-7)
Needham Heights (B-6,7)
Neponset (E,F-7)
Newton (B,C-5)
North Lexington (B-2)
North Weymouth (G,H-8)
Norwood (B-9)
Peabody (H-1)
Piety Corner (B-4)
Point of Pines (G-3)
Quincy (F-7)
Randolph (F-10)
Reading (D-1)
Revere (F-3)
Roxbury (D,E-6)
Saugus (F-2)
Shakerhill (C-2)
Somerville (E-4)
South Boston (E,F-5)
South Quincy (F-8)
Stoneham (E-2)
Swampscott (H-2)
Uphams Corner (E-6)
Wakefield (E-1)
Walpole (A-10)
Waltham (B-4)
Watertown (C,D-5)
Wellesley (A-6)
Weston (A-4,5)
Westwood (B-8)
Weymouth (G-9,10)
Winchester (C,D-2)
Winchester Highlands (D-2)
Winthrop (G-4)
Woburn (C-1)

MICHIGAN (pg. 64)

Acme (C-5)
Adrian (E-11)
Agnew (B-9)
Alanson (D-4)
Albion (D-10)
Alger (E-6)
Allegan (C-10)
Alma (E-8)
Alpena (F-5)
Ann Arbor (F-10)
Arthur (F-8)
Atlanta (E-5)
Au Sable (F-6)
Austin (C-2)
Bad Axe (G-7)
Baldwin (C-7)
Battle Creek (D-10)
Bay City (F-7,8)
Bay Port (F-7)
Belding (D-8,9)
Bendon (C-5)
Benton Harbor (B-10)
Benzonia (C-6)
Bessemer (A-2)
Beulah (C-6)
Big Rapids (C-7)
Bruce Crossing (A-2)
Burnside (G-8)
Burton (F-9)
Cadillac (C,D-6)
Carlshend (C-2)
Caro (F-8)
Carrollton (F-8)
Casnovia (C-8)
Cedar (C-5)
Charlevoix (D-4)
Charlotte (D-9)
Cheboygan (E-4)
Chelsea (E-10)
Chesaning (E-8)
Chesterfield (G-9)
Clare (D-7)
Clarkston (F-9)
Clinton (E,F-10)
Clio (F-8)
Coldwater (D-11)
Comstock Park (C-9)
Cooper Harbor (B-1)
Corinne (D-2)
Corunna (E-9)
Crystal Falls (B-2)
Curran (F-5)
Davison (F-9)
Dearborn (G-10)
Detroit (F,G-9,10)
Drayton Plains (F-9)
Drummond (E-2)
Dukes (C-2)
Dundee (F-11)
Eagle River (B-1)
East Grand Rapids (C-9)
East Jordan (D-5)
East Lansing (E-9)
Elberta (B-6)
Elmer (G-8)
Emmett (G-9)
Escanaba (C-2)
Fairview (E-5)
Ferrysburg (B-8)
Flint (F-8,9)
Flushing (F-9)
Frankfort (B-5)
Fruitport (B-8)
Gaylord (E-5)
Gladwin (E-7)
Grand Haven (B-9)
Grand Rapids (C-9)
Grawn (C-5)
Grayling (D-5,6)
Greenville (D-8)
Hale (F-6)
Harbor Beach (G-7)
Harrison (D-7)
Harrisville (F-5)
Hastings (D-9)
Hillsdale (E-11)
Holland (B-9)
Holt (E-9)
Homer (D-10)
Honor (C-5)
Houghton (B-1)
Howell (F-9)
Hubbell (B-1)
Imlay City (G-9)
Ionia (D-9)
Iron Mountain (B-2)
Ithaca (E-8)
Jackson (E-10)
Jones (C-11)
Jonesville (D,E-11)
Kalamazoo (C-10)
Kalkaska (D-5)
Lachine (F-5)
Lake Ann (C-5)
Lake City (D-6)
Lake Linden (B-1)
Lakeview (D-8)
Lansing (E-9)
Lapeer (F-8)
Levering (D-4)
Lexington (G-8)
Little Lake (C-2)
Lowell (D-9)
Ludington (B-7)
L'Anse (B-1)
Mackinaw City (E-3)
Mancelona (D-5)
Manistee (B-6)
Manistique (D-2)
Manton (D-6)
Maple City (C-5)
Marlette (G-8)
Marquette (C-2)
Marysville (H-8)
Mason (E-9)
Menominee (C-3)
Mesick (C-6)
Midland (E-7)
Mio (E-5)
Monroe (F-11)
Mottville (C-11)
Mount Pleasant (D-8)
Munising (C-2)
Muskegon (B-8)
Muskegon Heights (B-8)
New Buffalo (A-11)
New Era (B-8)
Newberry (D-2)
Newport (F-11)
Niles (B-11)
Northport (C-5)
Norton Shores (B-8)
Onaway (E-4)
Ontonagon (A-1)
Oscoda (F-6)
Otisville (F-8)
Owosso (E-9)
Parkdale (B-6)
Paw Paw (C-10)
Peck (G-8)
Petoskey (D-4)
Pontiac (F-9)
Port Austin (G-7)
Port Huron (G,H-9)
Port Sanilac (G-8)
Portage (C-10)
Prudenville (E-6)
Reed City (C-7)
Remus (D-7)
Richland (C-10)
Richville (F-8)
Rogers City (F-4)
Roseville (G-10)
Royal Oak (G-10)
Saginaw (E,F-8)
Sandusky (G-8)
Sault Ste. Marie (E-2)
Scottdale (B-10)
Scottville (B-7)
Seney (D-2)
Silver City (A-1)
Six Lakes (D-7)
Skandia (C-2)
Somerset (E-10)
South Haven (B-10)
Southfield (F-9)
Spring Lake (C-8)
St. Clair Shores (G-10)
St. Ignace (D-2)
St. Johns (E-9)
St. Joseph (B-10)
St. Louis (E-8)
Standish (E,F-7)
Sterling Heights (G-9)
Sturgis (C,D-11)
Swartz Creek (F-9)
Tawas City (F-6)
Tecumseh (E,F-11)
Tekonsha (D-10)
Three Rivers (C-11)
Traverse City (C-5)
Trout Lake (D-2)
Walker (C-9)
Watersmeet (A-2)
Webberville (E-9)
West Branch (E-6)
White Cloud (C-8)
Woodbury (D-9)
Ypsilanti (F-10)

Detroit (pg. 68)

Allen Park (D-5)
Auburn Hills (C,D-1)
Belleville (A-6)
Berkley (D-2)
Beverly Hills (C-2)
Birmingham (C-2)
Center Line (E-2,3)
Clawson (D-2)
Dearborn (D-4)
Dearborn Heights (C-4)
East Detroit (F-3)
Ecorse (D-5)
Farmington (B-3)
Farmington Hills (B-2)
Ferndale (D,E-3)
Fraser (F-2)
Garden City (B-4)
Grosse Point Farms (F-3,4)
Grosse Pointe Park (F-4)
Grosse Pointe Woods (F,G-3)
Grosse Pointe (F-4)
Hamtramck (E-3,4)
Harper Woods (F-3)
Hazel Park (E-3)
Highland Park (D,E-3)
Inkster (B,C-5)
Lincoln Park (D-5)
Livonia (B-3)
Madison Heights (D,E-2)
Melvindale (D-5)
Mount Clemens (F,G-1)
Northville (A-3)
Novi (A-3)
Oak Park (D-3)
Orchard Lake Village (B-1)
Plymouth (A-4)
Pontiac (C-1)
Redford (B,C-3,4)
River Rouge (D-5)
Rochester Hills (D-1)
Romulus (B-5)
Roseville (F-2)
Royal Oak (D-2)
Southfield (C-3)
Southgate (C,D-6)
St. Clair Shores (F,G-2)
Sterling Heights (E,F-1)
Taylor (C-6)
Troy (D-1)
Union Lake (A-1)
Utica (E-1)
Warren (E-3)
Wayne (B-5)
Westland (B-4)
Windsor (E,F-4,5)
Wyandotte (D-6)

MINNESOTA (pg. 76)

Ada (A-6)
Aitkin (D-7)
Akeley (C-6)
Albert Lea (E-11)
Andover (E-9)
Anoka (D-9)
Apple Valley (E-9)
Austin (E-11)
Bemidji (B-5)
Benson (B-8)
Big Falls (D-4)
Blaine (E-9)
Bloomington (E-9)
Blue Earth (D-11)
Brainerd (D-7)
Branch (E-8)
Breckenridge (A-7)
Brownton (D-9)
Burnsville (E-9)
Cass Lake (C-6)
Cloquet (E-6)
Cook (E-5)
Coon Rapids (E-9)
Cottage Grove (E-9)
Crookston (A-5)
Crosby (D-7)
Dakota (G-10)
Deer River (D-6)
Detroit Lakes (B-6)
Donaldson (A-4)
Doran (A-7)
Duluth (F-6)
Eden Prairie (D-9)
Elk River (D-8)
Ely (F-5)
Fairmont (C-11)
Faribault (E-10)
Fergus Falls (B-7)
Floodwood (E-6)
Forest Lake (E-8)
Fosston (B-5)
Garrison (D-7)
Graceville (A-8)
Grand Falls (D-4)
Grand Marais (G-5)
Grand Rapids (D-6)
Granite Falls (B-9)
Hader (E-10)
Hassman (D-7)
Hastings (E-9)
Heiberg (B-6)
Hibbing (E-5,6)
Hill City (D-6)
Hokah (G-11)
Hutchinson (C,D-9)
Illgen City (G-6)
International Falls (D-4)
Inver Grove Heights (E-9)
Jackson (C-11)
Karlstad (A-4)
Kasson (E-10)
Lake Benton (B-10)
Lake City (F-10)
Lakeville (E-9)
Little Falls (D-8)
Luverne (B-11)
Madelia (C-10)
Mahnomen (B-6)
Mankato (D-10)
Maple Grove (D-9)
Maplewood (E-9)
Marcoux (B-5)
Marion (F-10)
Marshall (B-10)
McGrath (E-7)
Milaca (D-8)
Minneapolis (D,E-9)
Minnetonka (D-9)
Montevideo (B-9)
Moorhead (A-6)
Moose Lake (E-7)
Mora (E-8)
Morris (B-8)
Motley (C-7)
Mounds View (E-9)
New Ulm (C-10)
Northfield (E-10)
Northome (D-5)
Olivia (C-9)
Ortonville (A-8)
Owatonna (E-10)
Park Rapids (C-6)
Pelland (D-4)
Peyla (E-5)
Pine City (E-8)
Pipestone (A,B-10)
Pliny (E-7)
Plymouth (D-9)
Preston (F-11)
Princeton (D-8)
Ramsey (D-8)
Red Wing (E-9)
Remer (D-6)
Richfield (E-9)
Rochester (E,F-10)
Roseville (E-9)
Sanborn (C-10)
Sauk Centre (C-8)
Shakopee (D-9)
Shoreview (E-9)
Slayton (B-10)
Spring Valley (F-11)
St. Cloud (D-8)
St. Louis Park (E-9)
St. Paul (E-9)
Stillwater (E-9)
Talmoon (D-5)
Thief River Falls (B-4)
Togo (E-5)
Two Harbors (F-6)
Virginia (E-5)
Wadena (C-7)
Walker (C-6)
Wanamingo (E-10)
Warren (A-4)
Warroad (C-2)
White Bear Lake (E-9)
Willmar (C-9)
Windom (C-11)
Winona (F-10)
Worthington (B-11)
Zumbro Falls (F-10)
Zumbrota (E-10)

Minneapolis (pg. 76)

Arden Hills (G-1)
Bloomington (E,F-3)
Brooklyn Center (E,F-1)
Brooklyn Park (E,F-1)
Columbia Heights (F-1,2)
Crystal (E,F-2)
Eagan (G-3)
Eden Prarie (E-3)
Edina (E,F-2)
Falcon Heights (G-2)
Fridley (F-1)
Golden Valley (E,F-2)
Hopkins (E-2)
Inver Grove Heights (G,H-3)
Little Canada (G-2)
Maple Grove (E-1)
Maplewood (H-2)
Mendota Heights (G-3)
Minneapolis (F,G-2)
Minnetonka (E-2)
Mounds View (F-1)
New Brighton (F-1)
New Hope (E-1,2)
North St. Paul (H-2)
Oakdale (H-2)
Plymouth (E-2)
Richfield (F-3)
Roseville (G-2)
Shoreview (G-1)
Spring Lake Park (F-1)
St. Louis Park (E,F-2,3)
St. Paul Park (H-3)
Vadnais Heights (G-1)
West St. Paul (G-3)
White Bear Lake (H-1)
Woodbury (H-3)

MISSISSIPPI (pg. 41)

Aberdeen (G-3)
Ackerman (F-4)
Amory (G-3)
Batesville (D-2)
Bay Springs (E,F-7)
Bay St. Louis (E-11)
Beaumont (F-9)
Belzoni (C-5)
Biloxi (F-11)
Booneville (G-2)
Bovina (C-6)
Brandon (D-7)
Brookhaven (C-8)
Brooklyn (F-9)
Brooksville (G-5)
Bruce (E-3)
Bude (C-8)
Calhoun City (E-3)
Canton (D-6)
Carthage (E-6)
Cayuga (C-7)
Centreville (B-9)
Charleston (D-3)
Clarksdale (C-2)
Cleveland (C-3)
Clinton (D-6)
Collins (E-8)
Columbia (D-9)
Columbus (G-4)
Corinth (G-1)
Crossroads (E-10)
Crystal Springs (D-7)
Daleville (G-6)
De Kalb (G-6)
Durant (E-5)
D'Iberville (F-10,11)
Eupora (F-4)
Fayette (B-8)
Flora (D-6)
Florence (D-7)
Forest (E-6)
Foxworth (D-9)
Fulton (G-2)
Gautier (G-11)
Georgetown (D-7)
Glendale (E-9)
Gloster (B,C-9)
Greenville (B-4)
Greenwood (D-4)
Grenada (E-3)
Gulfport (F-11)
Hamilton (G-3)
Hattiesburg (E-9)
Hazelhurst (D-7)
Holcomb (D-3)
Hollandale (C-5)
Holly Springs (E-1)
Houston (F-3)
Indianola (C-4)
Iuka (G-1)
Jackson (D-6)
Kosciusko (E-5)
Laurel (F-8)
Le Tourneau (B-7)
Leland (C-4)
Liberty (B,C-9)
Long Beach (F-11)
Louisville (F-5)
Lucedale (G-10)
Lumberton (E-9)
Lyman (F-10)
Macon (G-5)
Magee (E-7)
Marks (D-2)
Mathiston (F-4)
Maybank (E-8)
Mayhew (G-4)
McComb (C-9)
McLaurin (F-9)
Mendenhall (D-7)
Meridian (G-6)
Minter City (D-3)
Mize (E-7,8)
Monticello (D-8)
Moss Point (G-11)
Natchez (B-8)
New Albany (F-2)
New Houlka (E,F-3)
Newton (F-6)
Oak Grove (E-9)
Oakland (D-3)
Ocean Springs (F-11)
Ofahoma (E-6)
Okolona (G-3)
Osyka (C-9)
Oxford (E-2)
Pachuta (F-7)
Palmer (F-9)
Parchman (C-3)
Pascagoula (G-11)
Pearl (D-7)
Petal (F-9)
Philadelphia (F-6)
Picayune (E-10)
Pontotoc (F-2)
Poplarville (E-10)
Port Gibson (B-7)
Porterville (G-6)
Prentiss (D-8)
Puckett (E-7)
Quitman (F-7)
Raleigh (E-7)
Redwood (C-6)
Rich (C-2)
Richland (D-7)
Richton (F-9)
Ripley (F-1)
Rolling Fork (C-5)
Rosedale (B,C-3)
Roxie (B-8)
Ruleville (C-3)
Savage (D-2)
Scooba (G-5)
Senatobia (D-2)
Southaven (D-1)
Starkville (F-4)
State Line (G-8)
Steens (G-4)
Tchula (D-5)
Tunica (C-2)
Tupelo (F,G-2)
Tutwiler (C,D-3)
Tylertown (D-9)
Utica (C-7)
Vaiden (E-4)
Van Vleet (F-3)
Vicksburg (C-6)
Walnut (F-1)
Waltersville (C-6)
Washington (B-8)
Water Valley (D,E-3)
Waynesboro (G-8)
Webb (D-3)
West Gulf Port (F-11)
West Point (G-4)
Whites (G-4)
Wiggins (F-10)
Winona (E-4)
Woodville (B-9)
Yazoo City (C-5)

MISSOURI (pg. 77)

Adrian (B-4)
Affton (G-4)
Alton (F-6)
Anderson (B-6)
Aurora (C-6)
Ava (D-6)
Ballwin (G-4)
Belton (B-3)
Bethany (C-1)
Big Piney (E-5)
Bixby (F-5)
Blue Springs (B-3)
Bolivar (C-5)
Boonville (D-3)
Bowling Green (F-3)
Brookfield (D-2)
Brumley (D-4)
Buffalo (D-5)
Butler (B-4)
Caledonia (F-5)
Camdenton (D-4)
Cameron (B-2)
Canton (E-1)
Cape Girardeau (H-5)
Carrollton (C-3)
Carthage (B-6)
Cassville (C-6)
Charleston (H-6)
Chesterfield (F-3)
Chillicothe (C-2)
Clinton (C-4)
Collins (C-5)
Columbia (D-3)
Concordia (C-3)
Creve Coeur (G-3)
Cuba (F-4)
De Soto (F-4)
Devil's Elbow (E-5)
DeWitt (C-3)
Dexter (G-6)
Dongola (G-6)
Doniphan (F-6)
Drake (E-4)
Duke (E-5)
Edina (E-2)
Eldon (D-4)
Eldorado Springs (C-5)
Excelsior Springs (B-3)
Fair Grove (D-5)
Farmington (G-5)
Fayette (D-3)
Festus (G-4)
Florissant (G-3)
Fredericktown (G-5)
Fulton (E-3)
Gainesville (D-6)
Garwood (F-6)
Gladstone (B-3)
Glover (F-5)
Golden City (B-5)
Gower (B-2)
Grandview (B-3)
Grant City (B-1)
Green Ridge (C-4)
Greenfield (C-5)
Greenwood (B-3)
Hayti (H-7)
Hannibal (F-2)
Hartville (D-6)
Hermann (E-3)
Independence (B-3)
Ironton (F-5)
Jefferson City (E-4)
Joplin (B-6)
Kansas City (B-3)
Kennett (G-7)
Kingdom City (E-3)
Kirksville (D-1)
Knob Noster (C-3)
Lamar (B-5)
Lancaster (D-1)
Laquey (D-5)
Lebanon (D-5)
Leeton (C-4)
Lee's Summit (B-3)
Lewistown (E-2)
Lexington (C-3)
Liberty (B-3)
Licking (E-5)
Linn (E-4)
Louisiana (F-2)
Lynchburg (E-5)
Macon (D-2)
Malden (G-7)
Mansfield (D-6)
Marble Hill (G-5)
Marshall (C-3)
Marshfield (D-5)
Maryville (B-1)
Memphis (E-1)
Mexico (E-3)
Milan (D-1)
Moberly (D-2)
Monett (C-6)
Monroe City (E-2)
Monsterrat (C-3)
Montgomery City (E-3)
Mound City (A-1)
Mount Vernon (C-6)
Neosho (B-6)
Nevada (B-5)
New London (E,F-2)
New Madrid (H-6)
Odessa (C-3)
Osage Beach (D-4)
Osceola (C-4)
Overland (G-3)
Ozark (C,D-6)
O'Fallon (F-3)
Paris (E-2)
Patton (G-5)
Perryville (G-5)
Piedmont (F-6)
Pleasant Hill (B-3)
Polo (B,C-2)
Poplar Bluff (G-6)
Potosi (F-5)
Preston (C-5)
Princeton (C-1)
Raytown (B-3)
Richmond (C-3)
Rolla (E-5)
Sainte Genevieve (G-4)
Salem (E-5)
Sappington (G-4)
Savannah (B-2)
Sedalia (C-4)
Shelbina (E-2)
Sikeston (H-6)
Spanish Lake (G-3)
Springfield (C-6)
St. Charles (G-3)
St. Clair (F-4)
St. Joseph (B-2)
St. Louis (G-3,4)
St. Peters (F-3)
Stanberry (B-1)
Steelville (F-5)
Stockton (C-5)
Sturgeon (D,E-3)
Success (E-5)
Sunrise Beach (D-4)
Tarkio (A-1)
Thayer (E-7)
Tipton (D-4)
Trenton (C-2)
Union Star (B-2)
Unionville (D-1)
Versailles (D-4)
Vienna (E-4)
Vista (C-4,5)
Walnut Shade (D-6)
Warrensburg (C-3)
Warsaw (C-4)
Washington (F-4)
Wayland (E-1)
Waynesville (E-5)
West Plains (E-6)
Willow Springs (E-6)
Winfield (F-3)
Winona (F-6)
Winston (B-2)

Branson (pg. 77)

Kansas City (pg. 77)

Belton (B,C-11)
Claycomo (C-8)
Edwardsville (A-9)
Gladstone (B-8)
Grandview (B,C-11)
Greenwood (D-11)
Houston Lake (B-8)
Independence (C-9)
Leawood (B-10)
Lee's Summit (C-11)
Lenexa (A-10)
Liberty (C-8)
Merriam (A-10)
Mission (B-10)
North Kansas City (B-9)
Northmoor (B-8)
Overland Park (A-10)
Parkville (A-8)
Platte Woods (A,B-8)
Pleasant Valley (B,C-8)
Prairie Village (B-10)
Raytown (C-10)
Riverside (B-8,9)
Roeland Park (B-9,10)
Shawnee (A-10)
Sugar Creek (C-9)
Unity Village (C-10)
Weatherby Lake (A-8)

St. Louis (pg. 77)

Bel-Ridge (E-9)
Bellefontaine Neighbors (F-8)
Berkeley (E-8)
Black Jack (E,F-8)
Brentwood (E-9)
Bridgeton (D-8)
Cahokia (F-10)
Centerville (F,G-10)
Clayton (E-9)
Cliff Cave (E-11)
Columbia (F-11)
Comstock (G-8)
Concord (D,E-11)
Crestwood (D,E-10)
Creve Coeur (D-9)
Delwood (E,F-8)
Des Peres (D-10)
Dupo (F-10)
East St. Louis (F-9,10)
Falling Springs (F-10)
Fenton (D-10)
Ferguson (E-8)
Florissant (E-8)
Frontenac (D-9)
Glendale (E-10)
Granite City (F-8,9)
Hazelwood (D,E-8)
Jennings (E,F-8)
Kirkwood (D-10)

Ladue (D,E-9)
Lemay (E-11)
Madison (F,G-9)
Maryland Heights (D-8,9)
Normandy (E-9)
Olivette (D,E-9)
Overland (D,E-9)
Pagedale (E-9)
Paulina Hills (D-11)
Pine Lawn (E-9)
Pontoon Beach (G-8)
Richmond Heights (E-9)
Riverview (F-8)
Shrewsbury (E-10)
Signal Hill (G-10)
South Roxana (G-7,8)
Spanish Lake (F-8)
St. Ann (D,E-9)
Sunset Hills (D-10)
University City (E-9)
Villa Hills (G-10)
Washington Park (G-9)
Webster Groves (E-10)
Westwood (D-9)
Wilbur Park (E-10)

MONTANA (pg. 91)

Aberdeen (H-7)
Alzada (K-7)
Anaconda (C-5)
Augusta (D-4)
Avon (D-5)
Babb (C-2)
Baker (K-5)
Belt (E-4)
Big Timber (F-6)
Big Sky (E-6)
Billings (G-6)
Black Eagle (E-3,4)
Blossburg (D-5)
Bozeman (E-6)
Bridger (G-6,7)
Broadus (J-6)
Brockway (I-4)
Browning (C-2)
Butte (D-5,6)
Cartersville (I-5)
Chester (E-2)
Chinook (G-2)
Circle (I,J-4)
Coffee Creek (F-4)
Cohagen (I-4)
Colstrip (I-6)
Columbia Falls (B-2)
Columbus (G-6)
Conrad (D-3)
Crow Agency (H-6)
Culbertson (J-3)
Custer (H-5)
Darby (B-5)
Decker (I-7)
Dillon (D-6)
Divide (C-6)
Drummond (C-5)
Elmo (B-3)
Ennis (D-6)
Epsie (J-6)
Eureka (B-2)
Fairview (K-3)
Fallon (J-4)
Forsyth (I-5)
Fort Benton (E-3)
Fort Peck (I-3)
Fort Belknap (G-2)
Gardiner (E-7)
Garrison (D-5)
Glasgow (I-3)
Glendive (J-4)
Grassrange (G-4)
Great Falls (E-4)
Hamilton (B-5)
Hardin (H-6)
Harlowton (F-5)
Havre (F-2)
Hays (G-3)
Helena (D-5)
Hungry Horse (C-2)
Huntley (G-6)
Ingomar (H-5)
Jordan (H-4)
Kalispell (B-3)
Lakeside (B-3)
Lame Deer (I-6)
Laurel (G-6)
Lavina (G-5)
Lewistown (F-4)
Libby (A-2)
Lima (D-7)
Lincoln (D-4)
Lindsay (J-4)
Livingston (E-6)
Lolo (B-4)
Lolo Hot Springs (B-5)
Malta (H-3)
Marysville (D-5)
Medicine Springs (B-6)
Miles City (I-5)
Missoula (B-4)
Moore (F-4)
Mosby (H-4)
Nashua (I-3)
Norris (D-6)
Noxon (A-3)
Olive (J-6)
Opheim (I-2)
Plains (B-4)
Plentywood (J-2)
Polson (B-3)
Ravalli (B-4)
Red Lodge (F,G-7)
Rexford (B-2)
Rock Springs (I-5)
Rockvale (G-6)
Ronan (B-3)
Rosebud (I-5)
Roundup (G-5)
Roy (G-4)
Sand Coulee (E-4)
Scobey (J-2)
Shelby (D-2)
Sidney (K-3)
Somers (B-3)
St. Mary (C-2)
St.Ignatius (B-4)
Stanford (F-4)
Sumatra (H-5)
Sun River (D-4)
Sunburst (D-2)
Superior (B-4)
Sweetgrass (D-2)
Terry (I-4)
Thompson Falls (A-3)
Three Forks (D,E-6)
Townsend (D,E-5)
Tracy (E-4)
Trout Creek (A-3)
Troy (A-2)
Twin Bridges (D-6)
Van Norman (I-4)
Vanada (H-5)
Vaughn (E-4)
Warren (G-7)
Westby (K-2)
West Glacier (C-2)
West Yellowstone (E-7)
White Fish (B-2)
Whitehall (D-6)
White Sulphur Springs (E-5)
Wibaux (K-4)
Wisdom (C-6)
Wolf Creek (D-4)
Wolf Point (J-3)

NEBRASKA (pg. 78)

Ainsworth (F-3)
Albion (H-4)
Alliance (B-4)
Alma (F-7)
Ansley (F-5)
Arabia (E-3)
Arapahoe (F-6)
Arthur (C,D-4)
Ashland (J-5)
Atkinson (G-3)
Auburn (J-6)
Aurora (H-6)
Bartlett (G-4)
Beatrice (I-6)
Belden (I-3)
Bellevue (J-5)
Benkelman (D-7)
Blair (J-4)
Blue Hill (G-6)
Brewster (F-4)
Bridgeport (B-4)
Broken Bow (F-5)
Brownlee (E-3)
Bruning (H-6)
Brunswick (H-3)
Burwell (F-4)
Butte (G-2)
Cairo (G-5)
Central City (H-5)
Chadron (B-2)
Columbus (I-5)
Crawford (B-3)
Creston (H-4)
Dawson (J-7)
Daykin (I-6)
Decatur (J-4)
Dorchester (I-6)
Dunning (E-4)
Ellsworth (C-4)
Elwood (F-6)
Enders (D-6)
Ericson (G-4)
Fairbury (I-7)
Fairmont (H-6)
Farnam (E-6)
Filley (J-6)
Franklin (G-7)
Fremont (J-5)
Genoa (H-5)
Gering (A-4)
Gordon (C-3)
Gothenburg (E-5)
Grand Island (G-5)
Grant (C-6)
Greenwood (I-5)
Harrisburg (A-4)
Harrison (A-3)
Hastings (G-6)
Hay Springs (B-3)
Hazard (G-5)
Hebron (H-7)
Hemingford (B-3)
Holdrege (F-6)
Hooper (I-4)
Hyannis (C-4)
Inman (G-3)
Johnstown (E-3)
Kearney (G-6)
Kimball (A-5)
La Vista (J-5)
Laurel (I-3)
Lewiston (J-6)
Lexington (F-6)
Lincoln (I-6)
Loup City (G-5)
Lyons (I-4)
Magnet (H-3)
Maywood (E-6)
McCook (E-7)
Memphis (J-5)
Merriman (C,D-2)
Minden (G-6)
Mitchell (A-4)
Mullen (D-4)
Murdock (J-5)
Nebraska City (J-6)
Neligh (H-4)
Newport (F-3)
Niobrara (H-3)
Norfolk (H-4)
North Bend (I-5)
North Platte (E-5)
Oconto (F-5)
Ogallala (C-5)
Omaha (J-5)
Ord (G-4)
Oshkosh (C-5)
O'Neill (G-3)
Papillion (J-5)
Pilger (I-4)
Plattsmouth (J-5)
Ponca (I-3)
Ragan (F-6)
Red Cloud (G-7)
Rose (F-4)
Schuyler (I-5)
Scottsbluff (A-4)
Seward (I-5)
Shelby (H-5)
Sidney (B-5)
South Bend (J-5)
South Sioux City (J-3)
Spalding (G-4)
Spencer (G-2)
Springview (F-3)
St. Paul (G-5)
Stapleton (E-5)
Stromsburg (H-5)
Superior (H-7)
Syracuse (J-6)
Taylor (F-4)
Tecumseh (J-6)
Thedford (E-4)
Trenton (D-7)
Tryon (D-5)
Upland (G-6)
Valentine (E-2)
Wahoo (I-5)
Wallace (D-6)
Wayne (I-3)
Wellfleet (E-6)
West Point (I-4)
Wood River (G-6)
Wynot (I-3)
York (H-5)

Omaha (pg. 78)

Bellevue (B-8)
Council Bluffs (B,C-7)
Elkhorn (A-7)
La Vista (B-8)
Omaha (B-7,8)
Papillion (B-8)

NEVADA (pg. 105)

Amargosa Valley (E-9)
Ash Springs (G-7)
Austin (E-4)
Basalt (C-7)
Battle Mountain (E-3)
Beatty (E-8)
Boulder City (G-10)
Carlin (F-3)
Carson City (B-5)
Coaldale (D-7)
Denio Junction (C-1)
Elko (F-3)
Ely (G-5)
Eureka (F-5)
Fallon (C-4)
Gardnerville (B-5)
Glendale (G-9)
Gypsum Cave (G-9)
Hawthorne (C-6)
Hazen (B-4)
Henderson (G-10)
Indian Springs (F-9)
Jean (G-10)
Lage's (G,H-4)
Las Vegas (G-9)
Laughlin (H-11)
Lovelock (C-3)
Major's Place (H-5)
McDermitt (D-1)
McGill (G-4)
Middle Gate (D-5)
Nixon (B-4)
North Las Vegas (G-9)
Oasis (H-2)
Pahrump (F-9)
Panaca (H-7)
Preston (G-5)
Reno (B-4)
Scotty's Junction (E-8)
Searchlight (G-10)
Sparks (B-4)
Tonopah (D,E-7)
Virginia City (B-5)
Wadsworth (B-4)
Warm Springs (F-6)
Wellington (B-5)
Wells (G-2)
Wendover (H-3)
West Wendover (H-3)
Winnemucca (D-2)
Yerington (B-5)

Las Vegas (pg. 105)

East Las Vegas (C-9,10)
North Las Vegas (B-9)
Paradise (B-10)
Sunrise Manor (C-9)
Winchester (B-10)

NEW HAMPSHIRE (pg. 21)

Alton (G-8)
Amherst (F-10)
Ashland (F-7)
Atkinson Depot (G-11)
Bath (E-6)
Bedford (F-10)
Belmont (F-8)
Bennett Corners (G-7)
Berlin (G-5)
Bloomfield (F-3)
Boscawen (F-9)
Canaan (D-8)
Candia Four Corners (G-10)
Canobie Lake (G-11)
Center Ossipee (G-7)
Chester (G-10)
Chichester (F-9)
Claremont (D-9)
Colebrook (F-3)
Concord (F-9)
Conway (G-6)
Danbury (E-8)
Deerfield (G-9)
Derry (G-10)
Dover (H-9)
Epping (G-10)
Epsom (G-9)
Errol (G-3)
Exeter (H-10)
Fitzwilliam (D-11)
Franklin (F-8)
Glen (G-6)
Goffstown (F-10)
Gorham (G-5)
Goshen (D-9)
Grantham (D-8)
Greenland (H-10)
Groveton (F-4)
Hampton (H-10)
Hampton Beach (H-10)
Hancock (E-10)
Hanover (D-7)
Haverhill (D-6)
Henniker (E-9)
Hillsboro Lower Village (E-10)
Hillsborough (E-9)
Holderness (F-7)
Hopkinton (F-9)
Hudson (F-11)
Keene (D-10)
Kidderville (F-3)
Kingston (G-10)
Laconia (F-8)
Lancaster (F-4)
Laskey Corner (G-8)
Lebanon (D-8)
Littleton (E-5)
Londonderry (F-10)
Manchester (F-10)
Marlow (D-9)
Martins Ferry (F-10)
Meredith (F-8)
Merrimack (F-10)
Milford (F-10,11)
Moultonborough (F-7)
Nashua (F-11)
New Boston (F-10)
Newport (D-9)
North Sutton (E-9)
North Walpole (D-10)
North Woodstock (F-6)
Northwood (G-9)
Ossipee (G-7)
Otterville (E-8)
Penacook (F-9)
Peterborough (E-10)
Pittsburg (F-2)
Plymouth (F-7)
Portsmouth (H-9)
Potter Place (E-8)
Redstone (G-6)
Rindge (E-11)
Rochester (G-9)
Salem (G-11)
Sanbornville (G-8)
Somersworth (H-9)
South Stoddard (D,E-10)
Suncook (F-9)
Twin Mountain (F-5)
Warren (E-7)
Wentworth (E-7)
West Hempstead (G-10)
West Lebanon (D-8)
West Milan (G-4)
West Ossipee (G-7)
West Rindge (E-11)
West Rumney (E-7)
West Stewartstown (F-3)
Whitefield (F-5)
Winchester (D-11)
Wolfeboro (G-8)
Woodsville (E-6)

NEW JERSEY (pg. 17)

Asbury Park (G-6)
Atlantic City (E-9)
Atsion (D-8)
Avalon (D-10)
Barnegat (F-8)
Barnegat Light (G-8)
Bayonne (G-4)
Beach Haven (F-9)
Beach Haven Heights (F-9)
Bellmawr (C-7)
Berkeley Heights (E-3)
Berlin (D-8)
Boonton (F-3)
Bricksboro (C-10)
Bridgeton (C-9)
Brigatine (F-9)
Browne Mills (E-7)
Burlington (D-6)
Burlington (E-5)
Buttzville (D-3)
Camden (C-7)
Cape May (D-11)
Cape May Lighthouse (C-11)
Chambers Corner (D-6)
Chatsworth (E-7)
Cherry Hill (D-7)
Chester (E-3)
Clifton (G-3)
Clinton (D-4)
Collingswood (C-7)
Collingwood Park (G-6)
Colts Neck (F-6)
Cookstown (E-6)
Dover (E-3)
Dumont (G-2)
East Windsor (E-5)
East Orange (F-3)
East Brunswick (E-4)
Eatontown (G-5)
Edison (E,F-4)
Egg Harbor City (E-9)
Elizabeth (F-4)
Englishtown (F-5)
Ewingville (D-5)
Fairview (D-6)
Flemington (D-4)
Florham Park (F-3)
Four Mile (E-7)
Freehold (F-5)
Frenchtown (C-4)
Glassboro (C-8)
Gloucester City (C-6,7)
Gordon's Corner (F-5)
Goshen (D-10)
Greenwich (B-9)
Hackettstown (D-3)
Hamburg (E-1)
Hamilton Square (E-5)
Hammonton (D-8)
Hawthorne (F,G-2)
Highland Park (E,F-4)
Hillsdale (G-2)
Holmde (F-5)
Hopatcong (E-2)
Hopewell (D-5)
Hornerstown (E-6)
Irvington (F-3)
Jersey City (G-3)
Jerseyville (F-5)
Keansburg (F-5)
Lakehurst (F-6)
Lakewood (F-6)
Lambertville (D-5)
Lindenwold (C-7)
Livingston (F-3)
Long Beach (F-8)
Long Branch (G-5)
Loveladies (F,G-8)
Lower Harmony (C-3)
Madison (E,F-3)
Mahwah (G-2)
Malaga (C-8)
Manahawkin (F-8)
Manville (E-4)
Maple Shade (D-7)
Medford Lakes (D-7)
Mercerville (E-5)
Metuchen (F-4)
Middlesex (E-4)
Millstone (E-4)
Millville (C-9)
Monmouth Beach (G-5)
Moorestown (D-7)
Morristown (E-3)
Mount Holly (D-6,7)
Mount Hope (E-2)
Mullica Hill (C-8)
Netcong (E-3)
New Brunswick (E-4)
New Egypt (E-6)
Newark (F-3)
Newfoundland (F-2)
Newton (D,E-2)
North Plainfield (E,F-4)
North Beach (F-8)
Northfield (E-9)
Oakland (F-2)
Ocean City (E-10)
Oceanport (G-5)
Paramus (G-2,3)
Passaic (G-3)
Paterson (F,G-2)
Pemberton (E-7)
Pennsauken (C-7)
Phillipsburg (C-3,4)
Plainfield (E,F-4)
Pleasantville (E-9)
Pluckemin (E-4)
Point Pleasant Beach (G-6)
Pole Tavern (B-8)
Polkville (C-2)
Pompton Lakes (F-2)
Port Norris (C-10)
Princeton (E-5)
Rahway (F-4)
Ramsey (F,G-2)
Red Lion (D-7)
Red Bank (G-5)
Ridgeway (F-6)
Ridgewood (F,G-2)
Ringwood (F-2)
Rio Grande (D-11)
Rockaway (E-3)
Rocktown (D-5)
Rocky Hill (E-5)
Ross Corner (E-2)
Salem (B-8)
Sayreville (F-5)
Sea Isle City (D-10)
Seaside Park (G-7)
Seaville (D-10)
Ship Bottom (F-8)
Shrewsbury (G-5)
Smithburg (F-6)
Somers Point (E-9,10)
Somerville (E-4)
South Dennis (D-10)
South River (F-5)
Spray Beach (F-8)
Summit (F-3)
Surf City (F-8)
Sussex (E-1)
Tabernacle (D-7)
Tinton Falls (G-5)
Toms River (F-7)
Trenton (D-6)
Tuckahoe (D-10)
Tuckerton (F-8)
Tuttles Corner (D-1)
Union (F-4)
Union City (G-3)
Ventor City (E-9)
Vienna (D-3)
Vineland (C,D-9)
Waldwick (G-2)
Wanaque (F-2)
Waretown (F-8)
Washington (D-3)
Wayne (F-2,3)
Westfield (F-4)
Westwood (G-2)
Whitesbog (E-7)
Wildwood (D-11)
Wildwood Crest (D-11)
Willingboro (D-6)
Woodbridge (F-4)
Woodbury (C-7)
Wrightstown (E-6)
Wyckoff (F-2)

NEW MEXICO (pg. 106)

Alamogordo (E-7)
Albuquerque (D-3,4)
Alma (A-6)
Amistad (H-2)
Animas (A-8)
Antelope Wells (A-9)
Anthony (D-8)
Apache Creek (A-5)
Arabela (F-6)
Artesia (G-7)
Aztec (B-1)
Bayard (B-7)
Bernalillo (D-3)
Black Lake (E-1)
Blanco (B-1)
Blanco Trading Post (B-2)
Bloomfield (B-2)
Capitan (E-6)
Caprock (G-6)
Capulin (G-1)
Carlsbad (G-7)
Carrizozo (E-6)
Chama (D-1)
Cimarron (F-1)
Clayton (H-1)
Clines Corners (E-4)
Cloudcroft (E-7)
Clovis (H-4,5)
Columbus (B-8)
Conchas (G-3)
Corona (E-5)
Counselors (C-2)
Coyote (D-2)
Crown Point (B-3)
Cuba (C-2)
Cuchillo (C-6)
Datil (B-5)
Deming (B-8)
Des Moines (G-1)
Dexter (F-6)
Duke (C-1)
Duran (E-4,5)
Eagle Nest (E-1)
Elida (G,H-5)
Encino (E-4)
Estancia (D-4)
Farley (G-2)
Farmington (B-1)
Fence Lake (A-4)
Folsom (G-1)
Fort Sumner (G-4)
Gallup (A-3)
Grants (B-3,4)
Grenville (G-1)
Hachita (B-8)
Hatch (C-7)
Hobbs (H-7)
Hondo (E-6)
Jal (H-8)
Kingston (B-7)
La Cueva (E-2)
Lakewood (G-7)
Las Cruces (D-8)
Las Vegas (E-3)
Loco Hills (G-7)
Logan (H-3)
Lordsburg (A-8)
Los Alamos (D-2)
Loving (G-8)
Lovington (H-7)
Magdalena (C-5)
Mayhill (E-7)
Mesa (F-5)
Moriarty (D-4)
Nara Visa (H-3)
Naschitti (A-2)
Newkirk (F-4)
Ocate (F-2)
Pinon (E-7)
Portales (H-5)
Quemado (A-5)
Questa (E-1)
Ranchvale (H-4)
Raton (F-1)
Reserve (A-6)
Rio Rancho (D-3)
Romeroville (E-3)
Roswell (F-6)
Roy (G-2)
Ruidoso (E-6)
San Antonio (C-5)
San Jon (H-3)
San Mateo (B-3)
Santa Rosa (F-4)
Sante Fe (D,E-3)
Sapello (E-3)
Sheep Springs (A-2)
Shiprock (A-1)
Silver City (B-7)
Socorro (C-5)
Solano (G-2)
Springer (F-2)
St. Vrain (H-5)
Taos (E-2)
Tatum (H-6)
Tierra Amarilla (D-1)
Tierra Monte (E-2)
Truth or Consequences (C-6,7)
Tucumcari (G-3)
Tularosa (E-7)
Tusas (D-1)
Vaughn (E-4)
Wagon Mound (F-2)
White Horse (B-3)
Willard (D-4)
Winston (B-6)

Albuquerque (pg. 106)

Armijo (D-11)
Corrales (D-9)
Five Points (D-11)
Rio Rancho (C,D-9)

NEW YORK (pg. 18-19)

Adams Center (I-4)
Addison (G-9)
Albany (N-7)
Albion (E-6)
Alder Creek (K-5)
Alexander (E-6)
Alexandria Bay (I-3)
Alton (H-6)
Amenia (N-9)
Amherst (D-6)
Amsterdam (M-6)
Antwerp (J-3)
Arcade (E-7)
Arlington (N-9)
Auburn (H-6)
Ballston Spa (N-6)
Batavia (E-6)
Bath (G-8)
Beacon (N-10)
Belmont (F-8)
Bergen (F-6)
Binghamton (J-8,9)
Boonville (K-5)
Brasher Falls (L-1)
Brighton (G-6)
Brockport (F-6)
Buffalo (D-6,7)
Cairo (M-8)
Calcium (J-3)
Cambridge (O-6)
Camden (J-5)
Canandaigua (G-6)
Canastota (J-6)
Candor (I-8)
Canton (K-2)
Cape Vincent (I-3)
Carmel (N-10)
Carthage (J-4)
Castile (F-7)
Catskill (N-8)
Cayuta (H-8)
Cazenovia (J-6)
Central Square (I-5)
Champlain (N-1)
Chateaugay (M-1)
Cheektowaga (D-6)
Chestertown (M,N-4)
Chenango Bridge (J-8)
Childwold (L-3)
Chittenango (J-6)
Clayton (I-3)
Clintondale (M-10)
Cobleskill (L-7)
Cochecton (K-10)
Cohoes (N-7)
Colonie (N-7)
Colton (K-2)
Comstock (N-5)
Cooperstown (K,L-7)
Corning (H-8)
Cortland (I-7)
Croghan (J-4)
Dannemora (N-1,2)
Dansville (F-7)
Deferiet (J-3)
De Kalb (K-2)
Delhi (L-8)
Depew (D-6)
Deposit (K-9)
DeWitt (I-6)
Downsville (K-9)
Dryden (I-7)
Dunkirk (C-7)
East Chatham (N-8)
East Fishkill (N-10)
East Aurora (D-7)
East Hampton (H-2)
Elizabethtown (N-3)
Ellenville (M-9)
Elmira (H-9)
Endicott (I-8,9)
Endwell (I-8,9)
Evan Mills (J-3)
Fairmount (I-6)
Felt Mills (J-3)
Fishkill (N-10)
Fosterdale (L-10)
Fredonia (C-8)
Fulton (I-5)
Garden City (C-3)
Gates (F-6)
Geneseo (F-7)
Geneva (H-6,7)
Georgetown (J-7)
Glens Falls (N-5)
Gloversville (M-6)
Goshen (M-10)
Gouverneur (J-3)
Gowanda (D-8)
Grand Gorge (L-8)
Granville (O-5)
Greece (F-6)
Greenwich (N-6)
Hamburg (D-7)
Hancock (K-9)
Hannibal (H-5)
Hague (N-4)
Harrisville (K-3)
Haverstraw (N-11)
Hemlock (G-7)
Herkimer (K-6)
Highland Falls (N-10)
Hillsdale (N-8)
Hoosick Falls (O-6)
Hornell (F-8)
Horseheads (H-8)
Houghton (E-8)
Hudson (N-8)
Indian Lake (M-4)
Irondequoit (G-6)
Ithaca (I-8)
Jamestown (C-8,9)
Jasper (G-8)
Jay (N-2)
Johnson City (J-8)
Johnstown (M-6)
Keene (N-3)
Kenmore (D-6)
Kennedy (D-8)
Kingston (M,N-9)
Lackawanna (D-7)
Lake George (N-5)
Lake Placid (M-3)
Lancaster (D-6)
Latham (N-7)
Le Roy (F-6)
Liberty (L-9)
Lima (F,G-6)
Liverpool (I-6)
Lockport (D-6)
Long Lake (L-4)
Loudonville (N-7)
Lowville (J-4)
Lyons Falls (K-4)
Lyons (H-6)
Malone (M-1)
Maplehurst (E-8)
Margaretville (L-8)
Masonville (K-8)
Massena (K-1)
Medina (E-6)
Mexico (I-5)
Middleburgh (M-7)
Middletown (M-10)
Middleville (K-6)
Millerton (N-9)
Monticello (L-10)
Morristown (J-2)
Morrisville (J-6)
Mt. Ivy (M,N-11)
Mt.Kisco (M-11)
Mt.Lodge (M-10)
Nanuet (N-11)
Natural Bridge (J-3)
New City (N-11)
New Lebanon (O-7)
New Berlin (K-7)
Newark (G-6)
Newburgh (M,N-10)
Newfane (D-5)
Niagara Falls (D-6)
North Syracuse (I-6)
North Tonawanda (D-6)
Norwich (J-7)
Nyack (N-11)
Ogdensburg (J-2)
Old Forge (K-4)
Olean (E-9)
Oneida (J-6)
Oneonta (K-8)
Ossining (N-11)
Oswego (I-5)
Ovid (H-7)
Owego (I-9)
Palmyra (G-6)
Pamelia Four Corners (J-3)
Paul Smiths (M-2)
Pearl River (M-11)
Penn Yan (H-7)
Petersburg (O-7)
Philadelphia (J-3)
Plattsburgh (N-2)
Pleasantville (N-11)
Point Breeze (E-5)
Poland (K-6)
Port Jervis (L-10)
Potsdam (K-2)
Poughkeepsie (N-9,10)
Pulaski (I-5)
Red Creek (H-6)
Rensselaer (N-7)
Richfield Springs (K-6,7)
Rochester (F,G-6)
Rockwood (L-6)
Rome (J-6)
Romulus (H-7)
Roscoe (L-9)
Rotterdam (M-7)
Sackets Harbor (I-4)
Salamanca (D-8)
Saranac Lake (M-3)
Saratoga Springs (N-6)
Savannah (H-6)
Schenectady (M,N-7)
Schoharie (M-7)
Schuylerville (N-6)
Seneca Falls (H-6)
Severance (N-4)
Sharon Springs (L-7)
Sherburne (J-7)
Sherman (B,C-8)
Sidney (K-8)
Skaneateles (I-6)
Sloansville (M-7)
Sloatsburg (M-11)
Solvay (I-6)
Speculator (M-5)
Spragueville (J-3)
Spring Valley (M-11)
Springville (D-7)
Stamford (L-8)
Stoney Point (N-11)
Suffern (M-11)
Syracuse (I-6)
Tarrytown (N-11)
Ticonderoga (N-4)
Tonawanda (D-6)
Troy (N-7)
Tupper Lake (L-3)
Underwood (N-3)
Utica (K-6)
Varysburg (E-7)
Vernon (J-6)
Vestal (I-9)
Waddington (K-1)
Walton (K-8)
Warrensburg (N-5)
Warsaw (E,F-7)
Wurtsboro (M-10)
Warwick (M-11)
Waterloo (H-6)
Watertown (I,J-4)
Waterville (K-6)
Watervliet (N-7)
Watkins Glen (H-8)
Wells (M-5)
Wellsville (F-9)
West Point (N-10)
Westfield (C-8)
Westport (N-3)
White Plains (N-11)
Whitney Point (I-8)
Williamson (G-6)
Woodbourne (L-9)
Wurtsboro (M-10)
Yorktown Heights (N-11)
Youngstown (D-5,6)

Buffalo-Niagara Falls (pg. 18)

Amherst (G,H-10)
Blassell (G-11)
Cheektowaga (H-10)
Depew (H-10)
East Aurora (H-11)
East Lancaster (H-10)
Hamburg (G-11)
Kenmore (G-10)
Lackawanna (G-11)
Lancaster (H-10)
Lockport (H-9)
Niagra Falls (F-9)
North Tonawanda (G-10)
Orchard Park (H-11)
Shooktown (H-9)
South Lockport (H-9)
Tonawanda (G-10)
Williamsville (G,H-10)

Downtown Manhattan (pg. 25)

Battery Park City (A-9)
Central Park (B,C-1,2)
Chelsea (B-5)
Chinatown (B,C-8)
East Village (C,D-6)
Financial District (A-9,10)
Garment District (B-4)
Gramercy (C-5)
Greenwich Village (B-7)
Jacob Javits Convention Center (A-3,4)
Lincoln Center (B-1,2)
Little Italy (B,C-7)
Lower East Side (C,D-7,8)
Midtown (C-3)
Murray Hill (D-4)
Rockefeller Center (C-3)
Soho (B-7)
Times Square (B-3)
Tribecca (B-8)
United Nations (D-3,4)
Upper East Side (C,D,E-1,2)
Upper West Side (A,B-1,2)
West Side (A,B-1,2)
West Village (A,B-6)
World Trade Center Site (A,B-8,9)

Long Island (pg. 23)

Babylon (D-3)
Bay Shore (D,E-3)
Bethpage (D-3)
Bridgehampton (G-2)
Center Moriches (F-2)
Centereach (E-2)
Central Islip (E-2)
Cold Spring Harbor (D-2)
Commack (D-2)
Coplague (D-3)
Cutchogue (G-1)
Deer Park (D-2,3)
East Quoque (F-2)
East Patchoque (E-3)
East Northport (D-2)
East Islip (F-3)
Eastport (F-2)
Fisher's Island (H-1)
Freeport (D-3)
Glen Cove (C-2)
Great Neck (C-2)
Greenport (G-1)
Hampton (G-2)
Harrison (C-2)
Hauppauge (E-2)
Holbrook (E-2)
Huntington (D-2)
Huntington Station (D-2)
Islip (E-3)
Lake Ronkonkoma (E-2)
Levittown (D-3)
Lindenhurst (D-3)
Long Beach (C-3)
Mamaroneck (C-2)
Manorville (F-2)
Massapequa Park (D-3)
Montauk (H-1)
Mount Vernon (C-2)
New Rochelle (C-2)
New York (B,C-2,3)
Orient (G-1)
Oyster bay (I-2)
Patchogue (E-2,3)
Peetskill (B-1)
Plainview (D-2)
Port Chester (C-2)
Port Jefferson Station (E-2)
Ridge (F-2)
Riverhead (F-2)
Rocky Point (E-2)
Ronkonkoma (E-2)
Rye (C-2)
Sag Harbor (G-1)
Sayville (E-3)
Selden (E-2)
Shirley (F-2)
Smithtown (D,E-2)
Southampton (G-2)
Southold (G-1)
St. James (E-2)
Wantagh (D-3)
Westhampton Beach (F-2)
Westhampton (F-2)
Wyandanch (D-3)
Yaphank (E-2)
Yonkers (C-2)

New York City (pg. 24)

Albertson (I-3,4)
Allwood (B-2)
Annadale (A,B-8)
Astoria (E-3,4)
Athenia (B-2)
Atlantic Beach (H-7)
Auburndale (G-4)
Baldwin (I,J-6)
Bay Ridge (D-6)
Baychester (F-2)
Bayonne (B,C-6)
Bayside (G-4)
Bayville (J-1)
Bedford-Stuyvesant (E-5)
Bellaire (G,H-5)
Belleville (B-3)
Bensonhurst (D,E-7)
Bergenfield (D-1)
Bloomfield (A-3)
Bogata (D-2)
Borough Park (D-6)
Breezy Point (E-7,8)
Brighton Beach (E-7)
Broadway (G-4)
Bronx (F-2)
Bronxville (F,G-1)
Brookdale (A,B-3)
Brooklyn (D,E-6)
Brownsville (E,F-5,6)
Bulls Head (B-7)
Cambria Heights (H-5)
Canarsie (E,F-6)
Carlstadt (C-2)
Carteret (A-7)
Cedar Grove (A-2)
Cedarhurst (H-6)
Charleston (A-8)
Cliffside Park (D-3)
Clifton (B-2)
College Point (F-3)
Coney Island (D-7)
Douglaston (G,H-4)
East Elmhurst (F-4)
East Hills (I-3)
East Meadow (J-5)
East New York (F-5,6)
East Orange (A-4)
East Rockaway (I-6)
East Rutherford (C-3)
Edgemere (G,H-7)
Elizabeth (A,B-6)
Elizabethport (B-6)
Elmont (H-5)
Elmwood Park (C-1)
Englewood (E-1)
Fair Lawn (B,C-1)
Flatbush (E-6)
Floral Park (H-5)
Flushing (G-4)
Fort Lee (D,E-2)
Freeport (J-6)
Fresh Meadows (G-4)
Garden City (I-4)
Garfield (C-2)
Glen Cove (I-2)
Gramercy Park (D,E-4)
Graniteville (B-6)
Grant City (C-7)
Grasselli (A-6,7)
Gravesend (E-7)
Great Kills (B-8)
Great Neck (H-3)
Greenvale (I,J-3)
Greenwich Village (D-4)
Guttenberg (D-3)
Hackensack (C,D-1,2)
Haledon (A-1)
Harlem (E-3)
Harrison (B-4)
Hasbrouck Heights (C-2)
Hempstead (I,J-5)
Hewlett Harbor (H,I-6)
Hillside (A-5)
Hillside (G-5)
Hoboken (D-4)
Inwood (E-2)
Irvington (A-4)
Jackson Heights (F-4)
Jamaica (G-5)
Jericho (J-3)
Jersey City (C,D-5)
Kearny (B,C-4)
Kew Gardens (F,G-5)
Kings Point (G,H-3)
Kingsbridge (E-1,2)
Larchmont (G,H-1)
Lattingtown (I,J-1)
Laurelton (G,H-5)
Lawrence (H-7)
Leonia (D-2)
Linden (A-6)
Little Falls (A-2)
Little Ferry (C,D-2)
Locust Manor (G-5)
Locust Valley (J-2)
Lodi (C-2)
Long Beach (I-7)
Long Island City (E-4)
Lynbrook (I-6)
Lyndhurst (B,C-3)
Malverne (H,I-5)
Manhasset (H-3)
Manhattan (D,E-3,4)
Maplewood (A-4)
Mariner's Harbor (B-6)
Maspeth (E,F-4,5)
Matinecock (J-2)
Maywood (C,D-1)
Merrick (J-5)
Mill Neck (J-2)
Mineola (I-4)
Montclair (A-3)
Morris Heights (E-2)
Morrisania (E,F-2,3)
Mott Haven (E-3)
Mount Vernon (F,G-1)
Munsey Park (H-3)
Muttontown (J-3)
New Hyde Park (H,I-4)
New Rochelle (G,H-1)
Newark (A,B-4)
North Arlington (C-3)
North Bergen (D-3)
North Caldwell (A-2)
North Hills (H,I-3)
North New Hyde Park (H-4)
Nutley (B-3)
Oceanside (I-6)
Orange (A-4)
Ozone Park (F,G-5)
Palisades Park (D-2)
Paramus (C,D-1)
Parkchester (F-2)
Passaic (B-2)
Paterson (B-1)
Pelham (G-1)
Pelham Manor (G-1)
Perth Amboy (A-8)
Pleasantdale (A-3)
Point Lookout (J-7)
Port Newark (B-5)
Port Richmond (B,C-6)
Port Washington (H,I-3)
Princess Bay (A,B-8)
Queens (F-5)
Queens Village (H-4,5)
Rahway (A-6)
Rego Park (F-4)
Richmondtown (B-7)
Ridgefield (D-2)
Ridgefield Park (D-2)
Ridgewood (E,F-5)
River Edge (C,D-1)
Riverdale (E,F-1)
Rochelle Park (C-1)
Rockville Center (I,6)
Roosevelt (J-5)
Roselle (A-6)
Rosell Park (A-5)
Roslyn (I-3)
Rutherford (C-2,3)

INSTALLATION ... MAP PAGE (COORDINATE); TEXT PAGE

INSTALLATION ... MAP PAGE (COORDINATE); TEXT PAGE

INSTALLATION ... MAP PAGE (COORDINATE); TEXT PAGE

INSTALLATION .... MAP PAGE (COORDINATE); TEXT PAGE

INSTALLATION .... MAP PAGE (COORDINATE); TEXT PAGE